RECEIVED

APR 29 2014

BROADVIEW LIBRARY

D0387014

NO LONGER PROPERTY OF SEATTLE PUBLIC LIBRARY

Also by Charles Marsh

Welcoming Justice,
with John M. Perkins

Wayward Christian Soldiers

The Beloved Community

The Last Days

God's Long Summer

Reclaiming Dietrich Bonhoeffer

STRANGE GLORY

STRANGE GLORY

A LIFE OF DIETRICH BONHOEFFER

~

Charles Marsh

Alfred A. Knopf · New York · 2014

THIS IS A BORZOI BOOK
PUBLISHED BY ALFRED A. KNOPF

Copyright © 2014 by Charles Marsh

All rights reserved. Published in the United States by Alfred A. Knopf,
a division of Random House LLC, New York, and in Canada by Random
House of Canada Limited, Toronto, Penguin Random House companies.

www.aaknopf.com

Knopf, Borzoi Books, and the colophon are registered trademarks of
Random House LLC.

Library of Congress Cataloging-in-Publication Data
Marsh, Charles, [date]
   Strange glory / by Charles Marsh. — First Edition.
        pages   cm
   Includes bibliographical references and index.
   ISBN 978-0-307-26981-2 (hardcover) — ISBN 978-0-385-35169-0
   (ebook) — ISBN 978-0-307-39038-7 (trade pbk.)
   1. Bonhoeffer, Dietrich, 1906–1945.   I. Title.
   BX4827.B57M37 2014
   230′.044092—dc23
   [B]
                                                  2013045873

Jacket image: Dietrich Bonhoeffer during the meeting of the
Management Committee of the World Alliance in Geneva, Switzerland,
August 1932. bpk, Berlin / Staatsbibliothek zu Berlin, Stiftung
Preussischer Kulturbesitz / Art Resource, N.Y.
Jacket design by Stephanie Ross

Manufactured in the United States of America
First Edition

FOR KAREN

It is a strange glory, the glory of this God.

— *Dietrich Bonhoeffer*, London Sermon, 1933

CONTENTS

~

STRANGE GLORY

1906–1923

~

Eternity's Child

W hen he was a young child, and his family rented a sprawling villa near the university clinics in Breslau, Dietrich Bonhoeffer and his twin sister, Sabine, lay awake at night trying to imagine eternity. The ritual eventually became a game, with each child concentrating on the word to clear the mind of distractions.[1] On funeral days, as horse-drawn hearses approached the cemetery that lay just to the north, the twins would watch from their bedroom window.[2]

Eternity. *Ewigkeit.*

Sabine found the word "very long and gruesome." Dietrich found it majestic: an "awesome word," he called it.

Sometimes he would picture himself on his deathbed, surrounded by family and friends, reclining on the threshold of heaven. He knew what his last words would be and sometimes rehearsed them aloud, though he dared not reveal them to anyone.[3] He hoped to welcome death as an expected guest—he did not want to be taken by surprise. But, sometimes, when he went to bed convinced that death would come that very night, he would grow light-headed, and the walls of his bedroom would reel about, as if he were at the axis of a carousel. He imagined himself rushing from sister to brother, from father to mother, pleading for help. The prospect of its happening now—of his vanishing tonight into the vast mysterium—felt so real he had to bite his tongue to reassure himself that he was still among the living. That he could feel mortal pain. At such moments, he worried that he suffered from an "incurable fear."[4]

When the twins got separate bedrooms they devised a code for keeping up their metaphysical games. Dietrich would drum lightly on the wall with his fingers, an "admonitory knock" announcing that it was time once again to ponder eternity. A further tap signaled a new reflection on the solemn theme, and so it went, back and forth, until one of them discerned the final silence[5]—usually it was Dietrich. And with the game concluded, he lay awake, the only light in his room coming from a pair of candle-lit crosses his mother had placed atop a corner table.[6] "When at night I go to bed, fourteen angels round my stead," he would hear her sing. He liked the idea very much: one angel "dressed in a little white cloak," standing by his bed, and others watching over children everywhere.[7]

Dietrich believed the nightly ritual spared him from "being devoured by Satan," Sabine later wrote, though there are few references to Satan in her brother's adult writings, early or late.[8] Ultimately, death would enthrall more than it frightened, and the devil would frighten him hardly at all.[9] "God does not want human beings to be afraid," he would one day preach to the congregation in a posh London suburb. God's only desire is that people "reach out 'passionately' and 'hungrily' for mercy and love and . . . grace."[10]

Unlike most Protestant theologians of the twentieth century, Dietrich Bonhoeffer was not the child of a minister. The sixth of eight children (his twin being the seventh), he was born on February 4, 1906, in Breslau, into a family of prodigiously talented humanists, who preferred spending religious holidays in the festive company of relatives and friends rather than in church. "Popguns, soldiers!" he wrote in his first letter to Father Christmas.[11] Over the years he would ask for musical instruments, suits of clothes, fur hats, shirts and ties, trips abroad, shoes for every occasion, and the works of Immanuel Kant and G. W. F. Hegel. His wishes were most often granted.

The family lived at 9 Birkenwäldchen Strasse in the affluent Breslau suburb of Scheitnig. Across the street a narrow park traced the bend in the Alte Oder River south beyond the Dombrücke to the city zoo and Bishop's Forests; to the north, a path cut through dense pine woods to the cemetery and to the psychiatry and nerve clinic, where Dietrich's father worked. Sabine recalled a summer afternoon when her twin

DIETRICH AND SABINE BONHOEFFER
IN 1914

brother disappeared after the call to dinner. It was during a heat wave in lower Silesia. Dietrich, tanned and sporting "a shock of flaxen hair," had been larking about in the backyard hoping to ward off the midges. Finally, he took shelter in a garden niche deep in the overgrown field between the rose arbor and the edge of the property. As his nursemaid stood on the veranda, repeating the dinner call, Dietrich paid no mind. Heedless of the heat and the fading light, he was content in the solitude of his secret place in the summer garden.[12]

With its thick walls, narrow windows, and piercing spires, the house stood on the eastern bank of the Alte Oder, off a cobblestone street abutting another narrow wood. Arches and corbels enlivened the brickwork, and touches of Gothic-Baroque appeared in the finials, overhangs, and trussing. A hipped roof and screened-in porch entry, with deep eaves and dormer and eyebrow windows, gave the impression of a Low German farmhouse extending whimsically in every direction.

But for the rose arbor and a small vegetable garden, both carefully tended, the backyard was left to grow wild, according to fashion. Hens and roosters skittered about the yard and across the aging tennis court. Goats and sheep roamed freely in and out of the stables and even into the house when the doors were left open. Dietrich's mother kept a children's zoo with "rabbits, guinea pigs, turtledoves, and squirrels," a terrarium with lizards, and snakes, and "collections of birds' eggs and mounted beetles and butterflies." In the shade of a linden tree, Dietrich's father and older brothers built a tree house on dark piers, a latticework affair with a small stage for skits. One summer, Dietrich helped those same older siblings dig an underground passageway from the arbor to a boulder. Beyond the family's three acres lay what the neighborhood children called "the wilderness." There the land rolled softy toward the river and into a bog where they collected algae, worms, lizards,

PAULA BONHOEFFER AND HER SEVEN CHILDREN

and bullfrogs for their terrariums and things to inspect under their microscopes.[13]

Word that the family was moving to Berlin, more than three hundred kilometers from Breslau, came as a surprise to the children and elicited grumbling in the ranks. In 1912, the year Dietrich turned six, Dr. Karl Bonhoeffer was offered the chair of neurology and psychology at Friedrich-Wilhelms-University in Berlin, a prestigious post overseeing the clinic for nervous and psychiatric disorders.[14] At Breslau, which had numbered Max Born, Erwin Schrödinger, Fritz Haber, and Otto Stern among its many Nobel laureates, his position had been more than respectable.[15] But Berlin offered greater prominence for Karl's clinical studies—along with a better salary and "more possibilities" for the children's development. And the metropolis of two million held great potential for cases of hysterics and addiction to study.[16]

At first, the family rented a place on the Brückenallee, a street that no longer exists, near the Tiergarten, the former royal hunting estate that had become a public park, where Dietrich and Sabine might see the kaiser's children also at play. Four years later, Dr. Bonhoeffer purchased a three-story Gründerzeit-Villa in Grunewald. The suburb had been the brainchild of Otto von Bismarck, the first chancellor of the German empire, who set aside a large parcel of pristine forest to be developed as a residential district. A colony of grand country houses in a variety of architectural styles, Grunewald, or "green forest," was the ideal *rus in urbe*, offering rural atmosphere within reach of urban amenities, while keeping the city's grittier aspects at bay. Scientists, statesmen, and scholars, filmmakers and movie stars, financiers and industrialists, all promenaded along the same leafy boulevards and mingled together at neighborhood soirées.[17] In the summer, canopies of linden and birch shaded the paved streets, and the woodlands to the south seemed to entwine the neighborhood's generously proportioned blocks. The writer Christopher Isherwood, who in the 1920s rented a flat in a noisy working-class urban district, called Grunewald a "millionaire's slum."[18]

The Bonhoeffers warmed to their new home at 14 Wangenheimstrasse. Though smaller than their rented Breslau villa, the house was elegant and lean, built in the style of a classic German country home, with a hip, shingled roof, a bow front dormer, and a clinker brick face on the basement socle. There was also a deep yard, a large veranda facing the garden, and an office suite for Dr. Bonhoeffer's home clinic.[19] On mild days, music drifting through the open windows could be heard in the garden of primroses and young bracken.[20] "An unobtrusive wealth and an uninhibited taste for pleasure and comfort," Bonhoeffer wrote in his unfinished autobiographical novel. "It wasn't so much the importance of the individual object that pleased the eye and warmed the heart as the solicitous care given to the whole."[21]

Inside, the plain cedar floors, crafted to the highest German standards, were well worn. A "thick, plaited mat covered the parquet floor" in the front hall, there being no need, as the lady of the house, Paula Bonhoeffer, saw it, for children "to run across Persian rugs before they knew how to keep their shoes clean." The appointments were simple and sturdy throughout, made to last of top-quality wood and fittings. Beyond the foyer was an enormous living room (twenty meters wide, twenty-five meters deep) that the Bonhoeffer family called simply *das Zimmer*, "the room," or, if necessary, *das grosse Zimmer*, "the big room," but never *der Salon*, the "parlor," which to Paula's ear sounded pretentious. A massive dining table, the wood engraved on all sides, could comfortably seat a dozen in chairs of dark Bavarian timber. On the sideboard, Julie Tafel Bonhoeffer, the children's grandmother, who lived in Tübingen until moving to Berlin with her housekeeper in 1925, kept an antique silver box from which she occasionally drew pieces of chocolate to treat the little ones.

Family portraits and austere landscapes, many now hanging in Munich's Neue Pinakothek or in Hamburg's Kunsthalle, graced the spacious rooms downstairs. Some of the paintings were by Franz von Lenbach, the brothers Achenbach, and Johann Wilhelm Schirmer, but most were the work of Dietrich's great-uncle, Leopold Graf von Kalckreuth, and his father, Stanislaus Graf von Kalckreuth. Of them all, Dietrich best liked the portrait of his great-grandfather August von Hase, over a corner sofa. In the painting, the aging provost, for decades a distinguished professor of church at Jena, kneels before a crucifix, holding an empty hourglass.[22]

With the help of a small army of servants—chambermaids, housekeepers, a cook and a gardener, a governess for each of the older children, a nurse for the small ones—Paula was praised for keeping a well-tuned, comfortable, and stimulating home. After the move to Berlin a receptionist for Dr. Bonhoeffer's private clinic, housed in two side rooms off the main floor, was also hired, as well as a chauffeur.[23]

The earliest German descendants of the Dutch clan van den Boenhoff left Nijmegen in 1513, settling in Schwäbisch Hall as goldsmiths, aldermen, and landowners. On the family seal a lion clutches some beans, against a blue field. Roughly translated, "Boenhoff" means "beanfield." But by the nineteenth century, the family had achieved prominence in law, medicine, and the Lutheran Church.[24]

Karl Bonhoeffer was the son of Judge Friedrich Ernst Philipp Tobias Bonhoeffer, a lawyer who served most of his life as president of the provincial court in Ulm.[25] A contrary and emotionally distant man, he was a "firm enemy of everything faddish and unnatural."[26] He abhorred buses and trains, remaining convinced that any journey of less than sixty kilometers was better undertaken on foot, when all the transfers and inevitable delays were factored in. This meant that, for holiday visits, Karl and his siblings would have to walk the forty kilometers from Tübingen to their grandparents' home in Stuttgart. Each spring the judge trekked alone through the Swabian Alps with a burlap bag of radish seeds, which he scattered Johnny Appleseed style, returning in the autumn to collect the harvest.

Karl Bonhoeffer inherited his father's exactitude and his aloofness, though not, it appears, his short temper. Outwardly gentler than the judge, Karl nevertheless demanded as much of his children as of himself. This was especially so of the way the children formulated their thoughts and expressed themselves. He expected precise and measured judgments, brooking no "spontaneous utterances" or banter in his home. Any child with something to say in the presence of adults had better choose his words carefully. Not that Karl was uninterested in his children's opinions; rather, he took pleasure in clarity of argument. A word spoken in haste or a half-baked thought made him visibly unhappy. He could bring a child to attention by asking, "*Was sagst du?*"—"What are you saying?"[27] He may never have raised his voice, but he rarely embraced or kissed his children.[28]

Karl subscribed to an enlightened skepticism toward the miraculous and the supernatural, toward any belief that contradicted the laws of reason. He accepted his wife's instructing the children in religion only in measured doses, and so long as it served a useful purpose. Nearly two decades of clinical work in empirical psychiatry and neurology had inclined him to think of religion as a tool that might sometimes help people order their lives and ward off chaos—although he felt there were better alternatives. He chose not to accompany his wife and younger children to the Lutheran Church of Grunewald they attended now and then, and he steered clear of the Sunday-afternoon social hours that Paula convened over coffee and cake, with hymns sung around the piano.[29] The twins' religious formation was of more importance to their mother than that of the older children, perhaps because of her awareness of the boy's spiritual predilections. Karl Bonhoeffer did not oppose baptisms and confirmations—if they included a celebration in a spring garden, he rather enjoyed them—but he preferred to keep the Sabbath in his own way. It was his custom, after the evening meal, to gather the family in the library and read aloud stories, poems, and letters. Theodor Fontane and Friedrich Schiller were his favorites, though he also read from Fyodor Dostoevsky, Hermann Hesse, and Fritz Reuter, the popular nineteenth-century chronicler of rural life. This was much more intellectually satisfying than religion, or psychoanalysis, which he criticized forthrightly for encouraging the same sort of meandering speech and speculative indulgences he found so insufferable.[30] "I understand nothing of that," he once said with a sigh after his wife had read the Advent story from the Gospel of Luke.[31] He was only too happy to delegate stories of angels and virgin births to her capable care.

Paula Bonhoeffer was the daughter of Karl Alfred von Hase and Clara Gräfin von Hase, née Countess Kalckreuth. Karl Alfred had been chaplain to the emperor at the Potsdam Garrison Church, and his father, the aforementioned nineteenth-century church historian of some distinction. Paula's blue eyes, blond hair, and open, confident face set a striking contrast to her husband's pursed lips and melancholy eyes.[32]

Until the family moved to Berlin, Paula had schooled the children herself in a room equipped with desks and chalkboards. Having passed the state teacher's examination in 1894, she was certified to teach in coeducational middle schools and in high schools for girls. Her views on teaching and child rearing were well informed and eclectic, and drew from the work of progressive educators and the latest research in moral and developmental psychology. She was especially fond of Rudolf Steiner, founder of the Waldorf School in Stuttgart, who prized individual discovery as the key to a well-formed mind. "Germans have their backbones broken twice in their lives," Paula said, "first in school and then in the army."[33] She required only that children be truthful in all things and comport themselves calmly with others. They should be held accountable for moral lapses but not expected to act like adults. And so, lies were punishable offenses, but torn clothes, windows accidentally broken, even trampled rosebushes were barely noticed at all.[34] Paula wanted her children to be confident in their aspirations as well as to take pleasure in the good fortune of friends. The point of discipline and order was to inspire free exploration and invention.

Besides not overseeing the education of eight children and the household staff of ten, Paula loved to plan elaborate parties and galas; indeed, she was known—not only in Grunewald but throughout the Berlin *Bildungsbürgertum*, the educated upper middle class—as an excellent hostess.[35] There were elaborate costumes and skits and musical numbers. Dietrich relished the preparations and the pageantry,

KARL AND PAULA BONHOEFFER,
CIRCA 1930

designing the invitations, decorating the rooms, and arranging the stage props. With his mother, he selected the music and directed the skits. With his sisters, he rehearsed his lines and his dance steps. Paula kept a cedar chest filled with wigs and colorful silken fabrics, and so his costume was always a particular concern. As a small child, he liked to wear a white party dress with a "blue silk petticoat underneath."[36] Later, at a costume party in the Wangenheimstrasse home, he dressed up as Cupid, shooting blunt arrows at the young couples.[37]

Despite differences in background and temperament, Paula and Karl Bonhoeffer agreed on the family essentials. Both were wholly unimpressed by the modish [or "trendy"] advice that parents become close friends with their children. Neither practiced corporal punishment. If a child questioned some decision, he was encouraged to explain his concern—and to do it precisely. Paula, though more approachable than Karl, was herself a force not to be trifled with.[38] To go with the religious rituals, she instilled a genteel and felicitous but dutiful Lutheran piety. (Bonhoeffer may have had his mother in mind when, in a fictional sketch, he portrayed an urbane middle-aged woman who went to church only as a "salutary discipline," suffering an "old windbag of a preacher" full of "sanctimonious prattle.")[39] But she fully shared her husband's faith in science, never hesitating to administer medications for whatever might ail the children. Over the course of his lifetime, Dietrich, like his siblings, would avail himself of various powders for aches and pains, sleeping pills as needed, and even stimulants for an extra boost in the middle of the day (or to forgo sleep and finish an assignment). He never traveled without an ample supply of medicaments in his shaving bag. A regular visitor would later allow that he had never seen pills flow so freely as in the Bonhoeffer home.

It would be a challenge for Dietrich to make his mark among his many talented siblings. The oldest, Karl-Friedrich, born in 1899, grasped the complexities of science with uncommon ease. The next in line, Walter, born the same year, would prove a gifted young writer and naturalist.[40] Klaus, born in 1901 and the brother closest to Dietrich in age, was a free spirit, though one with a sharp analytical mind; he once received a low mark in chemistry for refusing to put away his volume of Hegel during class.

Bonhoeffer's oldest sister, Ursula, born in 1902, inherited her father's zeal for clinical knowledge and would study social work until she married at the age of twenty-one. Ursel was followed by Christine in 1903, who like her brother Walter loved nature, receiving university honors in zoology. The eighth and youngest child, Susanne, born in 1909, three years after the twins, possessed rare emotional maturity and empathetic gifts. Had she not found fulfillment as a minister's wife, Susanne might well have followed in her father's footsteps and pursued a healing profession.[41]

From an early age, Dietrich was aware of his privilege and its obligations. But he was not troubled if, in the pursuit of things he considered just and true, he seemed egotistical as well as courageous—or that classmates sometimes found him arrogant. "No one dared get in his way when he stood up for someone else," he would write of his alter ego in the unfinished autobiographical novel. "Then he fought like a lion and was a fierce opponent." He might have acknowledged that his motivation to act was "less out of love for the individual than out of the need for responsibility at the core of his being."[42] But his peers, as he explained to his parents, were incapable of recognizing excellence, and were filled with envy. Only later in life would the sin of pride become a project for spiritual correction; in his school years, Bonhoeffer regarded his superior intellect as a plain fact.

This made even more vexing his inability to surpass the academic achievements of Maria Weigert, "the Jewish girl," who lived nearby in Grunewald. "Beautiful, brilliant and energetic," her teachers gushed. Dietrich wished his top-of-the-class status were not always qualified as "among the boys."[43] The daughter of a Berlin judge, and heir to a German banking fortune, Weigert remained best overall. It only made matters worse that Dietrich could not seem to get away from her. Even at the Individualist Club, the Bonhoeffers and the Weigerts often kept company together. Sometimes, along with other Grunewald friends, the families went on Sunday outings to the Müggelsee, a nearby lake; attired in their sturdy country clothes, they would meet in the Halensee train station—the women in Beiderwand dresses and the men in knickers, sack coats, and lace-up cap toes. Equipped with utensils, baskets of food, guitars, and other paraphernalia, the group would occupy an entire train car of the regional line.[44]

In a 1921 photograph of the Grunewald students in their classroom, the dark-haired Maria—one of only three girls in the class of fifteen—appears confident and at ease in her white blouse, bow, and dark skirt, gently smiling as she leans slightly on her desk. Dietrich, though three years younger, barely a teenager, already seems too big for his chair, dwarfing the boys seated next to him, with broad shoulders and a massive head.

In 1913, a year after moving to Berlin, while still renting the place near the crowded Tiergarten, the Bonhoeffers purchased a country home in Friedrichsbrunn, a village on the eastern ridge of the Harz Mountains. At first, the children were decidedly unimpressed. The move from Breslau had been bad enough. Now, with the woodsy Grunewald place still in the future, they were obliged to give up their rural retreat in Wölfelsgrund—a lovely spot with fruit trees and a large meadow and a cold stream nestled in a valley near the Bohemian border—for an old hunting lodge in an unfamiliar region. Getting to Friedrichsbrunn involved a three-hour train ride to Blankenburg and an additional half hour in two horse carriages up the mountainside through the dense spruce forest surrounding the hamlet. But the children soon discovered the many delights of the eastern Harz: excellent cross-country skiing in winter; lush, verdant hillsides and hiking trails in spring, and cool summer evenings.

The region was also rich in literary history, and in the library of the new house the Bonhoeffers created a special section dedicated to local authors. Theodor Fontane had lived in nearby Thale, the medieval village where his novel *Cécile* is set. In 1824, following a year of great discontent in his university studies, a restless young Heinrich Heine kept a journal of his wanderings through the mountains.[45] *The Harz Journey* (*Die Harzreise*) tells of "golden sunbeams" and "festive rays" pouring through "the dense greenery of the firs," and of "twittering birds," "rustling firs," and "streams splashing out of sight"; Heine would enjoy a "feeling of infinite bliss" elemented of the "green trees, thoughts, birdsong, melancholy, the blue of heaven, memory and fragrance twined together in sweet arabesques."[46]

Written a century after Heine's, Dietrich's own writings from Friedrichsbrunn convey a similar exuberance and longing. In the mornings, he read and wrote and played the piano. In the afternoons, he made for the hills to hike or simply to nap. On occasions when he and Sabine went walking with their mother, it was enough to listen quietly, as Paula spoke of literature, music, family matters, or education, and while deer grazed in the afternoon fields amid the sunlight's westering shadows. Sometimes the three followed a sloping path to the ridge called Pine Hill, and from a clearing in a thicket of heather bushes they would watch the sun set over "distant forests" and wooded meadows. At Pine Hill, a pair of birch benches was set against a wooden cross bearing an Old Testament inscription: "The souls of the righteous are in the hand of God and no torment will ever touch them."[47]

I n the summertime, Dietrich studied and cataloged the wild mushrooms he collected across the glades and meadows, taking "rapturous delight" just to pull them gently from the soil and identify them by name.[48] On day trips to the Bergrat Müller Pond, he carried empty tins to put them in, the arrangement being that his older sister Christine would grill the harvest for lunch if the younger children collected enough. A boulder in the upper meadow served as tabletop as Dietrich and his siblings feasted on "bright yellow chanterelles; chestnut browcaps; tall, feathered parasol mushrooms," as well as "handsome blue tricholomae; orange agaric; and countless pungent marasmi," and, in a pinch, "hardy edible porcini," which Christine served with new potatoes and brown bread. Eating the simple meal, luxuriating in the "the energy of forest, sun, water, each other's company . . . and freedom itself," the boy could sense "in the depths of his being" the infinite everywhere alive.[49]

Some evenings, children from the nearby villages joined the twins for games. Dietrich often surprised others with his fierce competitive streak, playing to win, at least when he perceived a fair match. And he was not infrequently a showy winner, one afternoon returning with a garland he had made for himself from wildflowers and cotton grass. When Klaus caught sight of his husky towheaded brother adorned like an ancient Olympian, he mocked him mercilessly. Dietrich quickly removed his laurels in embarrassment.[50]

Friedrichsbrunn would always remain a place to which Bonhoeffer felt emotionally connected, returning there throughout his life. For his grandmother Julie's ninetieth birthday, he escorted her and twenty guests on an eight-kilometer promenade through spruce and birch from Ramberg to Viktorshöhe, where a spectacular view of the hill and forest tumbling into the distant plains of Sachsen could be enjoyed from a massive timber-framed watchtower. In his last letters, written from a Gestapo prison, Bonhoeffer described the flooding memories of lying on his back "watching the clouds float across the blue sky in the breeze and listening to the sounds of the forest." Such memories and impressions, he said, no less than the places that inspired them—not only the eastern Harz but the central uplands (the Mittelgebirge) like the Thuringian Forest, and the Weser Uplands—"made me who I am."[51]

Those days in the Harz were languorous but ordered. Two servants and the housekeeper kept the cup candles burning on the windowsills, and lit the wall sconces and indoor lanterns when night fell. The firewood had been neatly stacked by the fireplace. The house would not be wired for electricity until 1943, and by then everything had come to ruin—the family gatherings, the musical evenings and the skit nights, the hiking parties to the *Feuerturm*, the days of reading and rest. Everything.

In March of 1918, Walter and Karl-Friedrich volunteered for military service in the Deutsches Heer, the land forces of the remaining monarchy.[52] It would prove to be the last year of the Great War. Like Karl-Friedrich, who left home with a knapsack full of physics books, Walter enlisted as an infantryman out of a sense of valor and idealism, his own kit including his books and notes on nature; unlike Karl-Friedrich, however, Walter did not return from the western front. During Lieutenant General Erich Ludendorff's Spring Offensive against the French and British, a shell exploded amid Walter's column.[53] Wounded in both legs, he languished in a field hospital before succumbing to infection on April 28, barely a month after his enlistment. Karl-Friedrich sustained injuries in the war as well, though his were slight.[54]

Walter was a gentle soul who loved the outdoors and was happiest at Friedrichsbrunn, where it was his custom to leave the house before sunrise with a thermos, binoculars, and notebook. He knew the local foresters by name and was always happy to join the townsmen on a hunt—though he could rarely bring himself to take aim at a deer or wild boar. He could easily spend hours listening to birdsong from a cluster of trees overlooking the meadow north of town, perfecting birdcalls on his whistle. A copy of Brehm's *Life of Animals* lay open on his desk as if it were a family Bible. Dietrich always felt closest to his older brother under the open skies.[55]

The family hardly knew how to respond to Walter's death, they who had experienced so little personal tragedy. Throughout the war years Dietrich had remained fairly indifferent to the deprivations of his countrymen. Amid the blight of the 1917 Turnip Winter, with its tremendous hardships of food shortages and rationing—the same year Ludendorff had rallied the nation for "total war"—Dietrich wrote his grandmother about a recent dinner party on Wangenheimstrasse featuring sausage soup, veal roast, flounder from Ostsee near Boltenhagen, fresh asparagus and carrots, fruit preserves, cheesecakes, and "very good wine"—"quite a lot" of it. Ham and eggs served with coffee, as well as bread and sweet butter, remained the standard for breakfast.[56]

Karl Bonhoeffer had turned fifty only a few weeks before that bright spring morning when a messenger delivered two telegrams, one concerning each son, to the Grunewald address. Sabine remembered her father turning ashen, retreating quickly into his study, where, for what seemed hours, he "sat bowed over . . . his face hidden in his hands."[57] No one had ever seen him so distraught or otherwise emotional. He would soon adopt a stoic frame of mind, keeping his grief to himself, but for many years he could not bear to remain in the room if Walter's name was mentioned; and for the next ten years, he would make no entries in his New Year's Eve journal, as he had always done before.[58]

The morning Walter left for war, Paula had run alongside the train as it slowly rolled out of the Thale station, telling her son over and over, "It's only space that separates us." After his death, she fell into a depression so severe that she ended up moving out of the house to spare the children the sight of her anguish. For more than a month in the home of the Schönes family, under the care of her husband and a colleague, Paula lay in bed, clutching Walter's last letter.[59] "Thinking of you with longing, my dears, every minute of the long days and nights," he had written from the field hospital. "Love from so far away."[60]

Twelve-year-old Dietrich was completely blindsided. At a dinner party in Friedrichsbrunn, he had serenaded Walter on the eve of his departure with a rendition of "Now, at the last, we say Godspeed on your journey," accompanying himself on the piano.[61] Bonhoeffer would later perceive in Walter's life "early fulfillment though death for a high purpose." At the time, though, it seemed that reality, once so beautiful and pure, was fractured. It could never be apprehended apart from sorrow; the seamless fabric of dailiness and eternity was torn asunder.[62] "Human nature, what has become of it?" his uncle von Hase said in the eulogy. "No sooner do the winds of death blow on it, than it returns to the earth in a single hour."[63]

Karl-Friedrich returned home from the war bitter and disillusioned, fiercely hostile to the monarchy, and declaring himself a socialist and an admirer of the English labor movement. He spouted Ludwig Feuerbach's critique of religion—that the idea of God is finally a projection of humanity's own longings for omniscience—and refused to take part in Advent services. Even more shocking to young Dietrich and Sabine, he openly criticized the family's musical evenings as bourgeois frippery on the part of people with no real talent. It was, Karl-Friedrich said, a waste of money better spent in support of working-class musicians.[64]

Not too long after Walter's death, Dietrich announced that he had decided to become a theologian.[65] Only thirteen years old, he had no doubt about the rightness of this path.

For a while there had been some talk of a career as a concert pianist. His skill as a sight reader made him everyone's favorite accompanist for Saturday musical evenings.[66] By the age of eight, he was playing chamber music with Karl-Friedrich on cello and Klaus on violin, and accompanying his mother, as she sang her beloved Gellert-Beethoven-Lieder—the spare, melancholy hymns inspired by the poetry of Christian Fürchtegott Gellert—and other Romantic songs. On Christmas Eve, the mother-and-son duo would perform in Carl August Peter Cornelius's Epiphany anthem, "The Three Kings," and also Advent hymns from the era of Alexander von Humboldt and Felix Mendelssohn: "The star shines out with a steadfast ray / The kings to Bethlehem make their way / And there in worship they bend the knee / As Mary's child in her lap they see."[67] As a gift to his parents on Pentecost Sunday, Dietrich composed a piece for voices based on Psalm 42, "Why art thou cast down, O my soul? . . . Hope thou in God." He would prove even more skillful as an arranger with his "trio setting" of Franz Schubert's "Gute Ruh"—"Rest Well"—from the popular nineteenth-century song cycle *Die schöne Müllerin*.[68] Ever eager to perform, he once brought his Boy Scout troop to attention with an animated rehearsal of his favorite impromptus.[69]

Yet he ultimately found his passion for music not as great as the one stirred whenever his thoughts turned to God, or simply when he read in one of his uncle von Hase's leather-bound volumes of theology. His decision was further validated by Leonid Kreutzer, the renowned teacher at the Berlin Music Conservatory, after Dietrich auditioned for one of the much-sought-after spots in the freshman class. Kreutzer knew the Bonhoeffers well, attending their musicals on occasion. He liked young Dietrich and was impressed enough by his technical proficiency to admit him into the conservatory. But he told the parents that the boy lacked "expressive color" and advised against a musical career. Nor was he convinced that Dietrich truly wanted to be a concert pianist or fully understood the demands of the discipline.[70]

The son's decision to become a theologian came as no great surprise to the mother. Paula had long recognized his attraction to ultimate questions. A family photograph captures the younger children "playing at baptisms" in the garden at Breslau. The face of the "wispy headed toddler in linen white knickers" seated beside his governess registers intense concentration, almost as if to say, *What a fine and solemn occasion.*

Sabine marveled at how ceremoniously her twin conducted himself, and compelled others to behave likewise, at their pretend church.[71] As mentioned, a very real religious inheritance was bequeathed Dietrich on his mother's side, his grandfather having been court chaplain to Wilhelm II at Potsdam, and his great-grandfather, the aged theologian in the painting, a colleague of Hegel's who was ever true to "the old true covenant of freedom and Christianity."[72] And at the Breslau salons hosted by Clara Kalckreuth von Hase, Paula's mother, theologians were as prized as artists and other scholars. Even in Bonhoeffer's paternal line, there were churchmen, some Swedenborgians, among the military officers, painters, sculptors, doctors, mayors, and counts.

None of this, however, mattered to Dietrich's older brothers when they learned of his plan. Not only was Karl-Friedrich by now an avowed socialist, but Klaus had become an ardent Weimar liberal, befriending Russian émigrés and writing treatises on international law. Both found religion a distraction from the urgent work of promoting equality and human rights. They were not merely surprised but also mortified at the news and, sounding very much like their father's sons, they warned that becoming a theologian would amount to a retreat from reality.

"*Look* at the church," they insisted. "A more paltry institution one can hardly imagine."[73]

Unmoved, Dietrich replied, "In that case, I shall reform it!"[74]

In 1921, at the age of fifteen, he read Eduard Meyer's two-volume *Origin and Beginning of Christianity*—with such excitement that he began signing his name, "Dietrich Bonhoeffer, theol."

K arl's salary in Berlin had permitted not only the country house at Friedrichsbrunn but also holidays for the entire family in resorts fashionable among the upper middle class. In Boltenhagen, a spa town on the Baltic Sea the Bonhoeffers particularly liked, Dietrich would play in the shallow waters near Breaker's Bridge, count jellyfish, build elaborate sandcastles with ramparts and moats. One summer afternoon in 1918, his attention was drawn by two seaplanes flying low, returning from patrol in the waters between Germany and Denmark. He was captivated by the sight and the roar of the engines as the two planes made their parallel ways beneath the midsummer sun. Suddenly the one nearer the coastline pulled up sharply, while the one farther at sea continued over Gross Schwansee toward the landing strip near the Pohnstorfer Moor. At first Dietrich thought that the first pilot was attempting some acrobatic maneuver, a stunt of the kind he had seen at the Grunewald air show. In fact, something had gone wrong. Not far into its steep climb, the first craft sputtered and stalled before entering into a wild downward spiral, finally crashing in a ball of flame only ten meters offshore.

With the other onlookers, Dietrich ran toward the crash site. Sections of the shattered wing, fuselage, and cockpit lay scattered in the shallow waters; soon, rescue workers arrived to carry away the pilot's gnarled and burned body.

Dietrich fell asleep quickly that night, exhausted by the day's events, but he woke up with a start sometime after midnight. He could not go to his mother—Paula had remained behind in Berlin, sending the three younger children on ahead in the care of their nurses. Outside, the dark sea churned in a violent gale. Sand blanketed the wicker chairs and tables, and the surf pounded the beach and surged over the castles and ramparts built earlier. As the wind caused an unfastened shutter to beat against the side of the house in loud, startling claps, the child sat up, as the image of the pilot's singed eyebrows returned to him and troubled his thoughts.[75]

Notwithstanding the disturbing events of that spring and summer, by the fall of 1918 Dietrich's journals and letters had once again become a chronicle of family contentment and privilege. He reports precocious reading—a Beethoven biography, Fontane's *Der Stechlin*, Wilhelm Raabe's *The Black Galley*, Hermann Hesse's *Knulp*, Willibald Alexis's *Der Werwolf*, Felix Dahn's *A Battle for Rome*, J. Teneromo's *Conversations with Tolstoy*, and Ferdinand von Raesfeld's novel *Hunting and War: A Novel from the Frontier*, inherited from Walter. The letters written during the month-long vacation are full of ruminations on his carefree pursuits. On Saturday afternoons, he and Sabine joined their mother for musical performances at the Staatsoper on Unter den Linden; otherwise, he was content to go with his governess, Kathe Horn, to a museum or gallery.[76]

Bonhoeffer's natural athleticism found an outlet in tennis, dance, and skiing, and he played the piano with vigor. But he had no interest in organized sports. Whatever their other rarefied tastes, most Grunewalders enjoyed the soccer matches of the home team, Berlin Hertha, as much as any of the thirty thousand who typically filled Gesundbrunnen Stadium (also known as the Plumpe, for the old-fashioned water pump that stood just outside the gates), singing beer songs and waving pennants. (Hertha had a good run from 1925 until 1933, playing in the national championship finals six times and taking home the Bundesliga title in 1930 and 1931.) The competitive streak Dietrich had shown from an early age, however, was not engaged by such spectacles.

DIETRICH BONHOEFFER AT GRUNEWALD GYMNASIUM, FOURTH
FROM THE RIGHT, 1920–21; MARIA WEIGERT IS FIFTH FROM LEFT,
SEATED TO THE RIGHT OF THE TEACHER WILLIBALD HEINIGER

As a student he channeled his extracurricular energies into the arts more than sports. As a high school senior, he played the lead in Goethe's *Egmont*, alongside Ulla Andreae, the niece of German Foreign Minister Walther Rathenau, playing Clärchen. Rathenau, who would be assassinated weeks later by ultranationalist military officers, attended the premiere. (Bonhoeffer reported to his grandmother how at school on the morning of June 24, 1922, he heard "a peculiar crack in the courtyard," not knowing it was gunfire or that "a pack of right-wing Bolshevik scoundrels" had ambushed his neighbor en route to the ministry.)[77] Theater remained a passion, as would any literary effort, studying languages (especially with his French teacher, Fräulein Lindauer) and sentimental novels.[78] He was always physically game, but his greatest thrills were of the mind, the senses, and, ultimately, the spirit.

Paula's schooling, with the help of some tutors, in the makeshift classroom off the kitchen, equipped each of her children admirably for the tumultuous years ahead. All excelled in high school and passed their college entrance exams before most of their classmates. But Dietrich was especially advanced, beginning secondary school at Friedrich-Werdersches Gymnasium before transferring to Grunewald Gymnasium in 1918 at the age of twelve. (When Sabine's time came to leave her mother's classroom, she would attend a small girls' school run by Fräulein Adelheid Mommsen, the daughter of the great classicist and Nobel laureate Theodor Mommsen.)[79] He proceeded to graduate from Grunewald by his seventeenth birthday, two years ahead of most in his class—German high schools typically take two or three years longer than the American system—and at a younger age than any of his siblings. Dietrich would complete his requirements for the *Abitur*, the national qualifying examination, in March 1923, receiving a diploma that guaranteed him a place at a German university. He scored high marks in all subjects except English and penmanship. Outside academics, he earned accolades in "Singing," though his highest grades overall were in gymnastics and behavior.[80] He had become fluent in Greek and Latin, competent in Hebrew and French. Over the next five years he would learn Italian, Spanish, and English. In his three-thousand-word matriculation essay, "Catullus and Horace as Lyric Poets," he chose Catullus, "the son of a wealthy, aristocratic family in Lombardy," who transforms "everything into passion," as his favorite. "The most impressive thoughts fade away," Bonhoeffer concluded, "but great emotions are eternal."[81]

CHAPTER TWO

1923–1924

~

"Italy Is Simply Inexhaustible"

Dietrich hatched his plan to make the Grand Tour as he lay in bed recovering from a concussion: on his eighteenth birthday he had slipped while ice skating with friends. He lived now in the university town of Tübingen, in one of the newer dwellings comprising a neighborhood near the train station. Frau Jäger's boardinghouse at 10 Uhlandstrasse had agreeably large windows and a garden.[1]

Though confined to his rooms, Dietrich appeared in good spirits when his parents arrived from Berlin, bearing gifts of writing paper, books, chocolates, tobacco, and an envelope of cash to spend as he wished. He had his sights set on a classical guitar at a music store in town. Still, there was something he had been wanting, "infinitely" more than even the "splendid instrument with the wonderful tone." He wanted to spend the summer in Italy. He was besotted at the thought: "the most fabulous thing that could happen to me." He allowed that "I can't even begin to imagine how great [it] would be."[2] Indeed, he would never be daunted by the inconceivable.

Dietrich had heard stories of his family's journeys to Italy. His great-grandfather Karl August von Hase, a lifelong friend of the Nazarenes (the painters who had ensconced themselves on the Pincian Hill), had made some twenty voyages to Rome in the early decades of the nineteenth century. It was on one of these trips that Hase made the acquaintance of Goethe, who was so favorably impressed as to offer him the prestigious post at the University of Jena.[3] Hase's sketchbooks, travel guides, and journals would circulate among his descendants over the years, inspiring new generations of travelers. They had the same effect on Dietrich as the sketches of the Forum and Palatine hanging in Walther Kranz's history classroom. Like most children of the Grunewald elite, Dietrich thrilled to the images of the sun-drenched

South and treasures of antiquity. What's more, young Dr. Czepan, under whose Latin tutelage the boy had so excelled, knew the Italian geography as well as his native Germany's.

It was only a matter of time, then, before Dietrich had resolved to make an *Italienreise* of his own.[4] And as he lay there convalescing, that resolution hardened.

"After thinking about it," he told his sister, "I want to do it so much that I can't imagine ever wanting to do it more than I do now."[5]

Plans fell quickly into place. Dietrich would join his brother Klaus, who was celebrating having passed the bar exam with a summer in Italy. Axel von Harnack, a Grunewald neighbor and son of the famous theologian Adolf von Harnack, had spent the fall semester in Rome and was eager to offer suggestions. Sabine had never been to Italy either, and though she was not invited to accompany her brothers, Dietrich encouraged her to "shower him with advice." But he also needed to enlist his twin for an urgent bit of business: persuading their parents that he was ready to travel on his own.[6] As yet he had not asked Karl and Paula's permission, let alone secured their support.

The moment of their visit was not the most opportune. Besides the skating accident and Dietrich's feverish state of mind, there was the fact that he had not yet finished a single university term. But knowing the force of his will, they listened with an open mind as he made his case.

"It is strange that the fees are less expensive for foreigners," he said. "Food and lodging are *both* very inexpensive and easy to find." Studying in Rome would definitely "*not* be more expensive than studying here. . . . Furthermore, many Germans live there." A fraternity brother was heading to Italy as well, and of course Klaus would never be far, whatever Dietrich got up to.[7] Finally, having worked the idea from every angle, Dietrich sighed in feigned exasperation, "You know, I am in a great quandary about how to transport my lute."

There was nothing he hadn't thought of: he already had the necessary two suitcases and a backpack, which he would check all the way through to Rome, "so I won't have to mail any packages" before leaving the country.[8] Perhaps that degree of ordered thought moved Dietrich's rationalist father. In any event, his parents agreed.

"Just think," he told Sabine, exultant, "I will be studying in Rome!"[9]

It had continued to be true that Dietrich's biggest concerns were not those of his nation. In the fall of 1923, when he matriculated at Tübingen, the German economy was succumbing to virulent hyperinflation. The French and Belgian armies had occupied the industrial Ruhr Valley after Germany had repeatedly defaulted on reparations for

World War I, as agreed in the Treaty of Versailles. Food riots broke out when German farmers stopped delivering produce to the cities.[10] Why should they bother, when paper money had become worthless? In turn, desperate urban workers looted the countryside, raiding farms to feed their families. Everywhere money disappeared like "water in the sand." Businesses failed, unemployment soared. The middle class exchanged furniture, clothing, jewelry, and art—whatever they could muster—for food and provisions. Cultural centers and charitable institutions, churches and hospitals were forced to close their doors for lack of funds. Within a two-year period, a tuberculosis outbreak spread to epidemic proportions, killing record numbers of people, while malnutrition, mental breakdowns, and suicides left few towns and cities untouched. As their means dwindled, thousands of students left school to look for work, almost always in vain.[11]

Dietrich, meanwhile, was still settling into college life. Shortly after arriving in Tübingen he discovered that he had outgrown his trousers. At seventeen he still had two inches yet to grow before reaching his adult height of six foot one. "The first thing I did was go shopping," he advised his parents, to whom, of course, the bills went. Not that he was ignorant of the national crisis; that would have been impossible. In the worst of it, a meal at the university refectory would cost a billion marks. For a loaf of bread he would need a half million. Dietrich would on occasion shell out fifteen billion marks to have a shirt laundered and starched. Saving where he could, he asked his older sister Christine, a student of zoology at Tübingen, to see to his routine laundry; she complied, though not happily. Nonetheless, he presented his mother with a wardrobe inventory to frame his requests for a new linen jacket and pants that might serve for warmer days in Friedrichsbrunn.[12] As for shoes, he felt he could get by with what he had, his sturdy pair of Haferlschuhe, which would be his staple for the school year, being in "excellent condition."

His cozy room at Frau Jäger's was always adorned with fresh-cut flowers. He liked the simplicity of his "four naked walls, table, bed, two chairs and two windows," choosing to do most of his reading and writing there, because "everything is quiet and no one interrupts you."[13] He would need to give the work his full attention, having matriculated in a faculty whose distinguished graduates included Philipp Melanchthon, G. W. F. Hegel, and Friedrich Wilhelm Schelling. A century earlier, Ferdinand Christian Baur had founded the influential Tübingen School of Theology, which promoted a critical analysis of the Bible grounded in history, the method of interpretation often called "higher criticism." By approaching the scriptures primarily as historical documents rather than revealed truth, the new critics sought to understand the biblical writings in their original contexts. As part of this modern perspective on ancient doctrine, Dietrich took classes with the New Testament scholar Adolf Schlatter, and with Jakob Wilhelm Hauer, an Indologist who would go on to found the notorious German Faith Movement.

Intensive though his studies were, they did not keep Dietrich from extracurricular activities. Joining Der Igel—the Hedgehog—he followed his father and his uncle Otto, both natives of Tübingen, who lived at the same fraternity during their first two university semesters, having been proud "Foxes" (as first-year pledges were called). Founded in 1871, Der Igel was known as a "black fraternity," since the first class of pledges had refused to take part in the elaborate ceremonies of the other associations or to don their garish attire. Rather than parade through the village in gowns of gold and purple like proud provincial squires of old, they sported robes "of black-grey, mouse-grey and silver-grey."[14] This dour preference notwithstanding, the Hedgehog's membership was drawn from the same upper middle class as the rest of the university; all venerated the same ideals of Bismarckian nobility, which in 1923 were chiefly martial virtue and a united Germany under Prussian rule. For his "body guard," which is to say, the upper classman who helped him navigate the complexities of pledge life, Dietrich was assigned Fritz Schmid, a student of natural science. Dietrich's older brothers had each spent a year at Tübingen. But in 1919 Karl-Friedrich, who had flirted with communism since his return from the war, refused to join a fraternity upon learning that most of his prospective brothers thought the labor strikes in Stuttgart and Munich should be suppressed.[15] Klaus condemned the student societies as undemocratic and woefully nationalistic, at best a distraction from his study of international law. But Dietrich didn't seem to mind the conservative posturing; anyway, he would let his earnest siblings worry about politics and human rights. Still, there would be at least one young dissident voice at the Hedgehog. During the academic year 1923–24, a certain "Fox Kordau" resigned on the grounds that fraternity life ran counter to the "spirit of Christianity." Kordau "had tried and had pretended" to meet expectations, but finally realized that his commitment to "practical Christianity" left him no option but to renounce "this painful compromise."[16]

But Bonhoeffer did not see what the fuss was about.[17] "I took the customary step for every dutiful son and became a Hedgehog," he explained in his statement of initiation.[18] And so, in Der Igel's sprawling mansion (which had once been christened Die Bierkirche, "the

Beer Church") on the "hill behind the squared-stone walls of the castle Twingia," with a fine view of the Neckar River at the southerly point where it encircled a trace of "beautiful green islands," Bonhoeffer luxuriated in the well-appointed music rooms and parlors. In the afternoons, he would accompany the chamber music trio on the grand piano, teaching himself how to play the lute in the course of his first year.

He also distinguished himself as a graceful dancer, preferring the open waltz, the quadrille, and the française. He also found time to take up fencing.[19]

In addition, there were three or four one-hour tennis matches every week, which by most reports he usually won. There was hiking in the Schönbuch Forest, where he sometimes visited the twelfth-century Cistercian monastery and the sunlit cliffs of the medieval village of Bebenhausen.[20] It is not certain whether Bonhoeffer participated in the monthly *Stocherkahnrennen*, the race of punting boats on the Neckar whose goal was only not to finish last—as each member of the losing crew had to drink a "half-litre of sun-warmed cod-liver oil."

The letters and journals of his freshman year are reports of a confident, occasionally temperamental, eighteen-year-old, happiest when playing the piano or the lute in the great hall, performing Schubert lieder and learning new folk dances.[21] Classmates spoke of an affable young scholar who excelled in academics while finding time for music and sports with enviable ease.

D uring the fall term of 1923, Bonhoeffer spent the last two weeks of November as an enlisted member of the Ulm Rifles Troop. All his fellow Foxes joined this training program of the Black Reichswehr. Try as he might, though, Bonhoeffer's brief foray into "quasi-military service" was not a success. Accustomed as he'd always been to governesses, tutors, and housekeepers, he had no gift for roughing it as a soldier must. On holidays in the eastern Harz, even when the family took their Sunday-afternoon walk to the *Feuertum*, the fire tower, at the forest's edge, some servant would come along to chaperone the children or serve a hearty picnic. On his second day at the Ulm training camp, Bonhoeffer was reprimanded for emptying his washbasin out the bathroom window (rather than in the nearby cesspool; his penalty was to scrub down the barracks with a toothbrush). While most of the other men spent free time playing cards or board games, Bonhoeffer read Kant and played the piano. Still, he did manage to learn the elements of shooting, and by the time camp ended, he had grown fond of his superiors and the camaraderie of the barracks.[22]

Proud of his accomplishment at Ulm—he had endured a Hedgehog rite of passage—he was nevertheless glad to be back at Frau Jäger's. As he told his parents, it was a relief to eat with a proper knife and fork and bathe with warm water.[23]

He left for Italy on the afternoon of April 3, 1924. Toting his leather-bound Baedeker, his pens, books, and writing paper, and his saratoga—as well as wardrobe for warmer climes—he appeared in every way the sophisticated traveler. In this *Italienreise*, Bonhoeffer was, as described, following family tradition, but he was also expressing a more personal desire to cross borders and make discoveries in his quest for originality.[24]

"Fantasy begins to transform itself into reality," he wrote in his journal, as the train crossed the Brenner Pass and headed north into the Italian Alps. He worried that reality would not meet his expectations, that he would be left disappointed; and he worried over the prospect that all his wishes would be fulfilled! In Bolzano while waiting for a transfer, Bonhoeffer found a quiet corner in a rose garden near the station, where the "red glow of sunset" over the "magnificently beautiful Dolomites" set a deliciously melancholy mood.[25] But by the time the train reached Bologna, he found himself happily drawn into spirited conversation with other passengers, mostly Italians. During a four-hour layover, he and his cabin mates would stream into the city streets—a banker, two tourists, and a Catholic theology student. Under "beautiful clear moonlight," they strolled along the Via Emilia to the Piazza Maggiore through arcades and porticos on a two a.m. walking tour of the "venerable former capital of Northern Etruria,"[26] standing under the shadows of La Garisenda, "the most towering of the leaning towers," all the way to the San Pietro Cathedral. Bonhoeffer was thrilled that his first attempts at real conversation in Italian had gone so well, pronouncing them in his journal "a great success."[27]

The train departed Bologna just after daybreak, reaching Rome in early afternoon, a twenty-four-hour journey in all. Bonhoeffer's jubilant mood was deflated somewhat by the shock of the routinely chaotic train station. As he hankered for a hot shower and a change of clothes, his first encounters in the Eternal City were with the sudden swarm of beggars and hucksters, followed by the "knavery" of an overly solicitous cabdriver and of a *pensione* desk clerk demanding full payment in advance for his stay, as well as for the previous two nights. Every logistical complication—and there were many—irritated him, and the kaleidoscope of new impressions left him disoriented. "It is confusing," he wrote. The "enormous bustle on the streets," traffic rushing by "at furious speeds," "cars with fascists throwing pamphlets," grown men shouting to one another across crowded piazzas, "women with baskets of flowers, colorful oil carts juggling through the masses with much screaming"—he was a long way from the Grunewald. The "later it gets," he wrote, "the greater the turmoil in the streets."[28]

Belying the stylized umbrage he takes in his *Tagebuch*, Bonhoeffer was soon having a wonderful time. By the end of the week, in fact, his diary entries suggest a state of near giddiness; and in the story told over the next six weeks, a series of revelatory and rapturous moments build to a crescendo of previously unimagined joy.

The Coliseum conveyed incredible "power and beauty." He lingered "in reverie" for an hour in the ancient arena, now "overgrown" and "entwined with the most luxurious vegetation," encircled by "palm trees, cypress, pine, herbs, and all sorts of grasses," the overgrowth only heightening the mystical splendor. "The great Pan is not dead," he wrote.[29] He visited the Forum, the Palatine, the triumphal arch of Emperor Septimius Severus, and the Pincio, in whose monastery his great-grandfather von Hase had sojourned among the Nazarenes. Every sight elicited a superlative. The Palatine was "the most beautiful place in Rome," graced by "magnificent grounds, spacious views," and traces of archaic houses and imperial palaces. The blend of humanist and Christian expression appealed to Bonhoeffer. In the weeks ensuing, he followed the way of his Baedeker: the Museo Nazionale Romano, the Pincio (again), Ponte Molle, the Trevi Fountain, the Santa Maria sopra Minerva, the Callixtus catacombs, the Via Appia, the Vatican, Trajan's Forum, the Villa Borghese, the Villa Farnesina, a flash of Titian, Raphael, Leonardo. It was all so intoxicating that he misplaced his travel money, precipitating a frantic search, retracing his steps, before he found it in his hotel room. The city's offerings seemed endless, though he did not rate every sight as sublime. He was disappointed, for instance, by the Capitoline, with its lumbering Renaissance style and "garish reconstruction." The "few old ruins" and "the grand freestanding staircase" should have been left undisturbed, he decided. The Pantheon's exterior surfaces and "uniform architectural structure" seemed compromised by "atrocious" interior renovations, thanks to Vatican impositions and all those sixteenth-century pontifs who "lacked any sense of style and good taste."[30] Good thing, he added, that Roman Catholicism was much greater than the popes and their minions. Bonhoeffer's Italian journals, with their mannered entries recorded after each day's brisk excursion, linger longingly on the churches. His brother Klaus, who'd joined him in Rome, gravitates to other interests. On one occasion, Klaus is seen entering a small chapel at Vespers, only to exit quickly. But Dietrich retreats to a small chapel at Vespers, following the canons' every move with rapt attention. In the Lateran Church, its apse lined with mosaics and open to the air, a "feeling of mystery" drew him toward a candle-lit alcove behind the confessional, where the "prophets of the Bernini school" kept their eternal silent watch.[31]

His Roman itinerary led to "magnificent cloisters" and vestigial nooks, and always to deeper mysteries. Entering the "magnificent old basilica" di San Paolo fuori le Mura just before sunset, Bonhoeffer felt himself immersed in unexampled purity and shadowy enchantment, the place "full of atmosphere" amid the "organ music and angelic singing from a darkened side chapel." He walked home along the Via Ostiense, as the fading daylight turned from yellow to red and blue. Large tatters of rosy clouds "emerged and shimmered across the sky," the "deep blue[s] of nightfall" transfiguring the "deep green cypresses and pines," so that houses along the way stood as if in the glory of Eden.[32] The Bonhoeffer brothers rented a room from a family named Joccas that spoke only Italian, though they might easily have found expatriate German or German-speaking landlords. Mealtimes in the boardinghouse were a veritable Tower of Babel, Dietrich said, with "Italians, Russians, Greeks, French, Britons"—and at least two Germans—sitting at the common table trying to make conversation.[33]

Sometimes, daunted by the effort required to be social, Dietrich took a book and dined alone in a trattoria. The affable Klaus never felt such a need. One night Dietrich met Maria Weigert for dinner near the Trevi Fountain. His former Grunewald classmate was spending the summer with relatives in Rome. After the two had enjoyed a "good robust wine," Dietrich bade his onetime rival good evening and retreated to an overturned pillar in the Forum to dream "magnificent

dreams." Like the young Goethe captured in Tischbein's portrait, recumbent among the ruins in the Roman Campagna, Bonhoeffer sat beside the three columns of the Temple of Castor and Pollux, with the blue darkness as "background for the glowing orange trees" of the Pincio.

He had shipped a small library from Berlin to Rome, but aside from a few stolen moments in cafés or before bedtime—he mentions one stormy morning spent "a little in Heiler" (presumably the Marburg theologian Friedrich Heiler), and also dipping into some Goethe, mostly *Faust*—he found little time for reading.[34] While taking in the city on foot, he read only until the skies cleared, preferring to devour—as he would put it— the book of experience. He did keep one actual book, the Baedeker, always within reach, and on occasion also consulted Jacob Burckhardt's guide to Italian painting. Burckhardt held that art should be met with a studied admiration tempered by a certain willful naïveté—and this combination inspired in Bonhoeffer no few sophomoric judgments: to the width of the mosaic arches at St. Maria Navicella he ascribed an "architecturally unflattering effect," and there was "nothing special" about the Santa Prassede—true perhaps if one considers only the plain stone wall and "rather inauspicious door" on the street.[35]

But such pseudo-intellectual hiccups—and there were but few— hardly diminish an abiding appreciation of the world's splendor, one then typical of the wellborn. It is the critic's prerogative, he said, to "arbitrarily interpret, interpret, and further interpret the artworks." But Bonhoeffer was content to approach beauty more as an expectant admirer. "I believe that interpretation is not necessary in art," he said.[36] In this refusal, he maintained an Aristotelian purity: intuition formed by refinement and learning was enough to apprehend the beautiful and

ROME CIRCA 1920

the good, which categories in classical times would have been considered transcendental.

H e was amazed by how naturally he adapted to the "different atmosphere" and made himself at home. Even the Santa Maria della Concezione dei Cappuccini on the Via Veneto—the place where the bones of four thousand friars lay in their famous crypt and desiccated corpses, draped in Franciscan habit, sat upright—seemed inviting. "Lit only by dim natural light seeping in through cracks"—the spectacle had once been savagely mocked by Martin Luther as a heap of "Pope's dung."

On Palm Sunday 1924, Bonhoeffer rose early and hurried to make the morning Mass at St. Peter's Basilica. He went in anticipation of a grand spectacle, which he had read about in his Baedeker and in Goethe; he was not expecting the profoundly meaningful experience that transpired.

In north German Lutheranism, Palm Sunday had come to represent a brief, oddly formal pause on the way to Easter Morning. But the Sunday Mass at St. Peter's proved much more than the mere baton passing it had become in the evangelical sprint to the resurrection. The service was "infused completely with the *expectation* of the Passion." Bonhoeffer found a place next to a young woman who invited him to follow along in her Latin missal, as she spoke the soft musical cadences of the liturgy; the creedal invocation of the Lord's conception and birth (*"qui conceptus est de spiritu sancto, natus ex Maria Virgine"*—"who by the power of the Holy Spirit became incarnate of the Virgin Mary"); the "tender and melodious" responses of the people. As the music and spoken word echoed in the vast candle-lit vault, the sun beaming in through the cupola, Bonhoeffer was seized by a thought that would remain the most enduring insight of his trip: "The universality of the church!"[37]

The final benediction left him wanting more. So after lunch it was on to the Chiesa del Gesù, the "magnificent church" near the Palazzo Altieri, which housed the crypt of St. Ignatius of Loyola. Bonhoeffer marveled at the multitude of "white-robed Jesuits," swaying like a "sea of flowers," who read passages from Lamentations, while large families waited their turn at the confessionals, "illuminated by slowly darkening altar candles."

During Vespers at the Trinità dei Monti, forty girls, "in a solemn procession wearing nun's habits with blue or green sashes," took vows of poverty, chastity, and obedience. They sang the canonical hour with "unbelievable simplicity, grace and great seriousness." There was "not a trace of routine to be observed," and the "whole thing gave one an unequalled impression of profound, guileless piety."[38] It was "worship in the true sense." Standing outside on the terrace above the Spanish steps, Bonhoeffer savored the "most magnificent view overlooking the domes of Rome," as the sky, bathed in the red light of the sunset, once again offered its intimation of ethereal glory. "*Magnifico!*" he sighed.

"It was the first day on which something of the reality of Catholicism began to dawn on me," he wrote in his journal.[39]

M ost of Bonhoeffer's Holy Week entries record his emotional reactions to the sweep of magnificent events, but in one intriguing exception he recounts a boy leaving the confessional with his father. From the vestibule, Bonhoeffer observed the pair make their way to the front altar to light a candle, only for the child to break off suddenly and return to the booth. Why had he done that?

The boy, Bonhoeffer was certain, had remembered an unconfessed sin.

Earlier that same day, Bonhoeffer had stood transfixed before *The Boy Extracting a Thorn*, a first-century sculpture in the Capitoline. The statue moved him as no other in the museum had, he said. Now, as he contemplated this child raised to be "excessively scrupulous," and longing for purity, Dietrich was outraged. He resolved that such heightened self-scrutiny, and the fear it bred of error, was the "worst crime one can commit against the young"—even more egregious "in relation to the church."[40] The church, he concluded, should teach its children that grace forgives all the sins—spoken and unspoken—of a contrite heart.

Four days later, on Holy Thursday, Bonhoeffer was back in St. Peter's for the early Mass. He returned in the afternoon for the great procession to the papal altar, after which the priests swept the altar clean, in a ritual of purification. The next day, Good Friday, he was again among the first to arrive for the early service, which was, he said, distinguished by the "extraordinarily festive adoration of the cross," before which the priests knelt, kissing it.[41]

By the afternoon Mass, he was following along with a missal of his own, a gift from his new friend, a Catholic seminarian by the name of Platte-Platenius (who had been among the train passengers taking in Bologna by moonlight). Into his notebook Bonhoeffer feverishly copied the "Christus factus," the "Benedictus" from the Gospel of St. Luke; and, once again, the Miserere, the beautiful penitential prayer in Psalm 51: "*Miserere mei, Deus, secundum magnam misericordiam tuam*," "Have mercy on me, O God, according to your steadfast love." He registered not a hint of Protestant discomfort when a doughy-faced castrato descended from amid the choir to sing three alto solos. In fact, the eunuch's song produced quite the opposite effect: "a peculiar rapturous ecstasy . . . thoroughly inhuman."[42]

Bonhoeffer held the missal close, as a catechumen might. "Every [word] flows from the main theme of the Mass; the sacrificial death and its continuous reenactment in the sacrificial Mass of communion."[43]

That same evening, he engaged in a rare theological debate. Amid the exhilarating pageantry of Holy Week there had hardly been occasion for more than the odd and fleeting defense of the Protestant faith. But Platte-Platenius provoked Bonhoeffer. The seminarian claimed that modern Catholicism remained "fundamentally the same as early Christianity," the creeds and councils of the Magisterium having moreover "clarified" and "made intelligent [*sic*] the essence of the faith." Bonhoeffer took the bait, replying with the conventional Reformation point of view: Catholicism had "falsified the original" and turned the effervescent spirituality of the early Christians into static dogma. In allowing the symbolic and doctrinal encrustations to fall away, Protestantism had restored Christianity to its primordial purity.

But that was as far as the duel of budding theologians went.[44] Fairly consumed by his desire to get to the next Mass on time, to worship in what Martin Luther had called the "synagogues of Satan," Bonhoeffer had no interest in an extended back-and-forth.[45] He would continue on his blissful way through the Eternal City: "*Das Stück Erde*," he wrote, "*dass ich so sehr liebe*" ("This piece of earth, that I so very much love").[46] His journal's only harsh words for Italian Catholicism— "The objective fact certainly never plays the most important part"—he would later cross out in black ink.[47] He would not, however, cross out his criticism of German Lutheranism as "*provinziell, nationalistisch und kleinbürgerlich*"—provincial, nationalistic, and small-minded.

When Bonhoeffer entered the Basilica of St. John Lateran for the Saturday consecration of fire and water, he found the baptismal font lavishly decorated and ringed by "delightfully lively" priests in "joyous expectation." The Gloria prayer of the Mass carried the promise but still not the fulfillment of the resurrection. It seemed an exquisite agony. As a child of the Reformation, he was unfamiliar with the long day of waiting, the no-man's-land of Holy Saturday. Pondering the mystery of that singular place, he imagined two types of Christian. One stands always in the expectation of "that which is coming." Gazing into eternity, he speaks eloquently of heaven's glories and the streets of gold but stumbles in the here and now—and "thus loses the objectivity needed for the present moment." The second type lives in the present moment "to an exceptional degree." He might be called the Christian existentialist, pensive and brooding, but he braves the extremes and grasps at the infinite in the mundane.[48] Bonhoeffer wanted to be in the company of the latter, immersed in the "objectivity of worldly grace," to abide with those "profound individuals" who, realizing that they have no "ultimate escape from earthly tasks and difficulties into the eternal, drink the earthly cup to the dregs."[49]

To Platte-Platenius, Bonhoeffer, with his insatiable appetite for dazzling religious spectacle, must have seemed ripe for conversion. He certainly treated him that way. But Bonhoeffer insisted that he was not on a search for greater religious authority. In fact he mentions church doctrine in his journal only to lament how Catholic dogma veils the beautiful and "ideal." Even a personal exchange with Pope Pius XI (although what Bonhoeffer called a "personal meeting" was in fact a chance encounter during a public audience) earned a dismissal: "Nothing special."

Nor was he enthralled to spectacle as such. At the city's Armenian church, the impression "was that of an eastern fairy-tale play." The whole ceremony proceeded with "enormous pomp," "skillful display," and dazzling colors. And the ritual of opening and closing the altar's curtain proposed yet another way of seeing the Easter story. But he was simply not transported as he was at any of the Catholic churches. On Easter Sunday, he attended the High Mass at St. Peter's with Platte-Platenius, marveling at the choir of the Sistine Chapel which was singing in full Paschal splendor. "One can hardly conceive of anything so magnificent." But after days of so many magnificent moments, Bonhoeffer realized with a heavy heart that Holy Week had drawn to an end, and with that time had come to leave Rome, this city that had grown "dearer and more familiar to me than any other." He would be returning in two weeks to settle in for another month, but for now he would venture on to Sicily. Following an afternoon performance of Beethoven's Violin Sonata No. 5, the Spring Sonata, Bonhoeffer returned to his room at Signora Joccas's to pack.[50]

He would depart the Eternal City feeling "supersaturated." But in the light of morning, and with his brother Klaus seated alongside him on the train, hunched over his maps and legends, Bonhoeffer's appetite for new prospects was whetted. Sipping a cup of coffee from his thermos he resolved that though the cupolas, twisted spires, and domes of Rome were now behind him, he must content himself with whatever delights and surprises might await him. He would not be disappointed. On April 28, 1924, he wrote Sabine to say that he and Klaus had reached Girgenti: "the temples situated by the sea," the sunsets "completely red" and "magnificent blue," the "sumptuous garden[s] filled with fruit trees," the "colossal cacti" overhanging the cliffs above the water, and "a sea, ranging in color from sky-to steel-blue," ever shimmering in the background—he gave it all its due.[51]

But even two days earlier while still in San Giovanni, tip of the boot, he wrote his twin of basking in the "unbelievably alluring sweet scents" of the gardens there, of feeling as if the "old veils" had been lifted from his mind and "much more beautiful things [had] become real." As if a new world had been "born in oneself."[52]

"Magnificent fog heralds the coming of the sun in fantastic colors," he wrote, "but it only heralds it. Quietly, but only in the remote distance, one anticipates what will be," until "finally the sun is there in all its magnificence."[53]

Before the end of the first day in Sicily, Dietrich and Klaus were swimming in the Africanuum with some other young men they had met on the way. "How sad that we can stay in one place for only 2 days," Dietrich wrote. "One could live here a long time."[54]

In Syracuse, older brother Klaus had struck up a conversation with an Italian soldier who said he could get the brothers "a visa to visit the colonies."[55] After perusing a map, Klaus, animated by "imaginative thoughts and thrilling travel prospects," persuaded Dietrich to join him on an unscheduled excursion to North Africa. On April 29, 1924, the brothers climbed aboard a freighter for Libya.[56] Neither had bothered to inform Karl and Paula of the plan.

They sailed into the Mediterranean among a "gaggle" of soldiers, immigrants, Turks, and Arabs, the cramped passenger quarters in steerage class a veritable traveling roadhouse. After a feast of meatballs and spaghetti, the men commenced a long night of merrymaking, with plenty of sweet wine, coffee, and cigarettes, and soon they had broken out in song. Dietrich strummed a guitar; Klaus took up someone's violin; others played horns or hit sticks together. One of them worked over a lute. They belted out songs of the sea, of romance and adventures. Dietrich and Klaus had never before been in such rowdy company, Dietrich generally disapproving of that sort of ambiance. But on this overnight voyage to Libya, the Bonhoeffer brothers caroused with abandon and, it would seem, to excess.

During a stop in Malta, Klaus rushed to the deck and, steadying himself against the railing, puked into the sea. But he would have no regrets, eventually telling his parents that though their quarters had not been as comfortable as second class, they were "certainly 10 times more interesting." Dietrich seemed to have fared better, or at least he kept the details to himself. At daybreak, he gazed toward the southern horizon until, as in a dream, the harbor of Tripoli appeared. Most biographers portray the fortnight in North Africa as an ordeal that Bonhoeffer sorely regretted. Disoriented and afraid in an unfamiliar culture, he returned to Palermo, it is said, as soon as possible, only then "able to breathe freely again."[57] It is also said that he never spoke about the trip to his family.

But letters and notes published in 2003—and photographs made public—reveal a less disagreeable experience. Bonhoeffer encountered a side of life on those distant shores utterly foreign to him, a whirlwind of strange impressions, sounds, and smells; but his responses to such novelties were those of an attentive, curious, and mostly generous observer, not the misgivings of a pampered tourist.[58] In 1924 Libya remained under Italian occupation, enforced at times by brutal oppression, and Bonhoeffer's comments are striking for their sympathy toward the native Muslims.

"What enrages most," he said, "is that a people like the Arabs, who have such a well-developed sense of tradition and culture, are to be transformed into slaves. When one sees that [they] are treated with great brutality and vulgarity by the Italian soldiers, one can understand their bitterness and callous fear." In Tripoli, the Bonhoeffers were picked up at the harbor by a fellow German. They were surprised to hear that news of their arrival had made the city's Italian newspaper,

PHOTO TAKEN BY DIETRICH BONHOEFFER OF CAMEL MARKET, TRIPOLI, LIBYA

Corriere di Tripoli. After checking into their hotel—an Arab building built in the European manner—the brothers, despite fatigue from the riotous night before, made their way through the sunbaked streets of the port city.[59]

That first morning they took a bus to visit an oasis market, where a "colorful throng of peculiar figures" and natives from the interior sold and traded wares. Impressed by the "incredible calm and precision" of the work and the unfamiliar rhythms of the place, Dietrich and Klaus appeared more intrigued than fretful, gamely absorbing the culture shock.[60]

"Even now it seems like a dream to me," Klaus wrote. "Arabs, Bedouins, and Negroes sitting on donkeys in great, picturesque white cloaks or with laden camels. The houses are low and chalk-white. The living quarters open onto the street. The artisans live in certain streets according to their professions. The streets are narrow in the inner city, unpaved, and very dusty; yet they are not dirty as they are in Italy. It is also a lot quieter."

Klaus continued, "The pictures of the market and of our walks to the sea were fabulously beautiful. Outside the city one sees Bedouin tents along with their inhabitants, to whose face and form the long white robes lend a brilliant appearance."[61]

If an open mind can be indicated by a willingness to cross borders and observe with respect, the brothers' notes from North Africa, despite the freight of some cultural bias, reveal something even more: a generous heart. Dietrich, no less than Klaus, allowed his intuitive judgments to be continually tested by strangers, and while their accounts may at times "mirror their ambivalent experience of both being tourists and acting as amateur ethnographers"—as the Bonhoeffer scholar Robert Steiner wrote in a fascinating analysis of the 1924 trip to Libya—they lack the defensive element, and, though written in a "telegraphic style," lay open a world.[62]

"Day before yesterday we drove into the interior of the country for 2 days with our acquaintance from Stuttgart. By chance a troop of Italian soldiers drove with us. They even took us with them by car a good bit of the way, about 2½ hours, and provided us with lodging. We found ourselves at the end of the earth. The elevation was 600–700 meters."

Another journey into the interior two days later by car took the brothers to the desert outpost of Gharyan, one hundred kilometers south of Tripoli on the edge of the Nafusa Mountains. Dietrich wrote,

As far as the scenery goes, the mountain range gives the impression of being very peculiar, but extraordinarily beautiful. Because a large group of Italians chanced to arrive on the same day as we did—I don't know why—great festival performances by the native blacks, Arabs, and Bedouins had been planned. Some of the performances involved fabulously clever tricks. The Bedouins' races with their amazing horses were very grand. At furious speeds they readied their rifles, shot, and then, as if it were all a game, hurled their rifles into the air and caught them. We took several pictures of this, as well as some of a very amusing Negro dance.

As the sun was setting we took a short walk. Several Arabs whom we met on our walk spoke to us. When they discovered that we were Germans they were incredibly friendly. They showed us a lot of things. Moreover, they said we were the first Germans who'd been there, and that was why they were so happy. It gets cold after sunset, especially compared to the day-time temperature, which is when the Gibli—the south wind—so hated by the natives—is blowing; [the temperature] has been known to reach 58 Celsius (136 F). In spite of the terrible heat one doesn't feel ill. The air is very dry, never humid, always windy.

Dietrich found the southern night sky "truly magnificent." The heavens "blazed in deep blues against the sharp contours of the mountains," strewn with "a few isolated . . . olive trees." When the stars appeared in "radiant light," the night sky flared against the vast and brilliant blackness. It was "wonderful."

In the early morning, he went to the window of his stone hut and watched as townswomen walked homeward in the "translucent" glow of sunrise. They had gone in darkness to milk the goats. Some men rode to the watering holes on donkeys, as caravans arrived with wares for the city markets. Crowds soon gathered there and in the tearooms, or stood around in the street, singing in monotone from the Koran to the accompaniment of tambourines. All the native people stopped and listened devoutly, Dietrich noted, and gave generously to the collection of alms that followed.

"I imagine that it was very similar in ancient Israel, where the situation was surely comparable."[63] After a full day in the Middle East, Dietrich said, "you are reminded in an astonishing way of Old Testament scenes and atmosphere." It seemed to the theology student that in general "an immense similarity" existed between Islam and the lifestyle and piety recorded in the Old Testament." In Islam, as in Judaism, everyday life and religion were not separated at all. "Even in the Catholic Church they are separated, for the most part." German Protestantism, on the other hand, was defined by the separation. "At home one just goes to church. When one returns a completely different life begins. It is thoroughly different for the Muslims."

After a brief meeting, Gharyan's *kadi*, the local Muslim judge, finding the Bonhoeffer brothers sympathetic, gave them permission to step inside the Great Mosque, so long as they removed their shoes and observed custom. "It would really be very interesting to study Islam on its own soil," Dietrich wrote later that evening, "to probe more fully the cultic and social aspects of the religion." He had been happy to oblige the *kadi* on the former but remained frustrated that his access to the prayer rooms had been limited.

Before returning to Tripoli, Dietrich and Klaus received an unexpected invitation to a "princely reception" in the tent of a Bedouin chief. Details remain vague on the events that followed. They may have tripped over political issues or caused an unintended slight. Dietrich also came down with a violent stomach bug, which surely could have exacerbated the situation. Whatever the case, the desert excursion ended abruptly, with the two finding themselves whisked "away in an [Italian] officer's car as unwelcome guests."[64] The diary offers no insight, though it is clear that Dietrich, in the end, could not fathom this new religious world, and to his great credit he would not pretend otherwise. Despite a habit, entirely contemporary, of trading in generalizations, he did not use his own misstep, whatever it may have been, as an excuse for blanket judgments. He remained instead a charitable if sometimes perplexed observer of the unfamiliar. He would leave under no illusion that his brief foray into Muslim lands had equipped him to understand.[65] He felt he was but a "completely empty container" into which "enormous quantities of the heaviest materials had been thrown."

On the voyage back to Italy, Dietrich described feeling as if fetters had been removed from his limbs. It was as if he had dodged a great disaster.

From a café in Syracuse, he wrote in his diary on May 10, 1924, that should he ever return to Africa, he would need to bring a more precise measure, or be reduced once again to speechlessness and passivity. "Real reinforcement through extensive study will be necessary," he allowed specifically of the Islamic world, "in order to avert the catastrophe, because what one has seen was enormous." His "journey to the end of the earth" had led finally to a certain interpretive defeat, which he accepted with humility and as an invitation to further education and enquiry.

That night in Syracuse, Dietrich sat with Klaus "for a long, long time" behind the ruins of a Greek stage overlooking the "flawless" Mediterranean, "smooth as glass" in the last light of day. In the gentle air of the spring evening, and the wordless company of his brother, Dietrich relished the "indescribably harmonious quality" of the moment.

"When night had finally fallen and the stars came out, we went swiftly on the path to Giardini. . . . We were home again."

The "European trees" and "the richness of the [Italian] soil" induced a "strange, happily excited mood." As Klaus left for Berlin, Dietrich would return to Rome for another month, noting in his journal that he could feel his heart beat when he saw "the old water conduits accompanying us to the walls of the city for the second time." It was good to be back at "the fulcrum of the European culture and European life," and like a weary traveler sitting down to a generously prepared meal, he heartily indulged his appetite for Western humanism over the four languorous weeks to come. Not that he'd had his fill of Catholic Rome, but there was also so much yet to discover about "the Rome of Antiquity," the "Rome of the Renaissance," and the "Rome of the Middle Ages"—and "of the present day.[66]

He feasted on Raphael, Michelangelo, da Vinci, Caravaggio, Botticelli, Valázquez, and Titian, on Guido Reni's "enchantingly beautiful" *Concert of Angels* in a side chapel of the St. Gregorio and on all the mosaics at the basilica of San Lorenzo fuori le Mura, the sacristy at Santa Maria in Cosmedin, and at Santi Cosma e Damiano. Enraptured again by the ceiling of the Sistine Chapel, he was still unable, he said, "to move beyond Adam." For in that immemorial icon, "man is about to awaken to life for the first time." The ceiling held a mirror to Bonhoeffer's own soul and body, coming to life in the glorious meadows and hills of Creation's first morning. The painting was so very lush and pure, he said. "In short, one can't express it."[67]

He also found a piano to play. At the villa of Signora Jocca on the Corso d'Italia, he entertained his hosts with Bach, Brahms, Mozart, and the Hungarian composer Ernst von Dohnányi. (Hans von Dohnányi, son of the composer, would later marry Dietrich's older sister, Christine.)

Toward the end of his stay, Bonhoeffer once again invited Maria Weigert to dinner, and the two precocious children of the Grunewald elite, Christian and Jew, eighteen and twenty years old, shared a bottle of white wine, a loaf of bread, and some cheese. There, in his "favorite trattoria" near the Trevi Fountain, listening to his former nemesis reflect on her own travels, and responding in kind, Bonhoeffer might have recognized that he too had traveled some distance in his emotional formation. Maria still came across as "a little too academic in her way of thinking," Bonhoeffer would tell his mother, but "her idiosyncrasies" made her "only slightly unpleasant to be with." He would allow that "Maria really seems to understand something about art," but on second thought added, "or should we just say that she really enjoys it?"[68] In any case, he probed the matter no further; his Italian journey had brought him many new insights, which for now he was content to enjoy as such. As for Platte-Platenius, who had begun his theological studies in Rome, there is no indication that Dietrich remained in touch with him. But the Catholic seminarian had correctly discerned the ultimate purpose of Bonhoeffer's journey; it had always been a spiritual one. Bonhoeffer later told a friend that he had been "tempted" to convert to Catholicism, "to the Roman variety," the one that meant beauty, exuberance, and grandeur.[69] The depths as well as the heights drew him: the pageantry of life and death. The sacraments of the ordinary, and the extraordinary. The kind that is "simply inexhaustible." "At end of my stay," he said, "I saw what Catholicism is, and once again, I became truly fond of it."[70]

One week later, Bonhoeffer took the "fateful steps over the Italian border" back into Germany to enroll in classes at the University of Berlin. Though he barely made it in time, arriving on the last day of registration, he was ready to be back in the great metropolis his family called home.

CHAPTER THREE

1924–1928

~

University Studies

"I haven't written to you for a fairly long time," Bonhoeffer wrote Sabine in June 1924. "The last time I did, I tarried in more beautiful regions."[1]

Sabine was visiting relatives in Breslau when her twin brother returned to begin his studies. While Italy had no doubt overwhelmed him with its magnificence, Berlin, he would find, still had a multitude of charms, especially in late spring. In Grunewald, the hyacinths and daffodils were in bloom, the warm air scented with linden blossoms. The gap year at Tübingen had served its purposes: Bonhoeffer had studied modern philosophy, systematic theology, church history, and biblical languages, attended Professor Karl Hasse's popular lectures on "Forms in Beethoven's Symphonies" and read political theory with Robert Wilbrandt.

Still, he had no wish to linger there. Dr. Karl Bonhoeffer had grown up speaking the region's dialect, so his children were familiar with its idioms. Dietrich was not especially bothered by that diminutive drawl, but he'd had enough of the provincial dress and folk festivals and the vexing rail service, with local trains stopping at so many backwaters of southwest Germany that it took five transfers to get as far as Freiburg. One year in the Schwäbische Alb was quite enough for him.[2]

Bonhoeffer had originally hoped to spend a few weeks in Friedrichsbrunn before the semester began, but he had already delayed his return to Berlin by extending his stay in Italy—spending nearly a week in Sienna—and then joining two Igel brothers for a *Wanderung* in the Black Forest. The first day of classes was fast approaching, and still he had not done the reading he had hoped to finish during the two-month sojourn in Italy. "I absolutely have to get some work done," he wrote Sabine.[3] When she returned to Berlin later in the month, Dietrich welcomed her with a bouquet of flowers and gifts from his travels. He was most excited about the guitar he had found in Rome—"a neo-politan with a bass string," in good condition and reasonably well built, although it was not actually a gift. He had purchased the instrument only after receiving money from Sabine in the mail. But the important thing was that she would now have her own guitar, and the two could play duets.[4]

But Sabine had some news that came as rather a shock: she was now engaged to Gerhard Leibholz, a Berliner of Jewish descent, five years her senior, who was completing a doctoral dissertation in legal philoso-phy. It would necessarily be a long engagement, since Dr. Bonhoeffer forbade any daughter of his from marrying before her twentieth birth-day, and Sabine was only eighteen. Paula Bonhoeffer agreed with her husband's rule. She also had concerns about her daughter's marrying a Jew—concerns centering on the practicalities of such a mixed marriage. Although Sabine's fiancé had been baptized into the Lutheran Church as a child, he had dark eyes and a prominent nose, and his grandparents were practicing Jews. His father, William Leibholz, a widower with a fairly secular outlook, owned textile factories near Berlin, and had raised his children in a villa on the Königssee. And no one of any Jewish background had ever married into the Bonhoeffer clan.[5] But "Gert," as he was known, "won the hearts of the family" with his expansive mind, his kindly manner, and his broad intellectual interests. Sabine was delighted when she overheard her father say, "Of all these young people who now come to the house, I really like talking to young Leib-holz best of all. He is both intelligent and unpretentious."[6]

Dietrich, of course, received the news of his sister's engagement with deliberate cheer, welcoming Gerhard as a brother-in-law. But the sudden shift in family relationships did not come "entirely without a sense of loss." The devotion of the twins to each other, "so deep as seldom to need any expression," was a basic element of life. In child-hood, "neither had needed any other intimacy"; at least Dietrich had neither sought nor found any other. That bond would remain strong over the years and across the distances that separated them, but for now attending the wonderful news was a sense of isolation for Dietrich.[7] He moved back into his parents' house and withdrew into his studies.

Shortly after the twins' twentieth birthday in 1926, Sabine and Leibholz were married by Parson Priebe at the Grunewald Evangelical Church. Dietrich makes no mention of the three-day celebration in his journals and letters, nor is he seen in any of the wedding pictures. Sabine, however, recalled how at the feast on the wedding eve, Dietrich appeared in his elegant attire and entertained the sixty guests with a song and dance by Max Bierbaum: "Ring-row-rosary, I dance with my wife." The next morning he offered a "solemn but festive" rendition of Grieg's "Hochzeitstag auf Troldhaugen."[8] He may have felt bereft, but he was in no way sulking.

The turn of the century had been a glorious time at Friedrich-Wilhelms. Still under the governance of the kaiser, the university had assembled an unrivaled theological faculty, including Adolf von Harnack, Karl Holl, and Reinhold Seeberg. These three luminaries of the Protestant liberal establishment were in a class of their own. But one would hardly expect less of the faculty that had been founded a century before, in 1809, by the great Romantic theologian Friedrich Schleiermacher, the beloved "prince of the church," whose funeral in February 1834 drew more than twenty thousand to Trinity Church and its surrounding gardens in the Friedrichstadt district. It was at Friedrich-Wilhelms University in Berlin that Hegel had accepted the chair in philosophy left vacant by the death of Johann Fichte, counting as his colleague his former roommate Friedrich Wilhelm Joseph Schelling, and as his future disciple Ludwig Feuerbach. By 1924, when Bonhoeffer matriculated, the theology faculty comprised nine senior scholars, most of whom had been tenured before the Great War, in addition to adjunct professors and lecturers.[9]

In his first term, Bonhoeffer attended two seminars directed by Holl, one in church history and the other on the creeds and confessions. Harnack remained the preeminent scholar of the Berlin school,

FRIEDRICH-WILHELMS UNIVERSITY, BERLIN

but he had formally retired and was thus exempt from academic obligations, though he still offered doctoral seminars. Now Holl, star of the so-called Lutheran Renaissance, and younger than Harnack by fifteen years, had begun attracting the brightest graduate students. Holl's book *What Did Luther Understand by Religion?* had become a theological sensation when it appeared in 1921, outselling the year's other conspicuous hit, the second edition of Karl Barth's *The Epistle to the Romans*—which launched the radical movement called dialectical theology. Holl's book on Luther went through two more printings in 1922, and was reissued in 1923 in a revised version. His classes filled up quickly.[10]

More than any other professor, Holl shaped Bonhoeffer's view of Martin Luther, the catalytic agent of the Protestant Reformation. Holl offered a sober account for colleagues and fellow churchmen who had become "drunk on [too much] Lutheran pathos": Luther did not belong only to Germans, he warned. Having captured the spirit of human enlightenment in its religious aspects, he had forged a truly universal Christian worldview. Holl's Lutheran Renaissance emphasized "new" and unique elements of Luther's theology, preferring his early radical themes—the freedom of a Christian, salvation by faith alone (*sola fide*), the priesthood of the believers. Some contemporary Catholic critics had found these themes to be symptoms of a diseased, oversexed soul and even, as in the case of Luther's so-called discovery of justification by faith, the fruit of a memorably productive bowel movement.[11]

Holl's aim was also to complement Wittenberg's Luther with Geneva's John Calvin, the other great Protestant Reformer and in this way to strive toward a more broadly conceived Reformation Christianity. Luther's worrisome tendency toward the otherworldly might well be balanced by Calvin's understanding of the "resolute permeation of the world with divine presence."[12] This approach of Holl's—teaching a Luther who was more open "to the confessional, cultural, and political traditions of churches beyond the German homeland"—was broadly appealing to his Berlin students and, in particular, to Dietrich Bonhoeffer, who already gravitated to a cosmopolitan evangelicalism and a spirituality beyond the Protestant-Catholic divide.[13] Nevertheless, it deserves mention that before beginning university studies, Bonhoeffer's ample notes on books and ideas betray strikingly little interest in Luther and the Protestant Reformation. He seemed to have been from the beginning a natural ecumenist.

Bonhoeffer enjoyed Holl's seminars immensely and would remain grateful for Holl's marvelous theme of duty transformed into joy "in the face of the majesty of God"—such a refreshing alternative to the stentorian moralism of many Protestant liberals. Still, when Bonhoeffer would later have occasion to remember his university years, his thoughts turned more often to Harnack, the most distinguished scholar of the German Protestant Church; it was he—Bonhoeffer said—who had inspired his student's pursuit of "truth born out of freedom." When the seventy-five-year-old professor emeritus announced a seminar on the history of Christian dogma for the fall term, Bonhoeffer was delighted.

Of the nine on the theological faculty, Harnack, a slender man with an elegant demeanor, moved most easily among the city's cultural elite. His house on Kunz-Buntschuh-Strasse in the Grunewald, where he often held his seminars, was but a three-minute walk from the Bonhoeffers' on Wangenheimstrasse. On days that found the professor on campus, Harnack and Bonhoeffer would often meet at the Halensee train station to share the commute to Berlin Mitte. The Harnacks and the Bonhoeffers had long maintained comfortable social ties; Harnack's sons Axel and Ernst, both graduates of the Grunewald Gymnasium, though a generation before Dietrich, shared Bonhoeffer's fondness for music and travel.

Harnack remained not only Germany's grand old man of Protestantism but also the most influential German scholar of religion throughout Europe and the English-speaking world; he was twice offered professorships at Harvard. When Harnack had moved from the University of Giessen to Berlin in 1888, within two terms his early-morning classes were regularly attended by more than four hundred students. His university-wide lectures of 1899–1900, published as the book *Was ist Christentum? (What Is Christianity?)*, had by now been issued in multiple editions and in numerous foreign languages. In his seminal studies of early Christianity he had argued that religion was the product of historical and social factors—rather than supernatural forces, as the church had traditionally claimed—and so was best studied in the rigorous field of historical-critical scholarship. Sifting through early church documents, especially those concerning the practices and beliefs of the first Christian communities and their responses to the story of Jesus, Harnack concluded that the essence of the gospel could be reduced to the simple but profound message that God is love. This truth predated the rise of church councils and synods and their formulation of doctrines and creeds; it should, Harnack taught, be reclaimed as the eternal and unchanging heart of the faith—reclaimed, one might say more pointedly, from the institutional church, which had taken a simple ecstatic fact and transformed it into a body of static dogma and abstruse metaphysics. Had the apostles, to take one striking example, responded to their surprising encounter with the resurrected Jesus by reciting creeds? No, they had responded in spontaneous outbursts of joy—even Thomas, whose doubts eventually gave way to worship and praise: "My Lord and my God!" (John 20:28). Indeed, the Gospel of Luke observes that the disciples found it difficult to believe "*because* of their joy and amazement"!

It should be the mission of Reformation Protestantism, said Harnack, to free the gospel "from these unessential accouterments." Historical criticism offered the means to winnow out the "husks" of stale traditions from the timeless "kernel" of the Christian message. "The essence of Christianity," Harnack wrote famously, "its element of permanent validity, addresses an essentially unchanging core of human nature that yearns for that 'presence of the eternal in time.'" The gospel's "simple satisfaction of this yearning was its self-authentication," satisfying "the human yearning for the presence of the eternal." Therefore, to speak of the essence of Christianity is to affirm the "heart's trusting submission to a loving God," love's power to inspire "the person toward a life enamored of the good, energized by grace and in the service of his neighbor." Jesus's divinity and power should then be affirmed as the practical consequence of his intimate relationship with "God as the Father and as his Father." In contrast to traditional formulations as Jesus as a supernatural being—the Son of God, the second person of the Trinity, the revelation of the transcendent Word—Harnack described Jesus as the man, unique above all others, who achieved fully realized "God consciousness."[14]

I n his first month of coursework Bonhoeffer established a comfortable rhythm. A brisk swim in the morning was followed by reading until lunch—unless he had a morning seminar. In the afternoons, he met with classmates to recite and discuss passages from primary sources in church history.[15] Harnack preferred an evening time for the weekly gathering of students at his home.

Theological studies at the University of Berlin meant a total immersion in the currents of Protestant liberal thought. Bonhoeffer read Hegel's *Lectures on the Philosophy of Religion*. He read Friedrich Schleiermacher's *On Religion: Speeches to Its Cultured Despisers*—the most beautiful of all works in German Romantic theology—which praises religion "as a sense and taste of the infinite," the ultimate source of all human striving toward beauty and goodness, these being deemed objective realities, in accordance with the early Christians' Platonic inheritance. He read Ernst Troeltsch's two-volume *The Social Teachings of the Christian Churches*, as well as Troeltsch's writings on Christian ethics. Dietrich wrote a "very interesting paper" (he told his mother) on the sociologist Max Weber's three-volume *Gesammelte Aufsätze zur Reli-gionssoziologie* (*Collected Essays on the Sociology of Religion*). "After Weber, I also propose to finish off Husserl—and . . . to tackle Schleiermacher thoroughly," Bonhoeffer confidently reported. He was as good as his word: in addition to Schleiermacher's writings on hermeneutics and aesthetics, Bonhoeffer plowed through Edmund Husserl's *Ideas: General Introduction to Pure Phenomenology*, admiring the Jewish philosopher's razor-sharp analysis of human cognition. Over the course of the next six years, Bonhoeffer would return often to Husserl's writings on epistemology, while also resuming his study of Hebrew begun in high school.

Bonhoeffer the student brought a broad curiosity into the highly specialized subject of systematic theology, attending lectures outside his department and, with remarkable ease, reading across disciplines—in philosophy, of course, but also in sociology, social theory, and psychology. But the disciplines in which he moved most freely remained those discussed over meals at home, in daily exchanges with his father or with his siblings, in-laws, and even Grunewald neighbors; these were medicine and natural sciences, jurisprudence, philosophy, and theology—all staples of the daily discourse of Berlin's academic elite.[16]

Klaus was also back and living at home. After the carefree days in Italy, he spent the summer months working on his doctoral thesis. Dietrich told his parents that Klaus seemed "stressed out." No wonder: he worked most mornings in his university office and then brought his files home in the afternoon. Refreshed by an hour's nap before dinner, Klaus would be in his room writing until well after midnight.[17]

Dietrich, meanwhile, as always made ample room for recreation and leisure. He took pride in being able to complete difficult assignments in a single sitting and then enjoy time that was his own. He might, as on one break, hike into the northernmost regions of Schleswig-Holstein, over the Dithmarschen flats and coastal plains, and through the "flat, verdant . . . meadowlands" that bordered the North Sea west of Kiel and Flensburg, the country feeling "lonesome and monotonous," he said, but in a good way. Indeed, he loved the solace of endless plains and landscapes whose sparseness seemed ethereal, the dissolving horizons, colorless heaths, and "magnificent blue skies."[18] With his friend Robert Held, he would hike all the way to Husum, the grey town by the sea, and there set sail for the islands of Langeness, Helgoland, and Sylt, returning to town alert and refreshed, tanned by the sun scarcely felt in the bracing wind of the rugged coastal terrain.

Not that he found his studies laborious; there is hardly a hint of drudgery in Bonhoeffer's accounts. Studying in concentrated blocks

came naturally and was no burden, especially as it left him time for outings in Berlin—the symphony and theater, musical evenings at home,
the cafés. Even when he needed to cram large amounts of material—
once over a weekend he had to plow through another Husserl opus, this
time the two-volume *Logical Investigations*—or recharge his Latin, he
did what each day required with relish.[19]

He formed a chamber quintet, recruiting two Igel brothers now
living in Berlin to play first violin and first cello and roping Klaus
in as second cello. Herr Rohloff, Sabine's violin teacher, completed
the ensemble. Dietrich, as the pianist, selected the pieces, wrote the
arrangements, and led rehearsals at the Bonhoeffers' house, where on
most Saturdays the quintet performed in the downstairs living room.[20]
These convivial gatherings were but a continuation of the life they'd
enjoyed as children, with Paula's musicales, fascinating guests, and
good things to eat.

I n those university years Dietrich found his closest friend in Walter Dress. Bonhoeffer and Dress shared an interest in books, ideas,
departmental gossip, and negotiating the Byzantine requirements of
the program. But Dress was also the student Bonhoeffer looked up to
most, and he relied on him heavily for advice. Their relationship serves
to remind us that, despite a formidable intellectual maturity, Dietrich
was also very much an eighteen-year-old adolescent male, living under
his parents' roof, enjoying the provisions of his attentive mother, and
given occasionally to an exasperating neediness. He had never had a
best friend in high school, and even before then, his siblings, especially
his brothers, had observed in him a certain reserve—a reserve they
sometimes took for snobbery.

One afternoon when his friend Dress was turned away at the front
door, Dietrich flew into a rage and berated "these pearls of maids," who
scurried about the rooms but could not follow an instruction as simple
as, "Let no one in the house *except* 'Mr. Dress.'" "*Ergo nostra culpa*," he
wrote Dress in a letter of apology, adding, "*odi profanum vulgus (ancillas!)*," an allusion to one of his favorite odes by Horace: "I hate the
unholy rabble." The reference to the "maids"—(*ancillas!*)—was Bonhoeffer's, not Horace's.[21]

Mostly Bonhoeffer would talk and Dress would listen. More precisely, Bonhoeffer would pepper Dress, two years his senior in the
program, with requests for advice on writing assignments, exams, and
the stringency of due dates. The solicitations were fierce and frequent,
extending also to purely academic matters. What, for instance, did
Walter know about "Luther's feelings for his work"? Bonhoeffer had

been assigned a paper on the subject and needed some ideas to get started. Did Walter understand "Luther's view of history"? Did Walter think Luther had a view of history? If he did, would Walter say it could be called a "dualistic view of history"? Did Walter consider Luther a dualistic thinker? What about the scholastic theologians—did they, in Walter's judgment, have a "view of history"? To these and other questions—all from a single letter in the spring of 1925, in which Dietrich also wishes Dress a quiet vacation—the younger student importuned the older to make "speedy reply."[22] If Dress showed uncommon patience, it was doubtless inspired by his pursuit of Dietrich's older sister Susi.[23]

When a speedy reply was not forthcoming, Dietrich wrote Dress again. "I tried to telephone you several times, because I haven't heard from you. I beg you please write me."

Bonhoeffer also needed to know what Professor Harnack looked for in a paper—and Professor Holl, too. What were their expectations? Anything Dress could tell him about Holl would be helpful. Bonhoeffer did not know when to stop.

Where does the saying "the servant should not know his master's secrets" come from?

Did Walter know the date of the first Hebrew exam?

How long is the average research paper?

"Please write me and please write soon: *Friedrichsbrunn*, Eastern Harz Mountains (near Suderode)!"[24] Dietrich had gone to the country house for a long weekend. That Dress was himself under the gun, writing his doctoral dissertation on the Italian humanist Marsilio Ficino, somehow escaped Dietrich's notice.

"You have not responded at all," he wrote in desperation. "Are you sick? Please call."[25]

Bonhoeffer would write two lengthy papers for Harnack.[26] In "Luther's Feelings About His Work," he argues that despite a general pessimism about the world, Luther maintained "inner religious certainty" that steadied him on his tumultuous journey through guilt and shame to the apprehension of unconditional grace, and "this is what we must remember." Upon reading Bonhoeffer's second paper, "The Jewish Element in First Clement: Its Content and Relationship to the Whole Letter," Harnack conveyed his hope that the uncommonly meticulous young scholar would one day become a church historian.[27] Bonhoeffer received the highest mark in the seminar.

Despite great admiration for Harnack and Holl, Bonhoeffer made a surprising decision when it came time to write his dissertation: he would work under the supervision of Professor Reinhold Seeberg.

His parents were especially taken aback. Paula thought her son should write his thesis under Holl, since Harnack no longer kept regular office hours; she told Dietrich as much. Although a generation separated Harnack and Holl, the latter commanded wide respect among intellectuals outside academic theology, and he was, moreover, a Berliner. Seeberg, whose expertise lay in the narrow field called "dogmatics," seemed provincial and unrefined, with his bushy peasant beard and right-wing politics. Among his colleagues, he had been the most vocal, "aggressive" supporter of total war—a "propaganda-maker" and "unapologetic nationalist," according to Dorothea Wendebourg in her history of the Berlin theological faculty. Seeberg hated the Weimar Republic, its liberal social policies and internationalist convictions; he did not much care much for Berlin, either.

But Dietrich did not want to be stamped as yet another disciple of the Lutheran Renaissance. While he respected Holl immensely, he found Seeberg more eclectic in his approach to theological studies, interested in both the practices of faith, and varieties of interpretations drawn from other disciplines. Unlike the celebrity theologians Holl and Harnack, there was no "Seeberg School," and this fact pleased Bonhoeffer and held out a promise of greater freedom. The rough-hewn Seeberg was also somewhat less attentive, and not even slightly deferential. In other words, he was, in Bonhoeffer's estimation, a perfect counterweight.[28]

Every graduate student in Berlin had studied Seeberg's five-volume *Text-book of the History of Doctrines*, and indeed Seeberg's work encompassed a wide range of theological doctrines and disputes, not promoting any in particular. Bonhoeffer would eventually go his own way in the dissertation, as Seeberg would matter-of-factly report. But he would not abandon his concern for the volitional, or ethical, dimensions of belief—how the human will expresses itself morally—a concern he shared with Seeberg. The most important dimension of human existence remained the social dimension, Seeberg taught, and it was precisely this focus on the practical reality of human fellowship that brought Bonhoeffer to his office.[29]

When Bonhoeffer telephoned Seeberg to talk about the thesis, Seeberg rang back promptly and suggested a meeting that very day. When he appeared, Bonhoeffer proposed his idea of "writing on the history of doctrine . . . as it relates to the subject of religious community." Seeberg was delighted. He said he had waited a long time for a student to work on such a subject, the lived experience of faith. It impressed Seeberg further that Bonhoeffer had come up with the theme on his own rather than asking that one be assigned to him, as was commonly done.

Seeberg asked Dietrich to assure his father that "everything would certainly go well." When Dietrich laughed awkwardly at discovering in this way that Dr. Bonhoeffer had already been in touch with the professor about the dissertation, Seeberg merely repeated his direction: he had "already seen" enough of Bonhoeffer's past work to safely make this pledge to the father.[30] In fact, starting in his sophomore year, Bonhoeffer would attend every one of Seeberg's seminars, of which there were six in all during his remaining time at the university.[31]

Then he discovered the writings of the contemporary Swiss theologian Karl Barth, and everything changed. By the fall of 1926, two years into his program at Berlin, Bonhoeffer had become more unassumingly confident, a less preening scholar. He had left behind the anxious teenager, by turns obsessed over minor details and eager to know about classes "in which one can do the least and can be absent the most." He had hit his stride, excelling in biblical and classical exegesis and church history. He could enter into the personal religiosity of great thinkers, as when writing on Luther's "primal experience" and "monastic struggles" and on Søren Kierkegaard's *The Sickness Unto Death*. Or extend his outlook beyond Western Christendom, as in a paper entitled "Dostoyevsky and the Russian Philosophers of Religion." Other papers confirmed impressive range and curiosity: besides "The Jewish Element in First Clement" (as mentioned), there was "The Historical and Pneumatological Interpretation of Scripture" (summer 1925, for Seeberg); "Reason and Revelation in Early Lutheran Dogmatics" (winter 1925–26, for Stolzenburg); "Luther's Views of the Holy Spirit According to the Disputations of 1535–1545" (winter 1925–26, for Holl); "The Doctrine of Life After Death and the Last Things in Early Protestant Dogmatics" (winter/spring 1926, also for Seeberg); and "The Fifteenth Chapter of the Gospel of John and the Apostle Paul" (summer 1926, for Deissmann). All these efforts earned high marks, and Bonhoeffer rose to the top of his class.

But it was not until a fine spring evening in 1926, when he presented Harnack with an essay on the occasion of the esteemed professor's seventy-fifth birthday, that Bonhoeffer's prodigious intellect and organizational acumen produced a work of truly luminous insight and astonishing promise. "Joy in Primitive Christianity" offered a close reading of the Greek New Testament, with particular attention to St. Paul's inviting expression "shared joy" (*synchairein* in the Greek). Paul coined the term to describe the disciples' rapturous first encounter with the risen Christ. Bonhoeffer argued deftly that, by this *synchairein*, Paul meant more than emotions or feelings, even those elicited by the Lord's appearance in the flesh after his crucifixion and burial. Rather, Paul's neologism signified an altogether new social reality, one inaugurated by the joy of the resurrection. Bonhoeffer had taken Harnack's central insight—ecstatic joy as the essence of the gospel—and given it a social dimension, a vitality that could be experienced, shared. If only the German church had reached the same understanding, untold human suffering might have been avoided.[32]

A review of Bonhoeffer's transcript reveals that he approached all the compulsory subjects with a uniform studiousness. Aside from church history and social ethics with Harnack, Holl, and Seeberg, he took courses in Old Testament with Professors Gressman, Sellin, and Biehle, and Licentiate Dr. Gallingand. His New Testament classes were taught by Lietzmann, Deissman, and Licentiates Bertramer and Michaelis; he took philosophy with Heinrich Maier, Spranger, and Rieffert; and practical theology and pastoral psychology with Wertheimer and Mahling. In all it was a course of study that provided "extensive theological education and methodological skills in all disciplines." Bonhoeffer was finding his voice as a young academic theologian, amid a faculty deeply formed by the canon of classical liberal Protestantism.[33]

During a bout with the flu in the winter semester, Bonhoeffer passed the time reading Barth and Henrik Ibsen intermittently. That spring of 1925 he gave his mother a copy of Barth's latest, and she read it alongside *Der Historismus und seine Überwindung* by Troeltsch, in whom Dietrich was starting to lose interest. Not long before, in May, Bonhoeffer himself had first read Barth's explosive new book, *The Word of God and the Word of Man*. Almost immediately an " 'entirely new' note crept into" his journals and other writings.[34]

Barth wrote theology with the ferocity of a soul on fire. He had studied in Berlin a decade earlier, when Harnack was at the height of his powers, and he had worked with Holl and Seeberg as well. But rather than complete his doctorate, Barth took a pastorate in a working-class parish of Safenwil, Switzerland—a region dominated by the textile industry. Going about the duties of a small-town vicar, Barth found himself sent back to scripture when the philosophical and literary understanding inculcated in him as a student failed to answer the everyday questions of his parishioners. Soon "the strange new world of the Bible" became his obsession, and the once-familiar landscape of his liberal inheritance felt suddenly alien to him.[35] The Bible—its stories and characters—pulsed with life and spoke across the centuries of the "God beyond God." Barth felt the exhilaration of being set loose on a journey without maps.

Had he not made theological writing into an art form, Barth might have produced novels as inventive as those of Thomas Mann or Robert

Musil; paintings with the emotive, intoxicating textures of Ernst Kirch-
ner or Max Beckmann; or perhaps even symphonies in the expressionist
style of Arthur Honegger or Arnold Schoenberg. But Barth's idiom was
theology, and in it he was as much an original as these others were in
theirs. For him, no intellectual pursuit could possibly match the thrill
and the terror of the bold and audacious venture to speak about God.
With Bibles and ancient commentaries spread open on his desk—and
with Mozart on the phonograph—Barth answered the singular vocation to give form to "all these puzzling words." Audacity would indeed
be his stock in trade. The second edition of his commentary *The Epistle
to the Romans* had been published in 1921, the same year that Holl's
brief study of Luther appeared and Harnack retired. With this radically revised version was fired a barrage of missiles, seemingly out of
nowhere, that transformed the landscape of modern theology for good,
taking dead aim at the German Protestant church, whose intimacy with
nationalist sentiment had aided the mischief that led finally to Versailles. In Barth's understanding, the Kingdom of God is not a reality
that stands alongside culture and history; it is the new, the different, the
unexpected, the *wholly other.* Recalling the week in the Swiss Alps during which he had written a major section of the commentary, that based
on Romans 1, Barth said, "It was often as though I were being looked at
by something from afar, from Asia Minor or Corinth, something very
ancient, early oriental, indefinably sunny, wild, original, that somehow
is hidden behind these sentences and is so ready to let itself be drawn
forth by ever new generations."[36]

Among the University of Berlin theological faculty, however,
Barth's new theology remained more a nuisance than an inspiration.
Bonhoeffer had learned of the two controversial books not on campus
but from his cousin Hans-Christoph von Hase, who had transferred
from the Göttingen mathematics program to theology after hearing
Barth lecture.[37] Borrowing his cousin's lecture notes, Dietrich meticulously transcribed them under the heading "Karl Barth, dictated notes
on 'Instruction on the Christian Religion.' "[38]

It may seem odd today that Barth's views should have been marked
out as being so radical and subversive, particularly since he referred
constantly to Jesus and wrote almost confidently about him, in a highly
sermonic style. But it was precisely because of his deliberate use of the
old orthodox phrases and terms that Barth cut so close to the bone. It
was very much his aim to re-motivate a language that had once been so
essential and familiar but which in practice—in churches, of course, but
also in the everyday use of Christians' conversation, and particularly
"in second-order technical theological reflection"—had been emptied

of its vitality. For a long time, perhaps for more than 250 years, Barth explained, that vitality and inner-sense had "been receding from natural familiarity, certainly in theological discourse."

Bonhoeffer most certainly heard Barth's name mentioned by Harnack, but it would have been with a derisive *pfft*, or an *aach!* Professor Harnack had recently found himself in a most unwelcome barbed exchange with his former student—an "all-but-dissertation student," no less—who had so implausibly become a cause célèbre with his sulphuric jeremiads against the liberal Protestant patriarchs. In that widely observed debate, Harnack had not emerged the winner.

It was the 1920 Students' Conference in Aarau, Switzerland. Barth had delivered a lecture—"Biblical Questions, Insights, and Vistas"— that combined expressionist word game and jeremiad against cultural Protestantism into a manifesto of neo-orthodoxy. "Jesus simply has nothing to do with religion," Barth began. The meaning of the life of Jesus is, rather, "the actuality of that which is never actually present in any religion—the actuality of the unapproachable, the unreachable, the incomprehensible, the realization of the possibility, which is not a matter of speculation: 'Behold I make all things new!' "[39] Religion exists as a human endeavor, a habit speaking about God by speaking of humanity in a loud voice, and in this manner religion, in Barth's estimation, stands in stark opposition to revelation. Which is to say, the affirmation of God, humankind, and the world given in the New Testament "is based exclusively upon the possibility of a new order absolutely beyond human thought." And as prerequisite to that new order, he continued, "there must come a crisis that denies all human thought."

Harnack was appalled. He criticized Barth as a "despiser of scientific theology" and challenged him to face the modern age without retreating into the irrational.

Though he knew of strong opposition on the Berlin faculty, Bonhoeffer made no secret of his admiration for Barth. Seeberg became aware of Bonhoeffer's shift away from the academic mainline when he read his essay "Is There a Difference Between the Historical and Pneumatic Interpretation of the Bible, and What Is the Position of Dogmatics on This Topic?" For the first time, Bonhoeffer received only an average grade. But Seeberg, who had been supremely pleased by Bonhoeffer's solicitations and probably took some pleasure in seeing his celebrated colleague, Harnack, publically skewered, acknowledged the courage of Bonhoeffer's dissent.

And so Dietrich Bonhoeffer became a rare bird in Berlin: a liberal who nevertheless admired Barth and felt strong affinities for the spirit of so-called dialectical theology, whose radical approach to

DIETRICH BONHOEFFER AS A
DOCTORATE STUDENT, BERLIN 1924

God's transcendence cast aside the natural explanations of everyone since Aquinas as well as the recondite metaphysics of Germany's brightest lights. Navigating his way between the two competing schools, Bonhoeffer showed himself to be notably diplomatic or dexterous or both; it was a minor miracle that he could draw freely from Barth without alienating the Berlin faculty. And in truth, however harshly they might criticize Barth, Bonhoeffer's advisers showed a greater generosity toward their young student's neo-orthodoxy than Barth, at the time, would have ever shown anyone under his direction who spoke kindly of the liberal Christ.[40]

Completing a dissertation—that crowning achievement in every doctoral education, intended to demonstrate a command of knowledge equal to making advances in the field—is not meant to be easy for anyone. It would not be for Bonhoeffer. Despite a well-furnished mind and prodigious gifts of concentration, he'd never attempted anything of that scale. Dissertations do not get written in a single sitting. And attempting to adapt his talents to the effort would frustrate him immensely; from the outset, he repeatedly found himself crossing out large sections of work and starting over.[41] Such dead ends were new to him.

In March of 1927, he retreated to the country house in Friedrichsbrunn, hoping to find inspiration in the fresh air of the Harz Mountains for what he liked to call (perhaps exhibiting the defense mechanism Freud had called denial) his "paper." It seemed the right thing to do. Spring was already "marching headlong into the birch trees near Treseburg and along Bergrat Müller' Pond," he told his parents. He could never remember a time when the weather in March had felt so summery. He thought of Rome and how nice it would be to enjoy an "Est Est Est," the popular white Italian wine, in his trattoria near the Trevi Fountain. But Friedrichsbrunn calmed his mind like no other place he knew.[42] So it was vexing that even here the "paper" would not write itself; still, he relished the quiet and simple days and would remain in the country until finishing a major portion of the job.

Under Seeberg's loose supervision, Bonhoeffer would produce a

380-page manuscript called "Sanctorum Communio"—"The Communion of Saints"—with a lumbering (but to his Lutheran readers,
reassuring) subtitle: "A Theological Study of the Sociology of the
Church." In the course of his research and writing, Bonhoeffer had
blithely presumed that his dissertation committee would not mind his
undergirding his thesis with sympathetic use of their Helvetic nemesis.
The Barthian flavors in the opening sections, if not in the very first
sentence, were impossible to ignore: "In this study, social philosophy
and sociology are employed in the service of theology." To be sure,
ideas about God, church, and Jesus Christ have a social intention, and
it is best to be clear about how doctrines take form in lived experience. But theological thinking bears a distinctive character—an inner
sense, logic, and vocabulary—which must be respected and which in
turn must inform the theologian's engagement with other disciplines
and realities. The liberals tended to reduce Christian doctrine to its
functionality in human matters, as if doctrines were true only to the
extent that they were useful. Bonhoeffer countered this trend by arguing that in "genuine Christian thought," it is "only on the basis . . .
of the church-community"—only in a conception of God tethered to
the social body, not through individual social or ethical experience—
that faith can be finally understood in its essence. Christ exists as community, Bonhoeffer would say—*Christus als Gemeinde existierend*. His
broadest claim in the dissertation, the significant but initially bland
assertion that theological commitments really matter, no doubt helped
him walk a tightrope between the liberals and the conservatives on the
faculty—though perhaps his cousin Hans-Christoph von Hase had a
better explanation for Dietrich's success: the dissertation, he suggested,
sailed through because the theologians did not understand all the sociology, while the sociologists were perplexed by the theology, and neither camp wanted to betray its ignorance.

Bonhoeffer may not have reformed the church as he'd promised
his skeptical brothers years earlier, but he was proposing significant
renovations. In forthright and measured prose, he examined the rickety
foundations of Germanic theology, found them wanting, and set about
building sounder ones. Cutting through academic jargon and theoretical architectonics, he asked a quite remarkable question: Where
within the reality of the world does the new life confessed by Christians become real? Barth had issued a defiant *Nein!* to Harnack, Rudolf
Bultmann, and all the modernists who spoke of God merely as a mode
or modulation of human experience, who sought cultural relevance at
the expense of faith's distinctive claims. But simple gainsaying was not
Bonhoeffer's intention. Rather, he hoped to bring new confessional

energies to the liberal tradition, to erect a surer footing for its honest and studious attention to social existence; or, put another way, he sought to re-accommodate the liberal tradition to the greater one, the two-thousand-year tradition of Christian orthodoxy. In this manner, he hoped also to temper Barth's dialectical transcendent and "wholly other" God by focusing on God's immanence in the concrete relationships of Christians in community, the patterns and practices of lived faith. Bonhoeffer thus made his debut on the theological scene as a mediating force.

His themes highlighted the uniqueness of his emerging vision and anticipated his life's work. *Christ, community*, and *concreteness*—these were the key words. Still, he would test the outer limits of the Protestant imagination in his quest for a deeper integration of revelation and reality; and the phrase he coined, *Christus als Gemeinde existierend*, suggested something like an ethical sacrament. It was the conviction that knowledge of God begins in personal encounter—appearing in the other, through the "enigmatic impenetrable Thou."[43] Forgiveness means forgiving people, Bonhoeffer said, and apart from the dynamic of personal encounter, the doctrine of the justification of sins vanishes into thin air. As he sought to rescue the experience of Christ from metaphysical abstraction and capture the fullness of embodied life for the church, Bonhoeffer appeared to be still under the spell of his Italian journey. "There is hardly a more moving sermon on Christ's church-community," Bonhoeffer wrote, "than the kyrie eleison in the B-minor Mass."

While his emotions were understandably muted, cast in a scholarly, often stilted prose, Bonhoeffer would occasionally speak directly from the heart.[44] When Barth read the published "Sanctorum Communio," he called it "a theological miracle," using the phrase *eine theologische Überraschung*—which might equally be translated as a "theological surprise" or paraphrased thus: "how astounding that anything so sympathetic to me would ever come out of Berlin." Barth applauded the twenty-one-year-old's audacity in recasting the story of modern theology from a perspective that was, well, *so* Barthian. But he also detected a quality of "homesickness"—a longing for the church catholic and its tangible consolations.

If "Sanctorum Communio" is indeed miraculous, it is so no less for its imaginative virtuosity than for the breadth of its ambition. One might even approach it as a thought experiment, posing this question: How might social existence (or "sociality," in Bonhoeffer's terminology) be transformed if this ideal of the body of Christ became the aspiration of every Christian? There is in these pages no mistaking the longing for a more embodied, vital, and dynamic Protestantism. Barth was astute to detect as well a slightly monkish air to the exercise, and it would not be the last time he worried aloud about Bonhoeffer's nostalgia for Rome. Aside from a young man's infatuation with the Holy See, however, it is not immediately clear what inspired his radiant vision of Christian community. A yearning for other forms of intimacy, perhaps? In Berlin he had never shown much interest in religious practice—that is, in going to church—and even now as a student in a Lutheran theology program, he rarely appeared at his parish church on Fürtwangler Strasse. The dissertation may be an impressive display of Bonhoeffer's intellectual powers and high confidence and it may betray perhaps even a hint of genius. Yet his "communion of the saints," the ultimate importance of the harmonious fellowship of I's and Thou's, may attest to more private longings: for friendship and acceptance.

"There is a word that evokes tremendous feelings of love and bliss among Catholics who hear it," Bonhoeffer said in one of his first sermons, preached in Berlin during the dissertation year. It is "a word that stirs in them the most profound depths of religious feeling ranging from the awe and dread of judgment to the bliss of God's presence, although it is also a word that assuredly evokes feelings of home for them, feelings of the sort only a child feels in gratitude, reverence, and self-surrendering love toward its mother, the feelings that come over us when after a long time away we once again enter our parents' home, our own childhood home." While the Bonhoeffers projected an image of the perfect family, with their music evenings, salons, madrigals, and nature outings, Dietrich often felt great loneliness. He had never really had a close friend "during his childhood and youth."[45] And now Sabine was marrying the son of a wealthy industrialist, one soon to become a judge and a professor. And so in this manner Dietrich seemed to be writing in hopes of finding a more enduring and attentive family.

But the year was 1927, by which time the chickens hatched at Versailles had already begun coming home to roost. With further national calamity in the near future, the patina of Weimar liberalism appeared to be thinning even for this scion of the Grunewald. Beneath the surface of Bonhoeffer's idealized community lurked an all-too-easy recourse to nationalism, a naive but firm attachment to the venerable tradition of German martial theology. Beneath his "four conceptual models of social basic-relation," the altruism of "vicarious representative action," and the lofty sentiment that "Christian love knows no limits," one finds dark and alarming ruminations. For all of Karl Barth's admonitory insistence in his *Epistle to the Romans* that the God of Christian revelation refuses alignment with any human culture, it may even appear at times in "Sanctorum Communio" that *das Reich Gottes*—the Spirit-infused fellowship of "the Kingdom of God"—exists finally for the glory of the German Reich.

In one most unsettling passage, Bonhoeffer draws a connection between the Israelites' self-understanding as the "people of God"—a people called by God, as it is written in the Old Testament (Exodus 19:5), to be a "peculiar treasure unto me above all people"—and the fate of Germany. Where a people "submitting in conscience to God's will" goes to war to fulfill its historical mission, the nation should proceed in the certainty, Bonhoeffer writes, that "it has been called upon by God" and "that history is to be made." In such circumstances, Germanic Christians must be reassured that "war is no longer murder."[46] Reading this, even the hawkish Seeberg would jot in the margins, "Ambiguous!"[47]

There are hints of Bonhoeffer's uneasy conscience, if only in the inescapable conflict between the "new creation"—which punctuates the dissertation of every reference to St. Paul's letters the new transnational identity of Christ's body—and the author's unexamined prejudices. At least Bonhoeffer rejected the popular idea that killing for the fatherland might be affirmed as an act of love—little comfort though that omission would be to Germany's neighbors. Unlike Harnack, Holl, and Seeberg, each of whom remained loyal to the proud tradition of German war theology, Bonhoeffer at least acknowledged the clashing differences of "the New and the Old Adam, and the authority of the gospel over the state in issues of war and peace."

Five years hence, Bonhoeffer would feel "disgust and shame" at these passages, confessing as much before an international audience of concerned churchmen: "War today, and therefore the next war, must be utterly *rejected* by the church."[48] But the weight of German exceptionalism and the spiritual veneration of military valor were not easy inheritances to disown. In nineteenth-century Protestant Prussia, no less a philosopher-patriot than Hegel resolved that his beloved *Machtstaat* (the "power state" that was the German imperium) had been chosen by God to rule the nations by example, fiat, or force.[49] It was God's nature to manifest his will in superior and powerful nations, which demonstrated their providential purpose by imposing their will on their neighbors, as the ancient Hebrews had done. By the end of the nineteenth century, the idea of Germany as such a "world-historical nation" had become as hallowed as the historicity of the biblical narratives.

In August 1914, ninety-three German theologians and religious leaders had proclaimed their support for the war policy of Wilhelm II, with the Berlin faculty leading the charge. The revered Harnack promoted a genteel nationalism in his felicitous Lutheran amalgam of church and state. The ideal of citizenship, he believed, remained "a high-spirited disposition . . . very closely akin to religion." He would even be proud to ghostwrite Kaiser Wilhelm's 1914 public address "To the German Peoples" calling for war mobilization. This was the point, too, at which Seeberg, who'd sought to make Luther more accessible to modern believers, showed himself a zealous "annexationist," quite certain that the seizure of Belgium and northern France would strengthen the German soul.[50] Seeberg believed he was fulfilling his spiritual vocation by helping the German people discern the powerful hand of God in the new forces gathering to propel Germany to greatness. Among the professoriate there were precious few willing dissenters from this conviction.[51] German Protestant theology from Schleiermacher to Harnack and Seeberg presumed the providential blessings of the warrior God.[52] Later, after Versailles, they would take comfort in imagining that the nation's defeat resembled Christ's humiliation on the cross. In this way, the God with whom they kept faith would resurrect the fatherland from the ashes, restoring it to its former glory.

Bonhoeffer submitted "Sanctorum Communio" to Seeberg and his other examiners on July 4, 1927. He had turned twenty-one years old in February, and while academic degrees at the time were conferred much earlier by comparison with today's standards, a doctorate at the age of twenty-one was, even then, extraordinary.[53]

Seeberg's official response was blandly favorable. "From beginning to end," he wrote, the thesis "is in accordance with its purposes." While praising Bonhoeffer's gifts in "systematic thinking" and his "intelligent discussion" of social philosophy and doctrine, he remarked that Bonhoeffer seemed determined "to discover his way on his own." In the brief written evaluation, Seeberg further noted mild "insufficiencies" without specifying them, but they were nothing to detract from the "many good qualities," including "the ingenious particularity of its view" and "inner concentration," and the author's "critical ability to cope with other views" and his "enthusiasm for Christianity." The allusions to Barth in "Sanctorum Communio" had been "neutralized by others" and in any case did not determine the whole. Seeberg did express a slight worry that Bonhoeffer's criticisms of Troeltsch and German liberalism lacked careful attention to the sources.[54]

In December 1927, Bonhoeffer successfully defended the dissertation in public, as required; the forum convened in the great hall on

Unter den Linden. He passed the doctoral examination summa cum laude and, following routine deliberations by his faculty advisers, was awarded a doctor of philosophy degree from the Friedrich-Wilhelms University of Berlin.

Walter Dress was asked for one more favor: to take care of the final paperwork and administrative logistics pertaining to the doctorate. In celebration of his accomplishment, Dietrich had planned a holiday on the North Sea island of Sylt and was eager to leave town.[55]

CHAPTER FOUR

1928–1929

~

"Greetings from the Matador"

H e had never been a stranger to restlessness: life had fairly bristled
with rousing tests and luxurious enchantments. Adventures always
seemed to present themselves, and he was happy to pursue them, especially if they led him to new locales. But even a life full of diversions
can, over years, reveal itself to be subject to unsuspected routines, until,
at long last, even the challenges and delights become predictable. And
so it was that, at the age of twenty-one, with a doctorate already in
hand, on the verge of a brilliant career, Dietrich Bonhoeffer discovered
boredom. He needed to try something very different.

One day in the early fall of 1927, he received a telephone call from
Max Diestel, superintendent of the Lutheran Church in Berlin. Diestel
offered Bonhoeffer the post of assistant vicar of the German congregation of Barcelona. Bonhoeffer was intrigued by the opportunity as a
way of completing his practicum, feeling his wish had been granted "to
stand on my own feet for an extended period, completely outside my
existing circle of acquaintances."[1] And though he had spent the spring
of 1924 in Italy, returning there for a summer holiday in 1926, he still
felt as if he had never traveled on his own. "It was simply necessary for
me to start from the beginning," he wrote. The actual work of parish ministry would remain a prospect he didn't relish: aside from two
required courses in practical theology with Friedrich Mahling, Bonhoeffer had never given much thought to pastoral service.[2] His dissertation may have focused on the church community, but he had been
reluctant to spend much time in church himself. But without even fully
understanding what was expected of him, Bonhoeffer accepted Diestel's offer. He really wanted to see Spain and saw no "persuasive reasons
not to go." He would "just let the decision resolve itself over time."[3]

———

Pastor Fritz Olbricht, a forty-five-year-old harried, heavyset Bavarian, was desperate for help. Ministering to a growing expatriate
population in Barcelona, he had already appealed for an assistant several times to the church authorities in Berlin. Finally, in the first week
of December 1927, he learned that he would be sent a young man who
had recently finished his doctorate. Olbricht knew nothing of Bonhoeffer, let alone his distinguished Berlin relations. He was happy just to
know that help was meant to arrive very soon.[4] Bonhoeffer, however,
did not share Olbricht's sense of urgency.

In his first letter to Barcelona, Bonhoeffer asked advice on assembling his new wardrobe. He'd heard that the weather in Barcelona
could be fickle. He was particularly keen to know what style and weight
of suiting Olbricht recommended—these choices must matter greatly
in the temperate zone. And would he need special athletic wear at the
clubs? He also enquired whether he might proceed with scheduling
some vacation time; he wanted to tour southern Spain with his brother
Klaus.[5] All this was in a letter he posted shortly before Christmas.

It would be a month before a flustered Olbricht found "some peace
and quiet to respond to [his] questions."[6] When he did, he was at pains
to make clear that Advent was the busiest season for most ministers, a
fact he had hoped the new man would have understood. Thus, he had
further hoped—indeed, expected—to have Bonhoeffer in Barcelona by
Christmas. When *was* he planning to arrive?

As to matters sartorial, Olbricht said he himself wore "the same
heavy overcoat" in Spain that he'd worn in Germany. The days offered
plenty of sunshine, even in winter, but houses were poorly heated, and
the night often brought bitter winds off the sea. Bring your "warm
underwear, heavy suits, and an overcoat," Olbricht advised.

Bonhoeffer wrote back to thank Olbricht, and, ignoring the question of when he would start, raised another about his dress: Would he
need dinner clothes, or "special evening wear"?

In answering the second letter, Olbricht said there might be occasion for a tail coat, but that, in his opinion, a dinner jacket would serve
better. In that bit of counsel the sarcasm is debatable, but not so in
the next: one item the new assistant should not neglect to bring was
his clerical robe.[7] Olbricht was even less patient concerning vacation
plans. Having hoped the new man would be in place for the height of
the season, he was dismayed now to learn that he should not expect
Bonhoeffer until the lull time of mid-January.

When, by the third week of January, Bonhoeffer had still not
reported for duty, Olbricht wrote again, this time in desperation: he
had booked passage to Majorca, where many of his parishioners had

second homes. But it was not a holiday: a parishioner had died in Palma, and Olbricht had to conduct the funeral service.

"A shame you're not here yet," Olbricht wrote, evidently straining to uphold his Christian charity. "Now, another service must be canceled."[8]

Finally, on the eighth of February, following two weeks of farewell parties with friends and family, Bonhoeffer boarded an overnight train in Berlin, settling into his sleeper to begin the journey to Barcelona. Even then, however, he did not travel directly to Spain. Realizing he had to change trains in Paris anyway, he thought it only sensible to linger there for a week's holiday. After all, he had never been to Paris.

Arriving at the Gare du Nord, he took a taxi to the Hôtel Beauséjour, at 99 rue de Ranelagh in the 16th arrondissement. The hotel, a favorite of German tourists, had been highly recommended by an old high school classmate. But soon Bonhoeffer would have cause to wonder whether he'd picked the most propitious time to visit. He endured seven days of cold rain. But he made the best of it, spending morning in the cafés reading, afternoons in the Louvre, and evenings at the opera. He would hear Giuseppe Verdi's *Rigoletto* and Georges Bizet's *Carmen*—both splendid performances.[9]

In Paris, as in Italy, Bonhoeffer felt himself drawn to the sensual spirituality of Roman Catholicism. He attended a "festive high mass at the basilica of Sacré Coeur," the imposing Romano-Byzantine church at the summit of Montmartre. Here, a new social perspective emerged, one very different from his experience in the Eternal City. Where the magnificent churches in and around the Holy See drew a predictably cosmopolitan range of worshippers, in Paris he saw more local color among those entering the fellowship of the saints. Afterward, he would write: "The people in the church were almost exclusively from [the neighborhood]; prostitutes and their men went to mass, submitted to all the ceremonies; it was an enormously impressive picture"; taking in the scene, Bonhoeffer said he could see quite clearly how close, "precisely by reason of their lot and offenses," these "heavily burdened people" remained to "the heart of the gospel."[10]

The "heavily burdened people" of Montmartre called to mind the denizens of Berlin's gritty Tauentzienstrasse, where the city's vital commercial center was ringed by its red-light district.[11] Before this, Bonhoeffer had never given much thought to the underclass. To be sure, Professor Friedrich Mahling had discussed the theology of what he called "urban ministry," encouraging his students to confront the special troubles of congregations suffering high unemployment. But

Grunewald had sheltered Dietrich from Berlin's beleaguered precincts. And his intellectual interests lay elsewhere.

But in the candle-lit Mass at Sacré Coeur, a flash of insight came to him. A rough and seedy area like this presented "an extremely fruitful field for church work." Breathing the rarefied air of Romantic theology, one might easily forget that the face of Christ was to be sought not only in majesty on high but also, perhaps more intimately, among the ordinary and the downtrodden.[12] Not that he was entirely innocent of a certain self-satisfied solemnity in viewing the lower classes at worship. But the fact remains that he had never before witnessed the intense communion of the poor with their God, never listened for the voice of the thief on the cross, crying, "Lord, remember me when thou comest into thy kingdom." The prostitute and the thief abode nearer "to the heart of the gospel" than the "vain man praying," Bonhoeffer—aged twenty-one, barely yet a man—at last understood in his inmost parts.

Shortly before sunrise on Tuesday, February 14, 1928, he boarded a train bound for Barcelona and fell into a deep sleep. When he awoke they were just outside the village of Narbonne, and as he lifted the window shade "the landscape verging on spring seemed right out of a fairy tale." He "suddenly felt transported to the area around Naples." Almond, peach, apricot, and mimosa trees shimmered in "radiant fields."[13] In the distance, the gothic spires of the then-unfinished Cathédrale Saint-Just et Saint-Pasteur stretched heavenward in the late-morning sun. At Narbonne, he moved into a luxury coach for the remaining 160 miles and enjoyed a hearty lunch with a good red wine. Nearing the border of Spain, he saw the snowy peaks of the Pyrenees rising in the west and the blue Iberian Sea glistening in the south. During a short stop in Port-la-Nouvelle, Bonhoeffer stood at the open window, feeling the warm salty air on his skin and admiring the "cloudless" sky. The "sun burned" bright as on a midsummer day.

He reached Barcelona early in the afternoon of February 15. Despite an unpleasant exchange with a rude customs official, he was soon walking through the archways of the Estació de França, into the bustling district of Sants-Montjuïc, where Olbricht was waiting in a car.[14]

Bonhoeffer moved into a boardinghouse at 59 Calle San Eusebio in the Gracias neighborhood. He had been offered accommodations with a German family but told Olbricht he would rather live "among the natives." He would soon grow fond of the innkeepers, three Spanish women, only a few years older than he was, who could not say "Señor Dietrich" without getting tongue-tied and giggling.[15]

The arrangements suited him well. The boardinghouse was on a quiet street, just a five-minute walk from the German-Lutheran compound at 2 Calle Moyá. His room, one flight up, was spacious and clean, with floors made of smooth local stone. There was a bed, a worktable, a pair of chairs, and a basin for washing. A fine view of the northern hills could be had on either of the two balconies, which absorbed the warmth of the morning sun and were shielded from the cold winds, so that even in winter he took his morning coffee outside. "The sky is a glorious blue," he wrote to his family, "and I can look out onto two small streets and the houses, which, except for the roofs, are completely white. Down below, little children yell and play in the street, and people passing by call out all sorts of things. On the whole, the picture bears a strong resemblance to southern Italy."[16]

He found a bar on the Mole, the strand of Barcelona's harbor, where he could have an aperitif and a half-dozen raw oysters for one and a half pesetas. He thought the Spanish white wines excellent, but with the oysters he preferred vermouth and soda water. He liked the café con leche, but found the Spanish cakes and pastries "too sweet and fluffy." When his room was too cold in the evening, he'd take his books to a neighborhood café with a woodstove. On milder days, he'd take a streetcar to the cafés on the Plaza Cataluña, to read the newspaper or watch the people go by.[17] He was pleased to be writing again in his journal—describing "the ethnic mix," the "strikingly austere, masculine facial features . . . of the otherwise small, delicate, sinewy people," the "extremely fat ones," and "children whom you might consider obese."[18]

POSTCARD OF THE "BARCELONA. PLAÇA REIAL" FROM DIETRICH BONHOEFFER

He also admired the mixing of the social orders, the way "prosperous, rich, petit bourgeois, and really poor-looking people . . . all mingled together."[19] It was quite different from Berlin's stratified café culture. In Barcelona's parks the air held the perfume of lemon and almond trees and the saltiness of the nearby sea.

Best of all were day trips into the Serra de Collserola, the mountains that framed the sea to the west. With a book and writing paper in his backpack, he could reach the mountains by the funicular but would usually hike up the winding trail to the top of the Tibidabo. Local legend had it that this dramatic peak, the highest of the western range, was where the devil had tempted Jesus, indicating the town and sea and hills, the whole world that lay below: "All these tibi dabo (I will give to you)." Bonhoeffer wrote his mother a letter from that spot, saying he was waiting for the devil to come but so far he had failed to turn up.[20]

"One evening up there recently," he continued, "I watched a sunset whose colors I will never forget. A blue and then at last a haze of perfect violet settled around the mountains, and through it one could see shimmering the peculiar contours of Montserrat, the holy Mountain of the grail; in the foreground there were enormous cacti and trees in bloom."[21]

On another occasion, he hiked into the Montseny, a mountainous beech forest some sixty kilometers northeast of the city. He wanted to see the abbey of Sant Miquel del Fai, before ascending the narrow, craggy paths to the Turó de l'Home and its majestic views of the rugged Catalonian coastal range.

The German colony of Barcelona numbered about six thousand, but fewer than three hundred belonged to the Lutheran congregation. Fewer still attended Sunday-morning services with any regularity. Fifty souls in the pews was considered a decent turnout.[22] Many parishioners, an affable lot overall, spent weekends at their seaside homes, the best off enjoying their villas in rich coastal enclaves. The global stock markets wouldn't crash until the following year, in 1929, and meanwhile there was high living to be enjoyed by the German expatriates, most of whom had been sent to Barcelona by a prospering firm back home or else were thriving capitalists in their own right.[23] The Lutheran parish mostly reflected the petit bourgeois sensibility of the larger German community; Bonhoeffer said he had never seen people so visibly impressed by their own wealth. He heard the director of the German bank boast about a recent gala for which ten thousand pesetas had been spent on the decorations alone. There was also the businessman who'd imported dancing girls from the Moulin Rouge for his lavish parties on the Mediterranean.[24] The ostentation of the locals was disquieting to the new pastor, but as he had not lost his well-bred taste for the finer things, he rarely declined an invitation.

In fact, as word spread through the expat community of Olbricht's dapper new assistant, Bonhoeffer's company became much sought after. Socializing with these new-money parishioners was, on the whole, "very pleasant," he wrote, though he was unaccustomed to their idea of conversation.[25] His life in Berlin had been an easy triangulation of university, family, and neighborhood, with no domain obliging him to make intellectual allowances for any other. But in Barcelona, Bonhoeffer was amused and no doubt a bit disappointed to find that even after two months, he had not met a single person with whom he could speak in the "Berlin-Grunewald style." The conversations lacked depth, and "he lived without any exchange of ideas." Still, he appreciated the hospitality of his parishioners and their many tender affirmations.

"Every evening last week was booked up with invitations and other things," he told his parents. "Yours truly has the advantage of being admitted everywhere, and even being a rather popular guest." Late-night meals—as was the Spanish style—took getting used to. Sometimes he would not return from a dinner party until two a.m.—could they believe it? He sang in the German choral ensemble and performed musical skits at the German Club. Though never one for card games, he took up "skat," which was popular among his compatriots. At the posh Club Pampaia, Bonhoeffer made his mark as a bon vivant and competitive tennis player (he had to ask his parents for the membership dues when he realized he couldn't afford them on his modest church stipend). When invited to the club's annual masquerade ball, however, he replied, atypically, with regrets, out of concern that the sight of the young pastor costumed for Fat Tuesday might "prompt some sort of dumb gossip." It seems unlikely, though, that any members of this parish would have been offended.

The parishioners' friendliness came with a benign disinterest in religion. Most felt toward the church the same blind loyalty as they did toward their sports teams and the German National Party—only in the case of the church, as Bonhoeffer observed, there was much less desire to get personally involved.[26] It may be that they had never been given much reason. The beleaguered vicar to whom Bonhoeffer had been seconded, "a large, raven-haired man in his early fifties," spoke "frightfully fast and indistinctly." He was cleverer than one might expect of a pastor, but "not elegant." He had "a good sense of humor" and was "anything but unctuous." These are the words of the new assistant. Following their first meeting, Bonhoeffer felt certain they would get along, but he seemed less sure of Olbricht's power to inspire: "I can't imagine yet how he will preach."[27]

Not that the new man came overly enflamed with the Spirit himself. If Bonhoeffer did not begrudge his new flock their religious apathy, it was because he understood their disaffection and their boredom, in a profound sense, sharing those feelings.[28] Indeed, the question then forming in his mind was whether Christianity—despite the bland outward cast it had assumed—could still become a vital and meaningful reality for people who had found better ways to spend a Sunday morning.

As assistant pastor, he would work mainly in the children's ministry and with the high school youth group. He also taught an occasional class at the German school. He enjoyed these assignments, since the spiritual formation of adolescents and children remained a mystery to him on many levels. He found "their stunning naiveté about religious questions" endearing, and their capacity to feel simultaneously trust and suspicion a worthy challenge.[29] Bonhoeffer's favorite Romantic poets celebrated the child's free and spontaneous nature—as had his own mother. But every theologian he had read either ignored or trivialized the spirituality of children, notwithstanding Jesus's famous admonition in Matthew 19:14, "Let the little children come to me and do not hinder them." Bonhoeffer's earliest comments on the subject may seem a bit awkward and pietistic, but they were grounded in scripture. "For, indeed, God is closer to children than to adults. Remaining pure means remaining a child, even after you have become a man."

To the Lutheran youth ministry Bonhoeffer brought a "blaze of intellect" and "confidence."[30] He was careful, being young himself, to avoid patronizing the young. He respectfully presented them with new ways of thinking—philosophy, theology, literature: everything that excited him—and expected mature and thoughtful responses such as would have been expected of him as a boy in Grunewald. Engaging the children and teenagers alike as natural thinkers, restless and searching, he was sure they would respond once their imaginations were sparked.

But young Germans coming of age in Spain had "experienced nothing, or very little, of war, revolution, and the painful aftermath of this period." They lived "well and comfortably" and enjoyed "perpetually good weather," spending most of their free time outdoors. It seemed that no one in his youth group had ever been confronted with serious intellectual issues; the result, Bonhoeffer allowed with a sigh, was a merry band of "lazybones, good-for-nothings, [and] precocious" children utterly lacking in curiosity or passion.[31] His father would have been appalled. But the pastor had his work cut out for him.

DIETRICH BONHOEFFER IN
BARCELONA, 1928

In his favor, the students were impressed with him, though not so much on account of his intellect as his sartorial flair. It seems Pastor Olbricht's teenage son was one of the first to notice Bonhoeffer's style, pronouncing it "modern and worthy of imitation."[32] The boy was especially taken with the assistant vicar's Panama hat, worn at a rakish angle; he asked his father if he could get one too. Bonhoeffer had also let his hair grow longer in Spain; with his sun-bleached curls and khaki linen suits, he projected an infectious joie de vivre.

Whatever the catalyst, the congregation and youth group did flourish under Bonhoeffer's direction. Just a few weeks after he'd begun conducting the liturgy and the children's service, attendance in the youth program grew to fifteen, having started at one.

"Girls up to the age of fourteen, boys on the average ten to eleven years old," he wrote in his journal. "The latter are wonderfully fresh and lively. I showed them the splendid things that the children's service could offer, and that caught fire. Have to see what happens next time. This session has virtually transformed me; the slight anxiety that I couldn't get going with the practical work has vanished."[33]

Bonhoeffer preached his first sermon on March 11, the second Sunday of Lent, 1928. He chose Romans 11:6 as his text: "And if by grace, then it is no more of works: otherwise grace is no more grace." This verse, like the whole of St. Paul's letter to the churches in Rome, was ever dear to German Protestants. The Lutheran Reformation of the sixteenth century turned on the epistle's theme of salvation *sola gratia*— coming to sinners through grace alone, a gift by no means deserved by reason of any works, and certainly not owing to any priestly mediation.

There was a palpable intensity to the sermon that seems to have taken some listeners by surprise, at least those who knew the pastor only from informal exchanges. It reveals Bonhoeffer reaching for a spiritual vitality permeating the totality of creation, beyond the familiar dualisms of the sacred and profane, of spirit and body, earth and heaven.

Karl Barth had written that the Christian should be more humanist than the humanist, more romantic than the romanticist, but also more precise than either—humanism gathers tremendous strength in the story of the Word made flesh. And precision is the proper ordering of doctrine and belief.

Like Barth, Bonhoeffer interprets the human condition in the light of the incarnation, the "great event" when God assumed human form in Jesus of Nazareth, and, as described in the Gospel of John, "We beheld his glory, the glory as of the only begotten of the Father, full of grace and truth." But Bonhoeffer was seeking the *precise* terms for a lived faith in the here and now, hungering, as he said in the sermon, for "eternity in the midst of time."

To be sure, the doctrine of *sola gratia*, that God alone forgives, justifies, and *saves* undeserving sinners, was the essential message of the Christian faith, at least in its Lutheran form. "If there is anything at all on this earth that, however seriously it may present itself, is not ultimately trivial or even comical, it is the fact of justification." But to apprehend the doctrine without its changing one from the inside— without experience of a metanoia, a spiritual change of heart—is to trivialize God's redemptive acts. Bonhoeffer wanted to awaken his flock to the wonder and power of the "new creation," the universe as redeemed when God took flesh. He told them, "Through [justification] our gaze is opened on the entire world, on that which is vain and that which matters; in [that state] we understand both ourselves and . . . God."[34] He wanted his congregation to feel the full force of the "great disruption" caused by an awareness of God's merciful gift. For justification was fact before ever being expressed as doctrine. Grace frees and forms, grace invites and involves. Grace calls the idle and the complacent, even the nouveaux riches, out of their spiritual lethargy into heightened knowledge of God. But grace has no use for the indifferent heart.

Bonhoeffer spoke of the unquiet soul described by St. Augustine in *The Confessions*: "You have made us for Yourself, O Lord, and our hearts are restless, until they find their rest in Thee." Throughout his life, sometimes at the prodding of others—more often, though, of his own accord—Bonhoeffer would agitate against the Lutheran habit of reducing the self to an empty vessel into which God merely poured his grace. To be sure, the spectacular anguish Luther, as a new monk, had felt at his own insufficiency—the crushing weight of fear before his encounter with the God of infinite mercy—seemed to Bonhoeffer unsustainable in the languor of a semitropical paradise; he was, in any case, nowhere near such an extreme. So it was, then, that in several of the seventeen sermons preached during his year in Barcelona, his efforts to focus and inspire would follow not the Reformer of Wittenberg but the fourth-century Bishop Augustine of Hippo, the impulse not one of guilt or shame but rather sparked by the intimations of mystery everywhere abounding.

"'Restless': this is the word that concerns us," Bonhoeffer said. "Restlessness is the characteristic distinguishing human beings from animals. Restlessness is the power that creates history and culture. Restlessness is the root of every spirit that uplifts itself toward morality; restlessness is—let us go ahead and say it—the most profound meaning and the lifeblood of all religion. Restlessness—not in any transitory human sense, in which all we find is nervousness and impatience—no, restlessness in the direction of the eternal . . . pointing toward the infinite."[35] Restlessness is the very condition induced by what he called "the great disturbance" and "the great disruption" occasioned by awareness of God, the source of freedom and movement. Guilt immobilizes and fear hollows out, but restlessness and desire open the self to God.[36]

Compared with the formal rigors of the doctoral dissertation, the Barcelona sermons are both literary and uninhibited. Bonhoeffer found writing them a great liberation, for the exercise drew on his musical gifts and artistic intuitions. Indeed these lyrical and expressive essays are among his most beautiful writings. A mystical current guides the pen.

In one delivered in April 1928, with the city glistening as it does in springtime, Bonhoeffer spoke of an "anxious . . . questioning for divine things," "a great loneliness [that] has come upon our age," and "an enormous distress of isolation and homelessness." He alluded to a "yearning for the time when once again God might abide among human beings. . . . A thirst for contact with divine things has come upon people, a burning thirst demanding to be quenched." The most important thing is "to keep our eyes open to see where we find God."[37]

At Pentecost, a sermon of incandescent beauty summoned "torches of divine fire, divine clarity, divine light in the midst of a world that has sunk into night, torches pointing toward the light, torches with which others can light their own torches, torches ignited by the magnificence of the divine glory—this is what Jesus wants to make out of us. To purify and enlighten and warm." He prayed for the day when "the divine fire alone illumines the world."

On a subsequent Sunday, in the quiet of summer, when many parishioners were away, he spoke of the vision of God—the beatific vision—and he remarked the intimacy between a righteous life and the radiance of the Lord. Faith means this: "to behold our home after wandering our whole life long, to throw ourselves on God's bosom and weep and rejoice the way a child does in its mother's arms." Faith "drinks God's light," craves "his clarity like living water." To behold the majesty of God is "to become a piece of eternity. . . . It means rejoicing along with the chorus of the redeemed in white robes. . . . Oh, what a great wealth, both of wisdom and of the knowledge of God—[for] from God and to Him and Through Him are all things."[38] In faith, "our gaze opens to the fullness of divine life in the world."[39]

On another such sparsely attended Sunday, in late August, Bonhoeffer invoked the mysterious word he used to whisper in his twin sister's ear at bedtime, a word that now soared through his preaching like a bird against the Catalan azure. "God has touched [our souls] from *eternity*—this is the love within us and the longing and the sacred restlessness and the responsibility and joy and pain. It is the divine breath breathed into transitory being."[40] Nothing else could subdue earthly time except "Eternity," and its "forceful luminous current."[41]

"If we think about the boundaries of the world, of time," the days shortening into fall, "something miraculous occurs. . . . The limits of the world, the end of the world," where "time loses its power to eternity; the world's ultimate reality, death, itself becomes something penultimate. . . . The transitory is subsumed within the perspective of eternity." Beyond the ephemeral and the dark stands "a sign from eternity, solemn and mighty, bathed in the radiance of the divine sun of grace and light—the cross. And there [God] hangs, his arms outstretched as if to embrace the entire world in love."[42]

Bonhoeffer's presence in the pulpit, like in his work among the faithful, was a relief to the desperately overburdened Olbricht. Even so, the latter did not entirely appreciate his assistant's grand style or the wunderkind's effulgence. As church attendance grew steadily, and the youth group flourished, Bonhoeffer happily accepted credit—and Olbricht became increasingly jealous. He took Bonhoeffer's aloofness as disrespect (which it may have been), and his grand style as arrogance (which in part it surely was). But the rector was in a bind. He could no longer do without the extra pair of hands, and so his reports back to Berlin could not have been sunnier.

Bonhoeffer was not unaware of the effect he was having. As he wrote his mother, Olbricht, glad at first, became jealous only "after my services were much better attended than his." It was then, too, that Olbricht stopped announcing "ahead of time who would be preaching," fearing Sunday attendance would vary depending on the homilist. In any event, strong attendance at Bonhoeffer's lectures on other days also irked Olbricht—though perhaps not as much as would the assistant's success with the nativity play: Bonhoeffer not only directed the pageant but took a starring role as Joseph. The rave reviews, Dietrich reported to Paula, precipitated "a clash" with Olbricht.[43]

Just as Bonhoeffer was unashamed of his privilege, he did not downplay his innate gifts. But nor did he exaggerate them. Later, allowing that the sin of pride had been a lifelong struggle, he would learn to restrain himself so as to put others at ease. But he would never disown the advantages of birth or pretend to have surpassed them. It was an aristocratic confidence, he would insist, that helped him see through propaganda and resist mediocrity. Be that as it may, in Barcelona, outside the forbearance of the family circle (or its power to take him down a peg), the prodigious gifts of Karl and Paula Bonhoeffer's sixth child often left others all too aware of their more modest endowments.

POSTCARD FROM DIETRICH BONHOEFFER FROM BARCELONA,
TO RÜDIGER SCHLEICHER

"Greetings from the matador," he wrote on a postcard home, with his face superimposed on that of a triumphant bullfighter, hovering above the dying beast.[44] It was typical of the unchecked braggadocio of his reports to Grunewald. So, too, was a distinct lack of charity toward Olbricht, as evident in letters not made public until the past decade.[45] Admittedly, they were never intended for eyes outside the family, but they are notably harsh and unforgiving.

He allowed as how his beleaguered senior colleague had "apparently hitherto done nothing by way of addressing the youth of the parish," to whom he related but awkwardly. He also found Olbricht intemperate, "quick to rant"—"never toward me," but "certainly toward women and children." Olbricht reportedly would scold a confirmand who had dared ask a question instead of quietly writing out his weekly assignment. Olbricht was unfriendly to non-Germans who visited the parish, but his "excitement was almost childish when he received birthday presents." His whole manner offended Bonhoeffer. So did his cast of mind. Olbricht was constantly swallowing phrases, "as if he were a bit embarrassed."[46] A fully formed sentence never passed from his lips. He rarely read, unless it was the newspaper or some nationalist tract, and he "studied even less." Perhaps by no coincidence, "his sermons are uninspired and scandalously boring!" One might have forgiven his performance in the pulpit, but "[h]is pastoral care is nonexistent, and his instruction hopelessly uncomprehending."[47] Bonhoeffer believed Olbricht had missed his true calling: "He would have been better suited as a forest ranger or an infantryman," Dietrich told his mother. Oh, and his parsonage lacked tasteful furnishings.

Had his situation been permanent, Bonhoeffer said, he would have raised these matters with Olbricht. But circumstances inspired his magnanimous silence, for the good of both men, it would seem. As it happened, "[We] never once discussed a theological question, let alone a religious one; we basically remained strangers, although we did like each other. He granted me all the freedom I wanted, and for that I was grateful to him."[48]

K laus Bonhoeffer arrived in Barcelona on Easter Sunday, April 8, 1928, for a two-month visit. As it was a fine spring day, his younger brother was especially surprised that Klaus came along to the morning service. Olbricht was away on one of his occasional ministries to the "diaspora," as he liked to call German Lutherans living throughout Spain. This afforded Bonhoeffer the chance to shine on the holiest day of the year.[49] Before a full house, including his bleary-eyed brother, Dietrich, sporting new robes for the occasion, held forth on a theme he always favored, "God's intervention *from* eternity."[50]

But he took a slightly different approach that Sunday. Easter is traditionally a day most churches welcome newcomers and members who rarely attend; the Lutheran church of Barcelona was no exception. And so for this special occasion, rather than read a prepared sermon, Bonhoeffer chose to preach extemporaneously from notes, in a flight of kataphatic optimism, on a passage from St. Paul's first letter to the

Corinthian church (I Corinthians 15:17): "And if Christ has not been raised, your faith is futile and you are still in your sins."

> A dangerous Easter text. For if we look at it more closely . . . it could possibly rob us of all our Easter joy . . . Christian festival . . . threatening . . . allow this assault to affect us, then joy of Easter.—supports [are] pulled away, meaningless- ness . . . illusory . . . Our life depends on Easter. We? . . . Text. "Resurrection"?—Easter question.—Spring enables to sense primal struggle between darkness and light . . . spring emerges from winter . . . all that is dark must become light . . . law of nature . . darkness and nothing . . . Humanity. Prometheus. Good Friday . . . God who became human crucified; God's Holy One dies . . . Transcendent event. Not immortality . . . not divine seed . . . If God's history ends on Good Friday . . . "Great Pan is dead." Easter message: God lives, Jesus raised—fullness of God—God's victory . . . a prologue of ultimate, ineffable things . . . the entire glory and power of God . . . Questions?[51]

Bonhoeffer seemed pleased with the results. Some of those present would later recall the sermon as expressive, poetic, and graceful. This was especially so in comparison with his usual efforts, which, most agreed, tended to be a little wordy, even though the young Berliner's elocution always made his countrymen proud.

That afternoon Dietrich and Klaus joined Hermann Thumm, a German teacher, at the Plaza de Toros for the Easter *corrida*, the most anticipated bullfight of the season. Dietrich was pleased to report to his parents that he had not been troubled by the blood sport, at least not "the way many people think they owe it to their central European civilization to be shocked." On the contrary, he found the "great spectacle" a fitting complement to Easter among the German Lutherans. "Glory and power" in the morning, "blood and cruelty" in the afternoon, he joked. Thirty thousand spectators whipped into an ecstatic frenzy: Spanish Catholicism made enviable room for the instincts to run wild. Far from shocked, Dietrich was enthralled.[52]

Two months later, on the Monday after Pentecost, Dietrich and Klaus left Barcelona for a three-week journey, the long-anticipated tour of southern Spain. It was to be at their parents' expense, and long before, Dietrich had composed a two-page list of necessities for their consideration.[53] In addition to cash, the list included socks and ties, a new tennis racket, and ticket upgrades. "If we were to travel third class the whole way," Dietrich explained, "we would be spending a great deal of time on the frightfully slow railways, would often have to travel for considerable hours at night, etc." As usual, his expenditures were approved.

If not quite the Grand Tour, their travels nonetheless followed a similar arc, from Madrid and Toledo to Seville, Ronda, and the Alboran Sea. On most days, the sun burned bright in a clear sky as the train cut through groves of olive trees or cork oaks, fields of agave or fig cactus. "The fragrance of oranges was intoxicating," Klaus wrote in his journal. "Roses, carnations, gillyflowers, and wisteria created an incredible lushness on the squares and balconies" of the villages. The brothers traveled by car along the coast, taking breaks to swim, picnic, and sunbathe. Otherwise, they covered themselves "like a pious Arab woman—with a single eye exposed—to cope with the scorching sun."[54]

From the port city of Algeciras, they hugged the shore all the way to Tarifa, where they crossed the Straits of Gibraltar by ferry for an overnight stay in Tétouan. This was to be their second visit to North Africa. But whereas on their Libyan excursion they had people to look up, in Morocco they knew no one at all. Still, they marveled at the ancient Arab city, bordered by orange groves, pomegranate orchards, and rows of almond and cypress trees. "Chills run up your spine when you hear [them] along the streets loudly reciting suras from the Qur'an," Klaus wrote. Dietrich photographed the marble fountains and ornate houses, and the camels ferrying cargo along brick boulevards lined with citrus trees.

Near the harbor, they found a room in a small hotel, a sparsely furnished space resembling the interior of a mosque, "with three Arabic archways, Saracen tiles and no light." The windows had been barred and faced an interior courtyard anyway. They didn't get much sleep during their one night in town, what with other guests rocking in their iron-framed beds before settling down to snore, to say nothing of the disturbance caused "by roosters crowing and by the penetrating songs of pious Muslims."[55] The next morning, the sight of the caliph riding under a baldachin, wearing a "strangely cordial, gentle, almost feminine smile" and drawn by magnificent, pompously harnessed horses, made a brief, favorable impression on the young men.[56] In all they spent less than twenty-four hours in Morocco before beginning the journey back to Barcelona.

Following the three-week sojourn, Dietrich and Klaus were closer than they had ever been, even as their journals revealed strikingly different sensibilities. Klaus, who would return home in June, spoke fondly of the beautiful girls of Seville, their long black hair adorned with fire-red carnations, as well as of the Picasso he had purchased in a

Madrid flea market: a mournful study of "degenerate women drinking absinthe," which a Berlin appraiser would later determine to be fake.[57] (The painting nonetheless remained in their parents' home until the winter of 1945, when it was destroyed during an air raid that took out several rooms of the house.) For his part, Dietrich returned under the spell of the "reddish radiant" sunset from the towers of the Alhambra, the nightingales' song, the fragrance of orange trees along the Andalusian plain, and his purchase of a "southern Spanish portrait of Christ" (which cost only seven marks), which was still hanging over his desk in Berlin the evening he was arrested by the Gestapo in 1943.[58]

Bonhoeffer's workload in Barcelona was lighter than at any time during his student days: he would preach an occasional Sunday sermon, and his youth ministry required no more than a few hours a week. Much of the time was filled poring over the four-hundred-page dissertation he had lugged to Spain, knowing that, sometime soon, he would need to revise the manuscript for publication—"to rewrite a great deal and delete an entire section," he estimated.[59] And he knew that further academic labors awaited him following his yearlong stint on the Mediterranean. To qualify for a university professorship, he would need to habilitate, to prove himself again, which meant a second dissertation. At the least, he had hoped to return to Berlin with a few pages of notes on the new project, but all he had to show by the time his brother left were the phrases *theology of childhood* and *the question of consciousness*. Since he would be expected to begin the *Habilitationsschrift* right upon his return to Berlin, he began to feel the pressure. But a decision to deliver a series of public lectures at the Lutheran church in Barcelona made any progress on the academic research exceedingly difficult.[60]

Whether it was the late nights, the ocean air, or the remoteness of university rigors, he could not say for sure, but he seemed amused at his lack of inclination to study. "A week has gone by without my having either the desire or the leisure for writing."[61] After a couple of hours at the office, or in the sacristy, taking periodic breaks to play the organ, he would leave for the day. Lunch, a hearty meal as served by the three señoritas at the boardinghouse, usually lasted from one thirty to three. Only then did Bonhoeffer try to get some work done. Every afternoon, he went to his room with reasonably good intentions—or so he told his parents. But as the sun began to warm his westward windows and the street life settled down for the siesta hour, he would surrender to "the temptation" more often than not. "[The] spirit is usually willing, but the flesh is weak," he explained. "I sink down onto my bed with a book, but soon it's all over."

Work seemed no more compelling after his nap. Usually, he'd grab his jacket and head out, often to the movies. For one peseta—if he entered at the matinee hour—he could watch "two or three, often even four films . . . shown one after the other." He found most of the offerings "incredibly dumb and boring," but he kept going, and the Spanish that he had studied in his free time in Berlin served him well enough in its native land. An exception was the 1926 adaption of *Don Quixote*, which featured the Danish Laurel-and-Hardy duo Pat and Patachon in a Spanish-Danish production.[62] Bonhoeffer, who had never read Cervantes's masterpiece, soon obtained a copy, and with it another excuse to put off his scholarly work.[63]

He wasn't hiding his indolence terribly much. Dr. Bonhoeffer was so alarmed by his son's dispatches that he spoke with Professor Harnack, who in turn counseled Dietrich to get started on his postdoctoral studies—reading and taking notes—and not wait until returning to Berlin. Dietrich ignored the advice. As spring turned to summer, the days lengthened, blotting out any hope of academic effort. By late May, the temperatures soared above 90 degrees Fahrenheit (low-mid-30s Celsius), and nightfall brought little relief. Barcelona was "simply too hot for serious scholarly work." He deleted some sections in his "Sanctorum Communio," at the insistence of his editor—but that, together with the two phrases noted above, was the sum of his labors. "You walk silently and slowly about the glaring, hot streets and look for a bit of shade," he explained to his superintendent in Berlin.[64] Even the pulpit was insufferable, built into a corner of the sanctuary that the late-morning sun struck with merciless force.[65]

The climate did at least stimulate his theatricality. One afternoon he returned to his rooms with what he called the "mid-summer tremors." He reported to his mother that his body had reached "the absolute boiling point for human flesh," forcing him to wrap himself in blankets with a pot of hot lemon tea and a handful of aspirin and sweat "out the entire afternoon." It was just as well to put the brakes on his scholarly ambitions, he said, at least momentarily, as "practical things need to be done." Indeed, while he might have sapped his academic energies beneath the "brilliant sun, sea and sky," Bonhoeffer nevertheless made a crucial discovery: an unexpected joy in practical ministry. He was good at it, too, involving himself in people's lives more directly—even on occasions when no champagne was served—and he seemed quite happy to concentrate his remaining months on parish life. At the same time, he made free-form sketches in his notebooks and experimented with different styles of theological writing. How might the experience of God be rendered if he let the old categories fall away?

"Theology constantly runs the risk of standardizing piety," he said, "that is, of restricting it through the enforcement of specific rules." He intended to test the limits.[66]

It was not only the ways of his stolid alma mater that left him unsatisfied and searching for a more expressive approach. All academic theology seemed to him of a piece. One day in Barcelona, Bonhoeffer picked up his copy of *The Word of God and the Word of Man* and became suddenly aware of the imperious tone of Barth's voice. The book had always been Bonhoeffer's favorite—he had once called it a liberation. But now the dizzying rhetorical heights, the cataclysmic effect of bringing the infinite crashing into the temporal—the audacity that had once so excited him—seemed unsubstantial, unable to hold a single real thing. "Barth has become quite dangerous for me personally," Bonhoeffer said, "a fact I sense with increasing clarity here in the life of the congregation." Now, when he met anyone possessed of "an extremely strong piety or even pietism," he found it increasingly difficult to distinguish between that person's ardor and Barth's ballyhooed audacity.[67] But there were of course other factors provoking Bonhoeffer's reconsideration of his intellectual habitus.[68]

Mediterranean Catholicism had impressed him with its peculiar energies. While Pastor Olbricht ranted broadly about papists, his assistant marveled at the lush, at times even untamed, spirituality of Catalonia. He was entranced by the exotic goings-on, where Olbricht derided the feast days as "all humbug," even convening a parish business meeting on the afternoon of Ash Wednesday; to Bonhoeffer's great dismay, this meant he would miss the "magnificent" street processions "where ashes, bones, and children's skeletons were hauled about by priests wearing habits from the Inquisition, black pointed cowls and all," in a ritual of penitent lamentation.[69]

As Lent came to an end, he would be sure not to miss any of the Spanish Holy Week. His Barcelona letters and journals paint a portrait of the young theologian as an exuberant and wide-eyed pilgrim. After Easter and Pentecost, there would be the astonishing "bustle" of the Corpus Christi feast, the celebratory adoration of the Holy Eucharist "with confetti, paper serpents, [and] wailing instruments" and parades of giants waving "grotesque flags" as they danced and begged for alms; everywhere people rushed about, "creaking and squealing" with their noisemakers or their own voices.[70] There were processions of local dignitaries, civil authorities, clergy, and choirboys; of the military and its marching band; of recently confirmed children in white bridal gowns that set "their dark faces quite apart"; and of other children costumed as saints, Joseph, or the *mater dolorosa*, the "mother of sorrows." There was a figure of Christ with a crown of thorns bearing the cross, and following behind a "whole host of small angels, then St. Anthony, then an ancient hermit. . . .

"Then the monstrance arrived, the ornate sunburst in which the Eucharistic host is kept, and everyone—priests, soldiers, angels, giants, entire families—went down on their knees until the vessel passed by; then suddenly paper serpents and confetti swirled from all directions onto the sacrament, and the archbishop strode placidly through the crowd. Another military band followed in the rear, bringing the procession to an end."[71]

Bonhoeffer followed the parade all the way to the cathedral, where a larger crowd gathered in the piazza in the twilight for the Benediction of the Blessed Sacrament. There he beheld a scene so "genuinely rare and beautiful" that he felt transported, he said, to "a period five hundred years ago."[72] The choirboys stood in their crimson robes under flickering lanterns, alongside them infantry and cavalrymen resplendently uniformed with "large, fantastic, warrior-like knight's helmets" and "people wearing multicolored garments." When the priests and monks, together with their pupils from the collegiate school, entered in "radiant white robes" through the "mighty main portal of the cathedral," the monstrance was at last returned to its home on the altar. In that "unique illumination" of lanterns and torches, as a breeze stirred the canopy over the bishop, and everyone knelt within the church and outside, Bonhoeffer had an intimation of paradise.[73] "Corpus Christi lasts eight days, so I'm hoping to see more," wrote the uncommon Lutheran.[74]

He would say that he felt as if "a theology of . . . spring and summer" were replacing "the Berlin winter theology."[75] For the pageantry of sun and sea and spangled sky described a new field of vision. One day, standing on his balcony, it occurred to him that he had reason to doubt "whether Barth could have written in Spain." In any event, the more elemental existence steadily worked its magic on him. "My theology is becoming more humanistic," he would conclude.

If his thinking about God was being stretched and shaken, certain habits of mind did not change at all. He would continue to cajole his parents for money.[76] To college friends back in Germany, he would still boast of his popularity with the younger set, his prowess on the tennis court, and the decadence of Mediterranean life, in which he indulged (within acceptable limits). He told one acquaintance, "I drink hardly any water, but rather exclusively wine."[77] To another he allowed that he spent most of his day in the bathtub.[78] And in conversations with his mother, he fretted mightily still over his wardrobe. He needed studs for his dress shirts. He could use some new shoes—a couple of extra pairs, in fact, because, as he said, "the general view is that one needs a lot of shoes here." He needed sports clothes suitable for the summer weather: he had been "shocked" to realize he had forgotten to pack his "mountain outfit."[79] He also needed new tennis whites and six pairs of crew socks of the same color, his club's rules requiring one to play completely in white.

At the same time, the year in Barcelona inevitably broadened his social awareness. Covetous of finery though he may have remained, he judged himself "ever more sensitive to the plight of those who really are in need and cannot be adequately supported." It angered him to see Olbricht speak gruffly to an indigent who'd stopped by the church asking for help. Beyond the comfortable sphere of the German colony, in neighborhoods to the south and directly east, on his daily walks or in the cafés or in the course of some pastoral effort, Bonhoeffer discovered a different cast of characters. He would describe them vividly and with tenderness of heart, these men and women with whom, at one time, he likely would have never "exchanged even a single word." In this way he met "vagabonds and vagrants, escaped convicts and foreign legionnaires." He met "German dancers from the musical revues," "lion tamers," and "other animal trainers who have run off from the Krone Circus during its Spanish tour." There were "German-speaking misfits," among them "contract killers wanted by the police." All of them had heard of the sympathetic Berliner and sought him out for counsel. Bonhoeffer grew to enjoy their company, too: the "criminal types," the "little people with modest goals and modest drives, who committed petty crimes," and those driven by wild, wayward passions—the "real people"! And the stories they told, vivid and honest "to the last detail," gripped him with a blunt force, as of the gospel's concern for the least of these his brethren. These people labored "more under grace than under wrath," Bonhoeffer was sure; and they were "a lot more interesting than the average church member."[80] In a letter to Helmut Rößler, a former classmate in Berlin, Bonhoeffer described himself as learning to accept people "the way they are, far from the masquerade of the 'Christian world.'"

As his society became more capacious and broad, he also discovered a larger and more varied inner world. That he—once the hothouse flower par excellence—could come to feel so truly at home in a strange country speaks to transformations both within and without.

In the second week of the new year, 1929, Bonhoeffer traveled by ferry to Majorca, some 150 miles south of Barcelona, to minister to the faithful there. He had hoped also to work on his last public lecture to be delivered in Barcelona later that month. But his plans were changed by the warm sun and sea and the fragrance of an early spring that hung in the air of the hotel courtyard, where he took his breakfast "without a coat!" The lecture would be put off until February so that he might make himself a late Christmas gift: "eight days of solitude" in the blue Balearic Sea.[81] Once he took care of his small pastoral obligation, he felt as if he had the whole island to himself: in the mountains, where he hiked snowy trails, and on the beaches of the southern coast, where he basked in warmth, listening to the rustle of the wild palms, with a book open in his lap.

His manuscript notes for the farewell lecture would not be assembled until his last weeks in Barcelona. It was good reason to panic, and so, as had been his custom in Berlin, he fired off a desperate plea for help to his friend and classmate Walter Dress. The request, not only for advice but for a copy of Paul Tillich's *Religious Situation*, went unanswered. This time he was on his own. Earlier in the fall, Bonhoeffer had announced a four-lecture series on an ambitious range of topics, though to date he had managed to deliver only two. His first talk, on the evening of November 13, 1928, was concerned with making special topics in Old Testament scholarship accessible to laypeople. "The Tragedy of the Prophetic and Its Lasting Meaning," he entitled that one (based on Bernhard Duhm's book, *Israels Propheten*); the small audience he drew answered him with polite applause and blank faces. The second lecture, "Jesus Christ and the Essence of Christianity"—this title playing on Harnack's famous *Essence of Christianity*—was not as basic as it sounded: in it he sacrificed accessibility to rhetorical experimentation as he advanced a withering critique of the Protestant liberal idea of "religion." He also relied heavily on Barth, who may not have been able to write in Barcelona but offered an abundance of pithy phrases for a theologian exposing the flaws of bourgeois peity. What religion amounted to was the creation of idols, the hubris of imagining that to speak of God one had only to speak of humanity in a thunderous voice. This anthropomorphic captivity of the God-concept was, lamentably, its essence, Bonhoeffer told the small audience of mostly laypeople. Against this background of human religion and its pantheon of false gods, Bonhoeffer argued that "the essence of Christianity" was, by contrast, to be found only in the story of a God "who traverses the path *to* human beings," the "eternal, transcendent God who comes with loving compassion for human beings, most of all for the unworthy, for the sinner." So it is that the church, its faith and its practices, must be retrieved from the trash heap of "post-Enlightenment secularization" and the gospel preached once more out of its original strangeness, and mystery.

Bonhoeffer continued,

> To the nineteenth- and twentieth-century mind, religion plays the part of the parlor, as it were, into which one doesn't mind withdrawing for a couple of hours, but from which one then immediately returns to one's business. One thing, however, is clear: namely, that we understand Christ only if we commit to Him in an abrupt either-or. He was not nailed to the cross as ornament or decoration for our lives. If we would have Him, we must recognize that He makes fundamental claims on our entire being. We scarcely understand Him if we make room for Him in merely one region of our spiritual life, but rather only if our life takes its orientation from him alone or, otherwise, if we speak a straightforward *no*. Of course, there are those not concerned with seriously considering the claims Christ makes on us with His question: Do you wish to make a complete commitment, or not? They should rather not get mixed up with Christianity at all; that would be better for Christianity, since such people no longer have anything in common with Christ. The religion of Christ is not the tidbit after the bread; it is the bread itself, or it is nothing.

Aside from such forthright evangelical convictions, much of Bonhoeffer's meandering account of modern theological thought required a fairly extensive knowledge of Western philosophy. It is unlikely that the expatriate parishioners who braved the cold November night to hear about the "essence of Christianity" were quite prepared to hear so much on Plato, Kant, and Nietzsche, let alone Goethe and the Buddha, Hellenistic religious syncretism and pagan mystery cults—of Antaeus, Attis, and Dionysus, as well as that of the Thracian-Phrygian god Sabazios—historical critical Bible scholarship, the anthroposophists, or Dostoyevsky.

Bonhoeffer's last Barcelona lecture, delivered on April 8, 1929, was one he would live to rue. For among its fundaments—belied by its prosaic title, "Basic Questions of a Christian Ethic"—was a nationalistic feeling for the fatherland. What Bonhoeffer came to regret was the lecture's having connected the individual's "immediate relationship with God" and an obedience to the will of the nation. Despite an expansive mind and wanderlust, he was still in the sway of an imposing cultural inheritance, and, as in his doctoral dissertation, the Christianity of the Germanic warrior tradition. Bonhoeffer acknowledged the centrality of Jesus Christ. The path from God to human beings "is the path of love in Christ, the path of the cross." Nevertheless, he portrayed Christ as a singularly ethereal being,[82] even as aspects of his Christian ethic appeared indistinguishable from Teutonic *Vaterlandsliebe*.

"Ethics is a matter of blood and a matter of history," Bonhoeffer said. "It did not simply descend to earth from heaven. Rather, it is a child of the earth, and for that reason its face changes with history as well as with the renewal of blood, with the transition between genera-tions."

Christians create their own ethics, a new Decalogue, law, and stan-dard, said the pastor, invoking by name Nietzsche's Superman.[83] The Christian must exist beyond good and evil as well, forming ethical real-ity "out of eternity," rejecting static principles and rules for the sake of passion, creativity, and life. The only law is "the law of freedom," Bon-hoeffer said on that evening, "bearing responsibility alone before God and oneself." For this reason, "even murder can be sanctified." What then of the Sermon on the Mount, Jesus' earliest teachings on citizen-ship in the kingdom of heaven—blessed are the meek, the merciful, the poor in spirit and pure in heart, and blessed are the peacemakers? Bonhoeffer sounded very much the child of Protestant modernism in his blithe contempt for the letter of the law. Applying the Beatitudes concretely to the present age is "meaningless" and "impracticable," Bonhoeffer said, and goes against "the spirit of Christ, who brought freedom from the law."[84]

But if even Christ's teachings are dismissed as legalisms, how then is a Christian to know right from wrong? He must, Bonhoeffer answered, discern God's will anew each and every day, open always to novelty, free in the spirit, anchored in the here and now. To those who would claim, "War is . . . murder. War is a crime. No Christian can go to war," the faithful German answers, on the contrary, that "when my own people" are attacked, the "commandment of love" is transcended, and the "Christian duty to fight" becomes the ethical-spiritual impera-tive—to fight "with strength and valor for the homeland!" It would be an "utter perversion," he adds, to imagine that "my first duty is to love my enemy."[85]

Bonhoeffer's appeal to the German *Volk* (translated as "people") is full of unwitting portent. For if the Holy Spirit is not to be sought in every person as a temple of the living God but in the fullness of the moment, as Bonhoeffer believes (to say nothing of the particularities of race, as he implies), then to kill for the "glory of the Fatherland" might well not be murder. But in any case, "love for my own people [*Volk*] will sanctify murder, will sanctify war," the pastor said, allowing, however improbably, that something of the same applied to Christians of any and every nation!

Now, it bears noting that Bonhoeffer's claim, despite the disquieting imagery of blood and earth, was consistent with traditional Christian teaching about *bellum iustum*, or just war, beginning with Augustine, who denied any good in peace when only violence could stop a grave sin. But Bonhoeffer spun the doctrine out in directions few had gone before. For not only does love justify murder when the victim is the enemy, but even the act of killing the enemy may itself be regarded as an act of *love*. The godly warrior prays for those he kills; and when he delivers their bodies to death, he prays for the fate of their souls, so that in leaving the fields of battle, he may be confident that the command-ment of love has been honored—not in word but in spirit.

What, then, is a Christian ethic? Could it be a radical freedom from every human law for the sake of some locally derived principle— for a Christ of the forest mists and majestic alpine vistas, the ambers warming the hearths of humble homes, and for the spirit that clings to monuments, cathedrals, and ancient buildings, binding earth, nation, and people in mystical-historic union? If so, it would then seem that "Christ existing as community," the expansive and liberating ideal of Bonhoeffer's dissertation, had omitted to mention some crucial restric-tions that, at least, should have appeared in agate type.

A few weeks later, Bonhoeffer packed his things for the journey back to Berlin. "My books are returning to the crate largely unread," he wrote. Not long before returning to Barcelona from Majorca, he had set his sights on this moment: "And now in less than three weeks I really will be sitting in the train," he wrote eagerly. But with the moment hav-ing come, he realized that the hours and the days had flown by, "almost too quickly."[86] For as he was taking down his tent, he felt the sting of having nearly mistaken his temporary dwelling for a home.

On his last Saturday night in Barcelona, Bonhoeffer attended a performance of *Carmen* at the Gran Teatre del Liceu on the cen-tral boulevard known as La Rambla. Don José, the most famous Span-ish tenor at the time, sang the lead. "Although the prices were indeed insane, I wanted to let you give me that for my birthday," Bonhoeffer told his mother.[87] Dietrich's new friend Hermann Thumm, a teacher in the German school, joined him (his ticket also courtesy of the Bon-hoeffers) in the gallery for what proved a splendid performance. At the age of twenty-two, Bonhoeffer had been a veteran devotee of the opera for more than a decade; and like most Berliners of his background, he never hesitated to offer seasoned judgments. This was his second time hearing *Carmen* in six months, the first having been on his extended Paris layover. But he found Don José's singing that night "something quite rare." Afterward, Dietrich and Thumm retreated to an all-night café and "enthused" so long over the music "that we didn't get to bed until 3:30 a.m."[88]

"With one eye weeping and one laughing," Bonhoeffer left Barcelona by train on the evening of Sunday, February 17. The city was shrouded in a silver haze, a "barbaric" chill having descended from the Tibidabo. It seemed a good time to be heading home. Ten days later, after a stop in Geneva to see Klaus (who still had a few months remaining on his *Wanderjahr*) and a two-day visit with relatives in Bavaria, Bonhoeffer arrived in Berlin to find his father's chauffeur waiting. The ride from the Tiergarten to Grunewald in the black Horch Sedan passed serenely, as streetlamps flickered against the wintry sky and snow began to fall. Soon enough, he would be drinking a family toast to the "healthy, happy reunion."[89]

CHAPTER FIVE

1929–1930

~

"Covered in the Moss of Tradition"

Among those glad to have Dietrich back was his university chum Franz Hildebrandt. There had been a time when student ennui could easily be treated by dialing "Pfalzburg 2616," the Bonhoeffers' number in Grunewald, or by the jolt of strong Machwitz coffee taken in Hildebrand's Charlottenburg apartment. Lately, though, the "familiar doldrums" of both young men could only be addressed in the staggered call and response of letter writing. "Who on earth invented these horrible mornings?" Franz had written Dietrich in Barcelona. His own theological studies, be they of Martin Kegel or G. W. F. Hegel, had left Franz suffering "the worst attacks of yawning." It would be good to be able to commiserate in person once again.

Bonhoeffer, for his part, had been happy to be back, at least at first. For once the family festivities were over and the comfort of familiar things had faded, he suffered a rude awakening to all that he had not missed in the least. In particular, the transition back into academia was alarmingly difficult. After twelve months of languorous weather among adoring parishioners, he faced a mountain of grunt work: a full schedule of examinations, graded lectures, research for the second dissertation, and vassalage to an aloof faculty. He may have assumed that the rhythms of Berlin would revive and remotivate his scholarly ambitions, but he experienced no such effect. Something felt different. To one returning from the warm Mediterranean air, scented of citrus and almond blossoms, the very atmosphere of the gray fortress on Unter den Linden on a late Friday morning spoke only of the old "winter theology."

"In the course of eight days, one world has sunk," he said, "and a new, or rather old, gray one, covered in the moss of tradition, stretches out its hand as if it were the most obvious thing in the world. . . . The air is close in Germany, close and musty enough to suffocate you, and everywhere it smells like sweat. But, then, what else can one do but go ahead and breathe this air and get on with everything?"[1]

Any hopes of intellectual creativity were dashed by the hard knocks of university custom; life as a postgraduate student amounted to little more than grading "excruciatingly dumb seminar papers!"[2] He felt not only bureaucratic confinement but a lack of vital connection. The theology faculty, bunkered in their overheated offices near the Hegelplatz, seemed more Olympian than ever. Perhaps things had always been this way, but after Spain all he could see were the drab hallways, a colorless sky, the oppressive lighting of classrooms.

"The intellectual overproduction has something repugnantly un-intellectual about it," he complained. And again he perceived the spiritual malaise as foul air: "To me it smells too strongly of sweat; that is not an impartial aesthetic judgment of the situation, but I fear that it is Germany's fated path, [and] that path is the murder of the 'spirit.'"[3] Barcelona, he realized, had launched him on an "unwitting search for truth"; he felt a fierce longing for reality, nothing less.

He might have run away, if he'd had the nerve. Back to Spain or Italy. Or, even better, to India, or to Palestine, both places he yearned to visit. But as the search for alternatives proved as futile as it was desperate, remaining in Berlin demanded "the most resolute energy and self-control." It was a depressing realization. "Everything seems so infinitely banal and dull," he said. "I never before noticed what nonsense people speak in the trams, on the street—shocking."[4]

Finally, he resolved to press on and finish the program within the year. "I will go ahead and do my qualifying work for lecturing," he said. And then what? Absence had made his heart grow fonder of things that now clearly added up to "nothing of particular consequence." He could only hope that the picture would brighten on the other side of post-doctoral study. Or would he discover that he could only be happy on journeys to new places?[5] Whatever the case, he vowed "never to forget that this kind of life is unworthy, regardless of whether one is able to overcome it or not."

How idyllic it had all seemed in Barcelona when Bonhoeffer wrote a long, ruminative letter to Adolf von Harnack, addressing him as "Your Excellency." He recalled "those early days" when the aging professor convened a seminar in his house in Grunewald, for several hours leading students in awesome readings of historical theology, always in the original language. Bonhoeffer would walk the short way heading toward the forest, to reach the Harnacks' three-story house on Kunz-Buntschuh-Strasse. They were on the outermost edge of the neighborhood, and on summer evenings the environs echoed with the sound of birdsong. Remembering those times "as if they were yesterday," Bonhoeffer longed to sit "again for but a single hour in your seminar circle or have one of those unforgettable conversations with you."[6] Indeed, he could throw himself into "purely practical work," because he was "accompanied by the hope" that in only six months, he would "have all that again," though he did pronounce himself grateful for the chance to live abroad, removed from so many things about which he had become a "bit obsessive."[7]

When, in February 1930, Bonhoeffer did return to Harnack's Thursday-afternoon seminar—this one on Augustine's *City of God*, the last the old professor would teach—he was not disappointed, though his satisfaction owed more to what he was able to confess than to what he heard. He told Harnack how over the course of the year in Barcelona, he had acquired "a measure of freedom from didactic doctrines" and learned to recognize "much more precisely the limited value of pure scholarship, that [insight] in turn providing the vantage from which to reexamine everything one has worked on." Bonhoeffer knew that no one could better appreciate such a confession than this venerable champion of free inquiry, whose surest legacy would be the summons to enlightenment, in the same spirit as Kant had challenged Germans at the end of the eighteenth century: "saperere aude," dare to think, dare to be wise. All knowledge and belief were properly subject to probing critique. That evening, as on every other, Harnack had shown in his varied excellences that nothing was more beautiful than freedom "to speak without reserve about that which moves us."

That Harnack hadn't changed was a comfort amid all the dislocation Bonhoeffer was feeling. Even the effort to "pick up the thread" of old friendships seemed thwarted, as one after another of his former classmates and companions married and started families.[8] In addition to Sabine and Gert Leibholz, who had by now been married for more than a year, his former governess Maria Horn, his beloved "Hörnchen," was now the wife of his high school classics teacher, Richard Czeppan. "Within the space of seven years there were six marriages in our family," Sabine wrote in a memoir; "between 1923 and 1929 my mother provided all the furniture and household necessities for the new homes of four daughters, as used to be the custom."[9] Bonhoeffer's response to these developments was gracious but wistful. In a congratulatory letter to his friend Hermann Thumm, on the latter's engagement to one Miss Gumprecht, he acknowledged the "slightly painful feeling of being the one left behind or abandoned." His gladness at his friend's contentment about "the big decision" was genuine, if not ebullient: "I have always seen something in friendship that transcends the normal course of events," he said, "and in this sense I am happy you have found what others must perhaps seek for a long time."[10] But as Bonhoeffer began to imagine a different fate for himself—and his gradual surrender to it—he beheld a somewhat melancholy self-portrait.[11]

To be sure, there was more awry in Germany in February of 1929 than the sorrows of young Dietrich. The Weimar Republic was in fast decline as the economy was engulfed by the same tidal wave then sweeping western Europe and the United States. Unemployment was soaring, and most German workers were quick to blame the Weimar government—as were right-wing demagogues, who took every advantage of the situation. Since the end of World War I, the Conservative Party in Germany had become less a political entity than a club for angry malcontents. The much-loathed Treaty of Versailles, which attributed responsibility for the Great War solely to Germany, had not ceased to be a rallying point for the embittered. The humiliation generally felt inspired the new young demagogues to agitate for a return to a more authoritarian order, and one began to hear calls to "reinstate the monarchy." When Gustav Stresemann, by then foreign minister but formerly chancellor, died suddenly in October 1929, the loss finally extinguished the liberal flame of his administration, and among the embers there smoldered once more a popular distrust of democracy.

Within the ivory tower at Unter den Linden, Bonhoeffer was offered the post of *Privatdozent*, or "voluntary lecturer." He would naturally have been placed under Reinhold Seeberg, but since he had retired the year before, Bonhoeffer was assigned to Wilhelm Lütgert, an expert in German Idealism, recently arrived from Halle. Teaching his own courses would not be possible until Bonhoeffer had completed the *Habilitation* thesis.

Ruminations on a "theology of the child" merged with plans for a more broadly philosophical project; a phrase he'd jotted down in his Spanish journals, *the question of consciousness*, continued to appear in his notes. What began slowly taking shape was an argument about the shortcomings of modern German philosophy. The central claim was that classical German thought—the tradition running from Kant through Hegel to Feuerbach—promoted a conception of the self that might best be called "world-constitutive." Human subjectivity had been ascribed colossal powers, which ultimately overwhelmed all others. This was to propose, in Bonhoeffer's view, the triumph of a totalitarian ego, reality overcome by an all-invasive self. The remedy Bonhoeffer put forward bears a striking resemblance to much contemporary Jewish philosophy, though he had not read Franz Rosenzweig or Emmanuel Lévinas, and only skimmed Martin Buber's *I and Thou.*

Even in retirement, Seeberg took an interest, expressing hope that Bonhoeffer would pursue a different topic: an "ethical history of dogma," for instance, one examining "why ethical problems receded so much in twelfth-century scholasticism." This would have the advantage, Seeberg continued, of presenting an occasion to evaluate "the presentation [of ethics] in John of Salisbury's 'Metalogicus.'" Equally, Bonhoeffer might consider a thesis on "the history of ethics from the perspective of the Sermon on the Mount." Seeberg thought that anything on ethics would be better than the proposed voyage over the dark seas of German ontology.

This advice only confirmed Bonhoeffer's belief that Seeberg—with his Conservative Party banners waving—was not the best adviser for the second dissertation. Bonhoeffer told his friend Helmut Rößler that a sermon preached recently by Seeberg had amounted to little more than "shallow religious babble for forty-five minutes." It had been "painful."[12] Bonhoeffer would never bother to respond to Seeberg's letter.[13]

For him there was no turning away from what he perceived as original investigation that also promised to explain the crosscurrents of his own experience. Fortunately, Lütgert would give him his head: Bonhoeffer could take on the whole of modern German thought under the supervision of a true expert.

"The child and theology" or "an exhaustive account of consciousness"—these were the themes that attracted him.[14] He'd pondered the two side by side until he decided to tackle both in the same work. The *Habilitationsschrift*, entitled "Act and Being," with the ponderous subtitle, "Transcendental Philosophy and Ontology in Systematic Theology," would be his last attempt to do theology according to the rules of the guild. The result was a dense, impatient tour de force. But unlike "Sanctorum Communio," which had involved so many rewrites and revisions, "Act and Being," for all its compression, almost wrote itself, flowing freely from the realization that he could address intellectual and personal frustrations while trying to understand God.

As a *Privatdozent*, Bonhoeffer did not have the luxury of an office, so he worked most days from his bedroom in Grunewald, only occasionally heading to campus to retrieve books from the university library, whose doors were closed for the lunch hour beginning at noon and then for the day at 5:00. His most productive stretch came during a three-week stay in Friedrichsbrunn. There, the sun-drenched days and cool evenings of September, the relaxing breaks in the late afternoon, afforded him the peace and quiet that made it "easy to get work done."[15] Still, there is a hint of desperation in the thesis, a fear of what he had got himself into. This, after all, was his intellectual inheritance, whose weight never seemed heavier than in his final year of study: the sum of all the desires expressed in German thought to live in pure and perpetual freedom. The entire thesis, which runs just over a hundred pages, was written in the summer and winter terms of 1929, an effort of less than six months from beginning to end.

Act and Being (published in September 1931 by C. Bertelsmann) is a defense of the numinous reality of God against the Idealist and Naturalist program to reduce all things to either subjective constructs or mere phenomena of nature. Although the prose often staggers under the weight of jargon, the argument steadily gathers force toward a stunning conclusion. More ambitious than "Sanctorum Communio," *Act and Being* is rather more successful, as well; the second dissertation (out of print for two decades until 1989, when the first scholarly English edition appeared in the *Dietrich Bonhoeffer Works* series) should be counted as one of the great theological achievements of the twentieth century.

The book begins with a series of "typological sketches": complex philosophical arguments packed into sections of six to eight pages, each representing roughly a dozen note cards of thought. In these sketches Bonhoeffer humanizes Hermann Cohen, Paul Natorp, Friedrich Brunstäd, Edmund Husserl, Max Scheler, Martin Heidegger, and Erich Przywara as each pertains to the "reality of God." Readers looking for careful analyses of the German philosophical pantheon will be disappointed; the concentration remains theological throughout.

Modern theology has reached an impasse, Bonhoeffer reasons, and until theologians take stock of the situation and reckon with the wrong turns, they will be forever stuck in the same place, repeating the old formulas. The author takes an almost omniscient view to tell the story of how theology went awry by imagining a visit with Kant, who is at his work desk in Königsberg, scribbling away at his new model of the human mind. In his great landmarks, *The Critique of Pure Reason* and *The Critique of Practical Reason*, Kant constructs a theory of knowledge that would dramatically influence the intellectual course of the West. He concedes the Enlightenment's revolutionary critique of the idea of God: what was once presumed to be the truest and surest of all beliefs is in fact riddled with uncertainty, its basis unknowable. Kant, however, had intended to save God from the death to which many Enlightenment thinkers thought to put him. A pious churchgoer, he rejected atheism by relocating God from the starry heavens above to the moral law within. While the idea of God might not be empirically true—

and indeed without an objective referent, transcending all experience, one must conclude that it is not true—the idea remains *truthful*, that is to say, beneficial to moral life: as an organizing principle of society, inspiring the pursuit of the good, warding off chaos. Kant's Copernican revolution thus launched the signal enterprise of liberal Protestant theology: If God is not metaphysically real, then what is God? And where is God?

Bonhoeffer surveys the two most popular responses to the Kantian tradition and to these central questions as debated in the early twentieth century. One side described the idea of God as pure transcendence; the other argued that it was the mind's own creation. With faith's intellectual despisers growing in number, liberal theologians of both stripes had worked hard to lodge God somewhere safer, the transcendental "I" or the transcendent "Thou" proving the most popular resorts, but never the twain did meet. What alternative did Bonhoeffer propose, then, as a way beyond the impasse of modern theology? He merged two principles: First, the Reformation's emphatic doctrine of revelation; it is only through God's prior utterance and action in the Bible that he can be known, and the God-idea spared from modernist reductionism. Second, he borrowed Catholicism's expansive doctrine of the sacred, the idea that God can be known by analogies to nature of human experience. From these two, Bonhoeffer effected a new synthesis of act and being. Neither purely transcendent nor subjectively immanent, the reality of God could be experienced in the social dimension. Ultimately, "Spirit" is to be found in the particular, in relational dynamics, and "precisely not in 'intellection.'"

And so, the hard conceptual work having been done, he offers his conclusion—a theological meditation on "the child," the idea he had been working on in Barcelona—almost as a closing benediction. The child is "the sigh of theology," a whisper "between eternity and eternity," a "quiet and prayerful conversation . . . with the father." The child sees himself in "the power of what 'future things' will bring," and he asks of God only that he might live more fully in the present. He exemplifies the "new creation," being "born out from the world's confines into the expanse of heaven." On that singular note ended the lesson.[16]

H e submitted the work on March 14, 1930, and a few weeks later he returned to Barcelona, traveling alone by first-class train for Thumm's wedding. He found the city in springtime as glorious as he remembered it, the lilacs in full bloom, the street vendors bringing the season's first strawberries to market. At the Tibidabo, Bonhoeffer watched the evening sun spread "overwhelmingly beautiful" colors across the sky. His former parishioners and friends received him so graciously it "almost seemed" as if he had never left.[17]

After the wedding, he traveled to the medieval village of Tossa de Mar on the Catalonian coast, hoping (he told his parents) to "rest up from the events in Barcelona." He spent his days alone, swimming or sunbathing, and enjoying the wines of the Valle del Cinca. In late afternoon, he would stroll into the village to watch the townspeople dance *sardanes*.[18] "My solitary lifestyle once more," he wrote.

Meanwhile, back in Berlin, Professor Lütgert, in his university office, shuffled his way through a pile of essays and theses. Among them was Bonhoeffer's "Act and Being."

Lütgert tendered a mostly positive evaluation on April 15, thus approving Bonhoeffer for the postdoctoral degree and the habilitation. No knowledgeable reader, he allowed, could fail to recognize that Bonhoeffer "understands how to preserve his independence amidst all the ideas he has adopted here."[19] As a specialist in German Idealism, Lütgert was surprisingly partial to the conclusion, which "powerfully expresses the deepest religious and theological interests of the author, and does so in a language that very clearly elevates itself above the abstract way of speaking in the epistemological part." The professor was, however, ultimately unconvinced that a conceptual unity had been woven from the argument's different threads.

At twenty-four, with two dissertations to his name—the major requirements for admission into German academe fulfilled—the way ahead for Bonhoeffer nevertheless remained uncertain. Having "preserved his independence" over all adopted ideas was not necessarily a formula for collegial goodwill. And only a few modest benefits actually came with the promotion; a successful habilitation carried no guarantee of a professorship. Lütgert asked the faculty's bursar to hire Bonhoeffer as a teaching assistant, offering a stipend of 150 marks a month.[20] Until now, he had worked without pay.[21] But the stipend—modest though it was—carried no guarantee of more stimulating work. The department was growing in size and with it the number of papers someone had to grade and students someone had to supervise.[22] Bonhoeffer would expend some effort in helping the theology department move into new quarters on Dorotheenstrasse, but other thankless tasks tested his devotion. Classmates were impressed by his remarkable skill at avoiding menial labor, such as the distribution and securing of keys to classrooms and the rearrangement and maintenance of the faculty library.[23]

Bonhoeffer was thinking about leaving Germany again. His brother Karl-Friedrich had spent two semesters as a visiting fellow in physics at the University of Chicago and spoke with bemused fascination of America's vast landscapes and singular energies. So upon receiving a letter of invitation from Henry Sloane Coffin, president of Union Theological Seminary in New York City, to apply for a postdoctoral fellowship, Bonhoeffer was quick to act. On March 10, 1930, good news arrived in a telegram from Coffin; it read simply, "Bonhoeffer accepted Union."[24]

There were only a few more hurdles to clear in his race at Friedrich-Wilhelms. He passed his second theological examination with a "grade of very good."[25] He presented the required catechesis on June 29, 1930, during the children's service at the Berlin-Grunewald Protestant Church.[26] Written in the standard form of questions posed and answers expected, a catechesis—the term rooted in a Greek word meaning "to echo"—instructs children on the basic tenets of the Christian faith.[27] Bonhoeffer's expounded on the fifth petition of the Lord's Prayer, "Forgive us our debts, as we forgive our debtors."[28] But unlike the classic catechisms of the church, Bonhoeffer's showed little concern for "the level of maturity of those to whom it is preached" (as he forthrightly acknowledged) and in this way produced a "tiring effect" (as his examiners forthrightly noted).[29] "Individual questions are not skillfully worded," the report read. "It is questionable whether he genuinely will succeed along the path he has taken here."[30]

On the other hand, the recitation earned rave reviews from its littler judges, who were riveted by the theatricality. The children may not have understood a word, but they sat in rapt attention listening to the mellifluous tones and "skillful presentation." The examiners duly noted their admiration for the ease with which Bonhoeffer related to the children.[31]

Bonhoeffer preached the mandatory trial sermon on July 20, 1930, at the Teltow Lutheran Church in southwest Berlin. This requirement tended to be a rather formal, artless exercise. Members of the ordination committee sat in the front pew with their pens and notebooks. In this case, they noted certain (unexplained) "text-critical problems" but were impressed by Bonhoeffer's manner of speaking, which they found dignified and confident. His oration showed appropriate emphases and was, at times, punctuated with "lively but not exaggerated gesticulation." While they thought he might want to "strengthen his voice in the lower registers," the judges praised Bonhoeffer for memorizing the entire script.[32]

Beyond satisfying the committee, however, something unexpected seems to have happened.

Bonhoeffer's sermon was based on three verses from St. Paul's letter to the churches in Thessalonica—to be exact, I Thessalonians 5:16–18. "Rejoice always, pray without ceasing," the epistle reads, "give thanks in all circumstances; for this is the will of God in Christ Jesus for you."

Max Diestel, the church superintendent in Berlin, who had been observing the performance with concern for the nuts and bolts—pitch and posture, delivery and design, and all the elements of the discipline called "homiletics"—allowed as how an experience of profound joy broke through the strictures of the occasion.[33] Bonhoeffer had preached with uncommon intensity and clarity. This was the message of the gospel, he said: "an abiding happiness, one that lasts a lifetime, one that does not dissipate when the happy times are over"—a "foundational" happiness.[34] "Go outside and see how children play and rejoice and are happy; see how the birds of the field fly high up to heaven and are joyous in the sun. Watch them, and then watch them again and again, and then rejoice with them, become like them, like a child that is joyous in its father's garden."

The sermon's "first imperative"—"rejoice always"—had stirred Bonhoeffer's imagination for years. Joy (*Freude*), as he rendered it in an essay contributed to a 1926 *Festschrift* for Harnack, sparkled to life as an "objective power," let loose by the resurrection, permeating creation with "unheard-of energy" and "turbulent impatience." Life animated by the Holy Spirit "effervesces in joy!" But four years later, in his trial sermon of 1930, he struck a different note: gospel-joy reaches into human experience from a "distant, unknown land," one far removed from the manly Germanic piety of "work and duty and seriousness and nothing else." The abiding joy and strange light of Christ is a light whose source lies always and everywhere in another country.[35] For they that say such things declare plainly that they seek a country.

There were two requirements remaining—the trial lecture and the inaugural lecture—both scheduled for July. "I have my hands full," he told Rößler.[36] The end was in sight, but the next two weeks would feel like an eternity.

"Right now through my open window," he said to Sabine, "I am listening to dance music at the Weigerts'. Solitary couples are walking about in the garden—just as in the old days!—And I long for nothing more than to join the dance!"[37]

The trial lecture was a ritual peculiar to German academe: the candidate presented his advisers with three possible topics, from which the advisers picked one. No one attended but the theological faculty. The *Probevorlesung*, which he would deliver before that elite audience on July 12, 1930, would be the penultimate exercise in the long slog of his theological education before the final public lecture.[38] He proposed these three topics: the significance of the sociological category for theology; the possibility of a dogmatic system; and the concept of dialectic in so-called dialectical theology. He had already covered the first in painstaking detail in "Sanctorum Communio." The second he'd explored in "Act and Being," only to conclude that dogmatic systems quashed the personal dimension. Anyway, the faculty selected the third topic, the "concept of dialectic," or, put another way, the recent writings of Karl Barth. The manuscript of the *Probevorlesung* has not been preserved. It is possible that it resembled the lecture Bonhoeffer would give months later in New York on the "Theology of Crisis," explaining in mostly uncritical fashion the basic themes in Barth's theology and sounding, for the first time, like an apologist for Barth. More likely, though, Bonhoeffer mined his recently completed thesis, with its stinging criticisms of Barth, to reassure his professors that he had not truly crossed the Rubicon.

For the inaugural lecture, the young scholar's public debut, he was free to choose any topic within his field.[39] "I would like to speak on 'The Anthropological Question in Contemporary Philosophy and Theology,'" Bonhoeffer told his examiners.[40] And so he did, in a wooden rehash of "Act and Being."[41] It was perfunctory exercise, hurriedly fulfilled, and its chief excellence was in making "Act and Being" read like a page-turner by comparison. The lecture, which he gave in the great hall of the university, is the least-inspired piece in Bonhoeffer's extensive body of work, yet it was received enthusiastically by his professors. The argument he developed in "Act and Being"—that real personhood originates always outside the self, in the contingent act of divine revelation—is recast in such a way as to expose its greatest weakness. The dynamic of faith, its sunlight and music and open skies, is squeezed into an empty formalism. "Every individual theological problem not only points to the reality of the church," he said in conclusion, but "in its entirety also recognizes itself as something that belongs solely to the church."[42] In his mind and heart, Bonhoeffer had already moved on.

Harnack died that summer at the age of seventy-nine. After a memorial service in Heidelberg, where he'd been living at the time of his death, the venerable professor's body was cremated in Berlin and his ashes interred in the Old Church Yard of St. Matthew's parish in Schöneberg, in a quiet grove near the marble crypts of the Brothers Grimm. On his headstone there was simply this: "Who hopes in the Lord cannot but rejoice." It was, said Bonhoeffer, the "great petition under which [he] lived his entire life."[43] With Harnack and Holl dead and Seeberg in retirement, the reign of Bonhoeffer's Protestant liberal forefathers was drawing to a close.

There was, naturally, also a Berlin memorial service for Harnack, this one held in one of the city's great cultural centers, the Goethe Hall, near the Alexanderplatz. Bonhoeffer spoke effusively of the "master"—of *"Wirklicher Geheimrat,"* "Your Excellency, Professor Harnack"—who inspired his students "in the struggle for truth" and to "a reverence for a life led in the spirit." At no point in the tribute was there to be heard even an echo of the theological controversies in which Harnack had been embroiled, not a word about the fateful exchanges with Barth that had left Protestantism a house divided. Of course, a memorial service is hardly the place. Still, Bonhoeffer's remarks ran to five typewritten pages, and the extant manuscript reveals copious handwritten notes and underlining for emphasis. Harnack, he truly felt, exemplified the ideal that "everything must be completely truthful and completely simple." Truth, freedom, and simplicity—a scholar's holy trinity.

In August 1930, Bonhoeffer spent three weeks in Friedrichsbrunn, basking in the fresh mountain air and freedom from deadlines. He still managed to work on his English for an hour each day, in preparation for his upcoming journey to America. But he would not resist the many sweet diversions offering themselves on the eve of his departure. "You really can't imagine a more restorative vacation," he told his parents. He awoke to birdsong, wandered the familiar hiking trails, and collected wild mushrooms in the glens beyond the village church. "There are an enormous number of mushrooms," he reported. "You could easily have a plate of them at every meal, as indeed, we often do." He took runs twice a day with his cousin Hans von Hase.[44] At sunset he went into the forest to watch for the deer. "It's incredibly nice being outside day after day. Being up here we always resolve to move to the Harz permanently." While he noted that times seemed tough for most local people, with so many unemployed and suffering material hardship, he remained grateful for the long, languorous days. "We are living an unbelievably lazy existence up here," he said.[45] Apart from practicing his English, he remained happily "disinclined" toward productive work.

When his brother Klaus asked him to preside at his wedding, he sent regrets. Having already agreed to serve as the master of ceremonies at the *Polterabend*, the festive gathering on the wedding eve, he insisted he could not do both. Now, even Klaus had joined the ranks of the betrothed, along with so many friends and acquaintances; he and Emmi Delbrück would be married on September 4, 1930, theirs a perfect match of strong wills and fierce minds.[46]

Back in June, when Bonhoeffer had first been approached about spending a year in the United States, the Berlin church administrator Adolf Deißmann had promptly written to Henry Sloane Coffin at Union, saying that their young star was "very eager to study American Theology and Church life."[47] In fact, nothing could have been farther from the truth. Bonhoeffer had never expressed any interest in the history or culture of the Americas. And his level of academic training already surpassed that of nearly all American Protestant theologians and clergy. To the extent that he thought about this prospect, it was as one more jaunt in his privileged life. The fellowship seemed a quick cure for the Berlin blues, to judge by Karl-Friedrich's tales of his own year in America. In any case, there would be no teaching obligations or degree requirements. He could take any classes that interested him, without the grim burden of grading papers.

There is, however, one intriguing indication that he might have harbored more particular hopes for the year ahead. The clue has a rather unexpected source. As part of his second theological examination, Bonhoeffer was asked to select Bible verses on which he might someday base a preaching series. He looked to the Epistle to the Hebrews, which describes what he called "God's path through history in the church of Christ."[48] The epistle's author recounts a dramatic age-old narrative of keeping faith, a great sweep from creation through the incarnation to the first Christian martyrs, until, at the beginning of chapter 12, he exhorts, "Therefore, since we are surrounded by so great a cloud of witnesses, let us throw off everything that hinders and the sin that so easily entangles, and let us run with perseverance the race marked out for us."

Bonhoeffer was captivated by the verses and by their vision of the *sanctorum communio*, the only spiritual society that could nourish and sustain one over the greatest race of all. Some months after his arrival in New York, he would write his friend Rößler an uncommonly sober letter stating that his purposes had become clear.[49] As he made his way in a new country with a strikingly unfamiliar religious culture, he was looking, he said, for *eine solche Wolke von Zeugen*: "such a cloud of witnesses."

CHAPTER SIX

1930–1931

~

"I Heard the Gospel Preached in the Negro Churches"

On September 6, 1930, Dietrich Bonhoeffer boarded the SS *Columbus* in the German port city of Bremen and set sail for America. Once again in transit, he felt the weight of the previous months lifting, as the inlet at Nordenham gave onto one new horizon after another.

"The ship is very quiet," he told his grandmother Julie Tafel Bonhoeffer, perhaps not surprising for a 32,000-ton merchant vessel, Germany's largest and fastest, though it had been surrendered to the Whitestar line as part of the war reparations. "The day was beautiful. Until now it's as if we had been on the Wannsee, totally calm."

The first night, he watched the distant lights of the Belgian coast glistening in the east, the full moon silvering the surface of the North Sea.

"From our deck you look about twelve meters or more down to the water, through which the ship cuts a deep furrow," he wrote to his mother. "My cabin seems not unfavorably located. It lies deep in the belly of the ship. I haven't actually seen my cabin mate yet. I've tried to get a picture of him from the items he has left about. The hat, the walking stick, and a novel by Seymour suggest an educated American to me. I hope he doesn't turn out to be an old German prole."[1] In truth, few "proles"—proletarians—could afford any of the rooms on the luxury liner.

Bonhoeffer shared the weeklong voyage with people of similar backgrounds. He passed leisurely days availing himself of the ship's abundant amenities. There were convivial exchanges with Aristid von Grosse, "the chemist and atomic scientist," who knew his brother Karl-Friedrich from professional circles and who could not stop remarking on the resemblance between the brothers.[2] Bonhoeffer also met the attractive Louise Schaefer Ern and her boy Richard, on their way home to Connecticut from Switzerland, where her daughter had remained behind to be "treated for meningitis at a homeopathic spa."³ A certain Dr. Edmund De Long Lucas, academic dean of a Presbyterian college in India (Lahore, before partition), revealed himself as Bonhoeffer's roommate, ending the mystery; he was traveling to the States on a short furlough from his duties at the mission school.⁴ It pleased the dean to share with Bonhoeffer a book he had written, *The Economic Life of a Punjab Village*, and stories of his years on the subcontinent.

Christened in 1924, *Columbus* was not only the largest and fastest but also the most lavishly appointed commercial vessel on the high seas. The handsome fare promised palatial luxury. A dozen crystal chandeliers and murals by the German artist E. R. Weiss graced an exterior ballroom for nighttime dancing. Massive double pillars holding the bronze busts of classical poets opened onto a "wainscoted Library" with built-in cedar bookcases and comfortable leather chairs. Bonhoeffer could take his meals in any of the ship's four dining halls, swim in the outdoor pool, or nap in the sun on the observation deck. His letters and notes are cast in the familiar tone of his earlier travel writings—florid and expectant.

The sea journey was "perfect" and "fabulously beautiful," he said. He did not know "where to begin writing about it all."⁵

On September 15, 1930, the New York City skyline emerged on the western horizon, a marvelous panorama punctuated by the 102-story Empire State Building, nearly completed. He had never seen a city so vast and imposing. He was met at Chelsea Harbor by his aunt Irma and uncle Harold Boericke, on his mother's side, who whisked him home to Philadelphia for a five-day visit. His yearlong sojourn began in a comfortable house in Drexel Hill, his cousins Ray, Betty, and Binkie showering him with attention, and his aunt and uncle treating him like royalty. There were mornings in the city clubs, excursions to museums and parks, and board games in the evening. "You can hardly believe you're so far from Europe here, so much is so similar," he said. The exception was golf, not a sport popular among Germans of his ilk, but he did spend a day trying to play. The Boerickes amused Bonhoeffer with stories of their new life in America—they still possessed the Berliners' wit—and when he was leaving they made him promise to come see them again.⁶

It was in the third week of September that Bonhoeffer moved into his dormitory at the corner of 121st Street and Broadway. He marveled at the George Washington Bridge glistening over the Hudson, the building crews then working around the clock on its latticework of beams and cables in the final weeks of construction. The city was full of such wonders. The art deco Chrysler Building, with its steel gargoyles and thousand-foot pinnacle, had just been completed in May. Bonhoeffer came to feel excited about the year ahead.

In 1930 Union Theological Seminary was the proud flagship institution of liberal Protestant theology in North America. Students were there to become pastors or pursue some other ministry. A few became professors, but it was all in a spirit of service to humanity. Most seminarians still hailed from the Northeast, though the student body was now more diverse than at any time in its hundred-year history, including African Americans, Asian Americans, women, and poor whites from the rural South.[7] Henry Sloane Coffin, the seminary's president since 1926, charted a steady course triangulating his old-money connections, Ivy League erudition, and infectious Protestant optimism. Formerly minister of Madison Avenue Church, Coffin was a self-described "liberal evangelical." He got his start serving a Bronx mission, preaching hope to the destitute "over a meat market with a chopping block for a pulpit."[8]

In the twelve courses he took as a Sloan Fellow at Union, Bonhoeffer focused on philosophy of religion, theology, and social ethics; the subject matter was familiar but the institutional context altogether unlike anything he was accustomed to.[9] When he had written in the fellowship application that his aim was to better understand his "own particular scholarly discipline, systematic theology, as it has developed under completely different circumstances," he had no way of knowing that his discipline as practiced American style would be entirely unrecognizable. He was decidedly underwhelmed by a religious culture in which people fashioned their beliefs the same way a man ordered a car from the factory—according to taste and preference.

For this reason, Bonhoeffer arranged a special tutorial on the philosophy of William James, meeting every other week with Eugene W. Lyman. He considered Lyman, a graduate of Yale Divinity School who had also studied at the universities of Halle and Marburg, to be "a genuine representative of pure American philosophy"; in addition to the tutorial, he also attended Lyman's lecture course on the philosophy of religion, following a hunch that pragmatism explained much about Protestantism in the New World.[10] In the assessment he would file with his German supervisor, Bonhoeffer claimed to have read "almost the entire philosophical works of William James" as well as the major writings of John Dewey, Ralph Barton Perry, Bertrand Russell, Alfred North Whitehead, George Santayana, J. B. Watson, and Albert Knudson, along with the "behaviorist literature." But it was in James, especially *The Will to Believe* and *Varieties of Religious Experience*, that Bonhoeffer said he "found the key to modern theological language and conceptual forms of liberal enlightened Americans." This, he believed, was the intellectual source of the local compulsion "to hasten past difficult problems and to linger inordinately on things that are either self-evident or that without additional preparation cannot possibly be adequately addressed."[11] He would confide to Karl-Friedrich that he had "come to know American philosophy quite thoroughly," despite not having "gained much more faith in the whole business."[12] Truth is "essentially teleological, aimed at serving life," Dietrich remembered.[13]

While the pragmatic standard, he acknowledged, had no doubt produced an industrious society of inspired efficiency, the consequences for serious Christian theology were fairly devastating.

"The students—on the average twenty-five to thirty years old—are completely clueless with respect to what dogmatics is really about. They are not familiar with even the most basic questions." They become easily "intoxicated with liberal and humanistic phrases"; they talk a "blue streak," but often without the "slightest substantive foundation," blithely indifferent to the two thousand years of Christian thought. Railing against the Christian fundamentalists seemed to be the Union students' favorite pastime, Bonhoeffer said, "and yet basically [they] are not even up to their level."[14] Everyone "just blabs away so frightfully."[15]

"There is no theology here," he concluded flatly.

He noted with astonishment that he occasionally heard students—seminarians preparing for the ministry—ask "whether one really must preach about Christ."[16]

It was not that Bonhoeffer missed German theology. As his friend Franz Hildebrandt assured him with a homegrown irreverence, "There's nothing to report about Berlin theology that's any better." He recounted how "Dr. Dr. Dr. DeißmannDeißmann, Rector Magnificus, spent one and a half hours amid the constant applause from students (though at the end, the balcony was half empty) describing the fate of the New Testament." And what's more, Professor (Gerhard) Schwebel was "markedly inferior with his completely muddled discourse on the prospects and struggle of the church, authorities, school, and the merits of the Hohenzollern [imperial dynasty] and on the spirit of obedience in faith and of discipline."[17] Only in their correspondence could he and Dietrich hope to find "an oasis in the desert."[18]

Bonhoeffer was in fact less vexed by the theological modernism at Union than by the pervasive, willful (it would seem), if not blissful, naïveté that pervaded. In "Act and Being," his criticisms of the liberal tradition had in fact been restrained compared with the harsh judgments on Barth's "theological schizophrenia" and "over-determined" view of divine revelation—wherein Barth's "wholly other" God rode roughshod over his nature as a "socially and historically located" person in Jesus. No, the problem with Union students was not that they were liberals but that they were sloppy ones. In contrast to the German variety—"which in its better representatives doubtless was a genuinely vigorous phenomenon"—America's intellectual inheritance from the nineteenth century "has been dreadfully sentimentalized, and with an almost naïve know-it-all attitude." The Protestant liberalism professed at Union seemed but a friendly tweaking of the "Jamesian notion" of God, the old pragmatism slightly recast for progressive churchmen.[19] A case in point: during a class presentation on Martin Luther's "bondage of the will," his classmates laughed out loud. The spectacle of an educated person taking seriously the ruminations of a neurotic sixteenth-century monk struck them as comic.[20] The seminary "has forgotten what Christian theology in its very essence stands for," Bonhoeffer complained.[21] To be the virtuous man meant hardly more than to comport oneself as a "good fellow." Class discussions sounded like the blather of "first-semester freshmen!" Dogmatics was in "utter disarray."

In noting Bonhoeffer's reactions to Union, one should, of course, not forget how peevish he'd been about graduate school in Berlin, too. "I'm supposed to be intellectually creative and grade excruciatingly dumb seminar papers!" he had written of that airless realm overseen by the imperious air faculty of Dorotheenstrasse. Eventually, as the weeks passed in New York, he would learn to be amused and not merely appalled at his surroundings. After all, his notes and letters written on the eve of his journey suggest he expected just another fine jaunt in his charmed life. Still, just a few months earlier, while reflecting on Hebrews, he had expressed the hope of finding a spiritual community, having identified Hebrews 12:1—"Therefore, since we are surrounded by so great a cloud of witnesses"—as "the verse that culminates the saga of faith from creation to the first martyrs."[22] By the end of the fall semester at Union, he would still feel "bitterly disappointed."

Not that there weren't individuals who intrigued him—one in particular. From among a faculty of nearly forty, no one more fully embodied the ideals and energies of American social theology than the indefatigable Reinhold Niebuhr. Bonhoeffer had never met anyone like this excitable theologian-activist, a "dramatist of theological ideas in the public arena."[23] Validating Bonhoeffer's intuition, Niebuhr professed that the question of how to be in the world—how one analyzes

REINHOLD NIEBUHR, "DRAMATIST OF
THEOLOGICAL IDEAS IN THE PUBLIC ARENA"

the contemporary social situation and responds to its needs and conflicts— mattered more to theology than all the parsing of sacred doctrines.[24]

According to Niebuhr's concept of "Christian realism," which he'd been developing in seminars and lectures, all persons, believers or not, must never forget their extensive entanglements with the broken—indeed, he would insist, sinful—structures of the world. This realism began with the sober acceptance of there being no "final escape in historic existence from the contradictions in which human nature is involved."[25] Niebuhr's clear-eyed understanding of the dynamics of power and justice spoke to those searching for a way beyond liberal idealism and Victorian quietism, beyond utopianism and resignation.

Bonhoeffer took Niebuhr's courses during both semesters, and while he enjoyed the material—especially in the team-taught "Ethical Viewpoints in Modern Literature," which examined current events "in light of the principle of Christian ethics" and introduced him to the writings of James Weldon Johnson, Booker T. Washington, and W. E. B. Du Bois—he found Niebuhr's views positively bewildering. The man seemed to talk about everything but God.

One day, after a lively class discussion, Bonhoeffer approached Niebuhr and asked in exasperation, "Is this a theological school or a school for politicians?"[26]

Niebuhr was equally perplexed by the theological prodigy from Berlin and not shy about saying so (or much else). When Bonhoeffer claimed in a term paper that the "God of guidance" could be known only from the "God of justification," Niebuhr responded sharply that this conception of grace was too transcendent.[27] In vigorously Lutheran fashion, Bonhoeffer had been arguing that grace admitted no human effort to reach God; "man in all his ways" is ever "a sinner"—and one who cannot but offend the "glory that is God's alone." Niebuhr pushed him to think in more practical terms about the "God of guidance" in human reality. "In making grace as transcendent as you do," Niebuhr said, "I don't see how you can ascribe any ethical significance to it. Obedience to the will of God may be a religious experience, but it is not an ethical one until it issues in actions which can be socially valued."[28]

The son of a Lutheran minister from a midwestern immigrant community, Niebuhr had been thoroughly captivated by the Social Gospel movement since his first encounter with it while a student at Elmhurst College. That spirit had seized his slender frame and animated his piercing blue eyes, and he would remain ever ready to stand up for a righteous cause. Only two years out from his ministry in inner-city Detroit, he brought an "explosive sort of thinking" to the classroom. This effect, to quote one seminarian who would go on to become a labor organizer in the South, "kind of blew your mind."[29] Testimonials to Niebuhr's charisma and generosity spread rapidly among the rising generation of progressive churchmen. He was not only "young and radical and full of enthusiasm," but genuinely "interested in human problems"—in all, "a stimulating teacher, speaker and explorer."[30]

By the time Bonhoeffer arrived in New York in the fall of 1930, Niebuhr had started to rethink many of his fundamental convictions. In the 1920s, while still a pastor in Detroit, his preaching had been inspired by a robust blend of Social Gospel, Christian pacifism, and populist devotion to the underdog. But with his 1932 landmark *Moral Man and Immoral Society*, a book of "icy, aggressive and eerily omniscient" tone, there came an end to his idealistic ruminations on the Kingdom of God in America; he had concluded that human goodwill and effort would never be enough to usher in an age of perpetual peace.[31] While individuals (Moral Man) might be capable, on occasion, of altruistic and compassionate action, all groups and collectives (Immoral Society) remained, contrarily, unmoved by the mandates of love, or appeals to reason.[32]

Niebuhr was at his best when "analyzing the structures and behavior of political systems and offering theological interpretation" of events "as a basis for common action for a wide audience." In aspiring to greater public relevance, he tended to communicate his ideas in a manner that left his theological commitments unspoken. The public theologian, he understood, would inevitably be misunderstood at times, as would demurrals on doctrine's finer points, but he resolved nonetheless to be a circuit rider in "defense of the Christian faith in a secular age" while also making common cause with secular progressives in responsible action.[33] In an autobiographical essay, Niebuhr explained, "I have never been very competent in the nice points of pure theology; and I must confess that I have not been sufficiently interested heretofore to acquire the competence."[34]

Niebuhr would achieve celebrity by the end of the decade, so that by the 1950s any serious discussion of domestic or foreign policy had to make space for his Christian realist considerations. Yet his personal involvements in progressive social and racial organizing peaked in the years of Bonhoeffer's Sloan Fellowship at Union. The summer of 1931 would find Niebuhr rushing through a demanding schedule of lectures at southern Negro colleges and academies sponsored by the American Missionary Society. He was hoping, he said, to awaken quiescent black students to the activist energies of religious belief. His clarity concerning racial inequality would never be sharper, even during the civil rights era. In *Moral Man and Immoral Society*, Niebuhr put it plainly: "the white race in America will not admit the Negro to equal rights if it is not forced to do so." In numerous papers, published and unpublished, he would lament the travails of his seminary students as they tried to organize white and black tenant workers in the South. Moved by their suffering and self-sacrifice, he would often come to their public defense. But when many of these young radical Christians abandoned pragmatic piecemeal reform for doctrinaire Marxist radicalism, Niebuhr would become increasingly reluctant to offer his full support.[35]

Bonhoeffer would never acknowledge a theological debt to Niebuhr. His worries that Niebuhr's theology lacked confessional richness were basic and well founded. The two, nevertheless, would stay in touch over the next decade.[36] Bonhoeffer often wrote to him in German, which Niebuhr read well, though he replied in English. When, in the summer of 1939, Bonhoeffer found himself at a fateful crossroads, Niebuhr would offer him refuge in New York. Whatever their disagreements as to method, the vocation of public theologian as Niebuhr defined it excited Bonhoeffer and refreshed his perspective.[37] Niebuhr's influence can in fact be discerned every time, after 1933, that Bonhoeffer equates a faith deprived of ethics with dead religion, and holds that "costly" grace requires not that one become a saint, a genius, or a clever tactician but rather an honest, sober, and unflinching realist.[38] It is the Niebuhrian voice that resonates in Bonhoeffer's eventual resolve as a member of the German resistance "to speak of God at the center of life and address men and women . . . as responsible human beings."[39]

Bonhoeffer was both moved and inspired by Niebuhr—by the example of a theologian who engaged the social order with civil courage and ultimate honesty. For his part, Niebuhr found Bonhoeffer alto-

FROM LEFT: DIETRICH BONHOEFFER, HARRY WARD, REINHOLD NIEBUHR, PROFESSOR SWIFT, AND HENRY SLOANE COFFIN AT UNION THEOLOGICAL SEMINARY, NEW YORK, 1931

gether sympathetic, despite his imperious gaze during class and habit of slowly laying down his pen a few minutes after the lecture began. Niebuhr appreciated Bonhoeffer's prodigious intellect, his intensity and ardor; and he understood what a rare thing it was that a German theologian, with all his native prejudices, should choose to spend a year in America. Niebuhr was also confident that he could exert a positive influence on the restless twenty-four-year-old Berliner who held two doctorates to Niebuhr's none.[40]

Though outgoing by nature, Bonhoeffer, in the first weeks of the semester, preferred the company of the other European Sloan Fellows: Erwin Sutz, a theology student from a German-speaking canton in Switzerland, and Jean Lasserre, a Reformed French pastor from Lyons. While Sutz was fluent in French, Lasserre knew little German, and Bonhoeffer struggled with French. So when the three were together, they spoke English. Sutz and Lasserre, like Bonhoeffer, had attended humanistic secondary schools and believed that Americans were overly concerned about practicality, and too little about ideas for their own sake. "We were European[s] who liked to reflect before acting," Lasserre recalled, "while the Americans gave us the impression of wanting to act before [they] reflected." The trio's intellectual affinities inspired "frequent and intense" exchanges—debates on the finer points of doctrine sometimes lasting until two in the morning—that brought them "close together."[41] There was also music to share. As accomplished pianists both, Sutz and Bonhoeffer often played duets in the large Social Hall overlooking the quadrangle, Lasserre listening appreciatively.[42]

But their camaraderie remained decidedly more fragile than it may have appeared to their American classmates. Bonhoeffer was typical for most Germans of his generation. The widely loathed Article 231 in the 1919 Treaty of Versailles—attributing sole responsibility to Germany for the catastrophic Great War and imposing on Germany vast reparations and punitive measures—had embittered a nation already suffering under massive unemployment and runaway inflation. By 1930, popular resentment toward the treaty had served to unite republicans and nationalists alike "in a federation of self-pity." At first, Bonhoeffer, Lasserre, and Sutz danced around their conflicting views of Versailles, but over the course of the semester, they felt more comfortable discussing their disagreements, including the whole contentious matter of loyalty to nation, in an environment free of ghosts.

On a cold blustery weeknight, Bonhoeffer and Lasserre went to a Manhattan cinema to see *All Quiet on the Western Front*, which had been released the previous August. Based on the international bestselling book by German writer Erich Maria Remarque, the film follows a group of students—patriotic young men eager to defend the fatherland—as they enlist in the army, train for combat, and head resolutely to the front, where each encounters unimaginable horrors and perishes.

"The theatre was full," Lasserre said. "The audience was American but, since the film had been made from the German soldiers' point of view, everyone immediately sympathized with them. When French soldiers were killed on screen, the crowd laughed and applauded. On the other hand, when the German soldiers were wounded or killed, there was a great silence and a sense of deep emotion. This was a rather difficult experience for both of us because we were seated next to each other, he a German and I a Frenchman." Bonhoeffer seemed embarrassed by the portrayal. Of course, the experience was all the more perplexing since "the Americans had fought on the side of the French against the Germans."

From "a fraternal point of view," Lasserre continued, it moved him deeply to see how Bonhoeffer took pains to console him when the movie had ended.[43] "I was very affected and he was also affected, but because of me," Lasserre recalled. "I think it was there both of us discovered that the communion, the community of the Church is much more important than the national community."[44]

As the end of the fall semester drew near and Advent with it, Bonhoeffer was having an unusually hard time getting into the spirit of the season.[45] He had never spent Christmas apart from his family, and memories of past festivities that his mother planned with great care left him in a melancholy mood.

But homesickness did not account for the sum of his feelings. He wrote to his friend Helmut Rößler in Berlin to confess that his hope of finding a "cloud of witnesses" had "been bitterly disappointed."

"One feels like one is standing on an observation tower looking out over the whole world," he said, "and no matter where one looks, most of what one sees is infinitely depressing."

The "frivolous attitude" of the mainline churches in America had been vexing from the start, but now they seemed to hold a mirror to his soul. Monday-morning editions of the *New York Times*, with their page-three summaries of sermons preached the previous day, read like dispatches from the wasteland, with headlines conveying a Protestant establishment seeking relevance at all costs: "Jesus hides the Creeds," "Pastor urges strong values," "After all, it's character that counts," "Dr Fosdick urges his congregation to make the best of a bad mess."

"In New York, they preach about virtually everything," Bonhoeffer said, "except . . . the gospel of Jesus Christ."[46]

Dr. Harry Emerson Fosdick, rector of Riverside Church—the massive Gothic edifice that, together with the seminary, occupied a whole city block—reigned as the benevolent prince of the Protestant establishment. Bonhoeffer, however, had not heard of him before coming to America, though he knew the name Emerson from having read the New England transcendentalist who viewed God as coterminous with Nature's benevolent spirit. Following one Sunday at Riverside, the two thinkers were forever linked in the German's mind as artisans of the American deity. Fosdick preached "an ethical and social idealism borne by a faith in progress," and "in the place of the church as the congregation of believers in Christ there stands the church as a social corporation."[47] He meant to inspire harried urban sophisticates and awaken hopes for brighter tomorrows, bolstering resilience in anxious times, verve against the malaise, and a useful and industrious faith— all noble aims. But Fosdick's gospel was bereft of miracle, modernized and Americanized. "The sermon has been reduced to parenthetical church remarks about newspaper events," Bonhoeffer lamented.[48] At least Emerson sought communion with the supernatural pulses of the brooks, ponds, and forests.

And these critical observations came months before Bonhoeffer wandered into the sanctuary of St. Mark's in the Bowery for a Good

Friday service that featured hip-priest William Norman Guthrie unpacking the seven last words of Christ in a recitation inspired by Ezra Pound's *Cantos*. Guthrie was aiming for a more "convincing revelation of the Heroic Son of Man."[49] It could not have been farther from the Good Friday service at St. Peter's Basilica seven years earlier, with its "magnificent singing" and "extraordinarily festive adoration of the cross."[50] Having once been temporarily relieved of his "episcopal ministrations" (after staging a church dance to the Egyptian sun-god), Guthrie tempted fate again on Good Friday 1931, rejecting the cross altogether. "I do not want that kind of Christ," he said. A Christ sent to die for the sins of the world? No, Guthrie declared, "I deny the reconciliation of the Cross."[51] Instead he would treat his flock to a syncretistic smorgasbord of exotic tastings: a Brahmin priest intoning Hindu prayers, a Mohawk Indian in full body paint, a Zoroastrian holy man laboring over a fire ceremony, and a barefooted dance troupe from Barnard College improvising an Annunciation Day piece.[52]

For now, Bonhoeffer's dislocation would owe more to conventional American Christianity. "So thank God Christmas is coming just now in the middle of all this," Bonhoeffer wrote to his parents, "otherwise I would [fall completely into] despair."[53]

A ray of light came in an invitation to spend Christmas in Cuba as a guest teacher at the German school. With Sutz, his Swiss friend, he left New York on December 11, 1930, delighted to be out of the wintry city and see the landscape turn greener as the train rolled south. He told Sabine that while she would be enjoying a white Christmas in Berlin, he would be sweating "beneath the tropical sun."[54] From the port of Tampa, the two caught a regional train to Key West and there boarded the SS *Governor* for a seven-hour voyage over rough waters to Cuba. Over four days, they traveled thirteen hundred miles, covering the same distance that separates Berlin from the south of Spain.

The weather was "splendidly warm," Bonhoeffer reported from Havana: in the mid-eighties and clear. After "the recent icy, cold weeks in New York," the tropical gardens, which were "as green as in summer," and the blue sea close by were a balm for the soul.[55] Palm trees cast silhouettes in the late afternoon and created an "incomparably beautiful" effect. Hummingbirds flittered like butterflies.[56] Cuba was a sanctuary of birds—pelicans, cranes, herons, flamingos. And there were vultures as well!

During his brief tenure at the German school, where he taught religion classes in the last days of the semester, Bonhoeffer found time for leisurely walks through Havana and outings into the countryside.

"Huge pineapple fields, banana cultivation, sugar cane, tobacco plantations are all over the country. The streets are incredibly bad, and there are almost no pedestrian paths at all outside. All the mountain regions still seem to be completely undeveloped." He observed the human dimension as well: "The living conditions are the most primitive I have ever seen. They build windowless huts out of palm leaves and stalks and seem to use them only at night and for shade in the summer. The children often run around completely naked, and usually half naked."[57] The deprivations notwithstanding, Bonhoeffer said he found it striking "that the Spanish population apparently gets along much better with the Negroes than do the Americans."

He had great fun speaking Spanish again in Cuba. "And now that I am back here again, I notice how little joy the English language gives me." It sounded "so flat and superficial."[58]

On the fourth Sunday in Advent, December 21, 1930, he preached in the sun-flooded chapel of Havana's German Lutheran Church. The scriptural text was Deuteronomy 32:48–52, the moment in the Israelites' flight from bondage when Moses ascends Mount Nebo and views the lush Canaan valley, the promised land of milk and honey. "For you shall see the land before you, but you shall not go there, into the land that I am giving to the people of Israel." Whether the result of the balmy air, or the hypnotic light slanting through the open windows, or the congregants waving their pew fans in the thick Sunday heat—or simply his own indifference—Bonhoeffer's sermon was decidedly mediocre. In his white linen suit and tan derby shoes, the tanned and stylish German could not quite summon the beleaguered patriarch

DIETRICH BONHOEFFER AND ERWIN SUTZ
IN HAVANA, 1930.

sloughing through "disappointments, tribulations, defeats, apostasy and unfaithfulness."[59] God's promise to his chosen people "is a very serious matter," Bonhoeffer blandly proposed. "But Advent, too, is a serious matter; in fact, it is an enormously serious matter." The beloved before him responded accordingly.

In the last year of his life, on a hot summer day inside a Berlin prison, Bonhoeffer would remember the failed Havana sermon as a casualty of the "luxuriant tropical heat" and a time when he had nearly "succumbed to sun-worship." He was ever after on his guard in warm weather. "It was a genuine crisis, and a hint of it assails me every summer when I get to feel the sun," he said.[60] "I could hardly remember what I was really supposed to preach."

On the eve of his return to New York, he joined Sutz, who had spent most of his own time in Havana with family friends, for a stroll through the Paseo de Matti, the park in the center of the Prado, before retiring to the terrace of his guesthouse, the air sweet with the scent of butterfly flowers and morning glories. He was in a reflective mood. In a progress report to his superintendent in Berlin, Bonhoeffer posed a number of questions formed over the preceding four months in America, clarifying his hopes for the spring ahead.

The trip to Cuba had also occasioned a surprising discovery of the other America. "The separation of whites from blacks in the southern states really does make a rather shameful impression," he wrote after the train ride through the Deep South. The conditions were "really rather unbelievable." Segregation was enforced in so many unexpected ways: "separate railway cars, tramways, and buses south of Washington."[61] Bonhoeffer had studied this reality in his courses and had begun doing library research and some interviews, but Yuletide marked his first personal encounter with the institution of racism—and with the object of its oppression. Bonhoeffer had never seen so many black faces, but in Cuba, "Negroes and Negresses" constituted the majority.

His search for the elusive fellowship of authentic witness now took the form of questions raised by the fall semester: How can one speak authentically about Christianity? Where are Christian truth and its "criterion" to be found in actual experience? If the institutional churches should fall into utter chaos, how—and, again, where—might the gospel be seen, heard, felt, and embodied in the fullness of its mystery and power?[62] How does one understand the spiritual character of a nation that has "so inordinately many slogans about brotherhood, peace, and so on" but at the same time "legislates and practices racial segregation"?[63]

He returned to New York with a clear purpose for his remaining months in the U.S., and soon he and Sutz, as well as Lasserre, would be discussing the prospects for another trip into the Americas.

Before his arrival in New York from Germany in September 1930, Bonhoeffer had never had a conversation with a person of color. Once, on his ten-day excursion to Libya in late spring of 1924, he had noted in his journal the "Arabs, Bedouins, and Negroes sitting on donkeys in great, picturesque white cloaks," traversing the streets of Tripoli in a "colorful throng of peculiar figures." But that was the extent of his professed interest in race.

His teachers at Union introduced him to what the Swedish sociologist Gunnar Myrdal would later call the "American dilemma" via readings from Du Bois, Johnson, and the rest. Still, it was not until a seminarian named Franklin Fisher sought him out that he came to know a black man. And it was not until Fisher invited Bonhoeffer to join him for a Sunday-morning church service in Harlem that the German visitor had any experience of American preaching and worship that seemed to him authentic and vital. This first time he worshipped with black Christians would be a revelation. Fisher—the son of one A. C. L. Fisher, pastor of 16th Street Baptist in Birmingham and a graduate of Howard College (now Howard University)—had come to New York not only for the unique opportunities Union offered African American seminarians, but also to learn more about the Harlem Renaissance, then in full flower.[64] Assigned to the Abyssinian Baptist Church as a pastoral intern, Fisher would, with a gentle kindness, guide the stranger in a world foreign to most Americans, let alone Europeans. And Bonhoeffer was more than pleased to discover a tradition that stood "fairly untouched, indeed, avoided by the white church." It was the beginning of Bonhoeffer's intense, six-month immersion in American black Christianity and culture.

ABYSSINIAN BAPTIST CHURCH IN HARLEM

"Through my friendship with a Negro student at the seminary, I came together with a group of Negro boys each week and also visited them at home," he wrote, of what he understood as "one of my most important experiences in America." He knew that the access he enjoyed was rare, but at the same time, "the results of such an experience are, I must say, deeply distressing." It was to see "the real face of America, something that is hidden behind the veil of words in the American constitution that 'all men are created free and equal.' "[65] The image of the veil, it is well worth noting, Bonhoeffer borrowed from Du Bois's *The Souls of Black Folk*—a book he was reading for Niebuhr.[66]

It was not only the exuberance and "eruptive joy" of black church worship that excited Bonhoeffer, but the seriousness as well. Among his white northeastern classmates, he'd often had the sense of "talking with schoolboys." His conversations with Fisher and with other "Negroes and East Asian students," though in one way entirely new, were nevertheless reminiscent of exchanges in Berlin-Grunewald, the ideas percolating with intensity, concentration, and verve. The "reigning atmosphere" of white Protestant culture in America produced "inordinate confusion" and "lack of clarity" and always left Bonhoeffer "feeling depressed"; but his black interlocutors proved "never for a moment . . . boring."[67] "It really does seem to me that there is a great movement forming," he wrote in his notes, "and I do believe that the Negroes will still give the whites here considerably more than merely their folksongs."[68]

Abyssinian Baptist Church was founded in 1808 by Ethiopian immigrants and sea merchants who had severed ties with the First Baptist Church in lower Manhattan after failing in efforts to end its segregated seating practices. The dissenters would move several times in the following decades—from nearby 40 Worth Street, to 166 Waverly Place in Greenwich Village, to 242 West Fortieth Street—before purchasing land on 138th Street in Harlem between Lenox and Seventh Avenues. Shepherded by Adam Clayton Powell Sr., Abyssinian was the largest black church in the city, with some seven thousand members.[69] One New York writer called it the "symbolic capital of black America."[70] It could not have been more different from Fosdick's Riverside Church, and the difference was to Bonhoeffer a revelation.

A Union student from east Tennessee named Myles Horton met him after he returned from his first visit to Abyssinian. Bonhoeffer, Horton recalled, was in an expansive mood and eager to talk. Horton accompanied him on a most animate walk down Riverside Drive, the whole way Bonhoeffer speaking excitedly—in both English and German, which Horton did not understand—of the preaching, the congregants' participation, and "especially the singing of black spirituals." He conveyed the thrill of the flock voicing ascent with the preacher. Completely unguarded, at one point Bonhoeffer stopped abruptly and told Horton that his morning in Harlem was the only time "he had experienced true religion in the United States." Indeed, he had never seen such joy in worship anywhere before, certainly not in the melancholy north German plains. Bonhoeffer concluded that "only among blacks, who were oppressed, could there be any real religion in this country."[71]

His presence at Abyssinian that year coincided with important changes in Powell's vocation as an urban minister. A skilled administrator as well as an eloquent preacher, Powell had already been senior pastor at the neo-Gothic church for more than twenty years. But with the Great Depression sweeping over the neighborhoods of Harlem as hard as anywhere, he felt summoned to new convictions. For most of his ministry, he had traded comfortably on a notion of Christ as inaccessibly transcendent, the God-man in majesty. Lately, he had begun to dwell on Jesus as one who wandered into distressed and lonely places to share the struggles of the poor as a friend and counselor.[72] Bonhoeffer's later formulation of the "Christological incognito" bears the impress of

HARLEM IN THE GREAT DEPRESSION

Powell's decisive awakening, of Christ going incognito into the world, "an outcast among outcasts," hiding himself in weakness.[73]

Powell welcomed the German theologian into the full life of Abyssinian's community. In time, the stranger in tailored suit and silk tie would lead a Sunday school class for boys and a Wednesday-evening women's Bible study. He also assisted with the youth clubs and musical events, on one occasion even preaching from Powell's pulpit—a rare privilege.

It might well be remembered that in his dissertations, Bonhoeffer had mounted an acrid assault on the German philosophical tradition, hacking through the thickets and thorns of Hegelian dialectic in a desperate bid to rescue the sanctity of the social, relational self from a world-dominating "Transcendental Ego." While there is an undeniable beauty in those writings, in their unfolding and explication, they had come to seem to him algebraic and wintry. The opportunity to write a sermon for Abyssinian was something altogether different; even though that sermon has been lost, Bonhoeffer's remarks to a fellow German student shortly afterward survive. Rudolf Schade, who later taught at Niebuhr's alma mater, Elmhurst College, recalled his encounter with a "beaming and enthusiastic" Bonhoeffer trying to explain, in German, the emotional effect of hearing the black church folk generously answering his sermon with a chorus of "Amen"s and "Hallelujah"s and "Yes, Yes!"[74]

Paul Lehmann, an affable midwesterner (later to become professor of Christian ethics at Union), wondered whether his German classmate was spending too much time in Harlem. As early as October, Bonhoeffer had signed up for an outing to explore the neighborhood under the seminary's program called "Trip to Negro Centers of Life and Culture in Harlem." He compiled an extensive bibliography on "the Negro" through the Harlem Branch of the New York Public Library and collected articles on the race issue. With Fisher at his side, Bonhoeffer scoured Harlem's record shops for recordings of Negro spirituals, black gospel, and blues, most of which he would pack into a carrying case at the end of the school year and take home to Germany. The "spiritual songs of the southern Negroes represent some of the greatest artistic achievements in America," he told Lehmann, who would remain intrigued by how relentlessly Bonhoeffer pursued "the understanding of the [Negro] problem to its minutest detail through books and countless visits to Harlem." It was as if he had forged "a remarkable kind of identity with the Negro community."[75] By the mid-1930s, singing the Negro spirituals and listening to recordings of them would become a vital part of the dissident circles in Germany that gathered around Bonhoeffer.

Shortly after New Year's 1931, Fisher presented Bonhoeffer with a gift he would carry with him the rest of his life, a copy of Johnson's *Book of American Negro Spirituals* and sixty pieces of accompanying sheet music.[76] It seems unlikely that Fisher over the years cleaved as intimately to the gift Bonhoeffer offered in return, *Deutschland: Baukunst und Landschaft*, a slim edited volume on modern German architecture.[77]

Bonhoeffer never wrote an account of his Sunday mornings at Abyssinian. It is a frustrating fact, particularly in light of the ample ruminations of his Italian journals, stylized but evocative of inner life. Yet Abyssinian turned unquestionable Bonhoeffer outward and upward. In the "Negro church" he learned to see familiar things in a previously hidden dimension.[78] The scholar Ruth Zerner once astutely observed "that black worship, particularly in song, was so overwhelming and personal for [Bonhoeffer] that he found it difficult to analyze in writing."[79] Indeed, it left him simply, joyously, at a loss for words. On Thanksgiving 1930, he and Fisher, and two unidentified students—one black, one white—traveled by car to Washington, D.C. Fisher had relatives in the district. He showed Bonhoeffer the great monuments, the Capitol, the obelisk in tribute to the first president. He liked the way these landmarks were "all lined up and separated only by broad expanses of grass." But Bonhoeffer was most taken by the Lincoln Memorial, its

DIETRICH BONHOEFFER PHOTO
SUBMITTED WITH HIS APPLICATION
TO UNION SEMINARY, 1930

"enormously imposing" and exaggerated image of Lincoln, "ten or twenty times larger than life," and "brightly illumined at night, in a mighty hall." Bonhoeffer said he would not have believed Americans capable of such a thing. "The more I hear about Lincoln the more he interests me," he wrote to his parents. "He must have been a tremendous person."

It would appear, however, that the most enduring memories of Washington came of sojourning "entirely among the Negroes." American race relations were discussed in detail—not only with Fisher's relatives but with "leaders of the young Negro movement at Howard College," as Bonhoeffer noted in the same letter. And "their homes, by the way, were often strikingly well furnished." This company likely included the philosophy professor Alain Locke, whose influential 1925 anthology *The New Negro* epitomized the innovations in African American political thought and culture, those animating the Harlem Renaissance and larger trends in black intellectual life.

On Saturday, December 5, Bonhoeffer hurried back to New York City to hear the Philharmonic under Toscanini's direction, but after a week of intense exchanges and other experiences in the black life of the capital, he found the performance "dreadful" and "shallow." To be fair, Bonhoeffer had never much cared for the popular Italian maestro, who years earlier had been invited to supervise Germany's premier music festival, Bayreuth. "As if one of our own people could not have done it as well."

W hat became of Frank Fisher? In letters to Niebuhr after 1931, Bonhoeffer would ask after his "Negro friend," though the two would never see each other again. But on an evening in 1937, Bonhoeffer would tell a gathering of dissident Christians at an illegal seminary in northeast Pomerania that as he was preparing to leave New York at the end of his Sloan Fellowship year, Fisher implored him, "Make our sufferings known in Germany, tell them what is happening to us, and show them what we are like." Over beer and cigars, huddled around the fireplace in a sparsely furnished manor house, Bonhoeffer shared stories of his travels to Washington and through the Jim Crow South, read passages from African American literature, and led the Lutheran pastors in some of his favorite black spirituals.

After Union, Fisher would teach at Morehouse College before accepting the calling in 1948 to the West Hunter Street Baptist Church in Atlanta. It was a church of modest size and means on Atlanta's west side, but its proximity to the consortium of Atlanta black colleges and its significant membership of professionals gave it prestige and influence. Fisher is remembered as a minister who spoke with the precision of a theologian and dedicated his life to practical service in the congregation and community. Indeed, he helped build a vital and nurturing church in a city and region divided by race.[80]

In January 1957, Fisher was arrested with a hundred ministers from the "Law, Love and Liberation Movement," sometimes called the Triple L Campaign, for sitting in the whites-only section of Atlanta's city buses. Among their ranks was a young Baptist preacher who had traveled from his parish in Montgomery, Alabama, just for this purpose: Martin Luther King Jr. Atlanta's public transportation would remain segregated for another two years, but the Triple L Campaign, like many other protest movements in the South, had been inspired by the remarkable success of the Montgomery Bus Boycott, which the twenty-six-year-old King had led. The two Baptist preachers, King and Fisher, were soon thereafter linked as fellow travelers in the civil rights movement, and later that same year they combined their energies in launching the Southern Christian Leadership Conference, a social justice revival with a bold mission: "To Redeem the Soul of America." Fisher remained shepherd of the West Hunter flock until his death in 1960 at the age of fifty-one; he would be succeeded by a black Alabamian named Ralph Abernathy, on King's strong recommendation. It also bears noting that the irrepressible Vernon Johns, King's fearless predecessor at the Dexter Avenue Baptist Church in Montgomery, would preach his well-traveled sermon, "The Answer of Religion to the Riddle of Life," at the Union Seminary Chapel on February 4, 1931—Bonhoeffer's twenty-fifth birthday, though it is unknown whether he attended.[81]

In the remaining months of the spring semester, Bonhoeffer found his way into one other vibrant counterculture in progressive religious circles. Decades on, in 1976, the physicist Carl Friedrich von Weizsäcker would present a paper at the Dietrich Bonhoeffer Congress in Geneva (commemorating the seventieth anniversary of his birth), describing the pastor's life as a "journey to reality." If Bonhoeffer had remained an academic theologian, Weizsäcker wrote, "it seems to me that he would not have been able to resolve the problems he dealt with. In response to historical necessity, he freely chose a path that is more real."[82] That path, on which he first embarked during his American year, passed through not only the black church and the politically charged classrooms of Union but also, finally, circles of the American activist tradition—so that by the end "the real" had achieved the status of a sacrament.[83]

It was among Union's faculty and students that Bonhoeffer first encountered the scholarly activist cohort. Through these associations he would visit the tenement ministries of New York, engage with the Women's Trade Union League and the Workers' Education Bureau of America, taking notes on the labor movement, poverty, homelessness, crime, and the social mission of the churches. He met with officials from the American Civil Liberties Union, which after its founding in 1920 had focused mainly on the rights of conscientious objectors and on the protection of resident aliens from deportation.

All had connections with religious thinkers, Niebuhr foremost.

Since his arrival at Union in 1928, a cadre of social reformers had turned to him for moral and financial support, which, time and again, he provided graciously. Without his inspiration and practical assistance, historian Anthony Dunbar noted in his book *Against the Grain: Southern Radicals and Prophets, 1929–1950*, "these movements might not have existed or succeeded to the extent that they did."[84] Niebuhr's encouragement as well as his help with organizing and fund-raising are evident throughout the letters and exchanges among members of groups dating to this remarkably fertile period for American social theology.

Most of these men and women were earnestly seeking the Kingdom of God on earth. Clarence Jordan, one of the founders of the Koinonia Farm (the name from the Greek for "communion") in Americus, Georgia (where Habitat for Humanity later began), described the mission of his interracial cooperative farm as "a demonstration plot for the Kingdom." To be sure, these champions of the Social Gospel hardly had time to sift the implications of Niebuhr's developing "Christian realism," and its critique of such utopian aspirations. It speaks to his sensitivities and wisdom that even as he rejected as naive optimism many of the suppositions of the Social Gospel—that the age of perpetual peace was imminent—he still embraced the movement's transformative energies and never discouraged idealism among the grass roots, admiring the intent of these visionaries if not their understanding. In the same spirit, he also never failed to endorse experiments in radical community arising in the South and around the nation—even as hope for reform in this world was chastened by his own analysis.[85]

Bonhoeffer's personal knowledge of the American organizing tradition, however, came more directly through two largely forgotten teachers at Union, Harry Ward and Charles Webber. It also deepened in friendships with classmates whose social imaginations had been excited by the emerging Beloved Community, an international fellowship of peace that crossed national boundaries with the aim to unite all humanity.[86]

A Methodist minister, professor of practical theology, and "radical socialist" (Bonhoeffer's terse but apt description), Webber hailed from Osborne Mills, Michigan. He would become known to friends and foes alike as the chaplain of American organized labor. His book, *A History of the Development of Social Education in the United Neighborhood Houses of New York*, though unlikely summer reading in Friedrichsbrunn, was devoured by Bonhoeffer in New York. Webber was himself a skilled and tenacious organizer. His involvements were extensive: in the 1930s he held leadership positions in the Industrial Secretary for the Fellowship of Reconciliation, the Upper Mississippi Waterway Association, and the Amalgamated Clothing Workers of America in Richmond, Virginia, and in the 1950s and '60s he represented the National AFL-CIO to churches and religious organizations.

Webber's course, "Church and Community," which Bonhoeffer took in the fall semester, resembled what sometimes is called a "service-learning initiative," though it was much more than that. Webber used the class to introduce seminarians to the variety of lived theologies in a city facing the first year of the Great Depression, and to the variety of social ministries flourishing there. His subject was life, theology in practice; with Webber's guidance, Bonhoeffer and his classmates ventured out from the Union quadrangle into a metropolis abounding with innovative faith-based organizing.[87] There were "site visits" to dozens of New York churches and synagogues.

"In connection with a course of Mr. Webber's," Bonhoeffer wrote, "I paid a visit almost every week to one of these character-building agencies: settlements, Y.M.C.A., home missions, co-operative houses, playgrounds, children's courts, night schools, socialist schools, asylums, youth organizations, Association for advance of coloured people [*sic*]. . . . It is immensely impressive to see how much personal self-sacrifice there is, with how much devotion, energy and sense of responsibility the work is done."[88] That a professor would lead such efforts was nothing short of astounding.

Bonhoeffer would get deep into the weeds: visiting the National Women's Trade Union League and the Workers Education Bureau of America; studying labor problems, selective buying campaigns, civil rights, "restriction of profits," juvenile delinquency, and "the activity of the churches in these fields."[89] In proposing solutions, Webber drew on models and insights gleaned from the Southern Tenants Farmers Union, the Delta Cooperative, the American Civil Liberties Union, and the British Cooperative Movement, with whom he personally had worked. Upon returning to Berlin in the summer of 1931, Dietrich would tell his brother Karl-Friedrich that Germany needed an ACLU of its own.[90] Through his fieldwork with this now nearly forgotten professor of practical theology, Bonhoeffer envisioned a path from the classroom to the social reality, and many catchphrases of progressive American Protestantism began to pepper his sermons, writings, and letters.[91]

There was also Harry Ward, the Methodist activist and reformer, slightly older than Niebuhr and Webber and decidedly more ideological than any of his Union colleagues. Bonhoeffer referred to Ward as "Union's point man in the cause of the most radical socializing of Christianity."[92] In 1931, Ward was the seminary's best-known public intellectual—a status that changed abruptly when Niebuhr's *Moral Man and Immoral Society* was published the following year.[93] Widely known for his books—*Our Economic Morality*, the manifesto-like *Social Creed of the Churches* (which the body eventually known as the National Council of Churches would adopt as its platform), *The Gospel for a Working World*, and *Why War Morality?*, published in early spring 1931—Ward combined an old-time Methodist zeal for righteous action with a crusading Marxist critique of economic inequality.

Bonhoeffer took Ward's popular class, "Ethical Interpretations" (jointly taught with Niebuhr), designed to equip seminarians with the skills to interpret and evaluate "current events in light of the principles of Christian ethics." Students were required to read and analyze newspaper articles, political journals, government reports, and various legal documents—all from the perspective of "the Jesus of the proletariat." For Ward, this amounted to learning how to discern the social order in response to three essential questions: What are the facts? What do they mean? What should be done?[94]

Ward and Niebuhr would take dramatically different turns in the decade ahead: Niebuhr abandoning pacifism for Christian realism, and eventually becoming a Cold War anticommunist Democrat; Ward, meanwhile, hunkering down, as he saw things, in the trenches with Jesus and Marx, a defender of the "Soviet spirit" against all its enemies. His influence on mainline Protestantism would decline steadily as he turned hard toward a Leninist critique of capitalism, heralding the Soviet Union "as the repository for his hopes of humanity's ascension to a higher plane of spiritual and social life, atheism notwithstanding."[95]

But in 1931, when Bonhoeffer was their student, Ward and Niebuhr were united in their critique of American liberalism. The nation, in Ward's estimation, had become a "'cult of objectivity,' thriving on observation, experimentation and discussion" and producing a "paralysis of both the critical spirit and the moral will."[96] In the classroom, Bonhoeffer listened closely as Ward enunciated his singular version of Pascal's wager: Christians had the world to gain from living "as if" there existed an ethical God weighing every human action in the balance. This meant, at least for Ward, a socialist revolution.

Before that year in New York, Bonhoeffer had rarely discussed politics; when he had, it was mostly in response to his brothers, who, radicalized by the Great War, never missed an opportunity to butt heads on the finer points of the Weimar government or the morality of its democratic reforms. His friend Helmut Rößler had once complained of Bonhoeffer's inclination to escape into ethereal regions of "comprehensive" ideas and thus "avoid the murk and mists of boiling-hot politics."[97] Indeed, there is not even mention in his notes or letters of what was the lead item in the *New York Times* the day of his arrival: "Fascists Make Big Gains in Germany."[98] But, as it turned out, his querulous suspicion of God-deprived Union-style theology softened in the course of his interactions with (as he put it) "the contemporary representatives of the social gospel." He would come to regard "the sobriety and seriousness" of Niebuhr, Webber, and Ward as "irrefutable" as well as "determinative for me for a long time to come." He would never drop his charge that "Reformation Christianity" already included the same concerns without repudiating historical theology, which repudiation he would continue to regard as undermining the Social Gospel position. Yet his signal transformation in the course of that year—as he made his "turning from the phraseological to the real"—would always be linked to what he saw while at Union, both inside the classroom and out. There was for Bonhoeffer no longer an escape from this awareness: "something . . . was missing from German theology," as his cousin Hans-Christoph von Hase would later put it, "the grounding of theology in reality."

The Florida-born James Dombrowski was a white Methodist minister who attended Union and then Columbia University, where he earned a PhD in 1933 with a dissertation entitled "The Early Days of Christian Socialism in America."[99] But rather than pursue the academic career for which he had qualified, Dombrowski became an activist-scholar. Over the next three decades, he would direct the Southern Conference for Human Welfare (1942–46), edit the progressive *Southern Patriot* (1942–66), and—as executive director of the Southern Conference Educational Fund (1946–66)—work behind the scenes with many key figures of the 1956 Montgomery Bus Boycott, including E. D. Nixon, president of the Montgomery branch of the Brotherhood of Sleeping Car Porters and a leader of the NAACP. In these capacities, Dombrowski was of able service to a talented, if largely forgotten, generation of white southern progressives whose efforts broke ground for the coming civil rights movement: Howard "Buck" Kester, Constance West, Sherwood Eddy, Lillian Smith, J. R. Butler, Jessie Daniel Ames, Lucy Randolph Mason, Claude Williams, Elizabeth Gilman, and the aforementioned Myles Horton, who became, against all odds, one of Bonhoeffer's most trusted classmates. Almost to a man or woman, these southern radicals and prophets were connected with Union faculty and alumni in some form or fashion.

A country boy born and raised in the riverboat town of Savannah, Tennessee, Horton surely represents a type of divinity student inconceivable to Bonhoeffer before his year in America. His impoverished southern childhood would have fit well into James Agee and Walker Evans's landmark volume, *Let Us Now Praise Famous Men*. A product of Cumberland College, a school set up for poor whites in Appalachia, Horton had spent many a student summer working in vacation Bible schools in the mountains of east Tennessee. In an interview he would ascribe his admission to Union as owing to the seminary's need for a "token hillbilly." He remained intimidated by the "extremely high" intellectual level at Union, and its distance from his hardscrabble upbringing.[100]

In 1932 Reinhold Niebuhr would write a fund-raising letter to select patrons of progressive causes asking for support for the Southern Mountain School, a project inspired by his former students Horton and Dombrowski. The vision was to create an "experimental school specializing in education for fundamental social change."[101] In the 1930s and '40s, a golden age of progressive Protestant activism, the Highlander Folk School emerged as one of the most influential training centers, teaching southern workers to organize and helping launch the Congress of Industrial Organizations (CIO). In the 1950s, the school, by then under Myles Horton's direction, would switch focus from labor to the burgeoning civil rights movement and help train the generation of church-based organizers that included Rosa Parks, Ella Baker, and Martin Luther King Jr.

These Union personalities were among "the most radical Christians with whom Bonhoeffer ever associated," as the scholar Clifford Green notes. "They worked on urban and rural poverty, on racial justice and civil rights, on union organizing, on peacemaking, and many spent time in jails and prisons." By the end of his Sloan Fellowship, Bonhoeffer must also have recognized these men and women as being part of the greater "cloud of witnesses" he had longed for since the eve of his arrival in New York.

Bonhoeffer remained critical of the seminary's indifference to "all genuine theology," but his final assessments of the school's commitment to "radical socializing" were gentle and appreciative. For the same students who laughed out loud at mention of Luther's doctrine *sola gratia* were tireless workers in the vineyard, dressing the branches by which food, clothing, and shelter found the poor, extending the vine to the outmost highways and hedges, where the powerless dwelt and where righteous action was the highest of all virtues.[102]

On January 21, 1931, after several days abed with a nasty bout of the flu, Bonhoeffer wrote a birthday letter to Sabine. Once inseparable confidants, the twins had hardly exchanged a word in months. By now, she and Gerhard Leibholz had been married five years and already had two children, Marianne and Christiane, with another on the way. Bonhoeffer apologized for the fact that his letter would likely not reach Germany by their birthday of February 4: "It's so unnerving for me that we really are going to be twenty-five now," he also confessed. He explained about the flu and how it kept him from going to the post office, as well as buying the present he had picked out for her, though it was "nothing special."

"I don't quite know how I will spend the day," he said. "Several people have learned of the date and are demanding we have a birthday party, which I would give at the house of one of the married students. But perhaps I'll also find out there's something nice at the theater. Alas, I can't even raise a glass of wine to the occasion, since it's forbidden by federal law; how horribly tedious is this Prohibition business, which no one believes in."

He further allowed that his plans following the end of the term in May were still completely "up in the air." While he needed to return to Germany and figure out his options at the university, he really wanted to travel around the United States for four to six weeks, "perhaps through the South and West to Mexico." There was also the thought of going "all the way around the world, that is, especially to India, if my money lasts and I can find someone to come along and if Germany doesn't yank me back first." At all events, he would be home again by the end of June. The plan that finally came together would take him across the United States and Mexico; India would have to wait. When he drew in Lasserre and Sutz, the three could not manage to fix an exact itinerary, though all agreed that Mexico would be the goal.[103] With that much settled, Bonhoeffer began to feel the rush he always felt when a trip was in prospect.

And as usual, he attributed to his escape high-minded purpose: "I want to have a look at church conditions in the South, which allegedly can still be quite peculiar, and get to know the situation of the Negroes in a bit more detail," he wrote to his brother Karl-Friedrich. "[I]t really does seem to me that there is a great movement forming."[104]

They would leave the week after Easter.

Since his whirlwind tour of Rome during Holy Week four years earlier, Eastertide had always been associated with unsurpassed beauty. Easter Sunday 1931, however, would mark a change. Bonhoeffer had never heard of requiring the faithful to buy tickets for Easter services, but such was the practice at Abyssinian—as he would discover too late. Being unable to get a seat for the Sunday-morning service left him with a sour taste as he ended his involvement with the black church. "Nothing left," he reported, "but to go hear a famous rabbi who preaches every Sunday morning in the largest concert hall before a full audience."

The Free Synagogue of Manhattan (which met at the Universalist Church of Eternal Hope on West Eighty-first Street) routinely drew more than a thousand people to hear Rabbi Stephen Wise. The openness to all comers was appealing. "Pewless and dueless," was how the synagogue's first president, Henry Morgenthau Sr., explained it; unlike most synagogues there were no pews set aside for members and no annual fee. At the time there were sixteen vibrant synagogues in Berlin to serve the Jewish population of 120,000, but this service in New York was Bonhoeffer's first time worshipping together with Jews. He was grateful to hear Wise deliver an "extremely effective sermon" on building a "city of God" upon the five boroughs of New York—one of peace "to which the Messiah would then truly be able to come."

The next Tuesday, May 5, 1931, with "a tent and a little money," four unlikely companions sputtered out of New York City in a secondhand Oldsmobile. Just a half hour outside town they were met by the rolling hills of Essex County, ablaze with early wildflowers. In addition to the fellow Europeans Sutz and Lasserre there was the American, Paul Lehmann, along for the ride as far as Chicago. Bonhoeffer was at the wheel. He had never before held a driver's license, and had it not been for Lehmann's wife, Marion, he would never have obtained one in New York. The private instructor he'd hired praised his handling of the car, but officials at New York City's Department of Motor Vehicles had a different impression. After he'd failed the road test, Marion advised him to slip the examiner a five-dollar bill. The German strongly objected and promptly failed the test again. On his third try, he reluctantly offered up the bribe; he passed.[105]

Only a smattering of postcards survive as clues, but driving options were limited in 1931. It appears that the men took Highway 22 West in Newark and from there drove through Reading, Harrisburg, Altoona, and Pittsburgh.

A postcard marked "Portland," a hamlet in the heart of the Slate Belt, informs Grunewald that after covering one hundred miles in three hours (in surprisingly light traffic), Bonhoeffer and his mates had arrived in the mountains of Pennsylvania, where they stopped to have lunch and "enjoy the lovely surroundings and the beautiful, warm weather!"

From there, Highway 30 West was a straight shot to Akron, Fort

Wayne, and Gary. And then Chicago: here the gregarious Lehmann bade the others farewell and was dropped off at Elmhurst College, where he had lined up a summer teaching job (his father being the president). The Oldsmobile then followed Highway 66 west out of Chicago through Springfield to St. Louis; Highway 61 south to Memphis; and Highway 51 through the small north Mississippi towns of Senatobia, Batesville, Grenada, and Winona, on to Jackson and then to Hammond, Louisiana. They got all the way to New Orleans, nearly a thousand miles in two days, with only Bonhoeffer and Lasserre licensed to drive. None of them cared much for the Crescent City or the state over which Governor Huey P. Long ruled. The Great Depression had been no gentler on New Orleans than on the urban centers up north, to which it had laid waste. The visitors counted scores of empty warehouses in the once-booming port city of seventy thousand. Now, only crime was booming. Bonhoeffer navigated the cramped streets of the French Quarter to drop Sutz off at the old town harbor. The "Swiss fellow" had made arrangements to take a ship back to New York.

Running behind schedule to make a church conference in Mexico City, Bonhoeffer and Lasserre quit New Orleans in haste and rolled toward the Texas state line. It appears, however—and there's no explanation in the letters of this detour of some several hundred miles—that rather than taking Highway 90 directly west toward Houston, the two men drove northeast on Highway 8 to Shreveport, and from there drove due west on 80 to Dallas. Perhaps they got their signals crossed and kept driving north in Baton Rouge. Either way, vast distances still lay ahead. With Bonhoeffer doing most of the driving, there was no time to keep a journal or write letters home. The quartet had dwindled to a fellowship of two. Bonhoeffer did get off another postcard, but only because the car broke down on the outskirts of Fort Worth, just before exit-

DIETRICH BONHOEFFER'S POSTCARD FROM WACO, TEXAS, TO THE ERN FAMILY

BONHOEFFER'S POSTCARD OF PIRAMIDE DE TEOPANZOLCO IN MEXICO,
SENT TO THE ERN FAMILY

ing onto Highway 96. He wrote to reassure Louise and Richard Ern, the mother and child from Connecticut, who had come to the United States on the SS *Columbus* with him, that all was going well and that despite their car troubles—"the part from the shaft to the fan . . . broke off," meaning, one would assume, the carburetor needed fixing, and they had to buy two new tires—the "car is now driving admirably." He and Lasserre had seen "a great deal of the country" and were enjoying the fragrant southern air.

Another postcard, with a color shot of a Longhorn bull, dated May 16, 1931, informs his grandmother Julie that the hill country of south-central Texas recalled the Harz Mountains in springtime—"fresh," "untouched," "beautiful country." He had also seen "the great areas where entire cities quickly emerged and people made their money overnight." Rest assured, "We are doing wonderfully."

On May 17, he wrote the Erns again from the border town of Laredo to say that he had never experienced anything like the soupy cauldron of south Texas heat, with temperatures into the mid-nineties—and it was still May. But otherwise everything was going well. There were well-built roads out there. And after sunset, the huge prairie sky remained incandescent for nearly an hour.

The young Ern would receive a picture of the Aztec ruins in Cuernavaca, with news that the travelers had just been sitting on that very pyramid, listening to an Indian shepherd boy tell stories about his life in the mountains. "There are apparently a great many poor people here. They often live in tiny huts, and the children often wear only shirts or nothing at all. The people look nice and are quite friendly."[106]

In Laredo, Bonhoeffer and Lasserre boarded a train for Mexico City, to give the car a rest. For nearly a week they would explore "Mexico's strange intermediate culture, with its Spanish Catholic and native Indian elements so curiously and provocatively combined."[107] The conference organizers invited the two Europeans to share their observations of North America and any lessons learned in the course of the year. It delighted Lasserre to hear Bonhoeffer speak of his new understanding of the Sermon on the Mount and Jesus's command-ment of peace. The "example of Christ," it seems, had been much dis-cussed over long hours on the road and under night skies in campsites. Bonhoeffer had made strong arguments against Christian pacifism. Lasserre's impression—a correct one, no doubt—was that despite his friend's "comprehensive knowledge" of the Christian tradition and his erudition, a "peace ethic" was "something completely new to him." But then Lasserre's moral imagination was fairly littered with unfamiliar and provocative notions: the limits of obedience to nation, the seduc-tions and treacheries of the war god Mars, the subversive power of Christ's passion.[108] Bonhoeffer had answered him with counterclaims from the German war tradition. Still, in unhurried rehearsals on this journey in the "southern latitudes," he was beginning to learn the lan-guage of peace.

There are no further dispatches from the road. The two men drove twelve, fourteen, even sixteen hours a day, stopping only to make clumsy attempts at cooking meat over campfires, or to search, often frantically and without luck, for a motel room. Occasionally they enjoyed a hot shower and a bed, but mostly they were roughing it in the wild.

In 1971, Lasserre would recall the night he and Bonhoeffer pitched their tent in a quiet pine grove, little suspecting that they had tres-passed "the dormitory of a herd of swine." Just before dawn, Lasserre awoke to "ferocious snoring" and worried that Bonhoeffer had taken ill, only to find him "sleeping peacefully as a child." Stretched alongside him, though, halfway into Dietrich's tent, lay an enormous sow, also sleeping, if not as quietly.

Heading back to New York, they collected the Oldsmobile and drove directly to New Orleans, but then instead of retracing the same course home—north to St. Louis and Chicago and then back east—they took a different route. Beyond Lake Pontchartrain, Highway 11 ran straight into the heart of the Jim Crow South. Crossing the Missis-

AFRICAN AMERICAN HOUSING, LAUREL, MISSISSIPPI;
LIBRARY OF CONGRESS

sippi border, Bonhoeffer and Lasserre followed the two-lane blacktop through Slidell, Lumberton, Hattiesburg, Laurel, Meridian, Tusca-loosa. Ninety-five miles outside of Birmingham, while driving through the town of Fort Payne, they would have passed the exit for Route 35 North and, had they followed this road for thirty miles, arrived in Scottsboro, the north Alabama town, where, that very month, nine young black men were successively convicted, amid an angry mob, of raping two white women on a freight train. From Fort Payne, Highway 11 sliced through the northwest corner of Georgia on toward Chat-tanooga and Knoxville with the Great Smoky Mountains to the east.

The pair took a break in Virginia's southwest, the hamlet of Wytheville, where any local would have recommended they try the "World Famous SKEETERDOG," as one sign described it. They con-tinued on to Roanoke, Staunton, and Harrisonburg and then through Hagerstown and Harrisburg. Highway 22 East took them to Reading, Newark, and home at last.

All told, they had covered four thousand miles in seven weeks, not counting the twelve hundred on Mexican trains.

While Bonhoeffer, as we have seen, kept no journal of the trip, he seems to have jotted down some notes along the way. Impressions of the South, with studied observations of race relations, appear in the year-end report to his supervisor in Berlin. At times they are quite arresting, these terse remarks on *blood laws, mob rule, sterilizations, land seizures.* Bonhoeffer lamented a world "darker than [a] thousand midnights"

RURAL BLACK CHURCH, CIRCA 1930

and Scottsboro's "terrible miscarriage of justice." He had previously observed racial animus in New York City: once, while waiting for a table at a Manhattan diner, he and Fisher had been rudely shooed off by the owner. But "the way the southerners talk about the Negroes," Bonhoeffer wrote, "is simply repugnant ... and the pastors are no better than the others."[109] The report also reveals that on a Sunday morning in May, somewhere east of New Orleans and south of Knoxville, Bonhoeffer and Lasserre worshipped in a rural black church. With an "enormous intensity of feeling" the gospel was preached with conviction and power and interrupted by cries of joy. It was proof that "one really could still hear someone talk . . . about sin and grace and the love of God and ultimate hope." And beyond the preaching, Bonhoeffer *felt* churched deep in his bones, in the spirituals, in the "strange mixture of reserved melancholy" and the ecstatic joy "in the soul of the Negro." It was as if these rural folk, by some synthetic power and spiritual genius, had earthed emotion, intensity, and feeling in the sorrowful joy of Jesus. Bonhoeffer awakened to fresh spiritual energies in what he called "the church of the outcasts of America."[110]

Back in New York, he reexamined "The Black Christ," Countee Cullen's poem from 1929, which Niebuhr had assigned in his spring course. It was now with a new comprehension that Bonhoeffer read of a black man tortured and hanged by a southern mob. What is his crime? He has loved the earth and its delights, and he has defended his lover, who is white, from the wrath of a white man. For this he pays with his life. This death by hanging from a tree is brutally reminiscent of "Calvary in Palestine" and the many trees on which God "should swing, world without end, in suffering."[111] When Bonhoeffer writes of "the black Christ" being led into the field by a "white Christ," he refers to the astonishing paradox of Cullen's poem: the black man, lynched for his love of worldly pleasure, becomes, in his suffering, the Anointed One.

———

In America, Bonhoeffer's quest for a true Christian fellowship led him to a place where he was—to borrow from C. S. Lewis—"surprised by joy." (Lewis, who at fifteen had pronounced himself "very angry at God for not existing," would become a Christian that very spring, following a late-night walk with J. R. R. Tolkien.) In Karl Barth's *The Word of God and the Word of Man*, which years earlier had awakened Bonhoeffer from his liberal slumber, the author ponders the prospect of ever hearing the gospel anew after the era of religion—of hearing, amid the din and clutter of modernity, as if for the first time, the Eternal Word. Written in the aftermath of the Great War, a century of hopes for enlightened self-expansion lay in ruins. The world turned with "disquiet, disorder, and distress in forms minute and gross, obscure and evident."[112] Those keepers of the old order might take refuge on eternally green islands of security, pitching their tent in lands of self-righteousness, of man-made morality and religion and nation. But true Christian hope was elsewhere to be found. "We must take the trouble to go off far enough to hear the Word again," Barth implored.

Bonhoeffer now knew himself able to go that distance, for, as he said, "I heard the gospel preached in the Negro churches."

When, on June 20, 1931, Bonhoeffer embarked on his return to Germany, it was with a new perspective on his vocation as theologian and pastor. He was ready at last to put away childish things, foremost his professional ambitions, and begin to search the Christian and Jewish traditions for inspiration to peacemaking, dissent, and civil courage. The technical terminology faded steadily from his writing, giving way to a language more direct and expressive of lived faith, animated by his own will to discern God's in "the anxious middle." "It is the problem of concreteness that at present so occupies me," he wrote upon his return to Berlin—this from the young theologian who ten months earlier had found American pragmatism such an affront to Germanic exactitude.[113]

Far from another careless jaunt in a different culture, the American year would prove itself a forcing shed for a season of immense growth. Made alert to "a new kind of moral passion," Bonhoeffer could now see his way to a more demanding and complex faith.[114] His sojourn in an unfamiliar world, "an uninterrupted assault of new experiences," had furnished him with courage "to loosen boundaries between inner and outer, between emotion and reason, between thought and action."[115] "I don't think I've ever changed so much," he wrote, "except perhaps at the time of my first impressions abroad and under the first conscious influence of father's personality."[116] Beyond any expectation, this year had set his "entire thinking on a track from which it has not yet deviated and never will."[117] And how his understanding of the Lutheran doctrine of justification shifted in dramatic ways. No longer would he speak of grace as a transcendent idea but as a divine verdict requiring obedience and action. The American social theology, which had seemed so devoid of miracle, had remade him into a theologian of the concrete.

CHAPTER SEVEN

1931–1933

~

"Under the Constraint of Grace"

H ere I am sitting in the park in front of the University," Bonhoeffer wrote to Erwin Sutz, his Union classmate traveling companion, now back home in his canton of Zurich. Bonhoeffer was not at home, having gone to Bonn with a special purpose. "Barth lectures this morning. I took a short talk with him [a while ago]. This evening there is a discussion at his house with [monks] from Maria Laach. I'm looking forward to it immensely."[1]

It was indeed with immense anticipation that Bonhoeffer had traveled to the birthplace of Beethoven to meet Karl Barth for the first time. The Swiss theologian had moved from Münster a year ago to assume Bonn's post in Reformed Theology, which was being funded by American Presbyterians eager to promote Calvinism in the land of Luther.

Bonhoeffer's parents had hoped he would join them for a short holiday at their country house. He'd been back only a few weeks from his eventful nine months in America, which encompassed not only the academic year at Union Theological but more than five thousand miles of additional wandering by car, train, and ship. The Bonhoeffers were naturally hoping to spend a little time with their globe-trotting son.

But Bonhoeffer was on a pilgrimage of sorts, and as much as he adored his parents and the house in the east-

THE RADICAL THEOLOGIAN
KARL BARTH

ern Harz Mountains, nothing could have been more compelling now than the prospect of a rendezvous with Herr Professor Barth.

Bonhoeffer was much taken aback when the two finally met. In photographs, Barth was the picture of refinement, with his lean and elegant face. But on his first entrance into the lecture hall, "he looked dreadful," according to Bonhoeffer. He was disheveled, evidently paying little attention to his dress, and he had a hacking cough from a recent illness, aggravated further by his pipe smoking. He made an altogether sickly impression for such a lively mind. "Does Barth always look so bad?" Bonhoeffer asked Sutz, who, having studied at Göttingen, had arranged Bonhoeffer's visit.[2]

There are several good reasons why the answer was likely no. Barth was still recovering from a bout of diphtheria when the seven a.m. seminar began meeting. And having recently begun work on the first volume of his *Church Dogmatics*, he was beginning to grasp the enormity of the effort that lay ahead. Rebuilding the crumbling edifice of Christian orthodoxy was the work of a lifetime, and Barth had already turned forty-nine earlier that year.

Barth's summer course had been announced as "Prolegomena to the Study of Dogmatics."[3] He had a wry sense of humor, and may have considered the pseudo-Kantian title a little joke of sorts. There is no doubt that he found the habit of theological throat clearing tiresome in the extreme. Dogmatics required the twin virtues of audacity and precision in its aim to speak of the righteous and holy God. "[I] abhor profoundly the spectacle of theology constantly trying above all to adjust to the philosophy of its age," he had said in a heated exchange with Adolf von Harnack.[4] His methodology went something like: "Get to the point."

And so, at seven o'clock sharp, five days a week, following a short reading from scripture and a hymn, Barth got straight to work on the doctrines themselves, although he could rarely make short work of getting to the point. He'd lecture for three hours every morning from manuscripts on which he'd labored meticulously, often into the wee hours. Once, after moving to Basel, Barth had agonized all night over the doctrine of divine sovereignty only to cancel class that day, finding himself still unable to state the matter to his satisfaction. He lectured on Christology, the Trinity, the incarnation, the resurrection, and the divine attributes. But his acts of will were ultimately empirical, not subjective: his intent was to stand inside "the strange new world of the Bible" and let its "wild and crooked tree" grow freely, without constraint.[5]

Bonhoeffer, customarily a late riser, didn't mind the early hour, so eager was he to hear Barth. And if Barth was slightly off his game, Bonhoeffer did not notice. The performance was riveting: "He really is all there. I have never seen anything like it before." Barth's grand aura colored his exchanges with the students, who were both territorial and uncommonly deferential to the master.[6] For his part, Bonhoeffer—despite his two doctoral dissertations where Barth (like Niebuhr) had none—felt a sudden fear of being exposed as a "theological bastard." Among the Berlin faculty, Bonhoeffer's eclectic views were benignly tolerated. He was the scion of the Berlin intelligentsia and its encouragement of youthful exploration of unfamiliar landscapes. Such exploration was deemed essential to humanistic learning. Then, in America, where Christians ordered up their theology à la carte, he found that all potentially useful ideas remained on the table until pragmatically rejected. Having expected to find in the New World a parallel order to which he might compare his learning, Bonhoeffer had found a tabula rasa, at first unsettling but finally thrilling.

Bonn was different.

"No Negro passes 'for white,'" Bonhoeffer said. Images of his road trip through Mississippi and Alabama returned to him as an apt description of his life among the Barth epigones. In Bonn no less than in Birmingham, the keepers of the gate will "examine your finger nails and the soles of your feet," he said. The Barth circle kept vigilant guard over its dominion. "Up till now they've still shown me no hospitality as the stranger," he noted.[7]

And for the first week, as the morning seminar concluded at ten o'clock (normally his waking hour) and the other students hurried off together, Bonhoeffer found himself at loose ends in a city he found rather bland. He filled the time reviewing class notes; reading "some really interesting and lucid books"—works of economics he may have picked up in New York; checking the proofs of his book *Act and Being*, reading Barth's *Ethics II*; strolling about; and writing letters.[8]

"I am all alone here," he confessed to Sutz.[9]

"How nice it would be if you were here!" he told his New York friend Paul Lehmann. "I am completely alone . . . and waste the day quite fruitlessly. . . . In the meantime live ἐν ἐλπίδι—[in hope]."

One day, after class, Bonhoeffer locked horns with Barth, if only a bit.[10] Over tea in the professor's office, the two were discussing the proper relationship between theology and ethics. The disagreement turned on issues similar to those that had sparked Bonhoeffer's lively exchanges with Reinhold Niebuhr in New York, but the way Bonhoeffer was discussing them now gives further evidence of his theological transformations during the American year.

Barth was explaining his understanding of theology's peculiar place among the academic disciplines: theology is the science that ventures to speak a word about God ... the second-order reflection on the church's primary speech and practice, the writing that seeks to capture the bird in flight, to speak the impossible. Bonhoeffer asked what this had to do with reality.

The student agreed with the master on most of the basics: the theologian must be a servant of the church, and the basis for thinking truthfully about God is Jesus Christ. But Bonhoeffer was now living with the conviction that theologians must be willing to speak clearly and have a personal stake in their claims. He found Barth impervious to the ethical and social dimensions of doctrine—in fact, irritatingly so.

Barth responded with equal candor. Christian theology bore no responsibility to change society, he said. Theology makes nothing happen in the ordinary sense, and that's as it should be. He accused Bonhoeffer of "turning grace into a principle" and "thereby bludgeoning everything else to death."[11]

I n New York, Niebuhr had criticized Bonhoeffer's exposition of the doctrine of justification in a term paper. The young scholar's formulation was certainly familiar to Niebuhr from his own Lutheran upbringing, but he was now convinced—as he told Bonhoeffer in no uncertain terms—that without ethical content the doctrine remained inert and lifeless. Bonhoeffer's conception of grace was altogether transcendent, Niebuhr had complained.[12] It was godly mercy devoid of ethics.

Indeed in America, in the company of radical Christians, Social Gospel reformers, and African American churchmen, Bonhoeffer had felt, for the first time, the vitality of theology practiced closer to the field where the seeds are sown. The light of the world, he now believed, must illumine the heart to intervene with hope of repairing the world in all its brokenness.

Now, in Bonn, Barth was attacking him from the other direction: Bonhoeffer was too eager to apply the doctrine of grace to ethics, to make the social connection. His view was, Barth explained, not transcendent *enough*!

Over tea, Bonhoeffer bit his tongue, but later that evening he wondered to Sutz, "[J]ust why should one *not* bludgeon everything else to death?"[13]

Though Bonhoeffer did worry about the impression he had made. He would be relieved to hear from a classmate that Barth had thoroughly enjoyed the exchange. The contrarian voice was perfectly welcome, and when the seminar resumed the next day, Barth asked

Bonhoeffer to introduce himself to the other students. There soon followed an invitation to dine with the professor at home.

"Barth [is much] better than his books," Bonhoeffer wrote afterward. "There is with him an openness, a readiness for any objection which should hit the mark."

Bonhoeffer would leave Bonn very grateful for the opportunity to have heard Barth elaborating on his position and also opining on a variety of related subjects. Over the three weeks there had been "many real bons mots" to savor, leading Bonhoeffer to confess that his initial impressions of the Barth circle had probably been too harsh. Those students were, after all, people really interested in Jesus Christ and wrestling as best they could with their "pride of knowledge." They were less buttoned up than they had at first appeared; at an end-of-semester party, in fact, they performed a play written by Barth at the age of fifteen in the style of Schiller: *Leonardo Montenuova, oder Freiheit und Liebe* (*Leonardo Montenuova, or Freedom and Love*). Still, Bonhoeffer did not regret that it was time to go back home.[14]

B onhoeffer's plan, such as he had ever had one, was to become ordained to the ministry and work two part-time jobs: one as a chaplain at Berlin's Technical University and the other as an unpaid lecturer in the theology department at Friedrich-Wilhelms University, where he'd done his doctorate. Even with the dissertations, successful comps, and prestigious fellowship at Union, these two unglamorous options were, at the time, the best he could hope for in Germany's hidebound academe, particularly in a straitened economy. And neither came with an office. There was a bright side, however: he had two months free before the fall semester began. As we have seen, the long break usually meant a leisurely stay in the eastern Harz and some time on the Baltic Sea, as well as more exotic travels.

Sutz proposed a hiking expedition in the Alps, after which Bonhoeffer could join him in Zurich for a few days. His Swiss friend liked the idea of communing with his former Union classmate for tranquil reading and talk, far from the bustle of Broadway and 121st Street. But Bonhoeffer declined the kind offer, expressing the hope that Sutz would enjoy the mountain-air solitude without him.[15]

Bonhoeffer had landed an invitation to visit Cambridge, England, for an ecumenical conference called (in the chirpy parlance of still-emergent ecumenism) the World Alliance for Promoting International Friendship Through the Churches. Founded in 1914, the alliance sought to encourage world peace through inter-church and

BONHOEFFER RELAXING WITH AN ECUMENICAL COLLEAGUE
ALONG THE BALTIC SEA

inter-denominational action—or talk, at least. Bonhoeffer was eager to attend, as the burgeoning ecumenical scene appealed to his cosmopolitan sensibility, and after persuading his parents to cover the attendance fee (five marks a day), he caught a plane to the United Kingdom.

"My sojourn in America," he said later, "made one thing clear to me: the absolute necessity of co-operation" among the churches of the nations.[16] "When will it be," he would ask in the conclusion to his conference report, "that Christianity says the right word at the right time?"[17]

In Cambridge, Bonhoeffer distinguished himself as a brilliant young bridge builder. His initial contribution was to insist that the movement set itself on firmer theological footing, this point being made in response to certain Anglo-American delegates who had seemed (as he might now have expected) more interested in results than convictions and rather too syncretistic as well. Bonhoeffer listened, debated, and negotiated as one in possession of that rarest theological gift—the ability to lay aside doctrinal objections for the sake of a higher good, that good being the affirmation of the global, ecumenical church. Legitimate points of dispute had surfaced, many of which could have easily derailed the proceedings. But Bonhoeffer recognized that behind creedal disputes lay the urgent mandates of peace and the attendant need to create practicable initiatives for local congregations; delegates needed to find common ground and the concrete means by which all Christians might, with one voice, proclaim Jesus the Prince of Peace prophesied in Isaiah. This was the ultimate mission of the church in the nations of the West.[18] "The real key to Bonhoeffer's message," as the ecumenist Willem Visser 't Hooft recalled, was his "hunger and thirst for reality, for living the Christian life and not merely talking about it."[19]

Though not as consequential as his year in New York, the week in Cambridge had its own profound impression on Bonhoeffer and his "turning from the phraseological to the real." As a budding academic theologian he'd once sung the glories of the Prussian army and lamented the "shame of Versailles" alongside his fellow German Protestant liberals. Now he was wholeheartedly affirming a "unanimous message to the churches of the world." Full of the spirit of a unified Christendom, he called for a substantial reduction of military armaments of all kinds, for a reasonable and just coexistence between the nations under arms, and for freedom for all nations from military aggression.[20] After the conference, Bonhoeffer said he felt as if he had taken a leap into the unknown.

Indeed, on the home front, at least among those paying attention, Bonhoeffer's remarks in England, the once and future enemy of the fatherland, were met with a frost. Professors Paul Althaus of Erlangen and Emmanuel Hirsch of Göttingen coauthored a scathing response in the daily called the *Hamburger Nachrichten*, decrying the closing of the German Protestant mind. Holders of prestigious chairs at two of the nation's finest universities, the duo declared in no uncertain terms that given the current state of affairs there could "be no understanding between us Germans and the nations that were victorious in the World War." It was a view by no means extremist in the national context, but rather the norm, as was the claim that any German who believed other-wise was effectively disowning his "destiny and his birthright."[21]

Bonhoeffer's hymns to a worldwide Christian fellowship and his leap into the global ecumenical movement put him, as never before, on a clear collision course with the German church, which appeared ever more eager to quash internationalism as a threat to the Fatherland.[22]

"I just cannot see how to get things right . . . in the unprecedented situation of our public life," Bonhoeffer said. "The cheap consolation that I am doing the best I can, and that there are people who would in fact do much worse, unfortunately is just not sufficient."[23]

On a clear autumn day in 1931, Bonhoeffer finally returned to Berlin. It was time to start the new semester. When he arrived at the Anhalter Bahnhof, the yellow-brick train station on the Wilhelm-strasse, his father's chauffeur was waiting in a black Mercedes.

Bonhoeffer was energized by the week in Cambridge and equally by the prospect of leaving Germany again very soon—before the end of the month, as it turned out. The ecumenical movement, to which he had remained indifferent in his student years, now figured vitally in his desire to live a life more open to the world. His wanderlust had found its means of fulfillment and a worthy justification. In the next year he would join his new brethren for gatherings in Amsterdam, London, Prague, Chamonix, Čiernohorské kúpele, Gland, and (on multiple occasions) Geneva.[24]

His itinerary allowed him a transient escape from the inescapable realities that would attend his eventual homecoming: the two dreary part-time jobs overhung with uncertainty about more meaningful employment. And there was as well the ever-worsening national climate.

While Dietrich was still in America, his brother Klaus had sent him a grim report on recent developments in Germany.[25] "People are flirting with fascism," his brother wrote. If the "radical wave" of right-wing sentiment captured even the

DIETRICH BONHOEFFER AT AN
ECUMENICAL YOUTH CONFERENCE
IN GENEVA, 1932

educated classes, Klaus feared, soon it would be all over "for this nation of poets and thinkers."[26] Bonhoeffer's friend Helmut Rößler had also warned of a "purified, glowing national pride" linking arms with "a new paganism."[27]

Sure enough, the next two years would put Bonhoeffer's new cosmopolitan convictions to the test.[28] But the new realities would reach him more personally not long after he had moved back into his old room in Berlin-Grunewald.

The Berlin Technical University, a *Hochschule* for the applied sciences, was housed in a neo-Renaissance edifice occupying a forlorn stretch of easternmost Charlottenburg. Bonhoeffer's offer, as chaplain, to lead a theological discussion group met with exactly zero interest among the future engineers of Germany. He told his brother Karl-Friedrich of feeling like a housewife who puts a special effort into her cooking "only to see it gobbled up indifferently." Would, however, that they had cared to consume his fare in any fashion.

In the first week of the fall semester, a single malcontent twice tore down the fliers Bonhoeffer had taken pains to produce and post on all the campus kiosks. The first occasion had prompted the chaplain to write a "letter of concern" before re-plastering the same kiosks. When the culprit struck yet again, Bonhoeffer responded with another round of fliers and another letter, this one much less pastoral: "To the fellow student who has now felt compelled to remove this notice for the third time! Why so secretive and why always the same joke, or why so terribly angry?" And then, a plea: "Why not come round to see me sometime?"[29]

Attempts to host lectures, prayer services, and Bible studies likewise ran aground, along with his every high-minded summons to "really concentrate on the gospel and not get sidetracked." Any remaining hope was dashed when not a single student showed up for the first meeting of his discussion group, "The Crisis of the State and the Gospel." Morning devotions, too, were canceled for lack of demand, and during office hours he sat at a temporary desk waiting, usually in vain, for a visitor.[30] The few who did come to see him typically wanted help with their finances. There was one exception: he seems to have caught the attention of a fraternity that agreed to a discussion on ecclesiology—so long as it met in a beer hall near the Alexanderplatz and Bonhoeffer picked up the tab.

Not one to be easily discouraged, Bonhoeffer sustained himself by feeling more insulted than demoralized by the philistines at the TU.

He decided to turn to his other situation at Berlin University, his alma mater.

The job of *Privatdozent* at Berlin University resembled the post— one might say plight—of an academic lecturer at a medieval university. Whatever income he received depended wholly on the good graces of his students, whose attendance was voluntary.[31] Students paid whatever they wished; or, if they saw fit, they paid nothing. A barrage of new duties placed a great burden upon even his capacious energies, as he struggled to find projects and relationships that brought him into contact with people outside the academy. He managed to offer guest lectures and doctoral seminars; he gave public talks, prepared candidates for confirmation, graded papers, and preached sermons.

For years Bonhoeffer had moved at an exhilarating pace: in his university studies in Tübingen and Berlin and in his travels to Rome, Barcelona, New York, Cuba, England, and Mexico. But now he was back in a city that felt to him increasingly spectral. And he was only in his mid-twenties. What he tasted was the shock that comes of reckoning for the first time with the wages of one's dissent. He belonged to a faculty whose politics he no longer shared and a church whose preaching he found stultifying and dull—and a pervasive loneliness overtook him. To Sutz he confessed feeling "dreadfully [alone] even sitting in a whole crowd of people."[32]

The situation led Bonhoeffer into a season of new self-examination. At one point in that unsettled autumn of 1931, he decided he would rather be known as a Christian than a theologian. In the latter guise, his evolving ideas on the Lutheran doctrine of justification made increasingly uncomfortable demands on his academics and ministry. More than ever, he was desperate to understand how the Christian should act "under the constraint of grace" in obedience to Jesus, what it meant in the warp and woof of lived experience, to confess Jesus Christ as Lord and Savior.

In September, Bonhoeffer's second book, *Act and Being*, appeared, drawing a small scattering of favorable notices, which he promptly dismissed as "far too scanty a recompense."[33] Weighing this second dissertation in his hands, Bonhoeffer pronounced it "an altogether disagreeable product." His article "The Christian Idea of God," which appeared in the *Journal of Religion*, one of the premier North American theological quarterlies, left him "disgusted and ashamed."[34] In fact, extensive editing of the English translation produced fairly mediocre results, the heavy scaffolding of academic God-speak producing an effect as claustrophobic as the midday trains.

He told Sutz, "Sometimes I wish that I could go somewhere into the country to get out of the way of everything that is wanted and expected of me."[35] In the company of the Barthians in Bonn, he had felt like "an illegitimate among thoroughbreds," but among the Berlin professoriate, he struggled to breathe. "My theological core is becoming suspect," he said, "and they obviously feel they have nursed a snail on their breast."[36] He concluded finally that there was no one in Berlin "who can teach the elements of a vital Christian theology." He would make a desperate bid to get the faculty to lure Barth away from Bonn—"Barth is really someone from whom poor, desolate Berlin could learn a thing or two about God," he wrote to Sutz—but that effort was unavailing, like so many others.

In an Ascension Day sermon, he described authentic faith as an orphaned existence. He asked how a person "torn by homesickness" can rejoice in life; how a dissident Christian can bear the rejection he must inevitably face. Perhaps remembering in particular the example of the black churches in America, Bonhoeffer expressed hope that the greater church might itself find the strength to bear the weight of its outcasts, even as it sought, in an era of propaganda and mediocrity, to bear joyful witness to the truth.

Bonhoeffer had written in one essay that Christ means freedom— freedom from "the lie that I am the only one there, that I am the center of the world."[37] And so his feeling around the theology department must have been that of captivity, and the desolate absence of the Lord. "I hardly ever see [any] of the professors," he said. "But I'm not especially sorry about that."

The massive gray-stone fortress on Unter den Linden had all the charm of a mausoleum. The affable liberal men who had once filled the ranks of the faculty—like Harnack, Bonhoeffer's beloved teacher—had been replaced by colorless time-servers, who rarely extended a hand.

"Luckily I have my practical work," Bonhoeffer said.[38]

On the fifteenth of November, 1931, Dietrich Bonhoeffer was ordained to the ministry at St. Matthias Church near the Potsdamer Platz. It was not an especially memorable occasion. But he was now eligible to preach and administer the sacraments.

In his sermons from the time immediately thereafter, he spoke of the psalmist, whose felicitous piety had been rudely unsettled by his encounter with the living God.[39] He said that the church must exist under the constraint that its first order of business was to proclaim "the words of Christ that there should be peace."[40] He admonished those dearly beloved to subsist without hesitation on the truthfulness of

God's promises. To have faith was to live "totally" and unreservedly in the company of Jesus.[41] He launched into a recitation of the Beatitudes, Jesus's longest and most radical teaching on the extremes to which he calls his followers. "Blessed are those who hunger and thirst for righteousness, for they will be filled. . . . Blessed are those who are persecuted because of righteousness, for theirs is the kingdom of heaven."

These words were to be acted on in perfect trust and single-mindedness.[42] Toward that very end, Bonhoeffer had begun to practice certain devotional disciplines, following the daily readings in the Moravian prayer book that his governess had given him as a child, and listening to his collection of Negro spirituals and gospel standards, which was never far away. At the same time, he affirmed the Christian faith's blood kinship with Judaism and Jesus's lineage in the House of David. The strange, new world of the Bible (as Barth had called the countercultural impulse of the gospel) was at work on his own thoughts too, building brick by brick and over years a cathedral of new understanding.

In February 1932, Bonhoeffer finally left home. A second-floor room let by a master baker named Heide at 61 Oderberger Strasse in the Prenzlauer Berg neighborhood became his first German home away from Grunewald. It was not nearly so congenial, this working-class neighborhood in northeast Berlin, to which the district superintendent had assigned him when his chaplaincy at the Technical University was over. But Bonhoeffer had requested the post as a pastoral assistant at Zionskirche, the church around the corner; the assignment could not have pleased him more. "It's just about the worst part of Berlin," he said to Sutz, "with the most difficult social and political conditions."

Indeed, after his full-immersion baptism in Harlem, this move to an urban parish felt like a homecoming of sorts, except that the fifty teenage boys who fell under his supervision, sons of unemployed factory workers, proved more unruly than any child he had taught at the relatively genteel Abyssinian Baptist. "They behaved like mad things, completely crazy," Bonhoeffer said of the youth group.

But he discovered soon enough that boys could be brought to attention by the telling of Bible stories, the more dramatic the better. Bonhoeffer obliged, with an old reliable theatrical flair, offering "simple Biblical stuff with emphasis [on] the eschatological passages." The result usually produced "absolute quiet," he found, and he was pleased—and, even more, relieved. He told Sutz he was no longer afraid of meeting the same fate as his unfortunate predecessor, who had dropped dead on the job.

Moving into a neighborhood hit hard by factory closings to be near his fifty new confirmands, visiting the boys and their families in massive public housing blocks, praying for the barely accommodated as they struggled amid "indescribable poverty, disorder, and immorality," teaching teenagers in crisis the proper "care of the soul"—this was at last the "real work" he had longed for.[43]

The outlook for the winter ahead was "perfectly horrible," with as many as seven million Germans likely to be out of work. "The misery is frightful," Bonhoeffer said, "and the most terrible thing of all is the hopelessness of this situation." The nation was on the verge of a complete breakdown. "We will know how much we need the church, especially during the next winter," he said, "but what should its message be, and in any case will anyone bother to listen?"

In the second semester, Bonhoeffer started inviting his confirmands, in groups of two and three, to Herr Heide's boardinghouse, where he served them supper, read them scripture or recounted Bible stories, played for them recordings of classical music and Negro spirituals, even taught them chess. Sometimes he would tell a story from his travels. Evenings usually concluded with "a short spell of catechizing." He marveled at the power of the spoken word of scripture—only slightly enhanced by his own rhetorical flourishes—to render the young ruffians spellbound, sitting before him agape.[44]

No dramatic conversions or revival took place; the boys were simply paying the Word full attention, its proper due. But that was miracle enough. "Perhaps the foundation has been laid for a faith that will grow."[45]

In their ardor, he saw evidence of divine protection; the refusal to collapse under duress was their "great—and I think also moral—power of resistance."[46] Bonhoeffer found himself moved by these people on the margins, "far away from the masquerade of the 'Christian world' "—the "little people" who lived "more under grace than under wrath."[47]

The youth ministry in inner-city Berlin made Bonhoeffer acutely aware of the limitations of his training. Home visits left him with the feeling that he would have been better prepared had he studied chemistry instead of theology. "It sometimes seems to me that all our work on the care of souls comes to grief."[48] The eloquent scion of Grunewald found himself often at a loss for the right thing to say.

Parish life became the joyful counterpart to the grind at the university: "Christ existing as community." This notion that he had developed in his dissertations had remained mostly notional—now he was living it, together with the working-class parishioners of Zionskirche. "What a liberation!" he said.[49]

As an early Easter present for his confirmation class, he took them hiking on trails around the family house in Friedrichsbrunn. "Except for one broken window pane everything is still intact," he reassured his parents. On the happy occasion of the boys' having memorized the catechism, he threw a party, celebrating with "sausages, cake and cigarettes."[50]

Young Dietrich had been confirmed in the well-heeled parish church of Berlin-Grunewald, though he rarely darkened its doors. Even during the year of his ordination exams, he had attended services only sporadically.

"I came to the Bible for the first time," he would later say of these strange months following his return from America, as a "new and unexpected meaning broke through [scripture's] ancient words and phrases."[51] The Moravian prayer book became the source of his daily readings; the devotional disciplines he performed with relish. On four rolling acres near Biesenthal, thirty kilometers north of Berlin, which his parents had given him, he had a hut built, rather hermetic, but it served when he organized spiritual retreats for the youth group. He encouraged the confirmands to read scripture with prayerful concern for the church and an attention to God's will. He spoke of a communal life of "obedience and prayer." Observing Bonhoeffer's new fervor, some family members and friends grew worried. Colleagues at the university joked of such monkish ways practiced within their ranks. But the Sermon on the Mount had moved to the center of his thinking and there it would remain, he with it: Bonhoeffer was simply haunted by the simplicity and directness of Jesus's teachings, the concreteness of His demands, "their objectivity."[52]

His homilies and other church talks kept returning to the same profound question: What kind of theologian and pastor—*what kind of Christian*—must we encourage for the uncertain years ahead? And it worked in the other context, too: despite his alienation from the rest of the faculty, Bonhoeffer's question, and his manner of seeking to answer it in class, was received by some students as a welcome break from business as usual. He was, he could discern, not entirely alone there.

Wolf-Dieter Zimmermann had arrived at the university the cynical son of a minister. His first taste of the theology department had bored him "infinitely." There was "the pedantic juggling [of] Greek words," Professor Ernst Sellin's "formalistic" dealings with the book of Isaiah, rote translation of medieval texts (never mind "what they meant, how they were related to God's actions"), and all those "theological concepts [that] seemed meaningless . . . and gave me no guidance." So when Zimmermann heard from a fellow student about a young *Privatdozent* doing something different, he went to see.

Zimmermann attended the first lecture in Bonhoeffer's course "The Nature of the Church."[53] The "disheartening sight" of the sparsely attended class—only a smattering of students in the large hall—gave Zimmermann pause. He wondered whether he should withdraw, feigning to have entered the wrong room, but he "stayed out of curiosity," and would be glad of it. "A young scholar stepped to the rostrum with a light, quick step, a man with very fair, rather thin hair, a broad face, rimless glasses with a golden bridge. After a few words of welcome he explained the meaning and structure of the lecture, in a firm, slightly throaty way of speaking. Then he opened his manuscript and began."

Bonhoeffer allowed as how it had become not so unusual lately to hear people ask whether the church still had any relevance, whether they still needed God. But this question, he said, was wrongly put. The paramount concern is in fact "whether we are willing to offer our lives to the church and the world, for this is what God desires."[54]

Every sentence hit its mark, Zimmermann thought. Bonhoeffer spoke directly to the issue most deeply troubling the young man.[55]

Not that Bonhoeffer had turned difficult ideas into easy formulas. His appeal was not as a popularizer. He lectured from meticulously written notes, venturing undaunted over the fields of ecclesiology, philosophical theology, biblical exegetics, and church history. But within that intricate intellectual scaffolding, as Bonhoeffer constructed it, was a space where existential questions of faith and life—the most urgent questions of all, though largely ignored by academic theologians—became inescapable: "Where is God? How does God meet us and what does God expect from us?"[56]

And then, in a different voice, he explained. To answer these questions one must begin with the Christian's most elemental concern: "Who is this Jesus Christ, the one who encounters us in the Word of God?"

Within two months of his installation in Prenzlauer Berg, more than a hundred students regularly attended church events. And at Unter den Linden—in Berlin-Mitte, barely a half mile away though a world apart—a small circle of university students was coalescing around the young assistant professor, attracted to his peculiar combination of substance and style: a ponderous, pastoral theologian who could move mountains, it seemed, but returned always to first things. He spoke of God, Jesus Christ, and the church in ways that sounded truly radical.[57]

When, at the end of the fall semester 1932, Bonhoeffer proposed that the class find a more congenial place to meet than the cavernous lecture hall at the university, Zimmermann offered his modest rooms in the attic of his father's parsonage at the Königstor near the Alexanderplatz.

Twelve students and their teacher gathered there, "sitting on every possible piece of furniture." The seminar usually ran for three hours, the air thick with tobacco smoke. Topics ranged from the sacraments to salvation to ethics, but it was not so much the subject matter that made the gatherings unforgettable; it was the way Bonhoeffer addressed persons with an ardent, inspiring respect. And always the sessions included prayer and song: Bach, romantic lieder, Negro spirituals.

"What was far more important for us," one student recalled, "was working together to find clear ways of thinking," practicing simplicity, "learning not to slink off into side-issues, or to be satisfied prematurely with cheap and easy answers."[58]

E ducating theologians and pastors in a nation on the eve of enormous and catastrophic changes placed great demands on teacher and student alike. Bonhoeffer had no intention of offering intellectual shortcuts. Seeing the world anew through the peace of Christ summoned every available resource. If "pure, abstract theorizing" could illuminate concrete reality, his habit was to gently rub his brow and do the hard work—that is, to use philosophical terminology if it helped clarify the point and its application to life.[59] As his student Albert Schönherr later confessed, the idiosyncratic gesture always drew his attention to the professor's "big, Kant-like forehead."

Seminars concluded with a gentle "*Danke*" and the invitation to reconvene at a nearby café to take up other subjects—which might range from current politics to reminiscences of Spanish bullfights.[60]

As Bonhoeffer welcomed newcomers and transient visitors each week, the class grew beyond the point of fitting comfortably in Zimmermann's attic rooms. So the teacher decided that they would return to campus. Now, however, all the seats in the hall were filled, and it was not uncommon to find more than two hundred students sitting at rapt attention.[61] More than fifty regularly joined his "open evenings," at which the week's lectures were freely discussed, "untethered to the syllabus or assigned topics."[62]

Newcomers, and there were always some, having heard of his intensity at the podium, were often taken aback by the sound of his voice, high and slightly tremulous, "like a choirboy's."[63]

Zimmermann later found the record of his own impressions. "In old papers I have noted down about him: 'Near and far away at the same time,' 'keeping a distinguished distance and yet ready and open.' 'He has immense powers which are also immensely disciplined.' Conflicts were experienced and borne by him in an almost 'holy' way."

Bonhoeffer's aspect was indeed not that of a man burdened by study. He was, in fact, six foot one, broad shouldered, with a well-built, athletic frame. With his ruddy complexion, he looked more like a champion skier than a scholar.

"We followed his words with such attention that one could hear the flies humming," another student recounted. "Sometimes, when we laid our pens down after a lecture, we were literally perspiring."[64]

No doubt the effect owed to his lack of sentimentality as well as his deft and well-furnished mind; each was evident both at the lectern and in the rousing "table talk" after the work was done. But the students were drawn by something less abstract, too: the fact of his personal bearing. Bonhoeffer still lived as a bon vivant each day, as if to show that the pursuit of God could also inspire a rich and multilayered worldliness. Some hermetic disciplines notwithstanding, he was never one for sackcloth and ashes. The good things of this world, too, were full of God's glory. Bonhoeffer would later describe a humanism of the incarnation in terms of the musical concept of polyphony, and propose that the fullness of the risen Lord enabled an actual clarity of sight. He would not banish altogether the specialized elements of his earlier academic writing, the technical concerns and the philosophical principles. These would always remain in his tool box, but only as tools for shaping, as needed, the brick and mortar of a more expressive language, out of which he tried to build a dwelling place habitable by anyone.

For Bonhoeffer had become involved in humankind not only in the philosophical theologian's way but in the practical theologian's way, too. Every man, as John Donne wrote, was "a piece of the continent." And this solicitude for the individual, this care for the whole person, was especially uncommon in a professor. As one of his students would later report, in general "no one took any responsibility for nurturing the spiritual life."[65] Unless one sought out a chaplain or pastor, one was "entirely on his own." With Bonhoeffer, it was different.

In a photograph from a retreat to the village of Prebelow, Bonhoeffer appears younger than most of his charges, even though attired more carefully, his beige tweed vest, white collared shirt, and necktie paired with hiking boots to the knee for the requisite sprezzatura. He fairly beams a gentle confidence. On closer inspection, his blond hair, swept casually to the side, is already thinning, but he betrays not a care in the world, as one young man in the front row, his eyebrows mirthfully raised, serenades the company on a flute. Two women lean together, one enfolding the other loosely in her arms. Another lad crouches alongside Bonhoeffer holding a stick comically in his teeth.[66] If not exactly the choir of the saints, this fellowship of theological bohemians has nothing dour about it. *Homo theologicus* is *homo ludens*, a holy communion of joy and play.

BONHOEFFER AND BERLIN STUDENTS ENJOYING FREE TIME IN PREBELOW, 1932

Bonhoeffer would remain an outsider to the tenured faculty between 1931 and 1933—indeed, until he was finally removed from his post of unpaid adjunct in 1937. A certain distance between him and his colleagues, guarded from both directions, would always define his place in the academy. Nevertheless, in the special time between his return from America in 1931 and Hitler's rise to the chancellorship on January 30, 1933, Bonhoeffer became an unlikely, albeit minor, celebrity of the Berlin avant-garde. The voice he gave to a prevalent spiritual restlessness spoke to students and pastors but also to artists and intellectuals.

The novelists Ernst Wiechert and Frank Thiess were among a coterie of writers who invited Bonhoeffer to their salons in Berlin-Mitte.[67] Once, even the enigmatic bachelor Hans Schwarz opened his rooms, with their black-papered walls, for an evening with the artist Ernst Barlach. Barlach's reputation had soared in these Weimar years, thanks to his intriguing wood carvings of the weak and infirm and his

ALEXANDERPLATZ, BERLIN, 1932. IN THE BACKGROUND CONSTRUCTION OF THE
U-BAHN (SUBWAY) IN FRONT OF THE GEORGENKIRCHE

gnarled bronze sculptures. Barlach's play about a hedonistic squire who
contemplates suicide had recently premiered at the Staatstheater.

Bonhoeffer's own aesthetics reflected the forthright and conservative bourgeois taste of his family. And so he would mostly ignore
the Expressionist novelties of Hermann Hesse, Max Beckmann, Stefan Zweig, Arnold Schoenberg, and Arthur Honegger, notwithstanding an almost expressionist flavor in his theology: whether in sermons
or essays, it merged familiar images and ancient convictions with bold
new shapes and slashing strokes, to keenly subversive effect.[68] Indeed,
Bonhoeffer's meditations on the cross make an inescapable demand on
the listener—one every bit as unsettling as George Grosz's *Christ on
the Cross Surrounded by Soldiers*, Barlach's *Blind Beggar on Crutches*, Max
Beckmann's *Resurrection*, or Lovis Corinth's *Red Christ*.

"If we speak of Jesus Christ as God," Bonhoeffer said in his lectures, "we may not say of him that he is representative of an idea of
God, which possesses the characteristics of omniscience or omnipotence (there is no such thing as this [ethereal] divine nature!); rather,
we must speak of his weakness, his manger, his cross. This man is no
abstract God."[69]

"It is difficult to characterize the Bonhoeffer of those Berlin years,"
Zimmermann would recall. "My memory has retained some moments

of that time, whereas others have hardened into concepts, unconsciously. With astonishment I learned that he was a committed socialist and a pacifist." The revelation came as a shock to this son of a German pastor, who had been raised on a strict diet of Luther's doctrine of the two kingdoms. Bonhoeffer's alternative understanding seemed to Zimmermann so extreme that for a while the student altogether mistrusted the teacher's views on Christian ethics.[70]

Reading Bonhoeffer's book *Creation and Fall* brings one into the *Grosser Saal*—the great hall—on Unter den Linden to hear the twenty-six-year-old's discourse on the first book of the Bible. His lectures on Genesis began Tuesday, November 8, 1932, and would not end until Tuesday, February 21, 1933, spanning a fateful winter of rancorous discontent, as mass revolts by Nazi partisans brought a violent end to the Weimar Republic and, in its wake, ushered in Adolf Hitler, who, but three weeks into his dictatorship, opened the first concentration camps for enemies of the state.[71]

The Genesis lectures were focused on the holiness of God—God as giver of all good gifts, the beginning and the ending of creation's story. Though entirely free of theoretical armature and scholarly throat clearing, these lectures remain the most ponderous of all Bonhoeffer's writings. The style introduces a concentration altogether different from that of his earlier work. *Creation and Fall* is expressionistic and poetical, meditative and devotional, but also a ruthless rending of veils. It is the work of a Christian dissident awakening to his strange habitation in "the anxious middle."[72]

Creation and Fall resembled no other course in the curriculum. Only indirect attention was paid to debates proper to the guild; the published volume lacks footnotes. No contemporary of Bonhoeffer's is mentioned by name. *Creation and Fall* is a dazzling, cyclonic utterance, one not to be mistaken for a systematic or historical effort. Wrought out of densely textured prose, in five-hundred-word bursts, the narrative in flow, in the emergence of structure, delineates a space for contemplation, full of awe at the righteousness and transcendent mystery of the Creator.

In the beginning God created. In the beginning there was only God, indivisible and triune. And in the beginning God created the heavens and the earth. "Not that first God was and then God created, but that in the beginning God created."

The beginning defines the essential insight that only God is God; that God creates out of freedom, not necessity; that the creature exists in proper relation to this truth only by accepting the insuperable limit it imposes. This distinction, between the Creator and his creatures, must guide our thoughts and actions in all subsequent things, for it is only from the anxious middle—existence between Eden and the Apocalypse—that we can try to discern the truth about the beginning.[73]

"We do not know of this beginning by stepping outside the middle and becoming a beginning in ourselves," Bonhoeffer taught. The boast of our being masters of any new beginning is "accomplished only by means of a lie," although there were deceptions far graver than this. Humankind would love to turn back to its origins, to a "land of magnificent rivers and trees full of fruit."[74] But we cannot, and this realization—that we are ultimately powerless in the face of our absolute beginning, incapable of mastering the origin for all the cunning of warriors and demigods—is our great humiliation. It is the exile's terror, the thought that cannot be suffered in silence.

Those in the lecture hall could not have easily missed the political resonance, the notes of defiance, in these brooding meditations on sin. He had opened the Bible to unleash the living word against a church and nation on the threshold of catastrophic apostasy.[75] "The absurd, perpetual state of being thrown back upon the invisible God," he said, "no one can withstand it any longer."[76]

The joyful, unscripted sojourns of people cleaving to Christ in an idolatrous age—here was the only remedy for egotism and delusion. Bonhoeffer said that beyond reading the Bible as God's word to us, the time had come to begin reading it "against ourselves as well," accepting the word's power to implicate us as well as to redeem us.[77]

He never discussed his spiritual life from the pulpit or podium. He regarded self-revelation in sermons as a vanity, if not a vulgarity. But he could not hide having undergone a profound change in the past two years.

"I no longer believe in the university," he would confess amid the tumult of these horrible years, a horrible year. "In fact I never really have believed in it."[78]

CHAPTER EIGHT

1933

~

Theological Storm
Troopers on the March

It was the beginning of 1933, and Bonhoeffer was still enjoying the long Christmas break from the university. Having moved back into his parents' house on Wangenheimstrasse, he worked every morning from his bedroom, his notes carefully arranged on the oak writing table that had been his desk since boyhood. With a westward view of the neighbor's frozen garden, he wrote lectures and sermons with the familiar economy of effort, though now with the aid of a new Alder, his first typewriter. He had finally "entered the technical age," as he told his Swiss friend Erwin Sutz.[1]

Afternoons were set aside for naps, meeting friends over coffee, writing letters. Weather permitting, there was skiing on the well-marked trails of the Grunewald. Most evenings, he went into the city for a concert or a play. Musical nights at the Bonhoeffers' continued a pleasant Saturday ritual. During a short stay in Friedrichsbrunn, he lolled about reading Heine and Hegel.

But for the chances of an older candidate named Pätzol, Bonhoeffer thought himself a shoo-in for the pastorship of St. Bartholomew's Church in the east Berlin parish of Friedrichshain. His internship in the inner city had left him eager for a new clerical assignment to balance his academic work. But not long before classes resumed at the university in the second week of January, he would be passed over for the job.

A little over two weeks later, on January 30, the unimaginable happened. There had been signs: on the very day that Bonhoeffer's Genesis lectures had turned to the story of Cain—second son of Adam and Eve, who jealously murders his brother, Abel, to become the first "destroyer of life"—the storm troopers had appeared in the streets, bearing "their hideous rubber truncheons, their drums and flags." On that day, too, Adolf Hitler, a German citizen for less than a year, had been appointed by President Paul von Hindenburg as the new Reich chancellor. Nothing would ever be the same in the wake of that—not the world of the mind or the world of politics; not Europe or the world outside it. A city once contoured by the "hopeless, godless vacancy of satisfied faces" was transformed suddenly with an enormous sense of purpose.[2] Now was "the time of massed armies," "the restlessness of turbulent mobs," of "wars and rumors of war"; "the time of huge throngs moving over the face of the earth, of technicians planning grandiose feats of destruction," a time of "suspicion, hatred and distrust."[3] Bonhoeffer's life was now set on a collision course with Hitler's.

In the Protestant faculties and congregations, churchmen of fixed and iron-hard purpose, who called themselves the Deutsche Christen, the "German Christians," were pledging their loyalty to the fatherland. They claimed that God had chosen a new Israel, the German *Volk*; that the Christian doctrine of revelation had brought about the disinheritance of the Jews and that Jesus Christ had abrogated Israel's ancient covenant. They wanted a strong church of muscular virtues—a manly church, *eine männliche Kirche*—unified by German ideals. They even convinced themselves that Jesus was not a Jew. They boasted of their mission in the most inspiring terms imaginable: as the completion of Martin Luther's work. Revival was in the air.[4]

As a practical matter, this meant that the German Christians would pursue a fully assimilated *Volkskirche*, a national church based on common blood. Following the sixteenth-century principle of *cuius regio, eius religio* ("whose realm, his religion"), the German Protestant Church had long made room for non-Lutheran confessions. Of the twenty-eight regional churches—the *Landeskirchen*—extant at the beginning of 1933, twenty adhered to Lutheran tradition, two were Reformed, or Calvinist, and the other six were United, or combined—among them the Old Prussian Union Church, which included congregations in Berlin. The dispensation worked out under the Holy Roman Emperor Charles V had allowed German Protestants significant freedom as to their liturgical practices—such as whether to sprinkle the head of the catechumen or to immerse him fully in the baptistery; whether to baptize babies or only adults, according to confessional tradition—all this latitude and more while still enjoying "full membership in the national church." The unity of the regional Protestant churches lay mainly in their common Reformation heritage. But with the groundswell of national renewal, the German Christians reached beyond theological differences for a unity even sturdier than that of common confession, a unity based on ethnic uniformity.[5]

On February 1, two days into Hitler's rule, Bonhoeffer delivered an address broadcast on Berlin's Rundfunk radio station just after the rush hour, when the cafés and coffeehouses were most crowded and tuning in.[6] No recording of the radio talk exists, although he gave two addresses on the same subject shortly thereafter, reading from scripts that do survive, one at the Technical University and the other at the College of Political Science. Both scripts contain the same withering critique of the *Führerprinzip*, the Führer principle, the notion that political authority should flow from the top of the government down— that is, from the Führer.[7] Speaking as a pastor and a theologian, Bonhoeffer sounded very much like a diagnostician examining the nation's soul. He was still his father's child, offering his measured, almost clinical, observations.

Germany's defeat in World War I had obliterated the Protestant liberal optimism of the nineteenth century, and with it the congenial bonds of throne and Providence. Having come of age at a point when "the once well-established Western world was coming apart at the seams," a generation of lost souls—with plenty of anger in common— had wandered in darkness, unable to find their bearings. This generation had put its hope in technology, in the masses, and in the collective. It had sought ballast in resignation, meaning in meaninglessness. "Inanimate objects appeared to emerge from this collapse as victors," said Bonhoeffer. But nothing had been as consoling as denial. Reeling between fantasy and self-loathing, a generation in flight from actual circumstances found escape in a "metaphysic of reality." It had repudiated finitude and fact for an ever-expanding cosmos, whose banner would become the *Blutfahne*, the blood flag. The metaphysical turn welcomed "any development and construction." It was the ordinariness of things that was unbearable in these postwar years, the insatiable hunger for new horizons. Promising a new day—one of freedom from debts, from limits, and from shame—the metaphysic of reality overwhelmed the responsibility to reason. Frustrated by the constraints of time and history, Germans had imagined and embraced a reality without natural limits, one based on this new imaginary principle.

Bonhoeffer explained how German Protestants had desperately recast the Christian narrative of guilt and salvation as the story of Germany's defeat and rebirth: World War I and the shame of Versailles followed by the gift of Hitler and the rebirth of the fatherland. Salvation depends on a savior, but the Jew of Nazareth was not what the times required. Into this void entered the *Führerprinzip*, with the promise of a national atonement. "Freedom from debt, limit, and shame implied a new kind of human being," Bonhoeffer continued, a world-constitutive ego, an epochal self, the *Übermensch*, who aligns himself with "the forces of the eternal and divine," ordering "his state, his economy, his community accordingly."

With preternatural cunning, Hitler exploited the collective humiliation and the "great and unacknowledged void" in the German soul.[8] "Hitler's rhetoric was religious," Bonhoeffer said. "He dissolved politics in a religious aura, and all the theological terms which had been previously secularized" had now become "the great standards of his appeal." Hitler promised deliverance and redemption, rebirth and salvation, and in so doing denounced the Reich's enemies as godless and satanic. "He did all that in the name of Providence, for he believed that Providence had chosen him to deliver the German people."[9] In this exceedingly prescient address, delivered within weeks of Hitler's ascent to power, Bonhoeffer warned Germany that "everyone who misappropriates the eternal law and concedes responsibility to a Superman will in the end be destroyed by him." Bonhoeffer would begin speaking of Hitler as the Antichrist.

After ten minutes his radio address was cut off in mid-sentence, but a short essay believed to be the basis of the address was published the following week in *Der Angriff*, the Berlin daily established by Joseph Goebbels as a propaganda weapon taking aim at the degenerate opposition. Bonhoeffer's dissent served as fair warning of the struggle ahead.

Bonhoeffer and Reinhold Niebuhr had lost touch since Bonhoeffer's American year in 1931. But in the days following the January 1933 elections, Bonhoeffer's thoughts returned to Niebuhr and his American associates—indeed to all the social theologians who had preached ultimate honesty and ethical realism as hallmarks of authentic faith. Ostensibly to endorse his cousin Hans-Christoph von Hase's application for the Sloan Fellowship at Union, Bonhoeffer would write to Niebuhr in the first week of February: "Fit, open, sociable, approachable, with an independent mind," Bonhoeffer said of Hans-Christoph, who would eventually be accepted. But Bonhoeffer also took the opportunity to reconnect with Niebuhr at a time when the American's recent writings on Christian realism and the immoral structure of mass society had become urgent and undeniable.

Bonhoeffer began communicating with church figures of several other nations about the developments in Germany.[10] His notes, memos, and letters comprise his first unlawful actions, being violations of the Malicious Practices Act, passed in the wake of the Reichstag fire. Marinus van der Lubbe, the young communist who torched the government building, claimed to have acted alone. But typically, Hitler seized the moment. On February 28, 1933, the day following the blaze, he persuaded President Hindenburg to enact the Reichstag Fire Decree and to suspend the Weimar constitution. Under his new emergency powers, the Führer declared that the arson represented an attempted communist putsch. The subsequent trials, though travesties, gathered popular support for his curtailment of civil liberties and ban on publications unfriendly to the Nazi regime. Under the Enabling Act (in March), Hitler and his cabinet obtained power to enact laws without the Reichstag's approval: *Gleichschaltung*—the assimilation of all institutions and persons into Nazi ideals—was at last triumphant. The same week, in a scenic Bavarian town fifteen miles northeast of Munich, on the grounds of a former munitions plant, a concentration camp was established. The town was Dachau.[11] In response to the Nazi assault on civil liberties—which included the suspension of *habeas corpus*, freedom of the press, the right of free association and public assembly, free speech, and protection from unreasonable search and seizure— Bonhoeffer spoke out in defense of the liberal parliamentary state, now in ruin. He consulted his brother-in-law Gerhard Leibholz, a legal philosopher at Göttingen, and his brother Klaus, an attorney in Berlin, who held a doctorate in jurisprudence. (Leibholz had taught law at the University of Greifswald from 1931 until 1933, before taking the post at Göttingen, where in 1935 he would be removed, as a Jew, under the Nazi race laws, thereafter moving his family to England.)[12] Bonhoeffer would never write a political treatise, and his later, scattered ruminations on the future of Germany (in letters and other writings after 1940) seem to favor monarchy over democracy. But in his addresses of 1933, he consistently defended Weimar's democratic constitution and civil liberties. As the scholar Ernst-Albert Scharffenorth explains, the argument Bonhoeffer advanced throughout the year was unprecedented in the history of German Protestantism: namely, "that if mere objection alone could not prevent the state from turning justice into injustice and order into disorder, the church was obliged to abandon such 'indirect' political action and employ 'direct' political means."[13]

Bonhoeffer recognized that a "terrible barbarization of our culture" had begun. The nation was reeling under the spell of hysterical longings, magical incantations, warrior fanaticism, and "all manner of public exorcism." As he told Niebuhr, "here, too, we will need to create a Civil Liberties Union"; the future of the church had "seldom looked so gloomy."[14]

It was with renewed gratitude for the lessons learned in America that he asked Niebuhr to convey greetings to Union friends, especially to James Dombrowski, who had recently joined the staff of the High-lander Folk School, a radical Christian organizing hub in Monteagle, Tennessee, and who—as Bonhoeffer pointed out—had never returned the German visitor's term paper on Negro literature. Could Niebuhr track that down? It was not mere academic vanity on Bonhoeffer's part; he wanted to refer to the essay as he aligned with the German church of the outcasts.

On April 3, 1933, Paula Bonhoeffer wrote to her eldest daughter, Christine, with a mother's heavy heart, concerned for Dietrich's well-being. While he appeared to his students and friends as a rock of strength, at home he had grown sullen and withdrawn. For the first time, Bonhoeffer's mother did not know how to respond to her fair-haired and sensitive child, now a twenty-seven-year-old theologian and minister torn between the moral mandates of his new faith and the quietism of ordinary Lutheranism.

The Aryan paragraph was passed by the Reichstag on April 7. This calamitous decree and the adjuvant Law for the Reconstitution of the Civil Service ordered the removal of all Jews, persons of any Jewish descent, and other designated undesirables from civil service, including the churches, both Catholic and Protestant. The church action was justified by the fact that all churches received government funding. Both Catholics (who comprised about a third of the population) and Protestants (who represented most of the rest) paid taxes in support of pastoral functions—baptisms, weddings, funerals, and other services. But in the jubilant thrall of the *Führerprinzip*, it was the German Protestant Church that would become the German Christians' target for total nazification. The Deutsche Christen were moved by a perverse conceit disguised as an evangelistic crusade: they were supposedly bringing the Christian faith to the Nazis, who seemed to be veering toward paganism. Acting in the name of Luther's doctrines of the two kingdoms—that God has established two kingdoms (*zwei Reiche*): the kingdom of the earth, which he rules through human government and law; and the kingdom of heaven, which he directs by grace and through the church—the German Christians determined to achieve an accommodation (however tortured) of the Führer principle and the Aryan paragraph under church law. And this they would do in a spirit of obedience to God![15] Under this accommodation, baptized Jews, being a different race altogether, could no longer serve in the German Protestant Church, whose identity was now rooted in ethnicity, or racial sameness, rather than in the confession of Christ as Lord.

Such willful complicity gave Hitler, and his religious liaisons, full authority to assimilate the twenty-eight independent Protestant *Landeskirchen* into a unified Reich Church. The lines between church and state—regionally defined since the Reformation—were now radically redrawn, as church leaders submitted to the political momentum to form a single, national, *völkisch* church.[16]

The change was not accomplished without struggle. Hitler's appointment of his old friend Ludwig Müller as special representative to the churches set off a rush of behind-the-scenes "maneuvering" as the distinct and often competing regional churches jockeyed for advantage, aroused at the prospect of a unified national church under a single Reich bishop (*Reichsbischof*). Moderates had their hopes on Friedrich von Bodelschwingh, the widely respected director of the Bethel Health Center and son of its founder. But Müller seemed rather confident that "the honor would fall to him." As the historian Robert Ericksen reconstructs the confusing chain of events to follow, the first round went to Bodelschwingh, who gathered the most votes from the regional church councils.[17] Müller and his allies among the radical Deutsche Christen were outraged. They called in the brown-shirted, paramilitary storm troopers—the *Sturmabteilung*, or SA—to intimidate Bodelschwingh's staff, also persuading the Prussian cultural minister, Bernhard Rust, to appoint a state commissar for the regional church. Finding himself in a hopeless position, Bodelschwingh resigned from his bishopric at the end of June. The election was then thrown open to a vote of the full church membership.

On the evening of July 22, Hitler made a surprise radio broadcast, asking for support for Müller. The next day, with Bodelschwingh out of the way and many unfamiliar faces among the delegates, Müller drew more than 70 percent of the vote.[18] In addition to electing new leadership, the church approved the Aryan paragraph.

Bonhoeffer might not have believed it, had he not seen the march to this point for himself. Three weeks earlier he had attended a public rally in the cavernous Auditorium Maximum on the campus of Berlin University. The packed house included professors, church officials, ministers, and students exchanging heady proposals for "the church's mission in the new political order." Advocates of assimilation and the church's submission to the Reich dominated discussion with aggressive and virulent speeches. Only a small contingent of moderates expressed an opposing view:[19] Lutheran tradition, they said, required the church to preserve its independence from the state in all times and places. But no one spoke to the plain fact that the gospel was under assault. Bonhoeffer, who had been standing quietly with some students near the back, could no longer contain his anger. Interrupting the chair, he took a step forward and shouted for attention. As the eyes of several hundred German churchmen turned toward him, he declared that if God leads the church to wage war for her soul, God will honor only those who fight for her integrity.[20] "God, not human beings, makes the church what it is"—a foretaste of the perfect peace to come in the presence of Christ. The exclusion of converted Jews from the communion, Bonhoeffer insisted, meant the church "loses Christ Himself."[21]

The next week students from Berlin University would gather at midnight in the plaza surrounding the Hegel Memorial to salute the new Reich chancellor with a thunderous "*Heil Hitler!*"

Indeed, by July 23, when the synod met in Berlin to elect new representatives, devotion to Hitler had become tantamount to godliness. The Nazi Party issued orders that every delegate had to vote the full slate of Deutsche Christen tenets. Hitler, who at the time happened to be attending the Bayreuth Music Festival—the annual celebration of Richard Wagner's operas staged in the Bavarian Alps, featuring that year a production of *Parsifal* directed by Richard Strauss—took a moment to speak on live radio. In raspy and "convoluted" remarks, Hitler explained that, with God, he, as Führer, stood squarely on the side of the German Christians.[22] For the fate of the church remained inseparably bound, he said, to the "rebirth of the German nation." "*Heil Hitler!*" responded the audience, the whole message brought to the airwaves live and without interruption.[23]

When "the Bavarians and the gray old men" did finally convene, it was a showy display of martial piety. The ecclesial overlords of the German Evangelical Church processed into the General Synod in their purple vestments, the storm troopers providing a phalanx of evil vergers. The synod chair, who according to several witnesses appeared to be drunk, asked the delegates, "Who wishes to speak?," only to bark out immediately thereafter, "No discussion!" Bonhoeffer's attempt to voice opposition to the Aryan paragraph was "met with jeering and catcalls."

In the course of the evening, all resolutions proposing the church's adoption of the Aryan paragraph and other points of Nazi policy were passed unanimously. Even more astonishing to Bonhoeffer: the barrel-chested Ludwig Müller—a man of "mediocre and supercilious talents," a "former nonentity," and Hitler's preening sycophant—was unanimously elected as the new regional bishop. He would be promoted to *Reichsbischof* by year's end. Not allowed to vote in the election, Bonhoeffer exited the hall with his fellow dissidents.

Müller's election set in motion the nazification of the German Evangelical Church, igniting the long but futile *Kirchenkampf,* and the movement of dissident Christians to protect the regional churches (the *Landeskirchen*) against the imposition of Nazi will.[24] Enamored of his new powers, Müller summoned every available resource to further unify the German church, which would in turn confer "the monarchical title of *Summus Episcopus* [supreme bishop]" on the Führer.[25] Müller's docile mind, his bureaucratic fanaticism, and a raging inferiority complex would be put to good use in the coming years.

By the end of 1933, more than 90 percent of the student body of the Berlin theology department had joined the National Socialist Party. Most of Bonhoeffer's colleagues wore the bronze Nazi badge on their lapels. The dean of the faculty, Erich Seeberg—whose father, Reinhold, had directed Bonhoeffer's doctoral dissertation "Sanctorum Communio"—draped a swastika banner over the front entrance of the gray fortress at Unter den Linden.

Bonhoeffer was uncertain about how to respond. "We are about to witness a great reorganization of the churches," he said, and even "the most intelligent people have totally lost both their heads and their Bible."[26] He felt the growing demands of the situation bearing down like a great weight upon him, making it exceedingly difficult to concentrate on academic work, even on vacation or over long weekends in Friedrichsbrunn.

He thanked Sutz for his friendship and asked for his prayers; the thought of Sutz engaged in a quiet pastorate in Switzerland brought him joy—if also a little envy.

Though navigating the church bureaucracy and his department seemed more bewildering than ever, Bonhoeffer showed perfect clarity regarding the larger national developments, particularly the Aryan paragraph. Within two weeks of its passage, he'd completed his first written statement of protest, "The Church and the Jewish Question." The statement, which had begun circulating in mimeographed form on April 15, appeared in print later that spring in *Vormarsch*, a Protestant monthly journal of politics and culture.

Bonhoeffer proposed a three-pronged rejoinder to the loathsome Nazi ruling: the church should question the legitimacy of the state's actions; the church should assist the victims of such action "even if they do not belong to the Christian community"; and the church should take direct political action of its own "not just to bandage the victims upon the wheel," but to break the spokes of the wheel if necessary.[27] That last step, clearly the most subversive of the three, should, he stressed, be taken "only if the state failed in its function of creating law and order." But even his first two proposals—of challenging the legitimacy of the Aryan paragraph and affirming the church's "unconditional obligation" to all victims of society, irrespective of religion—violated the pastoral oath now required of every minister under law: that he support and uphold the laws of the Reich. In opposition to the German Christian movement, and specifically to its crusade against baptized Jews—of which there were approximately 350,0000 in Nazi Germany—Bonhoeffer pronounced that any person who refused to worship with Christians of Jewish descent "cannot be denied [the option] of leaving the church."[28] Later in the year Bonhoeffer would reiterate that position and his claim that anyone wishing to remove Jewish Christians might as well wish to remove Christ.[29]

It was, in context, a bold and undeniably courageous stand. Still, these criticisms were addressed to an ecclesial audience: they were not intended to be read by ordinary Germans, much less as incitement to mass protest. While he respected the rights of individuals and "humanitarian associations" to accuse the government of "crimes against humanity," he did not regard the church as a humanitarian association. Indeed, it was not one, according to civil law. Nor were Bonhoeffer's concerns about the application of the Aryan paragraph to the Jewish people—which is to say, to unbaptized Jews—explicitly stated in his April 15 tract.

The same week that Bonhoeffer's three-point broadside appeared, his sister Sabine asked him to conduct the funeral services for her father-in-law, William Leibholz, who had died on April 11. In addition to his success as a textile merchant, Leibholz, a member of the left-liberal German Democratic Party, had represented the Berlin-Wilmersdorf neighborhood as an alderman. The son of observant Jews, he had raised his own children in the German Protestant Church and identified himself as a Christian, although he had not been baptized.

Lutheran church polity prohibited ministers from officiating at the funerals of the unbaptized, Jewish or Christian; the only exception was made when a baby of communicant parents died before baptism. But with Paula's strong encouragement, Sabine told Dietrich in no uncertain terms that decency alone obliged him to a higher ethical standard. Neither mother nor daughter cared a wit for the finer points of Lutheran canon law. But Dietrich would not comply, deferring to the guidance of his supervisor, who cautioned against "conducting a funeral service for a Jew,"[30] even one who, like Herr Leibholz, had professed the Christian faith. Seven months on, while living in England, Bonhoeffer would write to Gert and Sabine, begging for forgiveness. He had been making notes for a sermon on Remembrance Sunday when he came upon a "beautiful text" from the book of Wisdom (3:3): "But the souls of the upright are in the hands of God, and no torment can touch them. To the unenlightened, they appeared to die, their departure was regarded as disaster, their leaving us like annihilation; but they are at peace." The "souls of the upright," he wrote in his notes, "their leaving us [is] like annihilation; but they are at peace."

The words from scripture tore into his conscience, as his mind was flooded with memories of that cruelest of Aprils. What a perfect choice the verse would have been for Gert's father, Bonhoeffer wrote his brother-in-law. And he confessed, "I can't think what made me behave as I did. I am tormented by the thought that I didn't do as you asked as a matter of course."

Bonhoeffer wondered, how could he have been so frightened at the time? "It must have seemed equally incomprehensible to all of you, and yet you said nothing." The decision would burden him into the small hours of the night, the shame remaining with him until his death. From that time he understood that his refusal was "the kind of thing one can never make up for."

"All I can ask then," Bonhoeffer said, "is that you forgive my weakness. I know for certain that I ought to have behaved differently."[31]

Bonhoeffer's grandmother Julie had set a different example. On an afternoon in mid-April, she was met by a cordon of SA brownshirts standing at the entrance of the Kaufhaus des Westens—the "department store of the West." They'd been dispatched to enforce a boycott of Jewish businesses, the posh store being the property of a prominent Jewish family of the Grunewald. Without hesitation, or thought for polity, ecclesial or otherwise, the ninety-one-year-old walked past the brownshirts and did her shopping.

Toward the end of the month, Bonhoeffer wrote for a second time against the Aryan paragraph: "The Jewish-Christian Question as *Status Confessionis*." The phrase, which in Latin means a "confessional situation," denotes a moment in which the church, "in order to be true to itself and its message, must distinguish as *clearly as possible* between truth and error." The issue of whether the Aryan paragraph constituted such an occasion for the German Evangelical Church figured centrally from the beginning of the *Kirchenkampf*, and would bitterly divide moderates from those radicals who would eventually form the breakaway Confessing Church. Christians may inevitably disagree on the application of doctrine to particular public policies or social practice, "[b]ut there are some issues so fateful that no dissimulation or compromise is possible, and there is no longer a basis for negotiation." Bonhoeffer believed that the Aryan paragraph presented just such a fateful issue.[32]

The matter of excluding Jewish Christians from communion and worship challenged the very identity of the church as a Christian body, imposing a test of conscience on its leaders.[33] "How can he who holds a church office administer that office knowing that there are in the communion brethren of lesser rights to whom such office is not open because of their race? Will he not then best safeguard his Christianity and his churchliness by preferring to be where the most despised brethren are, and no longer at the head of the table, 'among those who would be first'?" Bonhoeffer emboldened his earlier formulation of the church's sine qua non, arguing that a racial prerequisite for Christian fellowship tears the church away from her "sole foundation" in Jesus Christ.[34] "It is therefore an ecclesiastical impossibility to exclude," Bonhoeffer wrote, "as a matter of principle, Jewish Christian members from any offices of the Church." Put another way, the church, insofar as it bars Jewish Christians, ceases to embody Christ, without whom it is no church at all.[35] Aryanism was thus not merely a heresy but a kind of deicide.

As reports of the April boycotts of Jewish-owned businesses circulated in the international press, religious leaders abroad fully expected their German brethren to denounce the Nazi laws.[36] For more than a decade, ecumenists such as Visser 't Hooft, Pierre Maury in Geneva, and Henry Smith Leiper had met periodically with the German church leadership to discuss confessional unity, to exchange ideas, and to worship together. But German Protestants fell into line behind the Berlin church superintendent, Otto Dibelius, who defended the boycott and asked defiantly why foreign Christians had suddenly taken such a keen interest in protecting "Judaism in Germany."[37] Bonhoeffer was alone in denouncing the National Socialist captivity of the German Protestant Church.

Every summer tempest begins as "a little cloud out of the sea, like a man's hand," as it says in I Kings 18. Few indeed were those Elijahs who could see it before "the heaven was black with clouds and wind, and there was a great rain."[38]

As the non-Nazi church movement gathered momentum, the international churches and ecumenical bodies (most of them associates of what would after the war become the World Council of Churches, the WCC) were forced to reckon with an urgent and—as it turned out—surprisingly controversial matter: "whose version of events in Germany was to be trusted. Was it the official account of the German Evangelical Church, "represented ecumenically abroad at the time by Bishop Theodor Heckel," an outspoken and unapologetic Nazi, or that of the Young Reformation Group—soon to be renamed the Pastors' Emergency League, and within only months after that to become the Confessing Church?[39]

Absent Bonhoeffer, the ecumenical movement might have reached different conclusions. He communicated the German situation in detail to the churches abroad, delving into ecclesial matters, political events, and perceptions of Hitler's ambitions. His purpose "was not just to convey information . . . but to encourage and in some cases orchestrate foreign protest against Nazi policies."[40] Yet even Bonhoeffer's reports and the knowledge that the German Protestant Church was aligning itself with the Nazi regime would fail to inspire the WCC and its affiliates to cut their ties or affirm the churchly authority of dissident pastors. Ecumenical leaders would repeat the same sorry excuse over the next five years: that the German Protestant Church, despite its swift and unapologetic pledge to Hitler, remained the legitimate representative of German Protestantism.

As to Bonhoeffer's denunciations of the regime's anti-Jewish policies, one sobering fact bears repeating: his response to the events of April 1933, though forthright and courageous, applied strictly to Jews who had converted to Christianity—and more specifically to Jews baptized in the German Evangelical Church.[41] His April memoranda even allowed certain exceptions to the full communion of Jewish Christians, contradicting St. Paul's canonical teaching on the unity of all believers—"you are all one person in Christ Jesus . . . there is neither Jew nor Gentile, slave nor master, male nor female." The apostle is, nevertheless, invoked in one rather bizarre formulation alluding to Paul's instruction of the Christians in Rome "to consider your weaker brethren." Where Paul has in mind Christians who cannot manage certain ascetical disciplines, who carry on drinking alcohol or eating meat, Bonhoeffer quite awkwardly applies the wisdom to the presence of Jewish Christian pastors in a "predominantly 'German Christian' parish." Germans who felt uncomfortable around Jews, who "found them disagreeable," might themselves become spiritually "distracted" by their presence, thereby requiring the special consideration due a "weaker brother."

Bonhoeffer seemed to be seeking balance between the ecclesiastical principle of congregational freedom and the hope that gentle pastoral persuasion might awaken the desire for reconciliation in segregated churches. But in the meantime, for the sake of the gospel, one might need to indulge an anti-Semite in his prejudices, his weakness. Whether a Jewish Christian pastor, teacher, or leader was to be tolerated was a matter to be decided by each congregation for itself.[42]

Such equivocations notwithstanding, Bonhoeffer never wavered in his view that such feelings about converts born Jewish "violated" the church's essential nature; the sincerity or well-intentioned efforts of individual members could not alter the fact of their having "forfeited the blessing of God." He seems to have been playing for time, wishfully trying to keep the communion together long enough for all the laity to see the light. But as to the German Protestant establishment, their perdition seemed a foregone conclusion. The church was not *only* corrupt and corrupted; it had severed its ties with historic Christianity. An avalanche of confrontations and conflicts emboldened Bonhoeffer's ties to the ecumenical movement and his critical perspective on the German situation.[43]

In May, Bonhoeffer delivered what would prove his last lectures as a member of the theology department. His position as *Privatdozent*— untenured and not eligible for tenure—had not changed since 1931, although Professor Wilhelm Lütgert had eventually arranged a modest monthly stipend. At eight a.m. sharp on Wednesdays and Saturdays (not quite as early as Karl Barth's Bonn seminar but still challenging for a late riser), more than a hundred students would gather in the great hall in Berlin Mitte to hear Bonhoeffer speak with unexampled excitement on what it means to encounter Jesus Christ.[44] The instructor advanced a provocative claim: Christology—the doctrine of Jesus Christ, the historic and creedal affirmation of the Son as the second person of the Trinity—was the last truth separating the churches from barbarism. The truth concerning Christ's nature and person placed moral demands on humanity and the individual. Such was the inevitable consequence of God's having taken flesh to dwell among the rest of humanity as an outcast, reviled and rejected. And it was Bonhoeffer's hope that this Christological understanding would expose the heresies of the German Christian movement with the effect of subverting it. All this was part of his larger effort to preserve the mysteries of the faith from profanation and misuse.[45]

A s Bonhoeffer had intuited long before reaching adulthood, theology matters. From its very origins, Christianity had been a theological faith, obliging men and women to seek and affirm the Godhead, such as one could comprehend the incomprehensible. And the God one sought to know was the God of Abraham, Isaac, and Jacob, no less than it was Christ. Christianity was rooted in the theological traditions of ancient Israel, which was unified by its historical credos and affirmations of faith. To refuse the purposes of theological understanding, and its attendant mandate of self-examination, was not merely to neglect the distinctive claims of the faith and tradition but to turn one's back on revelation itself. The true Christian was obliged to possess a reasoned understanding of the faith, and to express it in a manner honoring the mystery of the triune God; this was incumbent upon every person who assents to the truth of the gospel, and never more so than in such a moment of crisis.

"No pretheological era has been discovered in the New Testament or in the history of the Christian community," wrote the historian John Leith. But it was precisely a "nontheological Christianity" that was on offer from the German church in the attempted fusion of Christianity with racial sentiment, which they called, with unintended perversity, *positives Christentum*—positive Christianity.[46]

The Christology lectures show Bonhoeffer at his most dexterous in articulating the elements of the faith. But they belie the intensity with which he applied himself to the task; he spent more time in preparation for that course than for any other he had taught. That effort was not wasted. As the biographer Ferdinand Schlingensiepen correctly observes, Bonhoeffer's work "from this point forward was ever nourished by these lectures," and "Christology became the mystical center of his thought." Faced with the ruins of German Protestantism, he could not have understood more clearly that the way Christians imagine Jesus Christ determines the totality of their worldview.[47]

As the German church marched to the clashing strains of Nazi war anthems, both pagan and pseudo-Christian, the orthodox understanding of Christ, which "begins in silence," directed Bonhoeffer onto a different path—one of recognizing dissent as a spiritual discipline. Indeed, the potential for treason in his doctrinal meditations did not go unnoticed by most listeners in the large hall. Departing from traditional debates concerning the nature of Christ, with their metaphysical accounts of divine-human commingling and speculations on how Christ could be both divine and man, Bonhoeffer began with the question, *Who is Christ?* Christology exists as a field of study first and foremost in response to the personal encounter of the other; the "I" as it meets the ultimate "Thou." In these lectures he did not draw explicitly from the Jewish philosopher Martin Buber, though he'd now read Buber's *I and Thou* with admiration, citing it elsewhere. Buber's emphatic concern for the living dialogue, and for the freedom it confers from tyranny, nevertheless fed Bonhoeffer's distinctly Christian view of revelation. Who is Christ? The question arose not out of some human will to power, but from humility and silence. Who is the Christ who encounters us in word, sacrament, and suffering? To speak faithfully of Jesus Christ and to obey his teachings is to embrace the idea of "God who was born in a stable because there was no room for him in the inn."

"We have the Exalted One only as the Crucified," Bonhoeffer said, "the Sinless One only as the one laden with [our] guilt, the Risen One only as the Humiliated One."[48] It was just such an essential and stark duality toward which Paul had directed the Corinthians when he resolved to know nothing "except Jesus Christ, and Him crucified."

During his year in America, Bonhoeffer had found the presence of Christ to be most palpable among those living on the margins. But it is not until these Christology lectures of 1933 that the "outcast Christ" enters his scholarly vocabulary, as he speaks of the "Christological incognito." With the swastika replacing the cross in the "great and glorious holy storm of present-day Volk happenings," Bonhoeffer was drawn to the Christ who sojourns in the world as a beggar among beggars. In places of exclusion and distress, there is Christ, he said, as friend, brother, savior.[49] "Christ enters the world of sin and death of his own free will," Bonhoeffer said. "He enters it in such a way as to conceal himself in weakness, not to be known. . . . He goes incognito, as a beggar among beggars, as an outcast among the outcast, a figure to despair among the despairing, dying among the dying . . . a sinner among sinners."[50] The Christological incognito offends the "magical picture of the world" no less than the self-sufficiency of bourgeois Protestantism.

Christ is the center of reality. The same Christ who is present in "Word, sacrament, and community" is the center of "human existence, history and nature," Bonhoeffer said.[51]

On April 21, 1933, the philosopher Martin Heidegger was elected rector of the University of Freiburg. He assumed the post the following day and ten days thereafter became member #312589 of the Nazi Party.[52] On May 27, he delivered his *Rektoratsrede*, his inaugural address, entitled "The Self-Assertion of the German University" ("Die Selbstbehauptung der deutschen Universität"), heralding the National Socialist triumph as a glorious revolution of spirit, and an epochal turning point in the history of Being.[53] "As a nation of singers, poets, and thinkers," Heidegger said, the Germans dream of a world of purity and inner fullness—of autumn suns of the Black Forest bathing the mountain ranges and forests in glorious clear light; and yet only "when misery and wretchedness dealt them inhuman blows" (read: the defeat of World War I and the humiliation of Versailles) did there well up in their ranks "the longing for a new rising, for a new Reich, and therefore for a new life."[54] He esteemed hardness and force as virtues, despised Weimar democracy, and fairly worshipped Hitler as the inauguration—or "instantiation"—of some long-anticipated ethnic renewal.[55] Heidegger would resign the rectorship on April 23, 1934, though he'd remain a member of the Nazi Party until the end of the war, never to apologize, discuss, or otherwise explain his support of Hitler, taking his reasons to the grave.

In the year of Heidegger's *Rektoratsrede*, Bonhoeffer—on his way to becoming the nation's most notorious theological dissident—told his students that humanity's only hope lay in the baby born to unwed Jewish parents in a desolate byway of Bethlehem.[56]

On May 17, Bonhoeffer wrote to the minister and social worker Friedrich Siegmund-Schultze, long one of the rare beacons of Berlin's urban ministries. Seeking out the working class and the unemployed, he had established such bodies as the Ulmenhof Adult Education Center (in 1927), to provide education for young workers. But in the Nazi campaign to rid the nation of communists and their sympathizers, he became a prime target of Gestapo repression. The Ulmenhof center and other programs of his were shut down in spring of 1933.

Bonhoeffer sought Siegmund-Schultze's advice on "a personal matter." A Jewish sociologist by the name of Landshut had been working as a graduate assistant at the University of Hamburg. There, he had made the acquaintance of Hans von Dohnányi, Bonhoeffer's brother-in-law, who also served as the legal adviser to the Reich Court president. As a result of the Aryan laws, Landshut had fallen on hard times. After the Nazis suspended his academic adviser—the economist Eduard Heimann, also a Jew—Landshut was thrown into limbo, no longer able to pursue the requirements for a university post. In any case, his prominent Jewish features, Bonhoeffer believed, now made an appointment anywhere unlikely.[57] Though he'd been earning only a meager stipend, its withdrawal had left Landshut without any income or meaningful employment. His wife, furthermore, suffered from heart trouble, and the couple had three small children.

Having met Landshut on a recent trip to Hamburg, Bonhoeffer praised him as a person of "the purest scholarship and integrity." In 1914, at the age of seventeen, Landshut had volunteered for combat duty and spent four years on the front. "He is a man who feels completely German and is not yet able to contemplate looking for a job outside Germany," Bonhoeffer said. His recent book, *Kritik der Soziologie*, showed evidence of a disciplined and judicious mind. Whereas Heimann, as a full professor, had been able to immigrate to the United States, taking a teaching position at the New School for Social Research in New York, Landshut could not. He lacked the necessary credentials, and besides there was his wife's failing health; Landshut needed to stay put.

Bonhoeffer asked Siegmund-Schultze to wrack his brain to find Landshut a post—even if it meant "something completely outside his profession." Might he introduce Landshut to officials at the Jewish Welfare Association, which had offices in Berlin and Hamburg, perhaps help him meet with the directors? Might the minister himself also meet with Landshut to discuss his problem? "For myself and those in my family, who are close friends of Landshut, it matters very much what happens to him, and I should not like to have failed to ask you earnestly for any help you might be able to provide him."

Siegmund-Schultze's response would be disappointing. He advised Bonhoeffer to have Landshut contact the Central Welfare Office for German Jews, judging this approach likelier to bear fruit. He may have been right. Siegmund-Schultze's campaign against unemployment and his efforts to build bridges between the churches and the trade unions had rendered association with him toxic amid the Nazi campaign of repression against communists and their sympathizers. The next month, storm troopers would seize the shuttered Ulmenhof center in Berlin, forcing the minister to flee with his family to Switzerland. Landshut succeeded in emigrating to Palestine in 1933, where he flourished as a scholar and teacher; he returned to Germany after the war and died in 1968.[58]

The theological faculties offered no sanctuary either. On the evening of May 10, 1933, the first day of the summer semester, students and professors joined members of the local *Sturmabteilung* around a bonfire at the Opernplatz in the shadows of the Humboldt monument. Albert Einstein and Thomas Mann, Sigmund Freud and Walther Rathenau, Stefan Zweig, Erich Maria Remarque, and Hermann Hesse were among the authors whose names were read aloud in a litany of protest against those who defied "the national will to live." The mob threw hundreds of volumes—seized from libraries, synagogues, and churches—onto the massive fire. Also destroyed were the works of Heinrich Heine, a writer of Jewish descent, who a century earlier had foreshadowed the hell to come: "Where they burn books, they will ultimately also burn people."[59]

I no longer believe in the university," Bonhoeffer had said.
It had indeed come to this. Most of Bonhoeffer's colleagues and former classmates, and a majority of the students—even many still attending his lectures—were on board with Hitler's racial-ethnic *völkisch* vision and were now card-carrying members of the Nazi Party (the Nationalsozialistische Deutsche Arbeiterpartei).[60] Seeberg, the forty-five-year-old dean of the theology faculty, readily championed the mandates of the Aryan paragraph; at age seventy-four, the dean's father had made an easy transition from old-school nationalist to new-

order Nazi, whose cause he served proudly at his Institute for Social Ethics.[61] Professors Caius Fabricius and Arnold Stolzenburg had joined the party in 1932. Under the younger Seeberg, party membership and loyalty became decisive criteria for tenure in the department.[62]

Similar pressures existed at other universities, though precious few responded with a defiant "*Nein.*" In Bonn, Barth quibbled over the new requirement to begin each class with a "*Sieg Heil!*" and was stripped of his chair. Frankfurt theologian Paul Tillich lost his job after delivering numerous public speeches and addresses critical of Hitler.[63] In 1937, New Testament scholar Günther Bornkamm lost his *venia legendi* at the University of Königsberg and did not return to academic life until after the war. And later, Helmut Thielicke was fired from his theology professorship in Heidelberg.

I n his May 28 sermon at the Kaiser Wilhelm Memorial Church in the Tiergarten neighborhood, Bonhoeffer likened the crisis in the German churches to the story of Moses and Aaron, the Hebrew patriarchs and brothers of the tribe of Levi. Most dissenting Christians remained uncertain about how to respond to the German Christians and which policies should be resisted or rejected. While most dissidents opposed application of the Aryan paragraph to the church, others supported the new German state. Some even endorsed the creation of a Reich bishop. It was "against this backdrop" that Bonhoeffer spoke of the "two churches of Moses and Aaron," which in his telling represented the demarcations of "idolatry and faithfulness." "The church of Aaron, while priestly and popular, was idolatrous. The church of Moses was the church of the prophet and of the demanding, judging Word of God."[64] Bonhoeffer drew the distinction as sharply as he could: on one side stood Aaron, maker of idols, and on the other, Moses, God's righteous patriarch. Though they belonged to the same people, the same tribe and clan, it was through Moses's guidance only, through the "church of Moses," that Israel was saved.

"Moses, the first prophet, and Aaron, the first priest; Moses, the one called out by God, the one chosen without regard for his person, the man who was slow of tongue, the servant of God who lived only by listening to the word of his Lord; Aaron, the man with the purple robe and the sacred crown, the priest who had been consecrated and sanctified, who was supposed to keep the people worshipping God." Moses stood alone "way up on the terrifying mountain," between "life and death with the thunder and lightning," called to receive God's covenant with Israel; while "down in the valley, Aaron in his 'sacred crown and garish robes of purple,'" catered to the people's impatience, pretending to be God's ambassador. "Take the gold rings from your wives, [Aaron] said, strip the gold adornments from your sons and your daughters; bring them to me." Nothing was spared; everything precious was thrown into the smelting cauldron, enough to form the likeness of a calf. "Then the frenzy began," the ecstatic veneration of the idol, the earth exploding with marches and festivals; "and the church of Aaron sat down to eat and drink, and rose up to revel." When Moses came down from the mountain and saw what the people had become, he ordered the idol ground to dust and the dust mixed with water and the mixture drunk as gall.

On this morning in May, Bonhoeffer asked the timorous beloved, who would lead them without Moses?

By June, German Protestant leaders were united in their praise of the Nazi regime. "Christ has come to us through Adolf Hitler," one minister gushed. "Through his power, his honesty, his faith and his idealism . . . the Redeemer has found us, [and] we know the Savior today has come!"[65] Passion and vigor, a brash and cocksure manliness, a Führer whose countenance fairly radiated these virtues—a nation was smitten. It felt good to be a German, again.

The Young Reformation Movement, formed in April, asked Bonhoeffer to deliver the plenary address at a conspicuous public forum; the hope was to call attention to the German Christians and their tyrannical capture of church authority. The event was held on June 22, in the spacious new assembly hall at Berlin University. "Bonhoeffer, for whom opposition to the Aryan paragraph had become the touchstone" for action, surprised even fellow dissidents by calling upon the assembly to pass a binding resolution establishing itself a "convened church council." Nothing less was acceptable; he demanded a decisive verdict, grounded in scripture and doctrine, leveled squarely against the pharisaical elites. It was clear to Bonhoeffer that both the "Jewish question" and "the ecumenical imperative of peace" required a "doctrinal decision by the collective church in response to Christ's binding command." But few were persuaded by Bonhoeffer's "unexpected" and "unpopular" declaration.

There were exceptions. A young Christian dissident named Gertrude Staewen was taken with the radical proposal. A social worker who'd followed Bonhoeffer's public lectures but who had been vacationing on the Baltic coast at the time of the Berlin forum, Staewen wrote to him on June 26, as soon as friends told her what she had missed. Considering the "Babylonian confusion of Christian discourse," Staewen said, the convocation of a binding council had become "really necessary."[66]

The German Christian movement did not so much destroy as emerge from the ruins of the once-grand Protestant liberal architectonic. It was perhaps a predictable dénouement for a tradition that increasingly turned theology into anthropology, surrendering the disciplined language of belief to the habit of speaking about God as if of human nature writ large.

Protestant liberalism—as the story goes—had begun with Immanuel Kant and his two devastating tomes, *The Critique of Pure Reason* and *The Critique of Practical Reason*, both appearing at the end of the eighteenth century. In these books' trenchant analysis of the human mind and its ways of organizing experience, Kant reached a conclusion that would dramatically alter the course of theological and philosophical thought in the West. His claim: that the idea of God is uncertain and unknowable, since the idea of God, much less *God himself*, does not appear in space and time, to become an object of experience.[67] Nevertheless, the idea of God remains useful, Kant would even say truthful, insofar as it brings order to moral experience.

Over the next century, Protestant liberalism would flourish, proffering its various creative responses to this radical reduction. In all instances, metaphysical knowledge, the doctrines and beliefs of the church, once held to be reliable and certain, persisted only as lessons, props, and modulations—that is, as useful tools for human understanding. They were denied their traditional transcendent value as truth (indeed, the notion of there being any such thing as truth had been drawn toward a conceptual precipice from which it would eventually fall).

The greatest liberal theologian of the era, Friedrich Schleiermacher, would try mightily to rescue the reality of the numinous from the maw of a Kantian reality limited to the world as conveyed to the senses. In his book *On Religion: Speeches to Its Cultured Despisers*, Schleiermacher's exquisite prose (rendered so well in the novelist George Eliot's English translation) expresses hope that Kant's critique might inspire high and sublime thoughts of religion as "the sense and taste for the Infinite." Still, the ship of Christian orthodoxy had run aground.[68] And ever after, its claims to truth would be subject to modernity's suspicious scrutiny.

Following Kant, the radical critiques of religion developed by Feuerbach, Marx, and Freud demonstrated the far-reaching consequences of the intellectual shift. Feuerbach judged the beliefs of the Christian faith to be mere human projections. Scared to acknowledge their own boundless potential, humans had naively projected their infinite value onto a screen of transcendence and named that image God. Marx decried religion an "opiate of the masses," a drug that constrains freedom and keeps the working class servile. From his vantage point in the analyst's chair, Freud diagnosed religion as a neurotic symptom, a "universal obsessional neurosis," which might be relieved by greater self-knowledge. In this manner, Schleiermacher's definition of religion as the "holy wedlock of the Universe with the incarnated Reason for a creative, productive embrace" was just what the psychoanalyst would expect of a north German Pietist with a hankering for maternal intimacy.[69] Religion could, at best, help emotionally feeble men cope with irrational needs, Freud reasoned.

It must be allowed that these three radical critiques have something in common: all assume that questions of human nature and the rest of reality are best answered in a scientific, nontheistic fashion. That was not traditionally the way of theology, of course, and for good reason. But the makers of Protestant liberalism wanted to carve out a space within this new modern world for religion. Claiming, however, that knowledge of God must be based on some mode or dimension of human experience (beauty, moral order, inner bliss, political loyalty), Protestant liberal thought lead to a theological dead end. Indeed, it lead to the conclusion that God is but an extension of human experience, a projection of human need and longing. The liberal theologians tried so hard to accommodate the gospel to the modern world that they ended up surrendering the faith "to the patterns, forces, and movements of human history and civilization" and to an "uncritical and irresponsible subservience" to these patterns, forces, and movements.[70] This would be Karl Barth's critique, the incitement for his neo-orthodox reclamation of a transcendent God. For him and his sympathizers, liberal Protestantism had drained the Christian gospel until it was no more than a principle, a set of moral values, a cultural or political program. The church could not live such a bloodless life.

In a way, the German Christians were merely carrying on the work of their Protestant liberal forebears, recasting doctrine according to social utility. One target of their assault on historic Christianity was the clause in the Nicene Creed known as the *filioque*, which had been brought to Germany by Charlemagne at the end of the eighth century in the fight against paganism, though the church in Rome would not adopt it for another two hundred years. When it did, the Latin phrase meaning "and (from) the Son," *filioque*—by which the Holy Spirit is understood to proceed from the Father *and from the Son*—would for the next millennium be the cornerstone of how the Western church understood the nature of the triune God of Father, Son, and Holy Spirit.

In their formulations of Trinitarian doctrine, the church fathers were at pains to work out the relations among the three parts of the Godhead; once the Son was established as the only begotten of the Father, the Spirit's affiliation could not remain undefined lest it become its own judge and justification, which is precisely what had happened. And so the Spirit would be said in the West to proceed from both Father and Son. In the East, meanwhile, the Orthodox churches would insist on procession from the Father alone, in accordance with the Greek text of Christianity's pivotal fourth-century Council of Nicea; the doctrine would become the stuff of Christianity's fifteenth-century Great Schism. But through it all, the *filioque* dogma would endure in the West—at least before the German Christians.

But the clerics of the German Christian Church would recast the Holy Spirit as an ethos instead of a person: "a nature spirit, a folk spirit, Germanness in its essence."[71] And in Nazi political theology the "third article of the Trinity" would be replaced with an "ethno-national" ideal. No less blasphemously, the Spirit was supposed to proceed from the Führer as well as the Father, and from nature, history, and nation.

Bonhoeffer pronounced the Nazi doctrine a heresy. The German Christians hailed their creed as "undegenerate Christianity."[72]

Theology has always mattered: the heretical turn of the German Christians can be directly connected with the catastrophe that followed. Bonhoeffer's friend Julius Rieger, director of the seminary in Naumburg, would describe the political consequences, and the genealogy, of theological error this way: "The crypt is below, the cathedral on top of it. . . . First nature's grace, then Christ's grace. First creation, then redemption. . . . It is a struggle between Germanic folk religiosity and the church. . . . This all goes back to liberal theology."[73]

With the explosive force of their Nazi theological artillery, the German Christians pounded the uncooperative doctrines of the church into submission—and usually beyond recognition. The doctrine of the cross was now understood to mean that "public interest comes before self-interest."[74] The church represented the communal expression of the German genius. The savior whom Paul had called "the first-born of the dead" was now the first of the storm troopers.

On July 17, 1933, Bonhoeffer wrote to Sutz in Switzerland to apologize for being a bad correspondent. "Please forgive me," he said, "but I think you know yourself why it had to be so." He had been completely absorbed with all that was happening in the church. "We are now about to come to a decision," Bonhoeffer said, "which I think will be of the utmost church-political significance. There is no doubt in my mind that the victory will go to the German Christians, and this will very quickly bring into view the contours of the new church, and the question will be whether we can even support it as the church. I am afraid, though, that we are crumbling gradually but steadily, that we no longer have the strength to act together. Then we will be back to small, unauthorized gatherings."

Bonhoeffer asked Sutz's counsel, but not before asking, only half in jest, whether Sutz might be able to find him a "nice professorship . . . there in Switzerland."

On July 23, 1933, the German Christians prevailed in the elections for representatives to local parish councils.[75] It was in the north and east of Germany that the National Socialist Party drew its strongest support: German Christians held large majorities among the clergy and laity of the Old Prussian Union, nearly 75 percent of the vote of the regional church that included Berlin and Wittenberg. After the elections in June, which secured the synod leadership, the German Christians assumed control of seven of the union's eight provincial branches. Only Westphalia "retained a non–German Christian majority," though this was less the result of dissent in the parishes than of "an intentionally undemocratic filtering system that protected higher synods from the Nazi sympathizers."[76] Beyond the domain of the Old Prussian Union, ecclesial loyalty to the National Socialists solidified rapidly, as *Gleichschaltung* was carried on with ever-greater force. Having taken control of church leadership, the most militant of the Deutsche Christen now had a new purpose: the consolidation of the Lutheran Church and the Nazi state.

The elections of July 23 had heralded a great spiritual surrender to the world-epochal mission of the Führer.

H itler was, of course, not a Protestant. Like Heidegger, he was a lapsed Roman Catholic who sought to remake the world into a liturgy of his own design. On a more practical level, Hitler needed the churches' cooperation, and so on July 14, he ordered the Protestant leadership to elect a new bishop and to do it on July 23.[77] He had no doubt that his machinations would lead to the consecration of the credulous Ludwig Müller.

With only a fortnight's notice, the German Christians launched a frenzied national publicity campaign to lay the groundwork for victory. Large rallies were held on university campuses where students had been coached to break out in "spontaneous" support of Müller. As Bonhoeffer biographer Schlingensiepen writes, " 'Spontaneous' was one of the Nazis' favorite words for actions planned by the Party. Years later, boys who had dutifully attended Hitler Youth meetings would be asked what those meetings entailed; they would be given to reply, 'We practiced spontaneous applause.' "[78]

It was during these days leading to the episcopal election that Bonhoeffer received his first visit from the Gestapo, most likely in response to a letter he'd circulated, "To Members and Friends of the Young Reformation Movement." Bonhoeffer had written to dissenting ministers and urged them to be on the alert for party members and sympathizers visiting their churches. He asked the pastors to let him know "*immediately* when interference of any kind occurs in their congregations or in others known to them." Interference would appear at his door shortly thereafter in the form of two Nazi security agents, come to warn Bonhoeffer to cease and desist in his efforts to block Müller's election; should he fail to comply, he would be sent to a concentration camp.[79] Bonhoeffer in turn instructed his comrades in the Young Reformation Group to "to destroy all privately produced leaflets and to distribute only those received from our Reich office."

On August 5, with the German Evangelical Church now under the leadership of Müller, Bonhoeffer traveled to the city of Bielefeld, just north of Teutoburg Forest in Westphalia, to meet with fellow dissenting ministers at the charity hospital called Bethel. The town by the same name was built around the hospital, which had been established by the church in 1867 to care for those suffering "seizure afflictions" and which now nursed the physically disabled, as well as those suffering from a variety of mental disorders. Physicians, nurses, ministers, staff, and patients all lived together on the hospital grounds.[80]

A theological school nearby was sympathetic to the Young Reformation Group, which made Bethel a safe place to work from. The goal was to hammer out a theological statement that would clarify the basis for their dissent and thus to draft a confession "suitable for our times." The group convening in Bethel wanted their statement to register protest as well as give encouragement to those pastors—the "lonely warriors"—trying faithfully to serve their parishes under the new constraints.

At an opening service on August 15, the theologians and pastors were joined for worship in the redbrick church on Zion Hill by the hospital staff and patients. The evening made a deep impression on Bonhoeffer. After such a rancorous summer, it was good for the brethren to gather and to sing hymns and hear the Word preached to "elderly tramps who'd wandered in from the country roads," to "children from the lab school," the hospital doctors, chaplains, families from the village, epileptics, deaconesses and nurses standing by to watch any patient suffering from seizures, to catch them should they suffer one and fall.

"Here we have a part of the church that still knows what the church can be concerned with and what it cannot," Bonhoeffer wrote to his grandmother Julie.[81] He'd had a sudden vision of Rembrandt's etching *The Hundred Guilder Print*, always one of his favorites by the Dutch master. It depicts chapter 19 of the Gospel of Matthew, in which Jesus heals the sick, debates the Pharisees, and bids them to let the little ones come to him. "Today in church was the first time it really struck me," Bonhoeffer wrote, reflecting upon how Jesus not only conferred special grace on the infirm and the weak but favored them. In the same reflection, in a rare but commodious turn to non-Western religions, Bonhoeffer is also reminded of the Buddha, whose conversion from the worldly life of a prince to one of contemplative discipline, some have said, was inspired "by an encounter with a desperately sick person." That encounter may have also inspired the Buddha's declaration to his disciples that "he who attends the sick, attends me," wisdom inescapably familiar to readers of Matthew 25:40: "Truly, I say to you, as you did it to one of the least of these my brothers, you did it to me." "What utter madness that some people today think that the sick can or ought to be legally eliminated," Bonhoeffer wrote.

After a productive week, the pastoral group had completed a draft of a new confession. It affirmed as basic tenets both the Lordship of Jesus Christ and the Abrahamic origins of Christianity—and also that the denial of either amounted to the renunciation of one's baptism. The divine election of Israel was built on a promise that shall never be broken; therefore, "[God] continues to preserve a 'holy remnant' of Israel after the flesh, which can be neither absorbed into another nation by emancipation and assimilation . . . nor be exterminated by Pharaoh-like measures." The Bethel Confession, as it came to be known, stated that the "holy remnant" of Israel bears "the indelible stamp of the chosen people." It further allows that no nation can be commissioned to take revenge on the Jews for the execution at Golgotha. It decries "the attempt to deprive the German Evangelical Church of its promise by the attempt to change it into a national church of Christians by Aryan descent."[82] Bonhoeffer wrote that draft in collaboration with a number of others: his former Berlin classmate Hermann Sasse, who had recently become a professor of church history at the University of Erlangen;

Gerhard Stratenwerth, a staff member at Bethel; and several associates of Karl Barth—George Merz, the managing editor of the radical journal *Between the Times* (*Zwischen den Zeiten*) and godfather of Barth's son Matthias; Hans Fischer, a pastor in Bochum and former student of Barth's in Münster; and Wilhelm Vischer, an Old Testament scholar in residence at Bethel who would later be one of Barth's colleagues at the University of Basel. It ended with a call for the immediate repeal of the Aryan paragraph.[83]

Although this, as with any theological collaboration, produced heated debate, Bonhoeffer was pleased with the breadth and clarity of the results, given here:

> The facts of salvation history to which the Scriptures bear witness (i.e., the election of Israel and the condemnation of its sin, the revelation of the Law of Moses, the incarnation, the teachings and deeds of Jesus Christ, his death on the cross and his resurrection, the founding of the church) are unique revelatory acts of God, which the church has to proclaim as such and as valid for us today as well. In accordance with the confessions of the Protestant churches of the Reformation period, we reject the false doctrine, in whatever form it may occur, that Christ may also testify to himself outside the Scriptures and without them. We reject the false doctrine that presents the history of salvation as a parable, for example, that the election of Israel as God's chosen people can be applied to any other people, or perhaps to all peoples. This is a denial of the uniqueness and the historicity of God's revelation.
>
> For the same reason we reject the false doctrine that recognizes the Old Testament only as the Bible of Jesus, that is, of the original Christian church, and recognizes its validity only in that context (religious anti-Semitism).
>
> We reject the false doctrine that says we confess Jesus as our Lord because of his heroic devotion. He is our Lord only because he is sent by our Father, the Son and Savior crucified and resurrected for us. With the confessions we hereby reject the error of the new Arians, "that Christ is not true, essential God by nature, of one eternal divine essence with God the Father and the Holy Spirit, but that he is merely adorned with divine majesty under and alongside God the Father."
>
> God glorifies his overflowing faithfulness in remaining true to Israel according to the flesh.

The Bethel Confession, especially in this first draft, before falling into the hands of critics and redactors in subsequent editorial sessions, exemplified Christian orthodoxy's subversive potential in the face of an idolatrous regime.

Bonhoeffer returned to Berlin convinced that the "big, *völkisch* national church" of German Protestantism could no longer "be reconciled with Christianity." The church in Germany would stand or fall by its position on the "Jewish question." The real issue was "Germanism or Christianity," "and the sooner the conflict comes out in the open, the better." The pursuit of a purely Germanic Christianity could only be called "a violation of the gospel," which was to say, a heresy. Bonhoeffer had spoken hard words. And the recriminations would come quickly. When they did, he would find strength in the fellowship of dissenters at home and abroad. In a meeting of its General Synod on September 5 and 6, the Old Prussian Union, which included Berlin and Potsdam, became the first regional church to adopt the Aryan paragraph. A vote by the entire Reich Church was scheduled later in the month at the National Synod in Wittenberg.

"By adopting the Aryan paragraph," Bonhoeffer told Barth, "the Evangelical Church of the Old Prussian Union has separated itself from the church of Christ. We are now awaiting an answer as to whether the pastors who have signed this statement are to be dismissed, or whether one need not worry about saying this sort of thing. Several of us are now very drawn to the idea of a free church."[84]

Bonhoeffer was taken aback, however, when Barth disagreed sharply with his position on the Aryan paragraph and its centrality in the Bethel Confession. Still living in Bonn—he would not move his family to Switzerland until summer 1935—the elder theologian opined that the Reich Church's adoption of the anti-Jewish clause, though regrettable, did not rise to the level of a theological crisis. The German Protestant Church was doubtless built on a foundation of theological errors—about that Barth wholeheartedly agreed—but he did not think the time had come for schism.

Bonhoeffer's charge of apostasy seemed rather premature, if not careless.[85] Barth believed that the church's adoption of the Aryan paragraph should be condemned as bad policy, but Bonhoeffer had gone too far in saying that the church would live or die by its position on the anti-Jewish measures. The Aryan paragraph was simply not a theological matter. Barth proposed a more cautious path for dissenting Christians: they must remain faithful to the German Evangelical Church while being *in statu confessionis*. The most severe posture of protest short of breaking away, *status confessionis* typically excludes those deemed in error from the communion sacrament and the pulpit.

Barth had not acquiesced in the least to the German Christians. He regarded the movement with utter contempt. But a Christian theologian's sole responsibility, he maintained, is to tend the church's dogmatics. The necessity of this exclusive focus he would soon try to explain in his 1934 manifesto "Theological Existence Today," written shortly before his move to Basel. Now more than ever, he wrote, theology must be done with single-minded respect, "as if nothing else were happening." Bonhoeffer's conviction that the Aryan paragraph was saturated with theological meaning betrayed a rather blinkered functional view of the theological enterprise.

Barth would later change his mind and come to regret the tepidness and legalism of his response. But in the summer of 1933, he preferred to wait and see, investing his energies in the writing of church dogmatics. In his grand scheme, it was theological liberalism that remained the archnemesis. National Socialism was but a sorry application of flawed doctrine. He had condemned the German Christians from the first, but his condemnation lacked teeth. "It will be worthwhile," he told Bonhoeffer, "to resolve not to think in terms of tactics at this point, but in spiritual terms." Barth said he was in "favor of waiting to see what comes." Bonhoeffer and his fellow dissidents at Bethel would do better to let the "evil decision" run its course, Barth advised. "Let the factual situation it has created speak for itself." More manifest opposition "should await something more doctrinally decisive than the Aryan Clause," by itself not reason enough to abandon "the sinking ship."[86] If there were to be schism, Barth said, let it come from the other side.

Bonhoeffer, however, was of a mind not to be changed: he continued to think it unconscionable that any Christian theologian would sit still in the face of the Nazi idols and not do his utmost to smash them. As he'd learned in America, conscience must have its correlatives in conduct. In this case it demanded acting on the judgment that assents to the Aryan paragraph amounted to the renunciation of the faith. It meant precipitating the resignations of the Nazi clerics from office, "beginning immediately," and thus the transfer of ecclesial authority to non-Nazi Protestants.[87] Barth's call to a *status confessionis* amounted to little more than evasion of responsibility. Now was no time for technical niceties. Neither was Bonhoeffer content to use the present crisis as an occasion to settle a theological score with the liberal tradition. Embrace of the Aryan paragraph meant that "even the apostles of Jesus Christ, and moreover the Lord himself, who in the flesh was a son of David," had been expelled from the German church.

"I know there are many who await your opinion," Bonhoeffer wrote to Barth in a letter dated September 9, 1933, "and I also know that most think you will counsel us to wait until we are thrown out. However, some of us have already been thrown out, namely, the Jewish Christians, and the same will soon happen to the others." The paragraph, he still contended, had separated "the Prussian church from Christianity" and "committed blasphemy against the Holy Spirit, which cannot be forgiven in either this world or the next."[88]

Barth did have one valid point as to the territory of theology. Prior Lutheran confessions had made no mention of race. That the Bethel Confession ventured into such territory bespeaks the force of Bonhoeffer's dissent and also of his insight that Nazi ideology turned now more on ethnic identity than religion.[89]

Bonhoeffer left Bethel hoping that the declaration would be received gratefully by ministers of conscience and by the faithful. Indeed, by year's end, six thousand ministers would pledge support for what came to be called the Pastors' Emergency League. A consensus was emerging among the non-Nazi clergy that a formal institutional identity was needed, as the dissident Christian community came to be seen as the true Protestant church in Germany.

In the third week of September, Bonhoeffer traveled with his Berlin colleague Julius Richter to Sofia, Bulgaria, for a conference of the World Alliance for International Friendship Through the Churches.[90] He was relieved to be out of Germany and in the company of fellow ecumenists. The conference was convening at the palatial Grand Hotel overlooking the city gardens, "with its marquee inscribed in girders on the steep, gabled roof," and its spacious ballroom, ornate interiors, and vast art collection—a stark and doubtless pleasing contrast to the ominous matters at hand.

The plight of minorities around the world, both Christian and non-Christian, was taken up in Sofia at great length. Among the resolutions passed was an appeal on behalf of Iraq's persecuted Assyrian Christian minority, mainly in the northern areas of Dohuk and Zakho.

By the end of the week, a consensus had emerged that racial discrimination, "whether because of color or on other grounds," in any form and any place, constituted "a great danger to peace and the welfare of humanity." While affirming the transnational and multiracial identity of their Christian faith, they gave equal attention to the broader matter of universal human rights. The resolution condemned all "discrimination or hierarchy among religions or nations" and specifically the "treatment that people of Jewish ancestry and association have suffered in Germany." It also included a confession of guilt for "our many sins of transgression against our brothers of other races and colour."[91] In response to "the State measures against the Jews in Germany," the British delegation, above all others, pressed for the use of the word "deplore" in the response to the Nazi view of the "Jewish race [as] a race of inferior status."[92]

In a private report to Bishop George Bell, dated October 5, 1933, the Danish ecumenist Ove Ammundsen, professor at Copenhagen and bishop of Hadersleben, offered his thoughts on the proceedings in Sofia: "The German delegates were Prof. Richter [member of the German Protestant mission board and of the World Alliance for Promoting International Friendship]; and the young *Privatdozent* at Berlin, Dr. Bonhoeffer. He is a splendid fellow, sincere, utterly earnest, determined not to compromise with antibiblical measures. He is on the left wing of the opposition." Both Bonhoeffer and Richter had voted for the resolution.[93]

Upon his return to Berlin on September 22, Bonhoeffer was handed a written reprimand from the Foreign Ministry—in the person of one bureaucrat named "Clodius"—charging him and Richter with international "incitement against the Fatherland."[94] The letter warned that any further criticism of the German Christians would be treated as high treason.[95] For its part, the Bulgarian press—under control of the authoritarian monarchy that had been Germany's ally in the Great War and would be again—echoed the sentiments of its national synod, emphasizing repeatedly "that the church should concern itself with things other than politics."[96] Bonhoeffer was undeterred. He defended the Sofia resolution as an expression of the pure and unadulterated gospel and would not retreat from any part of the wording—or, "disowning not a word of it."[97]

One week later, on a clear morning in late September, emboldened by the week in Sofia, Bonhoeffer decided to take his fledgling band of anti-Nazi agitators to the heart of the Lutheran establishment. It would be his last effort to stem the rising tide of Aryan Christianity before accepting a pastorate in London, although this autumnal journey to Luther-Stadt Wittenberg more nearly resembled a road trip of theological pranksters than an organized protest, including street theater, knavery, heckling, and preaching in public places. No less eccentric was the means of conveyance. The elder Dr. Bonhoeffer's black Mercedes and his personal chauffeur were enlisted for the ride south along the Berliner Chaussee and through the vast pine forests near Beelitz to the national Lutheran Synod. Besides Bonhoeffer's friends

Gertrud Staewen and Franz Hildebrandt, the back seat of the limousine was occupied by boxes upon boxes of a pamphlet entitled "To the National Synod of the German Evangelical Church."

Attending as unofficial representatives of the dissenting church, the three friends couched their protest against the "false church," in the authority of none less than Martin Luther, who, 450 years earlier, from the pulpit of the Castle Church at Wittenberg, had denounced the "Babylonian Captivity" of the German nation.[98] At stake in this "grave hour" was not just the church's freedom from political oppression but also the very truth of the gospel. Of course, the official church had likewise invoked its own Lutheran authority and lineage.

Upon arrival, the three Berliners wasted no time plastering the town with their pamphlet, affixing it to trees, telephone poles, buildings, and kiosks. They even sneaked into official church headquarters and scattered copies on the desks and seminar tables. On the town square they handed them out to passersby. "Appeals without any printer's name, minutes, communiqués, details, etc., are being circulated," wrote a concerned minister in the hastily dispatched reply appearing in the church paper *Evangelium im Dritten Reich* (*The Gospel in the Third Reich*). "But with unerring certainty and calm, our leaders will take steps."[99]

Indeed they would, as the Berliners watched in astonishment the scene unfolding on the cobblestone streets around Wittenberg's town

REICH BISHOP LUDWIG MÜLLER,
GERMAN PROTESTANT NATIONAL SYNOD IN WITTENBERG

center. There the first "teaching platoon" of the Augustusburg Leadership College in Saxony—the "theological storm troopers," as they called themselves—had assembled to stand guard for the future Reich bishop as he entered the Castle Church. Bearing their rucksacks like infantrymen, uniformed in field gray, with the purple cross and runes of the *Schutzstaffel* (SS) emblazoned on their arms, they might have been comical but for their deadly earnestness. Stationed in the choir loft, they would present an impressive martial discipline throughout the services.

Standing over Luther's tomb inside the sanctuary, Karl Fezer, once a respectable theologian at Tübingen, now a German Christian, proclaimed that Müller had been unanimously elected as the first Reich bishop by the representatives of the regional churches.[100] The bishop seized the reins with the confidence of a man in tune with providence. "The old has come to an end," he thundered into the candle-lit recesses of the church. "The new world has begun."[101]

All of Wittenberg had risen to its feet in celebration, one of the young Nazi clerics recalled. "A splendid sun again smiles from the cloudless sky, and the bells ring festively. [The] flags of the SA storm groups from Wittenberg, the flags of the Protestant youth organizations, of the craft guilds, of the associations; the theological faculties in festive robes, the clergy of Luther's city in gowns, the members of the Synod, the Lutherans in brown shirts, the bishops of the German Landeskirchen with the golden pectoral crosses of their office, and the man whom all eyes seek in awe: the future Reich Bishop Ludwig Müller."

When Müller declared that the time had now come for redeeming the soul of the people, Bonhoeffer, seated in the balcony, is said to have let out a "short sharp laugh."[102]

But it was like the voice of one crying in the desert. Bonhoeffer hardly doubted the German Christian's ultimate victory. The question was not how to save the German Protestant establishment but "whether Christians of conscience would be able to carry through on the promise and support the new church as the one true Lutheran church in Germany."[103] Even about that smaller goal, he was in doubt. He feared that already the fellowship of dissent was "crumbling gradually but steadily," and that soon the opposition would "no longer have the strength to act together." What, then, remained but the catacombs, or some version of those subterranean passages where the ancient Christians buried their dead and worshipped in secret under pagan rule. So much for the *Kirchenkampf*.

Müller won the bishopric in a landslide. The opposition's case, which Bonhoeffer had been prepared to deliver, was tabled without debate. The synod would not, however, vote on the Aryan paragraph, and thus the race laws were never officially adopted by the unified Reich Church. While this no doubt dismayed the zealots who wanted immediate application of the Aryan paragraph to all congregations, it was in fact the Reich Church's Foreign Office that quietly lobbied against official adoption, arguing that such an action would only create an unnecessary distraction. And, in a surprising but shrewd maneuver, Hitler entered, which is to say ended, the debate, by forbidding ecclesial leaders from endorsing the Aryan paragraph as church policy. There was no good reason to put the compliant bishops in the embarrassing position of answering to an angry minority, since most regional synods had adopted the Aryan laws anyway, and thus victory went decisively to the German Christians.[104] Inside the Castle Church, the clergy raised their right hands to solemnly swear in unison their loyalty to their new *Reichsbischof* and the Nazi state.

The testimonial of one German Christian pastor in attendance captures the tremendous optimism of the national church reborn: "27 September 1933! A splendid sun again smiles from the cloudless sky, and the bells ring festively and ceremonially. All of Wittenberg is on its feet. Shortly after eleven o'clock the huge procession starts to move to the Stadtkirche: the flags of the SA storm groups from Wittenberg, the flags of the Protestant youth organizations, of the craft guilds, of the associations; the theological faculties in festive robbers, the clergy of Luther's city in gowns, the members of the Synod, the Lutherans in brown shirts, the bishops of the German Landeskirchen with the golden pectoral crosses of their office, and—the man whom all eyes seek in awe, inquiringly and full of hope: the future Reich Bishop Ludwig Müller."

Bonhoeffer's high hopes for the Bethel Confession had by now been chastened not only by the crush of events but also by the negative response of pastors and theologians to whom the "August version" had been presented. After the gathering at Bethel, Bodelschwingh had reached out to an extended circle of more than twenty dissenting pastors and theologians with the urgent request "to review it, make suggestions, return their changes by September 15," after which their work on the final version would begin with an eye toward presenting at the October meeting. This wider circle of churchmen happened to include the scholar Paul Althaus, who had expressed an interest in attending the next dissident synod, this one at Barmen the following May, but was in fact only months away from joining the Nazi Party. From his distinguished chair in Göttingen, Althaus broke abruptly with the dissenting church; in his lectures and writings he would begin promoting a vision of the Reich Church as "a unity constituted by blood relations," lending an influential voice to the Nazi Protestant majority.[105]

In October 1933, Bonhoeffer and Hans Fischer, a Lutheran pastor in Bochum, returned to Bethel for a second editorial consultation; they would spend several long days sequestered in the seminary, working through a revised version. Fischer would later recall the "authority with which [Bonhoeffer] examined and worked through the criticisms contained in those opinions he had solicited."[106] One would have hardly guessed that, in a letter written earlier that month, even before having seen the respondents' copious suggestions, he had lamented to Barth that "the Bethel confession, into which I truly had poured heart and soul, has met with almost no understanding." Bonhoeffer would not attend the third editorial meeting in Bethel. He had rather abruptly decided to leave Germany, accepting an offer to serve as pastor of two German congregations in London. (He had already left when he wrote that downcast letter to Barth.) When he finally read the heavily redacted final version, his worst suspicions would be confirmed. On November 6, Merz told Bodelschwingh that the work had been completed, but he felt it "urgently necessary" that the final version be sent to Bonhoeffer in London and to Professor Sasse in Erlangen, another member of the original group. Both had been involved with the declaration since the beginning, explained Merz, so "we really can't send this out into the world without considering their opinions once more."[107]

Bonhoeffer's response to the "November version" has been lost, but George Merz's summary of Bonhoeffer's disapprobation has not. "No mere trifle, but rather a catastrophe," Bonhoeffer is reported to have said. He found the revisions deplorable, and on December 5, Merz would tell Martin Niemöller that "Bonhoeffer has resolutely rejected the reworked version and opposes its being published in the present form."[108] Niemöller was a celebrated World War I submarine commander and recipient of the Iron Cross who now shepherded the affluent St. Anne's Church in the leafy suburb of Dahlem; he opposed the state's intrusions into church affairs, though he had voted for the Nazi Party in the 1933 elections. Exploiting his power over the younger churchmen at Bethel as well as Bonhoeffer's departure for London, Althaus, the forty-five-year-old Göttingen professor, had taken a red pen to Bonhoeffer's forthright and reverential defense of Judaism; all criticisms of the Aryan paragraph were deleted. And the most important points of the confession had, Bonhoeffer felt, been eviscerated. "To the section on the State, sycophantic riders had been added concerning 'joyful collaboration' in its aims, and likewise, a paragraph on sharing responsibility for the country's guilt had been changed into participation by the Church 'in her country's glory and guilt.'"[109]

More an opportunist than a quisling, Althaus, in less than a year, had come to the conclusion that National Socialism was not simply another political party, but a spiritually virile movement that transcended politics. In this manner, the Third Reich would revivify the moral values and discipline undermined by Weimar's culture of license and experimentation. Althaus's interpretation of revelation no doubt inspired his nationalist pieties; the Word of God, he argued, is understood more effectively through the lens of "general revelation" than "specific," preferring to emphasize God's self-revelation in history, nation, race, and culture rather than the primacy of Jesus Christ. God's word to humanity, he said, "equals the situation at any given moment. . . . Obedience toward God consists of accepting one's allotted position in life as handed down by years of tradition."[110] Although Althaus imagined himself a mediating theologian—striking a balance between the Deutsche Christen and the dissenting congregations—his conviction that Germany's political renewal depended on Christian principles made such a rule finally impossible.

What had begun as a bold and concrete statement of faith in dissent had succumbed to the torpor of conscience by committee. "Too many cooks spoil the broth," Bonhoeffer told Justin Rieger.[111] In fact, it was hard not to see it as proof that the dissenters' resolve was crumbling as feared.

Bonhoeffer had stumbled awkwardly on the "Jewish question" earlier in the spring, but by the end of the year he'd concluded that it could only be justly answered in favor of God's eternal election of Israel. And so it was particularly distressing to discover that his comrades, with few exceptions, believed otherwise.

The decision to take the pastorate in London was undoubtedly born of frustration, if not despair. As he'd confessed to Barth, the reception of the Bethel Confession had come as a blow and one that had left him altogether uncertain about his future in Germany. He would not throw caution to the wind and cut his ties with everyone who disagreed with him. Rather, he requested and received a leave of absence from his department. He held out the hope of returning when his country had regained some measure of stability. He was delighted to hear a rumor that his name had been mentioned for an open chair in systematic theology; perhaps he would not be stuck forever in the quagmire of *Privatdozent*.[112] He was trying to sort through conflicting ambitions, to trust his heart but to be realistic as well. Erich Seeberg, the Nazi dean of the faculty, had also expressed a hope that Bonhoeffer's move would only be temporary.[113] Bonhoeffer found Seeberg's words oddly reassuring.

But when the theologian Arthur Titius learned of Bonhoeffer's move, he told his colleagues in Berlin, "It is a great pity that our best hope in the faculty is being wasted on the church struggle." Titius may have sat on the sidelines as the church imploded around him, but he seems to have understood the purpose of Bonhoeffer's leave better than anyone.

Through word and deed in the wake of the great upheaval, Bonhoeffer had landed himself in a strange and precarious place. All things were in flux. And he was no exception. "You have become a different person," the Berlin pastor Wolfgang Schlunk told him on the eve of his departure. Wishing Bonhoeffer well in England, Schlunk offered his teacher some sobering insight: "It will be difficult for you to go on working in the church, and outside the church there will hardly be any possible employment left for you in Germany." Indeed, he said, it was only a matter of time before the university would "chase you out."[114]

CHAPTER NINE

1933–1935: LONDON

~

Crying in the Wilderness

One night during Bonhoeffer's first weeks in London, at a dinner party in his Sydenham flat, he played a piano duet with the wife of a friend. It was a Beethoven concerto, one he knew quite well. Suddenly, to everyone's surprise, Dietrich abandoned the music as written and began improvising "in an entirely different key." A faint smile appeared in the corners of his mouth as he spun outward; and then, without missing a beat, he lunged back for the keys. Soon the same mischievous spirit had possessed his guests, who were roaring with laughter. When the duet was over, the performance was answered with resounding applause, at which Dietrich nodded appreciatively, seeming "genuinely and wholeheartedly involved" in the moment. For all that weighed on his mind, he remained, as one guest that night put it, a man of "endless surprises."[1]

In November of 1933 Bonhoeffer began his eighteen-month assignment in the eastern suburbs of London. He would take over two of the six German churches in the greater London area: St. George's Lutheran and St. Paul's Aldgate East.[2] St. George's stood on Dacres Road, in Whitechapel, on a wooded lot near the train station about halfway between the Forest Hill and Sydenham stops. St. Paul's, a community dating to the eighteenth century, was housed at that time in a building in Goulston Street, near the Aldgate. Bonhoeffer's predecessor there, a kindly Swabian named Friedrich Singer, had come to London from a German church in Newcastle but had recently returned to Germany.[3]

This would be Bonhoeffer's first and only experience of living in a church manse, as it was indeed his one and only tenure as a minister in charge. The parsonage was a three-story Victorian house near the top of Manor Mount Road in Forest Hill, in the borough

ST. GEORGE'S LUTHERAN CHURCH,
SYDENHAM, LONDON

of Lewisham. Bonhoeffer occupied the large rooms on the top floor, while the main rooms of the parlor level were used by a German school. He liked his spacious quarters, with their pleasant view of the hills. Still, life on his own lacked for most of the comforts of his parents' house. With its bland double-fronted exterior, the parsonage possessed neither the architectural refinement to be found elsewhere in London nor any of the natural simplicity and elegance of the Grunewald house. The rooms behind the grim facade were, moreover, quite drafty, pitifully under-heated. The presence of the parish's verger, with his solitary digs in the basement, added little personal warmth.[4]

A decade earlier, an addition had been built onto the house, but no proper foundation had been laid for it, so stepping from the old part into the new always felt like boarding a ship amid a heavy swell.[5] Such careless construction was of a piece with the flimsy windows, the warped floorboards, and the useless ancient heating pipes. "Cold, damp air penetrated through the windows," recalled Wolf-Dieter Zimmermann, who visited from Berlin.[6] Even the warmer seasons were uncomfortable. Bonhoeffer's morning bath, once a beloved daily ritual, became a perfunctory splash of cold water. He was constantly fighting off colds and fevers during the first months. But he soldiered on merrily, hardly bothered even by a mischief of mice that had lodged themselves in upper rooms, where they could multiply so fruitfully.[7]

In the first week of December 1933, as he was still unpacking—he had shipped large sections of his library, his wardrobe, his phonograph and record collection, even his grand piano—a high fog descended on London. The mass of cold, wet, and sooty air trapped beneath an impenetrably warm sky produced a "midnight at mid-day" effect. The sun turned pale red and finally disappeared, Bonhoeffer told his parents.

When his piano arrived separately by van one morning, he was amused to discover that the Bechstein grand he'd received for his fifteenth birthday would not fit through the narrow front doors. After studying the situation with the movers, the principal of the German school, and a few passersby, he helped construct an elaborate system of pulleys to hoist the piano up to the third story, where he would arrange a makeshift music room. It was to celebrate this successful feat of engineering that Bonhoeffer threw the aforementioned dinner party. By the end of his first month, music nights would be a weekly ritual in the otherwise drowsy suburban manse, combining singers and musicians from the parish with visiting friends from Germany. He would single-handedly revive the languishing St. George's choir and, later, in the fall of 1934, lend his own voice to a London chorus's performance of Brahms's German Requiem.[8]

As pastor of two parishes, Bonhoeffer conducted services twice every Sunday, and while he usually preached the same sermon to both congregations, he prepared for each occasion with the same care and attention he'd given to his academic lectures.

And there was much else to do besides. During his year in Barcelona, Bonhoeffer, as assistant, had shared the responsibility of ministering to a congregation of 120. The London situation was quite different. Despite a growing German expatriate community, neither St. George's nor St. Paul's provided an assistant. Bonhoeffer would claim he'd never worked so hard, wondering to his grandmother "how so much could be going on in such a small congregation."[9] (Perhaps it was justice for his having kept Olbrecht waiting past Advent!) But it didn't seem a hardship: the work was gratifying and perhaps not as onerous as reported. Visiting friends were relieved to find him in excellent spirits—and with more spare time than he'd adverted to.

In total, he had charge of several hundred souls, although the average attendance at St. George's was only thirty to forty, and only slightly higher at St. Paul's. But the numbers don't tell the whole story. The two congregations differed sharply as to their makeup and expectations. St. George's, Sydenham, resembled the Barcelona parish, composed mainly of small business owners, industrialists, diplomats, and other professionals.[10] When ground was broken in the 1880s, the German ambassador had laid the cornerstone during a celebration that included champagne and a full orchestra.[11] Soon a Gothic chapel of red brick and Doulting limestone would rise there, featuring a bell tower and a hundred-foot spire, the building hailed in the *Sydenham and Penge Gazette* as an "ornament to the locality." St. Paul's German Church in London's East End, by contrast, served a distinctly lower-middle-class population of bakers, butchers, and artisans. It was not as grand as St. George's or Barcelona, but it was also not as downtrodden as the parish he'd served in Berlin. He would move comfortably between his two communities.[12]

S hortly after his arrival in October, Bonhoeffer wrote a letter to Karl Barth that he knew was long overdue and would not be well received.

Since having formed a relationship with Barth in Bonn the summer after touring America, Bonhoeffer had felt himself obliged to keep the master apprised of any decisions taken in response to the church struggle in Germany. Indeed, Barth could be proprietary about the younger theologians he'd taken under his wing, even those, like Bonhoeffer, who had never studied with him. There is no denying that the relationship between them was special. As Mary Bosanqut wrote in the first published biography of Bonhoeffer, "they recognized each other over the heads of the theological academics." But while they would feel a lasting mutual regard, "it was never to warm into complete trust."[13] Bonhoeffer may have been too quick to regard himself as Barth's equal, though Barth may have been too quick to presume that Bonhoeffer (fourteen years younger) was not. One might imagine anyway that a man who'd made it his life's work to reconceive the whole canon of the church's doctrine and resuscitate its orthodoxy would not stand on ceremony or become exercised about another's career choices. As it happened, Barth was livid to learn secondhand of Bonhoeffer's decision to leave Germany, pronouncing it abrupt and irresponsible. His florid letter took the form of a fatherly dressing down. You have no business playing Elijah under the juniper tree or Jonah under the gourd vine, he said in essence. "Get back to your post in Berlin straightaway!"[14]

Barth could well appreciate that Bonhoeffer, like his peers, was "suffering under the enormous pressure of 'making straight paths for your feet,' through the present chaotic situation." But, he insisted, we are nevertheless called "to man our positions *in and with* our uncertainty, even if we stumble and go astray ten or a hundred times over."

There is a certain note of self-pity in the Swiss theologian's rebuke: "Why weren't you [in Germany] pulling on the rope that I, virtually alone, could hardly budge?" he asked. "How could you not be here all the time, when there is so much at stake?"

And: "What in the world do you suppose you are doing or hoping to do there?"

He couldn't conceive how the young man, so full of conviction, could think it a "good time to go into the wilderness for a spell, and simply work as a pastor, as unobtrusively as possible"? Not in the face of the inescapable facts: that "you are a German, that your church's house is on fire, that you know enough, and can express what you know well enough, to be of help." These facts obliged Bonhoeffer "to return to your post by the next ship!"[15] Get back to Berlin with all guns blazing, Barth demanded.

But the reprimand misfired.

Barth would remain the younger man's touchstone of Christian orthodoxy, a standard for theological precision and doctrinal fidelity to be admired and aimed for. Bonhoeffer could even tolerate the paroxysms of paternalism, the admonitions amply delivered with blustering certainty. But his tact would be to thank Barth for his advice without taking it.

He'd tried to preempt Barth's predictable disapproval in his letter of late October 1933, saying he had meant to write him six weeks earlier while still finalizing his plans. "I must beg your pardon," he wrote, hoping for the same respect in return, but—to be sure—not seeking approval.[16] In fact, in posting such a late dispatch, Bonhoeffer made the point rather clearly, that his deferential entreaties notwithstanding, he did not expect Barth to understand his decision to move to England.[17] He would even wonder whether Barth's singular vocation of doing theology "as if nothing else were happening" were not ultimately founded on a certain demurral on moral perplexity particular to Swiss Germans.

In fact, Bonhoeffer had not remotely abandoned his allies in the Pastors' Emergency League. Although no longer on the front lines, he spoke every day with colleagues in Berlin during his first month abroad. He also spoke daily with his mother, who had begun attending St. Anne's Church, Dahlem. The vicar, Martin Niemöller, had been elected in September head of the *Pfarrernotbund*, as the Pastors' Emergency League was known in Germany before it became the Confessing Church. Bonhoeffer's telephone bills were so high he usually had to borrow money from his parents to pay them—though, admittedly, that was nothing new. On one occasion a sympathetic clerk at the post office, where phone bills were settled, reduced the amount due by half.[18] Still, Bonhoeffer was not unaware of the impression left by his going to London. In a letter to Erwin Sutz, then serving a Reformed parish in the Swiss mountain village of Wiesendangen, he acknowledged that some fellow dissidents saw the move as a sign of quietism and retreat.[19]

As his travels attest, however, the reality was quite different. He attended the League of Nations in Geneva on October 14, 1933. Then, on January 31, 1934, he traveled to Paris for a meeting of the ecumenical youth commission. The following month, in February, he met with the Council of Brethren in Hanover before going to Berlin, where he caught the flu and had to recuperate at his parents' house. Although he would skip the May 29 meeting in Barmen—at which the Pastors'

Emergency League officially became the Confessing Church and the Barmen Declaration was drafted—he would return to Berlin on June 18 for meetings with Niemöller and Karl Koch. In late August he would spend two warm, sunny weeks on the island of Fanö, off southern Denmark. But even that was not what it might seem: an ecumenical conference was taking place there, and Bonhoeffer convened student seminars on the sand dunes along the Baltic coast. Not long after, in the first week of September 1934, Bonhoeffer would cross the English Channel once again for meetings with the French-German-British youth conference, squeezing in a visit with Jean Lasserre, his old friend from Union, at Lasserre's parents' house in the coal-mining town of Bruay in northwest France.[20]

Bonhoeffer traveled to the continent on average once a month for the duration of his London pastorate, and when he was not traveling, his thoughts were never far from his ecumenical brethren or the "lonely warriors" of the Confessing Church. Keeping up with colleagues abroad might take him to an alpine hotel or seaside resort, but the days, typically packed with meetings, were taxing all the same. Some were even miserable, owing to the recurrent respiratory infections suffered during his London residency. Under the hectic regime of frequent travels and late dinners, to say nothing of all the meats and pastries lavished on him by parishioners, Bonhoeffer suffered another misery as well, this for the first time in his life: he gained nearly fifteen pounds.

Though his comments had grown steadily more critical of the Reich Church, only once was he called back to Berlin to account for something he'd preached or published. The high consistory councilor, one Theodor Heckel, asked him whether he intended to continue on this path, which could lead only to "national indiscipline." At their meeting, Heckel ordered Bonhoeffer to refrain from all further ecumenical activity and to sign a pledge of compliance, which he set before the young pastor on the table between them.[21] Bonhoeffer refused to sign the pledge but feigned surprise at the high councilor's rebuke, promising to think about the demand in the coming days. But two weeks' reflection would not change his mind: again he allowed that he was unable "to sign such a revocation as you are asking of me." Bonhoeffer said he could see no "compelling reason" to suspend "this purely ecclesiological, theological, ecumenical work to which I have been committed for years." The unpleasant flight he had taken at the crack of dawn on March 5 to see Heckel would be, he vowed to himself, his "last act of obedience" toward his ecclesial superiors.[22]

Back in London, Bonhoeffer realized that the German church struggle must also be pursued by means less flamboyant than frontal assault, internecine debate, and published declarations.[23] He would work painstakingly to draw individual German pastors and congregations in England over to the side of the Confessing Church; to tutor members of the ecumenical movement on the German situation; to assist the refugees of Nazi Germany, who were relocating to England in growing numbers; and in his own parishes, to illuminate a way of being Christian apart from the sealed worlds of the nationalist churches.

Music parlor, salon, bachelor pad, and now hostel: his digs on Manor Mount, those two rooms of the top floor, evolved with the necessities of the situation. In those eighteen months, they would see a parade of Germans, including "a vast number of visitors, mostly Jews, who know me from somewhere and who need something." Amid this steady traffic, Bonhoeffer said, he had hardly the chance to be lonely.[24]

Franz Hildebrandt was one of the first to call.[25] It was, in fact, one week into his planned three-month visit that the Barthian missive landed in Sydenham. Though not personally acquainted with the Swiss master, Hildebrandt had his own vexed relationship to him, having written critically of Barth in a book called *Das lutherische Prinzip* (*The Lutheran Principle*) (1931). When Barth learned that Hildebrandt too was in London, he sent his greetings (via Bonhoeffer) to the man who "is supposed to have said some nasty things about me."[26] Barth would carry on claiming, improbably, that he himself had never read the critique.

Hildebrandt had been working as an assistant pastor in Kleinmachnow before his own sudden departure from the fatherland. Like Bonhoeffer, he firmly believed that in the face of the Aryan paragraph faithful Christians were obliged to make a total break from the apostate national church. "We must be radical on all points, including the Aryan paragraph," the two had written in one joint statement.[27] "Radical" in this context meant calling for the immediate resignation of Nazi pastors and theologians.

But while Bonhoeffer had chosen to come to London, Hildebrandt had run out of options in Germany. His mother was of the Sellingers, a prominent family of Jewish Berliners, mostly merchants and industrialists. And so Hildebrandt came to England with no plan but to "follow Bonhoeffer into the foreseeable future, as his guest at his new home, and then see what to do."[28] For his part, despite the trying circumstances, Bonhoeffer was delighted to be sharing his flat with a good friend and intellectual sparring partner. Indeed the two, whom Zimmermann had described as happily locked in a "state of permanent dispute," would pick up where they had left off, arguing for hours about literature, music, art, politics, and, of course, theology.[29] Butting heads over the history of ideas, Hildebrandt defended the German idealist tradition from the Barthian attack, while Bonhoeffer, sympathetic to Eberhard Grisebach and Martin Buber, argued for the priority of the personal encounter. Hildebrandt supported the Protestant Christians People's Party in the Reichstag elections of 1933, while Bonhoeffer argued that only the Catholic Center Party had half a chance of defeating Hitler.[30] The exchanges were "serious but good humored, aggressive and witty" and continued amid "all the day's events and meetings."[31] For Bonhoeffer and Hildebrandt it was like being graduate students again.

The mornings began late with a "sumptuous" breakfast and a copy of the London *Times*, both delivered by the housekeeper at eleven o'clock. Afterward, Bonhoeffer went about his daily tasks and worked on his sermons, until two o'clock, when he'd join Hildebrandt for a light lunch back at the parsonage. The ensuing discussion and debate would end only when the two finally sat down at the piano. Evenings were for the theater and the cinema, followed by drinks and dinner and more conversation, often continuing well after midnight, the flow of meditation, music, theology, and storytelling, "all following one another, blending into one another—till 2 or 3 a.m."[32]

Julius Rieger became another familiar face at the Church Hill parsonage. A fellow Lutheran pastor who had been assigned to the Seaman's Ministry in London, Rieger had met Bonhoeffer at the 1931 World Alliance conference in Cambridge, but it was not until 1934, the same year that Rieger would establish a relief center for German Jewish refugees in England, that a friendship formed.[33] The two pastors regarded each other as "excellent sounding boards for sermons and parish goings-on." And under Rieger's influence, Bonhoeffer got over his long-held disdain for middlebrow art, at least as far as movies were concerned. Once a week, schedules permitting, Bonhoeffer and Rieger caught a thriller or western at a Piccadilly Circus cinema, followed by a late dinner at the Shanghai Restaurant in Soho, a popular Burmese spot near the Charing Cross station. On nights when they craved home cooking, they went to Schmidt's in Charlotte Street, washing down generous portions of Bavarian fare with German beer. Occasionally they might take high tea at the New Criterion.[34]

Expected and unexpected, friends and acquaintances came and went, sometimes staying only overnight, sometimes for weeks, in the tiny flat. At some point in that first London year, the housekeeper suffered a complete nervous breakdown and was institutionalized—a case of "religious madness," Bonhoeffer pronounced with a sigh—the truly vexing result that for quite some time, "we had nobody to help us at all."[35]

In late March 1934, the dismal winter yielded to the English spring, and the resplendent burst of life delighted Bonhoeffer with its fragrances and colors. From the café in nearby Horniman Park or his own second-floor windows he could admire the verdant vistas southward to Kent and Surrey and "northwards across London as far as Hampstead Heath."[36] The season came as a "revelation." There were days when nature's newness could make him forget "everything else," when forests and fields, as far as the eye could see, were blanketed with wild rhododendrons and bluebells—a "triumphant" flower he had seen before only in the hill country of south-central Texas.[37] Clear days and a certain angle of light recalled his student days in Rome seven years earlier. But the bad news from Germany continued unabated.

An undeniable urgency entered Bonhoeffer's preaching in London. His sermons followed the liturgical year—Reformation Day, the German *Totensonntag*, Remembrance Sunday, Advent, New Year, Lent, Easter, Pentecost—but they were unpredictable in other ways. He spoke with an unsettling directness, and he would readily deviate from the theme of the season and the text from the lectionary if the times called for it.

Shortly after returning from America, Bonhoeffer had pronounced the German Evangelical Church "a wreath of blossoms," ornate and funereal.[38] But by the time he delivered his farewell sermon in London on March 10, 1935, he had resolved that "with single-minded purpose, Nat[ional] Socialism has brought about the end of the church in Germany."[39]

"Bonhoeffer the preacher made few concessions to his hearers," Keith Clements wrote in his fascinating study of the London year. He did not assume a professorial air or flaunt his erudition; with few exceptions his language was forthright and gin clear, lacking his accustomed flourishes. Still, he sought to evoke the effects of human encounter with the divine, and to stir a heightened sense of expectancy. He'd been rereading his Kierkegaard, the mournful Dane's feverish mediation on St. Paul's admonition to "work out your salvation with fear and trembling." In Kierkegaard's book by that name, faith is presented as a leap into the unknown, and the eschatology is pervasive. "God is coming! Are you ready?" Bonhoeffer asked the congregation. It is unlikely that very few could claim to be, or that they shared the preacher's intensity, or noticed the pains he took to connect with them. Bonhoeffer's sermons were meticulously handwritten and often typed out in complete manuscripts. Twenty-three such manuscripts—"comprising just fragments in two cases"—have survived; five were originally preached in English. Though attendance was spotty, Bonhoeffer preached as if to the whole world. His first sermons, coinciding with the beginning of Advent 1933, sounded the clanging cymbals of the Father's in-breaking decision: "For God so loved the world that he gave his only begotten son . . ." But not to be forgotten was that this decision summoned each individual to make a decision of his own. It was the Kierkegaardian either/or: Shall I pick up my cross and follow Jesus, or remain mired in idolatry and despair?[40]

On December 3, the first day of Advent, his starting point was Luke 21:28, the absurd venture of hope in a time of abandonment: "Now when these things begin to take place, look up, and raise your heads, because your redemption is drawing near."

"Can we hear it now, the knocking, the driving, the [striving] forward?" he asked. "Can we feel something inside ourselves longing to leap up, to free itself and open itself to the coming of Christ? Do we sense that we are not just talking in images here, but that something is really happening, that human souls are being raised up, shaken, broken open, and healed? That heaven is bending towards the earth; that the earth is trembling, and people are desperate with fear and apprehension as well as hope and joy?"[41]

And then: "Do you want to be redeemed? That is the one great, decisive question that Advent puts to us. Does there burn within us any ember of longing, of recognition of what redemption could mean? If not, then what do we ask of Advent? What do we want from Christmas? . . . a little sentimentality, a little uplift within . . . a nice atmosphere?

"But if there is something in us that cares to know, that is set afire by these words, something in us that believes these words—if we feel that once more, once more in our lives, there could be a complete turning to God, to Christ—then why not just be obedient and listen and hear the word that is offered us, called out to us, shouted into our ears?

"Take courage, fear not, do not be worried or anxious. . . . Christ is coming."[42]

In the autumn of 1934, Bonhoeffer preached a series of four sermons on 1 Corinthians 13, the hymn about love that has become such a staple of wedding ceremonies. "Love is patient, love is kind. It does not envy, it does not boast. . . . Love never fails." Bonhoeffer arranged the series so that the final installment would fall on Reformation Sunday, taking up the last verse of the chapter: "So faith, hope, love abide; but the greatest of these is *love*."[43]

That he chose it for that holiday is, of course, no coincidence. This was no simple plea for fellow feeling. Though the point may have well been lost on the congregation, Bonhoeffer was making a case for the necessity of love in connecting Luther's great doctrine of "justification by faith" with righteous action in the here and now. Luther's dogma of *sola fidei* must mean "something more than lazy piety or abstract intellectualism," he insisted.[44] Works have no redemptive power of their own, but faith, hope, and—above all—love oblige us to act nonetheless.

"And the church that calls a people to belief in Christ," he emphasized, "must itself be, in the midst of that people, the burning fire of love, the nucleus of reconciliation, the source of the fire in which all hate is consumed, and the proud and hateful are transformed into the loving."[45]

The churches of the German Reformation have taught many marvelous things about Christian freedom and the triumph of grace, he insisted, but these churches have not built loving hearts. Look around you, Bonhoeffer implored the faithful, look at the German church and nation. He referred to the Protestant youth groups and to Reich Bishop Müller's "decree concerning the restoration of order." The declaration, which came to be called the "muzzling decree," prohibited pastors from mentioning in sermons or discussing with parishioners any matter related to the church crisis. Violation of the decree would result in suspension, salary cuts, and, pending disciplinary hearings, dismissal from the ranks of the ordained clergy. Niemöller, he reminded them, had been sent into forced retirement and the worst was still to come.[46] The Reich educational ministry had dismissed Barth from his post in Bonn.[47] The theological faculties were now peddling a corrupt Aryan faith. "Is it not obvious? They have not made people who love!"

"It does nobody any good professing to believe in Christ without first being reconciled with his brother or sister—including the nonbeliever, his brethren of another race, the marginalized, or outcast," he explained.[48]

"[Even f]aith and hope as they enter into eternity are molded into the shape of love. In the end everything must become love," said Bonhoeffer. "Perfection's name is love."[49]

He would finally be introduced to George Bell on November 21, 1933. The bishop of Chichester was one of Britain's most respected ecumenists, and though Bonhoeffer had heard him speak at a 1932 ecumenical conference in Geneva—earlier that year Bell had been elected president of the Universal Christian Council for Life and Work—the two had never met.[50] Nevertheless, Bonhoeffer had been so impressed by Bell's address that he translated, with the help of his students Elisabeth Reinke and Berta Schulze, the bishop's *Brief Sketch of the Church of England* into German. In Bell Bonhoeffer perceived a kindred spirit and a likely ally for the Confessing Church: earlier in the fall, Bell, on behalf of the Church of England, had formally protested the German Protestant Church's acceptance of the Aryan paragraph.[51]

Despite differences—Bell at forty-eight was a "sagacious, broad-minded catholic Anglican," while Bonhoeffer, twenty-seven, was a fastidious neo-orthodox Berlin Lutheran—their common commitment to the ecumenical church brought them together. And as in so many of Bonhoeffer's friendships, there was also a shared love of music and theater. Bell had composed several hymns in the Anglican songbook, including a well-known anthem of Christian unity: "Christ Is the King! O Friends, Rejoice." As dean of Canterbury Cathedral from 1925 to 1929, Bell launched the Canterbury Arts Festival, which, funded by the church trust, would go on to commission T. S. Eliot's *Murder in the Cathedral*. In time, the two churchmen would discover further commonalities. Both, it turned out, were born on February 4, and each had lost an older brother in the Great War.[52]

Their meeting in Chichester on November 21, 1933, marked the beginning of an intense friendship, Bonhoeffer coming to regard Bell as his most loyal British ally in the *Kirchenkampf*, and Bell relying on Bonhoeffer as a trustworthy source on the situation in Germany.[53] Things there were going from bad to worse. A week earlier, on November 13, 1933, in the Berlin Sports Palace, the German Christian Faith Movement had staged what turned out to be a spectacular and grotesque stadium crusade for the soul of the Aryan nation. The message of Teutonic religiosity had never before enjoyed such wide exposure. Nor had it ever been so perversely enunciated.[54]

In addition to the audience of twenty thousand members, there was a contingent of foreign journalists. Before this overflow crowd, Reinhold Krause, leader of the Nazi Party in Berlin, derided the Old Testament as a book about miserly Jews, pimps, and cattle dealers that should be ripped out of the Bible and mentioned only as a foil representing a tyrannized faith.[55] Hymns, liturgy, and preaching must, Krause said in his keynote address, serve and quicken the spirit of pure Germanism. He demanded that the cross be removed from churches and that the colorful banners that draped church halls and sanctuaries, those marking feasts in the Christian calendar, be replaced by the red and black of swastikas. The Aryan paragraph must be "implemented everywhere without exception," he said, and all traces of "Jewish influences" purged from the Christian religion. Included among those texts requiring such radical redactions were the writings of the "Jew Rabbi," Paul of Tarsus.[56]

Despite the general enthusiasm for the *Führerprinzip* in the Sports Palace, the huffy Krause, a former high school teacher, delivered a screed so unremitting in its raw anti-Semitic virulence that even some German Christians walked out in disgust. The night would prove a colossal diplomatic imbroglio for Hitler's church sycophants, and Hitler lashed out, promptly relieving Krause of his duties. Though the Führer may have credited the sentiment, such raging animus on the world stage was not what was wanted for the capital preparing to host the 1936 Olympic Games. Repudiated even by Müller and other German Christians, Krause, in his bitterness, would form an organization called the German People's Church Movement. This body would take the Deutsche Christen mission of reconciling Christianity and Nazism to new, hitherto unimagined extremes of heresy, with its sole thesis that a pure German faith "means the end of the Christian church."[57] Krause's group would soon align itself with Wilhelm Hauer's German Faith Movement, in which a Teutonic-Hindu concoction of Aryanism would replace Christianity as the German *Volk*'s proper religion.

As a further consequence of such perverse extremism, the German Christian movement temporarily lost momentum among ordinary Germans, and the Confessing Church saw its membership soar to six thousand by the end of the year. But the dissenters' position would never again be as strong.

Müller and his German Christian crew were embarrassed but hardly vanquished by Krause's Sports Palace harangue. Redoubling his efforts to win back Hitler's trust, the Reich bishop would again prove his excellence as a lackey. In a bold and devious move, he consolidated the Evangelical Youth Ministry and the Hitler Youth, effectively turning every organization for young Protestant youth into a chapter of the Hitlerjugend. Hitler would be pleased with Müller's skillful implementation of this delicate maneuver, which, in fact, had been the Führer's brainchild.

The historian Doris Bergen, whose work on the "twisted cross" of Nazi religion has cast a penetrating light on the shadowy German Christian movement, once noted that the quest for racial purity was not simply a matter of ecclesial housecleaning, nor was it a mere rhetorical strategy. "Members of the movement acted on their words," Bergen observes, "and in the context of a brutal anti-Semitic state, those actions took on terrible significance. . . . Through their request for an anti-Jewish church, the German Christians endorsed, imitated, and profited from the crimes of the Third Reich."[58]

The Stuttgart-based *Deutsche Theologie* had been recently launched as the mouthpiece of the Nazi theologians, with a distinguished editorial board including such scholars as Hermann Wolfgang Beyer, Heinrich Bornkamm, Karl Fezer, Friedrich Gogarten, Emanuel Hirsch, and Gerhard Kittel. A special issue on Martin Luther had appeared in November.[59] The editors did not state as their purpose the promotion of Nazi theology. Actually, in contrast to the vitriol of Krause and an emerging neo-pagan faction their mission now seemed conservative—saving time-honored Lutheran practices from the twin toxins of popular rage and dissident church protest. Their aim was to create a safe home for traditionalists within the mercurial Reich Church.

For the short term at least, Müller not only survived the Sports Palace debacle but emerged a hardened and more cunning leader of the Reich Church. Fortified in this way, he next set his sights directly on the Confessing Church and its brash young spokesman in England. Indeed, far from being the wilderness in which Barth had imagined Bonhoeffer to be wandering, London would equip the young pastor with a host of new relationships and resources that would make him a much greater thorn in the side of the Reich Church. By the summer of 1934, support for the dissenting church among the German congregations of England would be consolidated, and Bonhoeffer would skillfully use his influence in ecumenical circles to frame the *Kirchenkampf* as a choice between the true church (the Confessing Church) and the cult of the Antichrist (the German Christians). But he would first have to contend with the angry clerics manning the bishopric in Berlin.

For when Müller finally understood what was happening in November 1933, he unleashed a pack of ecclesial watchdogs to England. Their mission was to make a quick assessment, contain the damage, and bring Bonhoeffer to heel. They also had ambitions to persuade the leaders in the Church of England, in particular the college of bishops, of their responsibility to attend Müller's installation as the first Reich bishop, the ceremony scheduled for December 3, 1933, at the Berlin Cathedral. (In fact, turbulence in the church was such that it would not take place until September 23 of the following year.)[60]

Leading the pack was the thirty-four-year-old Joachim Hossenfelder, the "brisk, slick, pomaded" bishop of Berlin-Brandenburg.[61] A member of the Nazi Party and a spirited ambassador of the German Christians, Hossenfelder liked to describe the salvation of the German people through Hitler as proof of God's reality in the modern world. In fact, he had been the one who proudly called the German Christian

Faith to "the storm troopers of the church," declaring that both forces struggled in the spirit of National Socialism "for the manly external and internal realization of the Third Reich."[62] Trailing just behind Hossenfelder was Karl Fezer, a scholar of solid mediocrity who in addition to serving on the editorial board of *Deutsche Theologie* had, in the wake of his endorsement of Hitler, been promoted to full professor at Tübingen and then to rector of the university.[63] As a result of the national "coordination" of civil society—the "bringing into line" with Nazi ideals—venerable theological faculties such as Tübingen and Berlin were now staffed, with a few notable exceptions, largely by second-rate talents. But these Nazi clerical grandees would persuade no one of the rightness of their cause, and their mission to win British sympathies proved a complete failure.

There was no meeting of the minds at Lambeth Palace. The mid-level church administrators to whom the Germans were allowed perfunctory access refused any part of the German Christian movement—indeed, they were offended by the presumption that they might feel otherwise. The presiding archbishop of Canterbury had been briefed by George Bell, but he needed no warning that the Reich Church would exploit even the most informal acknowledgment. And so no official meeting with leaders of the church hierarchy was granted, and the gates of Lambeth Palace remained closed to the delegation. At a gathering hosted by the German ambassador, Hossenfelder rambled incoherently about the German genius to the few Britons in attendance. So obtuse was the man that he couldn't comprehend the repeated refusal of his offer to make a speech in a German parish hall where the trustees included "a number of prominent Jews." The mission's sole bit of good luck was that the English press took almost no notice of it.[64]

On the eve of their return to Berlin, the Germans were feted by members of the Oxford Group. Its founder, an eccentric American evangelist named Frank Buchman, was driven by the dual mission of persuading young men to abstain from masturbation and leading Hitler to Jesus. Believing he could turn Hitler into a born-again Christian if only he could meet him, Buchman was desperate for an introduction to the Führer—hence the party for his emissaries.[65] The German leader, it may be said, appealed to the American's ideal of rugged individualism: Hitler seemed to Buchman a man's man, who by sheer will had concentrated epochal powers at his command. He was missing only one thing: a personal relationship with Christ. Buchman was awed at the potential of "a twice-born Führer": if it could only be made to happen, "every last, bewildering problem" would be solved overnight.[66]

Such a notion was ideal fodder for Reinhold Niebuhr's brand of moral realism. Upon reading in the *New York World-Telegram* of Buchman's campaign to convert Hitler, he called it the "most unbelievably naïve" thing he had ever heard. Bonhoeffer also thought it perverse to imagine that one could change Hitler by praying for his soul.[67] In any case, the Berlin delegation's evening with Buchman left both parties frustrated: Hossenfelder would not promise Buchman a hearing with the Führer, and the Germans learned to their dismay that the Oxford Group had not a shred of influence over the Church of England.[68] Hossenfelder and Fezer returned to Berlin anticipating Bishop Müller's certain fury.

Müller came to understand that muting Bonhoeffer's dissident voice was vital to his own survival at the head of the Nazi church. For this purpose he now turned to Theodor Heckel, the dour, conniving head of the Church Foreign Office of the German Evangelical Church, the man in charge of maintaining "unity" between the church authorities at home and German congregations abroad. Heckel had collaborated with Müller in drafting the muzzling decree of January 4, 1934, which made criticism of the Nazi state and church a violation of ecclesial law, subject to prosecution in the civil courts.[69]

Heckel had once felt kindly toward Bonhoeffer. In fact, he had supported the Young Reformation Movement, another seedling of the Confessing Church, when it was founded in 1933. But as would happen with other Bavarian churchmen promoted to Berlin, Heckel's admiration for Bonhoeffer's intellect and skill eventually gave way to envy. And the young pastor's blithe disregard of the muzzling decree did not help matters, inflaming Heckel's natural resentment of Berlin elitism. Proceeding under his new policing powers—and a fantasy of greater powers still—Heckel declared Bonhoeffer a *Staatsfeind*, an enemy of the state. He would now act against the young dissident with the full resources of his office.[70]

Upon his arrival in London, Heckel summoned Bonhoeffer to a meeting at the Savoy Hotel, where the bishop was to be found flanked by two brownshirts. Deploying pedantic legalism, thinly veiled threats, and outright lies, Heckel laid down the law, repeating the stern warnings he'd issued in his letter of the month before: all German pastors serving abroad must affirm their "*unconditional loyalty to the Third Reich and its Führer.*" He noted Bonhoeffer's failure to comply with the decree and accused him of "intrigue involving criticism of state, Volk, or movement." Any further criticism, he warned, would be considered an attack on the authority of the Third Reich and treated as criminal, as treason. Then, somewhat more paternally, he allowed that it was not for the younger man to reason why, but "to carry out his duties in a forthright manner," like a good soldier.[71]

The worst of it from Bonhoeffer's point of view was Heckel's utter failure even to acknowledge the theological tension at the heart of the church struggle. Realizing he had been summoned for nothing more than a bureaucratic dressing down, with an ultimatum attached, Bonhoeffer walked out of the Savoy, vowing never to waste any more time with this "fine pack of scoundrels."[72]

Like Hossenfelder before him, Heckel would return to Berlin empty-handed. Not only were the gates of Lambeth Palace shut in his face, but a minister of his own confession had defied the bishop's effort at correction.[73] Having stormed the shores of England to strong-arm an oath of allegiance from the German pastors abroad, he left with a vote of no confidence from Reich Bishop Müller and a six-point repudiation of his failed mission.[74]

The gates at Lambeth would eventually admit one German pastor, but not one Müller would approve. The next month, the archbishop of Canterbury invited Bonhoeffer to join him for tea. Cosmo Gordon Lang, born in 1864, could hardly be counted among the most dynamic or inspirational primates in the history of the Anglican Communion. His enthronement, it was said, had "pleased everybody, and alarmed nobody." Lang had spent two decades as the archbishop of York, showing himself an efficient and amiable member of the House of Lords with a generously Anglo-Catholic sensibility. "But by the time he succeeded Randall Davidson at Canterbury in 1928, he appeared tired and slow of movement, and he was often incapacitated by illness. He had not, however, lost his vigorous commitment to ecumenical unity."[75] Lang was proud to be numbered among the architects of the 1920 "Appeal to All Christian People," issued by the Lambeth Conference.[76]

The archbishop's interview with Bonhoeffer lasted forty-five minutes. Bonhoeffer gave Lang an account of recent developments in Germany, whereupon Lang assured him that the Church of England would never recognize the authority of the Reich Church. Nor would he be receiving Heckel or any Nazi official. Lang was appalled at what he heard and expressed the hope that he and Bonhoeffer would meet again soon. In the coming months—in letters to the London *Times*, in speeches, and in communiqués with German ambassadors—the archbishop would reiterate his profound "disgust at the treatment of Christians and Jews in Nazi Germany."[77]

The sympathetic exchange with a global Christian leader came as much-needed encouragement. These were difficult days, overhung with uncertainty. To be sure, Bonhoeffer felt little anxiety in disobeying the Reich bishop's gag order or in being branded a disgrace to his Holy Order. He had always found church bureaucrats an annoying lot. And he was truly indignant that men of such colossal mediocrity had risen to positions of leadership. Still, though now become a ship of fools, the German church had always been his religious home. Christian worship was necessarily communal from its inception. Despite Anglican support and ecumenical solidarities, this break must have felt like something of a step into the abyss. But he'd been left no choice.

By May 1934, the official crest of the Reich Church hierarchy had been transformed: in addition to a new cross, the Luther rose—the sacred heart enfolded into a white rose—was now entwined with the swastika. In June, Müller announced that charges of high treason would be brought against any minister who discussed German church matters with non-German churchmen. Effectively an intensification of the muzzling decree, this move directly targeted members of the Confessing Church, making their ecumenical efforts a crime punishable by death.

Bonhoeffer had not at first planned to attend the Ecumenical Youth Conference on the Danish island of Fanö. But his recent encounters with the "scoundrels" from Berlin had convinced him that the German Evangelical Church could no longer claim legitimate ecclesial authority. And so he secured a place on the program. After then sparring with the conference planners over their decision to seat the German Christians as well, he was granted a second time slot, whereupon he decided to attend despite the presence of the Nazi delegation. He had for some time looked forward to a three-week holiday in Friedrichsbrunn; now he would also make his first trip to Denmark. At Fanö he would declare that the time had come for the international churches to "state openly which of the two 'churches' in Germany" they were prepared to recognize. Neutrality was no longer a tenable option.[78]

The loathsome presence of the Reich Church delegation would prove a blessing in disguise; the appearance of Heckel and his stammering band would do more for the cause of the dissenting church than even Bonhoeffer's eloquent pronouncements. The delegation's performance was a study in absurdist stagecraft. Heckel got the show started with a presentation that ran for an hour and a half; piling one sentence fragment upon another, his paper naturally omitted to mention the German church conflict. Two days later, he took to the stage again with a talk on "church and state," which the *Times* would describe as "a brilliant ascent into the stratosphere of pure ecclesiastical dogma."[79] It was not meant as a compliment.

When word reached church headquarters in Berlin that Heckel had fallen flat, Müller hurriedly deputized an untested colleague and church scrivener named Birnbaum, putting him on the next plane to Copenhagen. Unfortunately, in their rushed attempt at damage control Müller's crew did not think through the logistics. Copenhagen lies some three hundred kilometers east of Fanö; arriving in the capital late in the day, Birnbaum missed the last scheduled flight to the island. Phone calls back to Berlin produced a flood of recriminations, telegrams, and more phone calls, before, finally, a seaplane was chartered to convey Birnbaum to the meeting.

Coming in as the conference was winding down, the delegate from Berlin discovered that he had been allotted just fifteen minutes to speak. In his diary, Rieger describes Birnbaum's speech, delivered in halting, percussive exhalations, as "an absurd rigmarole about his personal experiences with people who became Christians because they were National Socialists."[80] As a novice, Birnbaum may have felt relieved not to have been granted more time to embarrass himself, but the fifteen-minute slot was clearly another affront to Müller—further proof that the ecumenical churches did not appreciate the complexities of the German situation.

In fact, they understood only too well. On August 30, 1934, the conference repudiated the assertions of the German Christians, resolving that autocratic church rule, coercion, and the suppression of free discussion "were incompatible with the true nature of the Christian Faith." It was with "grave anxiety" that they remarked the German Christian assault on the basic principles of Christian freedom. The delegates further pledged "to maintain close fellowship" only with the dissident church and to offer its ministers prayers and heartfelt support.[81]

However, the statement stopped short of recognizing the Confessing Church as the true German Protestant communion. For the time being, they would affirm the Confessing Church as a courageous and prophetic movement, though not as a legitimate church body. This demurral came about despite one of the most stirring—indeed, prophetic—addresses of Bonhoeffer's ministry, which he delivered with perfect confidence, as though he were the official spokesman of the movement.

In his room, the windows open to the brisk North Sea air, he poured his heart and soul into the speeches. The address, titled "The Church and the Peoples of the World," was delivered on August 28, 1934. It was more sermon than lecture, based on a verse in Psalm 85, "I will hear what God the Lord will speak: for he will speak peace unto his people, and to his saints." Bonhoeffer expounded on the community of Christ beyond nation, race, and tribe—an "ecumenical Christendom." He spoke of a day when the church would resolve to become an agent of the promised peace rather than another force of violence. He spoke of communities that had been formed by the ethic of Christ, times when Christians obeyed Christ's commandments "without question." And he imagined a day when the church would again be, as in apostolic times, "at one and the same time in all peoples, yet beyond all boundaries, whether national, political, social, or racial." He was speaking not so much to the tragedy unfolding in Germany as to the larger problem of the church's loss of the primal spiritual unity upon which it was founded. Ecumenism was in this sense not so much a progressive notion as a pervasive orthodox one, an acknowledgment that all who profess Christ are bound together "through the commandment of the one Lord Christ, whose Word they hear, more inseparably than men are bound by all the ties of common history, of blood, of class and of language." For such a church, "peace is more holy, more inviolable than the most revered words and works of the natural world." Such people are unashamed to call for eternal peace, indeed see no "escape from the commandment of Christ [that they] be instruments of peace."

"The hour is late. The world is choked with weapons, and dreadful is the mistrust peering from all men's eyes. The trumpets of war may blow tomorrow," he pleaded. "Who knows if we shall see each other again in another year? What are we waiting for?

"Peace must be dared," he said. "Peace is the great venture."[82]

Christ is peace.

The address was answered with a standing ovation, but there was no official endorsement of any of its recommendations.

T he week in Denmark was a strange blend of languor and intensity. The climate and landscape beckoned one to idleness, but sessions ran into the late hours, the days beginning with morning prayers an hour before breakfast. Bonhoeffer found very little time to write letters, but a small collection of black-and-white photographs survive, attesting to the ambience. In one, Bonhoeffer, looking vigorous and tanned, sits atop a dune in a linen jacket and narrow dark tie, rehearsing his talk, as two men sit attentively on either side, and two women lean comfortably against the warm sand to his right.[83] He would still be revising that address minutes before taking the podium.[84] One Swedish student is reported to have asked him what he would do if Germany declared war on the Allies. Bonhoeffer let a handful of sand run through his fingers and then turned directly to the student. "I pray that God will give me the strength not to take up arms," Bonhoeffer said.[85]

Together with his meditations on eternal peace Bonhoeffer offered

DIETRICH BONHOEFFER WITH THEOLOGICAL STUDENTS
ON THE SAND DUNES NEAR FANÖ, DENMARK, IN 1934

concrete proposals for the churches in western Europe. The villainy of the Reich Church would not be obscured in the vapors of an eschatological dreamscape. He proposed the formation of church groups that would, he hoped, create legally acceptable alternatives to military service; others to study the factors leading to war and to work to neutralize them; groups to propagate the language of peace through teaching, preaching, and prayer, making such language a more routine feature of the church's distinctive voice; and groups to promote Bible study in full awareness of the commandments of Christ. In what would prove his first major pacifist pronouncement, Bonhoeffer, refusing the Christian tradition of just war first expounded by Augustine, would declare that "[f]or Christians, any military service except in the ambulance corps, and any preparation for war, is forbidden."[86]

A cadre of German students that would come to be known as the Deutsches Fanö carried this message from Denmark to Berlin, Tübingen, and Heidelberg, circulating and discussing the speeches and addresses of that summer. It was heartening to Bonhoeffer to see young men and women so eager "to take seriously the Christian message of peace," particularly considering "the steadily growing martial spirit" that prevailed in the university faculties and the churches. The Fanö group might well prove the seeds of a renewed church, he thought. During a visit to Berlin after the Danish meeting, Bonhoeffer was introduced to "students of various nationalities" meeting "under the auspices of the youth commission" in the house of a Swedish minister named Forell. Only a "clear and uncompromising stand," Bonhoeffer told them, could expose the heresy of "the conservative Christianity" serving not Jesus Christ but the "present Reichswehr (imperial defenses) and its industrial regime." He would be delighted to discover in Berlin "that a group of young Christians are seriously considering the possibility of starting a small Christian community, some kind of settlement inspired by the Sermon on the Mount." The same group, he added, "would also make a definite stand for peace by conscientious objection." The question then remains to only answer whether, in case of war, service [even] in a sanitary unit would be justifiable in Christian terms."[87]

Paul Althaus, the esteemed pastor-professor turned zealous Nazi, responded by saying he would not stand by idly and let Bonhoeffer promote "his Christian radicalism." In the name of Jesus and the Sermon on the Mount, Bonhoeffer, he charged, seemed intent on confusing Christians "with regard to the law, nation, government, and military service."[88] Such a piety lacking toughness and strength must be firmly rejected.

Of course, Bonhoeffer had not always been sympathetic to the philosophy of pacifism. As an assistant pastor in Barcelona, one will remember, he had blithely intoned the rhetoric of blood, soil, and fatherland, paying homage to the old Germanic war gods. Far from merely hewing to the tradition of Augustine and Aquinas, and their view of just war in the case of self-defense, he had also claimed territorial expansion and conquest as legitimate *casus belli*. The influence of his brothers, so disillusioned by the Great War, had not altered his views. But more recently, friendships with Christian pacifists like Lasserre and Hildebrandt, and of course his encounters a few years earlier with Christian peacemakers in America, had inspired new ways of reading scripture. These encounters had awakened Bonhoeffer to an intimate relationship with scripture that privileged Jesus' moral teachings and its fierce summation in the Sermon on the Mount.

To be sure, Karl Barth had written a fairly vertiginous account of the righteousness of God and the quaking of the tower of Babel, and despite the complicated and sometimes contentious exchanges of the two men, Barth, Bonhoeffer believed, had discerned the theological quandary of the hour with razor-sharp clarity. How might it be possible to experience the reality of God amid the prevailing idolatry? And who is God? Is God the continuation of blood and soil, humanity rendered in a loud voice? It was Barth's defiant "*Nein!*" that first shook Bonhoef-

fer out of his Protestant liberal slumber. No—this was the way of idolatry. God is the One who comes to humanity from a "wholly different"
source, Barth claimed, whose history reproaches "with its own distinct
grounds, possibilities and hypotheses," who lifts our sights "to the open
portals of a new world," to the peace that passes all understanding.
Still, Bonhoeffer pressed Barth's triumphal narrative into the straighter
way of the cross and the intimacy of discipleship. Obedience to Christ's
peace commandment represented the opposite of Nazism.[89]

By the time he came to Fanö his pacifism was fully formed. The
physicist Herbert Jehle, who'd attended Bonhoeffer's 1932 lectures and
heard him preach at Berlin's Dreifaltigkeitskirche, called on him often
in London. "I was in Cambridge and came to visit . . . I'm sure 30 to 50
times," Jehle said. "I became a pacifist exclusively through Dietrich."[90]
Upon returning to Germany after his Cambridge postdoctorate, Jehle
would join the Quakers, rejecting numerous employment offers in the
rearmament industry, before at last declaring himself a conscientious
objector. By 1940, this tall lanky scholar with "an ample golden beard
and a sparkle in his eyes"—the son of a decorated German general,
to boot—was arrested and sent to the Gurs concentration camp. He
would survive the imprisonment, later immigrating to America.

Bonhoeffer's London calling notwithstanding, on July 4, 1934, members of the Old Prussian Union Council of Brethren who were
unhappy by their regional church's alignment with the Reich Church
approached him with the offer to direct a seminary in Finkenwalde,
near the city of Stettin, some one hundred kilometers northwest of
Berlin. Bonhoeffer had long lamented the German educational system
for clergy, his view of academic theology routinely expressed in meta-
phors of confinement and asphyxiation. But his embrace of the offer
was no doubt inspired by the strenuous Christological disciplines that
now accompanied all his comings and goings.

To support the training of ministers drawn from the ranks of men
who hadn't been nazified, the nascent Confessing Church had adopted
five languishing seminaries mostly in rural areas just slightly beyond
the scope of Gestapo surveillance. Funded by the direct contributions
of sympathetic Christians, these institutions were able to maintain an
unusual degree of independence from the state as "Nazi-free spaces." It
seemed to Bonhoeffer a supremely worthy purpose, and a logical next
step in the mission still revealing itself to him. Bonhoeffer asked the parish council for a six-month leave of absence, explaining that he needed
"to answer a call from the leadership of the Confessing Church," and
his request was granted.[91]

To his older brother Karl-Friedrich, a committed atheist and anti-Nazi, he offered a frank explanation. "Perhaps I seem to you rather fanatical," Bonhoeffer said. "I myself sometimes worry about that. But to be honest, I know that the day when I become more 'reasonable,' I shall have to chuck my entire theology. When I first started in theology, my idea of it was quite different—rather more academic, probably. Now it has turned into something else altogether. But I do believe that at last, for the first time in my life, I am on the right track. And I am often quite happy about that. My only anxiety is that fear of what others may think will bog me down and keep me from moving forward. I think I am right to say that true inner clarity and honesty will come only by starting to take the Sermon on the Mount seriously. In it alone is the force that can blow all this hocus-pocus sky-high. . . . The restoration of the church must surely depend on a new kind of monasticism, which has nothing in common with its former self but proposes a life of uncompromising discipleship, following Christ according to the Sermon on the Mount. I believe the time has come to gather the people together and do this."[92]

In October, Bonhoeffer told Bishop Bell he wanted to visit as many alternative seminaries and peace centers as he could during his final months in England and to take a few days to hike in the Lake Country or climb Ben Nevis in Scotland. For the work ahead, he was eager to learn more about Anglican and Free Church experiments in Christian community, and "very anxious to have some acquaintance with our methods," observed Bell, who graciously made the necessary introductions. Among those Bonhoeffer sought out was Father E. K. Talbot, the superior of the Community of the Resurrection in Mirfield.[93] Nestled on twenty-two acres in West Yorkshire, Mirfield was an Anglican monastery operated according to a variation on the Benedictine Rule. Life revolved around the daily office—in the course of which the brothers prayed through the entirety of the acrostic Psalm 119—as well as work on behalf of the poor and unemployed. Five of the six founders of Mirfield were members of the Christian Social Union, and their judgment had figured prominently in "the decision to settle in the industrial north, between Wakefield and Huddersfield."[94] Bonhoeffer's experience there would deepen his "already strong attachment to the Psalter," and in particular to Psalm 119, the longest of all the songs, which "increasingly held him captive with its reiterated plea of the one who wants only to be allowed to live as a sojourner on the earth" and to fulfill the "beloved commands of the Lord."[95]

The tour of peace communities and alternative seminaries also took Bonhoeffer to Charles Spurgeon's Baptist College on South Norwood

Hill, the Society of St. John the Evangelist in Oxford, the Society of the Sacred Mission in Kelham, the Quaker community of Woodbrooke in Selly Oak (which he visited twice), and Cowley. He had already seen Richmond Methodist College in the western suburbs of London the previous autumn.[96] There, a seminarian noted in his diary on October 4, 1934, the visit by "Dietrich Bonhoeffer of the University of Berlin, one of the leading young Barthian theologians and one of the most important figures in the German Church situation"; true to his reputation, the young pastor gave a "splendid talk" on those matters and others.[97]

Although they differed in their forms, tone, and sources, these communities shared a commitment to the mysteries of faith. Mirfield, Cowley, and Kelham were products of late-nineteenth-century Anglo-Catholicism.[98] Woodbrooke had been established in 1903 in Selly Oak, near Birmingham, when the chocolate magnate George Cadbury donated his estate to the Quakers to found a peace community and education center. Each had its own rule of order.

On his visit to Cowley, Bonhoeffer reached for a cigarette in his pocket only to be told that smoking was forbidden. It was startling news for one who hailed from a nation of smokers and never left home without a supply of good German tobacco. At Mirfield, on the other hand, the habit was allowed, and among the brotherhood of Kelham, where the superior was a smoker, tobacco seemed de rigueur.[99] The director of Kelham, Father Herbert Kelly, was a chain smoker of uncommon enthusiasm. His black monk's habit appeared permanently covered in gray ash, and an even stranger custom could be daily observed at his lectern, where he kept a squat metal pail holding a flammable liquid into which he frequently dipped a long wooden stick that served as an elaborate cigarette match. The chain-smoking abbot told Bonhoeffer he found the strength to traverse the ascetical way through the daily acceptance of his weakness. "I can do it, because I cannot." The answer made sense to Bonhoeffer.[100]

Bonhoeffer was pleasantly surprised to discover that some communities found virtue in spontaneity and play, regarding leisure as a means of soul craft. A photograph from Mirfield shows Bonhoeffer in a sharp tweed suit preparing to serve in a game of ping-pong.[101] At times, he seemed as thrilled by the sight of Anglican monks enjoying sport—tennis, soccer, cricket, even rugby—in the afternoon as by the solemnities of compline and the simplicity of communal life.

Not all the monastics Bonhoeffer met credited his appreciation of the cloistered life. The year before, for instance, he had crossed

BONHOEFFER PLAYING PING PONG

paths with Hardy Arnold, a member of the Bruderhof settlement, who was taking summer courses in education at the University of Birmingham. Founded in 1922 by a pacifist theologian and Anabaptist minister named Eberhard Arnold, Bruderhof was forty kilometers northeast of Frankfurt, near the German village of Hessen. There the initiates pursued a kind of Christian communism, seeking to emulate the earliest Christian communities as described in Acts: people of "one heart and mind" who were "sharing all things in common," renouncing private property and all violence or coercion.

Arnold was pleased to share the story of Bruderhof with Bonhoeffer and his two companions, Rieger and Rudolf Weckerling. As Arnold told a friend later in the day, "Bonhoeffer was so very impressed with what I had to tell him." Nonetheless he found the Berlin intellectual the least sympathetic of the three. He was put off not only by Bonhoeffer's dandyism (a whiff of preciousness, lacking a certain deference), but also by how he expressed his hopes of founding a community of brothers based entirely on the Sermon on the Mount—as if he were contemplating some enchantment or thematic work of art rather than the lived faith as Arnold understood it.[102]

To Arnold, who had spent his entire life at Bruderhof, Bonhoeffer's zeal for the monastic life seemed far too romantic: he had seen many young men entranced by the idea of community and the common purse, only to become disillusioned or distracted. Bonhoeffer was delighted when Arnold gave him a chapter from a book by his father (*Innerland: A Guide into the Heart of the Gospel*), which described the Holy Spirit as "the sap of life that brings unity to the living organism called the church."[103] But Bruderhof's peasant-agrarian mysticism was simply not what Bonhoeffer was hoping to create in northern Germany. His own vision was rather more like a monastic Friedrichsbrunn. He imagined a fellowship of men, single-minded in their ardor

PHOTOGRAPH OF BONHOEFFER
TAKEN BY ERNST CROMWELL ON
BEN NEVIS, SCOTLAND, 1935

and devotion for Jesus, sharing books and music and meals, practicing the daily hours and offering intercessory prayers, and, as needed, taking breaks for tennis or hikes or excursions to the shore, as well as evenings around the piano. It was an especially vivid way of answering the dissident call, with a perfect circle of friends, though it was not everyone's idea of orienting their lives completely to Christ.

To Julius Rieger, who accompanied Bonhoeffer on the tour, the hourly prayers, the contemplative disciplines, common-table fellowship, reading the Psalter, corporate worship, learning to see the other under the mercies of the Holy Shepherd—these practices seemed a spiritual "straight jacket." And to most of his Confessing Church colleagues, they would have seemed an antiquated frivolity. But to Bonhoeffer, who had long admired the "secret strength of silence" (among other disciplines dating from before the Reformation), and who had no fear of introspection or paradox, these practices were positively energizing. In this, too, he did not fit the mold of traditional Lutheran piety.[104]

Shortly before Christmas 1934, a letter arrived at the London parsonage addressed to "Pastor Lic. Dietrich Bonhoeffer, Esq." It was from Mahatma Gandhi. A few years earlier, in a time when he felt overwhelmed by the demands of his inner-city youth ministry, Bonhoeffer had joked with Anneliese Schnurmann, a Jewish friend who'd recently made a financial contribution to his work, that he had half a mind to take her gift and run off with it to India. Bonhoeffer had written to Gandhi earlier that year, asking advice and inquiring whether it might be possible to visit the Mahatma's Sarbamati Ashram in northwest India.[105] But he had not expected a personal reply, certainly not one addressing him as "dear friend." Gandhi advised Bonhoeffer that the answers to his questions could be found by coming to India, "the sooner the better." Of course, he and his companion, Herbert Jehle, a Quaker and physicist who had taken theology classes in Berlin, would have to cover their travel expenses, but if Bonhoeffer could manage to live on a vegetarian diet, his living costs would be next to nothing. There was also the question of "how the climate here agrees with you." These considerations aside, Gandhi promised that as long as he was not out of the country or in jail, he would find time for the German theologian.[106]

It was a generous offer considering that Gandhi was then at the height of his powers at home and abroad—Winston Churchill's snarky dismissal of the "half-naked fakir" notwithstanding. It was the most intense period of the "inter-war constitutional debate" on the future of India, leading up to the passage of the India Act of 1935, a fact surely not lost on Bonhoeffer. The wish to visit Gandhi marks a crucial stage in Bonhoeffer's growth as theologian and pastor.[107] He had read the Mahatma's memoir long before coming to England, during his time in New York City, where he'd discussed it with Lasserre, Sutz, and the Union pacifists. He "had wanted to get to know India personally," Rieger observed. He was particularly drawn to the principle of *satyagraha*, nonviolent resistance, as a complement to the Sermon on the Mount. Gandhi, Bonhoeffer came to believe, showed more respect for the teachings of Jesus than most Christians did.[108] In their works of mercy and justice, those "heathen Christians" performed acts of true grace, as Bonhoeffer explained in a London sermon on Luke 13:1–5.[109] Like Martin Luther King Jr. a generation later, Bonhoeffer was looking to Gandhi's India for more than a moral exemplar and an effective means of civil activism.

Facing the pounding waves of hypocrisy and corruption unleashed by the German Protestant Church, Bonhoeffer had begun to feel a certain fatigue with Western Christianity—even as he accepted the challenge to purge its German manifestations of so many lies.[110] "In the West Christianity is approaching its end," he lamented.[111] What had begun as longings unfulfilled by Lutheranism, leading him to the basilicas of Rome and the convents of Britain, eventually brought Bonhoeffer to a point where he seemed no longer inclined to assert the superiority of the Christian religion, at least not as it was now lived. Hence the rather paradoxical coincidence of an eagerness to meet Gandhi and the intensification of his devotion to the Sermon on the Mount as God's will.

"Christianity did in fact come from the East originally," Bonhoeffer wrote his grandmother Julie on May 22, 1934, "but it has become so westernized and so permeated by civilized thought that, as we can now see, it is almost lost to us." He further confided to her that he had by now "little confidence left in the church opposition," having decided that, in any case, the truth of Jesus Christ could best be learned through witness and righteous action—a most heterodox turn for a man formed in a confession traditionally so unified, and so dogmatic in its disdain for the value of works.[112] This most learned of Lutherans was now prepared to allow that the "heathen" Gandhi gave uncommonly vivid expression to "the strange and slow journey that leads through repentance to the new life."[113]

In the end, Bonhoeffer would forego the opportunity to visit India. The decision illuminates a fundamental tension, or perhaps more precisely a clearer sense of calling, in his outlook. Tempted though he might be to take flight to some exotic clime (which he would likely have indulged in his younger days, particularly if oppressed by the judgment of some mediocrity at the reigns of authority), he simply could not justify a sixth-month sojourn with Gandhi. For all its faults, the house of the church was indeed burning. Even if it had lost its legitimacy, he was not prepared to consign the whole body of Christ in Germany to perdition, as long as a few righteous souls, however outnumbered, remained. Abraham, after all, had persuaded the Lord to spare Sodom for the sake of ten righteous men there. Bonhoeffer could do no less for his own people. And so it was, that after eighteen months of absence and incessant reflection, the very sense of responsibility that Barth had tried to drum into him beckoned Dietrich Bonhoeffer home.

There was also the matter of a growing self-knowledge respecting his vocation. "I have always wanted to be a pastor," he had written to Barth at the beginning of his London tenure, defending his decision to answer that call. But had he?[114] As we have seen, his earliest report to his grandmother Julie expressed amazement at the volume of work involved in ministering to even a small parish.[115] He'd made himself present as required, as far as we know. He happily sang with the choir at St. Paul's and tried to improve the music at Sydenham, though with limited success. He introduced the new German hymnbook for overseas congregations and tried to attend faithfully the Monday-morning meeting of ministers of Forest Hill. He oversaw confirmation classes and performed baptisms, and also performed baptisms and also attending the parties to follow. He officiated at numerous funerals and at least one wedding. At first, it had all been rather exhilarating, allowing him to bear the cold water and drafty rooms of the parsonage.

When Julius Rieger's wife gave birth to their second child, Bonhoeffer bought the entire stock of cornflowers and marguerites in a Forest Hill florist and carried the large bouquet with him as he negotiated two tram transfers on his way to their flat. Even so, in London Bonhoeffer would succumb to weariness at pastoral ministry, a feeling he had previously managed to avoid. The last-minute scurrying to find "flower-arrangers for the altar or someone to pump the organ," or to recruit actors for the nativity plays and other pageants; the constant haggling over church reports and budgets—there seemed no end to such drudgery. Increasingly the demands of shepherding a flock of German expatriates felt like a great distraction from a truer, more urgent calling.[116]

For fourscore years now, the Barmen Declaration, primarily the work of Barth during a synod of the Confessing Church held May 29–31, 1934, in the city of Barmen-Wuppertal in Rhine-Westphalia, has served the Protestant world as an inspiring example of radical Christian conviction and courageous dissent, a ray of light in those darkest of times. In his classic *Creeds of the Churches: A Reader in Christian Doctrine from the Biblical to the Present*, the scholar John H. Leith calls it "a witness, a battle cry."[117] The London *Times* ran the full text on June 4, less than a week after the synod concluded, and translations soon followed in newspapers and church periodicals throughout western Europe and the English-speaking world. Bonhoeffer had skipped the conference but signed the declaration. But even as he promoted the declaration to his ecumenical allies, he remained suspicious of many of his cosignatories.

He'd seen the dilution from which such group statements typically suffered. The preceding autumn, he had abruptly abandoned work on the Bethel Confession after discovering that all references to the Aryan paragraph and the Jewish people had been omitted from the final draft. The Barmen Declaration was in some ways just a forthright and single-minded affirmation of the Lordship of Jesus Christ according to scripture and tradition: " 'I am the way, and the truth, and the life; no one comes to the Father, but by me.' (John 14.6). 'Truly, truly, I say to you, he who does not enter the sheepfold by the door, but climbs in by another way, that man is a thief and a robber. . . . I am the door; if anyone enters by me, he will be saved.' (John 10:1, 9)." But it was also an exercise in subversive indirection. Reflecting on John 14:6, for instance, it says, "Jesus Christ, as he is attested to us in Holy Scripture, is the one Word of God whom we have to hear, and whom we have to trust and obey in life and in death. We reject the false doctrine that the Church could and should recognize as a source of its proclamation, beyond and besides this one Word of God, any other events, powers, historic figures and truths as God's revelation."[118] It was bold as far as it went. And yet in Bonhoeffer's estimation, the statement remained intolerably evasive on the concrete issues, never once mentioning the Aryan paragraph, just as years later the Confessing Church would demur on the burning of synagogues, the deportation of Jews and other non-Aryans to the concentration camps, or the extermination of people with physical or mental disabilities.

Bonhoeffer did not hold Barth solely responsible for this demurral on concrete applications. The master's articulation of Christ's Lordship was principled and daring. It no doubt unleashed iconoclastic energies; if Christ is Lord, Hitler is not. Still, in Bonhoeffer's judgment the extraordinary circumstances called for more, especially on the "Jewish question," which had been sometimes referred to as the "Jewish Problem." Barth would later allow that his omitting to mention it or the Aryan paragraph had been calculated to maximize support among the delegates: no text foregrounding these contentious issues, he explained, "would have been acceptable even to the Confessing Church, given the atmosphere at the time."[119] Still, he admitted that the matter could have been handled better.

And Barth's calculations were not merely concerned with whipping up support. He had been put under house arrest earlier in the year in Bonn, where he had taught since 1930, and his days as a professor at a German university were numbered. Bonhoeffer understood the limitations under which the Swiss theologian was operating.

Bonhoeffer was less forgiving, however, of another type of "dissident" that gravitated toward the Barmen Synod—the kind that found Barth's abstracted theology a convenient excuse for avoiding hard realities and choices. Barmen had exposed one of the Confessing Church's dirty little secrets: some of its members were card-carrying members of the Nazi Party who were merely put off by the crude pronouncements of Reich Bishop Müller's bumptious lackeys. The "naive, starry-eyed idealists like Niemöller," Bonhoeffer said, "still think they are the real National Socialists."[120] Though Niemöller would soon become one of the German resistance's most recognizable faces, Bonhoeffer saw through the Dahlem cleric's delusional hope of preserving the sacred freedoms of the church while affirming the political authority of Hitler.

From the perspective of men like that, Barmen's insistent focus on the theme of Lordship was palatable as the least radical reaction to awkward circumstances. It offered the thunder of righteousness without precipitating irreconcilable schism in the communion.

Not that it was entirely toothless. The declaration did refute many of the German Christian teachings, its six theses affirming the primacy of the traditional confessions and scripture. There was also a repudiation of Nazi interference in church governance, an absolute call for independence from the state's "ideological and political convictions." Finally, the declaration unambiguously rejected the Führer principle, the very foundation of the dictatorship. But in sum Barmen never amounted to more than a statement for *potential* political resistance, as Victoria Barnett has carefully shown in her definitive study of the Confessing Church, *For the Soul of My People*. It illuminated what could be seen as "a first step" toward a true confrontation but did not in itself constitute real defiance.[121]

Ultimately, Bonhoeffer would be glad to have skipped the Barmen Synod. For him, dogmatic proclamation would never be enough, and he believed that every confession of Christ as Lord must bear concretely on the immediate work of peace. Obedience could not be separated from confession. The kingdom of heaven does not suffer lip service.

Bonhoeffer would countenance no strategic compromise. He would stand or fall as a true dissident, certain of his judgment that the German Protestant Church had forfeited its membership in the body of Christ, and he engaged the church crisis from this radical position. "Those who knowingly separate themselves from the Confessing Church in Germany, separate themselves from salvation," Bonhoeffer said.[122] As he told Henri-Louis Henriod, secretary general of the World Alliance in Geneva, the Confessing Church must affirm and boldly act upon its claim of being the "*only theologically and legally legitimate Evangelical Church in Germany*."[123] For the hour was late, and "the lines have been drawn somewhere else entirely," Bonhoeffer said.[124] "And while I'm working with the church opposition with all my might, it's perfectly clear to me that *this* opposition is only a very temporary transitional phase on the way to an opposition of a very different kind, and that very few of those involved in this preliminary skirmish are going to be there for that second struggle."[125] The second struggle would be for regeneration, a new way of being Christian, which he believed demanded a modern monasticism, and it would be finally for conspiracy and tyrannicide: "I believe that all of Christendom should be praying with us for the coming of resistance 'to the point of shedding blood' and for the finding of people who can suffer it through. Simply suffering is what it will be about, not parries, blows, or thrusts such as may still be allowed and possible in the preliminary battles; the real struggle that perhaps lies ahead must be one of simply suffering through in faith."[126] It was with this understanding—that German Christians had made a Faustian bargain with Hitler—that Bonhoeffer had titled one of his sermons "The Church Is Dead."

Perhaps he meant only the German Protestant Church. For Bonhoeffer placed a great burden on the ecumenical movement to carry high the cross and lead the nations toward peace and a lasting fellowship. As he said in Denmark, "Only the one great Ecumenical Council of the Holy Church of Christ can speak out so that the world, though it gnash its teeth, will have to hear, and the peoples will rejoice as the Church of Christ in Christ's name takes weapons from their sons' hands, forbids war, and proclaims the peace of Christ against the raging world."[127] In the late summer of 1934, on the windswept island of Fanö, he had dared to imagine a world thus inundated by joyous evangelical fervor. His words were sublime and subversive, a cathedral of solemn hopes rising above the clamorous earth. But the burden of creating it was to prove more than the ecumenical church could bear. He would come to see that he had asked too much of this world, was too quick to pronounce the last word. Events would soon deliver him to a chastened hope for "something greater than the half-spoken word, not the final and decisive word, but the word before the last."[128]

"Perhaps this will amaze you," Bonhoeffer wrote to Sutz, "[but] it is my belief that the Sermon on the Mount will be the deciding word on this whole affair."[129]

On February 11, 1935, the church council of St. Paul's, Sydenham, convened for a quarterly meeting. Following a reading from scripture and a prayer, the minutes were signed and approved. Then the treasurer presented the account books, which were examined and found to be in order. Bonhoeffer asked that a special collection for winter aid be approved; German refugees were coming to England in ever-larger numbers, and the need was great. The pastor then requested six months of leave "to answer a call from the leadership of the Confessing Church in Germany to set up a theological seminary." The request was met with the council's full forbearance; it was decided that the leave would run from March 15 to September 15, for which Bonhoeffer offered heartfelt thanks. "The meeting was adjourned with a prayer at 8:30 p.m."[130]

CHAPTER TEN

1935–1937

~

"A New Kind of Monasticism"

In April of 1935, Dietrich Bonhoeffer arrived at the seacoast town of Zingst. It was hardly a terra incognita. He had spent summer holidays with his family near the Baltic Sea and later, as an undergraduate, trekked with classmates through Lübeck, Timmendorf, Plön, and along the trails of Dithmarschen, where the land is flat and green. And so, quite naturally, as he pondered where to set his experiment in evangelical monasticism, his musings led him to the sparse places of the northern shores, the vast inlands and the endless plains that dissolved into the horizon.[1] It was here that he would establish a seminary for preachers of the Confessing Church.

He was not unaware of the venture's eccentricity. As Bonhoeffer confessed to his agnostic brother Karl-Friedrich, it bothered him "that you really find all these ideas of mine completely mad": the restoration of the church, a new monasticism, a life of uncompromising discipleship "according to the Sermon on the Mount."

The communities Bonhoeffer had visited in England were housed in stately manors on well-kept grounds, with funds from church trusts and philanthropic societies supporting them. The first class of what would officially be known as the Emergency Teaching Seminary of the Confessing Church, on the other hand, was initially lodged in an unheated timber-framed structure surrounded by windswept outbuildings and low-thatched huts that looked like outcroppings of the craggy coast. Bonhoeffer could not have been more pleased with the arrangements. The sand dunes, only a hundred meters away, were the perfect setting for devotional readings, morning prayers, and afternoon naps. When the weather turned warm enough, Bonhoeffer would reconvene classes to a hollow in the dunes and lead a discussion on the day's readings or speak on scripture and doctrine accompanied by the rhythms of the sea nearby. One student recalled a day when Bonhoeffer abandoned the curriculum altogether and instead conducted a choral piece for four voices by Josquin des Prez.[2]

Across the channel to the east lay the island of Hiddensee and the greater expanse of Rügen beyond. The Bodden chain, the Fischland-Darss Peninsula, and the fortressed town of Barth framed the southern horizon.[3]

But warm days were few and far between on Europe's northern coasts. A clear June morning might yield suddenly to gray sheets of rain and bracing winds. By summer's end, huts warmed only by the sun were uninhabitable. It became obvious to Bonhoeffer and everyone with him that life in the rugged Zingsthof would not be feasible beyond September. And so he and his twenty-three students decamped to a local youth hostel to plan the next move. It was not long before providence smiled on them. Nearby in Pomerania—the Baltic south-coastal region lying between the Recknitz River near Stralsund and the mouth of the Vistula River, near the port city of Gdańsk—a shuttered school for preachers had become available. The village itself, Finkenwalde, lay just east of the Oder River, 250 kilometers northeast of Berlin and 380 kilometers north of Bieslou.[4] From the city of Stettin (now Szczecin, Poland), it was a half-hour drive, or one stop on the eastbound train. The school was set on thirty well-tended acres. It had proper classrooms and reliable heating. In close proximity there was also the abandoned, ramshackle estate of the von Katte family. Bonhoeffer liked that, too: "Simple but on a grand scale, near the forest" was how he described it.[5]

AS THE DIRECTOR OF THE NEW CONFESSING
CHURCH SEMINARY IN ZINGST
ON THE BALTIC SEA

Everyone agreed that the central room, with its large stone fireplace, would serve as the common room; and on either side, a lecture hall and the refectory. The main building of the seminary was well constructed and spacious but in a shabby state—a "veritable pigsty," one student complained. And so the seminarians, most of them in their twenties and from rural parishes, rolled up their sleeves and went to work cleaning and renovating. They scrubbed the floors, painted the "stained and peeling walls, washed the dirty windows and repaired the broken ones, mended the roof and the cracked plaster on the ceilings, and overhauled the plumbing." Outside they worked hard to rescue not only the garden but the house itself from the encroaching weeds and brush, which had crept up the windows. Bonhoeffer instructed the men to set aside one corner of the yard as a vegetable garden and assigned a group to hoe and plant.[6] The men also transformed the gym into a chapel with "whitewash, wood from packing cases and hessian," and across the wall they draped a banner with the Greek word "*Hapax*" in gold letters: "Once and for all."[7]

Bonhoeffer's friends, colleagues, and family responded generously to his petitions for help with the restoration. The Protestant congregation in the nearby village of Stolp donated the tables for the seminar room. The chairs came from members of the Confessing Church in Köslin. And the founder made his personal library available to the students, with the exception of books he himself had written (most students would complete their tuition never knowing that Bonhoeffer had published two important monographs). In his own way of helping the monkish evangelicals, Karl Bonhoeffer bought his son a new 1936 Audi convertible—an Auto Union, to be exact, the precursor to the German brand—which would serve him well.

Bonhoeffer was notably upbeat about the progress when writing to his British acquaintance Ernst Cromwell on July 2, 1935: "We managed to put the house here in order by ourselves, without outside help, and to equip it, for the time being, for our work. Farms in the countryside have been sending us all sorts of food stuffs. We could have made good use of your help these days! Now we have a great cook, aged 78, and two unemployed 14 or 15-year-old-boys to help her."[8]

On a warm and clear Sunday in late September 1935, a Prussian aristocrat named Ruth von Kleist-Retzow arrived for the morning service at Finkenwalde, accompanied by six children, ranging in age from ten to seventeen—two were her own, two were grandchildren of Otto von Bismarck, and two were from the family of Hans-Werner von Wedemeyer, who would one day become Bonhoeffer's kinsman, almost. In a simple Geneva gown, with his Luther Bible tucked under his arm, Bonhoeffer greeted the visitors and ushered them to the front of the chapel.[9] Kleist-Retzow was so impressed by his preaching that she soon adopted Finkenwalde as her home parish. Within the week she had obtained copies of Bonhoeffer's sermons, articles, and books (including the two dissertations), invited him to teach confirmation classes to her nieces and nephews, and begun introducing him to other wealthy families who disliked the boorish führer. After a tour of the seminary, she arranged for the delivery of furniture, rugs, musical instruments, and a variety of other appointments, which she insisted the house needed. Concerned that Bonhoeffer himself lacked a proper work space for his writing, she converted two rooms in her nearby Restow estate into a guest suite and studio. Some historians have called Ruth von Kleist-Retzow the "matriarch of the resistance," but during the two years of the Finkenwalde community, her concern was simply to ward off all "the dangerous forces that were poised" to attack her new pastor and friend.[10]

Bonhoeffer, for his part, felt an affinity with Kleist-Retzow from the start. He appreciated her high-born Prussian sensibility, her forthrightness, and her fierce independence.[11] A woman of fervent and deliberate piety, Kleist-Retzow cared deeply about the renewal of the church and supported the neo-orthodox movement in German theology. After reading Barth's "The Christian as Witness," she said, her heart leapt with gladness. She relished her theological discussions with Bonhoeffer and was grateful for the concern he showed for her welfare. That he would grant an old lady a little room in his life seemed to her "a great gift."

Like Bonhoeffer's mother and many others in the German nobility, Kleist-Retzow saw through the artifice of the new regime and recognized the "decay at its roots." Although she had close relations fighting on behalf of the Reich, she saw their service as the dutiful expression of a by-gone martial valor. As for herself, like Bonhoeffer's grandmother, Kleist-Retzow would, if necessary, readily defy the orders of the "brown demons filling the streets."[12]

But it was faith, not birthright, from which she drew her strength. She believed firmly in a church of the pure gospel and that "suffering is victory in faith." Over the next two years, that

BONHOEFFER AND HIS NEW AUDI

conviction would be tested: she would lose her son-in-law and all four grandsons on the Russian front.[13] Her only daughter she would lose to the Nazis, after the girl became a virulent anti-Semite during her studies in Berlin.

By late June of 1935, the Emergency Pastors' Seminary, or simply Finkenwalde, was suitably restored, now resembling a hunting lodge, a more-than-comfortable home for the young director, his twenty-three charges, and Peter Onnasch, the son of the regional church superintendent, who would serve as general administrator.[14] Bonhoeffer decorated the front entry hall with reproductions of Albrecht Dürer's four apostles and "a simple but beautiful chandelier." He also hung his beloved "*brassaro*" there, the "wonderful old Spanish portrait of Christ" that he had purchased at the monastery of San Lorenzo de El Escorial during his Barcelona pastorate, the simplicity of the image always drawing him back into the sixteenth century.

He kept the original window curtains. The dining room came to resemble a monastic refectory, with two massive wooden tables and a podium for the *lectio*, the ancient monastic practice that Bonhoeffer introduced to these young Protestant men under the less papish guise of a pleasing mealtime ritual (still it elicited a smattering of complaints). Bonhoeffer made the common room the building's "crowning glory." In this spacious salon, giving onto the garden, the "brothers" conversed, played records on his gramophone, sang hymns, and, following an old Bonhoeffer family rubric, performed skits and staged musicales.[15] For these, there was live music; Bonhoeffer had succeeded in securing the donation of not one but two grand pianos. "The times when Bonhoeffer and a student sat down together to play a piano concerto," Albrecht Schönherr, one of the seminarians, recalled, "were among the highlights of our life together."[16]

Studies were conducted in groups of three. The little chambers with views of the garden, formerly used as bedrooms, were now equipped with writing desks, shelves, and chairs for this purpose. As for sleep, twenty-five cots were arranged in two rows in the large bunkroom. Bonhoeffer kept a private room above the garage with a view of the slope to the Oder Estuary.[17]

The first session at Finkenwalde began on August 26, 1935, and would continue through the second week of October. For those who had never heard Bonhoeffer speak, and even those who had known him at Friedrich-Wilhelms University (about half the class), his lectures at Finkenwalde came as a revelation. The students soon understood that "they were not there simply to learn new techniques of preaching and instruction" but as initiates into a new manner of being a Christian. Dissent and resistance, they were taught, required spiritual nourishment: prayer, Bible study, and meditation on the essential matters to expand the moral imagination. Bonhoeffer, whose insatiable hunger for intimate fellowship had led him to this lovely tract of land in upper Pomerania, now made community his art, with beauty and discipline as complementary elements. By design, each day would begin and end in quiet meditation. The brethren would rise and proceed in silence to the dining room for prayers; there, in the early-morning light, they would sit until God had spoken some word for the day into their hearts—or until a half hour had passed. Then morning praises were sung. After hymns, the men read antiphonally from the Psalter. There followed a reading from the New Testament, and prayers, sometimes from the prayer book, otherwise extemporized. Morning worship concluded with another hymn, after which, upholding the Benedictine *taciturnitas*, the men would return to their bunk room in silence to make their beds and "put their things in order."

After breakfast, devotional exercises began, with two or three men sharing a room, each in his own carrel. For the first half of this period, they were to meditate on scripture. Bonhoeffer instructed them to center their thoughts for an entire week on a single passage, not for some purpose of exegesis—as would have been expected in the universities—or even for homiletic inspiration, but "to discover what the verses had to say" in the quiet of the morning. "Is there not in these repetitions of the same thought," Bonhoeffer said, "the tremendous suggestion that every word of prayer must penetrate to a depth of the heart accessible only through ceaseless iteration?"[18]

"We were to pray over it, to think of our life in its light," one student recalled, "and to use it as a basis for intercession on behalf of our brethren, our families, and all whom we knew to be in special need or difficulty." Only then, in the late morning, did the men begin the day's academic work, assembling in the dining room for lectures and seminars. Bonhoeffer's assignments were unlike any they had been given before. "Listen to what the formularies of the sixteenth century mean for us in the twentieth," instructed one of the lessons. Or: "By way of an incisive and thoroughgoing exegesis of the opening chapters of the Book of Acts, reflect on what God wills and hopes for his church." Another: "Why is it that a Christianity expressing itself only in the spiritual realm can never be thought obedient to Christ's summons to discipleship?" Half the answer was to understand that these were not really subjective exercises; the theological turn to life required distinct interpretive skills and rhetorical effects best achieved in preaching, but there was only one right answer. Bonhoeffer asked the students to submit drafts of sermons, which he read carefully, subjecting each "to searching but brotherly criticism." He then used their drafts for group discussions on the proper role of preaching and instruction in a dissident church.

Bonhoeffer did not shy away from offering his own sermons as exemplars of the genre. Preaching meant proclaiming the Word in the clear and measured exposition of scripture. His own idiom, he felt, had evolved to the point of banishing every trace of rhetorical manipulation. With the calculated deceit of Hitler's histrionics saturating the airwaves, truth's answer demanded simplicity. Bonhoeffer preached from a deep well of refined erudition, and he would not let his voice overrun thought. He never told stories or offered anecdotes. "In spite of this, or perhaps because of it, [his sermons] were extraordinarily impressive," Schönherr recalled. "There was not one word too many. Only the matter itself was spoken, sometimes in such a compressed way that what he had to say seemed almost forced out."[19]

After morning studies, the brothers had a half hour of free time before assembling in the chapel for song. Few shared Bonhoeffer's passion for music—many were musically illiterate—but they all participated in the singing. Bonhoeffer gave them no choice. Music was the theological language par excellence. "The hymns of the ancient church, of the Reformers, of the Bohemian brethren," the songs of those "who had lived and suffered through the Thirty Years' War," especially those written by Paul Gerhardt, they "all came alive for us," Wolf-Dieter Zimmermann said, "and we felt them to be our own. They mirrored our situation, they echoed our praise, they voiced our petitions, they articulated our repentance. In this group experience the church became once again a living reality for us, without boundaries of time or place, and we became increasingly conscious of being her members, men committed to her service, come what might."[20]

An unstructured interlude between lunch and teatime would be followed by the homework period in the late afternoon, dinner, and—on most weekday evenings—special lectures and topical conversations. Bonhoeffer introduced the rite of compline, the prayers before sleep, as the bookend of the monastic day; held at nine thirty, the evening office took "much the same form" as morning prayers. The hour as described in the Roman Breviary, which Bonhoeffer had likely read, was typically divided this way: the introduction, the psalmody (often accompanied by anthems), the hymn, the *capitulum*, the response, the gospel canticle, the prayer, and the benediction. After the blessing, Bonhoeffer instructed the brothers to maintain the "great silence" until bedtime, "for God's word was to be the last of the day just as it had been the first."[21]

Often described as an illegal or underground action, the seminary at Finkenwalde nevertheless operated for a time without state opposition. The regional church that supported the school, the Old Prussian Union, included many of the congregations least hospitable to the German Christians. With the university faculties thoroughly nazified, such seminaries—especially Finkenwalde—became remarkably fertile centers of confessional theology, while they lasted. A "younger generation of theologians," wrote Bonhoeffer hopefully, longed for something more than slogans and abstractions, more than new wine in old wineskins. "The damage done to the credibility of our preaching by our life and by our [hesitation and] uncertainty," Bonhoeffer said, "compels us to think again and to embark upon new practical ventures." The church having betrayed its mission, its only renewal was in a return to first things. His hope was that Finkenwalde would flourish as a place marrying the theological quest for "concrete, down-to-earth life together" and the "common regard for the commandments."[22]

For one or two semesters, Finkenwalde students took courses in practical ministry. In addition to biblical studies and preaching, practical ministry included instruction on performing baptisms, weddings, and funerals; visiting parishioners in hospitals and at home; as well as administering church budgets and programs—all the nuts and bolts of parish life. Years earlier Bonhoeffer had made no secret of his disdain for the requirement that all university students spend a term in a preacher's seminary. He even succeeded in avoiding it himself, in recognition of "his previous scholarly training, evidenced especially in his postdoctoral thesis."[23] Now, however, he could see its value.

While Finkenwalde operated within the ecclesial structures of the German Protestant Church, the decision to study with Bonhoeffer carried real risks. Only two months after classes began, the Old Prussian Union Council decided that the Confessing Church might call itself a "confessional movement" or "confessional front," but it did not have the legitimate status of *Kirche* (church). Thus study with Bonhoeffer became a badge of dissent, and in the eyes of the church authorities it was to mark oneself out as a "radical fanatic" and a disloyal German. Such pastors might sometimes be called "Dahlemites," after the posh Berlin suburb of Dahlem, indeed Martin Niemöller's parish, where a coterie of dissenting ministers had defied the Reich Church and proclaimed the Confessing Church the one true Lutheran church in Germany. Dahlem was also known popularly as a neighborhood of American expatriates and diplomats. Consul Fulton, for example, among others at the American embassy, was a member of the Berlin-Dahlem Lutheran congregation.[24] Thus the better informed among the parents of Finkenwalde seminarians would suffer "considerable anxiety" to see their sons depart for Pomerania, even if the family was not political or expressly disenchanted with the Reich. Finkenwalde would be unable—and little wished—to escape notice as the dispenser of a rival theology and instruction in a time when the church was a captive and instrument of the Nazi state.

The pedagogical structure was vital to the formation of the dissenting consciousness. "The next generation of pastors, these days, ought to be trained entirely in church-monastic schools," Bonhoeffer told his Union Seminary friend Erwin Sutz, "where the pure doctrine, the Sermon on the Mount, and worship are taken seriously—none of which are at the university and cannot be under the present circumstances." The avoidance of the Nazi contagion required nothing short of hermetic quarantine. Amid this winter of godlessness it was only in such a monastic greenhouse that the "pure doctrine" of the Sermon on the Mount could take root.

"In my days at a German university," recalled the Finkenwalde student Paul F. W. Busing, "no one took any responsibility for nurturing the spiritual life."[25]

There weren't many alternatives. The preachers' seminaries had all but vanished by 1935. Pastors were now trained almost exclusively in the university faculties, which had become bastions of Nazi propaganda. But as Bonhoeffer had been disillusioned to observe, even before the upheavals of 1933, the spiritual disciplines had never figured prominently in German theological training, the contemplative dimensions of Christian life having long been "confined to conventicles or sects." This attenuation in concern for the soul was in some sense an ineluctable outcome of the Reformation and the Enlightenment's religious legacy.

Among the twenty-three in Finkenwalde's first class was a slender, gentle young man, a minister's son named Eberhard Bethge. Aside from those who had taken classes with Bonhoeffer in Berlin—about half of the first class—most other Finkenwaldeans knew little if anything of the Berlin theologian. This included Bethge, who hailed from a rural backwater in Saxony. He had studied at Wittenberg for a time, but, having been expelled for voicing support for the Confessing Church, he needed to complete his ordination process elsewhere.[26] Finkenwalde was one of his few options.[27]

Their first afternoon together had been a festive affair. The day was bright and clear, the conversation anticipating the new semester. As the students gathered on the lawn for the opening reception, Bethge asked one of his new classmates when Pastor Bonhoeffer was expected to arrive. The student smiled and nodded in the direction of a tanned, blond-haired fellow in a white linen suit. "That's Bonhoeffer," he said, "the sporty dresser." Bonhoeffer may be the only monk ever so described by his brothers.

At twenty-nine, Bonhoeffer was three years older than Bethge, but he looked younger. Bethge introduced himself and the two men chatted briefly, sipping white wine on the summer lawn. Within a few weeks they had become inseparable, and Bonhoeffer would think of Bethge as "my daring, trusting spirit." In the company of other acquaintances, Bonhoeffer's conversation was narrower than it had been in years past, ranging mostly between the theological and the political, especially the *Kirchenkampf*. Everything was different with Bethge. Bonhoeffer had had intense friendships before—with Jean Lasserre, Erwin Sutz, and Franz Hildebrandt, for instance—but this was a closeness unlike any other.

In his unfinished novel, Bonhoeffer describes the camaraderie of Christoph and Ulrich, two persons who had grown into such perfect union that they knew each other "down to the most minute detail of their behavior, opinions, interests, abilities, and innate characteristics."[28] Bonhoeffer had never felt such a bond with a female, with the exception of his twin, Sabine. But her marriage had relegated her to the ranks of those near him whom he nevertheless held at a certain distance. This unguarded closeness was something different, and felt exhilarating. Some seminarians, indeed, wondered whether Bonhoeffer had fallen in love with the boyish country pastor. At times, as one might expect, it became a source of resentment among the brethren that Bethge had become the *"ausgesprochener Liebling des Chefs"*—the chief's clear favorite. When one student joked that Bethge had become the "representative of the Führer," he did not have Hitler in mind. The unflattering epithet arose in part because Bonhoeffer insisted that no brother ever speak of a fellow ordinand—or of the chief himself—in his absence, and "if this should happen, that he, the ordinand or Bonhoeffer, be told about it immediately afterwards."[29]

Eight years later, after one of their last evening visits while Bonhoeffer was in prison, he would write of "the advantage of having nearly every day for eight years experienced every event together, discussed every thought," for then "one needs only a second to know how things are for the other, and actually even that second is unnecessary."[30]

In Finkenwalde's music room Bonhoeffer played piano accompaniment to Bethge's delicate tenor. He taught Bethge, a son of the manse, to love Chopin and Brahms. In return, Bethge inspired Bonhoeffer, scion of the *Bildungsbürgertum*—the humanist haute bourgeoisie—to appreciate the choral music of the Reformation. Heinrich Schütz, Bethge's favorite church composer, would become Bonhoeffer's as well. And by the end of the school year, Bonhoeffer asked Bethge to become his confessor—another Protestant adaptation of Catholic sacrament, whereby brothers gained a clearer conscience, if not absolution. After the Gestapo closed Finkenwalde on September 28, 1937, until shortly before Bonhoeffer's arrest in April 1943, he and Bethge would remain together, when in Berlin sharing a bedroom in Bonhoeffer's parents' home on Marienburger Allee. They also kept a joint bank account, signed Christmas cards from "Dietrich and Eberhard," fussed over gifts they gave together, planned elaborate vacations, and endured numerous quarrels. Karl and Paula Bonhoeffer, as well as their children and their families, kept any reservations they had about the duo to themselves, and soon welcomed "Herr Bethge" into the family circle.

At the end of the first session, Bonhoeffer told his family that the experiment in community had been the most joyful and richest time of his life. He omitted to mention, however, that it had not been easy—or, for that matter, entirely successful.

As an experiment in Protestant monasticism—at its root, something of a contradiction in terms, Luther's teaching having closed far more monasteries than it founded—Finkenwalde needed to square the self-abnegation of the cloister with the individual freedom implicit in the Reformation view of Christian community. But in the first months, Bonhoeffer spoke more about being "bound together by brotherly admonition and discipline and open confession" than about freedom.[31] Most students, coming from conventionally Lutheran middle-class families, were uneasy at the strict ordering of spiritual life—and with Bonhoeffer's style of leadership, for that matter. For while he expected the brethren to follow the program he'd designed, he could on occasion cancel classes and direct everyone to the meadow, if the mood struck him. Thus life at Finkenwalde ultimately seemed to depend less on age-old cenobitic custom than on the director's whims.[32]

Many had Sunday duties in their home parishes. But for those who remained over the weekend, Bonhoeffer held a Saturday-morning service in the chapel. The sermon was preached by Bonhoeffer or a student he'd designated; later, Wilhelm Rott, whose arrival doubled the size of the faculty, would preach as well. Communion, it was decided, would be celebrated once a month in the custom of nineteenth-century Lutheranism—Luther himself having advised daily celebration of the Eucharist—and the men's preparation to receive the sacrament began Saturday afternoon with another period of house silence, according to Bonhoeffer's preference.

Bonhoeffer did reinstitute various or forgotten lost practices Luther the monk had approved: for example, the *mutuum colloquium et consolatio fratrum*, conversation and confession in fellowship. There were readings from the Psalms and the gospel during morning prayers and evensong in the form of a *lectio continua*. But later, when Bonhoeffer wanted to read the Bible aloud during meals after the fashion of medieval monks, his brethren at Finkenwalde voiced strong opposition. Exceptionally, Bonhoeffer capitulated, at least as to scripture, but not as to mealtime reading in general. He would carry on enforcing the practice, though with lighter, often more humanist, fare: Adalbert Stifter's short fiction, Georges Bernanos's *Diary of a Country Priest*, Mozart's memoir of his journey to Prague, and a collection of *Judenbuche*. He also managed to squeeze in, without protest, Agnes von Zahn-Harnack's biography of her father, Adolf, the church historian.

Based on little personal experience in ascetical living, Bonhoeffer's plan for raising up a generation of radical Christ-followers who had been fed on the pure gospel met with a fair amount of skepticism and grumbling in its early days. Besides the loyal Bethge, few seminarians found "the strict liturgical ordering of their day" to their liking, or could see much point to it.[33] "There was too much 'must' for us," one student grumbled. Likewise, Gerhard Ebeling, who would become a prominent postwar theologian, complained about the oppressively Jesuitical air and left after one semester. Having come in search of knowledge and answers, most were frustrated to discover only "emptiness in ourselves and in the texts."[34]

One complaint perhaps stood for them all: "A full half hour of silent meditation is torture: the mind moves around, memories flicker into consciousness, dreams awaken, angers flare up."[35] Perhaps the age could only be healed by a return to ancient manners of devotion, but perhaps, too, it was not possible to un-ring the bell of German Protestant tradition.

Bonhoeffer listened to the criticisms and made a few adjustments. On the problem of drifting thoughts, he encouraged the acceptance of distractions as inherent to devotional life. Reverie, daydreaming—fold them into your prayer, he advised. Trying to fight them off was a losing battle anyway! "Things have to come out in the open," Bonhoeffer said.[36]

Another accommodation lifted the burden of solitary meditation. They could form contemplative pairs or clusters and cohabit the same solitude—although the discipline of silence must still prevail. "Teaching about Christ begins in silence," Bonhoeffer had taught in his 1933 Christology lectures.[37] Christian thought and action emerge from the encounter with Jesus Christ, in stillness before the Word. For we must discover a silence "that brings clarification, purification and apprehension of this essential thing," he told the brothers—a holy silence. Holy silence reawakens and refreshes, making strange once more the mystery of the Word.

But if lost rigors and pregnant silences were essential to regenerate the pastorate, the laity, he understood, were in need of somewhat different spiritual medicine. Bonhoeffer did not blame nineteenth-century liberalism so much as generalized lethargy for the prevalence of moribund congregations, and he knew mere exhortations to concentrate on the Word alone would not retrieve the lost churches. What was needed, rather, was a thoughtful, disciplined attention to scripture, illuminating its relevance to the present circumstances; only this would ward off rigidity and quietism. Sermon exercises at Finkenwalde often sought to develop precisely such pastoral application: How did a given gospel pericope suggest courses of action and ways of engaging the world? Bonhoeffer instructed the seminarians to write their answers in the form of theses. "Then the various drafts were read aloud, [after which] Bonhoeffer showed the students his own version." The assigned verses might also be drawn from the Hebrew Bible—the prophets, the praises, or the poetry of exile.[38] Any text, he insisted, must be preached so as to enable the hearer to receive a blessing, and a word of instruction.[39]

Finkenwalde would remain, even after its rocky first months, a mostly improvised community.[40] Among the disciplines that would persist as first conceived was the daily requirement of manual labor, with renovations to the house and gardening taking up most of the time. Also unrevised, though perhaps not unremarked, was Bonhoeffer's custom of excusing himself from such work—leaving its direction to Friedrich Onnasch. Bonhoeffer thought his time was better spent getting to know the wealthy landowners in the region, introducing the provincial nobility to the seminary and winning their support. There were also weekly trips home to Berlin, for which purpose Karl had first given him a sedan before the convertible, though occasionally Karl would still send his own Mercedes and driver. Bethge often accompanied Bonhoeffer on these trips as well as on shorter excursions to Stargard, Penkun, Pölitz, and Gullnow. On warm, clear days, Bonhoeffer would take the top down and steer the Audi toward the eastern countryside, past the vast yellow seas of blossoming rapeseed that appeared in springtime or the explosion of sunflowers in summer, or along the gravel roads around Lake Dalie and into the Oder Delta—these were some of his favorite excursions.

The conspicuous adoption of Bethge as his favorite perhaps speaks to Bonhoeffer's uncertainty or inexperience as an evangelical abbot; constitutionally disdainful of authority, he made up rules as he went along and broke others on a whim, even once suspending the ascetic way altogether to throw a masquerade party. For all their complaints about the arbitrariness of monastic rigor, Finkenwaldeans were never required to take vows of poverty, chastity, or obedience. They were free to marry—indeed, some were married—or to leave the community whenever they wished, returning if they wanted to. They were, in short, subject only to Bonhoeffer's own selective application of a far more demanding life. Finkenwalde ultimately existed as the canvas on which he aspired to render his personal ideal of a Christian community.

He encouraged the ordinands to make time for recreation and on warm afternoons led the charge to the tennis courts, to the nearby forest, or to the beach, a short drive from the seminary. He was often first to strip off his clothes and plunge into the bracing waters of the Baltic Sea. But was it feasible for contemplative discipline to be such a ready complement of leisure? Could play exist as the counterpoint to discipline? And what of the sibling rivalry between eros and agape? Bonhoeffer asked many questions and sometimes made conflicting demands and proffered contradictory assertions. In his lectures to the young seminarians on Christian community, he spoke of the "dark love," "disordered desire," and "uncontrollable tyranny" of eros, which yearns "to force the other into one's own sphere of power," and contrasted it to the clear, bright light of agape-love, which illuminates the other in its strangeness, releases him from the ego's clutch, and lets him be whole in its difference. Bonhoeffer was speaking of how Christ-centered relation enables genuine community and, indirectly, of Nazism's perverse morality, although he might have also been unwittingly interrogating his own internal struggles, in particular, the quandary of finding himself smitten by a younger man, who was also a student.

The formula worked for some. The young clergyman Gerhard Lehne told Bonhoeffer that he had finally found a world that embraced much of what he loved and longed for: "straightforward theological work" in a community "where no unpleasant notice was taken of one's limitations, but where the work was made a pleasure; and with it all, open-mindedness and love for everything that still makes this fallen creation lovable." Sitting down with the other students over their afternoon coffee, sharing fresh bread with sweet butter and jam—it was finally these "peripheral things," Lehne said, "that increased my delight in what is central."[41]

Though the controversy surrounding the daily disciplines would never be resolved to everyone's satisfaction, Bonhoeffer felt increasingly comfortable imposing his own enthusiasm for sport and recreation on the community. Like worship, it should not be an exceptional activity but a natural part of the day. No lectures or schoolwork were scheduled on Sunday, which Bonhoeffer set aside not for mere rest but for music and games—with bridge and trivia quizzes being the most popular. And never one to hide his lamp under a bushel, he made a show of his prowess at tennis and ping-pong, which have rarely assumed such importance in monastic living. In sport as in all things, when he played, he played to win.

But he did not stand on ceremony. He asked to be addressed as Pastor Bonhoeffer, or simply "brother." But the informality was difficult for well-reared young Germans to accept; the students felt more comfortable calling him "Mr. Principal," which he greatly disliked, though not as much as he would have "der Führer," had he known. Try as he might to put the ordinands at ease, he could be intimidating, as by now he knew only too well. Once, when a seminarian accidently knocked a Byzantine-style icon from the wall and tried in vain to glue the pieces of it back together, Bonhoeffer said, "Such things do happen; do not take it tragically; one must accept facts."[42] In time, "Herr Pastor" would prevail as honorific, which seemed a good enough compromise, though some eventually warmed to "Brother Bonhoeffer"; and the number of those using "*du*" (the familiar form of "you") with him would also increase in time.

And recollections, too, would grow fonder: "Thus for two years, mostly after lunch and before making the rounds through the 'halls' of the seminary, 'Brother Dietrich', who always had time for his brethren, sat on the steps of the small stairway which led to the inspector's room. The picture is unforgettable: the small wooden staircase, the man sitting on it with crossed legs, reaching now and then for a cigarette, or accepting a cup of coffee poured out of the only coffee machine in the house. He had been in Berlin yesterday; he told us about it. Late in the evening when he came home, he gave those who waited for him one of his exciting reports about the deviations and embroilments of church committees, about spiritual and worldly affairs, politics of the Church and of the State, about those who stood firm, those who wavered and those who fell."

Still, there were times when he lost sight of just how imposing his personality could be. He worked hard to direct his forceful nature toward preaching and lecturing, table conversation, prayer and confession; but in the close quarters of monastic life, he could not always mask his raw emotions or contain his eruptive temper. The latter Bonhoeffer would confess to Bethge in detail, and in the coming years Bethge was often to bear the brunt of it.

A student called Johannes Goebel recounts one evening when Bonhoeffer was at the piano, as Goebel and a few others listened from a corner of the room. It may have been Beethoven or Chopin that Herr Pastor was playing. What Goebel would never forget, though, was the sudden "expression of natural force," primal and feral, that possessed Bonhoeffer. The effect resembled his London improvization, but it was no joke now. He appeared transformed. He sat before the keyboard not poised and erect, as was his custom, but as if clinging to a cliff, "as a pupil" would never "have been allowed to sit." He hammered the keys as if with a force beyond his control, improvising wildly. And then just as "abruptly as he had begun," Bonhoeffer stopped playing, collected himself, and left the room. The scene burned itself indelibly into Goebel's memory, leaving behind the dramatic, often startling contrast of what Goebel would ever after recall as the "essential Bonhoeffer" and the volcanic alter ego.[43]

With disarming simplicity, Bonhoeffer asked his students to think together with him as he explored anew the question, What does it mean to be a Christian? Leading them in reading the gospels, he would in fact manage to provoke many of them, perhaps for the first time, to feel the singular immediacy of discipleship in Christ, the summons and its redemptive answer: "As Jesus passed by, he saw Levi the son of Alphaeus sitting at the receipt of custom, and said unto him, Follow me. And he arose and followed him."

To teach others how to answer that invitation, Bonhoeffer borrowed yet another form of Catholic devotion, *imitatio Christi*, the imitation of Christ. In his 1933 Berlin lectures on creation and sin, he had taught that listening to the Word of God was no passive thing, but one requiring *exercitium*—exercise and practice—not unlike learning a piece of music. *Exercitium* had, in fact, been a term of art in monasticism at least since the fifteenth century, when Thomas à Kempis's devotional handbook *The Imitation of Christ* described "the pious practices [*exercitia*] suitable to a good monk," aspiring to be Christ-like.

When he visited Rome years before, Bonhoeffer's exchanges with Jesuits had also led him to study *The Spiritual Exercises* of St. Ignatius of Loyola, an even more regimented devotional prescription. And so in developing his Finkenwalde lectures on discipleship (which would ultimately be gathered in his famous book by that name) Bonhoeffer imagined his own guidance as "exercises actualizing the Sermon on the Mount." Their composition was one of his most joyous efforts, perhaps because it spoke to the most elemental needs of those seeking Christ. "Everything depends on the urgent invitation to take that first step into what is still an unknown, a new situation."[44]

Discipleship would evolve into a polemic against the Lutheran tendency to portray faith as a refuge from obedience. Indeed, modern Protestant thought, in its most influential forms, had abandoned the realm of fact and "public truth" for a private sphere in which faith was the sole requirement for salvation. Bonhoeffer sought to redefine the meaning of Luther's *sola fide* and *sola gratia*, too, moderating what had become their absolutism. From the disciple's first hearing of the call to his picking up his cross and following, his existence was properly one of concrete acts, of *lived* devotion to Jesus. Such a life necessarily integrated private and public, the inner and the outer reality—hearing *and* following: there was no other way of being a Christian. Neither the church nor its sacrament could relieve the individual of the weight of his decision (Luther had understood that well). But that decision necessarily implied a leap into a new world, a degree of personal responsibility for the here and now that Protestant thinking had effectively abjured. And so in reconsidering the obligations of discipleship the book was revolutionary.

Revolutionary in context, at least; in the larger scheme of the Christian tradition, it was rather quite orthodox. As in the gospel narratives, there is no grace without obedience; no remission of sin without the turning away from sin toward truth; no freedom without the burden of the cross. "Neither do I condemn thee," Jesus told the woman taken in adultery. "Go and sin no more." The terms of grace are quite explicit.

Jesus' call is not answered in the form of a doctrinal formulation, not even in "a spoken confession of faith. Rather, it is the immediate deed. . . . Nothing precedes, and nothing follows except the obedience of the called."[45]

In German, Bonhoeffer's book was called *Nachfolge*, or "Follow me"—a title that perfectly captures the intended immediacy of its message. The first English translation appeared in an abridged version in 1948 as *The Cost of Discipleship*, and this would remain the title of all subsequent English editions until the editors of the *Dietrich Bonhoeffer*

Works opted for the more precise *Discipleship* in their 1996 scholarly edition. Although more faithful to the German, *Discipleship* mutes the book's singular intensities. The word *Nachfolge* is an imperative. Jesus said to Simon Peter and his brother Andrew, "Whoever wishes to follow me must take up his cross daily and '*folge mir nach*.'" As Bonhoeffer wrote, "The bridges are torn down, and the followers simply move ahead. A call to discipleship thus immediately creates a new situation.[46] Imagine Søren Kierkegaard's vertiginous *Fear and Trembling*—a book Bonhoeffer carried with him during these months—translated as *Faith*, or Martin Luther's tortured treatise *The Bondage of the Will* reduced to blunt abstraction.

The lectures constituted the core of Finkenwalde's curriculum, although *Nachfolge* would not be published until 1937, after the seminary had been shut down. Karl Barth famously wrote in the final section of his thirteen-volume *Church Dogmatics* that as he turned his attention to a theology of discipleship, he was inclined to do no more than reproduce long passages from Bonhoeffer's account and let the matter stand at that. Still, the book is a reflection of the church *in extremis*. Bonhoeffer would come to acknowledge certain dangers of such a fraught exegesis, which laid upon the individual soul not just his cross but the weight of the world, the entire crisis of the Christian community. The will to make oneself an exemplar of faith could become too easily a recipe for a tortured soul or, worse, for an unforgiving perfectionism and sanctimonious bravado. It lacked balance. But it was addressed to the crisis at hand.

Bonhoeffer would worry, too, that his emphasis on the immediacy of action in following Jesus Christ proposed a hollowed-out version of the individual self. When Christ calls a person, he bids him to come and lose his worldly life to gain the life eternal. There is no reflection upon this invitation. And perhaps no such discipleship is to be found outside the gospels, in which those called leave their nets to follow Jesus and become fishers of men without a moment's hesitation.[47] The "vocabulary and perspective" of Bonhoeffer's ideal thus banishes "all other modulations in and forms of theology," refusing any other way of understanding the Christian faith in its essence.[48]

Still, Bonhoeffer would stand by his ideal. These, he felt, were the right words spoken at the right time, when only a rare ardor and rectitude, an almost saintly support of suffering on the part of all the faithful, could save the church. For ultimately, what was at peril was not so many individual souls as the very body of Christ. In this sense, it was well to remember that "Discipleship . . . does not create constitutions and decrees, but brings human beings into relation with one another."[49] The promise for those who follow Christ is that "they will become members of the community of the cross." They will become "people of the mediator, people linked together by the cross, and thus by a way that leads to suffering." It is when the community is most in jeopardy that the cost exacted from the individual is greatest. Jesus goes ahead of his people to Jerusalem, and "those following him are overcome with amazement and fear at the way to which he has called them." But they will go all the same.[50]

Such were the conditions of what Bonhoeffer would call "costly grace," the only kind one can seek when the world has become the desert. This desert world of costly grace he compares to Bach's *St. Matthew's Passion*. What is most "beautiful" in the oratorio is that "all the music's own beauty in and for itself is sacrificed, is 'denied' for the sake of Christ, that the music here only comes to itself through Jesus Christ and does not desire to be anything for itself but everything for Jesus Christ." The "beauty" denied is "the true and only possible beauty" in the community of Christ.[51] It delighted Bonhoeffer to learn that Bach sometimes wrote *Jesu Juva* and *Soli Deo Gloria* ("Jesus, help me" and "for the glory of God alone") at the top of his manuscripts. Discipleship is creative participation in the glory of Christ and in his suffering. "To be called, to go forth and to sing a beautiful song—this is true christology!"

Bonhoeffer celebrated his thirtieth birthday on February 4, 1936, in the company of Bethge and the other brethren, as he had come to call his students. Around a roaring fire in the great hall, he told stories of his journeys abroad. He spoke for the first time of his friendship with Franklin Fisher, the black man who'd been his classmate in New York and was now a pastor in Atlanta. Fisher, Bonhoeffer confessed in this intimate setting, had guided him into shared life with a people in whom one sensed "the integrity of unaffected creativity, born of a mysterious combination of suffering and humour."[52] It was an unfamiliar and radiant manner of being human that Fisher had revealed to him, and Bonhoeffer said he could never forget Fisher's final plea that he make the story of that people known in Germany. He played his recordings of Negro hymns and taught the brothers his favorites: "Go Down Moses," "Swing Low, Sweet Chariot," and "There Is a Balm in Gilead." "We were so joyful and so earnest, and focused," Wilhelm Rott recalled tenderly. Rott had arrived recently in Finkenwalde to serve as a kind of academic dean, coordinating curriculum and study groups, and covering Bonhoeffer's classes when he was away. He would be among the last to come and among the first to go.

There were times when "a unifying arc swung from music and play to quietude and prayer," when the seminarians understood the importance of the "innermost concentration" for which they were being prepared. And these were the best of times.

It was in the fullness of shared life with the Finkenwalde brethren that Bonhoeffer broke off an epistolary friendship with his third cousin, Elizabeth Zinn, whom he had met seven years earlier in Berlin and who bore a striking resemblance to his twin sister, Sabine. In fact, Zinn had written a doctoral dissertation under Wilhelm Lütgert, the same scholar of German Idealism who directed Bonhoeffer's habilitation thesis on the concepts of act and being in contemporary theology. Zinn wrote on the eighteenth-century Swedenborgian F. C. Oetinger, who despite strong theosophical leanings remained in full standing as a Lutheran pastor and church superintendent.[53] It has been reported by some biographers that Bonhoeffer and Zinn had begun discussing marriage in their letters and even had a brief engagement, although there are no extant letters that support this claim. What is certain, however, is that shortly after meeting Bethge and assembling the brethren in the monastic fellowship in Finkenwalde, Bonhoeffer felt decidedly more drawn toward "uncompromising" friendships than to marriage.

Determined though Bonhoeffer was to promote engagement with the world, the monastic life inevitably and by design has the effect of making the world seem far away, at least intermittently. So it might have seemed, when on May 1, 1935, a scant eight months after the death of President Hindenburg and Hitler's consolidation of dictatorial powers, the führer announced Germany's rearmament at Berlin's Tempelhof airfield. Far from recognizing the news as further evidence of a threat engulfing their country, many of the men at Finkenwalde, like most Germans, glowed with pride to hear the news of Germany's reemergence as a military power. The "shame of Versailles" would finally be lifted. When, after Hitler's speech, Bonhoeffer asked whether a Christian could object to war, there ensued a heated debate.

Their remove from the moral reality must have given Bonhoeffer to believe that a huge amount of work still lay ahead. "The majority of brothers would not accept the idea of Christians refusing to serve in war."[54] In fact, the ordinands had joined Bonhoeffer's school unaware of his pacifism, which they would discover only through these developments. As traditional Lutherans most of them would continue to believe that Christians were obliged to serve their country in war, even if the government had fallen into dictatorship. While they opposed the

Nazi regime, they saw no reason for the church to be unpatriotic. Most saw their community's political opposition as a potential moderating force, not a hotbed of treasonous sentiment, which could only rob it of legitimacy. From this perspective, pacifism posed a threat to the viability of the opposition.

In July 1936, Pastor Johannes Pecina and Willi Brandenburg, comrades in the Confessing Church, were among the first of the nearly one hundred of its ministers to be arrested under a law criminalizing all activities associated with non-"assimilated" (non-Nazi) churches and organizations. The first Finkenwaldean to be arrested was Wilhelm Rott, the Tübingen- and Berlin-trained theologian two years younger than Bonhoeffer. In an essay published that same year, "What is 'Positive Christianity,'" he had criticized Nazi ideology forthrightly but had limited his objections to the treatment of Jewish Christians. That was enough to land him in prison.

Several months earlier, on December 1, 1935, a front-page story in the Stettin evening paper had reported an ominous development: the chief of the SS and Minister of the Interior Heinrich Himmler had signed a decree making "all examinations held before courts of the Confessing Church invalid, all training centers set up by that church subject to closure, and all participants in them liable to punishment." The arrests to follow marked an escalation of threat and action against the dissenting pastorate.[55] By extension they were also an announcement that any personal affiliation with Bonhoeffer, the church's most visible figure, was tantamount to treason. Prayers of intercession for the arrested pastors became a daily ritual at Finkenwalde. Bonhoeffer would travel frequently with Bethge, and other brothers as well, to visit the prisoners in the Sonnenburg concentration camp near Küstrin in the Neumark, undeterred by the evident fact that the net was beginning to tighten. His brethren had by now realized, of course, that there was no way of being a patriotic dissenting churchman.

On the morning in January 1936 of Rott's release after several months in jail, Bonhoeffer and Bethge sat in the Audi outside the gates, waiting. As soon as his colleague, haggard but composed, reached the car, Bonhoeffer presented him with tickets for a performance of *Don Giovanni* taking place that night in Berlin. Rott had enough time to return with them to Finkenwalde to pick up a suit of clothes and an overnight bag. The three would spend a night on the town to celebrate his freedom. Rott recalled that on the journey Bonhoeffer spoke to him in grim terms about the political crisis, but during dinner at

Rheinhardt's following the performance at the Kroll Opera House, the conversation was only of happy subjects: music and theology and the delights of the great city.

On August 1, 1936, the games of the 11th Olympiad opened in Berlin. Berlin had won the bid to play host over Barcelona in 1931, when Hitler's intentions were still open to speculation. Now the Games would be the führer's opportunity to show the risen German state to the whole world. With the help of his propaganda chief, Joseph Goebbels, he spared no expense in projecting the illusion of a free, Christian nation.[56] The new Olympic stadium, along with nine additional sporting venues, were constructed at a staggering cost of twenty-five million marks; a hundred million marks more was spent transforming the city into a gleaming new Rome, with elevated train lines, subways, and even new streets built throughout the western half to ease traffic around the center of action.

The complex of event sites throughout northern Berlin-Grunewald would be called the Reichssportfeld. But the jewel in the crown was the Olympiastadion, created by Werner and Walter March according to Hitler's exacting specifications. With seating for 110,000, it was the largest sports arena ever constructed, and featured an imperial chamber for Hitler and guest dignitaries. Lesser mortals entered through a phalanx of brawny statues carved by the Nazi sculptors Josef Thorak and Arno Breker.

Also in Roman fashion, a ten-mile "Via Triumphalis" led from Alexanderplatz along Unter den Linden into the Reichssportfeld. It was the route along which the Olympic torch would travel its final miles from Greece into the German capital. The torch, which the ingenuity of German chemists ensured would continue burning through any amount of wind and rain, was borne by a golden-haired Berliner named Schlingen. As he approached the Olympiastadion to ignite the Olympic Flame within, men of the SS and the SA raised their arms in salute.

With the intent of camouflaging its racist policies, the German government removed its most visible anti-Jewish banners and encouraged the compliant local press to tone down their rhetoric during the two weeks of the Olympiad.[57] So while iconography of the Nazi state remained visible around Berlin, the cruder and more explicit public markers of the regime's animus were temporarily warehoused. In anticipation of the international guests, the yellow benches in the Tiergarten that signaled an acceptable place for Jews to sit had been repainted, and public notices prohibiting Jews to enter public buildings were removed. Members of Nazi organizations were told momentarily to suspend anti-Jewish conduct and displays. This meant a hiatus, too, for popular racist publications, such as *Der Stürmer*, Julius Streicher's weekly, with its vicious screeds and cartoons of strong-jawed SA men crushing "reptiles, rodents, vampires and spiders identified by Stars of David" and illustrations of "Jewish-looking" men, with grotesque physiognomies, stalking blond Aryan women.[58] As to the actual population, the city made every effort to remove from its streets anyone deemed unsightly.[59]

At the same time, organizers were aware that many visitors would be keen to sample the city's famous sex clubs, cabarets, and bathhouses. Although most such establishments had been shut down as vestiges of Weimar decadence and the degeneracy of certain racial types, the restrictions were temporarily lifted, putting, among other unloved Berliners, about seven thousand prostitutes back to work. Himmler even suspended Paragraph 175 of the Nazi penal code, which criminalized homosexuality, allowing once-popular gay bars to reopen for the Games. "We must be more charming than the Parisians, more easygoing than the Vietnamese, more vivacious than the Romans, more cosmopolitan than London, and more practical than New York," the magazine *Der Angriff* explained.[60] Applied to fashion and etiquette, these cultural aspirations gave women the freedom to wear hemlines five centimeters higher than normal.

David Clay Large writes in his history of the city of Berlin,

> Some foreign reporters remained skeptical about the show of civility they witnessed during the games.... William Shirer, who covered the Olympics for CBS News, understood that the Nazis had "put up a very good front for the general visitors." Most of the foreign press, however, were taken in by the friendly atmosphere and organizational virtuosity. Both the *New York Times* and the *New York Herald Tribune* spoke of a warm welcome surpassing anything the Americans had ever experienced at an Olympiad. Frederic T. Birchall of the *Times*, praised the stadium as a structure "built for the ages, revealing the farsighted vision" of its creators. The *British Daily Mail* declared that no festival could be more splendid than the one taking place in Berlin, and gushed that visitors would find the city "magical." The *World of Sports*, also British, proposed that if visitors could forget their "prejudices" and the "rumors" about Nazi Germany, they would take away an experience of "lasting good" based on "the friendship of the sporting youth of the world."

Even journalists from France, which had been shocked most by Germany's recent remilitarization of the Rhineland, expressed admiration for the cordiality of the Olympic hosts, noting with particular gratitude that Berliners had shouted "Vive la France!" on the French team's arrival.[61]

As part of the campaign to project an image of openness and toleration, the Reich Church invited Bonhoeffer to preach in an enormous tent erected near the Olympic stadium and to give a half-hour lecture on "the inner life of the German Protestant Church since Reformation." "They want to publish a booklet with our pictures for propaganda reasons," Bonhoeffer told Bethge, who would not join him in Berlin until the second week. "I think this is ridiculous and dishonorable and I will definitely not send them anything."

Despite abominating the regime's transparent efforts at image control, even Bonhoeffer could not help feeling genuinely excited about the Olympic Games themselves. Over the years, he had traveled abroad frequently for the solace of unfamiliar spaces, to satisfy his craving for new and diverse worlds. Now his hometown was to be for a time the crossroads of the world. He bought tickets for track and field events, and as a surprise for two Finkenwalde students who had never been on an airplane, made arrangements for a chartered flight from Stettin to Berlin. His parents' new home on Marienburger Allee, fifteen minutes on foot from the Reichssportfeld, would make the perfect base for his band. Bonhoeffer happily filled his days with sporting events and all the related festivities in the Olympic village and beyond.

But he missed the most talked-about events of the 1936 Olympics, when Jesse Owens, a black sprinter born in Oakville, Alabama, defeated the German Luz Long in the long jump, on his way to collecting an unimaginable four gold medals. Regarding reports that Hitler had refused to acknowledge Owens's victories and shake his hand, Owens replied, "When I passed the Chancellor he arose, waved his hand at me, and I waved back at him." Owens denied that Hitler snubbed him. "It was FDR who snubbed me," he said. "The president didn't even send me a telegram." Hitler, to be fair, did not congratulate any winning athlete.

In every way, the Reich was the greatest victor of the Olympiad. Despite Owens's haul, the host nation captured the most medals— eighty-nine in all, including thirty-three gold: useful proof of Aryan superiority—and the excellent organization and festive atmosphere were universally praised. Forty-nine national teams had traveled to Berlin, more than for any previous Games, and the major events were broadcast live internationally—another first in Olympic history. Frederick T. Birchall wrote for the *New York Times* that the 1936 Games had returned Germany "to the fold of nations" and restored a human face to its maligned citizens.[62] The whole world owed Hitler and the German people a debt of gratitude. The U.S. team—including its eighteen black athletes, who had been welcomed by the home crowds with polite applause—came in a respectable second in the collection of medals, taking home fifty-six in all. Although Jews and other non-Aryans had been banned from competing for Germany, nine Jewish athletes from other countries won medals, including five Hungarian Jews. Seven Jewish men represented the American team in Berlin. "Hitler is one of the greatest, if not the greatest, political leaders in the world today," Birchall gushed in his *Times* piece, earning the right to the gold medal for hyperbole, "and the Germans themselves are a wholly peaceful people who deserve the best the world can give them."

Bonhoeffer's summer rehabilitation was short-lived. Although he had declined the invitation to preach, he did agree to give a lecture at the Church of Paul the Apostle on August 5. He was surprised to be met by an overflow audience, to whom he proceeded to speak with perilous candor of the Confessing Church, Finkenwalde, and the German church crisis. The talk was well received by the many international guests present and promptly condemned by Reich officials.

On the day Owens sprinted to his second gold medal, Bonhoeffer heard from Erich Seeberg, the Nazi dean of the theology faculty at Friedrich-Wilhelms—and son of Reinhold Seeberg, Bonhoeffer's dissertation adviser, who had died in 1935—that his adjunct position had been terminated. His affiliation with the university was finally severed. But even recognizing the decision as a predictable consequence of his outspokenness—an inevitable cost of discipleship—he panicked. Perhaps it was the shock of losing his remaining ties to the academic guild: he would no longer be able to think of himself as a member of the professoriate, however tenuous that relationship had always been. Until now, he was not merely a teacher of humble parsons in an unaccredited seminary, but also a controversial figure in the grand old faculty that had once included Adolf von Harnack and Friedrich Schleiermacher. His conspicuous marginality there had been of use to him. Now he feared becoming irrelevant. On the basis of what status could he now claim a public voice?

The closing of the doors at Unter der Linden happened with a distinct want of ceremony. The termination letter was drafted and signed by Bengt Seeberg, a junior faculty member and as rabid a National Socialist as his father, the dean. On behalf of the student council, he asked the university "to consider the legal situation and remove Bonhoeffer for causing disorder in connection with the Confessing Church." Copies were submitted to the rector and the dean; a note was placed in Bonhoeffer's file. The case was closed.

No one protested the decision; in fact, most faculty members seemed unaware that Bonhoeffer had even returned from London. The 250 kilometers between Finkenwalde and Berlin was not conducive to collegial ties, though Bonhoeffer had hardly been inclined before to socialize with the sorry characters now holding the faculty's distinguished chairs. In fact, his extensive correspondence from these years does not mention the name of a single colleague.

The Reich Church's withdrawal of Bonhoeffer's authority to teach had even broader consequences than the end of his adjunct post: it barred him from any faculty, seminary, or institution supported by a church. This prohibition included Finkenwalde, since the seminary remained under the general auspices of the state church. It was at this point that Bonhoeffer's supervision of the training there became an illegal activity.

Bethge had been away on a church assignment for most of July, called back to his home in Saxony to help resolve "a bitter struggle between the Confessing congregation in Helbra and its German Christian–led church council."[63] "I miss you often," Bonhoeffer wrote to him on July 29, 1936. "Receiving your letters always makes me very happy!"

In Bethge's absence, Bonhoeffer put together a schedule of speaking engagements and ecumenical conferences on which he hoped his friend would join him, as a vacation for them both. He had already been invited to an ecumenical meeting in Chambry, France, by the Provisional Administration of the Confessing Church, and also to another event in Geneva.[64] But the logistics were complicated. Bonhoeffer needed to arrange things so that Bethge's presence as traveling companion and assistant would appear necessary. He wanted to show Bethge some of the places that had once brought him great happiness: "Switzerland or South Germany? Do you know Lake Constance?" he asked. "Or—dare I think about this—the Italian lakes?!"

"The heart is more deceitful than anything else; and is desperately sick. . . . The semester," he added, "is coming to an end, and I miss you often."[65]

But a series of awkward exchanges reveal some serious misunderstandings between them. Bonhoeffer had become, Bethge felt, a "demanding friend," and their back-and-forth over travel details show

how the friendship, ever more ambiguous and confusing, was affecting the other relationships each of them had.[66]

Problems started when Bethge invited his cousin Gerhard Vibrans along without asking Bonhoeffer's permission. Dietrich's measured initial response could not disguise his profound dismay. "It wouldn't be easy for three people," he said. Even if he could borrow money from his parents to cover Bethge's costs, he would not have enough for the cousin, not even if he drew upon the joint bank account he and Bethge had recently opened. "We are pretty much at the end [of that]."

Then Bonhoeffer grew more plainly irritated. If Bethge insisted on bringing his cousin on a vacation clearly intended for the teacher and his student, then Bethge must explain to Vibrans in no uncertain terms that every consequent decision and change of plan would inevitably bring on more disputes and conflicts. It wouldn't be a pleasant scene— "and *you* have to take the responsibility!"

In any event, Vibrans would have to find his own accommodations. Bonhoeffer had no time for such details, particularly as he was starting to feel pressure about the upcoming conference. The sessions, he complained, would no doubt prove difficult and stressful, and he simply wanted his proven assistant with him.

Had Bethge misread the offer?

Whatever the case, Eberhard refused to withdraw the invitation to his cousin and even asked his younger brother Hans to come along as well. Bethge seemed intent on adding to their party. And so, seeing that his friend was of a mind not to be deterred, Bonhoeffer tried an appeal grounded in more prosaic concerns. "About the car," he said, "the axle will be scraping along as it is with three people. It will be worse with four. . . . And then over the mountains!"[67]

He reminded Bethge that he wanted to show him Italy, if only "for 2–3 days." Bethge had appeared eager for that leg of the trip when it was first discussed. "But it will be much more complicated if we are a party of four," Bonhoeffer said. "Maybe they can go with us to middle or south Germany. And then we pick them up again. The route back is via Hessen-Nassau, so we should meet them somewhere in the Frankfurt area."

Not to be overlooked either: the trip would also be "naturally somewhat noisier" with Hans along—but "I do not wish to stand in the way," Bonhoeffer wrote, now resorting to perfect passive-aggressive rationality.

Hans Bethge would eventually bow out for financial reasons. And so, faced now with the original intruder, Bonhoeffer tried to make the proposition as meager for him as possible. As he told Bethge, the nature of his conference duties would make Bethge's presence at all events necessary, and there would be no place for Vibrans. If the cousin still cared to come along, he should plan to meet teacher and pupil sometime between the end of the conference and the start of their pure holiday time.

When this was agreed, the clouds lifted: "I am happy that everything is working out," Bonhoeffer said. "Now I am starting to look forward to Monday." He apologized for creating "tremendous problems" for Hans and Vibrans, but he put it all down to an honest desire to avoid other difficulties, unnecessary as they were unforeseen.

He also reasserted their closeness with some friendly advice: "Regarding the dress-code: please take the light travel suit with the two pairs of pants, and also the blackish one. I don't think you will need the blue one. But if it's not uncomfortable for you, it doesn't burden us in the car. I will take along a black one. A coat is not necessary [but I'll bring one just in case]. If I find a second one, I will take it along for you. Otherwise we will wear the one in turns."

The Chambry conference would confirm all of Bonhoeffer's worst fears about the ecumenical movement. With precious few exceptions, the church leaders chose "not to take sides and insisted that they would accept delegates from all adversaries in the church struggle, thus ending up with halfhearted resolutions that did little to clarify the church situation in Germany." Uncharacteristically, Bonhoeffer remained silent throughout the conference, "lacking enthusiasm" for the debates, apparently exhausted and distressed by the rush of events.[68]

It therefore came as a welcome relief, when, on August 25, he did take Bethge (without the cousin) to Italy, a tour that would end in Rome. "Once again entranced by St. Peter's," Bethge later wrote, "he sought to reveal the beauty of the magnificent building to his companion." But seeing in all the Italian cities the martial posters boasting of victory in Abyssinia gave both men a grim foretaste of what was coming at home. Returning to Finkenwalde on September 13, Bonhoeffer was greeted with urgent administrative matters and the case of one critically ill student—whom he "nursed back to health with paternal efficiency," Bethge recalled.[69] For a month, Bonhoeffer's prolific letter writing—to Bethge, of course, but to everyone else as well—came to a near standstill.[70]

In 1937, Dr. Karl Bonhoeffer was Berlin's preeminent neurologist and empirical psychiatrist, arguably the dean of the German psychiatric establishment. That same year, the Charity Hospital celebrated his silver jubilee as the director of the psychiatric clinic. He'd officially retired on April 1, 1936, but agreed to remain in place until a successor had been found. The occasion of his final lecture drew his three sons back to Berlin, along with the nation's leading lights in neurology, psychiatry, and brain science. In a photograph taken shortly thereafter, Dr. Bonhoeffer, in his white lab coat, is conversing with his colleagues as brother Karl-Friedrich and Bethge wait to speak with him, alongside Dietrich intently studying large diagrams of the human brain.

That summer, Bonhoeffer gave his own last lectures at Finkenwalde. He spoke not of the mind but of the soul and its need for community. The lectures would become his most widely read book, a minor commercial success, published under the title *Gemeinsames Leben* (*Life Together*).[71] But while still directing the seminary, he would be far too busy to convert his manuscripts into anything resembling a book; with Bethge's assistance, that job would be finished some months after the Gestapo had shut down the community. During the effort, the two would stay in an empty house in Göttingen belonging to Sabine and her husband, Gerhard Leibholz. *Gemeinsames Leben* was written "in a single stretch of four short weeks in late September and October of 1938," composed at a steady, even leisurely pace, but not without distractions. Bonhoeffer and Bethge both preferred to sleep late if they could; workdays began around eleven o'clock and ended in the midafternoon, with a nap. In the evenings, they attended concerts at the Kassel Music Festival.

Now a devotional classic, *Life Together* would be widely translated, read, and studied as a introduction to the spiritual disciplines—at times even as an instructional manual for Christian community. Read in its historical context, however, the five short chapters represent a poignant meditation on all that had been lost, its aim to capture in narrative a lightning flash of eternity. Israel's Diaspora has become the condition of Christ's disciples. To follow Jesus is to live in exile, for Christ's body is broken and scattered.[72] The world is the wilderness in which the Christian is ordained to wander, from which there is no escape. This is humanity's curse and promise: God's people are dispersed into the farthest corners, but in each Jesus meets us as friend and fellow stranger.

Life Together belongs to the genre of monastic literature that has its origins in the seventh-century *Rule of Saint Benedict*, but the book's literal frame of reference is the experiment of Finkenwalde. Bonhoeffer recalls his far-flung brothers' coming together, their daily life as one body, until their communion is broken, scattering them "like seed unto all the kingdoms of the earth." The "clamorous desire for something more" inevitably turns the gift into a possession; the simple, fragile presence of the other is obliterated for the sake of a "dream world." But

KARL BONHOEFFER, FERDINAND SAUERBRUCH, DIETRICH BONHOEFFER,
AND EBERHARD BETHGE, 1938

"Christian brotherhood" is "not an ideal which we must realize"; it is "a reality created by God in Christ in which we may [only] participate." The basis of genuine community is "the clear, manifest Word of God in Jesus Christ."[73] "God hates visionary dreaming!"

Despite the book's vivid sermonic prose and eventual popular resonance, the lectures at Finkenwalde were greeted with mixed reviews, some students finding them "laborious, not brilliant."[74] The young historian Wilhelm Niesel, who had not heard Bonhoeffer lecture since the 1933 Christology seminar, had taken the train up from Berlin. He expressed his surprise with "the dryness of style and effect." The talks were forthright to a fault, if not slightly parochial. The circle had been drawn so tight that a theologian unacquainted with the experiment in Pomerania—the dissident Niesel, for example—felt out of place. He asked Bonhoeffer afterward whether so much concentration on spiritual things left any room for pleasure. What about the cinema, for instance? Bonhoeffer must have thought it odd, given his own well-attested inclination to leisure; he tried to reassure the visitor, who remained nevertheless "suspicious of so much 'spiritualism.'"[75]

Perhaps to prove his point, the next morning Bonhoeffer invited Niesel on a rowing expedition on the Oder Sound. He wanted him better to understand the strenuous tone of the lectures, and had an idea of how to make that happen. When the two rowers reached the far shore, Bonhoeffer led Niesel up a small hill to a clearing from which they could see in the distance a vast field and the "runways of a nearby squadron." German fighter planes were taking off and landing, and soldiers moved hurriedly in purposeful patterns, like so many ants. Bonhoeffer spoke of a new generation of Germans in training, whose disciplines were formed "for a kingdom . . . of hardness and cruelty." It would be necessary, he explained, to propose a superior discipline if the Nazis were to be defeated.

"You have to be stronger than these tormentors that you find everywhere today," said Major von Bremer in Bonhoeffer's novel.[76]

Rowing back across the lake in the afternoon, Niesel, now indeed more at ease, had an intriguing story of his own to tell. He recounted an afternoon nearly twenty years before, when the rowing club of his school in Friedrichswerder was resting outside the boathouse of the Kleiner Wannsee following afternoon practice. Most of the other clubs had also finished training for the day. As Niesel and his teammates were heading off for coffee at the nearby Kohlhasenbrück Restaurant, a loud commotion drew their attention to a boat manned by a crew of two, a boat not yet docked and spinning in circles. "Behind the helmsman," Niesel said, "we saw the 'keelson,' a fat boy in a white sweater."[77] After a flurry of desperate measures (and scattered laughter on the shore), the boat appeared finally to be making landfall when everything went awry. The two on board, unable to jump to the pier, lost their balance, falling backward into the water, and the boat capsized. Niesel asked Bonhoeffer whether he knew anything about "that [soggy] little heap in the white sweater," who had talked his way into the crew despite total inexperience. Bonhoeffer nodded appreciatively, and the two laughed about the overconfident boy Dietrich had been.

In February 1937, during the fourth year of Hitler's reign, the Ministry of the Interior issued an order against naming from the pulpit anyone who had been removed from his position or who had left the Reich Church by reason of conscience. This was, in effect, a ban on intercessory prayer, the practice in Christian communities of praying for individual members or concerns of the parish, which petitions were also usually circulated in newsletters and other printed matter. Such prohibitions were aimed specifically at Confessing Church congregations and their so-called illegal pastors hired for "emergency" service. Indeed, most of the seminarians coming out of Finkenwalde, then only two years in operation, fit the description.

It was now also "forbidden to hold church services and gatherings on emergency church premises or in secular spaces."

It was further forbidden for congregations affiliated with the Confessing Church to take up offerings during worship services.

Without prior approval of the overseers of the Editorial Law, it was forbidden to make carbon or mimeograph copies of any parish communiqués, including newsletters, sermons, and letters to parishioners—any publications that fostered a sense of belonging.

The force of these restrictions brought the practices of the dissenting congregations to a halt. Especially painful was the ban on intercessory prayers, which were central to life at Finkenwalde, since Bonhoeffer had long regarded the discipline of pleading with God as necessary to ignite the moral imagination of individuals and communities. "The congregational prayer has long sent shivers down my spine," he had said in Barcelona years before. He was speaking of an experience of "incomparable beauty" when the children and young people of his church had prayed for him before the whole congregation. He felt that the act transformed the face of the petitioner into the face of one for whom Christ died. Intercessory prayer was "the purifying bath into which the individual and the community must enter every day."[78]

There followed in short order a massive wave of harassment and arrests of men who had been at Finkenwalde or followers of any non-Nazi ministers. Wilhelm Niesel, Gerhard Jacobi, Hermann Ehlers, and Wilhelm von Armin Lützow were detained by the secret police for preaching as Confessing Church ministers.

A friend of Bonhoeffer's, Hermann Stöhr of Stettin, secretary of the Germany Fellowship of Reconciliation, was taken by the SS and executed for being a "conscientious objector," a status he claimed based on his own reading of the Sermon on the Mount. Martin Niemöller would see his passport revoked and his lectures in Berlin banned. Any student caught attending them would be expelled. But far worse lay ahead for Niemöller. On July 1, 1937, while Bonhoeffer and Bethge were visiting him at his Dahlem parsonage, a black Gestapo Mercedes pulled up outside the church. The pastor watched from the living-room window as the officers approached the front door. Bethge and Bonhoeffer were ordered to remain as the Gestapo searched the house for seven hours. Paula Bonhoeffer, who had become a parishioner of Dahlem, got word of what was happening and, with her husband, drove quickly to the scene. For the next several hours, Bonhoeffer's parents circled Königin-Luise-Strasse in their car, peering anxiously every time they passed the front of the house. The search might have continued late into the night had one officer not detected, behind a painting, a wall safe containing thirty thousand marks. The funds, belonging to the Pastors' Emergency League, were seized. The Gestapo also carted

Niemöller away. And the next day he was sent to the Sachsenhausen concentration camp, his crime, "misuse of the pulpit."

Else Niemöller would face the next seven years without her husband, but the kindness of the Dahlem congregation—even after church officials removed the family from the manse—would sustain her. The evening of the arrest, as she sat in her living room alone trying to make sense of the day's events, the melodious strains of choral music broke the silence of the darkness, growing louder and louder still. Having learned of Niemöller's arrest, the women's choir had come to offer the comfort of song.[79]

When, two years earlier, in June of 1935, Barth had been removed from his post at the University of Bonn, he'd lashed out not only at Hitler but also against the Confessing Church leadership, which had shown, in his opinion, "no heart for the millions who are suffering unjustly" and had "nothing to say about the simplest questions of public honesty." Neither had the Confessing Church "spoken out on the most simple matters of public integrity. And if and when it does speak, it is always on its own behalf."[80]

It was a harsh criticism, especially from an academic theologian who had been willing to take the oath of allegiance to Hitler—though with a caveat: "as long as I can be responsible as a Christian." Whether this addition had been proclaimed in a whisper, a shout, or alone in his chamber, Barth would not say. But no qualification of any kind was acceptable to the Reich Church; Barth was soon dismissed. By the fall of 1936, he was safely ensconced in the chair of Reformed Theology at the University of Basel, from which he proceeded to issue a steady stream of suggestions, rarely solicited, to his beleaguered colleagues mired in the trenches of the church struggle. Barth would pass the remainder of his career in Switzerland, attended by his exceedingly loyal wife, Nelly, and his strikingly beautiful assistant, Charlotte von Kirschbaum, who came to occupy a room in the professor's home. That she would remain the theologian's lover until his death in 1968 is perhaps a final testament to his ardent embrace of Trinitarian thought."

Still, Bonhoeffer received Barth's every communication appreciatively, both those addressed to the plenitude of the dissident pastorate and to him personally; he bravely breasted the pontifical certitudes and the occasional reprimand—ever grateful for Barth's attention, genuinely convinced that the master's most important contribution to the resistance was his tireless work on the magisterial *Church Dogmatics*.

As the Gestapo moved on Hitler's orders to quash all remaining activities of the Confessing Church, Bonhoeffer chose a psalm of vengeance as the biblical text for one of his final sermons at Finkenwalde. It is significant that he "did not reject the Psalms of vengeance, as Christians have sometimes done, on the grounds that they reflected an earlier stage in God's relationship to humanity and contradicted the love-ethic of the gospel."[81] As a student of the Psalter he would never take such a view. He hoped rather that Christians would learn to read the so-called "imprecatory" songs—those of judgment and condemnation—as accusations in the voice of Jesus the Jew against injustice and innocent sufferings, the anguished utterances of the "crucified Lord."

"No, we sinners are not praying this song of vengeance," Bonhoeffer explained in condemnation of Hitler. "[I]nnocence itself is praying it."

September 1937 brought another decree from Heinrich Himmler: the Fifth Implementation Decree for the Law to Restore Order to the German Evangelical Church. This one outlawed the preachers' seminaries, the surviving handful of which had heretofore been the only alternative to the theological faculties for pastoral training. Bonhoeffer and Bethge were on holiday in Bavaria when a caravan of black sedans bearing the Nazi insignia and an SS unit arrived at Finkenwalde. The now twenty-seven ordinands were all arrested within the month. All five dissenting seminaries would be closed and boarded up by December.

"The enormous masquerade of evil" had finally reached into Pomerania. For the Finkenwalde brethren who had been living in *gemeinsames Leben* there would be no further days according the daily Christian hours. And for Bonhoeffer, this action brought an end to the happiest two years of his life.

Though under the heavy boot, he would continue to look for other means of training ministers in the Confessing Church—even as he began to consider more direct strategies of resistance and confrontation. In a final effort to keep alive the flame of dissident faith, he turned to the old and mostly forgotten practice of pastoral apprenticeships. It was an idea as clever and inspired as it was desperate. And for a while it worked. Small groups of pastoral novices were assigned to willing congregations, allowing theological life as practiced at Finkenwalde to continue on a different scale, beyond the range of state surveillance. Despite Himmler's prohibition of all religious activities "outside the immediate control" of the Reich Church, there would be, for a time, no legal challenges to the apprenticeships.[82] Bonhoeffer's vision of a *Sammelvikaria*—the nineteenth-century model of a collective pastorate—amounted, under the present circumstances, to an underground network, a sort of virtual seminary, assigning ordinands to dissident pastors still at large. Not all students would have real contact with their parish or even their mentor, but guidance would be communicated to them.

In the absence of a Confessing churchman to draw the Nazis' attention, brothers in the collective pastorates could still live together in a common house, maintaining—or "persevering in," as Bonhoeffer liked to say—the same spiritual disciplines learned in the seminaries: the liturgy of hours, intercessory prayer, and corporate worship, all now illegal, of course. In practice, this usually amounted to groups of seven to ten men keeping the ancient ways in the face of the present profanations.[83]

Two collective pastorates formed in the vicinity of Finkenwalde, one in the "rambling, wind-battered parsonage" in Schlawe, a town of ten thousand souls in Gross Schlönwitz near the Baltic Sea, the other in Köslin, a city of thirty thousand, twelve miles inland. The latter was the parish that had donated the chairs for Finkenwalde; it was also where Friedrich Onnasch, former seminary provost, now served as pastor.[84] As many as ten seminarians lived together in Onnasch's spacious manse, where secret classes were held, and where Bonhoeffer and Bethge kept a separate guest room for their visits.[85] The illicit classes involved mainly the shared reading and interpretation of scripture. Each ordinand was required to register with and "inform local authorities of the parish pastor to whom he had been apprenticed." In most instances the men complied. Bonhoeffer listed the parsonage of Block in Schlawe as his own official place of residence. "Work, meditation, worship, preaching, and biblical study remained central to the life of the ordinands in the collective pastorates."[86] But the pressure was kept up. In April 1939, the collective in Schlawe had to "relocate to nearby Sigurdshof in an empty house on the edge of the estate of a Confessing Church sympathizer."

Bonhoeffer's efforts to keep alive the spirit of Finkenwalde met with redoubled state suppression. By 1938, Hitler's lip service to the idea of the churches as "the last hope of protecting Christianity from godless Bolshevism" had outlived its political usefulness. He had never truly believed that Germany needed faith in anything more than the Nazi state's "unified principle that could explain everything." Ultimately, Nazism's all-consuming perspective could not coexist with any other form of religion; even the German Christians were at last regarded as competitors to be eliminated. Hitler, in fact, would reject not only the doctrines of the church but also the neo-pagan *völkisch* religiosity his movement had engendered and fed off of. He came to view the esoteric practices increasingly popular among a small but zealous Nazi coterie to be as distracting as Christianity. To him the essence of faith would remain the willingness to fight, and such had already been galvanized. "In a manly time of struggle," proclaimed one German Christian pastor at a Frankfurt rally in homage to the Führer, "one cannot get by with effeminate and sweet talk of peace."[87] Alas, men like him were by now preaching to the converted.

Harried by an escalation of arrests, imprisonments, and conscriptions, the collective pastorates slowly disintegrated. Bonhoeffer would carry on as an "itinerant preacher" in the northern provinces, homeless and with muted vocation, but ever grateful for the presence of Bethge. He still had the Audi, but had lately acquired a motorcycle, too; on clear days he would make the journey between Köslin and Schlawe with Bethge behind him astride the saddle. The two had become "perfectly complementary."[88] Bonhoeffer's electricity quickened Bethge's mild manner, while Bethge's steadiness moderated Bonhoeffer's dynamism, becoming for him "a hiding place from the wind . . . as the shadow of a great rock in a weary land."[89]

The story of the Confessing Church might best be described not as one of rise and fall but as "a brief energetic moment of vision and hope, followed by a gradual, poignant dissolution."[90]

THE HOME OF THE COLLECTIVE PASTORATE IN SIZURD IN 1939

CHAPTER ELEVEN

1938–1940

~

"I Must Be a Sojourner and a Stranger"

During a weeklong stay in Sigurdshof, Bonhoeffer was reading Psalm 119, the longest of the Psalms, indeed the longest chapter in the Bible. A collection of interwoven meditations on the precepts, works, and promises of God, the psalm is an elaborate acrostic corresponding to the Hebrew alphabet. Bonhoeffer would later send coded messages to fellow conspirators using the same device, but during this snowbound week in January 1939, together again with Bethge, he was fixated on the meaning of the nineteenth and twentieth verses: "I am a sojourner on the earth; hide not thy commandments from me. My soul is consumed with longing."

"The earth that nourishes me has a right to my work and my strength," Bonhoeffer wrote. "It is not fitting that I should despise the earth on which I have my life; I owe it faithfulness and gratitude. I must not dream away my earthly life with thoughts of heaven and thereby evade my lot—to be perforce a sojourner and a stranger—and with it God's call into this world of strangers. There is a very godless homesickness for the other world, and it will certainly create no homecoming. I am to be a sojourner, with everything that entails. I must not close my heart indifferent to the earth's problems, sorrows and joys; rather I am to wait patiently for the redemption of the divine promise—truly wait, and not rob myself of it in advance by wishing and dreaming."[1]

Sigurdshof was the last place Bonhoeffer would teach theology. He had retained the designation "collective pastorate" for this final experiment in communal life, but the reality—five unmarried pastors covertly ordering their lives around the liturgical day, each under the cloud of conscription—more nearly resembled the desolate rendering of the Christ-follower as exile in *Life Together*.

For many years—and with fierce concentration—Bonhoeffer had

stressed the distinctive speech and practices of Christian discipleship. The first step was inescapably a leap into the unknown. His shepherding of students and clergy had been ever infused with the urgencies of the Christian difference. But now he began to dwell upon being *in the earth* and one's relation to it, a notion disfigured in the Aryan cult practice of venerating home, hearth, blood, and soil. So many horrors had transpired in the course of human history precisely because Christians had turned their eyes upward or, worse, abandoned the narrow path— the way of the cross—for some imagined ladder of ascent. Bonhoeffer determined now to teach how a Christian dissident should think about his sojourn *on earth*.

The conscription cloud hung over him, too; though he had privately resolved never to serve in Hitler's army, he fretted about the public ramifications of his decision—not so much for his own life as for those of his Finkenwalde brothers, many of whom did not share his objection of conscience but would nevertheless be implicated in his views by association. His name had recently been added to the list of pastors banned from Berlin—banned not simply from preaching there, but even from entering the city, to his parents' great dismay. In March 1938, on one rainy night, Bonhoeffer and Bethge made a journey into the Thuringia, "the green heartland of the nation," driving from a point southwest of Berlin toward Erfurt. What Bonhoeffer saw along the way sickened him. Nazi banners draped on homes, buildings, and churches had by now become a familiar affront. But as the Wartburg Castle came into view, Bonhoeffer saw that the cross staked on the entrance had been replaced by a monstrous swastika, flood lit. In this fortress blending Romanesque and Gothic styles, which loomed over the Eisenach River, Luther had once occupied a sparsely furnished room while translating the entire New Testament in a feverish ten-week stretch. Even more depressing for Bonhoeffer: although this was Holy Week, most of his countrymen were celebrating the *Anschluss*, Hitler's annexation by force of neighboring Austria. There could have been no more compelling evidence that the German Christian drive to complete the work of Martin Luther had begun in earnest.[2] "In that I defend myself against Judaism," read Hitler's oft-quoted boast in *Mein Kampf*, "I am fighting for the work of the Lord."[3]

In disgust, the two men abruptly aborted their journey, diverting to the refuge of the Bonhoeffer country house in Friedrichsbrunn.

By the summer of 1938, the Bonhoeffers, like nearly all German dissidents, had become convinced that unless the Nazi regime was toppled, its expansionism would plunge all of Europe into war. Like many, too, they felt personally imperiled by a new slate of racial laws,

EBERHARD BETHGE AND DIETRICH BONHOEFFER
AT THE COLLECTIVE PASTORATE IN GROSS SCHLÖNWITZ

under which the passports of Jews would be required to carry the letter J. Since Gerhard Leibholz, husband of Bonhoeffer's twin, Sabine, was of Jewish descent, the couple, together with their two daughters, would join the thousands trying to flee Germany before the borders of every nation unfriendly to the Reich were permanently sealed.

One of their daughters, Marianne, recalled their last months in Göttingen before escaping to England:

> In the summer of 1938 I gathered from tiny hints thrown out by my mother that my parents were definitely preparing to leave Germany. I was just eleven. I knew about the Czech crisis and that there might be a war, that the likelihood of war was growing every day, that we did not want to be caught in Germany in a war because then we would no longer be able to leave the country if necessary. I knew that any plans to leave should be kept absolutely secret, and that if my parents told so little they had their reasons. I watched for hints of anything unusual in our lives, and on days when I got a strong feeling that something ominous would soon happen, I put several large [and] small crosses in my diary, according to the strength of my suspicions.
>
> On August 23rd my parents went to Berlin for four days and Great-Aunt Elisabeth von Hase came to supervise the house-

hold. On August 31st my father went to Hamburg for the day, on September 4th my parents left for Berlin, returning late on September 8th with Uncle Dietrich Bonhoeffer and Pastor Eberhard Bethge. On all these days I put down huge crosses.

The morning of September 9th was gloriously sunny in Göttingen. As usual our Nanny woke my seven year old sister Christiane and me at half past six and began to help us dress for school. Suddenly my mother came into the night nursery in a great hurry and said, "You're not going to school today, we're going to Wiesbaden," and to our Nanny, "We'll be back on Monday. The children are to wear two sets of underclothes each."

Our car was very full, but packed to look as if we were going on a normal holiday. Christiane and I were bedded down in the back. Uncle Dietrich and "Uncle" Bethge had brought another car, Uncle Dietrich's, and intended to accompany us to the frontier, and during the drive my parents and the uncles sat in the front seats of the two cars, changing places frequently, so that all came to sit with us children in turns.

We stopped briefly in Göttingen where the men bought a giant torch for the journey. When we were out of the town my mother said, "We're not going to Wiesbaden, we're trying to get across the Swiss border tonight. They may close the frontier because of the crisis."

DIETRICH BONHOEFFER AND EBERHARD BETHGE TAKING A BREAK AT THE BALTIC SEA, 1938

The roof of our car was open, the sky was deep blue, the country-side looked marvelous in the hot sunshine. I felt there was complete solidarity between the four grown-ups. I knew that unaccustomed things would be asked of us children from now on but felt proud of now being allowed to share the real troubles of the adults. I thought that if I could do nothing against the Nazis myself I must at the very least co-operate with the grown-ups who could. Christiane and I spent most of the time singing in the car, folk songs and rather militant songs about freedom, my mother, Uncle Dietrich and "Uncle" Bethge singing with us. I enjoyed the various descants. Uncle Dietrich taught me a new round of *Über die Wellen gleitet der Kahn.*

During the drive my uncle seemed to me just as I always remember him: very strong and confident, immensely kind, cheerful and firm.

We stopped at Giessen and picnicked by the wayside. The grown-ups' mood did not strike me as depressed. Then all of a sudden they said it was getting late and that we must hurry. "We have to get across the frontier tonight, they may close it at any moment." We children settled in our car, our parents got in, and I remember Uncle Dietrich and "Uncle" Bethge waving farewell to us, until they became tiny and were cut off by a hill. The rest of the drive was no longer cheerful. My parents drove as fast as they could, we stopped talking so that they could concentrate. The atmosphere was tense.

We crossed the Swiss border late at night. Christiane and I pretended to be asleep and very angry at being wakened to discourage the German frontier guards from doing too much searching of the car. My mother had put on a long, very brown suede jacket, whose brownness was meant to pacify the German officials. They let our car through and the Swiss let us in. My parents were not to cross the German border again till after the war.[4]

In February 1938, Bonhoeffer, a dissident since Hitler's first appearance, made his first contact with the German resistance. His brother Klaus and his brother-in-law Hans von Dohnányi, who'd married Christine Bonhoeffer, introduced Dietrich to members of a conspiracy based in a section of German military intelligence called the *Abwehr.* Hans and Klaus had no doubts about the inevitability of war.

Son of the celebrated Hungarian pianist Ernö Dohnányi, Hans, now thirty-six, had been a schoolmate of Klaus and Dietrich's at the Grunewald Gymnasium. Ernö had belonged to Hungarian nobility; therefore it was important to him when he came to Berlin in 1905 as a teacher that the prefix "von," which indicated an aristocratic descent in Germany, be added to his name.

Early on, Hans had distinguished himself as a brilliant lawyer, appointed a public prosecutor at the age of twenty-nine and an *Ober-regierungsrat* (a high-level bureaucrat) at thirty-one, having made all the right choices. But in 1936 envious rivals at the Ministry of Justice had discovered a non-Aryan family member in his maternal line, and he had been hard put to obtain a ruling from Hitler to the effect that Minister Gürtner's valued aide should suffer "no detriment" owing to "doubts" surrounding his grandfather's pedigree. He would remain in office until 1938 but meantime could see the writing on the wall. As party to the state's most sensitive "legal" actions, Dohnányi was able to construct a chronicle of Nazi brutalities. "From murder and attempted murder in concentration camps," Christine would recall, "from the . . . abominations in those camps to garden variety foreign-exchange rackets run by Gauleiters [regional paramilitary leaders] and the distasteful goings-on in the higher reaches of the Hitler Youth and SA." Dohnányi's "chronicle" would bring to light a variety of iniquities and a system whose corruptions reached as high as the Führer. Since 1933, Dohnányi had exploited his position at the Ministry of Justice and access to the Nazi regime's confidential records to compile a "Chronicle of Shame," a day-by-day listing of war crimes, military plans, and genocidal actions and policies. "To Dohnanyi, the logical inference was that his elimination would rid the country of a moral cancer," explained Heinz Höhne.[5]

In April 20, 1938, Friedrich Werner, director of the Protestant consistory, used every legal, financial, and administrative power at his disposal to bring all refractory clergy into line with the Reich. True German faith—the manly de-Judaized faith of the kind that would be propagated in various research centers, such as Walter Grundmann's Institute for the Study of the Eradication of Jewish Influence on German Church Life (established on May 6, 1939, at Wartburg Castle in Eisenach), and in the theology faculties of the Nazi-controlled university faculties—must inspire a glorious surrender to the Führer. Reforms that Werner had earlier sought to implement "with a certain spontaneity" he now carried out by brute force, both bureaucratic and spiritual.[6] His pronouncement read:

> Whereas only those may be office bearers in the Church who are unswervingly loyal to the Führer, the people and the Reich, it is hereby decreed:
> Anyone who is called to a spiritual office is to affirm his loyal duty with the following oath: "I swear that I will be faithful and obedient to Adolf Hitler, the Führer of the German Reich and

people, that I will conscientiously observe the laws and carry out the duties of my office, so help me God."

The oath was administered to all new clergy, obviously. But even pastors who had been called before Werner's decree were required to take it, and it would apply retroactively, meaning that any dissident activity prior to the decree was deemed actionable. Refusing the oath subjected one to dismissal and criminal detention.[7] To some degree, the underlying idea was consistent with the traditional Lutheran doctrine of the two kingdoms: Christians must be obedient to the earthly authorities as unto God.[8] But Werner went to an unprecedented extreme, turning a doctrine that had historically yielded a variety of views on church-state matters into an absolutist principle: make a "personal commitment to the Führer under the solemn summons of God," and forge an "*intimate solidarity* with the Third Reich" and with the saintly man who both "created that community and embodies it."[9] "Submit to Hitler with a joyful heart, in gratitude, as pleasing to the Lord."

Werner viewed his decree as a personal gift to his Führer, who on April 20 celebrated his fiftieth birthday. Hitler, evidently moved, returned Werner's tribute with a worshipful word of his own. "My feeling as a Christian," he said, "points me to my Lord and Saviour as fighter. It points me to the man who once in loneliness, surrounded only by a few followers, recognized these Jews for what they were and summoned men to the fight against them and who—God's truth!—was greatest not as sufferer but as fighter. . . . As a Christian I have no duty to allow myself to be cheated, but I have the duty to be a fighter for truth and justice."[10]

On January 30, 1939, in a speech before the Reichstag, Hitler announced his objective of the total destruction of "the Jewish race in Europe." He did not say whether accomplishing that goal would complete the work of Luther, but his militant defense of Germany's aggressive foreign policy portended even greater devastation in pursuit of that larger purpose ascribed to Luther's twilight vision: a world without Jews.[11] "Set their synagogues and schools on fire," Luther had written in his 1543 work "The Jews and Their Lies," "and whatever will not burn, heap dirt upon and cover so that no human ever again will see a stone or a cinder of it."

Jewish-owned businesses in Germany were liquidated that month, and in March German troops invaded Czechoslovakia. In the Berlin Staatsbibliothek, the city library near the Philharmonie at the Potsdamer Platz, a file from the more than twenty-five cases of Bethge papers contains a document called "List of Confessional Pastors Subject to Measures of Oppression by Police and Church Authorities as of June, 1939."[12] This was not Dohnányi's "chronicle" but a report compiled by Dietrich and Eberhard from assorted letters, dispatches, and bulletins. Included in the list of the ministers recently detained in the concentration camps was an update on the Lutheran pastor Paul Schneider of the Rhineland, imprisoned in Buchenwald. He had been arrested for "resisting the order of expulsion from his parish" in his village of Dickenschied; his wife and their six small children were then evicted from the parsonage. With chilling frankness the document reports the way the case was closed: "[Schneider] has now died as a result of maltreatment. Age 38."

There was also Pastor Alfred Leikam, a twenty-three-year-old chaplain, imprisoned "for his active Christian work among young people and for circulating news about the Church situation."

Pastor Karl Steinbauer was taken from his church in Bavaria on March 28, 1939, and locked in a cell in the Sachsenhausen camp "for his fearless Christian witness and warnings against paganism." As a matter of conscience, he refused to offer proof of his Aryan descent when it was required as a condition for his continued work as a teacher.

There was also, of course, the case of Martin Niemöller, who was sent to Sachsenhausen—where, according to his own testimony, he remained "morally and physically unbroken."

TORCHLIGHT PARADE IN THE BERLIN OLYMPIC STADIUM,
SUMMER SOLSTICE DAY, JUNE 1938

The report further listed the following oppressive measures: "103 curtailed in their functions by reduction of salary and various restrictions of their activities; 10 prohibited to leave their residence; 37 prohibited to stay in certain districts. 44 prohibited to speak in public. 100 expelled from their parishes. 4 expelled and forced to reside in small places in the country. 30 subject to measures after the Intercession-Service during the September crisis 1938 (suspension from functions or reductions of salary)."[13]

Now infamous for its meticulous record keeping, the state documented an impressive decimation of the dissenting clergy. Trusting as we should that no "oppressive acts" escaped mention, we must also see that the majority of dissident pastors were brought to heel; relatively few were those who forced the state to make good on the threat of Werner's decree. And so the perseverance of these few would finally be overshadowed by the expediency of the many. The difficulty of holding out was not a new one in Christian history: "I shall strike the shepherd, and the sheep of the flock will be scattered abroad." When ministers of the Confessing Church met on June 11, 1938, for their final disputation on "the Jewish question," Bonhoeffer was depressed to learn that the majority had taken the oath of allegiance to Hitler: 60 percent in Rhineland, 70 percent in Brandenburg, 78 percent in Saxony, 80 percent in Pomerania, 82 percent in Silesia, 89 percent in Grenzmark.[14]

It would be giving the dissenting clergy the benefit of the doubt to say that they had retreated into the insularity of theological debates. Most members of the Confessing Church had in fact taken the oath of allegiance fully aware of the "impending order for all non-Aryans to have a large 'J' stamped on their identity cards." And for the sake of confessional peace they were even prepared to subscribe to the view of Hanns Kerrl, one of the few irenic German Christians, whom Hitler had appointed to run the new Ministry for Church Affairs around the time of the roundup of 1935 (after the feckless Müller had made such a hash of things). Kerrl praised the Führer "as the bearer of a new Revelation," in fact as "Germany's Jesus Christ."

Bonhoeffer had worried since 1933 that the Confessing Church was more concerned with ecclesial purity—which is to say, its own organizational autonomy—than with Hitler's world-scale epochal ambitions. On Jewish suffering and persecution, it would remain hopelessly, infuriatingly silent, if not indifferent.

Bonhoeffer had also long seen himself as the Christian voice to challenge Hitler directly, which made him perilously conspicuous, though it is not clear who else might have been willing or able to be that voice.

At a Confessing Church meeting in October 1938, he asked his colleagues whether, "instead of talking of the same old questions again and again" (by which he meant the now effectively irrelevant issue of the church's authority versus the state's), it would be better instead "to speak of that which truly is pressing on us: what the Confessing Church has to say to [this] question of church and synagogue?"[15] He would now moreover begin speaking of an equivalence before God of the church and the synagogue, between the body of Christ and the chosen people of Israel. It was, to say the least, a stretch of Christian Orthodoxy, in which there is a clear view of the New Covenant of Christ as superseding the one God made with Moses. In Bonhoeffer's telling, the Jews—and not merely those who had become Christians—must be embraced as the "brothers of Christians," "children of the covenant," and the "children of Bethlehem," in their own right.[16] It is possible that his understanding of the question had truly evolved to such a point since his anguished refusal to officiate at the funeral of Sabine's father-in-law. Or he may have deemed this leap a moral necessity, however dogmatically dubious; he had always insisted on theology's obligation to respond to the here and now. Whatever the case, it was a claim that would set him at odds not only with the state but with most dissident Christians. He could have little hope for further solidarity with these brethren.

After Nazi gangs stormed Germany's synagogues and plundered Jewish-owned businesses, murdering scores and arresting thousands, in the Night of Broken Glass— Kristallnacht—Bonhoeffer underlined in his Luther Bible the haunting line from Psalm 74:8, "they burned all the meeting-places of God in the land," and added the date, "9.11.38," and alongside the next verse, "there is no longer any prophet," an exclamation mark.[17]

In 1939, with the Confessing Church movement in tatters, Bonhoeffer would take another leap, into a new sphere of action, meeting with members of the Berlin resistance to discuss a most audacious plan.[18]

The "lure of the political": that is what Bethge would later ascribe to the solicitations of Klaus Bonhoeffer and Hans von Dohnányi's proposal following the Confessing Church's effective demise. Indeed Bonhoeffer's decision to shift the focus of his activism from the church-based opposition to the mostly secular resistance, or Widerstand, was born of a great disappointment, not only with his fellow German dissident Christians but with the ecumenical movement: despite campaigning for nearly five years, he had been unable to persuade the leaders of the influential Faith and Order Commission—which had been founded by American Episcopalians shortly after the 1910 World Missionary Conference in Edinburgh to promote ecumenical understanding of the global churches—to acknowledge the dissenting body *as a church*. Now, with the Confessing Church having forfeited the theological high ground it could once claim, Bonhoeffer decided that the time was ripe for a new kind of engagement, a bolder vocation.

He would, however, make a final effort at solidarity with the dissident Christians at home and the Protestant churches abroad, calling on Leonard Hodgson in Oxford. Hodgson, a distinguished Anglican theologian, was secretary of the Commission on Faith and Order; he and Bonhoeffer had met twice since 1935 to discuss the crisis in the German Protestant church. Now, writing in English, Bonhoeffer expressed his concern that the "Confessional" pastors in Germany were "becoming cut off from our foreign friends." Certainly this intensifying sense of isolation was the result of the censorship, travel restrictions, and speaking bans under which Bonhoeffer and other pastors found themselves.[19] But that was not what Bonhoeffer wanted to talk about. The leaders of the ecumenical movement still recognized the Reich Church as the only legitimate Protestant church in Germany. Bonhoeffer pled for Hodgson's intercession to secure the "permanent representation" of the Confessing Church in the "oecumenic [*sic*] movement." If the Reich Church's legitimacy could be challenged, perhaps there was hope yet for the Confessing Church, if only as a scattering of beleaguered collective pastorates across the north German plains. Perhaps the body of Christ in exile was its true mission all along.

During a meeting in London at the end of March 1939, Bonhoeffer told Hodgson he needed the "theological help of other churches in order to bear the burden of responsibilities which God has laid upon us." He could have gone on at length about the insights "which God has given us anew during the last years,"[20] but as time was of the essence, Bonhoeffer got straight to his request: he wanted Hodgson to approve the creation of a permanent German secretary to represent the World Alliance in Geneva. Bonhoeffer was under no illusions about the effect of such representation. He surely did not think it would put any political pressure on Hitler. But the affirmation of the Confessing Church *as a church* was, at a minimum, what the Christian dissidents in Germany needed just to survive at all. Hodgson was unmoved. Whatever its sins, the Reich Church remained the only legitimate Protestant communion in Germany, controlling the faith's infrastructure and institutions and thereby holding sole authority to administer the sacraments in accordance with canon law. The matter, Hodgson insisted, was beyond his control. Bonhoeffer found this response pharisaical and pedantic, though not surprising. Two years earlier, Hodgson had refused to bend to Bonhoeffer's petition that he unseat the Reich Church representatives at international church synods. Now, in March 1939, he was justifying himself with the same canonical casuistry, though with notably less sympathy and patience. The dispiriting exchange would only confirm Bonhoeffer in his suspicions that the ecumenical movement had folded its hand vis-à-vis the German church crisis.

When Hitler's army occupied Prague, the same month, most Germans were content to believe that their nation's growing territorial demands could be achieved without bloodshed, through a "skillful combination of intimidation with infiltration and propaganda." But the Bonhoeffers and their dissident circle "were convinced that Hitler's military policies meant that European war was inevitable, and in all probability imminent."[21] If so, Bonhoeffer would be called for military service within a year. And so it was, as his disgust with ecclesial bureaucrats abroad exacerbated his anxieties about refusing conscription, he decided to leave Berlin for his second visit to America.[22]

Reinhold Niebuhr had had his own sharp disagreements with leaders of the ecumenical movement. He was outraged to discover that he had not been consulted about the request to Hodgson or any member of the Commission on Faith and Order. For, as he assured Bonhoeffer, he would have sided with the Confessing Church without reservation. Nonetheless, he was now more concerned about the escalating persecution of dissenting Christians in Germany than with WCC protocol. In fact, despite theological differences—Bonhoeffer for all his new realism remaining fairly neo-orthodox—Niebuhr was still the young German's most ardent supporter on the American scene, writing numerous dispatches in the *Christian Century*, *Dissent*, and his own magazine, *Christianity and Crisis*, on the Confessing Church. As a result of Niebuhr's efforts, Bonhoeffer was now known throughout Protestant circles as the courageous, lonely voice crying out against the Nazi church, and as founder of an illegal seminary. With recent reports from Germany telling of a steady increase in crackdowns and mass arrests, Niebuhr had concluded that Bonhoeffer's only hope for avoiding prison was swift flight to the United States. But neither Niebuhr nor Bonhoeffer's other America contacts knew that a year earlier, he had taken "the first step" into the resistance and its plot of tyrannicide.

In the spring of 1939, Niebuhr had taken a leave from Union Theological Seminary to prepare to deliver the prestigious Gifford Lectures at the University of Edinburgh. Niebuhr was but the fifth American who had been invited to give these annual lectures on "natural theology" endowed in 1888 by Lord Gifford with a gift of 80,000 pounds sterling.[23] The other four Americans had been William James, Josiah

Royce, John Dewey, and William Hocking. Niebuhr's talks would lead to his book *The Nature and Destiny of Man*. On a trip to London to visit Sabine and Gert, Bonhoeffer, joined by Bethge, spent a few days in April with the Niebuhrs on the northeast coast. Niebuhr's wife, the former Ursula Mary Keppel-Compton, was a native of Southampton who had earned a double first at Oxford. She had heard a lot about Bonhoeffer from her husband and others who followed the German situation. When she finally met him, something in Bonhoeffer's bearing and style convinced her immediately of his pomposity. It was not only the manner in which he sat on a "very inartistic sofa, updating Reinie on the situation in Germany."[24] Bonhoeffer was "too Teutonic," "too Prussian," Ursula said, for her tastes.[25]

Bonhoeffer and Bethge returned to London, spending their free days in the National Gallery. Niebuhr, meanwhile, dispatched an urgent memorandum to colleagues and church associates in America and abroad. Failure to secure a position for Bonhoeffer, he warned, boded ill for this man who "has done a great work for the church." To Paul Lehmann, one of Bonhoeffer's classmates in 1930–31 and now professor of Christian ethics at Union, Niebuhr confided that "there

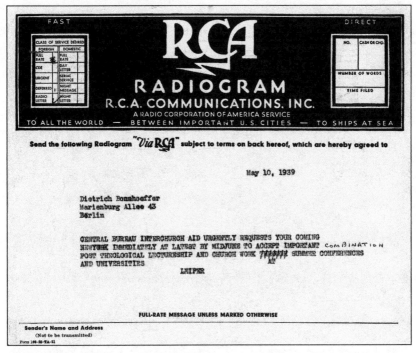

REINHOLD NIEBUHR'S LETTER TO HENRY SMITH LEIPER IN SUPPORT OF DIETRICH BONHOEFFER'S APPOINTMENT TO UNION THEOLOGICAL SEMINARY IN 1939

will be some difficulty getting [Bonhoeffer] out," but if they failed, he would surely land in a concentration camp. Even knowing little or nothing of Bonhoeffer's involvement with the resistance, Niebuhr was now aware from their meeting of Bonhoeffer's determination to refuse the draft. That alone would now constitute a crime punishable by death. For his own refusal, Hermann Stöhr, secretary of the Fellow-ship of Reconciliation, had been taken to an empty field near Stettin and shot in the back of the head.[26]

Niebuhr would succeed in arranging a position or, more precisely, a patchwork of part-time jobs—one with the German refugee program, another as an itinerant preacher, a third as a visiting professor. These would keep Bonhoeffer employed through the end of the year. Mean-while Niebuhr had hopes that a chair might be endowed to create a permanent place at Union.

The invitation came not a moment too soon. Back in Berlin, Bon-hoeffer heard from Klaus and Hans that war in Europe was indeed imminent; in May, a month after his meeting with Niebuhr in England, Bonhoeffer received the long dreaded call-up.

On a warm morning in June 1939, Bonhoeffer left Germany on his second journey to America.

"I'm flying over the Channel in the glow of a pink sunset," he wrote

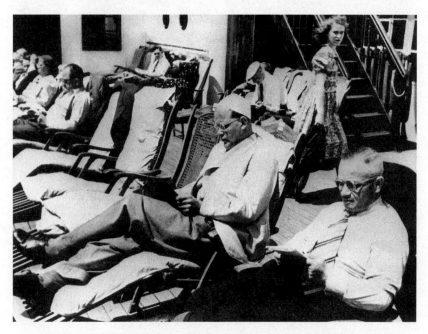

DIETRICH BONHOEFFER ON A SHIP TO AMERICA IN THE SUMMER OF 1939

to Bethge on June 4. "It is 10 o' clock, but still very bright. You will be tired and gone to bed now. . . . I am well."

After a weeklong layover in England, he boarded the *Bremen* for the five-day ocean voyage to New York. Pleased with his spacious cabin and the appointments of the ship, he read and napped in a lounge chair on the hardwood deck. He was content to be alone. "The weather is wonderful and the ocean is quiet," he told Bethge. "I will spend a lot of time thinking of you and all the others." "Today is Sunday. No worship service," he wrote from the deck of the luxury liner on the second day. The change in time zones had already prevented his taking part remotely in Bethge's worship "as it was happening"; the growing distance had already caused a clear new day to dawn in the mid-Atlantic. "But I am fully with you, today more than ever," Bonhoeffer said. "If only the doubts about my own path were overcome."[27]

He found New York much changed since his last visit nearly a decade before. The new Empire State Building had transformed the skyline, though it stood mostly tenant-less. Robert Moses's titanic public works program was evident, with new bridges and roadways in the works. In April the World's Fair had opened in Queens to great fanfare. In the Bronx, Lou Gehrig was playing in his last season for the Yankees; he would retire midsummer, having set the record for consecutive games played (2,130). The movie *The Wizard of Oz* premiered on August 17 at Loew's Capitol Theatre, almost without Judy Garland's iconic "Over the Rainbow," which, the producers feared, might slow down the story. John Steinbeck's *The Grapes of Wrath*, published by Viking Press, won the National Book Award and the Pulitzer Prize. Somewhat less conspicuously, an unabridged edition of *Mein Kampf* appeared for the first time in English.[28]

Bonhoeffer could not summon the sense of optimism and adventure and wonder that had attended his last sojourn in New York. The hard lessons of the previous years had brought him closer to Niebuhr's realism, and Harlem was no longer on his mind. At the World's Fair, his heart sank to see the "Temple of Religion," where, under an enormous tent, Christians and Jews were preaching in turns, as if in a circus act.

He arrived at Union Theological Seminary in the middle of the summer vacation, on the first day of a heat wave. The brick and limestone fortress sprawling between Broadway and Claremont Avenue on the city's Upper West Side was a world away from the rustic estate where Finkenwalde had not too long ago flourished, even further from the modest parish houses of the collective pastorates. He unpacked his bags in the room for visiting scholars—the "prophet's chamber," it was called. But what kind of prophet was he? At least he had plenty of space.

With the temperatures soaring into the high nineties, it was impossible to shut the windows—and with one giving onto the interior courtyard, the other onto Broadway, the street noise persisted until late at night, even then abating only little. The airlessness was enervating.

And so was the lack of society. Niebuhr had advised him to come to New York as soon as possible, which Bonhoeffer took to heart. But when he arrived in New York City on the morning of June 12, his American hosts, decent and thoughtful people, were nowhere to be found. Niebuhr was still in Scotland with his family, preparing for his Gifford Lectures, scheduled for September. The convivial Lehmanns had decamped to Indiana, where Paul held summer classes at Elmhurst College; he confessed that he was unsure when exactly he and his wife, Marion, would be back in town. Paul Tillich, who wholeheartedly supported Bonhoeffer's appointment, was sequestered in his Maine retreat, and in any case not involved in the details of the younger German's case. Though deeply grateful for the support of his American friends, Bonhoeffer, in his vulnerable state, was suffering their absence.

He passed the time by smoking cigarettes, reading, and taking walks. He visited the Metropolitan Museum, where he lingered over El Greco's *View of Toledo*, a "landscape . . . entirely in green," and Hans Memling's *Christ Giving His Blessing*. He tried to catch up on the latest American theology, and he thumbed through recent issues of the *Nation* and the *Christian Century*—including the column "How My Mind Has Changed," which he thought "instructive." He bought Niebuhr's newest book, *Interpretation of Christian Ethics*—which he found "filled with wrong and superficial statements"—and a volume titled *The Kingdom of God in America* by H. Richard Niebuhr, Reinhold's younger brother and a Yale theologian; that he found a little more palatable. In fact, he would borrow a few of its observations for his own final summation of American Christianity, an essay titled "Protestantism Without Reformation."[29] Still, he found all the books and articles ultimately uninspiring. "The decisive shift to the Word still does not seem to have been made," he concluded.

There was plenty of time to send postcards home. And every few days he rang Karl-Friedrich for a quick chat; his brother was in the final month of a sabbatical year at the University of Chicago. He made entries in his brown leather journal—a going-away present from Bethge. Never one to inventory his interior life, Bonhoeffer was left with few other options amid the shock of separation. Later in prison, on hot summer days in his stifling cell, he would tell his parents not to worry about him, seeing as how he had survived the heat of "Italy, Africa, Spain, Mexico—and perhaps worst of all in New York in July 1939."

As a sensitive child, he had always been content with small pleasures, whether accompanying his mother as they sang the Gellert-Beethoven songs, collecting wildflowers in the glades near his home, or reading stories aloud with Sabine after school in the garden. In his Union dormitory, he drank coffee, ate moderately, smoked immoderately, and sat at his desk with a floor fan, taking the little relief it offered.

He was able to make contact with a few acquaintances who didn't live according to the academic calendar.[30] Paul Griswold Macy—a scion of the Macy's department store fortune and a sturdy Protestant churchman—met Bonhoeffer on his first night in town for drinks at the Parkside Hotel. Another moneyed Manhattanite, Henry Smith Leiper, showed him around the Federal Council of Churches, an entire city block filled with ecumenical offices, and hosted a dinner party for him at a midtown restaurant. Bonhoeffer also reconnected with the theologian Henry van Dusen. Unfortunately, he found Van Dusen even less sympathetic than during his previous stay at Union, when the two quarreled over doctrine. "A poor and self-righteous theologian of the American mold," Bonhoeffer concluded. "I don't like him."

Coffin, the seminary president, invited Bonhoeffer to come with him by train to his country house in the Berkshires. Of all his New York acquaintances, Bonhoeffer liked Coffin, with his refreshing candor and deliberate piety, best of all. Bonhoeffer's admiration only grew as he discovered Coffin to be a clear and practical man who understood "the necessity of preaching the gospel with a generous conviction"—a side of him Bonhoeffer had missed the last time in New York. "Niebuhr preaches a half hour about the 'failure of man' and the last two minutes about the 'grace of God,'" Coffin said with a smile. At that Bonhoeffer could smile, too.

Bonhoeffer told his parents that the Connecticut countryside reminded him of the area around Friedrichsbrunn. He breathed a little easier on the porch of Coffin's Lakeland home, with a glass of cold gin and the "fresh and luxuriant" landscape rolling to the horizon.[31] He had never seen fireflies in the eastern Harz Mountains, but during the evening in the Berkshires, "thousands of fire-flies," along with "flying glow-worms," flashed against the fading daylight like shooting stars. "Quite a fantastic sight!" he wrote in his diary. Aiming to lift Bonhoeffer's clearly flagging spirits, the Coffins or their friends held dinner parties in their homes or took him to concerts and plays; ultimately, however, they would fail to relieve him of his apprehensions. The best efforts of these energetic men and their fine families could not overcome his acute sense of dislocation.[32] Everything felt freighted with melancholy.

A journal entry reads,

Since yesterday evening my thoughts cannot get away from Germany. . . . In the morning a car drive that was in itself beautiful, to a woman acquaintance in the countryside, i.e., in the mountains, became almost unbearable to me. One sat for an hour and chatted, not at all stupidly, but about matters that were so utterly trivial to me, whether a proper musical education is possible in New York, about raising children, etc. etc., and I could only think how usefully I might have spent these hours in Germany. . . .

In the evening the cinema: *Juarez* with P. Muni.[33] A good film. My thoughts were captured for a while. . . .

[But] this inactivity, or rather active pursuit of trivialities, is simply no longer bearable. I would have liked to take the next ship.

The situation at home, it was now clear, had depleted his lifelong love of idle pleasures to a remarkable degree. Dietrich had become consumingly serious.

Amid the outings and pleasantries and cocktail hours of the New York summer set, Bonhoeffer had found no time for Bible study and prayer, but this would change.

"All I need is Germany, the brethren," he lamented. "I do not understand why I am here."[34] He proposed to Bethge that they mark their first Sundays apart with the promise that "someday we will worship together in eternity." Bonhoeffer had already reached the conclusion that a year in America would be far too long—despite Niebuhr and Coffin's hopes that he would stay at least that long.

Back in Manhattan, he sought relief from the weight bearing down on him from the assurances of scripture. In the Bible's cold, sober comforts, there were no quick remedies to be found. But he wasn't seeking anything of the kind. He read Lamentations, the Psalms, and the Hebrew prophets. They spoke to the virtue of patience: "It is good that one should wait quietly for the salvation of the Lord" (Lamentations 3:26). As he had done at Finkenwalde, he followed the daily readings in the *Losungen*, the devotional book of the Moravian Brethren that his governess had given him as a child. He pondered the lines from Isaiah: "You are my servant, I have chosen you and not cast you off" (41:9). And Psalm 28:7: "The Lord is my strength and my shield; in him my heart trusts; so I am helped, and my heart exults, and with my song I give thanks to him." How excellent were the daily readings, he said. Despite the divide of an ocean, reading them in sync with Bethge and the brethren sustained a spiritual bond, one to overcome any earthly distance.

In the prophet's chamber, he wrote in fits and starts. Over the years he had rarely labored over assignments, sermons, books, or letters. Writing mostly involved the smooth transcription of well-organized thoughts. Now the subject seemed more complicated than even the mysteries of the Incarnate, Crucified, and Risen Christ. He was trying to understand himself.

"Is it cowardice and weakness to run away from the here and now? . . . I can hardly tear my thoughts away from Germany.

"I am [not] quite clear about my motives. Is that a sign of uncertainty, inner dishonesty, or is it a sign that God leads us over and beyond our own powers of discernment; or is it both?" Introspection, a new pursuit for him, had reduced him to probing the most elementary matters.

"I would not have thought it possible that at my age, after so many years abroad, one could get so dreadfully homesick. . . . The whole burden of self-reproach because of a wrong decision comes back again and almost overwhelms me."

It vexed Bonhoeffer, too, that Bethge seemed not to share his urgency to correspond, and he scolded his friend in his own voluminous epistolary outpourings. Bethge acknowledged with gratitude the "abundance of letters" coming from New York, while Bonhoeffer complained that he hardly received a thing. Bethge apologized and tried to explain, suggesting that some of his letters were getting lost in transit. He also worried that letters and photographs would only inflame Bonhoeffer's loneliness. Sometimes he pled that he was "so overworked" or even unwell. "I would really ask you to bear in mind what the new situation has demanded of me and not be angry, so that we can look forward to our reunion without ill thoughts." Bonhoeffer could easily fire off a letter and a postcard nearly every day; Bethge had no such spare time, having not been relieved of his pastoral duties and other obligations, and there being, besides, not much to report from Sigurdshof: "The weather is so bad. I was desperate to go to the Baltic Sea. But there is a storm. Not even tennis is an option right now. Ms. Pastor Gelhoff died unexpectedly. Cerebral hemorrhage or something similar." None of it was enough for Bonhoeffer.

"I wait for mail! It can hardly be endured. I will probably not stay long."

Meanwhile, the gospels' very own urgency was making itself felt:

"'Watch therefore, for ye know neither the day nor the hour wherein the Son of man cometh' (Mt 25:13). . . . God's word today states: 'See, I am coming soon—.' (Rev. 3:11). No time is to be lost, and here I am losing days, perhaps weeks. . . . I cannot be alone abroad. That is utterly clear to me."

Bonhoeffer did not seek out his old classmates. Although he stopped by the West Side YMCA on Fifty-seventh Street—to which he was introduced through Charles Webber's social ministry class—he did not worship at Abyssinian Baptist. Adam Clayton Powell Sr. had retired two years earlier, handing the mantle in 1938 to his ambitious twenty-nine-year-old son. But it was not the younger Powell who kept Bonhoeffer away. Bonhoeffer's search for a cloud of witnesses had been fulfilled in the fellowship of the brethren—here lay the love and burden of his heart and soul. The Harlem church had once nourished him, and invigorated his moral imagination, and for that he remained grateful. But the American dilemma had been overshadowed by German suffering in the joyful pursuit of his pastoral calling.

Bonhoeffer did ask about race relations—mentioning a "noon conversation with two students from southern states about the problems of blacks"—and he was saddened to learn that apart from the Castigan-Wagner Bill, an anti-lynching measure debated in both houses of Congress in 1934 but ultimately filibustered into oblivion, "nothing seems to have changed." Not until 1968 would federal statute outlaw lynching, a measure passed under the auspices of the Civil Rights Act.

He asked, too, about American Jews and noted in his journal the "great increase in anti-Semitism" in the United States. He had seen two advertisements in a local paper that read, "A mountain resort: '1000 feet—too high for Jews.'" And: "Gentiles preferred."

He heard a sermon at Riverside Church on Sunday, June 18, given not by Harry Emerson Fosdick but by Halford E. Luccock, professor of homiletics at Yale. Luccock ruminated on William James's phrase *accepting a horizon*, which Bonhoeffer found "discreet, opulent, [and] self-satisfied," recoiling from what seemed to him a veritable "temple of idolatry." The sermon left such a bad taste that he sought out another service the same night—somewhere he might hear the gospel preached, to clear his mind of Luccock's insipid remarks.[35] If accepting an ultimate horizon was the essence of religion, he said, then may a thousand Friedrich Nietzsches blossom. John McComb's evangelical sermon on "being conformed to Christ" at the Broadway Presbyterian Church was something of an improvement—but "what dreadful music."[36]

Bonhoeffer's final summation of mainline Protestantism, "Protestantism Without Reformation," would confirm many of his observations from a decade ago, but he could now barely conceal his disdain for American Christianity and its "I-centrism." Indeed, the essay fairly burns with contempt for the "denominations of America." "I am now reflecting often on whether it is true that America is the land without Reformation." Or even more bluntly: "God has granted its churches no Reformation." The American churches had surely produced thrifty churchmen, earnest theologians, and revivalist preachers, but they had failed as yet to reckon seriously with the "scandal of the Cross."

Some of his criticisms bore sharp resemblance to ones he had leveled against the German Christians. According to Bonhoeffer, the American Christian had never learned to trust God fully, or to know what it means to stand under the judgment of the Word, for he had never had to learn the lesson. Flight from persecution was the founding condition of the American religion; thus "the person and work of Jesus Christ" sink into the background and are not recognized "as the sole basis of radical judgment and radical forgiveness."[37] Where were the communities of "judgment and radical forgiveness?" he asked, despite having made no great effort to find them. Absent a Reformation crisis, when Christians might have been thrown back on the truth of the Word of God alone, American Protestants had preferred to claim "the right to forgo" suffering and "live out their faith in freedom without a struggle." Between fight and flight, flight had been the American experience, at least in matters spiritual.

The essay lumbers well beyond the limits of its usefulness, but ultimately the shortcomings of American Christianity are not its real concern anyway. Bonhoeffer was wrestling with a more general question about the options of "perseverance or flight in times of persecution." Having been talked into the latter by friends with the best of intentions, he was struggling to find his way back to the former, where, he knew, he would end up.

In Germany, baptisms now routinely concluded with the prayer that "this child will grow up to be like Adolph Hitler and [Heinrich] Himmler." The theology departments now existed for the sole purpose of building "a religious foundation for the new State ethics."[38] Bonhoeffer had provocatively claimed that the German Protestant who is not aligned with the Confessing Church is not a Christian; to this Martin Sasse, bishop of Thuringia, responded, "In Germany, there is no life except with the Führer." The German Christians had waged a seven-year campaign to make the churches safe for the Reich, winning virtually all their parishioners to the Nazi cause. What a pity for them that Hitler no longer cared.

By 1939, most high-ranking members of the regime, beginning with the Führer himself, were of the mind that Christianity was no different from Judaism in its enfeebling effects on the *Volk*. The religion of Jesus—a Jew, after all—was at last a "malignant, corrupting influence," a faith of and for the darker races, not compatible with the Aryan soul. Bonhoeffer had long argued that Christianity and Judaism were inseparable; in the end, the Nazis would agree, although with a grotesquely different purpose. The anti-Semitic journal *Der Stürmer* ran a cartoon of a Jewish man raising the hat of a Christian cleric over his head. There is no question of his race: he has an angular, attenuated nose and his bloated form is naked but for a crest with the star of David. He has also a tail and cloven hoofs. "The Church: Under good protection," the caption reads.

Bonhoeffer would continue to write from New York in fretful, revelatory bursts.

"I no longer know where I am."

"I cannot make out why I am here . . . whether the end will justify it."

"I cannot believe it is God's will that I should stay on here, in the event of war, without any particular assignment."

W hen the new visiting scholar first opened the doors of Union's "prophet's chamber" at the start of the fall semester, he would be taken aback by the mess, which no one had yet bothered to clean up after the prior tenant. An ashtray on the desk overflowed with cigarette stubs and burned matches. Crumpled writing papers, dozens and dozens of wadded-up sheets, lined the floor. The young scholar could make out a German word or two; otherwise the handwriting was illegible. Had he been able to decipher Bonhoeffer's pinched cursive, he might have learned the reason for the previous occupant's abrupt departure.

"Christians in Germany will face the terrible alternative of either willing the defeat of their nation in order that Christian civilization may survive, or willing the victory of the nation and thereby destroying our civilization," he had finally explained in a letter to Niebuhr. "I know which of these alternatives I must choose, but I cannot make that choice in security. . . . I have come to the conclusion that I made a mistake in coming to America."

It had long been Bonhoeffer's inclination, in the face of any approaching crisis, to let the logic of external events carry him forward or to withdraw from the scene as gracefully as he could. Either way, he always achieved the same result of managing to avoid decisive action. "Whenever there was a dilemma, I just left it in abeyance and—without really consciously dealing with it intensively—let it grow toward the clarity of a decision." For all his youthful rebelliousness against faculty sclerosis, for all his hungering after new things and places, for all his spadework in the ecumenical community for the Confessing Church, he'd been a mostly passive sort, ever bobbing and weaving amid the raining blows of authority, never standing still to face the consequences of real action. But the half summer in New York—June 12 through July 27, 1939—forged a new resolve. These six weeks of feverish prayer and self-examination enabled him to know his own heart. "Manhattan at night, the moon stands above the skyscrapers. It is very hot. The journey is over. I am glad that I was there, and glad that I am on my way home again."

He would join the struggle that would cost him his life. He would pray, and plot, for the defeat of his country. He would find clarity in responsible action and in the free decision to suffer. And he would be reunited with Bethge.

"I am happy to join you at the Baltic Sea," Dietrich wrote to Eberhard from the deck of the *Queen Mary*. "I am very much looking forward to it. Please see to it that we have nice lodgings. . . . I am very excited. It is beautiful: we can share many stories on the beach. . . . By the way, Sabine wants to give us the trip to Switzerland as a present, I think that's very nice of her. . . . What shall it be after the Baltic Sea? Do you want to have me or not? I would like to know. It won't be long and we will meditate together again."

Bonhoeffer made the strange discovery that in all the decisions, he had always obscured his own motives. He wondered whether it was something characterological, "a sign of lack of clarity, inner dishonesty." Or did it rather mean that "we are *led* beyond that which we can discern, or is it both?" Whatever the case, he was certain now, perhaps for the first time, that the decision was fully his own.

"Since I have been on the ship, the interior conflict about my future has ceased. I can think about the abbreviated time in America without self-reproach. Passage for the day: 'It is good for me that I have been humbled; that I might learn thy statutes' (Psalm 119:71). From my favorite psalm one of my favorite verses." The ship landed at Southampton, giving him the chance to call on Sabine and Gert once more, but then it was on to the fatherland.

Bonhoeffer's story after his return to Germany in July 1939 and before his arrest on April 5, 1943, undoubtedly marked a new stage in his life; but much of it remains a mystery to be solved. He necessarily entered into a covert resistance, practicing carefully calculated duplicity in the pursuit of one objective: Hitler's demise.[39] This new way, too, engaged his philosophical bent: What does it mean, he pondered, to tell the truth?

Whatever the attendant travails, the next three years, most of that time shared with Bethge, proved singularly fulfilling. He would describe them to Sabine "as great abundance for us." Moving his home base in Pomerania every few months, he traveled secretly from one eastern German village to another, supervising his remaining students, "the brethren" who had not yet been called to the front. With the outbreak of hostilities in September—ahead of the invasion of Poland there had been military mobilization and the signing of the Molotov-Ribbentrop pact—pressures "intensified in a new way."[40] Under increased police surveillance, Bonhoeffer rarely preached or spoke in public, and he was forbidden to publish. The villages of eastern Pomerania were teeming with German infantry awaiting deployment to Poland. All these restrictions complicated his daily plans with Bethge during those months.

On the afternoon of June 19, 1940, Bonhoeffer and Bethge were sitting in a café on the Baltic seaside when news reached them that France had surrendered to Germany. In an instant everyone rose to their feet in celebration, and some, clambering onto chairs and table, with outstretched arms, began to sing "Die Fahne Hoch"—"The Flag on High"—the Nazi Party anthem also known as the Horst Wessel Song. Making a good show, Bonhoeffer joined in, shooting a triumphant *"Heil Hitler"* for emphasis. When Bethge objected, Dietrich leaned into him and demanded, "Are you crazy? Raise your arm!" Later, when they were alone, Bonhoeffer explained that in the days ahead they would suffer many risks for "many different things, but not for that salute!"[41]

Hitler's massive ground and air assault would soon unleash a storm of death and destruction whereby German forces overwhelmed the Polish army, and forced the surrender of Warsaw on September 28 of the previous year. England, followed in short order by France, Australia, and New Zealand, had declared war on Germany in response to this aggression as it was getting under way on September 3. By now, however, Poland lay smoldering.

One factor in his abortive decision to go to America had not changed: he still lived under imminent threat of call-up to active combat duty. Protestant clergymen were receiving their orders every day in large numbers; nearly all theology students and seminarians would be sent to the front within the year. Bonhoeffer applied to the Reich Church for an army chaplaincy—this seemed like a fea-

DIETRICH BONHOEFFER AND HIS SISTER SABINE IN WHAT WOULD BE
THEIR LAST VISIT, ENGLAND, SUMMER 1939

sible way to avoid killing on behalf of the Reich. Church officials waited six months to inform him that his request was denied. And so he accepted an assignment in the office of the *Abwehr*, the German military intelligence. This decision, and his dual role as a secret agent in the resistance—while continuing to mentor young seminarians and pastors—would sow great confusion among those who knew Bonhoeffer; as a way of staying out of the army, however, the *Abwehr* allowed him to avoid doing violence on the Reich's behalf, while also maintaining his contacts with the outside world. The exact dates of Bonhoeffer's entry into the resistance are unclear—his progress was incremental, with no formal commitment—but it is certain that in the fall of 1939 he made his first contact with Hans Oster, the resistance leader who was also an Army general and deputy chief of the *Abwehr*.[42] By the time the German military invaded Poland on September 1, Bonhoeffer had already expressed his willingness to be involved somehow in Oster's plans, which centered on a military coup.[43]

His service in the conspiracy notwithstanding, on June 5, 1940, Bonhoeffer's fears were realized when he was summoned to the military recruitment station in Schlawe. After a medical examination, he was officially pronounced "KV," which meant "fit for military service."[44] It was now only a matter of time.

In a conversation with Dohnányi in late July, Bonhoeffer finally decided to serve as a *V-Mann* (*Verbindungsmann*, or secret agent) in military intelligence under Wilhelm Canaris, the chief and anti-Nazi conspirator of whom Oster was a close confidant. Bonhoeffer would use the position to gather what news he could, heard and overheard, regarding German military plans, and disseminate it through his network of conspirators. Through his extensive ecumenical contacts, he would also try to keep the Allies apprised of resistance activities in the hopes of garnering international support for a non-Nazi government to follow the planned coup. Bonhoeffer's intention to avoid the draft had led him along a circuitous path to the singular assignment as a counterintelligence agent, but it had been successful. His involvement with the *Abwehr* released him from combat duty.

He seemed to be worming his way in without notice, when in September 1940 the Reich Central Security Office informed him that after a thorough review of his activities since 1935, the office had reached the verdict that his teaching and preaching constituted an "activity subverting the people."[45] He would be required "to report regularly to police in the village of Schlawe, near Finkenwalde, which had become his official place of residence."[46] This amounted to a ban on living in Berlin, which he had sought to avoid by establishing residence elsewhere— first at a cottage in Pomerania and then in a guest room in Königsberg. Bonhoeffer took these restrictions in stride. The ban on public speaking covered speech anywhere in the Reich, not just Berlin. Bonhoeffer was surprised to learn that a small student gathering he had recently led one evening in Blöstau had been reported to the Gestapo. In this town on the outskirts of Königsberg, home to a university, Bonhoeffer expounded on the story of the rich young man in the Gospel of Luke, and conducted a worship service the following morning. That afternoon, he had been scheduled to give a lecture titled "The Problem of Death," but as he was chatting casually with students at the coffee hour following the service, a squad of Gestapo agents arrived and closed down the meeting.[47] Fifty years later, researchers working in a Berlin archive would discover that one of the six participants had been a Gestapo spy. The evening before, when Bonhoeffer preached the story of the rich man unwilling to forego earthly rewards and pick up the cross, the Gestapo informant thought Bonhoeffer's interpretation "in a way that seemed to register subversive intent." That claim would have been true in whatever time or place that parable was preached.

E ven before the war, some regime opponents within Germany had begun plotting an overthrow. This first plan, conceived during the Sudeten crisis in 1938, depended on the support of key figures within the German military. It would never be set in motion, however; with German victories in Poland and on the western front, the military leaders' appetite for such risks diminished. The resistance groups would have to find another way of showing their seriousness if they wished to win material support from abroad.[48]

During the first weeks of autumn 1940, after having made up his mind to join the conspiracy, but before having been accepted into the *Abwehr*, Bonhoeffer wrote a meditation that would eventually be included in his *Ethics:* "The Church . . . was silent when it should have cried out, because the blood of the innocent was crying aloud to heaven. . . . It has stood by while violence and wrong were being done under cover of . . . the name of Jesus Christ. . . . The Church confesses that it has witnessed the lawless application of brute force, the physical and spiritual suffering of countless innocent people, oppression, hatred, and murder, and that it has not found ways to hasten their aid."[49]

One trammel on the resistance was the difficulty of noncombatants being unable to travel outside Germany, even to neutral nations. Without his new position, he would have found himself stuck in the Reich with most of his associates. But as a civilian member of the *Abwehr*, he would serve as a courier and diplomat to the British government; he would take the opportunity to provide classified material to the Allies and lobby for their support of a coup attempt. The official reason for such an unlikely appointment to a Nazi counterintelligence post was the belief that Bonhoeffer's experiences abroad would help keep the *Abwehr* informed of political developments in the United States, England, and Sweden, in particular.

Most of his theological and pastoral colleagues abroad would remain unaware of his being a double agent and were understandably perplexed upon suddenly discovering his role in the Nazi government. Bonhoeffer understood the risk of inviting misunderstanding and suspicion. The best he could do under the circumstances was to ask his friends' patience and prayer and to express his hope that they not lose faith in him. But he would not offer more specific assurances.

Bonhoeffer undertook his move into active conspiracy without the blessings of the church—needless to say: the Reich Church controlled the institutional structures of German Lutheranism, and the Confessing Church, never recognized, lay in ruins. It is interesting to ask what the position of the dissident church would have been on this question, had it even won the acknowledgment it sought from the ecumenical movement. As it was, Bonhoeffer regarded his decision as naturally continuous with his pastoral vocation: he would serve as a theologian, pastor, and confessor in the resistance. And doing so he would be obliged to depend on his own resources. There was no precedent for a Lutheran minister to be involved in civil subversion as a duty of his office. Fortunately, at least for his cover, Bonhoeffer's new involvements "looked more like collaboration to some."

One who would take that view was Karl Barth. He could see no other reason for Bonhoeffer's freedom to travel outside Germany as the war raged on. During his September 1941 trip to Switzerland, Barth asked Bonhoeffer directly, "Why are you actually here?" It was a fair question—and one many colleagues and associates were asking privately. Offered Bonhoeffer's vague reassurances, Barth remained skeptical. As for Bonhoeffer's more cryptic allusions to a coup and the creation of a new government, Barth found them altogether delusional. Over the next two years Bonhoeffer would continue to hear from mutual acquaintances that the master in Basel could not for the life of him understand what this pacifistic evangelical monk was up to.

But how is it possible that Bonhoeffer—a professed anti-Nazi, beset with numerous bans and restrictions, the most indomitable voice of the Confessing Church—would have been given a position in military intelligence? How could the Nazis possibly have trusted him? Popular and scholarly accounts of the conspiracy have largely demurred in the face of these critical, and surely inescapable, questions.

The answer is twofold. First, there were his connections to Dohnányi, a commissioned major in military intelligence, and to Oster, the head of Department Z, the central department of the Military Intelligence Foreign Office in the army high command. Second, inside the Nazi bureaucracy, an intense rivalry had formed between the Gestapo and the *Abwehr;* the point of dispute was control over state intelligence. When high-ranking military officers learned from Gestapo sources that Bonhoeffer had been recruited as an *Abwehr* spy, they seized the opportunity not only for the obvious purpose—using his ecumenical contacts to gather information on foreign governments—but also to strengthen the military's hand within the regime: the prospect of such a useful operative was, however irrationally, irresistible despite the flashing red lights of his past activities. The *Abwehr* leadership therefore was deeply motivated to have him and succeeded in persuading the more suspicious Gestapo that Bonhoeffer's international stature would make him an "excellent collector of information." It was, one might suppose, conceivable that such a spirited young man had seen the light; in any case his ecumenical activities per se had posed no perceived threat to Reich security. And so he was waved through.

Regarding the question of why Bonhoeffer would have accepted Dohnányi's invitation, the reasons would be even more obvious in retrospect: on February 7, 1941, after seeking a deferment for two years, he would receive a classification excusing him from active military service.

His continuing activity among the international churches gave him plausible cover for his efforts as a Nazi spy; at the same time, his work as a Nazi spy disguised his work as a conspirator recruited by Oster, Canaris, Gisevius, and Dohnányi, for the purpose of undermining the Third Reich.[50] The conspirators were even more tolerant than the Nazis of his ties to the enemy, for they knew that the coup's success would depend on not only Allied support but especially a willingness to suspend "military action against Germany in the aftermath of a successful overthrow." The churches in the Allied countries were, after all, among the most trusted of national institutions; what better way to win over their governments than to persuade Bonhoeffer's "ecumenical contacts . . . to convince the allies that a post-Hitler government represented by disenchanted members of the German military could be trusted"? Dohnányi charged Bonhoeffer with this very task of communicating to the British and French and others that the resistance, with its deep roots in military and political leadership, was reliable. At the same time, the resisters were patriots. And so Bonhoeffer must also win assurances in return that neither Germany nor the plotters would suffer because of this subversive action. "The military members of the resistance wanted guarantees of German territorial integrity and of their own position as leaders of a postwar Germany."

But such assurances would never materialize. Bonhoeffer's communiqués via bishops and influential ecumenists, as well as the secret reports of other conspirators to members of the Allied intelligence, were received mainly with collective distrust. In the end, neither the Americans nor the British ever considered a German coup a serious plan worth supporting.[51]

The conspirators would carry on without foreign assistance, and in the end this isolation may have doomed their effort.

In the Nazi Reichsgau of Wartheland, the conquered province comprising greater Poland and its surrounding areas, the Reich's regional governor, Arthur Greiser, outlined his vision of a thoroughly assimilated and unified church in his "Thirteen Points" of March 14, 1940.

But by that time, Hitler's regime no longer cared that the churches had taken the oath to the Führer, affirmed the Aryan laws, excommunicated the Jewish Christians, thrown out the Old Testament, fashioned a Teutonic Christ, and done everything else imaginable to accommodate the regime. The "Thirteen Points" were intended as the finishing touches on the hideous process of *Gleichschaltung*, the assimilation of all German life under Nazi rule. But by criminalizing all activities associated with the churches, those who had forfeited the faith would only find themselves forfeited in turn.

Among the program's mandates was the prohibition of all youth groups dedicated to religious formation. Injunctions were issued against church offerings, the printing of church bulletins, calendars of the Christian year, monthly newsletters, sermons, or reports from missionaries abroad. Laypeople were forbidden to contribute directly to congregation life, so older men and women of all ages—all Germans not called to the front—were barred from "mak[ing] themselves available for pastoral care." The Gestapo forbade meetings in house churches, services in schools, and any religious activity on private property—all of which practices were common among the collective pastorates, as well as with rural parishes, where the loss of the local pastor meant that sacraments and the rest of church life came to an end. This purpose was effectively served by drafting the clergy en masse, not only from the Confessing Church but from the Reich Church as well. The life of the congregations could not continue without the leader: "I will strike the shepherd . . ."

The "Thirteen Points" also brought an abrupt end to the Lutheran Service of the Word, whereby a layperson read a sermon written by a minister in absentia, as well as to chaplaincy programs in church-run hospitals and to the religious formation of children. High school students seeking Bible study on school grounds were threatened with expulsion, even in church schools. If students and laypeople wanted to form a study group, they were permitted only if they chose a theme or book of direct service to the Reich, such as Friedrich Schmidt's best seller *Das Reich als Aufgabe—The Kingdom as a Task*, the first edition running to seven million copies—and devoted their attention to the Führer's apocalyptic hopes, the breaking away from all non-Aryan traditions, "the decisive destruction of the churches," the creation of "the inner conditions" for total victory—the triumph of the pure German will.

Bonhoeffer was left virtually alone to preserve the convictions of the old Confessing Church. Moving more deeply into his double identity of theologian and spy, he began to minister to both the conspirator and the collaborator alike. By the end of 1940, he had deftly fashioned the narrowest ledge on the church's ruined edifice as it leaned against the ghostly pillar of the resistance. From that tight spot he gave tireless voice to the embattled language of the gospel.

His Easter sermon of 1940 proclaimed in Stettin:

> The resurrection of Jesus Christ is God's Yes to Christ and his work of expiation. The cross was the end, the death of the Son of God, curse and judgment on all flesh. If the cross had been the last word about Jesus, then the world would be lost in death and damnation without hope; then the world would have triumphed over God. But God, who alone accomplished salvation for us—"all this is from God" (2 Cor. 5:18)—raised Christ from the dead. That was the new beginning that followed the end as a miracle from on high—not, like spring, according to a fixed law, but out of the incomparable freedom and power of God, which shatters death. "Holy Scripture plainly says / That death is swallowed up by death" (Luther). . . .
>
> The resurrection of Jesus Christ is God's Yes to us. Christ died for our sins; he was raised for our righteousness (Rom. 4:25). Christ's death was the death sentence upon us and our sins. If Christ had remained dead, this death sentence would still stand: "We would still be in our sins" (1 Cor. 15:17). Because, however, Christ is risen from the dead, our sentence has been lifted, and we are risen with Christ (1 Cor. 15). . . .
>
> The resurrection of Jesus Christ is God's Yes to the created being. What takes place here is not the destruction of life in the body but its new creation. The body of Jesus comes forth from the tomb, and the tomb is empty. . . . We know that God has judged the first creation and has brought about a new creation in the likeness of the first. It is not an idea of Christ that lives on, but the bodily Christ. This is God's Yes to the new creature in the midst of the old. In the resurrection, we acknowledge that God has forsaken the earth but has personally won it back. God has given it a new future, a new promise. The very earth God created bore the Son of God and his cross, and on this earth the Risen One appeared to his own, and to this earth Christ will come again on the last day. Those who affirm the resurrection of Christ in faith can no longer flee the world, nor can they still be enslaved by the world, for within the old creation they have perceived the new creation of God.[52]

CHAPTER TWELVE

1940–1941

~

"Christmas amid the Ruins"

A winter storm was blanketing the village of Ettal, sometimes in billowy down, sometimes as blinding white sheets. Every day "it snowed like crazy." Bonhoeffer had taken a room in the Hotel Ludwig der Bayer across the street from the Benedictine monastery, where he would live for the next three months. Throughout December 1940 and into the first weeks of January 1941, the snow would continue, covering hill and dale and house. A path cut from the hotel to the monastery disappeared amid the drifts seven and eight feet high. "Extraordinary!" Bonhoeffer wrote.[1]

There were nights when the distant roar of fighter planes signaled that the Allies had brought the fight to Munich, which lay a hundred kilometers to the north; there were nights when the shriek of the air raid alarms shattered the stillness, warning of attack even nearer. But in Ettal, Bonhoeffer was grateful for a chance to work on his new book, *Ethics*, in relative peace and tranquility. As far as the Reich was concerned, however, his base would remain Munich, where the wages of appeasement had recently been revealed.

Little is known of the house in Munich that he made his permanent residence. Oster and Dohnányi wanted Bonhoeffer stationed near Joseph Müller, the Catholic attorney who was negotiating on the conspiracy's behalf with the Vatican, and Bonhoeffer had family relations in Munich. He also needed an official address outside of Berlin to satisfy the Gestapo restrictions, and the place in Unertlstrasse served both purposes. The house belonged to his aunt Countess Christine von Kalckreuth, and it was actually in the eastern suburb of Schwabing. "Kalckreuth was a painter and graphic artist, who opened her home to young relatives attending the university in Munich and to her artist friends." On visits there in better times, Bonhoeffer had become acquainted with her brother Johannes, "a highly-regarded music critic."[2] Now, he would come to know Müller, who would introduce Bonhoeffer to the fellowship of kindred souls that made up his Bavarian network. Müller's strong ties to the Vatican proved helpful in convincing Pope Pius XII to vouch for the credibility of the conspiracy in his communiqués to the Western allies.[3]

Though he had waded into the conspiracy some months before, Bonhoeffer was in another sort of limbo, awaiting final clearance for service in the *Abwehr*. The intelligence service had not yet persuaded the Gestapo of his value, and so he remained subject to call-up at any time, pastoral exemptions having been discontinued the previous year. As a desperate measure to expedite his clearance, he tried to obtain membership in the Reich Chamber of Literature. Such membership depended on his demonstrating pure Aryan descent by means of an *Ahnenpass*, or certificate of ancestry. He wrote to his parents for help, saying he did not even know what an *Ahnenpass* was. "How do I get one?" he asked. As Paula worked on documenting their Aryan genealogy, Bonhoeffer tried to join another Nazi organization called the Nationalsozialistische Volkswohlfahrt, or National Socialist People's Welfare.[4] These efforts would come to naught, though it is fair to say that they relieved the suspicions of some officials concerning this dissident pastor who wanted to join military intelligence. Bonhoeffer had come to Munich from Königsberg, in East Prussia. Königsberg, the former imperial city, where the great Immanuel Kant had taught in the second half of the eighteenth century, had been Bonhoeffer's "home base" for the previous six months. He had led house groups, Bible studies, hosted by families willing to risk police scrutiny and arrest, and coordinated other "visiting pastorates" in East Prussia, checking in regularly with the Gestapo to reassure them of his new "official" residence outside Berlin. For a while Bonhoeffer stayed in the house at 18 Rhesastrasse that his parents had rented before he was born and that had since become a Protestant hostel. He liked East Prussia better than Pomerania, he told Karl and Paula, and found the people "more generous." "Königsberg too seems like a city in which one can live well, in contrast to Stettin." But there was no time now for putting down roots; "behind everything that we see," he said, "other experiences loom that fill our thoughts unceasingly, even into our dreams."[5] In July, he learned from a Gestapo agent that the SS had banned him from public speaking throughout the Reich.[6]

He packed his winter clothes and outdoor gear, his books, pens, and paper, and boarded the train for Bavaria. Before going, however, he wrote his "dear Mama" to let her know another bundle of laundry was

ETTAL BENEDICTINE MONASTERY

en route to Berlin. Throughout his peripatetic life after Finkenwalde, he had maintained a fresh wardrobe by mailing his laundry home to the help, who promptly cleaned and returned it via Deutsche Post.

In Munich, he would stay for the first few nights, where he had to check in with his *Abwehr* contacts, Müller among them. Otherwise he was on his own.

From his room at the Park Hotel, he wrote Bethge that it felt good to be in an unfamiliar city—that youthful urge had not left him entirely. His friend had begun work at the Gossner Mission in Berlin, primarily assisting displaced ministers of the Confessing Church, while preaching occasionally in the Dahlem parish.[7]

In the evening Bonhoeffer would go to the opera (there were performances of *Ariadne auf Naxos* and *Othello*) or to the grand Odeon for Bach's *Art of the Fugue*, or Beethoven's Sixth Symphony. He visited the museums in the Englischer Garten.[8] These were all pleasant diversions, but he missed Bethge very much. At the Altdorfer department store, Bonhoeffer purchased a hundred Christmas cards with a reproduction of Dürer's *Holy Night*—one of their favorite woodcuts—to send to each of his former seminarians.[9] Bonhoeffer joked to Bethge that this year he and his friend might inscribe their card "Christmas amid the ruins."[10] One morning, Bonhoeffer found two hundred marks tucked into the side pocket of his briefcase. He couldn't remember having put them there, but what a stroke of good fortune, he told Bethge. The money would come in handy on their Christmas trip—that is, if he could resist the temptation to buy Bethge "something very nice" in Munich, a fur wrap or a bottle of cognac, perhaps. The prospect of their reunion leavened his mood.[11] Though the dissident church had all but collapsed under the weight of its own bad faith, the end of Bonhoeffer's intense two-year experiment at Finkenwalde had seemed abrupt. It had come as part of a wave of police actions in March 1940 that dispersed the collective pastorates and unsettled the Council of Brethren of the Old Prussian Union, flushing out the last dens of non-conformity. Remarkably, internecine debates over ecclesial principle, though now mostly as an inconsequential exercise, would continue to be waged in the regional churches well into the war years. More practically, though, the end of the *Kirchenkampf* left Bonhoeffer in another kind of limbo: What did it mean to be a pastor without a church? Or, to serve a conspiracy in a spiritual role? To offer the sacraments in the ruin of a church? And what did it say about the institutional church that it had proved so entirely feckless in organizing opposition to Hitler?

Following a few nights at his official base of Munich, Bonhoeffer traveled south into the foothills of the Bavarian Alps, toward the town that would be his true base. He traveled to Ettal, where he lived as a guest of the fourteenth-century Benedictine monastery. While making frequent trips back to Munich, checking in with Müller and his lot, Bonhoeffer lived in the monastic village from November 1940 until February 1941, working in solitude on his *Ethics*, with the snow falling steadily. By the time he left, he had completed major sections on "ultimate and penultimate things" and had "crafted a robust affirmation of the nature and the integrity of all created life."[12]

Father Angelus Kupfer, Ettal's abbot, welcomed Bonhoeffer with a key to the cloister and the monastery library.[13] Bonhoeffer knew from earlier exchanges that Kupfer was familiar with his recent books, but he would be dumbfounded to learn that the monks read aloud from *Life Together* and *Discipleship* at mealtimes.[14] Having lived for years as a pariah among German Protestants, he now moved freely to the rhythms of cloister life once again, this time without the headaches of being the director. And so he was able to settle into a routine of reading, prayer, and writing.[15] Not that his stay in Ettal was entirely without distractions. He was constantly looking up from his manuscript to attend to his new secret activities as a theologian in the conspiracy, and he was often without his typewriter.[16] Nevertheless, he resolved that the most important thing now was to live in the present moment, with as much beauty, concentration, and inner stillness as he could sustain.

And meanwhile, he would wait for the *Abwehr* to pronounce on his position.

Just five days after his arrival in Ettal, his sister Christine von Dohnányi showed up with her two children. The boys and their mother had come seeking refuge from the bombing raids over Hamburg, where the family lived. Christoph and Klaus were enrolled in Ettal's secondary school, the well-regarded *Gymnasium*, with the intention, it seemed, that they would remain there indefinitely. The situation brought on natural obligations for Bonhoeffer. When Christine moved into an apartment in nearby Oberammergau, he kept a close eye on his nephews—even bringing Christoph, his godson, into his own room to care for him when he came down with the flu.[17] The distraction meant he would write fewer letters to the brethren, though he did remain in close touch with his parents, and of course with Bethge, the letters to him now reaching a new intensity.

"I have everything that one could desire," Bonhoeffer wrote. "The only things missing are a desk and what in these nearly six years has become a matter of course, the exchange of my impressions with you."[18]

There was time on some days for an afternoon hike on the snow-packed trail that traced the western ridge above the monastery. At the popular restaurant in the Hotel Ludwig der Bayer, Bonhoeffer had generous portions of Bavarian fare and sweet mahogany-brown Dunkelbier, which the monks had been brewing for four centuries. By the end of November, Abbot Kupfer had invited him to join the brotherhood for meals in the refectory. Bonhoeffer also attended Mass in the marble rotunda chapel. Everything about the monastery—its ornate altars, rococo sculptures, peasant woodcarvings, flying buttresses, the scene in the tympanum of the crucified Lord before whom the monastery's founding couple bowed—Emperor Louis the Bavarian and his wife Margaret—he found "wonderful."[19]

It did not matter that, as a Protestant, he could not receive communion: "I am still a guest here after all." The transcendent beauty of the Benedictine rites enthralled him all the same—such a welcome relief from the "dreadfully legalistic" Lutheran recitation of confessional. Pope Pius XII had issued a *motu proprio*, a kind of ad hoc decree, in which the Holy Father called on all Catholics to pray for peace in the Roman churches. Why should I not pray as well, Bonhoeffer wondered, and for all the churches, Roman and Protestant? So during Mass he prayed for the peace of the universal church and of the world.[20]

"This form of life is naturally not foreign to me," he told his parents, "and I experience its regularity and silence as extremely beneficial for my work."[21]

Bonhoeffer wrote Bethge every day, sometimes twice a day. He sent telegrams, and when possible—when the lines weren't down— spoke with him on the telephone, the uncertainty about Dietrich's conscription making the need for contact and its comfort more urgent. Bethge could not match Bonhoeffer's effort. But he wrote often, several times a week; and at Bonhoeffer's insistence, he offered more personal details than was his custom. In return Bonhoeffer sent gifts of tobacco, sausages, clothes, and books.

His letters to his parents, forthright though formal in their customary simplicity, reveal little. He remained the respectful son, circumspect, full of purpose, given to measured judgments. But with Bethge, it seemed, he felt—perhaps for the first time in his life—freedom from the lifelong pressure to present himself as an exemplar of propriety and probity. The guardedness had started at home: as if the call to ministry were not burden enough, his mother had once told him, "You are my most special one." He was ever vigilant to banish complacency of the kind God had sent the prophet Amos to warn the people of Israel. The Lord, it was to be remembered, had elected his people but was no respecter of persons.

To overcome the trial of their "unnatural" separation, the two must cleave only more closely to each other, Bonhoeffer told Bethge, who was living at the time in the Burckhardthaus in Berlin-Dahlem. "All sorts of external things are running through my head," Bonhoeffer said, and he wanted desperately to share them in person with his chosen confessor.[22]

Not all of Bonhoeffer's concerns were matters of life and death. There was, for example, the issue of Bethge's hopelessly provincial attire. From their first meeting, Bonhoeffer made his new friend's fashion sense—or lack thereof—a personal project. Although it seemed futile instilling some sense of style in the country boy from Saxony, Bonhoeffer never stopped trying. Even fearing that Bethge's own conscription was imminent—as it happened, Eberhard would manage to avoid the draft until August 1943—Bonhoeffer arranged with a Berlin haberdasher to furnish dress shirts, ties, a suit, and various outfits for special occasions; he also provided Bethge with some cash to make purchases on his own, once he got the hang of it.[23]

Then there was the business of their annual Christmas shopping. They'd been giving Christmas presents as a pair for several years, paying for them out of their bank account. At first, the practice created some awkwardness with some members of Bonhoeffer's family (these relating mostly to the logistics of reciprocity now that "Mr. Bethge" was on the list of recipients), but by 1940, Christmas presents from "Dietrich and Eberhard" had become a family tradition. Bethge kept the "household" accounts and paid their taxes, whereas Bonhoeffer decided how to spend the money; it had evolved into an efficient partnership, this mutual dependency.

As December approached, Bonhoeffer wrote to Bethge with his suggestions for gifts. Dietrich would purchase as many as he could on his weekly trips into Munich. He'd already acquired the perfect gift for his mother: a good-sized bag of sugar. With wartime rationing in effect, Bonhoeffer had "saved" his small daily portions from breakfasts at the monastery; now his mother would be able to prepare all the Christmas favorites, the *Kuchen* and *Süsses;* he was sure she'd be thrilled. For cousin Hans-Christoph von Hase, he was in search of the Furche edition of John Calvin's letters to the Huguenots; if that was not to be found in Munich, he would buy instead the first volume of Ricarda Huch's history of German art. Bonhoeffer thought they might forego gifts for their siblings this year, using the savings to do something special for the Finkenwalde families, the wives and children of those who had been called to the front.

He would need Bethge's help to round up the other items on the list: a copy of *German Satirical and Polemical Writing,* or an outdoor thermometer of fine quality, for his father. For his godchildren, a framed print of Stefan Lochner's *Birth of Christ.* As for Finkenwalde's faithful patron Ruth von Kleist-Retzow, he knew she would love nothing more than a sweet and thoughtful letter. As for Bethge's family, what about a copy of *Adelheid* for his aunt Lene—there was one on the shelf in their room at the Bonhoeffers' country house. And for Eberhard's mother, Elisabeth, Bonhoeffer thought a flask would be nice.[24]

Then there was his most urgent question: Would Bethge come to Ettal for Christmas? "I suggest you do," Bonhoeffer said, promising to introduce him to the brothers, and their Benedictine spirituality; then they could spend a day in Munich before taking the train to Friedrichsbrunn. They simply must be together, Bonhoeffer urged. Bethge could bring his mother, if he wanted. She had never been to Friedrichsbrunn, and now the house had heating and electricity. Still, it might be better if he and Eberhard kept Christmas alone; they could sleep by the fire, read books aloud to each other, and play the piano at all hours. When Bethge said yes, Bonhoeffer was ecstatic.[25]

"So we will be together as before!" he said.[26]

Not everything came off as Bonhoeffer had hoped. He was sorely vexed to learn that all the sleeping cars from Berlin had been commandeered by the military. It was a long ride—eleven hours—to Munich, and he wanted Eberhard to enjoy it in comfort. He even dispatched his father's chauffeur to try his luck at the station with agents of the Deutsche Bahn, but to no avail. With abject apologies, Dietrich recommended reading a volume of his favorite Henrik Ibsen plays—*The Wild Duck*, *A Doll's House*, and *Ghosts*—as a pleasant way to pass the time.[27] Bethge assured Bonhoeffer that he did not at all mind traveling second class, preferring it, in fact.

Bethge arrived in Ettal a few days before Christmas; suddenly, it seemed, the clipped days of the winter storms yielded to "wonderful weather for skiing." As he hadn't for some time, Bonhoeffer slept soundly—yes, like a baby, he said. Not even the sirens of the air raid watch kept the two from rising late in the morning, as was their preference.[28] After a languorous Christmas Eve dinner at the Ludwig der Bayer, Bonhoeffer and Bethge strolled to the monastery for the midnight Mass in the chapel there.[29]

After Christmas Day lunch in the refectory, Bonhoeffer sat down to write a letter to the brethren. On occasion, he would write to students and pastoral comrades collectively, inspired by the Pauline model of instruction and exhortation.[30]

In his hotel room, Bonhoeffer dictated the letter to Bethge, who typed it with plenty of sheets of carbon paper; later Bonhoeffer would address each copy in longhand. Bethge had fairly mastered the process since the previous year, when civilians "had been forbidden from sending publications to members of the armed forces." After the seizure of Finkenwalde's mimeograph machine, they began making carbons of newsletters on the typewriter, each of which Bonhoeffer would sign, like this Yuletide greeting, to give the impression not of something published but rather personal correspondence. It was a clever arrangement, since carbons did not count as publications under the strict terms of the publication ban.[31]

In the Christmas greeting of 1940, Bonhoeffer recalled the cataclysmic shock of World War I, the shattering of the old order, and the "ever new phases" of collective anger that followed. He asked, is our present situation significantly different? He thought it was, but only as an even "sharper clarification of our existence in this world." The eruption of villainy they were witnessing was unprecedented—that much was indisputable. But the Christian mission had not changed. He proposed an analogy from photography, asking the brethren to contemplate the way a time-lapse image makes visible, "in an ever more compressed and penetrating form, movements that would otherwise not be thus grasped by our vision." In such a way the new "war makes manifest . . . the essence of the 'world'"; revealing the perversions of idolatry in their infinite multiplicity, now apparent as never before with the human will unmoored from any moral constraints.

In such a time, the meaning of Advent assumes a heightened urgency: What other power but God's can arrest the "vast and unavoidable" inclination of the heart toward destruction? It is a difficult message that many find unfathomable: Jesus the Jew, born homeless in a manger, the son of God. "Unto us a child is born, unto us a son is given: and the government shall be upon his shoulder" (Isaiah 9:6). This is the message of Advent—that God comes among us, but as a stranger! What an outrage! What an insult! Germans, he warned, do not want a stranger for a savior. They want a "vacation from life," "a wisp of magic asking nothing and promising everything," each soul seeking "a vacation from myself." Having wished "to be transported into a fairy land," they now find their flight from reality stalling; thus is the "essence of the world" revealed in the "manifest reality" of the present age. Luther had long ago proclaimed the tormented ego to be the precursor of grace; in his Christmas message, Bonhoeffer likened his warrior-nation and the war to this self-imprisoned heart and thus invoked Luther's anguished account: Germany as the *cor cuvum in se*, the heart turned in on itself, standing in need of grace.[32]

But Bonhoeffer's probing analysis of a church without Christ, while theologically in line with Lutheran thought, is insular, even triumphalistic: Nazi tyranny as an occasion, a propaedeutic perhaps, for salvation. But the doctrine of original sin remained a pillar of Christian orthodoxy, nowhere looming larger than in Luther's justification by faith, to which Bonhoeffer's brethren were heirs. He drew on these themes to make sense of the world and his students' entanglements in its brutal arrangements. But how could a Christian—one such as Bonhoeffer—celebrate the coming of the Messiah, the God who would be mocked, scourged, and crucified as King of the Jews, while everywhere the Jews of Europe were beset with terror at the approach of the year that would see the first mass killings?

Proclaiming the truth of the gospel while pondering the end of

BONHOEFFER AND EBERHARD BETHGE MAKING MUSIC
AT ETTAL BENEDICTINE MONASTERY, DECEMBER 1940

Christianity, as he would do in the coming years; plotting the assassination of Hitler while affirming the ethics of pacifism; celebrating the
sacrament of marriage while binding his affections joyfully to another
man—Bonhoeffer came to embody some of the perplexing contradictions that modernity had imposed upon the faith. Yet he could not
be pried from his adherence to its essential orthodoxy: God holds the
world mercifully in his hands. This was the strange and glorious gospel that Bonhoeffer had taken vows to proclaim, despite little evidence
of what most of the world would recognize as "good news." Nothing,
however, could preempt grace's imminent intervention in the world:
"Salvation is at hand! The night is far spent; the day is at hand! The rule
of the world, already denied to its 'principalities and powers,' has been
laid on the shoulders of this child! God holds the world in his hands
and will never let it go."[33]

Sometimes, of course, the gospel can only be proclaimed in a whisper, within the echoing dark, from the anxious middle.

Over the next two years, his missives to the brethren would typically
begin on a more somber and plaintive note. He wrote as if offering a eulogy for fallen comrades, naming the dead. He would mourn
the loss of F. A. Preuß, Ulrich Nithack, Gerhard Schulze, and Konrad Bojack, men who with "earnestness and joy" "trusted in word and

sacrament," before they were killed on the eastern front. Many others would be called to the "heavenly congregation": Hans-Otto Georgii, Martin Franke of Pomerania; Engelke from Brandenburg; Heyse from Sachsen; Nicolaus from the Rhineland. "They have gone before us on the path that we shall all have to take at some point." More than half of Bonhoeffer's students would die in the war.[34]

In his courses and Bible studies, Bonhoeffer had taught pacifism as the way of the cross. He supported the notion of the conscientious objector, though never applying for that status himself. War had always been a reality impervious to grace. Discipleship formed the language of peace. But with few exceptions, his former seminarians had enlisted of their own will. In frank and open letters, they related to him the dizzying effect of immersion into sometimes barbaric warfare after following the spiritual discipline at Finkenwalde. He would never condemn any of those who took up arms for the Reich, neither those who submitted to the draft nor those who freely enlisted. Neither did he expect that the brethren would be torn between the freedom to love and the order to kill; there was no place on the battlefield for such rumination.

It was in response to the nightmarish reality as it unfolded that Bonhoeffer crafted his theodicy, his view of war as preparing the way for grace: How could God allow such things to happen to young German men, many of whom had no love of the Führer, and most of whom—speaking of those training for ministry—had acted only out of duty, letting their soul "be subject unto the higher powers," as St. Paul instructed? For both those brethren at war and those still in parish life, he offered the same encouragement: extend particular grace and mercy to those serving in the battle, especially those benumbed, even crazed, by the brutalities and the killing.

B onhoeffer told Bethge that the ethics manuscripts might be called *Preparing the Way* and *Arrival* (*Wegbereitung* and *Einzug*)—each a more evocative and daring title than those of his earlier books (*Discipleship* and *Life Together*)—or simply *Ethics*, as the book would be called on its posthumous publication.[35] Bonhoeffer found the work "dangerous" but endlessly "stimulating."[36] It felt like "a decisive break," he said. "Sometimes I think after this time, that Christianity will only live in a few people who have nothing to say."[37] Bethge confessed to being "startled" by aspects of the new work.[38]

His reading in Ettal reflected the shifting currents of his thought. He'd finally gotten around to George Santayana's *The Last Puritan: A Memoir in the Form of a Novel*, which he'd bought in New York during the hot summer of 1939. In that book, a professor of philosophy at Harvard recounts the story of a young man born into money who comes to realize that his exalted sense of duty often undermines his personal well-being. Bonhoeffer recognized himself in the character of Oliver Alden, the novel's protagonist. Oliver is "lonely, even ridiculous," forever pouring "himself out for every conceivable thing without being convinced of the inner meaning of that outpouring." Like Santayana's "last puritan," Bonhoeffer believed that he had never given himself permission to feel free—"free for the authentic and utterly unique pouring out of his life."[39] He had lived too much out of loyalty to the past or in expectation of future trials; he had been a prince of self-restraint. How lovely it would be "to surrender to the strong desires" of the present!

Bonhoeffer had also read Reinhold Schneider's *Power and Grace* (*Macht und Gnade*) with "great pleasure," recommending that Bethge buy it too, before it sold out: Schneider having been charged with subversive activity, his books were banned, not to be restocked. In any case it was not Schneider's view of the government but his dialogue between the artist and his demons that captivated Bonhoeffer.[40] There was also the American author Eric Knight's *This Above All*, a best-selling novel about a conscientious objector who abandons his post in the British army.[41]

Bonhoeffer had also brought with him to Bavaria his Braunfels edition of *Don Quixote*, and as always he was reading his Kant and also Ibsen, looking especially at the play *Brand* while in Ettal.[42] He read Fyodor Dostoyevsky's *The Brothers Karamazov* and Aldous Huxley's *Point Counter Point*. He managed to obtain as well the latest installment in Barth's *Church Dogmatics* (volume II/1), which pondered the question of God's identity: God's being, Barth explained, was in God's becoming.

On February 4, Bonhoeffer turned thirty-five years old. Naturally and as always, he spent part of the day reading the Bible, but now it was with a new freedom and clarity. He also listened to the music of Heinrich Schütz, sent by Bethge as a birthday gift. Schütz's compositions, inspired by Lutheran theology and the German polyphonic tradition, came as a great joy to Bonhoeffer.[43]

Drawn to the Baroque and Romantic periods, Bonhoeffer—until meeting Bethge—had given scant attention to this seventeenth-century composer and music-master to the royal court of Dresden, but after listening to *Kleine geistliche Konzerte* and *Symphoniae Sacrae*, he fell under the spell of Schütz's "whole rich world." Music nights with Eberhard were never complete without a rendition of "Bone Jesus," "Habe deine

Lust an dem Herren," or "Jubilate Deo omnis terra," with Bonhoeffer playing piano and Eberhard singing these clear, free songs that gave their lives "wholeness," as Bonhoeffer said.[44]

Snow had continued falling on Ettal until the end of January. The Christmas break in Friedrichsbrunn had been glorious, but now Bethge was back in Berlin. Filling the lonely hours proved difficult for Bonhoeffer after the month together. Resuming to write, he now pondered the meaning of "penultimate and ultimate things." He'd been inspired by his exchanges with the Benedictines on the Catholic tradition of natural theology. Now he would apply himself to defending the integrity of created life—of "natural and bodily life"—against the Nazi program of legalized euthanasia and eugenics.[45] Away from war and the noise, he drew analogies between God and nature: the divine spark luminous in the created order was "like the young boy who is speechless gazing upon his hero . . . like the man . . . calmed by the gaze of his beloved . . . like all of us who are silenced in reverence and awe at the heart of nature, under the starry heavens."[46]

When God became flesh in Jesus Christ, "the whole human race recover[ed] the dignity of the image of God," Bonhoeffer explained, upholding the theological significance of the human form, the bodily life perverted by Nazi ideology. "Therefore, any attack even on the least of these is an attack on Christ, who took the form of [humanity,] and in His own Person restored the image of God in all that bears a human form . . . 'my body'—not only in its achievements and over-comings but in its ordinariness and breakdowns—has 'the right to be preserved for the sake of the whole person.' "[47]

The human body, he continued, "is not intended only as protection against bad weather and the night, or as a place for offspring to develop. It is the space in which human beings may enjoy the pleasure of personal life secure with their loved ones and their possessions."[48]

Bodily life is meant for joy: "Eating and drinking not only sustain bodily health, but also the natural joy of bodily life." Clothing is not only a "necessary covering" for the body, but "an adornment" as well. Relaxation and leisure not only facilitate "the capacity for work," but also grace the body with the measure of rest and joy that is its due. "In its essential distance from all purposefulness, play is the clearest expression that bodily life is an end in itself."[49] Breaking from work one morning, Bonhoeffer wrote to Bethge, "Sometimes I am startled and fear that, the σάρξ ('flesh') is energetically engaged in this work apart from the Spirit."[50] The truth of this in his own life was revealing the truth of it in all.

B onhoeffer's emotional resources, it must be readily acknowledged, were not equal to his intellectual ones, even at this mature age. After he'd written all he could of a morning, the remains of the winter day typically seemed interminable. He began taking the regional train more frequently into Munich, meeting with resistance comrades, reporting as required to the Reich office, and inquiring as to his draft status. He went to the ballet—a "riveting" performance of Beethoven's *Creatures of Prometheus*—the symphony, and a few movies, which he found dismal. The German film industry now cranked out "terrible, pathetic, clichéd, phony, unreal, unhistorical, badly acted, kitsch!" He would also travel to Switzerland for his work in the conspiracy.[51]

In mid-February he suffered a nasty bout of scarlet fever. At the same time, he felt the net of circumstances tightening. The number of Ettalites called to military service had grown so that classes at the monastery school had to be canceled or combined. Reports of more brethren lost or in danger or under arrest arrived every day. "Gurtner's death hits us hard." "Gabriel-Halle is in Dachau." Herbert Jehle was detained by the Gestapo in southern France. "Neuhäulser suddenly became ill and went into the hospital," Bonhoeffer wrote. In the coded language of his letters, "going to the hospital" usually meant being sent to one of the concentration camps; in this instance, the Catholic priest Johannes Neuhäusler had been taken to Sachsenhausen.[52]

The reports also told of nervous breakdowns and suicides. Adding to the stress was Bonhoeffer's knowledge that his parents suffered "insurmountably under it all."[53] He had decided not to resist the draft if it came to that, mainly out of concern for what might consequently befall his family and friends, who would likely be charged with aiding and abetting criminal behavior. To be sure, after 1939 conscientious objection was no longer a legal option. To assert it was to invite the fate of his pacifist friend Hermann Stöhr and the Austrian Franz Jägerstätter (beatified in 2007 by Pope Benedict XVI), who were arrested and murdered by the Gestapo.

When finally accepted into the *Abwehr* in late October 1940, Bonhoeffer was granted the so-called UK, or *unabkömmlich*, status, meaning "indispensable" to state security and thereby exempt from military service. But his UK exemption would not take effect upon first joining the military intelligence, only after he started working as a courier "assigned to engage in covert talks with foreign church leaders who would communicate with Allied leaders." The exempt status also needed to be renewed periodically. And so he would remain ever fearful that it would be revoked. Bethge would remember that the entire time from 1940 until his arrest in February 1943 was "constantly accompanied by the struggle to renew the UK classifications."[54]

This was the first winter of the war, and it would be a season of many endings. "*Life Together* was my swan song," Bonhoeffer poignantly explained. Finkenwalde was now an abandoned building on a wintry plain in Pomerania. Even more disquieting, he began to fear that the ties to Bethge were fraying.[55]

Only in Bethge's company did Bonhoeffer relax his finely tuned rectitude and reveal his inmost fears and disappointments—and also the bits of humor he found in life amid the ruins. On hearing, for instance, that their beloved clavichord had a broken string, he told his friend not to worry, for "should a bomb fall on it, it is gone anyway, and if no bomb falls, we can still repair it later." He noted in another letter that in addition to the work on euthanasia and the penultimate-ultimate, he was making sketches for a short essay for one of the brethren on the "spa ministry"—or as he put it, "the spa ministry!" With Bethge he felt free to add the exclamation mark.[56]

Bethge's letters to Bonhoeffer were deferential and affectionate, but they did not convey the same urgency or reciprocate the other's emotional claims, certainly not to the latter's satisfaction. Nor were they as frequent: equally maddening. In trying to summarize their six-year relationship, Bonhoeffer would reach for an ever-deeper intimacy, whereas Bethge saw fit only to thank his mentor for "the secure feeling of knowing someone with whom counsel and solutions are to be found in all circumstances." In such measured terms would he sometimes also try to temper Bonhoeffer's solicitations, though to no avail. On one occasion he conveyed the wish that Bonhoeffer have many "good stimulating friends" in his life. But Bonhoeffer swatted away the suggestion with a quick reply. "One can well wish such a thing for oneself," he said. "And yet the human is created in such a way that we seek not the many but the one particular." The heart wants what the heart wants. Bonhoeffer celebrated their "anniversary," as he put it, by sending Bethge two long letters and an embarrassment of gifts: a fur-lined hat and money for a viola da gamba. "You really choose well," Bethge, no doubt blushing, replied. "And all the extra treats!"[57]

The generosity was totemic. There were relationships, Bonhoeffer said, in which the partners challenged each other to achieve their better selves, others that resembled "intrusive forays" into inner realms, and still others that remained distant, unfamiliar, and indifferent— "noncommittal chats which barely veil the distance, unfamiliarity."

But his relationship with Bethge was of a wholly different kind. He likened it to a conversation in which there existed "a mutual giving and receiving of gifts," where neither was ever domineering, violent, or indifferent; and to a "natural harmony" where all that "remains unspoken signifies a gesture pointing toward as yet undiscovered treasures, toward riches still hidden in the other which will be disclosed when the time is right."[58]

Bonhoeffer had always felt incomplete apart from Bethge. But now his declarations had become uninhibited and, in the dependency they revealed, inevitably tragic. Had anyone but Bethge ever witnessed the explosive temper for which Bonhoeffer often begged forgiveness? But unto whomsoever much is given, of him much shall be required. Bonhoeffer demanded of Bethge not only that he be a "faithful helper and advisor," "daring, trusting spirit," a source of "extraordinary joy," but also that he suffer the teacher's "severe tests" and "violent temper" with patience. "[This], I too abhor in myself and of which you have fortunately repeatedly and openly reminded me," he said.[59] But it is not only the lurking volcanic temper that inspired Bethge's increasingly hesitant tone and reserve in reply. The letters of that winter plead for a connection that Bethge was not willing to accept.

Bethge was not remotely unaware of being unable to match Bonhoeffer's affections. He knew he had become, on this account, a disappointment, and that knowledge saddened him. He would apologize for the infrequency of his letters, but Bonhoeffer would not complain now, straining toward a heightened intimacy, offering expressions of his unrequited ardor in the way of a man who believes the heart can be won by persuasion.

"The day is over," Bonhoeffer wrote to Bethge on February 4, moments after a long phone conversation between them. "[But] before I go to sleep I want to spend more time with you." The sound of Eberhard's voice, he said, had recalled "especially vivid" memories of birthdays past, when Bethge had made him the gift of a song, sung in his gentle tenor. The day had brought other pleasant moments as well. His parents had sent a nice letter, along with two cakes, a bottle of schnapps, and an azalea plant. He heard from his sisters and his godson. Still, nothing could compare to the joy of speaking with Eberhard, or of knowing that despite the geographical distance between them, the two had sung the same morning hymn and prayed the same prayers; their shared devotions and personal intercessions have given "meaning and substance" to this as to every day. That day's hymn was Bethge's favorite, Schütz's "Eile mich, Gott, zu erretten" ("Hasten to save me, O God"), and until he went to bed that night, Bonhoeffer carried the sheet music around with him, humming the lines to himself, he said, with "a warm and grateful heart."[60]

Bethge's birthday present would arrive a few days late, but when it came, Bonhoeffer was ecstatic. "I am utterly at a loss for words," he said. "It is truly beyond all bounds, completely impermissible, and nevertheless a tremendous joy." Bethge gave Bonhoeffer two silver cordial cups, a perfect complement for their after-dinner schnapps—"precious vessels intended for precious contents," mused Bonhoeffer, the perfect reminder of their many evenings together.

"I keep glancing at them in disbelief," Bonhoeffer continued. "Clearly you spent months searching and eventually turned your wallet inside out to give this joy to me. It is incredible that you even came upon such cups. Now they await a worthy inauguration, the chance to use them with you! . . . I shall drink the first glass to the constancy of our friendship." When Bonhoeffer took the cups to a farewell celebration for him at the monastery, one monk allowed that they looked like the ideal wedding present.[61]

On February 15, after the largest accumulation of snow in a decade, the skies cleared and the day dawned cold and blue. Bonhoeffer told Bethge that the two Benedictines who checked in on him most days wondered what had become of that "Bättge." "They always want me to greet you for them; it seems as if they think something of you—strange!"

"You see, you simply must come back," he said. "I miss having a partner. . . . I miss Finkenwalde."[62]

On February 19, 1941, Bonhoeffer announced that he had finally resolved some visa problems that had temporarily restricted his travel abroad and he would be leaving the monastery within a week. He planned to spend a few nights at the Europäischer Hof in Munich before heading for Switzerland on the 24th, on what would be his first real errand for the conspiracy. He hoped to return to Berlin after about a month—or as soon as he could collect his parents from Oberammergau, the village four kilometers south of Ettal, where Paula and Karl were vacationing.

"I hope you will pick us up in the Mercedes," Bonhoeffer said to Bethge. "I would be eager then to go with you to Friedrichsbrunn over Easter."[63]

Although that reunion was over a month away—it felt "so absurd," so long a time—the prospect allowed Bonhoeffer happily to work on the mundane preparations. Their mail should now be sent to the Bonhoeffers' house in Marienburger Allee, where they would once again share the second-floor studio. The books, supplies, and clothes that would be coming from Ettal by post should be taken directly upstairs. In all, he seemed indifferent to how the coming months would make unprecedented demands on his time and energies.[64]

The purpose of the March trip to Switzerland was the renewal of Bonhoeffer's "lines of communication with his international contacts." He managed to meet with two German émigrés—Friedrich Siegmund-Schultze, the Berlin social theologian living in exile in Basel, and Otto Salomon, his former editor at the publishing house Christian Kaiser Verlag, whom he visited in the scenic town of Rapperswil on Lake Zurich—and also with the ethicist Alfred de Quervain, who had settled in Canton Bern, the Dutch ecumenist Wilhelm Visser 't Hooft, director of the World and Life Council in Geneva, and others. It would have been inconceivable to go to Switzerland without seeing Erwin Sutz. Sutz had become the "mailbox" for Bonhoeffer's written exchanges with colleagues in England.[65] So the two former Union classmates, friends now for more than a decade, squeezed in an afternoon together in Rapperswil, where Sutz was still pastor of the Reformed church.

His covert agenda was packed, but Bonhoeffer did manage to squeeze in a brief tête-à-tête with Barth. As it turned out, the visit was not so well timed, which he gathered from the fretful demeanor of Barth's wife, Nelly, when she greeted him at the front door. Things were uneasy within the plain three-story house on Bruderholzallee, for the great Reformed theologian, who, as noted earlier, had single-handedly retrieved the language of Christian Orthodoxy from its modernist reductions, had performed an even more astonishing feat: he had managed to move his beautiful assistant, Charlotte von Kirschbaum, into the household.

Nelly led Bonhoeffer back to the staircase, covered in red carpet. "On the wall alongside them were prints of famous philosophers and theologians, ascending from Kant to Schleiermacher to Nietzsche . . . to Blumhardt to Wilhelm Hermann to Harnack."[66] Under the solemn gaze of Mozart and John Calvin, whose portraits hung at the same level above the doorway to the book-lined study, Barth from behind a small desk offered Bonhoeffer a seat, in what proved for both men, it would seem, an awkwardly formal exchange.

Even after Switzerland, the months ahead would be hectic for Bonhoeffer, consumed with travel, shifting plans, and impromptu meetings, but he wouldn't seem the least harried or unhappy. He had always felt rather at peace in the itinerant life, and it was no different now. In fact, it was as if the chaos relieved him of boredom, his greatest fear, and blotted out as well the expectations he felt from others. In perpetual motion, he lived with a heightened awareness of the fragility of things, and that awareness eased his inhibitions in a spirit of carpe diem as natural to the Christian as to the hedonist. "What remains for us is only the very narrow path," he wrote, "sometimes barely discernible, of taking each day as if it were the last and yet living it faithfully and responsibly as if there were yet to be a great future."[67] In a more strictly Christian way, he crafted the art of "inner dying," the *ars moriendi*, glimpsed eternity from a new perspective, and felt free to go as far as he could go into the world. He said he felt the grace of a steadying joy, a blessed stillness within, even in flight.[68]

Over drinks one spring evening with one of Barth's wealthy friends, Gerty Pestalozzi, on the balcony of his villa near Zurich, Bonhoeffer suddenly felt a profound sense of "refreshment and delight."[69] It was more than just the rush of alcohol and a fine view of the Zürichsee at sunset.

"The Christian . . . has no last line of escape into the eternal from earthly tasks and difficulties," he would write, "but, like Christ himself ('My God, why hast thou forsaken me?'), he must drink the earthly cup to the lees."[70]

This meant the obvious rituals of self-sacrifice—"being crucified with Christ," suffering for a just cause, crossing the threshold to treason in his case—but draining "the earthly cup" did not mean neglecting the daily, transitory tasks, even if the day's business was shopping for silk underwear in a Geneva haberdashery. It was indeed a stylish pair he'd found on the Rue du Marché; and he would tell Bethge about a fantasy of strolling along the Promenade de Luc in nothing but his shimmering golden briefs. He was reaching a place beyond simple spiritual ardor, where duty vanished into grace, and life seemed to him charged with longing for the things of this world, as well as thoughts of the next. Returning to Munich, he found awaiting him at the hotel a letter from Wilhelm Ihde, director of the Reich Chamber of Literature. Bonhoeffer recognized the name as that of a zealous Nazi and the author of mawkish historical tracts, whom Joseph Goebbels had recently appointed to enforce the Reich's publishing standards. Ihde was writing about Bonhoeffer's failure to submit *Discipleship* and *Life Together* for official approval, a violation subject to a fine of thirty marks.[71]

Bonhoeffer objected, promptly filing an appeal—no doubt intended to bolster his image as someone working dependably within the system. He also disputed Ihde's charge that the omission amounted to disloyalty. Furthermore, there was nothing subversive about the books, he said. *Discipleship* was "a purely scholarly work" and "everywhere acknowledged in theological circles" as such. The same holds for *Life Together*, which he wrote solely for theologians—for all his publications, in fact: "Not one" could be considered subversive or deserving of a fine.[72] Ihde denied the appeal, coming to the conclusion that, at least in this instance, would be shared by Bonhoeffer's most sympathetic readers: his writings were indeed subversive in effect.[73]

In *Discipleship*, Bonhoeffer had imagined the world as a vast and menacing realm of temptation and terror; against this the Christian must keep his vigilant watch, holding high the cross. In *Life Together*, Bonhoeffer had somewhat soothed the individual's wounds laid bare in *Discipleship*, applying the balm of beloved communion. But what would the likes of Ihde make of the new book he had not yet published?

Ethics marks a turning point in Bonhoeffer's thought, a step into new territory. Both daring and luminous, it refracts the "breakthroughs" of recent months and though the form is fragmentary, a coherent existential narrative emerges. He ponders the most difficult and urgent of questions. Might "extreme actions" be required of morally responsible people in extraordinary circumstances and exceptional cases? Why were there more humanists and atheists (like his brother Klaus or his cousin Hans) than Christians in the ranks of the resistance? How could the integrity of the person be preserved against dehumanizing technologies? How might the created holiness of all bodily life be safeguarded from Nazi eugenics and euthanasia laws? But *Ethics* is not an instructor's manual or a work of practical wisdom; it is best read as a collection of theological dispatches, albeit by a dissident theologian in the grip of what Bethge would call "the lure of the political." At more than three hundred pages, it is in every way Bonhoeffer's most mature work, and in every way bears the traumatic scars of its time.

Ethics reveals the shifting assumptions of a chastened believer; it is no less Christocentric than the earlier writings, but it is more open to Christ's presence in persons, places, and movements outside the church. As Bonhoeffer thought more carefully on the subject of "natural piety" and the category of the "natural" (both drawn from Catholic teaching), he found himself often running up against a strange but exhilarating notion: "unconscious Christianity." He was intrigued by certain unexplored possibilities in the classical Lutheran distinction between *fides directa* and *fides reflexa*—a distinction roughly corresponding, respectively, to a very visceral faith born of desire and a more reflective, conscious one, rooted in ascent. The duality was developed by Lutheran scholastics in the seventeenth century to explain how or whether a baptized infant could be said to have faith in Jesus Christ. Bonhoeffer, though not uninterested in the mysteries of infant baptism, invoked the terms for a different purpose.

The Confessing Church had finally cowered before the Führer. Its officials and caretakers of the Word had become bystanders to evil. By contrast, Bonhoeffer's new secular comrades in the resistance fastened themselves to the concrete reality with brave defiance. This puzzling divergence inspired Bonhoeffer to cultivate an appreciation of the "good people" and propose "the beatification of those who are persecuted for the sake of a just cause."[74] The world full of depravity and menace, as portrayed in *Discipleship*, might seem a more accurate reflection of the Zeitgeist. But in *Ethics*, Bonhoeffer moved well beyond such depictions, and their implied division between God and humankind; his goal was a singularly intense and all-pervading Christomorphic order, in which all reality conforms to the divine love, taking shape in the incarnation.

These are bold, far-ranging, and (singularly) confident speculations. Understood in relation to the inner life of a Christian conspirator, however, they represent an effort at self-understanding, instruction on the theology of shared human struggle, and a benediction for secular agents of grace. If they often seem at odds with traditional views of salvation, they nevertheless bespeak a generous hope, a Christological concentration leading to a greater inclusiveness. For in doing righteousness and justice, one creates a space that necessarily "belongs to God." It is a premise Bonhoeffer follows to an astonishing conclusion: in earlier times, he says, the church could preach that to find Christ a person must first be aware of himself as a sinner, like the publican and the harlot. But in the present time, it must be said, rather, that to find Christ a person must first seek to become righteous, like those, Christians and non-Christians alike, who strive and suffer for the sake of justice, truth, and humanity.

Those who come to the work of mercy and justice from places outside the church are animated by an energy that the church knows intimately but dares not seek to own. These unacknowledged "children of the church," as Bonhoeffer calls them, are as much part of the world to which God reconciled himself through Christ as any observant Christian.[75]

"During the time of their estrangement their appearance and their language" may have indeed changed a great deal, and "yet at the crucial moment the mother and the children once again recognized one another," Bonhoeffer wrote. "Reason, justice, culture, humanity and the other kindred concepts sought and found a new purpose and a new power in their origin," which thus led the "theologian in the resistance" to conclude gratefully that all good and righteous people are moved by the same grace that brings the baptized infant to faith through no conscious effort of its own.[76]

Crisis had induced—at least in Bonhoeffer's case—a more generous vision of the righteous and the just. Still, there remained the practical question of who but "the last gentlemen and gentlewomen of the era of Bismarck" would come to the defense of culture, humanity, justice, and reason.[77] In this, he was appealing to a different German tradition and value system, one entirely familiar to his fellow conspirators and their typically elite families. His appeal was to a time-honored sense of noblesse oblige. In this turn from the phraseological to the real, Bonhoeffer was proposing less the sacrifice of privilege than its reorganization on a higher plane. The conspiracy could only be led by the aristocrats, not of blood but of responsibility.

By "responsibility" Bonhoeffer meant an utmost attention and responsiveness to the whole of reality unified in Christ; this was Reinhold Niebuhr's Christian realism, but with Christ restored to its center. Honesty, humanity, toleration, authenticity, trust, faithfulness, steadfastness, patience, discipline, humility, modesty, contentment—these were the virtues of the Christian aristocrat, the fruit of the spirit in a post-metaphysical age. It is no surprise to see Bonhoeffer return to the theme of Christian humanism in his late writings—discipleship as the path to a consummate humanness. "Throwing oneself completely into the arms of God" meant living in the world as if there were no God but nevertheless doing his will, with a trust and fidelity beyond dependence and necessity and fear of judgment. This more than a quietist "imitation of Christ"—which Thomas à Kempis had identified with "contempt for the vanities of this world"—was the way to be properly human; this was where discipleship to Christ led. "It is not through the art of dying but through Christ's resurrection that a new and cleansing wind can blow through our present world," Bonhoeffer said. "If a few people really believed this and were guided by it in their earthly actions, a great deal would change."[78]

Ethics is a work of complex ambitions, among the foremost to offer theological resources to the men and women of the resistance. Its Christological notion of responsibility was a complement to the secular one, investing the word with transcendent power, and "a fullness of meaning that it does not acquire in everyday usage, even when it is placed extremely high on the scale of ethical values, as it was, for example, by Bismarck and Max Weber."[79] The conspirators and their families might be the last gentlefolk, the vestiges of a vanquished nobility—and the last human dam against the inundation of barbarism—but they needed Christ all the same. All the more so, in fact. It was a realization that would come naturally to some of them, like Bonhoeffer's brother Klaus, an atheist who spent his final months in prison pondering the mysteries of the gospel. Visiting Klaus in prison after he'd been sentenced to death, his older brother Karl-Friedrich noticed a copy of Bach's *Saint Matthew's Passion* in the cell. He expressed admiration "that Klaus could hear music just by reading the score," to which Klaus replied, "But the words, too, the words!"[80]

Bonhoeffer rehearsed the aristocratic virtues with native understanding. But he was under no illusions that these alone could fill the moral void created by the nazified church (a skepticism that Klaus and Dohnányi likely shared.) However inspiring and humbling his experience with secular members of the resistance, he knew very well that a highborn humanism could be as vacant as any kind. Bonhoeffer would never relent in his assault on bourgeois Christianity—the piety of "self-sufficient finitude," as Paul Tillich had once called late-nineteenth-century Protestant liberalism. But he was quick to add that the moral torpor of the upper classes had contributed more than its fair share to the rise of an evil regime.

In Bonhoeffer's unfinished novel, the child of a wealthy Berlin family remarks, "And who's responsible for this whole calamity? None other than the classes that set the tone." He meant those he had grown up with, the *Bildungsbürgertum*, the cultured elites, those everyone looked to "as a model for success in life," but who had shown themselves to be nothing but a "bunch of rotten, obsequious lackeys."[81] Had Germans in these late days become a soulless people, devoid of all qualities except "formality and compulsion and officiousness"?[82] Elsewhere in the novel, the character Renate, discussing the same subject with her friend Christoph, allows as how in her own social circles she often has the feeling of being choked to death. She refers to the very same "tired indifference" that Bonhoeffer believed had come to define the *Weltanschauung* of the educated classes. "Today is just like my experience a week ago when I rode the same train," Bonhoeffer observed on the train ride to Munich. "In every car there is on average only one person reading a book. Most are dozing off alone, half awake. Clearly almost all are retracting from some hectic pursuit. Now they have a couple of spare hours merely to brood dully to themselves, neither happy nor unhappy." This is the emblematic condition of the times: a state of apathetic waiting for some indeterminate future. It is not submission, rebellion, or defiance that weighs these people down, dulling their senses; it is this thing called "tired indifference." "Focusing on a book seems to belong to a past age."[83]

In the late summer 1941, Bonhoeffer's brother-in-law Hans von Dohnányi sketched out plans for the escape of seven Berlin Jews to safe haven in Switzerland. The group would be escorted through Gestapo checkpoints at the Swiss border near Basel under the guise of being secret agents for military intelligence.[84] It wasn't so preposterous: intelligence officers did occasionally use Jews as covert operatives. But the necessary documents would have to be forged.

Bonhoeffer's role was limited but strategically vital. He used his ecumenical contacts to arrange visas and sponsors for the seven. He would also introduce Wilhelm Schmidhuber of the Munich Military Intelligence Office to Alphons Koechlin, president of the Swiss Church Federation, who would facilitate the entry into Switzerland.[85] By the time the mission was executed on September 30, the size of the party would double to fourteen; the code name nevertheless remained Operation 7. Of the fourteen Jews secreted out, eleven were Jewish Christians.

Charlotte Friedenthal was one such baptized Jew. Bonhoeffer took a special interest in her case because she had worked for the Provisional Administration of the Confessing Church, in the office of Heinrich Grüber, the director of Jewish Christian affairs.[86] Bonhoeffer wrote to Koechlin in support of two other Jewish refugee women as well, Inge Jacobsen and Emil Zweig. But in Friedenthal he recognized certain qualities of his former Jewish neighbors in Grunewald—indeed, of his own family.[87]

Charlotte Friedenthal, then forty-nine, was born the daughter of a prominent judge in Bonhoeffer's hometown of Breslau, where she was baptized as a child. From January 1, 1934, to February 28, 1936, she had served as deputy director of the Protestant district welfare office of Berlin-Zehlendorf under Martin Niemöller. From March 2, 1936, until October 1937, she was with the Provisional Administration, becoming the personal secretary to Superintendent Albertz, the Reformed member of the administration. Her sister was married to Dr. Ernst Brieger, former chief of staff of the Tuberculosis Clinic of Breslau-Herrnprotsch, and until 1933 the only German member of the International Tuberculosis Committee. Friedenthal's brother was the prominent attorney Ernst Friedenthal, who, like Brieger, his brother-in-law, served as a decorated officer in the Great War before assuming the post of director of the Deutsche Zentral-Bodenbank AG. Since 1939, Friedenthal had been "registered for emigration to the United

States," but "no opportunity for this has materialized to date, and in addition she is so rooted in the church and in church work that up to this point the suggestion of emigration did not seem responsible to us. . . . Thus now the urgent request from Brother Albertz to take her into the Swiss church, where with all certainty she would prove to be a valuable, particularly well-informed, and collegial member."[88]

On September 5, Friedenthal would arrive safely in Basel,[89] the thirteen others crossing to safety there on September 30th. Encouraged by this success, Dohnányi hoped to coordinate a second rescue operation, but before long Gestapo agents had discovered the trail of money that rescuers had "sent abroad to the group of fourteen and other Jewish immigrants, and the plans were thwarted."

Bonhoeffer was delighted to hear of the success, though he had not been present for the actual border crossing. He had hurried on with Bethge for a two-week vacation on Lac Champex.

CHAPTER THIRTEEN

1941–1943

~

Killing the Madman

In 1935, with the whole brood having left the nest, Karl and Paula Bonhoeffer had moved from Berlin-Grunewald to Marienburger Allee 43 in Charlottenburg. The new house was of more modest proportions, the neighborhood closer to the Charity Hospital. Before long, Dietrich had laid claim to rooms on the second floor. And so it was that, after he and Eberhard had returned from their vacation in Switzerland in late September of 1941, the thirty-five-year-old pastor took up residence under his parents' roof once more. On his writing desk awaiting his arrival was a bottle of Danziger Goldwasser, his favorite schnapps, compliments of Eberhard, who'd arranged for its delivery by a mutual friend, having himself been called away on pastoral duties. Bonhoeffer doubtless treasured the thoughtfulness of the gesture, as he did Paula's regular attention to tidying his room, for which effort he occasionally left his mother thank-you notes.

In response to the recent Gestapo ban on his published work—predictable, as he'd already been prohibited from preaching and teaching—Bonhoeffer spent several hours each day writing.[1] Meanwhile, on the eastern front, German troops awaited Adolf Hitler's orders to invade Russia. Reichsführer-SS Himmler had issued the fateful orders prohibiting the emigration of Jews from Germany.

Bonhoeffer had returned to a capital in crisis. On September 5, 1941, German Jews had been ordered to wear a yellow Star of David; the first deportations east would begin the following month. The Gestapo had sent the deportation orders to the *Jüdische Gemeinde* (Jewish community) leaders, who in turn informed those selected for "relocation," but no one knew when the brownshirts would arrive. When they did appear—on October 16, between the hours of eight p.m. and midnight—the storm troopers gave the evacuees about an hour to collect their things before forcibly removing them from their homes. Some Jews, such as those who worked the night shift at the Siemens factory, were taken directly from their offices or warehouses to the transit stations.[2]

The Gestapo sometimes allowed them up to ninety minutes, or as little as fifteen. Meanwhile, a friend or family member would be obliged to fill out "the mandatory check lists and include a detailed inventory of the furniture, clothing and bank balances." Then the apartment would be sealed, the former residents ferried to the synagogue on Levetzow Street in Moabit (northeast of the Tiergarten, roughly a mile from Charlottenburg), which had been emptied in anticipation. No distinction was made between Jews and Jewish Christians. They all waited together in the synagogue until being herded onto cattle cars on Saturday, October 18.[3]

Sixty thousand Jews were deported by train from Berlin in the first three weeks of October 1941; almost all would eventually be killed in the extermination camps of occupied Poland. In the wake of the mass deportations, the Nazi block captains—low-level thugs who served as "local informants"—plastered the cities with warnings for the other neighborhoods. One flyer read, "Now you too will realize that every German who in any way supports a Jew out of false sentiment, even

JEWS DEPORTED TO CONCENTRATION CAMPS ON THE RUSSIAN-GERMAN FRONT

KARL AND PAULA'S NEW HOME AT MARIENBURGER ALLEE 43
IN BERLIN-CHARLOTTENBURG

merely through friendly encounter, commits a betrayal of our people."
Within that month of the first deportation of Berlin's Jews, the first gas
chambers were constructed in the concentration camp in Auschwitz.[4]

After the seizures of October 16, there would follow sixty-three
more deportations over the next three and a half years. By February
2, 1945, 116,000 of the 122,000 Jewish residents of Berlin were gone.

While recovering from a bout of pneumonia in the first weeks of
October, Bonhoeffer wrote one of several reports on the mass deportation of "Jewish Citizens" from Berlin. These reports, coauthored
with Friedrich Justus Perels, who had been a lawyer for the Confessing Church, were intended for Hans von Dohnányi, who was trying
to finish compiling his documentary of evidence of Nazi brutalities,
which he would present to General Ludwig Beck, the leader of the
German military opposition. Bonhoeffer likely also delivered a copy to
Geneva—the headquarters of both the World Alliance and the Universal Christian Council—this through his intermediary Hans Schönfeld.[5]

According to Bonhoeffer and Perels's account,

> More of these letters were sent out until October 18. Exact
> numbers are not known at this point. Persons of all ages are
> affected, even those who for months have been mobilized to
> work. . . . According to the reports, around fifteen hundred of

the letters mentioned above are said to have gone out to the first group, of whom not all had yet been deported. The criteria according to which the selection was made are not yet clear— for example, lodgers were affected but not the main tenant and vice versa.

We have heard of similar actions in other cities. It has been determined that on Tuesday, October 21, a transport is to leave the Rhineland (Cologne, Düsseldorf, Elberfeld) headed for Poland. It is said that in Berlin further transports are to leave on October 19 and 22 as well. In the Rhineland it was reported that fifty pounds of luggage, one hundred marks, and provisions for eight days were allowed to be brought along.[6]

The promise made by Gestapo officials that those affected by this action have the opportunity to seek new accommodations was a despicable lie. Baptized Jews were included in the round-up as well.[7]

Speer had only become head of armaments in 1942; until then, he functioned as the General Building Inspector for the Reich, where his spectacular projects included plans to redesign Berlin as the Welthauptstadt Germania, the "World Capital of Germania," showcased by a massive sprawl of fortress-like government and commercial buildings, spacious boulevards, and an ornamental lake encircled by Nazi statuary, all ordered along an East-West axis that climaxed to the oceanic Grand Hall, planned (had it been built) as the largest enclosed space in the world, enough to hold sixteen St. Peter's Domes. Emerging from a desert of stone, Germania would be the capital of the thousand year Reich.[8] Following the deportation the apartments were sealed by the block captains.

On November 22, Bonhoeffer had recovered enough to compose a Finkenwalde newsletter, informing the dispersed and shrinking brethren that two more of them, Edgar Engler and Robert Zenke, had been killed at the front. "It is very, very sad," Bonhoeffer wrote.[9] By early December, he felt up to resuming work on *Ethics*, installing himself at Klein Krössin, the Kleist estate in Kieckow owned by his friend Ruth von Kleist-Retzow, for this purpose. But on the fourth Sunday of Advent, he would return to Berlin for Christmas. He and Bethge celebrated their reunion with a rendition of "Es ging ein Sämann aus zu säen seinen Samen" ("The sower went out to sow his seed"), one of Heinrich Schütz's cantatas for voices and instruments. They would reprise the piece for Paula's birthday on December 30.

New Year's 1942 would see Bonhoeffer fully restored to health but anguished at word that more brethren had perished. In his sec-

ond pastoral letter in as many months, he informed his former seminarians that "our dear brothers Bruno Kerlin, Gerhard Vibrans, and
Gerhard Lehne . . . now sleep awaiting the great Easter Day of resurrection." The next month there would be more losses still: Christoph
Harhausen, Günther Christ, Wolfgang Krause, and Johannes Staedler;
Joachim Staude had been missing since August. The aforementioned
Vibrans was Eberhard's cousin—the same one who years earlier had
been the unintended cause of Bonhoeffer's jealous anger after being
invited by Bethge to join the pair on a trip to Switzerland—had been
vaporized by an air-strike bomb "just as he was about to sing with his
comrades from *Ein neues Lied.*"[10]

On January 20, 1942, in the third year of war, fifteen high-ranking
civil servants, SS, and party officials gathered on the Grosser
Wannsee, at Villa Minoux, the guesthouse of the Gestapo and the
Security Service in the southeast suburbs of Berlin. The narrow road
along the lake's southern shore connected the lavish summer homes of
Berlin's industrial and cultural elites. But of course it was not a summer
holiday that drew the Nazi caravan of black limousines to the snow-
covered road and finally to 56–58 Am Grossen Wannsee in the early
hours of that morning. Their purpose: to outline the "Final Solution of
the Jewish Question."[11]

Reinhard Heydrich, an ambitious thirty-eight-year-old navy officer
from an artistic Catholic family in Halle, had been personally selected
by Hitler as the chief executor of the mission. On September 24, 1941,
Hitler had appointed him Reich protector of Bohemia-Moravia, giving him the authority to crush the Czech resistance and to hasten the
deportations of Jews from the occupied Czech territories to Poland.[12]
By the time of the meeting on the Wannsee, just a few months later, he
had risen to become chief of the Reich Security Office, overseeing the
Gestapo, the general police force, and the homeland security service
(the *Sicherheitsdienst*, or SD) for all of Germany.[13]

In a calm and meticulous manner, Heydrich outlined "the expulsion of the Jews from the living space of the German people" and "from
every sphere of life of the German people."[14] For maximal efficiency as
specified in section II of the four-point Wannsee Protocol (drafted by
Heydrich and his assistant, Adolf Eichmann), the "organizational, policy and technical prerequisites for the Final Solution" would now need
to be coordinated by Himmler, the Reichsführer-SS, and Heydrich
himself as the chief of the SD.[15] Yet the Wannsee Protocol reached far
beyond the German-speaking nations, far beyond Europe, in fact, envi-
sioning a day when the entire world would be made free of Jews; when

all "enemies, parasites, and germs" (as Hitler called them) have been exterminated, there would reign a "supra-individual" Aryan purity.

The Swiss human rights commissioner Carl Jacob Burckhardt would later call Heydrich "the young evil god of death." His squinting, suspicious gaze could indeed produce a chilling effect, but there was nothing demonic, let alone godlike, in his background. Like the fifteen other participants—including SS Oberführer Gerhard Klopfer, Otto Hofmann, who ran the Office for Race and Settlement, and Nazi Foreign Minister Martin Luther—Heydrich, a classically trained violinist and competitive fencer, was a respectable scion of the educated German middle class. Two-thirds of those in attendance possessed a university degree, and more than half had earned a doctorate. The drafters of the Wannsee Protocol were also conspicuously young: half in their forties and five in their thirties.[16]

In the course of the meeting, Heydrich presented the various department heads a plan of unprecedented ambition, one to achieve the destruction of the entire Jewish population of Europe and French North Africa (Morocco, Algeria, and Tunisia). Those fit for labor might be assigned, temporarily, to roadwork and other construction projects, but there would be no ultimate exemptions from the Final Solution: the workers, too, would be annihilated once their work was done. As Mark Roseman notes in *The Villa, the Lake, the Meeting: Wannsee and the Final Solution*, "Despite the euphemism of evacuation, the minutes unmistakably contain a plan for genocide—formulated in sober, bureaucratic language, deliberated on in civilized surroundings in a once cosmopolitan suburb of Berlin."[17]

Police actions against Jews since 1933, Heydrich explained, had been woefully deficient, though not for want of effort: there had been the continual pogroms, the disease-infested ghettos, the campaigns of "relocation," the forced-labor camps, as well as various other strategies of legalized repression and humiliation. And as Soviet and Allied forces steadily pushed back the German lines in late 1942, most Jews in German-occupied Europe were being sent directly to the death camps if not murdered on the spot. Even so, by the time of the Wannsee Conference, with the war entering its third year, 75 percent of those European Jews eventually to be exterminated were still alive. Two years later, however, by Christmas 1943, the same percentage of the eventual six million would be dead. As Roseman writes, "Nineteen forty-two was the most astounding year of murder in the Holocaust, one of the most astounding years of murder in the whole history of mankind."[18] It was largely thanks to the villainous efficiency of Heydrich, who by the spring of 1943 managed to have five new killing centers up and running in occupied Poland.

The months between January 1942 and his arrest in April 1943 would be among the most wrenching for Bonhoeffer, the demands of discipleship becoming ever more difficult to reconcile with the duplicity he'd undertaken. He would concede uncertainty. He would renounce pretensions of saintliness. He would seek only to discern the responsible course of action. It meant learning to see "events from below" and banishing pious cant. Only by aspiring to be "simple, uncomplicated, and honest human beings" could he and his comrades navigate a way through the "great masquerade of evil," the ubiquitous fog of propaganda and deception. Still, his struggle would not end heroically.[19]

Three days after the Wannsee conference, Bonhoeffer and his brother Klaus, who was now the chief legal counsel of Lufthansa, met with Helmuth von Moltke, Ludwig von Guttenberg, and Klaus's brother-in-law Justus Delbrück, at the Venetia Hotel. The wider German resistance network was seeking various means of overthrowing the regime, but in Berlin the conspiracy focused solely on killing Hitler. It had been so ever since Hitler assumed the role of commander-in-chief, after removing the head of the army on December 19, 1941. Also present at the Venetia was the young lawyer Fabian von Schlabrendorff, adjutant to Henning von Tresckow, chief of staff of Army Group Centre, the force that carried out Operation Barbarosa, as the invasion of the Soviet Union was called. Bonhoeffer had been introduced to Schlabrendorff one year earlier at Klein Krössin. Now, as plans began to develop quickly, Bonhoeffer assured him and the others that, despite knowing nothing about guns and explosives, he was willing to "join any attempt on Hitler's life if such action were asked of him." His one condition was that he be given "sufficient warning" so that he might first officially sever his pastoral ties to the Confessing Church. Tyrannicide was a crime that the church would not condone—nor would he have wished it to.[20]

It must be allowed that prevailing views of Bonhoeffer's part in the resistance retain a certain gilt of hagiography. Even the assertion of his membership can be misleading; the resistance would remain a fluid entity, spread over numerous cells, mostly uncoordinated and unrelated. One might work on behalf of the general cause, but one could not join the movement as one might a club or political party. Bonhoeffer would indeed be drawn into treasonous conspiracy and pay for it with his life. But as the scholar Sabine Dramm argues in her seminal study of Bonhoeffer and the resistance, the actions for which he would be condemned are but "a component" in "the complex inner and outer developmental process of his life as a whole"; which is to say, his decisions are fraught with doubt and largely unscripted, as perhaps most heroic deeds are in retrospect. Nevertheless, to speak of Bonhoeffer as a hero is to promote an oversimplified understanding—in Dramm's words, a "bland interpretation," one that ill-serves the reality of his role or the complexity of his motivations, in particular his deep ambivalence about the proposed assassination.[21]

In her own forthright efforts to temper the heroic narrative, Victoria Barnett, a Bonhoeffer scholar and director of church relations at the United States Holocaust Museum, has claimed that Bonhoeffer acted more on the margins than at the center of the resistance, such as there was a center. His voluble opposition to Hitler was a stirring counterpoint to the compliant rhetoric of most Protestant ministers, paralyzed as they were by a typically Lutheran veneration of the state. His clarion eloquence would justly win him many admirers—among not only popular chroniclers but scholars as well. But it has also given rise to "a kind of mythology"—one that proposes a more dramatic and central involvement for Bonhoeffer than can be asserted by the evidence.[22]

Bonhoeffer received no financial compensation from the *Abwehr*. Whatever income he had during these years, modest to say the least, came from a half-time stipend from the Old Prussian Union, the so-called "love offerings" of wealthy friends, and, as ever, his parents. His duties as a conspirator were actually few, as were the fruits of his efforts. He played no active part in any of the assassination plots—which, by one count, numbered well over a hundred. There may even be some truth to Dramm's assertion that Dohnányi might have drawn his brother-in-law into the conspiracy for the sole purpose of securing the exemption from military service he so desperately wanted.[23] The point of such observations is not to detract from Bonhoeffer's contribution but, rather, to emphasize the peculiarity of his vocation as a minister to the conspirators, of his straining to establish within the chaos of the conspiracy a space for Christian reflection.[24]

Bonhoeffer himself would never imagine his actions as heroic in the least, describing himself as an "accomplice conscious of his guilt."[25] He offered the sacraments to traitors, subversives, and deserters. He prayed for the conspiracy, for the defeat of his nation. And when asked, he prayed with the conspirators. To those who had acquiesced to the imperative of killing Hitler, and even to those plotting the deed directly, he presented a priestly objectivity—more so than detachment. His flock ran the gamut from Christians, atheists, and chastened romantics; these were men and women whose courage and commitment to righteous action—to the good of humanity—existed beyond churchly constraints and exhortations. Bonhoeffer's distinctive contribution to this fellowship was to articulate with authority the moral justification for their goal, unsettling, as Robin Lovin has described it, the state's traditional claim upon the individual's absolute loyalty, a claim "based on patriotism and the sanctity of military oaths." Luther's Large Catechism had taught that only God or his governments on earth could justly take a life. It was for Bonhoeffer to stake out the moral ground for action that tradition condemned as the sin of murder.[26]

Meetings with Barth—with perhaps the one exception—had formed some of the most pleasant memories of his previous two trips to Switzerland. In the professor's study on the second floor of the plain house on Bruderholzallee, the two would ruminate over "history and eschatology," "Christian responsibility," the "forgiveness of sins," and other doctrinal matters, great and small. Bonhoeffer would leave Basel with "the confidence" that he would enjoy such stimulation again.

But in the past year, Barth had grown suspicious of Bonhoeffer's freedom to travel abroad, and then baffled by news of his affiliation with the *Abwehr*. Where once his travel and speech had been severely restricted, now suddenly, it seemed, he was free to go anywhere. His errands, Barth is reported to have said, were "unsettling as to [their] objectives." His third and final trip to Switzerland would thus occasion Barth's most serious doubts concerning "the circumstances of Bonhoeffer's visit."[27]

For his part, Bonhoeffer was not unaware of the impression he was leaving among all but the small circle of friends who knew what he was up to. He realized that in certain quarters it was whispered that he'd become a Nazi sympathizer. His ecumenical contacts alerted him that Barth was among his doubters, which claim, initially at least, Bonhoeffer was prepared to dismiss as "overinflated rumor."[28] When it was confirmed, however, Barth's suspicion hit him hard. Deeply embittered, Bonhoeffer wondered how his friend could possibly suspect him of having so compromised his theological convictions. In fact, such suspicion on Barth's part was not so unusual: after his ouster from Bonn, he tended to imagine anyone who disagreed with his dogmatic theology to be guilty of all kinds of mischief.

On May 17, 1942, Bonhoeffer complained in a letter to Barth that notably lacked the accustomed deferential tone. "It is most reprehensible to sow and encourage mistrust," he said. "Our duty is rather to foster and strengthen confidence wherever we can." Trust was the only thing left in a world consumed by "deception and lies." But under the "curse of suspicion," no friendship could be expected to survive. Bonhoeffer told Barth he could imagine no greater, rarer, or happier blessing than that of erring on the side of charity when a friend appears to be moving in strange ways.[29]

As a Swiss academic, Barth was an outsider to the German plotters, but that would not keep him from expressing sharp criticisms of the resistance, as he became aware of their plans. The Berlin conspirators operated with a naive confidence in the dissident members of the military: so he'd concluded in spring 1942, as if he were the first one to hold the view.[30] In fact, both the Allied governments and the majority of those in other parts of the German resistance had come to the same conclusion. But those like Dohnányi would continue to believe that only the critics had the luxury of criticism. As far as he was concerned, there was no better hope for overthrowing the Reich than the plan involving the upper echelons of the military.

Barth would never respond to Bonhoeffer's letter directly, being consumed with work on the latest volume of his *Church Dogmatics*. In March 1942, volume II/2, his monumental study of the doctrine of election (covering the thorny issue of divine predestination), had been rushed to press. "A number of unbound copies" would soon be smuggled into Germany—under the innocuous title *Calvin Studies*—one finding its way to Bonhoeffer. Now Barth was focused on the doctrine of creation, beginning with a "thorough-going exposition of the contents of the first two chapters of the Bible"; this minutely detailed work he would pursue with the music of Mozart "in my ears"—especially the flute concertos, *The Magic Flute*, and the horn and bassoon concertos.[31] Nevertheless, Barth knew he had injured Bonhoeffer, and he sought to reassure him, albeit through his assistant, Charlotte von Kirschbaum. Above all, Kirschbaum wrote, Bonhoeffer should be assured of a welcome in Barth's home no less gracious than he'd known before. Overnight accommodations, however, would need to be arranged elsewhere, as "we no longer have a guest bed here." Kirschbaum denied that Barth had even "for a second" distrusted Bonhoeffer and further claimed that despite whatever misgivings he may have had, the master had written "to you immediately and directly."[32] He had not provided grist for the rumor mill.

Bonhoeffer, needless to say, had never received any such communications. Still, he was thrilled to have a signed copy of *Church Dogmatics* II/2, carrying the galley proofs with him for a leisurely stay at a friend's summer cottage on Lake Geneva, and various other travels, often in the company of Bethge, to whom he read passages aloud.

Bonhoeffer and Barth would meet briefly on the afternoon of May 25. During their visit, news broke on BBC radio that Vyacheslav Molotov had arrived in London to sign the British-Soviet treaty.[33] When the presenter remarked that the treaty precluded either country from reaching a separate peace with Germany, Bonhoeffer said, "Well, now it's all over!"[34]

Through the spring of 1942, Bonhoeffer's base remained his parents' house on Marienburger Allee—at least this is where he kept his books, notes, and other worldly possessions. Three days after returning from Switzerland—this was his third trip to Zurich and Basel in the past year and would be his last—he traveled to Sweden on a small aircraft through a violent summer storm, where a secret meeting with George Bell had been arranged in the village of Sigtuna, twenty miles northwest of Stockholm. It was to prove mainly an exercise in solidarity, like most of his meetings, achieving no tangible result. But to the resistance, Bonhoeffer's ability to articulate with utmost clarity the state of the nation and of the conspiracy mattered greatly; for Dohnányi and the others believed that what their emissary said to Bell would be transmitted to the highest "levels of the British government." The job Dohnányi had entrusted to Bonhoeffer was, they thought, vital to the greater purpose of persuading the Allies to back the conspirators.

As it would turn out, Dohnányi and his colleagues had overestimated Bell's influence. Allied leaders were simply not interested in a German churchman's revelations about a planned coup d'état and the viable non-Nazi government to follow. Nor did they particularly care what the Anglican bishop of Chichester judged to be the best way of defeating "a monstrous tyranny."[35] To the extent that the Allied leadership paid any heed at all, they greeted the various "communiqués" from the German underground with suspicion and finally disdain, particularly the conspirators' demand for assurances "of German territorial integrity and of their own position as leaders of a postwar Germany."[36] From the Allied perspective, the very idea of altering, let alone suspending, their intricately laid military plans to place their hopes with a band of disaffected former Nazis was nothing short of ludicrous. Neither the Americans nor the British would ever seriously consider the option. That much became clear in January 1943, when, at the conclusion of the Casablanca Conference, Winston Churchill and Franklin Delano Roosevelt issued a joint announcement: the Allies would accept nothing less than Germany's unconditional surrender. Until that word arrived from Morocco, the Berlin circle would continue to chase the chimera of assistance from the Allies.

All the Sigtuna conferees stayed in the sprawling crème stucco villa set on a green hillside on the outskirts of the medieval village. The estate overlooking Lake Mälaren ordinarily housed the Nordic Folk School, founded in the nineteenth century by the Swedish pastor Manfred Björkquist to promote Christian spirituality and humanistic dialogue. It was not lost on Bonhoeffer, that the *Folk* in the Swedish *Folkhög-skola* (folk high school) conveyed quite a different meaning than the *Volk* of the reigning German idiom: not the nation destined to rule over all states but the folkish fellowship of peoples, of common humanity.

Apart from Bell, there were several other ecumenical leaders present, including representatives of the Scandinavian Protestant churches.[37] But it was to Bell alone—his most trusted ecumenical colleague—that Bonhoeffer confided the full details of the plot to kill Hitler. They broke away from the others, going to the nearby Nordic Ecumenical Institute, which had become a vital point of convergence during the years when the ties that bind the Nordic countries had frayed from one another and the ecumenical movement was being ground to a halt by the war." As he and Bell sat together, little did Bonhoeffer suspect the futility of this risk he was about to take. He asked Bell to ascertain whether the Allies would be prepared to negotiate with a new government; as he spoke, he grew excited at the prospect of a European reconciliation born of this coordinated effort.[38] On the night of May 30, the eve of the conference, as Bonhoeffer dined in Stockholm with Hans Schönfeld, his Geneva-based colleague, who'd joined him on the trip, the British Royal Air Force had conducted its first heavy bombing of Germany. The target had been Hamburg, but the mission was diverted to Cologne owing to heavy fog over the port city. Nearly a thousand airplanes rained fire over Rhein-Ruhr, obliterating thousands of houses and other buildings.

The news was not the only reason Bonhoeffer was glad to be in Sweden. He had happy memories of his earlier visit in 1939, shortly after his thirtieth birthday. A photo from that time shows him boarding a ferry to cross the Baltic with twenty-six students from Finkenwalde—all of them turned out like earnest young preachers in their bowlers, suits, ties, and secondhand trench coats (except for Bonhoeffer, of course). The students had managed to get passports from the local authorities, but they were not allowed to carry any German money with them. Most had never left their homeland and were full of apprehension. But their experiences in the homes and congregations of Swedish pastors and host families came as a great refreshment. By the time the party arrived in Stockholm on the night train from Lund, four newspapers in the capital and Uppsala had run stories on the German visitors, quoting Bonhoeffer's remarks about the "unforgettable days" and the "rich impressions" and "friendliness" of their encounters.[39] This trip, three years on, would not be so fondly remembered, once the naïveté of its premise—the hope of winning Allied support for the conspiracy—had been revealed. Nevertheless, the effort would represent Bonhoeffer's most daring mission as a participant in the resistance.[40]

Years later Bell would remember that Bonhoeffer and Schönfeld had told him in "great detail [of] the character and purposes of the German resistance." The briefing included the "names of the leading personalities," he said, "the same who were involved in the Hitler plot of 20 July 1944." It was then left to Bell to ascertain whether the Allied governments might be willing to accept a successful coup as evidence "that the whole Hitler regime had been destroyed"—thus clearing the way for a peace settlement with the new leadership.[41]

Upon returning to London, Bell dutifully conveyed Bonhoeffer's request (albeit in writing) to Anthony Eden, Churchill's secretary of state for war.[42] But in January 1941—nearly a year and a half before Bonhoeffer and Bell's exchange—Churchill had clearly stated England's intent to greet all inquiries about support for a German coup with "absolute silence." Since then, the prime minister's mind hadn't changed: he remained immovably committed to the Allied military strategy, as Eden well knew. And so when Eden did finally reply on July 17, 1942, he categorically told the bishop that "it would not be in the national interest for any reply whatever to be sent to [the two German pastors]" and that "no action could be taken" by the government.[43] Eden expressed sympathy for the dangers and difficulties faced by the opposition but allowed that they had given little evidence of seriousness.

In the months following the Sigtuna meeting, the United States Air Force would join the RAF's steady strategic bombing of German military assets.

As to its express purpose, the June meeting in Sigtuna came to nothing. But it was productive in another way: coupled with a visit by Moltke a month earlier, it created networks of communication that would contribute to the rescue of a significant number of Norwegian and Danish Jews in September 1943. Moltke's warning to his Danish friend Merete Bonnesen that the Nazis planned to transport Danish Jews to German camps sparked planning for rescue operations that would deliver 7,400 Norwegian and Danish Jews to safety in Sweden. But these rescue missions succeeded "thanks to the groundwork which the Sigtuna group had prepared through high level participants." In a fictitious diary that he had begun keeping while in the *Abwehr*, daily evidence of his supposed fidelity to the Reich, Bonhoeffer observed with feigned ruefulness that "theologically the German influence seems in recent times to have unfortunately diminished sharply in favour of the Anglo-Saxon."[44] Throughout February, Bonhoeffer kept this camouflage, or "pretended," diary (as Bethge much later explained to George Bell) to disguise the purpose of his trips abroad in case the Gestapo searched his parents' Charlottenburg home—and indeed this seemed inevitable after his *Abwehr* colleague Wilhelm Schmidhuber's arrest in late October 1942 for "currency violations."[45] (He had helped provide financial support to the Jews smuggled out of Germany in Operation 7.) Bonhoeffer represented his intention as being "to inform his countrymen still in power, that they are losing the ideological war in Sweden to democratic and freedom-loving British and Americans."[46]

From his upstairs room on Marienburger Allee or his studio at the Kleist-Retzow estate, on trains and planes, in hotel rooms, on retreats and in various hideaways, Bonhoeffer would continue throughout the summer of 1942 to work on *Ethics*. While striking a chastened note—"An ethicist cannot be a man who always knows better than others what is to be done and how it is to be done"[47]—Bonhoeffer's meditations nevertheless draw on the theological intensities of Barth's jubilant defense of God's sovereignty. Beyond all understanding, obedience to God remained a venture into the unknown—a journey without maps, a "total" and "unconditional" decision, guided by trust alone. On June 26, Bonhoeffer left Berlin for two weeks in Italy. Little is known of this trip. His bogus diary offers only the most pedestrian summaries of his movements, blandly describing places over which he had earlier rhapsodized. A part of him must have relished the irony of the exercise; at times the journal seems like an inside joke at the Gestapo's expense. "Main impressions: the Laocoön," he wrote. "Curious, until now the Laocoön never made any particular impression on me." He praises the xenophobic rector of the Collegium Germanicum as a "very collected, clear, smart old world officer" and ridicules a stupendously dull Nazi named Wilhelm Schmidhuber (who was, of course, Bonhoeffer's comrade) as a "bon vivant."[48]

When she first met Bonhoeffer in the fall of 1935, Maria von Wedemeyer was just a nine-year-old accompanying her grandmother, Ruth von Kleist-Retzow, to worship services and morning prayers at Finkenwalde. Before the Gestapo closed the seminary in 1937, Kleist-Retzow asked Bonhoeffer to instruct Maria, now eleven, and two other grandchildren for their imminent confirmation. But he did not meet Maria again until June 1942, when he paid a visit to

Kleist-Retzow on his return trip from Sweden. Whatever he knew of Wedemeyer in the intervening six years—apparently very little—he had learned from Kleist-Retzow.[49] Maria was the daughter of a provincial aristocrat with twenty thousand acres in Pomerania. She read Rilke, loved dancing and skiing, and rose to the call of the autumn hunt. She would have been expected to marry into the landed gentry and content herself as a nobleman's wife. But the "sprightly" teenager he met on the Kleist-Retzow estate in June 1942 charmed Dietrich with her clear blue eyes and confident smile. He noticed she bore a remarkable resemblance to his twin sister, Sabine, as a teenager. Bonhoeffer was smitten.

Still a very young man emotionally, Bonhoeffer was uncertain about how to proceed or what to make of his new affections. But he'd be equally perplexed by the feelings that were developing in the months before his reunion with Maria. On the train from Klein Krössin to Munich on June 25, 1942, he wrote Bethge a letter confessing that he felt as if he was "on the verge of some kind of breakthrough." He was not referring to his forthcoming encounter with Wedemeyer. He had in mind a new apprehension of himself, which he wanted to share with his best friend.[50]

He wanted Bethge to know that the arc connecting the disciple to the physical world extended farther than he had ever imagined. He felt singularly open to "the worldly [*weltlich*] realm"—intrigued and "amazed" by life. "I am living, and can live, for days without the Bible," he said. But when he opened his Bible again after an absence, he could hear and experience the "new and delightful . . . as never before." "Authenticity, life, freedom, and mercy" had acquired a new significance for him. A worldliness heretofore unknown was unexpectedly refreshing his spiritual being, and with it he felt a growing aversion to all things "religious." What a glorious discovery, the vast new spiritual energies he was feeling! It was an impulse to let things take their own course and try his best not to resist. It was his first intimation of spirituality outside the church.

Bonhoeffer does not mention his visit with Wedemeyer directly, though the letter makes clear that Bethge already knew of it— Bonhoeffer allows that he has not written to her and has no intention of doing so. He would even be content, he says, to go without seeing her again and simply savor "the pleasant thought of a few highly charged moments" in her company. Still, he knew himself well enough now to realize that pleasant thoughts would, sooner or later, "dissolve into the realm of unfulfilled fantasies"—a realm that, in his case, was "already well-populated."[51]

Indeed, little would follow on those "highly charged moments" for the next three months; there would be no visits, phone conversations, or correspondence. On October 31, Bonhoeffer sent Wedemeyer a letter of condolence on the death of her brother Maximilian, a casualty on the eastern front. Nothing more is said until November 27, when Bonhoeffer wrote Bethge to report on his recent stay at the Wedemeyers' estate in Pätzig. It had been an agreeable visit: contrary to his great fear "that the house would have an excessive spiritual tone, its style made a very pleasant impression—but it ended awkwardly." After learning of her daughter's correspondence with Bonhoeffer, Ruth von Wedemeyer expressed sharp disapproval of the familiarity between the thirty-six-year-old pastor, who appeared to Ruth temperamentally middle age, and her third child, who was barely eighteen.[52]

During these same three months, much had changed in Bethge's life. At the age of thirty-three, he had begun courting Renate Schleicher, Bonhoeffer's seventeen-year-old niece, who lived next door at 42 Marienburger Allee. As a child, Renate and her siblings had played in the garden beneath Bonhoeffer's second-floor window—and now she was being wooed by his closest friend and confessor. By the end of November, the pair were engaged, although Renate's parents—Ursula (Bonhoeffer's older sister) and Rüdiger Schleicher—did not approve of the match and insisted that the couple undergo a yearlong separation before carrying things any further.

Bonhoeffer couldn't help but notice that he'd worked himself into a parallel predicament. At thirty-six, he was closer in age to Maria's mother, Ruth von Wedemeyer, née von Kleist, than to Maria. Ruth was a tall, slim, dark-haired woman of forty-six whose husband, Hans, had been called out of retirement and sent to the eastern front, perishing in the Ukraine. With no knowledge of Eberhard and Renate's situation, Maria's mother imposed a one-year moratorium on the relationship with Bonhoeffer, as must have been a common remedy to protect girls not yet finished with their schooling. Though Bonhoeffer might be an eminent theologian and esteemed pastor of the Patzow faithful, the age difference and the peculiar cast of the courtship made Ruth von Wedemeyer uneasy. As it happened, Maria was said to have been perfectly "relieved and happy" about the delay.[53]

Bonhoeffer had never had a girlfriend. A long-distance friendship ten years earlier with a student named Elizabeth Zinn had dissolved in confusion; he then chose to pour his heart and soul into Finkenwalde. Zinn would go on to marry the New Testament scholar Günther Bornkamm. Through it all, Bonhoeffer's friendship with Bethge, now in its seventh year, had sustained him fully.

But Bethge's engagement to Schleicher, though deferred for a year, threw everything out of balance. Wedemeyer's fascination with Bonhoeffer, and the slow turning of his attention to her, were no doubt owing to an all-too-common desire for intimacy in those days of mounting personal losses for everyone. Her father had died in August, and before the year's end, she would also lose her brother and her two closest cousins. In the wake of such sorrows, Bonhoeffer's pastoral instincts drew him closer to the Wedemeyer and Kleist-Retzow families.

The announcement of Bonhoeffer and Wedemeyer's engagement on January 13, 1943, would come as a surprise to both families.[54] The Bonhoeffers knew that arrests were imminent; moreover, they had never met Maria. When, after Dietrich's arrest and imprisonment in April, Dr. Bonhoeffer finally did meet his son's intended, he found her "nice and intelligent." With "oval eyes" and a "noble provincial forehead," Maria reminded him of Robert Graf von Zedlitz-Trützschler, the former *Oberpräsident* of Silesia, Posnen, and Hessen, who was her maternal grandfather.[55] Observing his son's happiness with Eberhard for the previous seven years made it even more difficult to comprehend that this girl had become the object of his son's romantic attachment. On the other side, much as she admired Bonhoeffer, Wedemeyer's grandmother, Ruth von Kleist-Retzow, could not hide her displeasure. Had the flamboyant abbot of Finkenwalde, whose cause she had generously supported, really asked for the hand of her teenage granddaughter in marriage? Eventually, Wedemeyer's mother would tighten her original moratorium, forbidding all correspondence and phone calls until her daughter attained her majority. Bonhoeffer responded to the situation with "great sensitivity," Wedemeyer would later write. He complied with the decree to the last iota.[56]

From the start the engagement had been fraught with complications. The imposed separation, though accepted with equanimity—one might even say unwitting relief—cast the romance in an ethereal light. "I think that if I wanted to I could prevail. I can argue better than the others and could probably talk them into it. But that seems dreadful to me," Bonhoeffer gallantly reported to Bethge.[57] Theirs was, and would remain, an engagement of the spirit.[58] But by the time the two were finally allowed to write and then to see each other, Wedemeyer—known to friends as a free-spirited girl and unafraid to speak her mind—would address her fiancé as "Pastor Bonhoeffer."

In turn Bonhoeffer treated her like the confirmand she had been years earlier. She had found him pompous and even comical back then. Once, in class, he told the students he had learned his first ten sermons by heart and if they did not leave the room at once, and quietly, "he

MARIA VON WEDEMEYER
AROUND 1942

might be tempted to prove his claim!" He would in fact go on to flunk Wedemeyer, who was later to be confirmed by another pastor.[59]

In time, Wedemeyer grew easier in the engagement. She would opine on subjects great and small—literature, music, the art of painting Christmas ornaments, the peculiarities of provincial life. She was not afraid to sound silly or to offer a breezy aside, just to leave the dapper theologian (such a serious man, she sighed) wondering what would come out of her next.

She said she loved his book *Creation and Fall*, her favorite of all his writings. But it was not easy reading. So she mainly dipped into it at bedtime, and even then she could hardly finish a sentence before falling asleep. She meant no offense. The "beginning of a sentence often interests me a great deal." And the next morning, she would promise herself that she would do better that night; all day long she would look forward to reading more, but then "the same thing happens."[60]

Perhaps Bonhoeffer was intrigued by Wedemeyer's eager tone. But until the Nazis closed the prison doors on him, he quite often responded to her opinions with boyish sarcasm or professorial bravado. Occasionally, he even corrected her writing.

Maria was also the first person Bonhoeffer had ever known who did not speak of his father with reverential awe. She found Dr. Bonhoeffer imperious and distant, and she did not like the shape of his mouth: something about it made her sad. Karl-Friedrich, whom she also met on the same visit, did not fare much better. His hard laugh made her cringe and wonder whether he was mocking her or was merely a nervous type.

But Maria took immediately to Paula, who welcomed her into the family with quiet and affectionate purpose. Her unfailingly forthright manner and attention to little things put Wedemeyer at ease. She gave the girl eight small photographs of her son and prayed with her in the early mornings.

Wedemeyer liked the family's simple home, on the cul-de-sac with the garden in full bloom. In the room upstairs that Bonhoeffer had kept with Bethge, she lingered among the objects of her betrothed. "The desk where you wrote your books and letters to me, your armchair and ashtray, your shoes on the shelf and your favorite pictures"—all these things seemed so much a part of him. In this room, as in all the rooms of the house, she felt close to her fiancé, closer than she had ever felt in his presence.[61]

Bonhoeffer had visited her family's estate in the late fall of 1942, shortly before they announced their engagement. One Wedemeyer family custom that seems to have annoyed him was the running of laps around the property and "getting splashed with buckets of cold water by the servants"—this even before breakfast had been served.[62] He also found the family's hushed reverence for music and art rather precious; at the Bonhoeffers', where witty improvisation always carried the day, these were things to dive into playfully. The Wedemeyers' seasonal trips to town for the opera or theater had the air of pilgrimage about them.

Describing the couple years later, Renate Bethge would say that she never saw them together and that only after Bonhoeffer had gone to prison did she and other members of the Bonhoeffer family consider them a pair. Bonhoeffer's first biographer portrayed Wedemeyer as a "medium-sized," "not too slender" girl who "did not wear make-up."[63] But a photograph from the year of her engagement reveals the elegant face Karl had admired, with high cheekbones, dark eyebrows, and red lipstick. Bethge, who after the war became Bonhoeffer's Boswell, does not even introduce Maria until the very end of his thousand-page treatment.

Why did Dietrich Bonhoeffer pursue Maria von Wedemeyer? Bethge's engagement and his sudden withdrawal had come as a surprise. Bonhoeffer also took it as a test of his own mettle—his capacity for entering into and sustaining a romance with a woman and thus keeping pace, as it were, with the man who was his soul mate. If he could mirror the arrangement that Bethge had entered into with natural gladness, he might be able to remain close to his true companion. Such would prove wishful thinking, however; upon learning of Bethge's engagement, Bonhoeffer sought assurances from his friend that their own relations would not suffer any alienation, that they would continue to travel together, have new adventures inspired by the new arrangements. Bonhoeffer imagined a time after the war when the two couples would take joint holidays, in the course of which, at some point—and in one singularly fantastic example—the men would leave their wives behind and continue alone together to Palestine.[64] The thought of a life in the Holy Land with his friend was a frequent fantasy.

But Bethge harbored no such hopes for preserving their intimacy.

He told Bonhoeffer that things would inevitably change. For marriage was what "remains stable in all fleeting relationships." Bonhoeffer protested that "we should also include friendship among these stable things."[65] He told Bethge that their "attunement and familiarity" with each other, "achieved through years of not always frictionless practice," was "something we must never lose."[66] To this Bethge objected—in a bold and forthright manner that promptly ended the exchange: friendship was "completely determined and sustained by its own particular substance" and thus lacking stability in principle.[67] Marriage, on the other hand, stood on the firm ground of a formal, legal contract, ordained by God, and the outward respect this confers, giving it permanence, even amid the flux of such tumultuous days. And, Bethge added, "it gives me a sort of calm and makes me feel more manly."[68]

Bonhoeffer's engagement to Wedemeyer, finally proposed and accepted in letters exchanged in January 1943, would create its own impression of intimacy and permanence. But after his arrest and imprisonment in April of that year, Bonhoeffer understood that his marriage to Maria was never to happen. And it was his love for Bethge that would endure.

In November 1942, Bonhoeffer joined his former student Wolf-Dieter Zimmermann, his wife, and a few mutual friends for a weekend at Zimmermann's parsonage in Werder on the Havel. The town, twenty kilometers southeast of Berlin, one of the few surviving congregations of the Confessing Church, provided its pastor a wooden house on a hill overlooking the river. Among the handful of guests at the dinner table was Werner von Haeften, an old friend of Zimmermann's and now staff lieutenant of the army high command.

As Zimmermann recalled the evening of the first meal together, Haeften sat uncharacteristically silent, as the conversation ranged over literature and music and the challenges of heating the drafty wooden house. But as the dishes were being removed and coffee was served, Haeften—as if having reached the climax of some interior monologue—turned to Bonhoeffer and asked, "Shall I shoot?" When Bonhoeffer did not answer directly, Haeften added, "I can get inside the Führer's headquarters with my revolver. I know where and when the conferences take place. I can gain access."[69]

Haeften's question landed like a grenade. Zimmermann tried "to steer the conversation back to casual concerns and calm the others down." But Bonhoeffer wanted to pursue the matter.

He told Haeften that the "liquidation of Hitler" would accomplish nothing in and of itself. It might even make matters worse. The real objective of any assassination had to be "a change of circumstances, of the government." This standard, Bonhoeffer explained, that every action must yield specific political ends, was precisely what made work in the resistance so difficult; everyone involved labored under the constant pressure to prepare and review each step with the utmost care. He might have added: only thus could murder be justified.

The others at the table were eventually drawn into the discussion Bonhoeffer and Haeften would continue well past the dinner hour, about how best to lay the groundwork for a new government. Haeften was not satisfied with Bonhoeffer's answer, finding the approach too measured. Enough was now known about the brutalities of the Nazi regime. It was time to take action and suffer the consequences, whatever they might be.

Haeften was, in Zimmermann's judgment, a "gentle type—enthusiastic, idealistic, and a man of Christian convictions." But he was also from a distinguished family of military officers, and as such naturally preferred to hammer out a plan of attack rather than to muse on the proper conditions for a coup. "He kept asking questions, digging deeper," inviting Bonhoeffer to clarify. "Theoretical reflections" did not suffice in the current crisis. Given his proximity to the high command, he thought he might be one of the very few in a position to get the job done. With great emotion he confessed to the little gathering that he was able and ready. What did his own life matter compared to those of all who might be saved by removing the madman?

Bonhoeffer agreed with the need for concrete action but also stressed the need "to be discreet, to plan clearly, and then consider all unforeseen complications."

"But shall I?" Haeften asked again. "May I?"[70]

Bonhoeffer said he could not make the decision for him. Haeften would have to struggle with the question in his own conscience. But what was clear to Bonhoeffer—and this much he allowed forthrightly—was that no one could ever emerge from this situation morally innocent. By neither course—action or inaction—could one be spared guilt, but the Christian could take consolation in the knowledge that guilt is "always borne by Christ."[71] Bonhoeffer had not given Haeften a specific answer, but insofar as Haeften sought to know what was ethically permissible, the proposition that "both the no and the yes involve guilt" was as good as affirming the choice of assassination.[72]

The next week Haeften returned to his military duties. Two years later, as an aide-de-camp to Colonel Claus von Stauffenberg, he would play a key role in the July 20, 1944, attempt on Hitler's life. Later that same day, with sunlight streaming into the tribunal chamber in central Berlin, Haeften and his fellow conspirators would be condemned by General Friedrich Fromm. Shortly after the stroke of midnight, Gestapo agents led Haeften and three comrades into the courtyard of the army high command on Bendlerstrasse, where they were executed by a ten-man firing squad.[73] There was indeed no escaping guilt.

C hristmas would find Bonhoeffer with his family and with Bethge. It would be their last one together. Shortly before New Year's Day, Bonhoeffer wrote a letter to his closest comrades in the conspiracy: Dohnányi, Oster, and Bethge. The letter would come to be known by a name suggesting casual self-reflection: "After Ten Years: A Reckoning Made at New Years 1943." In substance, however, it is more like the profession of a worldly faith. "Are we still of any use?" he asks—"we" being the aristocrats of conscience, the cosmopolitan elites, the "children of the church."[74]

Bonhoeffer had been startled into a new way of thinking. The tumultuous years of resistance and conspiracy had created in him an irrepressible need for summing up and casting forward—and, as in one particularly luminous section of *Ethics*, "Christ and Good People," the need for a compassionate yet decisive rethinking of Christianity's exclusive claims.[75]

> Ten years is a long time in anyone's life. As time is the most valuable thing that we have, because it is the most irrevocable, the thought of any lost time troubles us whenever we look back. Time is lost in which we have failed to live a full human life, gain experience, learn, create, enjoy, and suffer; it is time that has not been filled up, but left empty. These last years have certainly not been like that. Our losses have been great and immeasurable, but time has not been lost. It is true that the knowledge and experience that were gained, and of which one did not become conscious until later, are only abstractions of reality, of life actually lived. But just as the capacity to forget is a gift of grace, so memory, the recalling of lessons we have learnt, is also a part of responsible living.[76]

Bonhoeffer surveys the ruins of the nation, the churches, and the vanquished ideals of the *Bildungsbürgertum*: "We have been silent witnesses of evil deeds. We have become cunning and learned the arts of obfuscation and equivocation. Experience has rendered us mistrustful of human beings, and often we have failed to speak to them a true and open word. Unbearable conflicts have worn us down or even made us cynical." He said he had learned "to see the great events of world history from below, from the perspective of the outcast, the suspect, the maltreated, the powerless, the oppressed and reviled, in short from the perspective of the suffering."[77] We have lost much, things far beyond measure, but the time has not been wasted. "Indeed, the insights and experiences we have gained and of which we have subsequently become aware are only abstractions of reality, of life itself. Yet just as the ability to forget is a gift of grace, so too is memory, the repetition of received teachings, part of responsible life. Who stands firm amidst the tumult and cataclysms?"[78]

"The huge masquerade of evil has thrown all ethical concepts into confusion," he confessed. "That evil should appear in the form of light, good deeds, historical necessity, social justice [as well as in] is absolutely bewildering for one coming from the world of ethical concepts that we have received. . . . The failure of '*the reasonable ones*'—those who think, with the best of intentions and in their naive misreading of reality, that with a bit of reason they can patch up a structure that has come out of joint—is apparent. With their ability to see impaired, they want to do justice on every side, only to be crushed by the colliding forces without having accomplished anything at all. Disappointed that the world is so unreasonable, they see themselves condemned to unproductiveness; they withdraw in resignation or helplessly fall victim to the stronger."

Bonhoeffer continues, "Who stands firm? Only the one whose ultimate standard is not his reason, his principles, conscience, freedom, or virtue; only the one who is prepared to sacrifice all of these when, in faith and in relationship to God alone, he is called to obedient and responsible action. Such a person is the responsible one, whose life is to be nothing but a response to God's question and call."[79]

Where are these responsible ones? Who are they? Bonhoeffer's answer is astonishing not only for its fierce defense of individual valor, but also for its echoes of Reinhold Niebuhr's Christian realism. Bonhoeffer longs for the virtues of civil courage and ultimate honesty. In the ten years since Hitler's ascent to power, there had been no shortage of heroism, bravery, and self-sacrifice. But civil courage, which is to say, the discipline of dissent, had been trampled beneath the mobs and the masses. The issue of ultimate responsibility had, in these dark circumstances, become a question "not [of] how I extricate myself heroically from a situation but [of how] a coming generation is to go on living." Then there is the seemingly prosaic matter of stupidity, which in Bonhoeffer's estimation is as dangerous an enemy of the good as evil itself. One may wage protest against evil; evil can be exposed and, *if need be*, overcome by force. But stupidity mounts a broad and insidious defense in this way: "Facts that contradict one's prejudgment simply need not be believed. . . . —and when facts are irrefutable they are just pushed aside as inconsequential, as incidental." Great caution is needed to challenge stupidity, for the hour had grown too late to change the stupid man through persuasion or inner transformation—even though in normal times it is true that internal liberation, "living responsibly before God," is the path to true freedom. "The fear of God is the beginning of wisdom," the Hebrew psalmist wrote. But now stupidity had become calcified in the Nazi herd and the mass structures of the Reich; as a result, the dictates of ultimate honesty—and indeed the application of unflinching Niebuhrian realism—led to the sober conclusion that the only remaining option was "external liberation." Until the day when external liberation has been achieved, Bonhoeffer wrote, "we must abandon all attempts to convince the stupid person [through reason]."[80]

And so there must be a return of aristocrats of conscience. "Nobility arises from and exists by sacrifice, courage, and a clear sense of what one owes oneself and others, by the self-evident expectation of the respect one is due, and by an equally self-evident observance of the same respect for those above and those below. At issue all along the line is the rediscovery of experiences of quality that have been buried under so much rubble, of an order based on quality." The social order he calls for sounds much like a bygone code of chivalry—by no coincidence, since that code arose with the ideal of the Christian warrior. But where the medieval knight saved the widow and the orphan from the infidel and the brute, in this day the danger was from the hollowing effects of totalitarianism and the leveling of all thought and feeling to the basest instincts. Against such a corruption, only quality could mount an adequate defense, but quality must cease to identify itself with privilege and rediscover the imperative of honor. This meant in social terms renouncing "the pursuit of position" and the cult of celebrity, in favor of "an opening upward and downward, particularly in the choice of one's friends, a delight in private life, and the courage for public life."

In cultural terms, the renewal of quality demanded a return from the newspaper and radio to the book, from feverishly acquisitive activity to contemplative leisure and stillness, from frenzy to composure, from the sensational to the reflective—"from the idol of virtuosity to art, from snobbery to modesty, from extravagance to moderation."[81]

No one person is, of course, "responsible for all of the world's injustice and suffering." No one person holds within him the powers to redress the world's sorrows. "We are not Christ. . . . We are not lords but instruments in the hands of the Lord of history; we can truly share only in a limited measure the suffering of others." Still, if we want to be cosmopolitan Christians, we must "take part in Christ's greatness of heart, in the responsible action that in freedom lays hold of the hour." "Inactive waiting," the curiosity of mere spectators, a dearth of imagination, empathy, sensitivity, and inner feeling—all these made plain the desperate need for a New Nobility, one possessed of "strong composure, unperturbed energy for work, and great capacity for suffering." What is woefully and critically wanting, Bonhoeffer teaches, is a "greatness of heart."[82]

"What remains for us is only the very narrow path, sometimes barely discernible, of taking each day as if it were the last and yet living it faithfully and responsibly as if there were yet to be a great future. 'Houses and fields and vineyards shall again be bought in this land,' Jeremiah is told to proclaim—in seeming contradiction of his prophecies of woe—just before the destruction of the holy city; in light of the utter deprivation of any future, those words were a divine sign and a pledge of a great, new future. To think and to act with an eye on the coming generation and to be ready to move on without fear and worry—that is the course that has, in practice, been forced upon us. To hold it courageously is not easy but necessary. . . . We still love life, but I believe that Death can no longer surprise us.

"Are we still of any use?" he asks again in conclusion.[83]

The conceptual precision of the philosophical theologian is unmistakable throughout—even as the essay smolders in the crucible of historical crisis, which promises that the future will be dark and personal goals will remain unfulfilled.[84] Equally unmistakable is Bonhoeffer's stance of self-censure. He was writing, once again, not for academic theologians but for his colleagues—his brethren in the conspiracy. "Nach Zehn Jahren"—"After Ten Years"—stands as the definitive reckoning for the Christian elites of the German resistance. And so its rhetoric is carefully generalized, anticipating that its readership might inadvertently come to include the Gestapo. Nevertheless, it proposes a clear way forward for the conscience of the disciple.

On February 18, 1943, Propaganda Minister Joseph Goebbels, once a scholar of German Romantic drama, proclaimed total war in a defiant speech at the Berlin Sports Palace. (It was an apt moment, as he had recently assumed the additional title of *Reichsbevollmächtigter für den totalen Kriegseinsatz an der Heimatfront*, the Reich Plenipotentiary for "Total War" on the Homefront.) That same day in Munich, the Gestapo arrested the university students Hans and Sophie Scholl, a brother and sister, for treason, condemning them to death. The conspiracy, as mentioned, had its flowerings not only in Berlin but throughout the nation; many brilliant and resourceful Germans had applied themselves to various efforts, and more than a hundred plots to overthrow the Führer have been documented. All the meticulously planned schemes would come to naught. But the Scholls were engaged in a different kind of resistance.

With a cadre of sympathetic friends, they often met in "an Italian wine shop" or in some dorm room to discuss how they might respond to Nazi atrocities. "They would recommend books to one another, read aloud, and hold talks"; eventually their opposition took the form of publishing subversive leaflets, which one day they scattered freely through the lecture halls and other buildings of the university. One leaflet distributed by their group, the White Rose, read, "Every word that comes from H's mouth is a lie. When he says peace, he means war, and when he blasphemously uses the name of the Almighty, he means the power of evil, the fallen angel, Satan. His mouth is the foul-smelling maw of Hell, and his might is at bottom accursed. . . . whoever today still doubts the reality, the existence of demonic powers, has failed by a wide margin to understand the metaphysical background of this war . . . the struggle against the demon, against the servants of the Antichrist." The brother and sister, along with four other members of the White Rose were beheaded just four days later, on February 22. By now, words alone could cost one his life.[85]

Bonhoeffer's involvement in the resistance would last until March 13, 1943. On that day, Fabian von Schlabrendorff smuggled a time bomb, disguised as bottles of cognac, onto an aircraft scheduled to carry Hitler back to Germany from the Army Center Headquarters in Smolensk. But the detonator failed—owing perhaps to the low temperatures inside the plane at altitude—and the plot was discovered.[86] When the knock on the front door came on the evening of April 4, 1943, Bonhoeffer was sitting at his desk in his upstairs room. Some of his writings, including parts of his unfinished *Ethics*, were hidden in the rafters. The fictitious diary he had kept to disguise his conspiratorial exertions lay on his desk. He surrendered to Gestapo agents and was led out of the house in handcuffs and into a black Mercedes waiting at the end of the walkway. He was thirty-seven years old.

Hans von Dohnányi was apprehended the same day, along with his wife, Christine von Dohnányi, Bonhoeffer's sister. In the following year, other intimates would be arrested: Klaus Bonhoeffer on October 1, 1944, their brother-in-law Rüdiger Schleicher on October 4, and Eberhard Bethge on October 30. The growing list of Bonhoeffer relations behind bars would lead the chief of the Gestapo to conclude in his summary of charges stemming from the failed July 20 officers' plot that "an entire circle of conspirators" had emanated from the Bonhoeffer house.

For now the charges against Bonhoeffer included offenses related to his UK classification, avoidance of military service, and various "minor" acts of subversion, among them assisting Confessing Church pastors and advising students on ways to avoid military service. The indictment further mentioned numerous illicit wartime activities related to his work in the Confessing Church.[87] What it did not include, however, was any charge of plotting to kill Hitler, or of taking part in Operation 7, or any other crimes of conspiracy or treason. Bonhoeffer would remain in prison for more than a year before his interrogators gained knowledge of these further illegal involvements.

What had become of Bonhoeffer's theology of nonviolence? During the *Kirchenkampf* of the previous decade, Bishop Theodor Heckel, head of the Reich Church's external relations, had denounced him as "a pacifist and enemy of the state." And an enemy of the state Bonhoeffer had surely remained. But was he still a pacifist? He prayed for the defeat of his country and the assassination of the Führer, and in praying *with* the conspirators, he conferred God's blessings on tyrannicide. Bishop Bell would recall that when he first heard Bonhoeffer refer to Hitler as the Antichrist, the remark was followed by an even more incendiary one: "We must therefore go on with our work and eliminate him whether he is successful or not." The answer is complicated, pragmatic, and, in its application, singularly, and finally, Lutheran: "sin and sin boldly"![88]

Bonhoeffer moved within an inescapable paradox; he gave his blessings to those who conspired to murder the Führer while affirming the essential nonviolence of the gospel. Responsible action meant killing the madman, even though such action violated God's commandment not to kill. How could it be otherwise? In the face of Hitler's atrocities, the way of nonviolence would bring inevitable guilt—both for the "uncontested" injustices and for the innocent lives that might have been saved. To act responsibly in these circumstances meant killing the madman if one could, even though such action violated God's commandment not to kill.

Was Bonhoeffer overthinking what should be a direct ethical mandate—destroying an evil regime to stop a genocide? As a Lutheran pastor, Bonhoeffer would have to navigate perilous (or at least, unfamiliar) theological terrain in order to reach the conclusion that permitted tyrannicide. In the face of Hitler's atrocities, the way of nonviolence would itself bring on inevitable guilt; for allowing injustices to go "uncontested" was to allow the loss of innocent life.[89] And so sin—whether through action or inaction—was a certainty.

In this connection it was useful to remember Luther's understanding of the working of grace. Humankind, despite its best efforts, was inevitably engulfed by sin, from which Christ's death on the cross offered the only redemption. It was for this reason—not out of perversity, as many Catholic critics would claim—that the father of the Reformation had reasoned that the Christian must sometimes "sin boldly." His counsel was not an incitement to wantonness but rather to heightened awareness that only Christ saves. One came to Christ a sinner in the best case. One could at least sin for the sake of righteousness. Bonhoeffer did not try to resolve the paradox by assuming moral innocence but accepted the paradox by incurring the guilt born out of responsible action.

Such reasoning would not, however, suffice to release Bonhoeffer from his moral conundrum, the perplexing choice between strict obedience to the Word and taking one's share of responsibility for the state of the kingdom on earth. He would continue to see himself in a *Grenzfall*—a borderline situation—pressed to discern moral exceptions to the commandment that no divine law had previously expounded and that only concrete reality could reveal. He would bear his uncertainty as a spiritual discipline, "with all its problematic elements," taking joy in suffering. Arriving at no real resolution, he would abandon any hope for innocence, incurring the guilt born of responsible action. Of the two evils, it was the one he could abide.

Bonhoeffer knew, of course, that he would not be the one to murder Hitler.[90] He had virtually no conception of the logistics involved—he barely knew how to hold a gun, his three-week training with the Ulm Rifle Club having been a comedy of errors. Still, he'd vowed on numerous occasions that he would not hesitate "to kill the madman" if he somehow had the chance. It was not bluster. It was his way, perhaps, of acknowledging the moral equivalence of aiding the assassin and actually pulling the trigger. Like responsibility, the stain of guilt seeped outward from the action precipitating it.

He thought of it this way: If he were walking along the Kurfürstendamm in Berlin, or Oxford Street in London, and he saw some lunatic plowing his car into the crowd, he could not stand idly on the sidewalk. He would not say to himself, "I am a pastor. I'll just wait to bury the dead afterward."[91] In whatever way he could, he would try to stop the lunatic driver. Honoring a peace ethic did not bind one to a radical pacifism, an indifference to exceptional and extreme circumstances. A peace ethic acknowledges that in historical existence certain extreme circumstances inevitably arise that require actions unacceptable in the pacifist's worldview—these are the so-called *Grenzfälle*, the extreme cases, the boundary situations. In such instances, the decision to use violence must be risked if the pure principles of peace block the way to responsible action and the relief of innocent suffering. "My peace I give unto you: not as the world giveth, give I unto you." So said Jesus on the night when he was given up. The heavenly peace is not won through a paralyzed acquiescence to villainy for the sake of an ideal. The kingdom is to those who take action: for these reasons, Bonhoeffer concluded that in the face of Hitler and the prevailing brutalities, only the violent shall bear it away.

CHAPTER FOURTEEN

1943–1945

~

"The Greatest of Feasts
on the Journey to Freedom"

I n a high-security holding cell the Gestapo reserved for dangerous criminals, Bonhoeffer slept fitfully his first night in prison. The threadbare blanket was little protection against the cold of an April rainstorm. In the next cell, another prisoner wept audibly.

Early the following morning, a slot in the door scratched open, and through it appeared a tiny portion of bread on a tin plate. The prison staff addressed the men as "scoundrels," "scum," "traitors," "swine." It would be four months before Bonhoeffer was even shown the warrant for his arrest.

Sometime toward the end of the first week, he was moved to an isolation cell on the top floor. He was not allowed books, newspapers, or tobacco; he could not write letters. Only after forty-eight hours was his Bible returned to him. "It had been searched to make sure I had not smuggled in a saw, a razor blade, or the like."

For the next twelve days, he would remain in solitary confinement, shackled hand and foot. The cell door opened only to admit food or for the removal of the latrine bucket. In all other respects, it was as if he weren't there, the staff answering no questions, meeting his every utterance with silent indifference. Nor was he permitted the regular half hour of free time in the prison yard allowed ordinary prisoners. Nights carried the muffled sobs of men broken by confinement, his new congregation.

Alone, Bonhoeffer prayed for his invisible neighbors, morning and night, pronouncing upon them his silent blessings. Although there was a sanctuary in the center of the prison grounds, religious services were forbidden in these years.[1] Later, when he was released from solitary confinement and finally allowed pen and paper, he would write prayers for the salvation of his fellow captives on sheets of paper bearing the watermark *Beroer 4b normal.* These he would mail to his parents, who, in turn, delivered them to the prison. The prayers were not jotted down "spontaneously" but composed "after extended meditation and experienced discipline."[2]

With the urgency of the psalmist he recited prayers by heart: "I am lonely, but you do not abandon me. I am restless, but with you there is peace." Or: "I thank you that you have brought this day to an end." He praised God for each new day, for granting him strength and allowing him to borrow hope from family and friends. But God would not bring down the walls of the prison as he had those of Jericho. Nor would a violent earthquake shake the foundations, freeing him as Paul and Silas were freed in Acts. Bonhoeffer knew this. And so in the first weeks, he fell into a deep despair. Over the years of the *Kirchenkampf*, he had observed holy silence and practiced the contemplative disciplines, but in solitary confinement, when silence was imposed, he did not feel the consoling presence of his beloved in Christ, only the cold surroundings of concrete and iron. It was overwhelming loss, to which no prayer or blessing seemed equal.

Scribbling anxious notes in his journal, he contemplated extreme measures: "Separation from people, from work, from the past, from the future, from marriage, from God . . . Smoke in the emptiness of time . . . The significance of illusion . . . I am already dead, draw a line, summing up." Suicide, another sin in most circumstances, had become a decent option for many conspirators, an honorable act of defiance.

His thoughts also turned to his aging parents, who were desperate with worry. "I do want you to be quite sure that I'm all right," he would tell them when at last he could write his first letter, on April 14, 1943; after that he was able to write them and his brother Karl-Friedrich every ten days. Prison, he assured them gallantly, was nothing more than a "steam bath for the soul."

"It is quite possible to satisfy one's morning appetite with dry bread—and by the way, I am also getting all kinds of good things—and the cot does not bother me in the least. Between eight at night and six in the morning, one can get plenty of sleep. I have, in fact, been particularly surprised that, from the first moment, I have almost never had a craving for cigarettes. . . . The considerable internal adjustment demanded by such an unexpected arrest and having to come to terms and put up with a completely new situation—all this makes physical needs completely secondary and unimportant. I am finding this a truly enriching experience."[3]

After nearly two weeks in isolation, Bonhoeffer was moved to a somewhat larger cell on the third floor, "a sweeping view across the prison yard to the pine forest," he told his parents. There, in cell block 25, Bonhoeffer spent the next eighteen months.

By April 14, 1943, Bonhoeffer had obtained stationery, his Bible, and a few things to read from the prison library. And by the end of April he was allowed to go outside for the half hour of fresh air; he told his parents of being allowed once again to smoke, of sometimes "even forgetting briefly" where he was: "Here in the prison yard a song thrush sings most wonderfully in the morning and now also at nightfall," he said.

On Sunday mornings, he could hear the church bells beckoning the faithful to morning worship in the neighborhood surrounding the prison. During air raids, when he was transferred to a second-floor cell, he could "look out just at the level of the church towers," which was "quite lovely." It moved him to think that some people—mostly the elderly—were still going to church; that amid the turmoil, preaching and the liturgy continued. He missed the music of church above all. "[Still] the wind sometimes bears fragments of hymns to me," he said.

Bonhoeffer did not know the full extent of his parents' anguish—that in the same roundup of suspected traitors, the Gestapo had seized his sister Christine and detained her in the police prison on Kaiserdamm on the charge of "aiding high treason," and that her husband, Hans von Dohnányi, had been incarcerated in the Berlin-Moabit military detention center at Lehrter Strasse. Christine was held for two weeks, after which charges against her were dropped; she was released on April 23.

He also did not know that his mother suffered fainting spells and had assumed a palsied demeanor, as she descended into the same darkness that had engulfed her twenty-two years earlier after her son Walter's death. "Everything just happened too suddenly," Paula said. Still, Bonhoeffer begged his parents' forgiveness for the grief he was no doubt causing them.

Sometimes he wrote two drafts of a letter home, trying "to formulate things so that they would not become sad." He told how, after the first two weeks' interrogations had ended, he had been treated much better and even had the time to read again. At first, he'd found it difficult to focus on his work, but by Holy Week, he had been able to give himself over to an "intensive study" of the Passion narrative, particularly John 17, in which Jesus offers his high priestly prayer: "Father, the hour is come; glorify thy Son, that thy Son also may glorify thee . . ."

He was getting some rest, too, he told them. After the hectic months preceding his arrest, it was a kind of relief going to bed at eight o'clock and looking forward to the stillness of the night. "I have dreams every night, and they are always pleasant."

He had even begun a "little study on 'The Feeling of Time.'" Perhaps not since his childhood meditations on eternity had temporal experience been so perplexing. The essay, he said, arose "out of the need to make my own past present to myself in a situation in which time could so easily appear 'empty' and 'lost.'" But that was not his immediate inspiration. A previous occupant of his cell had scribbled over the door, "In a hundred years it will all be over." That inscription overhung the chamber like some fatalistic needlepoint. Though, as he told his parents, he did not entirely agree with the sentiment, he did allow that there's a lot one could say on the subject.

Mornings after breakfast, from about seven o'clock until noon, were for writing. In the afternoon he read. "I always have all sorts of things to learn." If he had the energy, he would write again until dinner. "In the evening I am then tired enough to be glad to lie down, if not yet to sleep."

His dispatches home are mostly without complaint, but as in better times, he might seek help with his furnishings, his wardrobe, and the accoutrements of his grooming. The heels on his shoes were falling off. He would be grateful if his mother and father could send the newer brown pair or, even better, the high black lace-ups. He also requested his favorite brown suit, since the one he was wearing from the time of his arrest was now beyond soiled. Other necessities: a hairbrush, toiletries, a coat hanger, plenty of matches, a pipe with tobacco, a pouch for these, and also pipe cleaners, and some German cigarettes. And might they also stick a copy of Schelling's *Moral Philosophy*, volume 2, and Adalbert Stifter's novel *Indian Summer* in one of the parcels? As balm for their own suffering spirits, he proposed that the three of them—father, mother, and youngest son—commit to memory some of the great Reformation hymns.

Bonhoeffer indeed sought to spare his parents the worst of his experience, but his reports to Bethge are entirely unguarded. His first letter would, however, not be sent until November 18, 1943. Forbidden to correspond with anyone but a relation, he was able to do so with Bethge only thanks to a sympathetic Corporal Knobloch, who acted as a conduit for letters to Bethge during Bonhoeffer's detainment.[4] Knobloch, who appears to have been a churchman acquainted with Bonhoeffer's writings and may have heard him preach years earlier, would carry the letters home with him, posting them from his personal address. In turn, Bethge would send his letters to Knobloch, who delivered them to Bonhoeffer in prison.[5] "You are the only person who knows the *'acedia'-'tristitia'* that, with its ominous consequences, has often haunted me," he told his friend. Indeed, no one but Eberhard had observed this "melancholy of the heart," which could sometimes overwhelm Bonhoeffer.

At night, when he sat alone in his cell, by the light of a single candle (another luxury permitted him after the days of solitary confinement), he recalled the countless "evening conversations" he'd had with Bethge. "I imagine us sitting as in old times following supper (and the regular evening work) together in my room upstairs and smoking, occasionally playing chords on the clavichord and telling each other what the day has brought." There were "infinitely many questions" he wanted to ask—about Bethge's new military service, his travels, his pastoral work. What it felt like "being married." In September 1943, Bethge had received his call-up orders, and after basic training in Spandau, he entered the army an ordinary infantryman, stationed in Rignano, Italy. From there, his unit sometimes traveled south to Velletri, where in the distance he could see the Allied fleet near Nettuno and Anzio and could hear echoes of their furious shelling.[6] His job as *Schreiber*, or company clerk, kept him out of combat.[7]

Bonhoeffer also wanted to confess to Bethge, over the same imaginary dinner, "that despite everything I have written, it is horrible here."

Terrifying thoughts pursued him "well into the night." He coped with them only by "reciting countless hymn verses"—but even then, he would usually awaken with a sigh or a gasp, instead of a blessing or word of praise. "One becomes accustomed to the physical deprivations," he wrote, "in fact one lives for months at a time as if bodiless—almost too much so—but one never becomes accustomed to the psychic pressure. . . . I have the feeling that what I am seeing and hearing makes me years older, and the world often feels for me like a nauseating burden."[8]

Still, some thoughts were too dark to share even with Bethge. He'd conducted a brooding self-examination, recorded as "Notes I, May 1943" and "Notes II, May 1943," the fragments surfacing only after his death. It was these "notes" that constituted the "little study" he had blithely mentioned to his parents, though they are the thrashings of a very anguished soul.

The ravages of time—the gnawing of time . . .

. . .

—time as help—as torment, as enemy.
boredom as expression of despair.

. . .

> Separation—*from what is past and what is to come*
> "If you faint in the day of adversity, your strength being small"

. . .

> Prov. 31 laughs at the time to come
> Matt. 6 do not worry . . .
> waiting
> boredom

. . .

> continuity with the past and the future interrupted
> discontent—tension
> impatience
> yearning
> boredom
> night—deeply lonely
> apathy
> urge to be busy, variety, novelty
> dullness, tiredness, sleeping . . .
> Fantasizing, distortion of past and future
> suicide . . .
> the closing of the book,
> sum total.

The telegraphic lines eventually made their way to Bethge, who doubtless recognized the unifying sensibility. But when Bonhoeffer wrote them in May 1943, in clean Latin letters, they were like so many silent screams.[9]

During the two years between his arrest and his death, Bonhoeffer never stopped writing: there were letters, poems, prayers, drafts of novels, plays, and stories; there were outlines of future books and essays; aphorisms and exegeses of scripture; sketches on various themes. Collectively, his letters and prison papers document a great unburdening.[10]

He resisted the notion that he suffered in prison. To suggest that he was suffering, as some friends did, seemed like a "profanation" to him. The first weeks had been wretched, as he only obliquely revealed to his parents and more candidly to Bethge. Still, it would be a perverse "indulgence" to claim suffering—and he had no hankering after martyrdom. "These things must not be dramatized," Bonhoeffer cautioned. "A great deal here is horrible," he said, "but where is it otherwise?" The Jews suffered; the families of the fallen brethren suffered; the mental incompetents murdered by death squads had suffered; his anxious parents suffered. "No, suffering must be something quite different, must have a quite different dimension from what I have so far experienced."

Seven hundred men were housed in Berlin's Tegel prison. Most endured months of interrogation with no right to counsel. With few exceptions, their warders lacked common decency. The sick were beaten and tortured. Men in the throes of convulsions and other nervous seizures were left unattended. Every aspect of the place—the overflowing latrines, the endless repetition of the same questions, the chains and manacles—seemed designed to break the spirit.

But if any prisoner enjoyed special favors, it was Bonhoeffer. At first the prison officials were not aware that he was a Protestant theologian and pastor; nor did they recognize him as the son of the famous psychiatrist, Dr. Bonhoeffer, who, as a state employee, had received a dispensation from the Nazi Party to continue his directorship of Berlin's Charity Hospital through 1938. Nor did they know that this Pastor Bonhoeffer was the nephew of General Paul von Hase, former city commandant of Berlin. When these and other details came to light, the warden made sure Bonhoeffer got extra portions of food, hot coffee, and cigarettes. A few times a week, he was served his meals as the prison staff were, on china plates with silverware. The officials treated him with "exceptional politeness," Bonhoeffer said, "and some even came to apologize."[11]

On occasion, Captain Walter Maetz, the commandant of Tegel, called on Bonhoeffer and accompanied him on his walks in the prison yard. Maetz permitted Karl and Paula to bring their son "colorful bouquets of dahlias" and grapes from their garden, reminders of how beautiful "the world could be on these autumn days." His uncle Hase once visited, and the two drank champagne and talked for five hours.[12] Bonhoeffer told his father he found the new courtesies embarrassing: he refused the extra portions of food—although he was happy to accept the champagne, the cigarettes, and the other privileges.

On his wall he hung a reproduction of Dürer's *Apocalypse*—a rendering of Revelation 12:7, the battle between good and evil, with St. Michael leading the angels against the dragon.[13] On his table of cast iron he would place the flowers from his parents.

Set against the backdrop of the death camps, the complaints of a Lutheran pastor whose meals sometimes arrived on china with silver cutlery might well seem trivial. They did often seem to resemble the indignation of slighted nobility. But he did not intend to let little offenses pass unnoticed. A line ran from the particular to the general—from the petty humiliations to the colossal abuses of power. This was a lesson Bonhoeffer had been taught as a child, and one he would carry with him to the end.

And so, he protested the conditions mightily and with forthright contempt—confident that on account of his privilege precisely he was obliged to voice the concerns, great and small, of all. When the soup contained only a sliver of pork, he complained that the meat rations fell short of a proper diet. He complained that kitchen staff sliced the bread and sausage unevenly. Once he was so incensed at the skimpy portions that he summoned a prison guard to watch as Bonhoeffer weighed a wedge of bratwurst to prove it was fifteen grams, not the twenty-five required by law. He complained that the prison doctors and officers received heaping plates of meat with cream sauce, whereas the prisoners' meals on Sundays and holidays were "beneath contempt," "consisting of watery cabbage soup completely devoid of any fat, meat, or potatoes. On these days nobody will be checking on the food."[14] On winter nights, prison guards often put out the lights in the cells while forbidding inmates from lying in their cots until taps was played, thus forcing them to stand alone in darkness. Even worse was the lack of an air raid shelter for the general prison population; Tegel stood near the massive Borsig Fabrik, a machine works factory that had some priority as a target of British attacks. "The screams and frenzied struggles of the prisoners locked in their cells during a severe attack, some of whom are here only for very minor offenses or may even be innocent," Bonhoeffer wrote, "is unforgettable for anyone who has heard it." (He would never refer to the air attacks as "terror bombings," the term many Germans used to claim a moral equivalency between Nazi aggression and Allied attacks.) When the night skies were lit up by the green flares called "Christmas trees," launched to illuminate the targets of the RAF Pathfinders, Bonhoeffer spoke of the paradox of wrath and grace, reminded of the Old Testament prophet Amos's description of the divine wrath as an unquenchable fire.

Not since university days had he had so much time to read—even after his release from solitary confinement, he was still forced to remain in his cell for fourteen hours a day. Now able to return to his studies, he requested books in philosophy, science, art, political theory, history, and literature. The prison library had limited offerings, and so he read whatever his friends and family sent, devouring books, sometimes with scholarly purpose, sometimes on a whim. As a result, the bibliography of his internment is rather idiosyncratic. In addition to Stifter's novel, his favorites included Jeremias Gotthelf's *Geist und Geld*, the poems and stories of Theodor Fontane, and Carl Friedrich von Weizsäcker's *The World View of Physics*. He read Immanuel Kant's writings on anthropology and Wilhelm Dilthey's *Weltanschauung und Analyse des Menschen seit Renaissance und Reformation*, a study of humankind and the emerging worldview in Europe since the Renaissance and the Reformation. "I'm back to working with more concentration and am especially enjoying reading Dilthey," Bonhoeffer wrote to his parents. He read Walter Otto on Greek mythology, the Spanish philosopher José Ortega y Gasset on the philosophy of history, and Adolf von Harnack's history of the Royal Prussian Academy, which he found "beautiful indeed." He also immersed himself in Nicolai Hartmann's *Systematische Philosophie*, excited at the prospect of several weeks devoted to the German idealists.

A letter to Bethge describes the "random mixture" in which he had recently indulged: a history of Scotland Yard; a study of the origins of prostitution; a book by Hans Delbrück—though "the problems he deals with don't actually interest me"; Reinhold Schneider's sonnets— "of uneven quality, though some were very good." He had read "a huge English novel that goes from 1500 to the present"; Hugh Walpole's *Herries* novels; and the medical corps handbook, this so he might be prepared "for any eventuality."

DIETRICH BONHOEFFER IN BERLIN'S TEGEL PRISON IN THE SUMMER OF 1944

He read Dostoyevsky's "Totenhaus" (*Memoirs from the House of the Dead*), as he became "preoccupied" with the necessity of hope in a time when his hopes of release had disappeared. "I'm reading [Dostoyevsky] with great interest," he said, "and am impressed by the sympathy, devoid of any moralizing, that people outside show toward the inmates. Would this lack of moralizing, which comes from religiousness, perhaps be an essential characteristic of this people and would it help explain more recent events?" In his last letter, he would ask his parents to deliver H. Pestalozzi's

Lienhard und Gertrud and *Abendstunden eines Einsiedlers*, Paul Natorp's *Sozialpädagogik*, and Plutarch's *Große Männer: Biographien*, to the Gestapo prison at 8 Prinz-Albrecht-Strasse, to which he was moved on October 8, 1944, a windowless cell he would inhabit with one wrist chained to a heavy iron clasp.

He read most anything but theology—with one important exception. The latest installment in Karl Barth's *Church Dogmatics*, volume II/2, thrilled Bonhoeffer endlessly. This was the high point of Barth's opus. Indeed, many modern theologians have argued that II/2 displays such staggering genius that had Barth written nothing else, he would still deserve a place alongside Martin Luther and John Calvin in the Reformation pantheon. For in this volume Barth turned on its head the contentious doctrine of double predestination—that God had predestined some to salvation and others to hell. God's grace is irresistible, Barth said, concurring with the church fathers, and for this reason no finite reality could finally deny its saving power or hide from its reach. All humanity—past, present, and future—has been redeemed from the curse of sin by the death and resurrection of Jesus Christ; everyone was now the "elect man."[14] Comparing Barth's effort to the cathedrals of Rome, the symphonies of Mozart, Bonhoeffer found it altogether convincing. With meticulous detail and symphonic grandeur, Barth had captured the essence of God as love overabounding. Bonhoeffer would draw extensively from this volume in his prison writings.[15]

B onhoeffer's interrogation in the first months of his imprisonment proceeded under the command of Dr. Manfred Roeder, the Reich's senior military prosecutor. Appointed by Admiral Max Bastian, president of the Reich war court, Roeder would be the one to prosecute Dohnányi as well. In the background of these efforts stood the bitter rivalry between the Gestapo and the *Abwehr*, the Gestapo being eager to "discredit" the *Abwehr* by mounting "a corruption case against Dohnányi." Roeder's first objective in Bonhoeffer's case was to prove him guilty of evading military service. In pursuit of this objective Roeder would prove dogged.

At the end of July 1943, four months into his arrest, Bonhoeffer was finally notified of the charges against him, and, according to the terms of the indictment, he "appeared to be guilty" and "reasonably suspected in Berlin and in other places" on two counts: evasion of military duty, and assisting others in evading duty. Also itemized were numerous activities related to the Confessing Church. Notably absent was any mention of Operation 7, or of any other activity related to the resistance. Considering the crimes of which he would eventually stand

VIEW OF TEGEL PRISON YARD FROM BONHOEFFER'S CELL

accused, the charges of 1943 seem minor, certainly less serious than high treason. But they nevertheless left him subject to the violation of statute "§ 5 Section 1 No. 3 KSSVO,[2] § 74 RStGB," the crime of "subversion of military power" (*Wehrkraftzersetzung*, which can also be translated as "undermining military strength"), which was punishable by death. Horrified, Bonhoeffer answered the charges with defiance while also attempting to mitigate them.

"I do not need to tell you what even the fact of an indictment for subversion of the war effort means for me professionally and personally and for my family," he wrote Roeder in a huffy letter of August 2. "You know my professional and personal relationships well enough to appreciate [the effect]. If the law requires an indictment, then it must be issued; this I understand. That I did not expect it may be attributable to my deficient knowledge of the letter of the law, as well as to the fact that I have felt—and, following further consideration of what you told me on Friday, continue to feel—innocent of the charge." Ignorance of the law is never much of a defense; it was as if he had not yet realized the seriousness of his situation, or believed he could, by reason of his prominence, be forgiven an honest mistake. He closed, affably, "May I finally add to this something that actually goes without saying, that if in fact my work for Military Intelligence is no longer regarded as important I will immediately make myself available for another form of service."[16] Roeder would issue the formal indictment on September 21, taking no account of Bonhoeffer's letters to him, often signed with an ingratiating *"Heil Hitler!"* "Be strong. Admit nothing," Bonhoeffer told himself in preparation for the hearings. He had taken the precaution of memorizing a version of events, which he had constructed with Dohnányi and Joseph Müller.

On September 16, 1943, Kurt Wergein, an attorney and professor of legal philosophy, was appointed as Bonhoeffer's defense counsel. As Bonhoeffer wrote his parents on September 25, he was "really glad when first the authorization for the attorney and then the arrest warrant arrived. So the apparently aimless waiting may be coming to an end at last after all." He remained hopeful of a favorable outcome, still treating his predicament like a petty squabble: "Initially R. [Roeder] would have liked to finish me off; now he has been forced to content himself with an utterly ridiculous indictment that will garner him little prestige." Indeed, the possibility of his being "sentenced but released" still had some basis at the conclusion of the initial hearings.

There had been cause to worry when Roeder turned his attention to Operation 7. But when no evidence against him in that connection materialized, Roeder focused on the only availing issue: Bonhoeffer's UK classification.[17] Even so, the interrogations languished, and when a number of papers related to the case were destroyed in an air raid, Bonhoeffer's hopes of a "favorable outcome" rose.

In May 1944, he would be helped by Dohnányi's attempt at thwarting his own investigation by the Gestapo and delaying "a major hearing in his trial." With the July coup attempt in prospect, Dohnányi "deliberately infected himself with scarlet fever and diphtheria." His wife (Dietrich's sister), Christine, smuggled the pathogenic substance into the Buch military prison hospital with a concealed note that read "red paper and stain on the mug . . . = infected!" And the infection led to severe paralysis of his extremities, with Dohnányi being moved to military quarantine in Potsdam. As hoped, his trial was postponed, and with it the disclosure of anything that would incriminate Bonhoeffer. Roeder's investigations into the preacher's evasion of service ended with an entirely bureaucratic whimper: "The facts found relevant under criminal law were finally reduced to the fact that a legal UK classification had been granted by an unauthorized office."

In the short term, Bonhoeffer had successfully traversed a minefield. That the fanatically driven Roeder and Judge Advocate General Sack would uncover the more serious matter of his involvement in the conspiracy would remain a fear not realized. The name of Bonhoeffer would work its way into the enquiry but the evidence of complicity would remain obscured. It would take a different prosecutor working in the aftermath of July 20, 1944, to discover it and seal Bonhoeffer's fate.

Until then, he continued in guarded confidence of his acquittal and release. He wrote Bethge to say that the two would soon "see each other in freedom." Even if he had to spend Christmas 1943 alone in prison, he was hopeful now that, after New Year's, he would be reunited with his family, his fiancée, and his friend in the clear light of a winter morning.

More than a month later, in a letter of February 4, his thirty-eighth birthday, Bonhoeffer imagined himself and Bethge together once again, as in those bygone times that now stirred a stream of remembrance:

> Eight years ago in the evening, we were sitting around the fireplace together, and you . . . had given me the D major violin concerto, and we listened to it together. Then I had to tell you all stories about Harnack and times past, which for some reason you particularly enjoyed, and finally we decided definitely on the trip to Sweden. The year after that, you gave me the "September Bible," nicely inscribed, and the first name on the list was yours. Then followed Schlonwitz and Sigurdshof, celebrated in the company of a good many people who are no longer with us. The singing outside my door, the prayer during the worship service that you led on these days, the Claudius hymn, for which I thank Gerhard—all these are wonderful memories, which the dreadful atmosphere here cannot diminish. I am full of confidence that we shall celebrate your next birthday together, and who knows? perhaps even Easter! Then we'll get back to what is really our life's work, and there will be plenty of good work to do, and what we have been through in the meantime will not have been in vain. But we shall always be grateful to each other that we have been able to live through the present time in the way we are both doing. I know you are thinking of me today, and if these thoughts include not only memories of the past but also hope for a future together, even though it will be a changed one, then I am very happy.

"By then I will certainly be out," he said, "for, given the nonsense they are pinning on me, they will have to release me at the court appearance."

Surely, Bethge would be so resourceful as to wrangle a short leave from military duty for this joyous occasion, Bonhoeffer added.

I n prison, Bonhoeffer's thought took new directions, while at the same time attention to his first loves intensified, in the manner of a mature artist, layering brushstroke upon brushstroke.[18] He recalled his student years and his convivial exchanges with professors Adolf von Harnack and Karl Holl. He grew nostalgic for the vanished ideals of German liberalism. A decade had passed since he had last been a full-time member of the university. One of his final seminars in the summer of 1933 had been a line-by-line reading of Hegel's *Lecturers on the Philosophy of Religion*. Once again, he found nourishment in that "great scholarly tradition of the nineteenth century," even as its restrictive intellectual boundaries, once a kind of protection, collapsed gently before his fresh awakening to what he called the "polyphony of life."

He spoke of loss and of letting go, of academic careers unfulfilled, of engagements pending, of letters unfinished; sometimes the litany proved too much to contemplate: "I must break off for today."[19] But he knew he might easily have wound up one of those who'd been "torn to pieces by events and by questions." With that deliverance in mind, he opened himself to the inevitable incompleteness of things, accepting even the upheavals and intrusions with a disarming gratefulness.

"That which is fragmentary may point to a higher fulfillment," Bonhoeffer said, one "which can no longer be achieved by human effort." Strive though we might, the only work that mattered would be done by grace alone.

Filled with appreciation for the wholeness he had once known, Bonhoeffer turned to the small and sometimes broken things—not with resignation but with compassion.

A stanza that I came across from Storm resonates with this mood and echoes over and over in my consciousness, like a melody one can't get out of one's mind:

If outside it's all gone mad
in Christian ways or not
still is the world, this gorgeous world
entirely resilient.

A few fall flowers within view of his cell window, a half hour's exercise in the prison yard, a beautiful linden tree—minor glories were enough to confirm the transcendent one. He remembered the story of a man who had "a nightmare that a bomb might destroy everything" and who, upon waking, thought, How sad for the butterflies![20] In the end, Bonhoeffer said, "the world is summed up . . . in a few people one wants to see and with whom one wishes to be together."

On January 17, less than three months before his arrest, Dietrich and Maria had become engaged, though in deference to her mother they had kept the arrangement a secret. Upon his arrest, however, the news had become public.[21] Their brief romance is a tragic story, often told and nearly always embellished—as, for instance, in a BBC film adaption, which, in one scene, has Bonhoeffer and Wedemeyer stealing a kiss through the barbed-wire fence of the Flossenbürg concentration camp.

Bonhoeffer despised the way he came across in his letters to Wedemeyer—as "a paragon of virtue and a model of Christian behavior," like some ancient martyr—though he could hardly help it. But he was right about their overall effect. He often sounded like a father writing admonitory notes to his daughter. He needled her, too, as when he raised concerns about her fondness for Rilke. Sparing Wedemeyer accounts of his personal anguish, which he continued to convey unflinchingly to Bethge, Bonhoeffer bumbles along in search of solid footing. Eberhard remained "his daring, trusting spirit," *his friend*, while Maria was to be *his wife*. And therein lay the conflict; his awareness of each role intensified. His singular friendship with Bethge—now idealized more than ever—represented the joyful and freeing counterpart to marriage, which, so far as it entered his mind, had always been equated with duty, obligation, necessity, and law: an arrangement necessitated by original sin.

On August 28, 1944, even in the wake of the miserable failure of the officers' plot, and the summary executions of Claus von Stauffenberg, Friedrich Olbricht, Werner von Haeften, and Albrecht Mertz von Quirnheim the month before—he wrote a poem for Bethge's thirty-fifth birthday. This poem was called simply "The Friend."

> *Not from heavy soil, where blood and race and oath . . .*
> *but from the heart's free choosing,*
> *and from the spirit's free longing,*
> *needing no oath nor legal sanction.*
>
> *These were the sources of their affection.*
> *Playmates at first,*
> *On the spirit's long journeys into wondrous, faraway realms,*
> *which, veiled in the morning sun, gleam like gold,*
> *toward which in noonday heat the wispy clouds*

drift along in the blue sky,
[and] in the excitement of night, by lamplight,
beckon the seeker like hidden, secret treasures.

Theirs, he intoned, was a love that "no one planted," "no one watered," but "it grew freely and in cheerful confidence."

Like a clear, fresh wellspring
where the spirit cleanses itself from the day's dust,
where it cools itself after blazing heat
and steels itself in the hour of fatigue—
Like a fortress, where the spirit returns
after confusion and danger,
finding refuge, comfort, and strength.

Theirs was a love that lived "under the wide sky," unlike "things formed from weighty, earthy stuff." Stuff like labor, the sword, and marriage.

When the sirens howled their midnight cue,
Long and silent were my thoughts of you,
how you might be, old times when you were here. . . .

After a long silence, at half past one
comes the signal that the danger is done.
I took this as a friendly sign from on high
that all dangers are quietly passing you by. . . .
This is what the friend is to the friend.

Over the destiny of wife and husband—as the gloomy contrast is set—creeps the shadow of wrath, while the weight of sin presses against "the heavy soil of earth," to be borne by husband and wife on account of the first transgressors in the garden. Marriage commands. Marriage compels assent to doctrine. Marriage imposes alien laws. Marriage adjudicates an ancient curse. These, too, are notions to be found in the poem.

"The wife is to give birth to her children in pain, and the husband, in caring for his family, is to reap many thistles and thorns and must work by the sweat of his brow," Bonhoeffer wrote. The very wages of sin were these. "This burden is meant to lead husband and wife to call upon God and to remind them of their eternal destiny in God's kingdom."

There is no poetry in these grim postulations, also written for Bethge, but now as a kind of cautionary epithalamion. They can only be understood as an oblique reminder of the comparative bliss of friendship. With marriage comes "difficulties, impediments, obstacles, doubts, and hesitations." The holy estate of matrimony might be honorable, worthy of praise as "a decisive triumph," but the true fellowship of souls such as he and his friend enjoyed was a state of "unimaginable freedom and power," an ineffable lightness as against the leadenness of wedlock.

Renate and Eberhard would not read the sermon at their wedding, as its author intended; Dr. Bonhoeffer had mistakenly filed the manuscript away with his son's will. Still, the meditation gives evidence of Bonhoeffer's thinking on the subject as he tried to make a complicated emotional transition of his own, from Bethge to Wedemeyer. Whatever he felt in his heart of hearts, Bonhoeffer took the prospect of his marriage seriously for as long as he believed in the chance of his release. He wanted to discuss with Maria the details of the celebration, what text should be read, and the menu. They spoke of where they might live, how they might furnish their home, and the other logistics of cohabitation: Bonhoeffer thought, for instance, that he would be the better cook. Given time, he believed, he could assert his Pygmalion-like influence. He suggested that Wedemeyer improve her English, though she could not see a point in doing so. Wishing she shared his love of music, he insisted that she spend more time practicing the violin, which she seemed to play in a manner particular to the provincial nobility, plodding but with feeling.[22]

By the spring of 1944, Bonhoeffer had settled into regular rhythms of reading and writing. Alongside the dates on his letters, it was his custom to enter Latin designations for the Sundays, and he followed the readings and prayers of the hours in his *Losungen*, the Moravian prayer book his governess had given him as a child. Within the first six months, he had read the Old Testament through "two and a-half times."[23] He organized his days according to the church calendar and tried to infuse cell block 92 with monastic order, extending its gifts of hospitality to every part of the prison. "Waiting with Christ in Gethsemane"—this solemn phrase inspired the liturgical shape of his days: meditation, thanksgiving, intercessory prayer, praise, and lament. "If we are to learn what God promises, and what he fulfills, we must persevere in quiet meditation on the life, sayings, deeds, sufferings, and death of Jesus."[24] The first Christmas in prison, he'd hummed carols and hymns to himself; adorned his *Adventskranz* with a reproduction of

Filippo Lippi's *Nativity;* and "feasted on an ostrich egg."[25] He consoled fellow prisoners and guards alike. "Pastor, please pray that we have no alarm tonight!" a sergeant once whispered. Even the medical orderlies "became attached to him, and often sat up late talking with him in the sick quarters."

The failure of the July 20, 1944, coup attempt ushered in a new phase of Bonhoeffer's imprisonment. As the man responsible for issuing and receiving army reports and dispatches, Bethge from his post in Italy was the first in his unit to hear of the failed plot and "report it to his superiors."

In subsequent letters—the first dated the following day, July 21, 1944—Bonhoeffer expressed the hope that despite "his premonition of impending death," he might live to enjoy his relationship with Wedemeyer as much as he had once relished the one with Bethge. But not long thereafter the correspondence with Wedemeyer would come to an end, even as his letters to Bethge became charged with a new energy. A fresh awareness began to inform Bonhoeffer's writings, and it coincided with an intuition that, contrary to earlier optimism, he was not to get out alive.

There had been intimations of a theological transformation in earlier efforts. Still, when he read Bonhoeffer's meditations on a "religionless Christianity" and "a world come of age"—written between the spring of 1944 and Christmas, when they ended abruptly—Bethge expressed surprise and excitement. Questions that had been raised over the course of their long friendship resurfaced with "singular intensity" under "the impression of total war" and the expectation that it was only a matter of time before his involvement in a capital crime was uncovered. Now, Bonhoeffer invited Bethge to perform with him an intellectual pas de deux of exquisite intricacy, and Bethge gladly joined the dance that his longtime teacher would lead with flashes of inspiration and brilliance. For his part, Bethge, "whose different gifts complemented those of his friend, provided the critical sounding board."

Bonhoeffer attested to having undergone a "great liberation from guilt and self-doubt" during his final year in prison. What had stirred it? Discipline, control, and ardor—these were the qualities to which he had long aspired, and insofar as he'd attained them, they would sustain him until the end. But a new element had entered his being as well. Bonhoeffer discovered the value of *hilaritas*—good humor—as the quality of mind, body, and spirit most important to animating the greatest human achievements. "High-spirited self-confidence," speaking the Yes and the Amen in gleeful defiance of the Nothing, a cheerful audacity—"spread *hilaritas!*" Bonhoeffer directed Bethge, in a kind of eureka.

It was when he first read Barth's *Church Dogmatics* II/2, Bonhoeffer said, that *hilaritas* leapt off the page at him. And now that his eyes were opened, he discerned *hilaritas* shimmering and sparkling in all of humanity's beautiful and good creations: in the triumph of grace as narrated over five hundred pages in Barth's disputation of the God who *has saved all humanity* in the sacrifice of Jesus Christ, crucified, dead, and risen; in Raphael and Mozart; and in Walther von der Vogelweide, the Knight of Bamberg, Luther, Gotthold Lessing, Peter Paul Rubens, and Hugo Wolf, to name but a few. *Hilaritas* connoted boldness, audacity, and a "willingness to defy the world and popular opinion"; this one did by living out of the "firm conviction" that with his work one is giving the world something good, "even if the world is not pleased with it."

Ignited by *hilaritas*, Bonhoeffer opened his mind to "the knowledge accumulated over the years": the ancient church fathers Irenaeus and Augustine; the medieval philosopher Nicholas of Cusa; the Dutch jurist Hugo Grotius; the pillars of the Enlightenment, the Romantics, and the great system builders, Kant, Hegel, and Kierkegaard. Now, in his consciousness, all of these would coalesce into what remain some of the freshest, most vivid, and yet confounding theological meditations of the modern age.

The power of Bonhoeffer's prison writings lies precisely in their being unshackled to convention, the freedom he indulged in "trial combinations" and "lightning flashes" of spiritual insight.[26] It is as though Bonhoeffer's lifelong protest against the world-constitutive ego and its thought-systems had at last assumed the wholeness of literary form. From his cell, he had surveyed the story of modernity. "God as a working hypothesis" was no longer required, he said in accord with philosophical secularists—no longer required for science, politics, or morality (or even philosophy and religion), not for thought in any measure. What, then, shall the "anxious souls" do, Bonhoeffer asks? In the year before his death, he grasped an enlivening worldly godlessness that felt closer to the gospel than any formal religiosity he had known.

What is Christianity, or who is Christ for us today?" That is the question Bonhoeffer posed to Bethge in a letter of April 30. The language of Christian faith could no longer forestall its own death by a thousand equivocations.

"We are approaching a completely religionless age," Bonhoeffer wrote, "people as they are now simply cannot be religious anymore.

Even those who honestly describe themselves as 'religious' aren't really practicing that at all; they presumably mean something quite different by 'religious.'" The rickety scaffolding of Protestantism had tumbled finally to the ground in the wake of the German church's complicity with the Nazis; every attempt "to force it once again" into the shape of a powerful institution "will only delay its inescapable reckoning." Religion as it had been lived before was obsolete.

So shall we content ourselves, he asked, with longing to be "the last of the knights"? "How can Christ become Lord of the religionless as well? If religion is only the garb in which Christianity is clothed—and this garb has looked very different in different ages—what then is religionless Christianity?" How could one be a disciple, clothed not in the garb of tradition, but having, as Paul tells the Galatians, "put on Christ"?

Bonhoeffer's answers revealed a faith chastened by history, mindful of its failures and misuses—imprisoned by consequence!—yet abidingly and hilariously confident that Christ has broken the chains of death. In the meantime, the Christian witness shall be limited to prayer and righteous action. "All Christian thinking, talking, and organizing must be born anew, out of that prayer and action." Until the time that people will once again be able to speak the word of God "with power," the "Christian cause will be a quiet and hidden one."[27] These are not post-theistic ruminations, the kind made popular by the Death of God theologians and their merry riffs on the prison texts; rather, they are a sober assessment of the gospel's political captivity—and how to escape it.[28]

Though Hitler's Germany had been filled with festivals and assemblies, songs and melodies, to say nothing of an abundance of religious cant, these sounds and sights were not what the Lord required. "Take away from me the noise of your congregations, you who have turned justice into poison," fumed the Hebrew prophet Amos, also warning of a famine of the Word, a famine more devastating than a "famine of bread" or "thirsting for water"—a "famine . . . of hearing," a famine "of the words of the Lord."

> *They shall wander from sea to sea,*
> *And from north to east;*
> *They shall run to and fro, seeking the*
> *Word of the Lord,*
> *But they shall not find it.*

No peace or solitude can be found in a nation that "abhors the one who speaks the truth." Amid the clamor and self-congratulation of the chosen nation, it had become impossible to hear the Lion of Zion roar—in Israel as now in Germany. How could such idolatry be defeated? Bonhoeffer turned his attention to an ancient spiritual practice intended to guard the mysteries of faith, the so-called "arcane discipline." He had first used the term *arcanum* in his lecture series "The Essence of the Church," delivered in Berlin during the summer term of 1932. "Confession belongs in worship as *arcanum*," he said. "The confession is not to be screamed loudly in a propagandistic manner, it must be preserved as the sacred good of the church-community."[29] In his Finkenwalde lectures on preaching, he described the arcane discipline in the early church (under Origen) as "closed assemblies" that received the sacraments, the confession of faith, and the Lord's Prayer. In *Discipleship*, Bonhoeffer wrote specifically of the "discipline of the secret." The Lord himself had taught, "When thou prayest, enter into thy closet, and when thou hast shut thy door, pray to thy Father which is in secret; and thy Father which seeth in secret shall reward thee openly."

It was a great mistake, Bonhoeffer said, to think of theology's purpose as being the unveiling of the mystery, "to bring it down to the flat, ordinary wisdom of experience and reason!" Theology should, rather, as its sole mission aim to "preserve God's wonder as wonder, to understand, to defend, to glorify God's mystery as mystery." "In the arcanum," he said, "Christ takes everyone who really encounters him by the shoulder, turning them around to face their fellow human beings and the world."[30] Theology's task was to preserve the eternal mystery in a catastrophically demystified time.

B y the way, I notice more and more how much I am thinking and perceiving things in line with the Old Testament," Bonhoeffer had written to Bethge on December 5, 1943, the second Sunday of Advent. "In recent months I have been reading much more the Old than the New Testament." And then comes a kind of litany of beatitudes for the post-religious Christian:

> Only when one knows that the name of God may not be uttered may one sometimes speak the name of Jesus Christ.
> Only when one loves life and the earth so much that with it everything seems to be lost and at its end may one believe in the resurrection of the dead and a new world.
> Only when one accepts the law of God as binding for oneself may one perhaps sometimes speak of grace.
> And only when the wrath and vengeance of God against His

enemies are allowed to stand can something of forgiveness and the love of enemies touch our hearts. . . .

Why do people in the Old Testament vigorously and often lie (I have now collected the citations), kill, betray, rob, divorce, even fornicate (cf. Jesus's genealogy), doubt, and blaspheme and curse, to the glory of God, whereas in the New Testament there is none of this? "Preliminary stage" of religion? That is a very naïve explanation; after all, it is one and the same God.

Formed as a Christian in discipleship to Jesus, Bonhoeffer realized finally that genuine *humanness* would forever wander into abstraction if it were not anchored in the history, suffering, and religion of the Jews.

"Has not the individualistic question of saving personal souls almost faded away for most of us? Isn't it our impression that there are really more important things than this question (—perhaps not more important than this matter, but certainly more important than the question!?) . . . Does the question of saving one's soul even come up in the Old Testament? Isn't God's righteousness and kingdom on earth the center of everything? And isn't Rom. 3:24ff. the culmination of the view that God alone is righteous, rather than an individualistic doctrine of salvation? What matters is not the beyond but this world, how it is created and preserved, is given laws, reconciled, and renewed."

His faith had grown more at home in the Old Testament as he reached the extraordinary conclusion that "whoever wishes to be and perceive things too quickly and too directly in New Testament ways is to my mind no Christian." And with a new sense of worldly habitation were unleashed certain desires and energies, long restrained.

H e wrote to Bethge on May 30:

> I'm sitting alone upstairs. Everything is quiet in this building; a few birds are singing outside, and I can even hear the cuckoo in the distance. I find these long, warm summer evenings, which I'm living through here for the second time, rather trying. I long to be outside, and if I were not "reasonable," I might do something foolish. I wonder whether we have become too reasonable. When you've deliberately suppressed every desire for so long, it may have one of two bad results: either it burns you up inside, or it all gets so bottled up that one day there is a terrific explosion. . . . Perhaps you will say that one oughtn't to suppress one's desires, and I expect you would be right.

But look, this evening for example I couldn't dare to give really full rein to my imagination and picture myself and Maria at your house, sitting in the garden by the water and talking together into the night etc. etc. That is simply self-torture, and gives one physical pain. So I take refuge in thinking, in writing letters, in delighting in your good fortune, and curb my desires as a measure of self-protection. However paradoxical it may sound, it would be more selfless if I didn't need to be so afraid of my desires, and could give them free rein—but that is very difficult.[31]

He longed for an evening at Bethge's house and for Maria's company; he longed for desire's complete course, the "etc. etc." of sexual love, as he put it. Bonhoeffer felt open to those desires and to Bethge's counsel, spoken years earlier, he recalled, that he stop "beating them back."

On July 28, 1944, Bonhoeffer thanked Bethge for the humorous postcard from Italy—a photograph of a reluctant soldier reclining in the Umbrian countryside like the young Goethe. Bonhoeffer asked his friend if he might send a different image as well, an image that captured him—"all of you"—in a softer, more familiar pose, set against the Italian Alps, but natural and clear.

In January 1943, Bethge had been sent to the Italian front, "assigned to a small Military Intelligence unit of sixteen men in the Tenth Army under the command of General Heinrich von Vietinghoff." His unit was charged with supplying intelligence to the field marshal, although much of the time Bethge served as "chauffeur, secretary, and night watchman," an assignment whose relative safety was a great comfort to Bonhoeffer, who also took delight in the notion that his friend was stationed in the same countryside where, just four summers ago, the two had taken a "magnificent holiday." Having obtained a detailed map of the environs of Rome he imagined Bethge "driving around the now familiar roads, hearing the sounds of war not very far away, and looking down from the mountains to the sea. . . .

"I'm so glad you're stationed far away from the highway and that you've got a north-facing room and the countryside is so beautiful where you are. . . .

"You think that the Bible does not say much about health, happiness, strength, and so on," he continued. "I have thought that over again very carefully. I'm sure it is not true of the Old Testament in any case." For in the Hebrew Bible, the "mediating theological concept" between God and happiness is "that of human blessing, as far as I can see."

This mental picture of Bethge in Italy inspired Bonhoeffer to read the Song of Solomon. Over the years he had spent little time with these spiritual meditations on erotic love. Only once, during the vicariate in sunny Barcelona, had he taken up a passage from the Song in a sermon.[32] On November 28, 1928, he preached on 8:6b, "Love is strong as death," a sermon that has survived only as a fragment. The erotic element, while present, could not sustain the overpowering force of eternity, symbolized in the sermon by a man standing on the seashore, "as wave upon wave rolls in, breaks on the beach, and sinks away in the endless gray water; eternally one and ever another." In that homily, the Song becomes a lesson in the fleeting, ephemeral nature of human existence: "life is but a moment before the ancient, primal sea;" a wave that passes away even as it forms, eternity compressed into sexual desire.

"And we are unable to turn our gaze away," he said, "for hours on end we stare over the foamy crests, outward—to where?—we hardly know ourselves, but it draws our gaze into the endless distance, out to where the sun sinks into the sea, where the waves rise, and the soul stretches out, wants to know what the eyes cannot sense—wants to know about what is beyond the gray sea—or whether it just continues on eternally like this, without an end, without a beyond, a process of becoming and passing away with neither measure nor goal—and yet as intensively as it searches, it always sees the same drama . . . no hope . . . eternal hiddenness."

The physicality of desire recedes into the endless distance, where it belongs and where it must remain. The "urge to be together" as God intended inspires one instead toward what is "most gentle, profound, pure, purifying" and offers safe harbor from the body's startling contretemps.

In prison, by contrast, Bonhoeffer sang a song of earthly love— with no transcendent hiddenness or gazing into the endless distance. He said he did not share Diogenes' opinion that the "absence of desire is the highest joy and an empty barrel the ideal vessel." The Song of Solomon, the Hebrew Bible's hymn to sensual love, Bonhoeffer was discovering now to his sudden delight, in fact consecrated the flesh: "you really can't imagine a hotter, more sensual, and glowing love than the one spoken of here." He read the book through a Christly lens but without making a reflexive leap to the symbolic, such as has often been used to mask Christian fears of the body. Excited by the Old Testament's affirmation of "strong, erotic love," he questioned anyone who

would say that "the restraint of passion" denoted the disciple's prerogative. "Why is there no such restraint in the Old Testament?" he wrote.
"Israel is delivered out of Egypt so that it may live before God as God's
people on earth."

Shut inside a Gestapo prison, Bonhoeffer could hardly do more for
the Jews of Europe than to honor the story of Israel as a lesson for the
Christian church. Precisely because he was a man formed in whole-
hearted discipleship to Jesus, he realized that thinking about God
would forever lead into abstraction and idolatry if the thinking were not
anchored in the history, suffering, and religion of the Jews.

O n a hot summer afternoon, he sat in his cell in Tegel wearing a
pair of gym shorts and a dress shirt—both items he had bought
for Bethge in Stockholm. Bonhoeffer was spending another day mull-
ing over his "non-religious interpretation" of the Bible, but the "concrete bodily experience of heat" was overpowering, so he paused to
write to Bethge. The heat had awakened his "animal existence," "his
corporeal being," with a singular urgency—"not just to see the sun and
sip at it a little, but to experience it bodily." He longed "to feel again
the potencies of the sun," he said, and his memory ranged languorously
over summers past: with Klaus in Rome and Libya in 1923; the first
trip with Bethge to Naples in 1936, to the colors of the sun hitting the
Mediterranean, as observed on the ferry to Majorca; Christmas 1931 in
Cuba. He pondered "the romantic enthusiasm for the sun," the cult of
the sun-gods. "Does it make Goethe or Napoleon a sinner to say that
they weren't always faithful husbands?" Bonhoeffer asked abruptly.

Apropos of the "potencies of the sun" and the Berlin heat wave,
he made a pitch for "strong sins" and "sins of strength"—sins dared
for the sake of the other, for the purpose of "nurturing intimacy with
others." Bonhoeffer happily bade farewell to a caution mistaken for
sanctity and conversely the "perverse satisfaction in knowing that every
person has failings and weak spots." He thanked Bethge for his long-
suffering patience with his friend's many moods. He did not deserve
such patience, but he was grateful for it. "I have learned from you to
see so many things in a new way," he said. He might have said, more
precisely, "owing to you" rather than "from you," but that would not
have changed the ultimate consequence of their association, which was
this: finally, at the age of thirty-eight and with nothing left to lose, he
felt free from the yoke of scrupulous introspection. The Word of God
does not ally itself with the rebellion of mistrust, he said triumphantly,
but reigns in the strangest of glories.

———

On June 3, 1944, despite having no official guest privileges, Bethge visited Bonhoeffer in prison. Bethge had tried in vain to gain permission from the minister of corrections, but it took a bribe to a prison guard to win access on that June day—a favor which would likely have involved a case, if not a carton, of cigarettes and a bottle of schnapps.[33] Terms of the favor—which likely included a portion of meat, peaches, a wool scarf, and cash tucked into the pages of a book—were reached, and Bethge entered Tegel under the radar of standard protocol.[34]

Bethge was pleased to find his friend in good spirits. In the earshot of a noncommissioned prison official, the two mainly avoided talking about the conspiracy. Bonhoeffer was eager to discuss his recent theological sketches, although there were a few mundane concerns on his mind as well. He was slightly vexed that the slacks his sister Ursula had sent were not the ones he requested. "What I need are the light brown summer trousers," he said. Bethge should convey the urgency to his sister, since the only pair he had with him for the warm days was "ripping every which way." Then the two men broached a subject that had long been looming beneath the surface: namely, how to start wrapping up "the logistical loose-ends" of their long relationship, which proved exceedingly difficult in written correspondence. These included "the technical details of living together," "their shared bank account," and "other legal arrangements."[35] "If it would make things easier for Renate," Bonhoeffer had earlier told Bethge, "please don't hesitate to help yourself to my money!"

Bonhoeffer had long presumed responsibility for shaping his friend's future. And with this responsibility had often arisen doubts that what he was doing was best for Bethge. But now, in prison, when suddenly "almost all our possibilities to be involved" were cut off, there was "somewhere the awareness, behind all our fears for the other, that his life has now been placed wholly in better and stronger hands."

Now for a few more thoughts on our topic," Bonhoeffer wrote the next week, as if all that had been expressed centered on the new determinant. "Finally, the philosophical closing line: on one hand, the deism of Descartes: the world is a mechanism that keeps running by itself without God's intervention; on the other hand, Spinoza's pantheism: God is nature. Kant is basically a deist; Fichte and Hegel are pantheists. In every case the autonomy of human beings and the world is the goal of thought. . . . As a working hypothesis for morality, politics, and the natural sciences, God has been overcome and done away with, but also as a working hypothesis for philosophy and religion (Feuerbach!). It is a matter of intellectual integrity to drop this working hypothesis, or eliminate it as far as possible." Bonhoeffer hoped that people would seek God in what they know, rather than in what they do not know.

Is there any room left for God? Ask those who are anxious, Bonhoeffer replied, and since they don't have an answer, condemn the entire development of intellectual history that has led to this decisive question.

He had spoken with Bethge of the myriad ways to escape the narrow spaces of modernity: the notion of God as a working hypothesis, a deus ex machina that spares each protagonist the fate of hard questions.

There is, of course, no way back from a conceptual dead end, he reasoned. The only way forward was through Matthew 18:3—"through repentance, through *ultimate* honesty!"—a reborn seeking of God.

"We have rather to recognize that we have to live in the world— *etsi deus non daretur*," as if there were no God. And this is precisely what we do recognize—before God! "Living as if there were no God, before God"—this was the discipline of being in two worlds, with equal intensity. No more complicated than living in-the-world-but-not-of-the-world, no simpler than faith itself—indeed an art more difficult could not be conceived!

"God beyond necessity; beyond need," Bonhoeffer had said in a Barcelona sermon. "Servile, fearful, shirking complexity," he wrote in prison, "God does not want us to live that way.

"The same God who makes us to live in the world without the working hypothesis of God is the God before whom we stand continually." "Before God, and with God," we live without God, even as God draws closer to humanity in its new freedom. Faith begins not with the ascent to truthful propositions, the heart's modulations of trust, the Kierkegaardian leap or even with the "first step" of obedience; it begins with simple, grateful praise of God as the mystery of the world, who exists beyond necessity and desire.

The profound this-worldliness of Christianity"—Bonhoeffer first used the phrase in the letter to Bethge the day after the failed coup. In the last few years, he said, he had come to know and to understand more of this powerful notion. "The Christian is not a *homo religiosus*, but simply a human being, in the same way that Jesus was a human being." He did not mean "the shallow and banal this-worldliness of the enlightened, the bustling, the comfortable, or the lascivious," but rather a worldly concentration that involves the same discipline, skill, and patience of this difficult artwork—and "includes the ever-present knowledge of death and resurrection."

Bonhoeffer recalled a conversation with his friend Jean Lasserre during their road trip across America. The two had asked themselves what they most wanted of their lives. Lasserre, who would go on to be a pastor in Calais and a member of the French resistance, said he wanted to become a saint. Bonhoeffer had been impressed by this declaration and said it was quite likely that the man had done just that. But for himself Bonhoeffer expressed a different hope. He wanted only to learn to have faith.

Of course, Bonhoeffer had not for a long time "understood the depth of this antithesis": the mutual exclusivity of the two aspirations. He thought he could learn to have faith by trying to achieve spiritual perfection. "I suppose I wrote *Discipleship* at the end of this path," he admitted, acknowledging the dangers of that approach, "though I still stand by it."[36] Later on, however, he'd discovered, "and am still discovering to this day," that one only learns to have faith by entering into "the full this-worldliness of life."

He allowed that he was grateful to have been given these insights. "I know that it is only on the path that I have finally taken that I was able to learn this. So I am thinking gratefully and with peace of mind about past as well as present things." *Discipleship* was but a stage in the journey, one that he had now moved beyond.[37] After the war, it would comfort his family to read the prison letters and to know that the strenuous austerity of his writings of the 1930s had given way to a faith more open, munificent, and sensuous.

Until the events of July 20, 1944, the members of the Bonhoeffer circle remained guardedly hopeful that the criminal investigations of Dietrich would end in his acquittal. All that changed after the coup d'état failed.

On that afternoon, Colonel Claus Schenk Graf von Stauffenberg, a nobleman born in the family castle in the Bavarian town of Jettingen, carried a bomb into Hitler's headquarters in east Prussia. The July 20 plot drew from the highest levels of German society and government, including the so-called "Goerdeler Circle," led by the former mayor of Leipzig Carl Goerdeler and the diplomat Ulrich von Hassell; the "Kreisau Circle," clustering around Count Helmuth James von Moltke and his Silesian estate in Kreisau; and the *Abwehr* cell, headed by Hans Oster, Henning von Tresckow, and Colonel Stauffenberg. Other clusters remained informed of plans for the coup but without being directly involved with the assassination attempt. The Freiburg circle, for instance, with whom Bonhoeffer met several times, issued a memorandum that "sketched the contours of a post-Nazi government" and included "the first acknowledgment that the German people owed reparations to the Jews." These scions of the German nobility were joined by the trade unionists Wilhelm Leuschner and Julius Leber as well as by leaders of the Social Democrats.

The failure of the July 20 conspiracy brought to light the secret meetings and discussions, the traitorous deeds contemplated and attempted over the previous year; and in but a few days to follow, more than 170 people related to the plot were arrested, interrogated, in many instances tortured, and then brought before a commission of the Reich Central Security Office. Still, this hectic moment saw no immediate change in the circumstances of either Dohnányi or Bonhoeffer. And so the family took hope that their "early arrest could [yet] save them in the end," since no proof of complicity had yet been discovered. Over the next several weeks, however, Himmler's Gestapo, excited by an enraged Hitler, raided the homes and offices of everyone related to the conspiracy. They discovered letters, diaries, and other documents leading to further rounds of arrests, including arrests of conspirators involved in earlier plots. And yet: no connection to the coup attempt was imputed to Bonhoeffer.

On August 3, Bonhoeffer sent Bethge what he called "Outline for a Book." The four-page précis of another project never to be finished reveals the "exciting flash of recognition" that sparked his final writings; it also renders implausible any claim that he had not embarked on a distinctly new path of thought. Bonhoeffer had remained deeply concerned for Bethge's safety. He wrote of having heard about the "'tropical heat' in Italy," referring in code to the heavy fighting there and withdrawal of German troops. But he also meant the heat wave smothering most of western Europe. As temperatures in Berlin soared into the nineties and sweat flowed from his head onto the pages of his Dilthey, Bonhoeffer sank into a sweet reverie of his Italian travels with Bethge. There was the trip to Florence in the summer of 1936, a time when they had been poor, he recalled, and all he could give Bethge for his birthday had been "an evening of ice cream." As ever, he longed for the "clarifying conversations" of their best times together, but he remained hopeful that this new "kind of work" could take shape through their written exchanges and with much prayer. It excited him mightily that the book outlined in his letter would be their first real collaboration, and, not knowing this work would be his last, he eagerly solicited Bethge's ideas.

Bonhoeffer devoted much time to the project in the fall of 1944 and winter of 1945, and according to Bethge, he "had probably written a considerable amount before it became impossible to continue." But all that survives of the effort is the short sketch sent to Bethge, handwritten on August 3, 1944, in blue-black ink and, in parts, in old German script—along with lengthy and often cryptic sections of other letters, in which Bonhoeffer tested out his ideas.[38]

He imagined a short volume of a hundred pages—an essay, he called it, with three chapters—in which he would take inventory of Christianity in "a world come of age." Even the "Outline for a Book" indicates that he had in mind something with the urgency of a manifesto. Defying the idea of religion as a working hypothesis, as "a stopgap for our embarrassments," or a mode or modulation of human experience, Bonhoeffer proclaimed a God beyond human necessity. This brought him back to the basic question: Who is God?

"God is not primarily a general belief in God's omnipotence," he wrote in his notes for the first chapter. God is not a metaphysical proposition, or the being compared with which nothing greater can be conceived, or any such reality derived by the philosophers by inference, however sublime or inspiring. "That is not a genuine experience of God. That is but a prolongation of a piece of the world." What God is is "encounter with Jesus Christ," Bonhoeffer said—which is to say that a genuine experience of God only occurs in social terms, in the encounter with the Thou. God is the experience of a particular truth: "a transformation of human life is given in the fact that 'Jesus is there only for others.'" That is the only Christian prerogative (as it was also, importantly, the basic German Jewish conviction, minus the Christological dimension). Being a Christian, then, means participation in the story of Jesus: "a new life in 'being there-for-others,'" discovering transcendence in "the neighbor within reach in any given situation." "Human relationships are the most important thing," Bonhoeffer said. Needing nothing, "God allows himself to be served by us in all that is human."

Barth had once pictured the church as a structure with four sides open to the world, with practices of hospitality, forgiveness, and reconciliation as the marks of Christian devotion. In Bonhoeffer's "Outline for a Book," however, the structure collapses—the world having evolved beyond religion in the old sense—while the community of Christ, accepting exile as its lot, stands in solidarity with the distressed and the excluded. Bonhoeffer introduces the concept of "the hero whose creativity thrives on limitations."[39] Such a hero is one who cares for the lonely and the bereaved; attends to "the fatherless and widows in their affliction"; acts boldly against the powers of death in whatever form they take; renounces the desire to turn God into the summation of need and ambition; lives in humble gratitude for the opportunities of life; sings a hymn to "the small but journal wonders," to borrow from

W. H. Auden, whom Bonhoeffer is thought to have met briefly in New York in the summer of 1939.[40]

All other options had failed: German Protestantism had first sought legitimacy by defining a spiritual dimension beyond state intrusion. Lutheran orthodoxy had sought to redeem the church by making doctrinal rectitude the absolute measure of faith. The Confessing Church had affirmed the Lordship of Jesus Christ over all others and fought for the purity of the church. The ecumenical movement had rallied around the naive hope that Christ's peace would prevail in history. But none of these efforts could so much as dent the impregnable armor of the Nazi monolith—or save the Jews from mass slaughter. And so Bonhoeffer's final thoughts in prison came as an invitation to rethink the Christian witness and the church's complicity in war, mass death, and genocide.

During the Finkenwalde years, Bonhoeffer had discussed the need of "completely free, trained pastors" who would preach the Word of God and discern the spirits of the age. Such pastors would live closer to the ground, "immediately ready to serve . . . at the outbreak of any new emergency"—ready even to "renounce all the privileges of clergy, financial or otherwise." It had been Bonhoeffer's hope to inspire a new generation of rapid-response, free-floating churchmen equal to the exigencies of any mission. But Finkenwalde had long been boarded up, and with it went the emergency seminaries, houses of study, and other places of spiritual formation. Even a phalanx of pastors trained and deployed to meet these harrowing times were not equal to the emergency.

In *Machtstaat und Utopie*, a book Bonhoeffer had read with admiration, Gerhard Ritter said of the rulers of his utopian state that "they will not be isolated as a class for they will be continuously replaced by people advancing from lower levels." But they will be distinguished from the rabble "in their possession of elite intellectual gifts and moral maturity." The fate of Christianity in "a world come of age" depended in Bonhoeffer's view on just such a "new elite of people," with moral sensibilities shaped by "a view from below," forming an aristocracy of responsibility—a nobility of righteous doers and prayerful pilgrims. These "new elites" would enlist to the cause all who exhibit the highest values, safeguarding "in their silent deeds the besmirched words freedom, humanity, and toleration." Around "the silent sanctuary of lofty words, a new nobility will develop, must develop, in our time. The aristocrats of responsibility shall alone render the necessary judgments in a world come of age. Neither birth nor success, will be the foundation of this nobility, but humility, faith and sacrifice."[41] The Christian must hereafter live as if moving gently through a "quiet sanctuary"—and thus we come to an understanding of his religionless Christianity.

The whole edifice of institutional Christianity—what corresponded to religious life for nearly all who claimed to be religious—must be rebuilt from the ground up. The church must give away all its property! Pastors should take no salary but live on unforced donations and wages earned in some concurrent secular vocation. In this world, as in the apostolic age, clergy and laity alike would "participate in the worldly tasks of life in the community—not dominating but helping and serving." They will confess "in every calling that a life with Christ means to be there for others." They will not be afraid "to confront the vices of hubris, the worship of power, envy, and illusion" as "the roots of evil." They will praise the virtues of moderation, authenticity, trust, faithfulness, steadfastness, patience, discipline, humility, modesty, and "contentment." They will not underestimate the significance of human example (which has its origin in the humanity of Jesus, and is so important in Paul's writings!); for the Church's word gains weight and power not through concepts but by example."

It is exceedingly difficult to believe in God without a living example, Bonhoeffer said, although Protestantism had built its franchise on that very absence. Of this "I will write in more detail later," he said.

M ore than five thousand people would eventually be arrested on charges related to conspiracy, and of those at least two hundred would be executed. Not all those rounded up were actually connected with the July 20 plot, but the Gestapo used the occasion to settle scores with many whom it merely suspected of sympathizing with the opposition.

In the Nazi star chamber, Judge Roland Freisler bellowed and gesticulated wildly, shouting down the reasonable pleas of many men and women now victims of their conscience. Freisler had been a prisoner of war in Russia and a committed Bolshevik, before later becoming an ardent Nazi, and he greatly admired the "terror methods" of the Soviet vanguard, especially Andrei Vishinsky's performance during the Soviet purge trials of the 1930s. These he tried to emulate in Berlin.[42]

The vast tribunal chamber, draped with swastikas and overflowing with Nazi dignitaries, looked more like a Bavarian beer hall than a hall of justice.

On the opening day of the trials, Count von Moltke told the court that his decision to take part in the coup was a matter of conscience—based on his conviction that "the German position in Poland" was immoral. "My personal political experiences have caused me great problems," he continued, "because I worked to promote the German heritage in Poland. And since then I have experienced various changes in my attitude toward Poland."

This launched Freisler into the first of his tirades: "Are you blaming these various changes on National Socialism?" he barked.

"I was actually thinking of the many murders," Moltke answered quietly, "that occurred here and abroad."

"Murders! You really are a filthy louse," Freisler shouted. But Moltke continued speaking in a soft voice, his face lowered in concentrated thought.

"Are you cracking under your own villainy?" Freisler asked.

After a silence, Moltke tried once again to speak of the "murders," but Freisler interrupted him.

"Yes or no! Give a direct answer!"

"No," answered Moltke, raising his eyes directly to the court: "His own villainy" had not caused him to crack.

On September 20, Gestapo Commissioner Franz Sonderegger made a discovery that portended the worst for many members of the resistance in the *Abwehr*.[43] In an outpost of the military intelligence headquarters in the Berlin suburb of Zossen, numerous crates of documents had been stored for safekeeping during the air raids. It was here that Sonderegger—who, with Roeder, had been originally responsible for the arrests of Dohnányi and Bonhoeffer—came upon the *Abwehr*'s secret files. These files incriminated Dohnányi in the Stauffenberg plot beyond dispute; implicated, too, were his comrades in the Berlin circle, including Bonhoeffer. The papers found in "Portfolio Z"—the three "slips of paper"—did not link Bonhoeffer directly to the July 20 plot, but they contained one of his handwritten notes on the conscription of clergy for military service.[44] "It was an innocuous note but given the context of the Zossen files, a connection had finally been established between Bonhoeffer and the conspirators."

Reports of the discovery of the files spread quickly through the conspirators' network, reaching the Bonhoeffer family circle. Bonhoeffer's mother, Paula, who, shortly after the coup attempt, had expressed her great relief that no connection had been made to "our two," fell into a despair from which she would never fully recover. Word also reached Bonhoeffer in prison. This put an end to any remaining hopes for acquittal.

It was not Bonhoeffer's intention to die a martyr or otherwise submit to the verdict of the state. So his first response to the news was to launch an escape plan. Though designed some months earlier, the plan had been held in reserve until now.[45] With the help of a sympathetic guard—the reliable aforementioned Corporal Knobloch, who'd also arranged Bethge's visit—he would try to slip out and go underground, possibly to wait out the Führer's crumbling reign from a monk's cell in Ettal. It was "a desperate measure," perhaps, but not an especially complicated feat. On September 24, 1944, Renate Bethge, along with her parents, Rüdiger and Ursula (neé Bonhoeffer) Schleicher, rendezvoused with Knobloch in a Berlin suburb. They gave him a book of ration cards and a package of food and clothing and instructed him to keep the provisions in a storage shed "on an allotment garden" until Bonhoeffer's escape from Tegel.[46] But despite preparations, the plans would be abandoned.

On October 1, 1944, Klaus Bonhoeffer paced back and forth in his home. An arrest was imminent, he had learned, and suicide seemed the only honorable option in this darkest of hours. It was only through the intervention of his older sister, Ursula, that brought a distraught Klaus to his senses; he now understood that this way out represented a capitulation to Nazi terror and wasn't consistent with the family's principles.[47] His arrest came that afternoon. The next day, Knobloch visited Karl and Paula at Marienburger Allee to inform them that the escape plan had been aborted. Dietrich, rightly fearing retributions against his family, had decided to stay put.

Rüdiger Schleicher was arrested on October 4, and the day after that, Friedrich Justus Perels. Meanwhile, later that month, Bethge, as the clerk in charge of the Lissa post, was amazed to open a telegram ordering his own arrest and immediate deportation to Berlin. After anxious consideration, he decided to give it to his commanding officer, who, to Bethge's amazement, was not unduly worried about the directive, even though he was duty bound to send Bethge back to Berlin under guard. Bethge still had sufficient opportunity now to destroy the September letters from Bonhoeffer, making the one of August 23 the last of them to survive. The earlier letters survived because Karl and Paula buried them in canisters in the garden of their Charlottesburg home so Bethge could see them, too.[48] It seemed now far too dangerous for either of them to continue writing.

In October, Bethge was transferred from the Italian front to the Reich Central Security Office on Kurfürstenstrasse in Berlin before being sent to the Lehrter Strasse prison. Lehrter Strasse had been reserved for political prisoners implicated however remotely in the July 20 conspiracy. During the interrogations (undertaken in connection with investigations of Rüdiger Schleicher and Klaus Bonhoeffer), Bethge's contacts with Dohnányi, Perels, and Bonhoeffer were not discovered. Bethge would be charged only with the Confessing Church activities, his expressions of compassion toward Jews, his associations with conspiratorial visitors in the Schleicher home, and his failure to report such contacts. Formally discharged from the army, he was to appear before the People's Court for trial on May 15, 1945.

The Zossen files gave Roeder a new avenue for his interrogation of Dohnányi. As evidence not only of Dohnányi's involvement in the conspiracy but Bonhoeffer's as well, these documents provided the long-sought and until now elusive proof of high treason. Nevertheless, Dohnányi, Oster, and Wilhelm Canaris were able to argue that "these papers were official coded Military Intelligence materials"—not what they seemed. Remarkably, it was enough to make Roeder drop this line of interrogation, temporarily; so, at least for the moment, the Gestapo would remain unaware of Bonhoeffer's complicity. But Roeder would press on, aware of having in his possession, finally, evidence linking high-ranking members of the *Abwehr* to the conspiracy; he would have to work past the captives' denials to use it, but use it he would to bring his long investigation to a successful conclusion.

"Personally," he said later, "I never thought much of the Abwehr and took the view that all Abwehr officers should have been transferred after a year at most because of the many dangers besetting them, especially those of weak character."

"There's no one left to cover for you!" he snapped at Lieutenant Randolph von Breidbach, a conspirator and member of the *Abwehr*. "General Oster's finished, thanks to me. I'm going to clean the whole place out."

The same month, Bonhoeffer was transferred to the SS prison in the Reich Central Security Headquarters on Prinz-Albrecht-Strasse. In his cell at the epicenter of the terror there would be no more meals on china plates, nor would there be afternoon strolls with the commandant. Here began a descent into the hell of solitary confinement, torture, and concentration camps. The Bible that he had been allowed to keep in Tegel was confiscated; he was no longer allowed to correspond with Bethge. He could write to his parents, his brother Karl-Friedrich, and Maria, but only on rare occasions and according to strict guidelines; neither his parents nor his fiancée would ever again be allowed to see him. Only two short, heavily censored letters to his parents have survived.[49] Along with visiting privileges there came to an end all contact with the outside world.

Fabian von Schlabrendorff, a July 20 conspirator and Wedemeyer's first cousin, recalled his great surprise upon seeing Bonhoeffer in the subterranean corridor that had once housed the sculptors' studios of the School of Industrial Arts and Crafts. Acquainted since before the war, they had developed a profound mutual respect as comrades in the Berlin conspiracy. Some mornings later, the two arranged to take a shower together in a hidden niche of the washroom, and there informed "each other of their thoughts and experiences" as prisoners of conscience. Bonhoeffer spoke of his interrogations "and with what brutality the proceedings were carried through."[50] *Disgusting* was the word he used to describe the ordeal, which included, according to Schlabrendorff, Bonhoeffer's first acquaintance with intentional torture.

Between 1933 and 1945, nearly fifteen thousand political opponents of the Nazi Reich were detained in what one former prisoner called the "dark catacomb" at 8 Prinz-Albrecht-Strasse. It was Reinhard Heydrich himself who, while serving as head of the Political Police in Berlin, had designed the facility to affect "police custody of a very particular kind." "Heightened interrogations" took place on the upper floors of the south wing and were often conducted by Gestapo volunteers, who, having been passed over for ordinary posts, were keen to demonstrate—in these encounters with high-level political prisoners, these "traitors"—their freedom from all moral or legal inhibitions.

"Still he betrayed no sign of [suffering]," Schlabrendorff said. "He always cheered me up and comforted me.... Many little notes he slipped into my hands on which he had written biblical words of comfort and hope."[51] "Spread *hilaritas!*" Bonhoeffer told Schlabrendorff of his firm resolve: he would resist the Gestapo "to the end and would reveal nothing."[52]

Schlabrendorff, who survived the war, later recalled the horrific four-stage torture to which he was subjected that included iron spines pressed into his fingertips, stovepipes bored into his calves and thighs, a "procrustean bed" on which he was strapped and pulled from every side, and a full-body shackle that contained him as the interrogators beat him from behind with heavy clubs. "All the participants expressed their enjoyment in the form of derisive shouts," continued Schlabrendorff, who the next day, alone in his cell, suffered a near-fatal heart attack.[53]

A few days later, Bonhoeffer was transferred from cell 19 to 24, finding Schlabrendorff his neighbor in the adjoining cell. In further exchanges—once amid the confusion of an air raid—the two men agreed that the most plausible means of survival was to run out the clock, to create distractions that might slow the investigations as much as possible.[54] No one doubted that the end of the war was near. Other imprisoned conspirators had reached the same conclusion: they should probably "no longer hope for a quick release through a trial and acquittal," but rather they should "try to escape notice by keeping silent and 'vanishing into the sand.'"[55]

By Christmas, however, Bonhoeffer knew that his fate was sealed. In letters to his parents, and in one to Eberhard that evaded detection, written shortly before his disappearance into the black hole that was the Gestapo's network of torture chambers and concentration camps, he offered tender reassurances to his family, thanked Wedemeyer for her steadfastness, and bade farewell to Bethge, eternally grateful, he said, for "the liberating, fresh air" that had enabled so much freedom and growth. Awkward misunderstandings between them were now a thing of the past. Bethge had helped Bonhoeffer see how his artistic and creative side had been "suppressed" since childhood. He would never acknowledge a sexual desire for Bethge, nor would Bethge have welcomed its expression. Until the end, in fact, he would remain suspicious of inwardness and introspection; psychoanalytic accounts of the unconscious—for which his father the neurologist had little use either—he dismissed as the bad fruit of people who like to "busy themselves with themselves."[56] Back when he was reading Stifter's novel *Indian Summer*, when the captive life was like graduate school, he had remarked, "For me, Stifter's greatness lies in the fact that he refuses to pry into the inner realm of the person, that he respects the covering and regards the person only very discreetly from without, as it were, but not from within."[57] Bonhoeffer's relationship with Bethge had always strained toward the achievement of a romantic love, one ever chaste but complete in its complex aspirations.

Some friendships are built on competition, "in which the partners challenge each other," whereas others are filled with "intrusive forays and cheap disclosures." Still others descend into "noncommittal chats which barely veil the distance, unfamiliarity, and indifference between people." Bonhoeffer realized at last that what he'd shared with Bethge existed on a higher plane: their partnership had been "a mutual giving and receiving of gifts, [in which] there is neither violence nor indifference." What remained unspoken signified a gesture pointing toward as yet undiscovered treasures, toward riches still hidden in the other, which will be disclosed in the fullness of time. But the preciousness of those treasures would be in their contemplation rather than their possession. Theirs was a duet of "natural harmony," he liked to say, like all that is holy. And so everything that remained unfinished—"the loss of so many things"—rushed toward a "great liberation"; and this, like all the loves that he had given up, though first among them, had returned to him once more, transfigured in a final beatific surrender.

On his last day, though he knew it not as such, he joined others in singing Bach's cantata "Eine feste Burg ist unser Gott" ("A Mighty Fortress Is Our God"). He preferred to sing it briskly, with "bouncing rhythms," vivid tonic melodies, and appreciation of the delicate balance between what was above and what below:

> And though this world, with devils filled,
> should threaten to undo us;
> we will not fear, for God hath willed
> His truth to triumph through us.

He had sometimes let music slumber through his brain, section by section, "listening with his inner ear," especially to *St. Matthew's Passion*, which he thought Bach's most beautiful work. While in prison, he inscribed from memory the musical notations of sacred songs. Bethge had taught him to love Heinrich Schütz, the greatest German composer before Bach, who'd brought the sumptuous polychoral style of Venetian ceremonial song to seventeenth-century Lutheran church music. In prison he transcribed the staves of Schütz's "O bone Jesu"—from the *Kleine geistliche Konzerte*, a gentle meditation on the "restoration" of all earthy desire, tendered by the "kind Jesus, Word of the Father, Splendor of the Father's Glory, on whom the angels desire to gaze"— onto his final letters. "Nothing is lost," Bonhoeffer wrote alongside the meticulous notation, "in Christ all things are taken up, preserved, albeit in transfigured form, transparent, clear, liberated from the torment of self-serving demands," the joyance of recapitulation, "magnificent and consummately consoling."

Bonhoeffer would face death as he had lived, with tensile strength nourished from "a higher satisfaction," and he would die a celibate. "I've already seen and experienced more of life than you have," he wrote to Bethge, "except for one crucial experience that you have, which I still lack—but perhaps that's precisely why I have already had more of 'my fill of life' [*lebenssatt*] than you as yet."[58] He was not asking for pity, much less trying to shame Bethge for the contentment it was his good fortune to find. He wanted his friend "to be glad" of what he had, "which is truly the polyphony of life (forgive me for riding my newfound hobbyhorse!)." Neither did Bonhoeffer seem remorseful, neither regretting pleasures he had not enjoyed nor being contrite for his longings. But fears of oblivion were a different matter; the worst times were those when the past felt lost forever. "I want my life," he had whispered in the dark in the summer of 1944. "I demand my own life back. My past. You!"[59]

H is gift to his family on Christmas 1944 had been a poem titled "Von guten Mächten," or "From All Good Powers." Bonhoeffer sent a copy to Wedemeyer (who lived at the Bonhoeffers' Charlottenburg home from October 1944 until January 1945), which was hand-delivered by the police commissioner Franz Sonderegger as a favor to the family. His parents shared the poem with Bethge and with their daughters whose husbands were imprisoned—Ursula Schleicher, who lived next door in Charlottenburg, and Christine von Dohnányi.[60] This would mark Dietrich's last word to them, and one of his last bits of written expression before being deported from Berlin.[61] The city now lay in ruins: whole streets had "disappeared under piles of cascading rubble," smoke filled the air, and broken water lines created vast sheets of black ice. But still the Gestapo was about its work.

He told his parents the lines that had been running through his head for several days: seven verses of iambic pentameter (the standard of classical German sonnets), written in the sixth Advent season of the war.[62] Breathing mortal longings, "Von guten Mächten" is finally a prelude to eternity.

> *By faithful, quiet powers of good surrounded*
> *so wondrously consoled and sheltered here—*
> *I wish to live these days with you in spirit*
> *and with you enter into a new year.*
>
> *The old year still would try our hearts to torment,*
> *of evil times we still do bear the weight;*
> *salvation for which you did us create.*
>
> *And should you offer us the cup of suffering,*
> *though heavy, brimming full and bitter brand,*
> *we'll thankfully accept it, never flinching,*
> *from your good heart and your beloved hand.*
>
> *But should you wish now once again to give us*
> *the joys of this world and its glorious sun,*
> *then we'll recall anew what past times brought us*
> *and then our life belongs to you alone.*

The candles you have brought into our darkness,
let them today be burning warm and bright,
and if it's possible, do reunite us!
We know your light is shining through the night.

When now the quiet deepens all around us,
O, let our ears that fullest sound amaze
of this, your world, invisibly expanding
as all your children sing high hymns of praise.

By powers of good so wondrously protected,
we wait with confidence, befall what may.
God is with us at night and in the morning
and oh, most certainly on each new day.

It would be a fine thing if one could enter the New Year in the physical presence of his family and friends. "If it's possible, do reunite us!" he pleaded. If not, Thy will be done.

As he comprehended that death was imminent—his association with the July 20 conspirators having quashed any realistic hope of release—the voices of the past faded to the deepest quiet. What would take their place?

On the threshold of eternity, he heard a new song. The polyphony of life was indeed beautiful: the hissing glades and woodland murmurs at Friedrichsbrunn, the wind whispering through linden forests. Yet the music of the heavenly choirs, "invisibly expanding / as all your children sing high hymns of praise" of "your world," was that "fullest sound," engendering amazement.

"When it says in the old children's song about the angels: 'two who cover me, two who awaken me,'" he wrote in his last letter to Wedemeyer, "this protection night and day by invisible powers of good is something that we adults today need no less than the children."[63] Nothing gained or lost shall be forgotten; everywhere resounds "the Yes and the Amen." He asked her not to be anxious for his sake. "My past life is brim-full of God's goodness, and my sins are covered by the forgiving love of Christ crucified. I'm most thankful for the people I have met, and I only hope they will never have to grieve for me, but that they, too, will always be certain of, and thankful for, God's mercy and forgiveness."

In the hell that was the Gestapo interrogation prison, Bonhoeffer was graced with the visitation of angels. The "great invisible realm" had become now visible, and there remained no longer "any doubt about its real existence."[64]

Two weeks later, on January 17, 1945, in a letter to his parents, written in pencil, he turned to the matter of his personal effects. He asked his mother to give all his clothes to the *Volksopfer* public relief effort: his dinner jacket, his felt hats, his salt-and-pepper suit (which was too small anyway), the pair of brown loafers. He expressed confidence that by now his dear mama would have a better idea than he of what he still owned. "In short, give away whatever anyone might need, without a second thought."

The famous last words attributed to Bonhoeffer in the hour of his death—"This is not the end for me; it is the beginning of life"—are those of a British intelligence officer writing five years after the war.[65] They are an eloquent farewell, and true to Bonhoeffer's eschatological hopes, but the officer was not present when Bonhoeffer was summoned to the gallows in Flossenbürg. In any event, his last written words seem more fitting for the pastor who had come to feel uneasy with pious language: "Please drop off some stationery with the commissar."[66]

On the afternoon of February 7, 1945, Bonhoeffer was taken from Berlin and transported to an unknown destination. It was not until the next Wednesday, when an orderly refused delivery of his weekly parcels, that his family and fiancée realized "there was no longer a recipient for their gifts" at Tegel. His parents were frantic. "We have had no news of you since your departure," his father wrote, uncertain where to send the letter. "I hope that Christel may discover something today."[67] Christel (by which Dr. Bonhoeffer meant his daughter Christine) was dispatched to the Prinz-Albrecht-Strasse prison to ask about Dietrich's whereabouts, only to be turned away without answers.

A volume of Plutarch, *Große Griechen und Römer: Ausgewählte Lebensbilder* (*Great Greeks and Romans: Selected Portraits*), a gift from Karl-Friedrich for his thirty-ninth birthday, had remained with Bonhoeffer even after he was moved from Tegel on October 8, 1944, in the final chaotic six months of his life. With a blunt pencil he'd written his name and address in large letters in the front, back, and middle of the book, which he placed on a table in his cell as a kind of buoy during these chaotic final days.

On April 4, 1945, the diaries of Admiral Wilhelm Canaris, head of the *Abwehr*, were discovered by General Walter Buhle in a deserted safe at the Armed Forces Supreme Command headquarters, which had housed the *Abwehr* offices. Furious at what he read in them the next day, Hitler ordered the summary execution of all the imprisoned *Abwehr* conspirators. Himmler relayed the order directly to the Gestapo, who coordinated the hurried transfers.

By this time, Bonhoeffer had been in Buchenwald for two months. After being put on the bus to what turned out to be Stalag 13b in Weiden, Bonhoeffer told his friend and coconspirator Joseph Müller that he had stopped denying his role in "Canaris's political information service," and that indeed he had done everything in his power to avoid the draft. But when the transport bus arrived in Weiden—where more than twelve thousand refugees from the east now overwhelmed a town of 27,000 inhabitants—it was waved on due south, to Regensburg.

On April 8, in an abandoned schoolhouse in the village of Schönberg, in the far hinterlands of Bavaria, Bonhoeffer and a small group of prisoners celebrated the second Sunday of Easter with a short worship service. Bonhoeffer had expressed reluctance when Hermann Pünder, a Roman Catholic conspirator from the Rhineland and a former senior official in the Reich, had asked him to lead the service for the men, mostly Catholics. It was not simply that he was a Protestant minister—though despite his lifelong attraction to Catholicism he respected the limits of his evangelical ordination. Rather, Bonhoeffer was concerned about the effect the service might have on the morale of one of their company, a self-professed atheist. Only when the atheist insisted did Bonhoeffer oblige.[68] He read the scriptural passages from the daily *Losungen*, Isaiah 53:5 ("But he was pierced for our transgressions; he was crushed for our iniquities; upon him was the chastisement that brought us peace, and with his wounds we are healed") and 1 Peter 1:3 ("Blessed be the God and Father of our Lord Jesus Christ! According to his great mercy he has caused us to be born again to a living hope through the resurrection of Jesus Christ from the dead"). Not long after the service concluded, two guards arrived for him. "Prisoner Bonhoeffer, get ready and come with us!" one ordered.[69]

The SS transported him by bus to the concentration camp at Flossenbürg, a village in the Oberpfalz region of upper Bavaria near the border of Czechoslovakia, home to rich quarries and a ruined medieval castle. For three centuries granite had been mined in the stony ground of the Upper Palatinate Forest, so it was not surprising when the Nazis carved a concentration camp into a shallow valley on the outskirts of town. Since 1938 Flossenbürg had served the Third Reich, the German Stone and Building Works fabricating building materials by forced labor, quarrying granite for the Autobahn and the Reich party buildings.[70] Among the several thousand prisoners undergoing the SS-designed "work cure" were "vagabonds," "beggars," "pimps," "gypsies," and "antisocials," according to Himmler's protocol, along with the men who formed the Pink Triangle, the special section in Flossenbürg for homosexuals.

On the night of April 8, in a hurriedly convened court martial, SS Judge Otto Thorluck arraigned, convicted, and condemned Bonhoeffer. No witness gave testimony, and the accused was allowed no defense counsel.

The next morning, April 9, Bonhoeffer and five others, among them Canaris and Oster, were forced to undress and were led naked down the short steps from the detention barracks to the gallows that had been erected against a high brick wall. In this small courtyard more than a thousand people had been executed in the past year. Later, at a war crimes tribunal, H. Fischer Hüllstrung, the camp physician who attended to Bonhoeffer in his final hour, would say that he saw the pastor "bow to his knees and pray fervently to God"; he would add that, again, at the place of execution, Bonhoeffer had spoken a short prayer, this before ascending the last few steps, "brave composed. . . . [H]is death ensued after a few seconds."[71]

The disposition of Bonhoeffer's remains is unknown. Most of the dead at Flossenbürg were cremated in a facility in the valley just outside the walls of the camp. Photographs show the crematorium and the heap of ash that collected in the shape of a pyramid beside the building. As one of the "special" prisoners, whom the Nazis knew would be of great interest to the Allies, Bonhoeffer was likely cremated shortly after his death. Fabian von Schlabrendorff, stricken to see Bonhoeffer and his other comrades murdered, also suffered the horror of watching from his cell window as the bodies were burned on "piles of wood out in the open."[72] "His ashen remains may rest here, then," Schlabrendorff later speculated. The crematorium at Flossenbürg had broken down a few days earlier and was temporarily out of service.

But another possibility exists. When the Allies liberated the camp two weeks later, on April 23, they discovered piles of corpses. Writing in 1989, the American Leslie A. Thompson, chaplain of the 97th Infantry Division, recalled his arrival sometime after the liberation: "Two days later a mass burial ceremony was held for the unburied dead. The chosen site was a vacant area in the town of Flossenbürg. The Jewish chaplain gave the ceremony for the Jewish persons, the Catholic ceremony was given by Chaplain John Tivenan, and I gave the Protestant ceremony." The American officers in charge ordered the townspeople to attend. It is possible that Bonhoeffer was buried in one of these unmarked graves.

Evidence long available to scholars but often neglected in popular accounts contradicts Hüllstrung's story of Bonhoeffer's relatively merciful—or at least mercifully quick—end. There is in fact reason to believe that he and his fellow conspirators—Admiral Wilhelm Canaris, Canaris's deputy general Hans Oster, the military jurist General Karl Sack, General Friedrich von Rabenau, the businessman Theodor Strünck, and the resistance activist Ludwig Gehre—died a slow and

FLOSSENBÜRG CONCENTRATION CAMP, THE SITE OF BONHOEFFER'S EXECUTION

tortured death, after "prolonged barbarity."[73] The Danish commercial attaché and resistance organizer Jørgen L. F. Morgensen, one of Bonhoeffer's fellow prisoners in Flossenbürg, dismantled the prison doctor's claims in a narrative written shortly after the camp's liberation.[74] "Those who were sentenced to death were always murdered individually," Morgensen explained. "The prisoner was taken from his cell and lead to the washing rooms, where they undressed him and tied his arms behind his back with a strong paper-cord they had previously prepared. The nude prisoner was then led to the exit in the middle of the compound and forced to walk along the building on the outside, past the windows, to the canopied place of execution where the rope was waiting for them above the hooks on the wall." The executions of April 9, 1945, took an unusually long time: from six a.m. until noon.[75]

Though Morgensen was not an eyewitness, the day after Bonhoeffer's execution he saw in the prison courtyard an L-shaped hook, its long cantilevered arm culminating in a thick tip, in the prison courtyard. Bonhoeffer must have been hanged like "animals in a slaughterhouse," Morgensen concluded. "Under the weight of a normal person, the hook would be elastic, so that, given the appropriate length of rope the victim would slightly touch the ground. In this way the long duration of the hanging can be explained. I met one of the prison guards in the afternoon, who was still visibly thrilled."[76]

And the barbarism would not end all at once. On April 23, the same day the Americans liberated the concentration camp in Flossenbürg, Klaus Bonhoeffer and Rüdiger Schleicher were taken from the prison at Lehrter Strasse 3 and shot in cold blood by firing squad. By then the meadows and fields of Flossenbürg and the Upper Palatinate Forest had already greened in the warm sunshine of an early spring.

Schlabrendorff would owe his survival to a bookkeeping error. Distracted by the chaos engulfing the camp—as the Allied troops approached, and the remaining prisoners were hurriedly evacuated, either transported to Dachau or marched to death by the indefatigable SS—an administrator at Flossenbürg accidentally omitted Schlabrendorff's name from the killing roster. At first it appeared deserted. But as soldiers made their way inside, they discovered more than sixteen hundred critically ill men: Jews and other non-Aryans, political prisoners, and homosexuals, who had been abandoned in the evacuation. Thompson, accompanied by the American rabbi assigned to the XII Corps, reported seeing "a large cistern-like area with an opening about six or eight feet in diameter," full of charred bones, and then, farther toward the forest, a stack of decomposing bodies. "As I looked down," the minister said, "I prayed that God would have mercy on those who had been so mercilessly treated."[77]

B onhoeffer had always lived with premonitions of an early death. His cousin Hans-Christoph von Hase recalled a visit to Grunewald in spring 1929, when a twenty-three-year-old Dietrich, "sitting at the window of his study," suddenly declared, "I will not grow old; I'll die when I'm forty years old." Hase was taken aback by the remark, which seemed, with its hint of vanity and bravado, unbecoming a young theologian. He counseled his cousin to "give thanks to God for his robust health and energy" and anticipate a full and happy life. But gazing into the lush spring garden below, Bonhoeffer would not relent, only replying, "Yes, that's how it is."[78] He would share this premonition many times with friends and other relatives over the next decade. "In a more dangerous period in 1937," Gert Leibholz, Sabine's husband, visited him as he lay stricken with pneumonia at his parents' new house in Charlottenburg. From his sickbed, the young pastor prophesied, "You and I will not live long lives." As it happened, Leibholz would live to eighty, dying in 1984. "If I will that he tarry till I come, what is that to thee? Follow thou me."

By late May 1945, Bethge, who had been released from prison on April 25, was able to confirm the prisoners' deaths and convey the news to the families. Shortly after his arrest, Bonhoeffer had written his last will and testament, addressing the envelope: "To be delivered to my relatives in the case of my death." To his parents he offered his eternal gratitude. To his godchildren, six in all, he willed his Mexican rug, a painting by his great-uncle Leopold Kalckreuth, the jewelry box he'd purchased in Spain, his clavichord (if Christophe von Dohnányi "would take pleasure in it"), his baptismal watch, a gold pencil, a chair from Trent, the crucifixion scene painted on canvas, and books. To Maria Wedemeyer, who had made a desperate, futile attempt to find her fiancé in Flossenbürg—walking seven kilometers to the camp after spending two days on trains, only to be turned away "without any prospect of hearing anything"— Bonhoeffer left word that she could select an item among his belongings that she might "cherish as a remembrance."[79]

BONHOEFFER'S CELL, FLOSSENBURG CONCENTRATION CAMP. PHOTOGRAPH TAKEN BY THE AUTHOR, MARCH 2013

Bonhoeffer bequeathed the bulk of his worldly effects and his most precious possessions to Bethge: his library and Rembrandt Bible, the Dürer *Apostles*, his grand piano, the Audi and the motorcycle, the standing desk he'd used in Altdamm, the Chinese and all the Persian rugs, the Grunewald reproduction that hung over his bed in Finkenwalde ("where is that, by the way?"), his fountain pen, the Fra Angelico print, and one of his two icons. All these things, Bonhoeffer wrote to his friend, had "significance for their shared labor and life," since they had first met in 1935 on a summer evening near the Baltic Sea. Bethge should also have their six Indian scorpion spoons (which Paula Bonhoeffer was safeguarding in Charlottenburg), along with the alpine landscape by Stanislav Kalckreuth (Bonhoeffer's great-great-uncle, and Leopold's father), his entire life's savings, and whatever remained of his clothes.

Bonhoeffer left Bethge his letters and papers as well, hinting that one day they might deserve a fresh reading. "It would be very nice if you didn't throw away my theological letters," he said. "One writes some things in a more uninhibited and lively way in a letter than in a book, and in a conversation through letters I often have better ideas than when I'm writing for myself." At the time of Bonhoeffer's arrest in April 1943, his *Ethics* remained in preliminary drafts, and the writings that would be collected, under the title in English *Letters and Papers from Prison*, were still scattered throughout the family.

Bonhoeffer insisted finally that Bethge not bother himself with funeral arrangements. It would be quite appropriate if the surviving brethren took care of these details. Bonhoeffer offered these final lines to Eberhard with "the grateful awareness" of having lived richly and abundantly, in the certainty of forgiveness, and in the hope of eternal life.

ACKNOWLEDGMENTS

In 2007, I served as the Dietrich Bonhoeffer Visiting Professor at Humboldt University in Berlin. With a cozy office on Burgstrasse just across the River Spree from the Berliner Dom, soon enough I made my first trip to the Staatsbibliothek, the capacious city library designed by Hans Scharoun near the Potsdamer Platz, and there, with the kindly assistance of Dr. Jutta Weber, the director of special collections, gained access to the Dietrich Bonhoeffer archives. This collection, which had been recently obtained from the estate of Bonhoeffer's biographer and closest friend, Eberhard Bethge, filled more than twenty-five cases and included lectures, letters, books, photographs, notebooks, and journals; and while many appeared in the sixteen-volume *Dietrich Bonhoeffer Works*, the singularities of Bonhoeffer's life, the evidence of which I held in my hands—his registration papers for a new Audi convertible, a bank slip from the joint account he shared with Bethge, his file of magazine articles and pamphlets about African Americans, inventories of his wardrobe, and landscape photographs he made in Libya and Morocco—illuminated an intriguingly different character from the one I had carried with me since writing a doctoral dissertation on his philosophical thought nearly two decades earlier. I felt the gentle nudge into biography.

Since 2007, I have returned often to Europe, with Berlin as my home base, and with the goal of visiting the towns and regions where Bonhoeffer had lived and that influenced his journey from sheltered child of the Berlin-Grunewald to conspirator in a plot to kill Hitler. This meant trips to Breslau (now Wrocław, Poland), Tübingen, Rome, the Baltic seaboard and Pomeranian plains, Barcelona, London, Sigtuna-Stockholm, New York, Geneva, Ettal, Prague, Friedrichsbrunn in the eastern Harz Mountains, and the village and concentration camp of Flossenburg, where Bonhoeffer was executed on April 9, 1945. When circumstances forced me to cancel my trip to Tripoli and Tetouan, I turned to Brian L. McClaren's *Architecture and Tourism in Italian Colonial Libya* and Paul Bowles's memoirs for atmospherics on Bonhoeffer's two weeks in North Africa. The travels were rich and rewarding, but always the best part was returning to Berlin and to quiet and easygoing Prenzlauer Berg, my adopted neighborhood. I offer my heartfelt thanks to the friends and acquaintances in this wonderful city who helped make the difficult work so enjoyable: Kara and Wolfgang Huber, Helmut and Erika Reihlan, Christian Nowatsky, Theresa Clasen, Wim and Donata Wenders, Sibylle Tönnies, Webster Younce, and Tammy Murphy.

Time is indeed the writer and scholar's most precious commodity. But the time to read and write and amble through another person's story requires money as well; so I hope to be ever mindful—and appreciative—of the persons, institutions, and programs that allowed me to focus on large sections of the book with a minimum of distractions:

the John Simon Guggenheim Memorial Foundation for the award of a Fellowship in the Creative Arts in the fall of 2009;

the Lilly Endowment of Indianapolis, and especially Craig Dykstra, former vice president for religion at Lilly, and his successor, Chris Coble, apart from whose generous support the small village of students and scholars that clustered this project—and the countless discussions on matters Bonhoefferesque—would never have found structure or nourishment;

the dean of the College of Arts and Sciences at the University of Virginia, Meredith Woo, who offered encouragement when it was sorely needed and during her successful tenure inspired new institutional partnerships with Humboldt University, Berlin; and Cristina Della Coletta, associate dean for the arts and humanities, who coordinated logistical details for the research leaves, including a semester leave generously funded by the UVa Sesquicentennial Fellowship in the academic year 2011–12.

In 2010, the American Academy in Berlin honored me with the Ellen Maria Gorrissen Prize and a six-month writing residence. The daily exchanges with fellow scholars and writers in the Academy's beautiful research community on the Wannsee entertained as often as they inspired; and over the course of the term—and a winter that brought the longest stretch of days without direct sunlight in recent memory—I found the confidence to turn what had originated as a book on Bonhoeffer in America into a full life. I will forever treasure the convivial hours spent with Judith Wechsler, David Abraham, Jeffrey Chipps Smith, Andrew Norman, Camilo Vergara, Francisco Goldman, and the irrepressible Peter Wortsman. The Academy's remarkable staff unfailingly attended to every detail of my family's well-being and patiently answered my random, frequent questions. I trust I have not failed to note the hospitality of other staff members when I thank in particular Simone Donecker, Cornelia Peiper, R. J. Megill, Christina Wölpert, Alissa Burmeister, Peter Salamon, Malte Mau, Yolande Korb, Reinold Kegel, Stefan Czoske, Gabariela Schlickum, Andrew White, and the tenacious Gary Smith, the academy's executive director.

Gratitude is further due to the many friends who sustained my work in indirect but deeply felt ways: Mark Gornik, Jon Foreman, David Dark, Sarah Masen, Mark Edmundson, Mary Catherine Wimer, Locke Ogens, Richard Lee, Susan Holman, Ralph Luker, Daniel Berg, Carlene Bauer, Don Shriver, Diane McWhorter, Mick Watson, Stanley Hauerwas, Denise Giardina, Amy Laura Hall, Shea Tuttle, Kristina Garcia Wade, and Maran and Roy Hange. Numerous colleagues shared ideas and answered questions on topics related to German thought and history and to Bonhoeffer's extensive travels, among whom I wish to thank Alon Confino, Gene Rogers, Claudia Koonz, Paul Daffyd Jones, Michael Bray, Chuck Mathewes, Vigen Guroian, Heather Warren, Tal Howard, Chad Welmon, William McDonald, Jalane Schmidt, Asher Biemann, John Portman, and Ralph Luker.

Over the past two decades an international team of scholars under the auspices of the English Language Section of the International Bonhoeffer Society, along with the German Bonhoeffer Society, Gütersloher Verlagshaus, and Fortress Press, has produced the sixteen-volume complete works in German and English. Graced with marginalia, editorial essays, and a veritable trove of new research discoveries, these volumes have fortified Bonhoeffer's reputation as one of the most original religious thinkers of the modern age. Quite simply, this book could not have been written apart from the extraordinary accomplishments of the Dietrich Bonhoeffer Works Project as well as professional friendships with members of the International Bonhoeffer Society. Names of theologians and scholars involved in these endeavors appear throughout the notes of this book, but I wish to offer special thanks to those who went beyond their own editorial duties to share additional notes and perspectives: Victoria Barnett, Clifford Green, Geffrey Kelly, Michael Lukens, John De Gruchy, Mark Brocker, Stephen Plant, Larry Rasmussen, Keith Clements, Wayne Floyd, Andreas Pangritz, Glenn Stassen, John Godsey, Ralf Wüstenberg, Christiane Tietz, Jens Zimmermann, Martin Rumscheidt, Reggie Williams, Guy Carter, Leroy Walters, Christof Gestrich, Robert Steiner, Hans Pfeiffer, Klaus von Dohnányi, Jürgen-Lewin Hans von Schlabrendorff, Ferdinand Schlingensiepen and his son the documentary filmmaker Helmut, and Renate and Eberhard Bethge, who long before I ever considered biography shared with me stories of their beloved Dietrich over a marvelous lunch of chicken curry and Riesling in their home in Villiprot-Bonn.

I must also offer a hearty *vielen dank* to my graduate research assistants at the Project on Lived Theology for their tireless and often heroic efforts in tracking down documents, gathering and checking facts, and engaging me as intellectual comrades. Kris Norris, Rachel Butrum, Tim Hartman, A. J. Walton, Kelly Figueroa-Ray, Philip Lorish, Kendall Cox, and Roger Connaroe—these gifted young scholars and edifying critics have surely made the book better than it otherwise would have been. Resourceful and meticulous as readers and editors, Kelly, Kris, and Rachel, along with Jennifer Seidel in Charlottesville and Theresa Clasen in Berlin, helped me to the finish line in the final arduous months. And hats off to the numerous undergraduates who photocopied and transcribed German documents without complaint and at work-study wages, brave souls all.

Many librarians and archivists kindly responded to my frequent and sometimes impatient requests. I am deeply grateful to these hardworking women and men, and to the libraries and archives that made historical documents and photographs readily available:

Ruth Tonkiss Cameron, at the Burke Library Archives, Union Theological Seminary, Columbia University Libraries;

Jennifer Belt, Associate Permissions Director, Art Resource, New York, and her colleague Gerhard Gruitrooy;

Sabine Schumann, at the bpk Photo Agency in Berlin;

Jutta Weber, mentioned earlier, who—among her many responsibilities at the Staatsbibliothek—curates the Dietrich Bonhoeffer and Eberhard Bethge Papers;

Burckhard Scheffler, who magnanimously oversees research programs and events at the Bonhoeffer Haus in Charlottenburg-Berlin, even once allowing me to take a nap in Bonhoeffer's upstairs bedroom on an afternoon when I felt suddenly overwhelmed by jetlag.

My agent, Christy Fletcher, spirited this project along with her unrivaled verve and resoluteness and provided all the right suggestions and reassurances at crucial stages in the writing. I'm grateful to Christy and her colleagues at Fletcher and Company, Melissa Chinchillo, Rachel Crawford, and Sylvie Greenberg, for their good energies and excellent representation.

A more generous and involved editor than George Andreou at Knopf is difficult to imagine; my debt to him is incalculable. George helped bring the story into focus, and with his eye for detail and close attention to the line turned an excruciatingly long and unwieldy first draft into a more coherent narrative. I wish also to thank Juhea Kim, George's editorial assistant, for the carefulness and intelligence with which she helped move the manuscript through the various stages of editing. Together they gave me a new appreciation for the art of literary publishing.

My mother and father have spent much of the past twenty years serving English-speaking Protestant congregations in Europe, exemplifying in word and deed the "very profound compassion" of which Bonhoeffer wrote in his final prison letters. Their encouragement fills me with great gratitude and satisfaction.

Indeed I am blessed to have a family that not only indulged my writing and the selfish demands it inevitably makes, but joined me, when possible, in the adventure of research and travel. Henry Marsh, a tenth grader in the spring of 2007, has now embarked on a career in finance and economic development. Will flew the coop after his second Berlin residency to study English literature and write music. Still in high school, Nan, so beautiful, brilliant, and caring (if I might), keeps the home flames burning in her older brothers' absence. My wife, Karen Wright Marsh, remains my most fierce and loving advocate, a beacon of light through the long haul of research and writing and in the seasons of self-doubt. I dedicate this book to Karen with love and admiration.

NOTES

CHAPTER ONE Eternity's Child

1. Sabine Leibholz-Bonhoeffer, cited in Bethge, *Dietrich Bonhoeffer: A Biography*, p. 38.
2. Ibid., p. 14.
3. Sabine Leibholz-Bonhoeffer, cited in ibid., p. 38.
4. Bonhoeffer, "Literary Attempt on the Theme of 'Death,'" in Bonhoeffer, *DBW*, vol. 11, pp. 396–97.
5. Leibholz-Bonhoeffer, *The Bonhoeffers*, p. 32.
6. Sabine Leibholz-Bonhoeffer, cited in ibid., pp. 38–39.
7. Christian Gremmels, Renate Bethge, et al., in Bonhoeffer, *DBW*, vol. 8, p. 549.
8. Sabine Leibholz-Bonhoeffer, cited in Bethge, *Dietrich Bonhoeffer: A Biography*, p. 38.
9. In Martin Luther, Satan is everywhere, as readers of the sixteenth-century reformer can attest, lurking behind wayward thoughts, corrupt popes, perplexing sensations in the body, and other unknown and shadowy regions. With Bonhoeffer's contemporary Paul Tillich, Satan has been slain by modern psychology, but the "demonic" appears throughout, in opposition to the divine, in a never-ending dialectic of creativity and destruction. In his youthful notes and letters, Bonhoeffer gives little attention to the devil, but later he will speak of Satan and his legions in reference to Hitler, who is also called the "anti-Christ."
10. Bonhoeffer, "Sermon on 2 Corinthians 5:10, London, Repentance Day, November 19, 1933," in Bonhoeffer, *DBW*, vol. 13, p. 330.
11. Bethge, *Dietrich Bonhoeffer: A Biography*, p. 19.
12. Leibholz, "Childhood and Home," p. 19.
13. Bonhoeffer, *DBW*, vol. 7, p. 90.
14. Leibholz-Bonhoeffer, *The Bonhoeffers*, p. 11.
15. Haber would later supervise Karl-Friedrich's research at the Max Planck Institute.
16. Bethge, *Dietrich Bonhoeffer: A Biography*, pp. 21–23.
17. Schlingensiepen, *Dietrich Bonhoeffer*, p. 12.
18. Isherwood, *Goodbye to Berlin*, p. 16.
19. My gratitude to Theresa Clasen, Kerry Moror, and Mark Rylander for

architectural and historical detail on Berlin-Grunewald and fin de siècle Germany.

20. As was the case in the home of Max Planck, one block away on the same street. Herman, *Max Planck Monographie*, n.p.
21. Bonhoeffer, *DBW*, vol. 7, pp. 89–90.
22. Ibid., pp. 85–87.
23. Leibholz, "Childhood and Home," p. 20.
24. Bethge, *Bonhoeffer: A Life in Pictures*, p. 14.
25. Bosanquet, *The Life and Death of Dietrich Bonhoeffer*, p. 19.
26. Bethge, *Dietrich Bonhoeffer: A Biography*, p. 10.
27. Bethge, "Dietrich and Marie," p. 14.
28. Leibholz-Bonhoeffer, *The Bonhoeffers*, p. 58.
29. Bethge, "Dietrich and Marie," p. 14.
30. As a proponent of empirical psychology and neurology, Dr. Bonhoeffer remained cautious—"by nature astute and critical," said his colleague Robert Gaupp—in the treatment of addictions, depression, and hysteria. Sigmund Freud's biographer, Ernest Stanley Jones, claimed that under Karl Bonhoeffer's leadership, Berlin University became a "bastion against Freudian and Jungian psychoanalysis." But Karl Bonhoeffer appreciated certain insights from the practice of psychoanalysis: the dispassionate and concentrated attention to mental illness, "accompanied by scrupulous observation." Like his mentor at the University of Breslau, Carl Wernicke, Karl Bonhoeffer focused on the symptoms of impaired consciousness such as hysteria and delirium. Karl Bonhoeffer, though, was not at all an impersonal and detached physician. Sabine was once struck by how much more freely her father revealed himself to his patients than to his own children. Kindly, demanding, and aloof with his own family, Dr. Bonhoeffer brought "empathy and understanding" to his clinical relationships, and affection as well, and was, in turn, loved by his patients.
31. Bethge, *Dietrich Bonhoeffer: A Biography*, p. 36.
32. Leibholz-Bonhoeffer, *The Bonhoeffers*, p. 10.
33. Bethge, *Dietrich Bonhoeffer: A Life in Pictures*, p. 14.
34. Leibholz, "Childhood and Home," pp. 19–20.
35. Leibholz-Bonhoeffer, *The Bonhoeffers*, pp. 8–9.
36. Leibholz, "Childhood and Home," p. 19.
37. Ibid., p. 40.
38. Bethge, "Dietrich and Marie," p. 14.
39. Bonhoeffer, *DBW*, vol. 7, p. 74.
40. Bethge, *Dietrich Bonhoeffer: A Biography*, p. 18.
41. Leibholz-Bonhoeffer, *The Bonhoeffers*, pp. 49–50.
42. Bonhoeffer, *DBW*, vol. 7, p. 127.
43. Bonhoeffer, *DBW*, vol. 9, pp. 29, 31, 33.
44. Teresa Classen, conversation with the author.
45. *The Harz Journey* was published in book form as part of *Travel Pictures I*.

46. Heine, *The Harz Journey*, pp. 65, 82.
47. Bonhoeffer, *DBW*, vol. 7, p. 180.
48. Leibholz, "Childhood and Home," p. 25.
49. Bonhoeffer, *DBW*, vol. 7, pp. 97–98.
50. Leibholz-Bonhoeffer, *The Bonhoeffers*, pp. 33–34.
51. Bonhoeffer, *DBW*, vol. 8, p. 294.
52. Leibholz, "Childhood and Home," p. 30.
53. Karl Bonhoeffer cited in Leibholz-Bonhoeffer, *The Bonhoeffers*, p. 18.
54. Bethge, *Dietrich Bonhoeffer: A Biography*, p. 28.
55. Bonhoeffer, *DBW*, vol. 7, p. 93.
56. Bonhoeffer, *DBW*, vol. 9, pp. 19–20. In a February 9, 1920, letter, he mentioned bread ration coupons and a bicycle stolen from the home in Friedrichsbrunn.
57. Leibholz-Bonhoeffer, *The Bonhoeffers*, p. 17.
58. Schlingensiepen, *Dietrich Bonhoeffer*, p. 13.
59. Leibholz, "Childhood and Home," p. 30.
60. Schlingensiepen, *Dietrich Bonhoeffer*, p. 13.
61. Leibholz, "Childhood and Home," p. 30.
62. Bethge, "Editor's Afterword to the German Edition," p. 228.
63. Leibholz-Bonhoeffer, *The Bonhoeffers*, p. 19.
64. Bonhoeffer, *DBW*, vol. 7, p. 82.
65. In a curriculum vitae written for his fraternity at the University of Tübingen, where he spent his freshman year, Bonhoeffer wrote, "From the time that I was thirteen years old it was clear to me that I would study theology." Cited in von Hase, "'Turning Away from the Phraseological to the Real,'" p. 594.
66. Leibholz-Bonhoeffer, *The Bonhoeffers*, p. 34.
67. Translation mine. "The Gellert Lieder were composed during a tumultuous time in Beethoven's life; in an 1801 letter to Dr. Franz Wegeler we find the composer's first mention of the growing deafness that would eventually drive him into near isolation. This distress, combined with the disappointment of his unrequited love for a 'dear charming girl' (most likely the Countess Giulietta Guicciardi, a student of Beethoven and the dedicatee of the 'Moonlight' Sonata, op. 27, No. 2) may have induced his temporary attraction to religious subjects such as the Gellert poems, or Christus am Ölberg (Mount of Olives), composed in 1803." From "Ludwig Van Beethoven," http://www.classicalarchives.com/work/4590.html#tvf=tracks&tv=about (accessed March 22, 2011).
68. Bethge, *Dietrich Bonhoeffer: A Biography*, p. 25.
69. Bonhoeffer, *DBW*, vol. 9, p. 31.
70. Ibid., p. 46.
71. Bethge, *Dietrich Bonhoeffer: A Life in Pictures*, p. 24.
72. Karl August von Hase had gained considerable renown for his massive *The History of the Christian Church (Kirchengeschichte: Lehrbuch zunächst für*

akademische Vorlesungen, 1834), although his many writings also included popular and sympathetic biographies of St. Francis of Assisi, Catherine of Siena, Die Jungfrau von Orleans, Savonarola, and Thomas Münzer.

73. Eberhard Bethge, conversation with the author, May 1992.
74. Bethge, *Dietrich Bonhoeffer: A Biography*, p. 36.
75. Bonhoeffer, *DBW*, vol. 9, pp. 21–22.
76. Ibid., p. 46.
77. The "pack" was in fact two former military officers, members of the anti-democratic Organization Consul. Bonhoeffer, *DBW*, vol. 9, p. 49.
78. Ibid., p. 46.
79. Bonhoeffer-Leibholz, *The Bonhoeffers*, pp. 12–13.
80. Bonhoeffer, *DBW*, vol. 9, pp. 53–54.
81. Ibid., p. 214.

CHAPTER TWO "Italy Is Simply Inexhaustible"

1. As of 1915, Dr. Simon Hayum and his family lived at 15 Uhlandstrasse. In the same building, he and his cousin Dr. Julius Katz ran the largest law office in town. In 1929 his son Dr. Heinz Hayum joined the office. Dr. Simon Hayum got involved in many cases with public life in town as well as in the self-administration of the Jewish community. Between 1924 and 1935 he was on the steering committee of the Israeli Assembly of Württemberg; from 1919 until 1933 he was chairman of the Deutsche Demokratische Partei (DDP) at the city council as well as in the steering committee of the *Oberschulrat*. His generosity toward people in need was well known in town, yet already in 1933 he was a victim of anti-Jewish bullying. Immediately after the Nazis rose to power, Hayum was pressured into relinquishing his honorary civic office. In 1939, he and his family were forced to sell their large house to the city and emigrate, via Switzerland, to the United States. See "The Uhlandstrasse Story," http://www.tuebingen.de/19.html#142.243 (accessed May 2, 2013), my translation.
2. Bonhoeffer, *DBW*, vol. 9, p. 78.
3. Schlingensiepen, *Dietrich Bonhoeffer*, p. 21.
4. In the eighteenth century, Italy became the destination of choice for the "accomplished, consummate Traveller," the high point of the Grand Tour for the English and northern Europeans—and remained so throughout the nineteenth century. German fascination boomed in the wake of Johann Wolfgang von Goethe's best-selling *Italian Journey*, filled with beautifully rendered and inviting stories of his 1786 and 1787 travels. But after World War I, as a new German nationalism emerged, travels abroad lost their appeal, and all but the most devoted Italophiles vacationed within the fatherland. Even some members of the Bonhoeffer and von Hase families changed their routines, preferring instead such

fine sights as the Cathedral of Doberan, the graves of the Huns in the Wilseder highlands, and the pine-covered slopes on Kickelhahn.

5. Bonhoeffer, *DBW*, vol. 9, p. 78.
6. Ibid., pp. 78–79.
7. Ibid., p. 79.
8. Ibid., p. 81.
9. Ibid., p. 78.
10. Only after the occupation did Cuno actively decide to renege on all reparation payments. Whether Germany intentionally defaulted before the occupation is uncertain.
11. Barth and Thurneysen, *Revolutionary Theology in the Making*, p. 119.
12. Bonhoeffer, *DBW*, vol. 9, pp. 55, 64, 66, 61.
13. Ibid., p. 58.
14. Bethge, *Dietrich Bonhoeffer: A Biography*, p. 48.
15. Ibid., p. 49.
16. Wilhelm Dreier to Dietrich Bonhoeffer, in *DBW*, vol. 9, p. 131.
17. Bonhoeffer did not withdraw his membership in the fraternity until the middle of the next decade. By 1935, the Hedgehog had embraced the Nazi *Gleichschaltung*, with members parroting the view that Hitler's plan to "establish a system of totalitarian control and tight coordination over all aspects of society and commerce" should be celebrated as the fulfillment of an ancient German ideal. Bonhoeffer's resignation was noted in the 1936 fraternity bulletin. If he showed any sign of discontent in his student year, it was only in his slight impatience with provincial Swabia.
18. Bonhoeffer, *DBW*, vol. 9, p. 60.
19. Leibholz, "Childhood and Home," p. 26.
20. Eduard Mörike, "Urach Revisited," *Friedrich Hölderlin and Eduard Mörike, Selected Poems*, trans. and ed. Christopher Middleton (Chicago: University of Chicago Press, 1972), p. 137.
21. Robert Held cited in Pfeifer, "Editor's Afterword to the German Edition," p. 570.
22. Bethge, *Dietrich Bonhoeffer: A Biography*, pp. 51–52; Bonhoeffer, *DBW*, vol. 9, pp. 70–74.
23. Bonhoeffer, *DBW*, vol. 9, p. 74.
24. Goethe, *Italian Journey*, p. 128.
25. Bonhoeffer, *DBW*, vol. 9, p. 83.
26. Richard Francis Burton, *Etruscan Bologna* (London: Smith, Elder and Co., 1876), p. 4.
27. Bonhoeffer, *DBW*, vol. 9, pp. 83–85.
28. Ibid., pp. 83–84.
29. Ibid., p. 84.
30. Ibid., pp. 84–88.
31. Ibid., pp. 85–86.
32. Ibid.
33. Ibid., p. 87.

34. Ibid.
35. The church of Santa Prassede is "rich in treasures, but on entering it [it] is not so much this that strikes us, as the sensation of being in a well-loved parish church." Georgina Masson, *The Companion Guide to Rome* (New York: Harper and Row, 1965), p. 327.
36. Bonhoeffer, *DBW*, vol. 9, p. 103. He ridiculed the writings of Karl Scheffler and Wilhelm Worringer, two critics who wrote primarily on German art, and scoffed at most of the other critics he consulted as well.
37. Ibid.
38. Ibid., pp. 88–89.
39. Ibid., p. 89.
40. Ibid.
41. Ibid., p. 91.
42. Ibid.
43. Ibid., p. 111.
44. Ibid., p. 91.
45. For centuries, the Lutheran suspicion (if not abhorrence) of Rome had become part of the cultural inheritance of German Protestantism. At the time of Bonhoeffer's 1924 visit, the relationship between Catholics and Protestants could be summed up in the phrase *"Fremdheit und Scheu"*— strangeness and shyness. But unlike many Protestant pilgrims to Rome, Bonhoeffer was smitten by the Eternal City.
46. Bonhoeffer, *DBW*, vol. 9, pp. 88–89; Bethge, *Dietrich Bonhoeffer: Theologe—Christ—Zeitgenosse*, p. 85. On the same page Bethge observes, "Ihn hat die Ewige Stadt nicht wie andere protestantische Romfahrer entsetzt und abgestoßen; sie hat ihn im Gegenteil für immer mit Sehnsucht erfüllt."
47. Bonhoeffer, *DBW*, vol. 9, p. 91.
48. Ibid., p. 92.
49. Bonhoeffer, *Letters and Papers from Prison*, ed. Eberhard Bethge, p. 337.
50. Bonhoeffer, *DBW*, vol. 9, p. 93.
51. Ibid., p. 113.
52. Ibid., p. 95; Goethe, *Italian Journey*, p. 129.
53. Bonhoeffer, *DBW*, vol. 9, p. 95.
54. Ibid., p. 113.
55. From Klaus Bonhoeffer to his parents, ibid.
56. Ibid., p. 97.
57. Bonhoeffer, ibid., p. 98; Bethge, *Dietrich Bonhoeffer: A Biography*, p. 59.
58. Bonhoeffer, *DBW*, vol. 9, p. 116.
59. From Klaus Bonhoeffer to his parents, ibid., p. 114.
60. "The 10,000 Jews live in a special quarter. They have little in common with our German Jews or the Polish Jews." From Dietrich Bonhoeffer to his parents, ibid., p. 116.
61. From Klaus Bonhoeffer to his parents, ibid., pp. 113–15.
62. Steiner, "Desire and Transgression," p. 29.

63. Bonhoeffer, *DBW*, vol. 9, pp. 116–18.
64. Bonhoeffer, *DBW*, vol. 9, p. 97.
65. Robert Steiner's phrase; see "Desire and Transgression," p. 23.
66. Bonhoeffer, *DBW*, vol. 9, pp. 98–100.
67. Ibid., pp. 101–2.
68. Ibid., pp. 87, 104.
69. From Detlef Albers to Dietrich Bonhoeffer, April 14, 1929, in *DBW*, vol. 10, p. 181. Detlef Albers told Bonhoeffer that during a recent holiday he had seen a great deal of Spanish Catholicism and had found it chaotic and grim. "The Roman variety that tempted you to convert, I think, must have been quite different, for I really cannot possibly imagine such a temptation in my own case." In Bonhoeffer, *DBW*, vol. 10, p. 180.
70. Bonhoeffer, *DBW*, vol. 9, pp. 121, 112.

CHAPTER THREE University Studies

1. Bonhoeffer, *DBW*, vol. 9, p. 129.
2. Ibid., p. 51.
3. Ibid., p. 129.
4. Ibid., p. 123.
5. Bonhoeffer accompanied his twin sister, her husband Gert, and their two daughters, Marianne and Christine, "some of the way into exile" before the Leibholzes crossed the border near Basel into Switzerland. The family emigrated to England, where Gert obtained a faculty post at Oxford. Bethge, *Dietrich Bonhoeffer: A Life in Pictures*, p. 112. Four weeks after their flight from Germany, "on 5 October all non-Aryans' passports that were not stamped with a 'J' were declared invalid." Bethge, *Dietrich Bonhoeffer: A Biography*, p. 632.
6. Leibholz-Bonhoeffer, *The Bonhoeffers*, p. 55.
7. Bosanquet, *The Life and Death of Dietrich Bonhoeffer*, p. 54.
8. Leibholz-Bonhoeffer, *The Bonhoeffers*, pp. 56–57.
9. Wendebourg, "Dietrich Bonhoeffer und die Berliner Universität."
10. Bonhoeffer, *DBW*, vol. 9, pp. 144–46.
11. Kenneth Hagan, "Changes in the Understanding of Luther: The Development of the Young Luther," *Theological Studies* 29, no. 3 (1968): 477–79. The reference is to the polemical writings of Heinrich Denifle and Hartmann Grisar.
12. In this manner, Holl argued that "[o]nly both reformist movements, the Wittenberg movement and the Geneva movement, opened up the whole process of reformation." The Lutheran Renaissance illuminated "a step beyond Luther," which meant that in the face of nationalist movements, Protestant Christians should "keep developing the economic and legal order in such a way that respect to human dignity becomes evident everywhere." Hagan, "Changes in the Understanding of Luther."

13. Holl argued that the Reformation banner of *sola fidei*—God justifies sinners by faith alone—presupposed the life of the church community. Not only is justification rightly understood in the context of the church; the consequence of justification *is* the church. The church exists by grace alone.

14. Harnack, *Das Wesen des Christentums*.

15. Bonhoeffer, *DBW*, vol. 9, pp. 132–33.

16. Wendebourg, "Dietrich Bonhoeffer und die Berliner Universität."

17. Bonhoeffer, *DBW*, vol. 9, pp. 133, 135.

18. Ibid., pp. 137–38.

19. Ibid., p. 133.

20. Ibid., pp. 129–30.

21. Ibid., p. 161.

22. Ibid., pp. 144–45.

23. The two would marry in November 14, 1929.

24. Bonhoeffer, *DBW*, vol. 9, pp. 145–46, 150.

25. Ibid., p. 150.

26. Pfeifer, "Editor's Afterword to the German Edition," p. 572.

27. "B minor Mass for today's Repentance Day. For years it has been part of Repentance Day for me, just as the St. Matthew Passion is part of Good Friday. I remember quite clearly the evening I heard it for the first time. I was eighteen years old, was coming from a Harnack seminar in which he had discussed my first seminar paper very graciously and had expressed the hope I would someday become a church historian; I was still quite full with this when I entered the Philharmonic Hall; then the great 'Kyrie eleison' began, and at that moment everything else sank away completely. It was an indescribable impression." See Bonhoeffer, *DBW*, vol. 8, p. 177.

28. Bonhoeffer, *DBW*, vol. 9, pp. 146–49.

29. Weizsäcker, "Thoughts of a Nontheologian on Dietrich Bonhoeffer's Development," p. 163.

30. Bonhoeffer, *DBW*, vol. 9, pp. 148–49.

31. Wendebourg, "Dietrich Bonhoeffer und die Berliner Universität."

32. Bonhoeffer, *DBW*, vol. 9, pp. 148–49.

33. Ibid.

34. See Pfeifer in ibid., p. 148.

35. Barth, *The Word of God and the Word of Man*, p. 28.

36. Barth and Thurneysen, *Revolutionary Theology in the Making*, p. 43.

37. Von Hase, "'Turning Away from the Phraseological to the Real,'" p. 595.

38. Barth's lectures on Christian dogmatics during the summer semester of 1924 and the winter semester of 1924–25 comprised an early draft of the first volume of his *Doctrine of the Word of God: Prolegomena to Church Dogmatics*.

39. Barth, *The Word of God and the Word of Man*, pp. 59–60.

40. Ibid., p. 80. Nowhere did the disagreement between Harnack and Barth appear more sharply than at the 1920 Students' Conference in Aarua, Switzerland, where Barth delivered the lecture "Biblical Questions, Insights, and Vistas." With Harnack sitting in the audience, and in the company of old-guard liberals, Barth unleashed a full-scale attack on what he considered the central convictions of the liberal-historical school. "Jesus simply has nothing to do with religion," he said. Jesus was a radical and a revolutionary, who overturned moral conventions. Christianity was not about making the world more comfortable. The teaching of Jesus begins and ends with his proclamation of a new world actively invading the old world in judgment. "The affirmation of God, man, and the world given in the New Testament is based exclusively upon the possibility of a new order absolutely beyond human thought," he said, "and therefore, as prerequisite to that order, there must come a crisis that denies all human thought." Harnack was appalled by what he heard. In his published letter to the "Despisers of Scholarly Theology" on January 11, 1923, he challenged Barth to face the intellectual demands of the modern age. Under the pretense of a radical agenda, Harnack felt, Barth was retreating into the irrational and undoing all progress in religious thought.

41. Bonhoeffer, *DBW*, vol. 9, p. 166.

42. Ibid., pp. 171–72.

43. Bonhoeffer, *DBW*, vol. 10, p. 495.

44. Bonhoeffer, *DBW*, vol. 1, p. 120. The phrase Bonhoeffer used to describe the source of the distinctive social relation of the church is the kind of phrase academic theologians use to avoid the embarrassment of simplicity—"vicarious representative action." He had in mind his favorite of all of Luther's writings, "The Blessed Sacrament of the Holy and True Body of Christ, and the Brotherhoods" (1519), the passage that reads, "It is good if you find that you are becoming strong in the confidence of Christ and his dear saints, so that you are certain that they love and stand by you in all the trials of life and death." See Luther, *Luther's Works*, p. 72. Vicarious representation means simply this, Bonhoeffer concluded: the essence of Christianity is the grace of God revealed in community and the awakening of love in return.

45. Schlingensiepen, *Dietrich Bonhoeffer*, p. 60.

46. Bonhoeffer, *DBW*, vol. 1, p. 119.

47. Reinhold Seeberg, cited in editorial notes in Bonhoeffer, *DBW*, vol. 1, p. 119.

48. Bonhoeffer, *No Rusty Swords*, p. 170.

49. Moses, *The Reluctant Revolutionary*, p. 28.

50. Ibid., p. 32.

51. Ibid., p. 33.

52. Ibid., p. 10.

53. Bonhoeffer, *DBW*, vol. 9, p. 174.

54. Ibid., pp. 175–77.
55. Ibid., p. 177.

CHAPTER FOUR "Greetings from the Matador"

1. Bonhoeffer, *DBW*, vol. 10, p. 57.
2. "Friedrich Mahling came from the city mission; he was a man who could provide exact diagnoses and analyses of the effects of the social upheavals on the Church that started in the late years of the Kaiser's reign and lasted until the years after the World War. Inspired by the goal to keep up the Church of the People also in new times, he prepared his students in all fields of practical theology to fulfill their future profession as pastors in the face of new conditions. Only in 1920, the University established a new Chair for Mission Studies. It was held by Julius Richter, who had already been teaching for quite some time at the faculty and who had been granted an honorary doctorate. His five-volume *History of Missions* and an abundance of other publications about different stages and areas of the world mission in the past and present were Richter's instruments to give academic legitimacy to this young discipline. Furthermore, he was a former member of the Edinburgh World Missionary Conference in 1910 and consequently committed to the international ecumenical movement." Wendebourg, "Dietrich Bonhoeffer und die Berliner Universität."
3. Bonhoeffer, *DBW*, vol. 10, pp. 57–58.
4. Ibid., pp. 53–55, 60.
5. Ibid., pp. 53–55.
6. Ibid., p. 53.
7. Ibid.
8. Ibid., p. 54.
9. Ibid., p. 59.
10. Ibid.
11. Green cited in ibid., p. 69.
12. Bonhoeffer, ibid., p. 59.
13. First citation is my translation from the German. The second citation can be found in ibid.
14. Ibid., p. 66.
15. Ibid., p. 60.
16. Ibid., p. 67.
17. Ibid., p. 62.
18. Ibid., p. 82.
19. Ibid., p. 62.
20. Ibid., p. 70.
21. Ibid., pp. 70, 80.
22. Green, "Editor's Introduction to the English Edition," p. 4.

23. Bonhoeffer, *DBW*, vol. 10, p. 60.
24. Ibid., p. 69.
25. Green, "Editor's Introduction to the English Edition," pp. 4–5.
26. Bethge, *Dietrich Bonhoeffer: A Life in Pictures*, p. 47.
27. Bonhoeffer, *DBW*, vol. 10, p. 68.
28. Ibid., p. 174.
29. Ibid., p. 64.
30. Bosanquet, *The Life and Death of Dietrich Bonhoeffer*, p. 66.
31. Bonhoeffer, *DBW*, vol. 10, pp. 62–64.
32. Ibid., p. 61.
33. Ibid.
34. Ibid., p. 481.
35. Ibid.
36. Ibid., p. 483. Here in the restless heart, in the "great disturbance" and the "great disruption," emerges another path than guilt and shame, the path of God to human beings, the path of revelation and of grace, the path of Christ, the path of justification by grace alone.
37. Ibid., pp. 491–92.
38. Ibid., pp. 515–16.
39. Ibid., pp. 494–95.
40. Ibid., p. 501.
41. Ibid., p. 519.
42. Ibid., pp. 519–20.
43. Ibid., pp. 174–75.
44. Bethge, *Dietrich Bonhoeffer: A Life in Pictures*, p. 47.
45. Bonhoeffer, *DBW*, vol. 10, pp. 53–94.
46. Ibid.
47. Ibid., p. 174.
48. Ibid., pp. 174–75.
49. Ibid., p. 54.
50. Ibid., pp. 485–87.
51. Ibid., pp. 485–90.
52. Ibid., p. 83.
53. Dietrich wrote to his parents, "Now we are planning our trip to the south, and Klaus shocked me by telling me he was to withdraw money for the trip and for his stay here in Spain using a letter of credit. Briefly put, this is how things stand. I had 1000 pesetas here = 720 marks. From that, I withdrew 400 pesetas; 120 pesetas of that went for the athletic outfit (which is, however, quite respectable and is considered such a bargain that someone else is having one made as well), ca. 80 pesetas for our Montserrat outing (i.e., 15 marks each day, including travel), also tennis club, racket, socks over 100 pesetas, then I have to pay all sorts of dues, buy all sorts of things like ties, so that over time the 400 pesetas have simply run out, even though on a daily basis I get along on my salary. So there are still 600 pesetas here, i.e., 450 marks. The trip south and back

is 3,000 km and costs ca. 225 marks each. If we were to travel third class the whole way, we could save 75 marks, but we would be spending a great deal of time on the frightfully slow railways, would often have to travel for considerable hours at night, etc. Daily expenses will probably be an average of 10 marks, eighteen days = 180 marks, so that the whole thing will cost a bit over 400 marks for each of us. Was that approximately what you imagined, or not? Please write soon concerning this so that we can make arrangements. Klaus still has 500 marks here, so that we can go ahead and depart if that's all right with you, although it would be better if you could raise the limit on the letter of credit (which at the moment would be very advantageous given the low status of the peseta). . . . It would be very good if you write soon, considering all the preparations we can begin making only then." Ibid., p. 84.

54. Ibid., p. 98. Referenced in *DBW* as Tarragona.

55. Ibid., p. 94.

56. Ibid., p. 93. A "baldachin" is defined by Clifford Green in the notes as "[a] canopy, often richly embroidered, carried above the dignitary."

57. Ibid.

58. Ibid., pp. 95, 91.

59. Ibid., p. 122.

60. Green, "Editor's Introduction to the English Edition," p. 1.

61. Bonhoeffer, *DBW*, vol. 10, p. 61.

62. Ibid., p. 63. Bonhoeffer wrote, "During the afternoon I had no desire to work and so went to the movies with Mr. Thumm: *Don Quixote* was being shown. Because I had never read the novel, I couldn't really get a good overview of the content, so the film probably had some errors. Besides, like all Spanish films, endlessly long. The cinema is the cheapest form of entertainment here. For one peseta at the most, one is entertained for four consecutive hours. Two or three, often even four films are shown one after the other; the first are generally incredibly dumb and boring. Nonetheless this film did bring the problem of Don Quixote to my attention, and I will probably soon pick up the novel itself."

63. He returned to Don Quixote in his *Ethics* (*DBW*, vol. 6, pp. 51, 80) and in his prison writings (*DBW*, vol. 8, p. 42, 176, 303).

64. Bonhoeffer, *DBW*, vol. 10, p. 103.

65. Ibid., p. 112.

66. Ibid., p. 87.

67. Ibid.

68. Bonhoeffer already detected a hint of world suspicion and Christian triumphalism in Barth, without having yet met him, and for reasons that will become clearer over time, Bonhoeffer was truly bothered by it.

69. Ibid., p. 75.

70. Ibid., p. 106.

71. Ibid., pp. 98–99, 106.

72. Ibid., p. 99.

73. Ibid.
74. Ibid., p. 118; Clifford Green notes, "Probably St. Christopher, whose feast day was actually July 25." St. Christopher is the patron saint of travelers, and, as Bonhoeffer's report illustrates, he had been adopted in modern times by motorists in particular.
75. Bonhoeffer, ibid., p. 77.
76. Ibid., p. 84.
77. Ibid., p. 74.
78. Adolescent boredom: "As far as going swimming is concerned, things are rather awkward insofar as you have to walk a half-hour through the hot city, which is not particularly attractive and is also extremely boring if you are by yourself. But I have a bathtub with a shower head, in which I will spend most of the day." Ibid., pp. 102–3.
79. Ibid., p. 82.
80. Ibid., p. 110.
81. Ibid., pp. 165–66. He asked his sister to send him a copy of Paul Tillich— "Right away!!"—and to his Barcelona address, of course; he wanted to read Tillich in preparation of a fourth lecture, but it appears Bonhoeffer never gave a fourth lecture. Clifford Green cited in ibid., p. 157.
82. Ibid., p. 363.
83. He said, "Acting according to principles is unproductive and merely reflects or copies the law. Acting in freedom is creative. Christians draw the forms of their ethical activity out of eternity itself, as it were, put these forms with sovereignty in the world, as deed, as their own creations born of the freedom of God's children." Indeed, Nietzsche's Overman is not, as he imagined, the opposite of the Christian; without realizing it, Nietzsche imbued the Overman with many of the features of the free Christian as described and conceived by both Paul and Luther. Bonhoeffer states, "Traditional morals . . . can never provide the standards for the action of Christians." Ibid., pp. 366–67.
84. Ibid., p. 367.
85. Ibid., pp. 370–71.
86. Ibid., p. 156.
87. Ibid.
88. Ibid., p. 167.
89. Ibid., pp. 170–71.

CHAPTER FIVE "Covered in the Moss of Tradition"

1. Bonhoeffer correspondence with Detlef Albers, in Bonhoeffer, *DBW*, vol. 10, p. 177.
2. Ibid., p. 189.
3. Ibid., pp. 182–83.
4. Ibid., pp. 177–78.

5. Ibid., p. 178.

6. Bonhoeffer wrote to Harnack, "It is no accident that during recent weeks my thoughts have repeatedly been drawn to you and to your seminar as if by a magnet, since it is once again the anniversary of those early days in July, when for years you would take your seminar in the afternoon to Grunewald to give us a few hours, times that are surely as vivid for many others, as for me, as if they were only yesterday. And while during the course of the semester's work I had the chance to express modestly the gratitude I always feel toward you in an inconspicuous fashion through the actual attempts at collaboration, and because on several occasions over the past few years I was able to take the floor in the name of the seminar and speak to you openly about those unexpressed things that were on our hearts—words that were always as difficult for me—for who can find the right words for such things?—as I would like to have spoken them from my heart—for what is more beautiful than being permitted to speak without reserve about that which moves us? So, too, this year, when I am so distant from all that, such hours of gratitude often come upon me precisely at this time, and such hours should not be left unused. Here amid all my purely practical work, where as a scholar I am completely dependent on myself and my books, where I must live without any exchange of ideas in this regard, I think back to those hours in your house and to those afternoons in Grunewald with a certain sense of longing and melancholy, and often wish I could sit again for but a single hour in your seminar circle or have a conversation with you of the unforgettable kind that I remember from seminar celebrations, outings, and various other occasions. Only here have I come to realize completely what I had and what I have lost, both in a scholarly and in a human sense. But this realization is accompanied by the hope that it will not be much more than six months now, and I will have all that again, and today I am already looking forward to it. That said, the time I am spending here as an academic hermit, absorbed in so many new impressions from the practical side of life, does seem to have the potential to be quite fruitful in its own way. One gains distance from so many things with which one had become a bit obsessive, one acquires a measure of freedom from didactic doctrines and also learns to recognize much more precisely the limits of the value of pure scholarship; and in turn all that provides the point of departure from which one reexamines everything one has worked on. Hence I believe that my time here—precisely this time spent outside Germany—has a significance that I should make the most of. I am glad to be here but will also be glad to return home, for scholarship never releases those it has seized. I have very few others to thank besides you for the fact that it has seized me . . . that I remember from seminar celebrations, outings, and various other occasions." Ibid., p. 115.

7. Ibid.

8. Ibid., p. 179.

9. Leibholz-Bonhoeffer, *The Bonhoeffers*, p. 9.
10. Bonhoeffer, *DBW*, vol. 10, p. 190.
11. Ibid., p. 186.
12. Ibid., p. 205.
13. Reinhold Seeberg in ibid., p. 145.
14. Bonhoeffer, ibid., p. 103, emphasis mine. The birthday present—as attested by Bonhoeffer's letter to Susanne Bonhoeffer on June 20, 1928—was a piece of "Toledo handwork," a particular kind of embroidery (à jour or openwork pattern).
15. Ibid., p. 191.
16. Bonhoeffer, *DBW*, vol. 2, pp. 157–61.
17. Bonhoeffer, *DBW*, vol. 10, p. 209.
18. Ibid.
19. Ibid., p. 213. The report states, "Likewise, the comment in the curriculum vitae, that the author has followed the progress of dialectical theology with an active interest, is confirmed by this work. Its course is in a constant argument with dialectical theology, and the familiar concepts of this theology are recurring and to some extent adopted. In this respect, the dissertation is a very characteristic document of the interest that the younger generation of theologians takes in dialectical theology. Yet one cannot speak of a dependence here either, for occasionally there is also a very energetic objection to Barth (e.g., 94, 130, 132, 171). But one cannot fail to recognize the sympathy with Barth's religious standpoint, most especially with the eschatological standpoint, when, e.g., faith is described as determination by the future (178). Kohlbrugge is cited with absolute agreement (150, 153, 164). It cannot be denied that the author is a student of Reinhold Seeberg. Epistemologically he is explicitly tied to him (33, 38). Otherwise, too, the point of departure that the author has taken from Seeberg is expressed explicitly (97ff., 115, 1). But even here, the author intends to proceed beyond Seeberg's position" (pp. 210–11).
20. Wilhelm Lütgert to Adolf Grimme in ibid., pp. 215–16.
21. Ibid., p. 216. In fact, according to Clifford Green, "Bonhoeffer occupied the position of assistant from May 1 to July 31, 1929, for which he was paid 900.00 marks." Green cited in ibid.
22. "Bonhoeffer's talent for finding people to do things for him proved useful," Bethge said. Bethge, *Dietrich Bonhoeffer: A Biography*, p. 129.
23. Wilhelm Lütgert to Adolf Grimme in Bonhoeffer, *DBW*, vol. 10, p. 216.
24. Bonhoeffer, ibid., p. 206.
25. Ibid., p. 229.
26. Ibid., pp. 229–30.
27. Rahner, *Encyclopedia of Theology*, p. 173.
28. Bonhoeffer, *DBW*, vol. 10, pp. 558–71.
29. Ibid., pp. 558, 229.
30. Ibid., pp. 229–30.
31. Ibid., p. 233.

32. Ibid., pp. 230–31.
33. Ibid., p. 230.
34. Ibid., pp. 574–75.
35. Ibid.
36. Ibid., pp. 226–27.
37. Ibid., pp. 227–28.
38. Green, "Editor's Introduction to the English Edition," pp. 14–15.
39. For the trial lecture Bonhoeffer proposed the topics: (1) The significance of the sociological category for theology; (2) the possibility of a dogmatic system; and (3) the concept of dialectic in dialectical theology. He had covered the first topic over several hundred pages in "Sanctorum Communio." The second he had explored in "Act and Being," only to conclude that a dogmatic system drained the vitality out of Christian faith and practice (as any claim to systematic knowledge in the humanities tended to quash spontaneity and verve). The faculty picked the third topic, the "concept of dialectic in the so-called dialectical theology." Or, more simply stated, the theology of Karl Barth. The manuscript of the trial lecture has not been preserved, though it very likely resembled the same talk he gave several months later titled "Theology of Crisis," in which he outlined in fairly prosaic fashion the basic themes in Barth's theology. The fall lecture is intriguing in only one respect: Bonhoeffer put aside the criticisms of dialectical theology he had made in the second dissertation and spoke without reservation as an apologist for Barth to a skeptical audience. But it did appear that Bonhoeffer's attention had moved to other concerns. See ibid.
40. Bonhoeffer, *DBW*, vol. 10, p. 224.
41. Ibid., pp. 389–408.
42. Ibid., p. 408.
43. "Veni creator spiritus": found in Zahn-Harnack, *Adolf von Harnack*, p. 442.
44. A young man from Bonhoeffer's Barcelona youth group, the troubled Karl-Heinz Köttgen, had also joined the family for the holiday at Friedrichsbrunn.
45. Bonhoeffer, *DBW*, vol. 10, p. 238.
46. Ibid. See also note 2.
47. Ibid., p. 240.
48. Ibid., p. 385.
49. Ibid., p. 261.

CHAPTER SIX "I Heard the Gospel Preached in the Negro Churches"

1. Bonhoeffer, *DBW*, vol. 10, pp. 241–42. In note 5 on page 242 editor Clifford Green writes, "Bonhoeffer uses the German cognate 'Prolet,' short

for 'proletarian'; in addition to its class connotation, it can also mean 'lout' or 'clod.'"

2. Bonhoeffer, ibid., p. 242.

3. Eric Metaxas. *Bonhoeffer: Pastor, Martyr, Spy* (Nashville: Thomas Nelson, 2010), p. 97.

4. Bethge, *Dietrich Bonhoeffer: A Biography*, p. 147.

5. Bonhoeffer, *DBW*, vol. 10, p. 242.

6. Ibid., p. 243.

7. "Though occasionally Black students had attended the seminary since the mid-nineteenth century, the number significantly increased during Coffin's presidency. In the years 1926–33, for example, those who came to [Union] . . . included William H. King, Leroy J. Montgomery, J. Neal Hughley, Shelby A. Rooks, William E. Carrington, Claude L. Franklin, Colbert H. Pearson, M. Moran Weston, Charles E. Byrd, Porter W. Phillips, and Seth C. Edwards." Still, despite the new social mix of the student body, the majority of seminarians at Union remained northeastern white males. Although the number of women graduating from the seminary would increase in the Coffin years—in part because of the founding of the School of Sacred Music—Coffin was not particularly keen on the notion of a woman studying theology. As Robert Handy notes in his history of Union, a number (most) of the denominations served by the seminary did not permit the ordination of women. "When Doris Webster Havice—who entered the seminary the same year Niebuhr joined the faculty—asked Coffin for permission to complete her last year abroad (at New College, Edinburgh), Coffin responded gruffly, 'I will do everything in my power to get rid of you,' adding that the presence of women was 'hazardous' to the wellbeing of the school. Havice later earned a doctorate at Columbia University." Handy, *A History of Union Theological Seminary in New York*, p. 178.

8. Cited in ibid., pp. 161–62; see also Smylie, "Pastor, Educator, Ecumenist."

9. Green, "Editor's Introduction to the English Edition," p. 21.

10. Bonhoeffer, *DBW*, vol. 10, p. 310.

11. Ibid.

12. Ibid., pp. 293–94.

13. Ibid., pp. 310–11.

14. Ibid., p. 265.

15. Ibid., p. 294.

16. Ibid., p. 309.

17. From Franz Hildebrandt, in ibid., pp. 247–48.

18. Ibid., p. 246.

19. Ibid., p. 266.

20. Ibid., pp. 266, 309–10.

21. Ibid., pp. 309–10. Alexis de Tocqueville states, "The Americans, hav-

ing admitted the principal doctrines of the Christian religion without inquiry, are obliged to accept in like manner a great number of moral truths originating in it and connected with it." *Democracy in America*, p. 5. There is no indication that Bonhoeffer had read Tocqueville's landmark study.

22. Cited in Green, "Editor's Introduction to the English Edition," p. 17.

23. Larry Rasmussen, ed., *Reinhold Niebuhr: Theologian of Public Life* (Minneapolis: Fortress Press, 1991), p. 1.

24. These are Larry Rasmussen's words.

25. *Radical Religion*, 4 (Spring 1937), pp. 2–3.

26. Green, "Editor's Introduction to the English Edition," p. 23, note 115.

27. Bonhoeffer, *DBW*, vol. 10, p. 451, and Niebuhr cited by Clifford Green in ibid., note 13. Bonhoeffer, like Martin Luther King later, would say to Niebuhr that his conception of love was too transcendent. See Charles Marsh, *The Beloved Community: How Faith Shapes Social Justice, from the Civil Rights Movement to Today* (New York: Basic Books, 2005), pp. 40–41.

28. Bonhoeffer's course paper, "The Religious Experience of Grace and the Ethical Life," in Bonhoeffer, *DBW*, vol. 10, pp. 445–51. Bonhoeffer wrote on August 7, 1928, to his friend Helmut Rößler of the contrast between his former academic life as a student and his current life as the pastor of the German-speaking congregation: in the latter, "work and life genuinely converge, a synthesis that we all probably sought but hardly found in our student days—when one really lives one life rather than two, or better: half a life; it lends dignity to the work and objectivity to the worker, and a recognition of one's own limitations [*Grenzen*] of the sort acquired only within concrete life" (pp. 126–28). After returning to Berlin, Bonhoeffer wrote in a correspondence with Detlef Albers, the teacher of history and geography at the German Protestant school in Barcelona, "Perhaps today . . . 'spirit' [*Geist*] really is to be found in the particular, that is, precisely in the 'material,' in concretely given reality—and precisely not in 'intellectuality' [*Geistigkeit*]" (pp. 182–83).

29. Horton and Freire, *We Make the Road by Walking*, p. 43.

30. Horton, Kohl, and Kohl, *The Long Haul*, p. 35.

31. The historian Gary Dorrien refers to the tone of the book as "icy, aggressive and eerily omniscient." *Soul in Society*, p. 91.

32. Secular liberals appealed to reason and nature while Christian liberals appealed to love in their mutual struggles for justice; nevertheless, both, argued Niebuhr, were inadequate responses. The secular liberal appeal to reason and nature fails to grasp human sinfulness and the wide-reaching consequences of the Fall, especially its corruption of knowledge, while the Christian liberal appeal to love fails to grasp human sinfulness as its corruption of society and politics.

33. Rasmussen, "Introduction: A Public Theologian," pp. 2–3.

34. See http://www.religion-online.org/showchapter.asp?title=3279&C=2735 (accessed February 14, 2013).

35. Fox, *Reinhold Niebuhr*, pp. 128, 283.
36. His mention of Niebuhr in his progress report of the year is hardly a rousing endorsement: "Reinhold Niebuhr, one of the most significant and creative contemporary theologians in America, whose primary works one must know, if one is to have an overview of the theological situation." Bonhoeffer cited in Green, "Editor's Introduction to the English Edition," p. 539; written after his return from New York at the end of July 1939.
37. Rasmussen, "Introduction: A Public Theologian," p. 1.
38. "An Account at the Turn of the Year 1942–1943: After Ten Years," in Bonhoeffer, *Letters and Papers from Prison*, ed. Eberhard Bethge, p. 52.
39. Bonhoeffer, *DBW*, vol. 8, p. 24.
40. Ursula Niebuhr did not at all share her husband's affection for Bonhoeffer. She found him rather pretentious. What may have struck some of his fellow Union students as native confidence appeared to her as the arrogance of a pampered intellectual. "He was so much more densely and seriously educated than the other students," she said, and he carried "that knowledge proudly." Sifton, *The Serenity Prayer*, p. 136. It is not clear whether the Niebuhrs understood the extent to which Bonhoeffer's experiences in America changed his understanding of the theological vocation. Their daughter later described a Bonhoeffer who regarded as quaint his fellow students' involvement in progressive social ministries. Even by the year's end, he had not learned "that to put one's faith to the test of lived experience is to put one's life on the line" (p. 140). While the truth is that Bonhoeffer worried that the American seminarians' zealous participation in the social justice was poorly served by theologians whose articulations of the Christian faith were thinly veiled versions of American pragmatic philosophy. The American theologian Stanley Hauerwas would argue in his 2001 Gifford Lectures that Reinhold Niebuhr's Yale Divinity School thesis on William James, titled "The Validity and Certainty of Religious Knowledge," offers insight into not only James's pragmatic critique of religion but also Niebuhr's own Jamesian premises: the truth of Christian revelation, scripture, and tradition is the ability to generate myths that regulate and order religious and moral life. See Stanley Hauerwas, *With the Grain of the Universe: The Church's Witness and Natural Theology: Being the Gifford Lectures Delivered at the University of St. Andrews in 2001* (Grand Rapids, MI: Brazos Press, 2001).
41. Jean Lasserre cited in Kelly, "An Interview with Jean Lasserre."
42. Schlingensiepen, *Dietrich Bonhoeffer*, p. 67.
43. Nelson, "Friends He Met in America," p. 37. After 1931, the two unlikely friends met only twice. They exchanged letters throughout the 1930s and until Bonhoeffer's imprisonment in 1943. Unfortunately, Lasserre burned all but two of Bonhoeffer's letters. "Lasserre was a member of the French resistance, and it was too dangerous to retain his friend's correspondence," Nelson explained.

44. Jean Lasserre cited in Kelly, "An Interview with Jean Lasserre." Lasserre continued, "It was then that I noticed the Americans were for the most part children and weren't really aware of the situation. They sympathized with the German soldiers against whom they had fought a few years before and they practically ridiculed the misfortunes of the French soldiers." The film was released in August 1930 and won an Academy Award in November for Outstanding Motion Picture; it was based on the book by Erich Maria Remarque, *Westen nichts Neues* (German, 1928; English, 1929), which was assigned for the first class of the second-semester course "Ethical Viewpoints in Modern Literature" on the subject "War Literature." See Bonhoeffer, *DBW*, vol. 10, pp. 420–21.

45. Ibid., p. 261.

46. Ibid., pp. 312–13.

47. Ibid., p. 313.

48. Ibid., p. 266.

49. Green, "Editor's Introduction to the English Edition," pp. 23–24. Also see Bonhoeffer, *DBW*, vol. 10, pp. 316–17 and note 37 on 316.

50. Bonhoeffer, *DBW*, vol. 10, p. 91.

51. Ibid., pp. 316–17.

52. Green, "Editor's Introduction to the English Edition," p. 24.

53. Bonhoeffer, *DBW*, vol. 10, p. 261.

54. Ibid., p. 260.

55. Ibid., p. 265.

56. Ibid., pp. 268–69.

57. Ibid., p. 268.

58. Ibid., p. 269.

59. He preached two sermons in Havana, both on the same Sunday.

60. Bonhoeffer, *DBW*, vol. 10, p. 631.

61. Bonhoeffer, *DBW*, vol. 10, pp. 257–58. The Home Missions Council focused on all those missionary activities falling outside normal congregational life, especially social service work among Native Americans and migrant workers.

62. Ibid., p. 266.

63. Clifford Green notes that Bonhoeffer wrote those observations on January 2, 1931, to his brother Karl-Friedrich by hand on the stationery of "The Peninsular & Occidental Steamship Company—Havana—Port Tampa—Key West." That was the cruise ship he was traveling on in his return voyage to the United States after spending Christmas in Havana, Cuba. He found himself describing this "shameful impression" of white–black southern interaction in that letter while he was traveling through the South, in the middle of it. Green also indicates that Bonhoeffer was deeply disturbed by news of lynchings. In February of 1931, Bonhoeffer learned of a lynching that occurred on January 12, in Maryville, Missouri, when a black man was accused of rape, chained to a schoolhouse roof, and burned to death by a lynch mob. Two months later, in April of

1931, Bonhoeffer was again deeply disturbed by the story of the infamous Scottsboro case, in which "nine young black men were hastily convicted and condemned to death, after being accused," Bonhoeffer argued, "of raping a white girl of dubious reputation." He went on to describe it as another "terrible miscarriage of justice." Bonhoeffer, *DBW*, vol. 10, p. 269.

64. Locke had been the first African American Rhodes Scholar and a PhD graduate from Harvard, and was the chair of the philosophy department at Howard. Howard College had strong intellectual ties to Harlem. *The New Negro*, a book published in 1925 by philosophy professor Alain Locke, became the Bible of the Harlem Renaissance, inspiring students like Fisher to explore, affirm, and partake in this great flourishing of artistic and intellectual creativity/activity/life.

65. Bonhoeffer, *DBW*, vol. 10, p. 321.

66. See Reggie L. Williams, "Dietrich Bonhoeffer, the Harlem Renaissance, and the Black Christ," in *Bonhoeffer, Christ and Culture*, ed. Keith L. Johnson and Timothy L. Larsen (Downers Grove, IL: Intervarsity Press, 2012), pp. 59–73.

67. Bonhoeffer, *DBW*, vol. 10, p. 296.

68. Ibid., p. 293.

69. Bob Gore, *We've Come This Far: The Abyssinian Baptist Church, A Photographic Study* (New York: Steward, Tabori and Chang, 2001), p. 31.

70. Ibid.

71. Letter to Martin Rumscheidt, December 17, 1986, in the Bonhoeffer Collection, Union Theological Seminary. First published in the *Newsletter*, International Bonhoeffer Society, English Language Section, no. 39 (October 1988): 3–4.

72. In his short memoir: Clayton Powell Sr., *Upon This Rock* (New York: Abyssinian Baptist Church, 1949), p. 42.

73. Bonhoeffer, *DBW*, vol. 12, p. 356.

74. Zerner, "Dietrich Bonhoeffer's American Experiences," p. 269.

75. Paul Lehmann cited in von Hase, " 'Turning Away from the Phraseological to the Real,' " p. 597.

76. Green, "Editor's Introduction to the English Version," p. 141.

77. This information comes from Reggie L. Williams. His source was Dr. Valerie Fisher, one of Frank Fisher's daughters.

78. Clifford Green's achievement in his essay "Editor's Introduction to the English Edition" in *DBW*'s volume 10—and I would say the achievement of the recently published translation of volume 10 as a whole—is not only that of highlighting the important interconnections between progressive Christian organizing in America in the 1930s and Bonhoeffer's theological transformations. It is also his calling attention to "the thread" that links the New York experiences into a coherent life story. Evaluating Bonhoeffer's letters, sermons, essays, and lectures from the first American year, Green says that we must "discover and interpret"

422 | NOTES PAGES 119–122

statements from this period, as well as from the prison letters more than a decade later, in which Bonhoeffer "describes the significance of these years for his own sense of vocation and his theological development." In Tegel prison in 1944, as we saw at the beginning, Bonhoeffer recalled the first American visit as one of the three decisive and transformative influences in his life. "It was then that I turned from [the phraseological to the real]." The thread that weaves through Bonhoeffer's development in these years and over the coming decade, giving his life personal and spiritual coherence, is, as Clifford Green argues, precisely this journey from the "phraseological to the real."

79. Zerner, "Dietrich Bonhoeffer's American Experiences," p. 11.

80. Abernathy would later say that King tried to replace Fisher with his former Montgomery cohort "even before Dr. Fisher had been laid to rest." Abernathy said he was amazed at how quickly he would move to get me into an Atlanta pulpit when the opportunity seemed to present itself." Ralph Abernathy, *And the Walls Came Tumbling Down* (New York: Harper and Row, 1989), p. 195.

81. Thanks to Ralph Luker for this fascinating discovery. In correspondence with the author, Luker wrote, "Johns preached at Union on 'The Answer of Religion to the Riddle of Life.' I've got a footnote that runs to a page and a half about the tradition of 'riddle of life' preaching in 20th century American Protestantism. Nearly everyone you can think of—Fosdick, MLK, Sockman, etc., had a 'riddle' sermon. Because of peculiar details of attribution, I suspect that John Haynes Holmes heard Johns at UTS and got his own 'riddle' reference there. I would be surprised if Bonhoeffer didn't hear that Johns sermon. I've tried several times to no avail to find out from archivists at UTS whether there's a 1931 student newspaper or any documentation about the Johns sermon. If Bonhoeffer writes about 'Is the Universe Friendly?,' he's tapping into a lively discussion around Union and in American Protestant pulpits, black *and* white."

82. Weizsäcker, "Thoughts of a Nontheologian on Dietrich Bonhoeffer's Development," p. 270.

83. The philosopher Richard Rorty called this tradition "the reformist left" in his Harvard Massey Lectures, published in the superb volume *Achieving our Country: Leftist Thought in Twentieth-Century America.*

84. Dunbar, *Against the Grain,* p. 41.

85. For more on the intentional community movement in the United States, see Tracy Elaine K'Meyer, *Interracialism and Christian Community in the Postwar South: The Story of Koinonia Farm* (Charlottesville, VA: University Press of Virginia, 1997); Marguerite Guzman Bouvard, *The Intentional Community Movement: Building a Moral World* (Port Washington, NY: Kennikat Press, 1975); and Martin B. Duberman's excellent study, *Black Mountain: An Exploration in Community* (Garden City, NY: Anchor Press, 1973).

86. Duke, *In the Trenches with Jesus and Marx.* See Frank Adams, *James A.*

Dombrowski: An American Heretic, 1897–1983 (Knoxville, TN: University of Tennessee Press, 1992).

87. Bosanquet, *The Life and Death of Dietrich Bonhoeffer*, p. 84.

88. Bonhoeffer cited in ibid.

89. Bethge, *Dietrich Bonhoeffer: A Biography*, p. 162.

90. Ibid.

91. "Christian Socialism," *Time*, May 11, 1931. Union was not Bonhoeffer's first exposure to practical theology. In an article on the theology faculty at Berlin during Bonhoeffer's student years, Dorothea Wendebourg explains, "He not only attended Mahling's cyclical lectures, but also his course on homiletics, and twice the catechetical seminar." Mahling had served on Bonhoeffer's dissertation committee. "On the one hand, this corresponded to his church commitment that becomes obvious also to his interest in catechetics, his work with children's services and youth groups." Mahling was interested in the question of how modern industrial and urban life created new challenges for the church's mission and work. Still, Bonhoeffer had little interest in practical theology as a subdiscipline of theology, even though his intellectual interests inclined ever more toward the practical consequences of theological commitments.

92. Bonhoeffer cited in Duke, *In the Trenches with Jesus and Marx*, p. 142.

93. The first version of the Social Creed was adopted by the Federal Council of the Churches in Christ in America on December 4, 1908; the second version was adopted on December 9, 1912.

94. Handy, *A History of Union Theological Seminary*, p. 191.

95. Doug Rassinow, "The Radicalization of the Social Gospel: Harry F. Ward and the Search for a New Social Order, 1898–1936," *Religion and American Culture: A Journal of Interpretation* 15, no. 1 (winter 2005): 63–106.

96. Duke, *In the Trenches with Jesus and Marx*, p. 144.

97. Helmut Rößler cited in ibid., p. 283.

98. Guido Enderis, special cable to the *New York Times*, September 15, 1930: "Fascists Make Big Gains in Germany, Communists Also Increase Strength as Moderates Drop in Reich Election; Socialists Remain in Lead," http://select.nytimes.com/gst/abstract.html?res=F00811F83C55 147A93C7A81782D85F448385F9 (accessed October 10, 2013).

99. See Adams, *James A. Dombrowski*. His dissertation was published as *The Early Days of Christian Socialism in America* (New York: Columbia University Press, 1936).

100. Horton, Kohl, and Kohl, *The Long Haul*, p. 35.

101. Dale Jacobs in Dale Jacobs, ed., *The Myles Horton Reader: Education for Social Change* (Knoxville, TN: University of Tennessee Press, 2003), p. 33.

102. Duke, *In the Trenches with Jesus and Marx*, p. 142.

103. Bonhoeffer, *DBW*, vol. 10, p. 296.

104. Ibid., p. 293.

105. "U.S. Route 1," from Wikipedia: "One of the many changes made to the system before the final numbering was adopted in 1926 involved US 1 in Maine. The 1925 plan had assigned Route 1 to the shorter inland route (Route 15) between Houlton and Bangor, while Route 2 followed the longer coastal route via Calais. In the system as adopted in 1926, US 2 instead took the inland route, while US 1 followed the coast, absorbing all of the former Routes 24 and 1 in New England. Many local and regional relocations, often onto parallel superhighways, were made in the early days of US 1; this included the four-lane divided Route 25 in New Jersey, completed in 1932 with the opening of the Pulaski Skyway, and a bypass of Bangor involving the Waldo-Hancock Bridge, opened in 1931. The Overseas Highway from Miami to Key West was completed in 1938, and soon became a southern extension of US 1." See http://en.wikipedia.org/wiki/U.S._Route_1 (accessed October 10, 2013).
106. Bonhoeffer, *DBW*, vol. 10, p. 304.
107. Bosanquet, *The Life and Death of Dietrich Bonhoeffer*, p. 90.
108. Phrases comes from Lasserre, *War and the Gospel*, pp. 35ff.
109. Bonhoeffer, *DBW*, vol. 10, p. 269.
110. W.E.B. Du Bois was a major figure in what Bonhoeffer referred to as "the young Negro movement." Du Bois's lament resonates in Bonhoeffer's sober observations of the "racial question"/"Negro problem": "Why did God make me an outcast and a stranger in mine own house?" See Reggie L. Williams, "Christ-Centered Empathetic Resistance: The Influence of Harlem Renaissance Theology on the Incarnational Ethics of Dietrich Bonhoeffer," doctoral dissertation, Fuller Theological Seminary, 2012, p. 34.
111. Reggie L. Williams notes that "of the numerous works by Harlem Renaissance writers that Bonhoeffer read, and wrote about, this poem by Cullen is the only Harlem Renaissance literary work that Bonhoeffer directly referenced by name." Ibid.
112. Barth, *The Word of God and the Word of Man*, pp. 11–12.
113. Bonhoeffer, *DBW*, vol. 10, p. 305. In his probing scholarship on the American year, Hans Pfeifer has shown that "continuity and change" are not only meaningful criteria for understanding the relation between the early and late Bonhoeffer—a concern that scholars have emphasized over the past several decades—but are thematic structures in every phase of his life. In this manner, continuity and change present "a significant key to understanding his entire work." Full of unexpected surprises, Bonhoeffer's experiences in America were marked by recognizable patterns of thought and action—by desires, habits, and various intricacies of character—unique to his story. See Pfeifer, "Editor's Afterword to the German Edition," p. 578. Clifford Green notes that in 1938, Bonhoeffer mentioned to Paul Lehmann that he continued to stay in contact with Erwin Sutz, and that Jean Lasserre had married. "And what about Joe Moor, Franklin Fisher, Klein, Dombrowski," Bonhoeffer asked. See

Green, "Editor's Introduction to the English Edition," p. 33. See also Pfeifer, "Learning Faith and Ethical Commitment in the Context of Spiritual Training Groups," pp. 251–78.

114. In the late 1980s, a young historian named David Nelson Duke studied Bonhoeffer's year in New York. Professor Duke died of cancer in 1992 and the work remained unfinished. But in his two essays, along with his notes and chapter fragments, Duke gave ample evidence of his thesis that Bonhoeffer's year in America cultivated in him "a new kind of moral passion." See Duke, "The Experiment of an Ethic of Radical Justice."

115. Zerner, "Dietrich Bonhoeffer's American Experiences," pp. 261–82.

116. Bonhoeffer, *Letters and Papers from Prison*, ed. Eberhard Bethge, p. 358.

117. Bonhoeffer, *DBW*, vol. 16, pp. 367–68.

CHAPTER SEVEN "Under the Constraint of Grace"

1. Bonhoeffer, *No Rusty Swords*, p. 119.

2. Ibid.

3. Some disagreement exists on the title of the summer seminar; the "Introduction to Schleiermacher's *Glaubenslehre* (Doctrine of Faith)" has also been given as the subject.

4. Barth and Bultmann, *Karl Barth–Rudolf Bultmann Letters, 1922–1966*, p. 41.

5. Ibid., p. 40.

6. Ibid., p. 120.

7. Bonhoeffer, *No Rusty Swords*, p. 120.

8. Ibid., p. 122.

9. Ibid., p. 119.

10. Ibid., p. 121.

11. Bonhoeffer cited in Tödt, Tödt, Feil, and Green, "Editors' Afterword to the German Edition," p. 411.

12. Bonhoeffer, *DBW*, vol. 10, p. 451.

13. Bonhoeffer cited in Tödt, Tödt, Feil, and Green, "Editors' Afterword to the German Edition," p. 411, note 7.

14. Bonhoeffer, *DBW*, vol. 11, p. 40.

15. Ibid., p. 122.

16. Bonhoeffer cited in Bosanquet, *The Life and Death of Dietrich Bonhoeffer*, p. 98.

17. Bonhoeffer, *No Rusty Swords*, p. 139.

18. Scharffenorth, "Editor's Afterword to the German Edition," pp. 490–94.

19. Willem Adolf Visser 't Hooft, "Foreword," in J. Martin Bailey and Douglas Gilbert, *The Steps of Bonhoeffer: A Pictorial Album* (New York: Macmillan, 1969), pp. v–vi.

20. Bonhoeffer, *No Rusty Swords*, p. 136. Bonhoeffer sought to frame the language of peace in the context of the dynamic God-human encounter. In

contrast to the Anglo-Saxon view (represented at the World Alliance) that international peace was an ideal, an absolute, a "final order of perfection, valid in itself," an inevitable "part of the Kingdom of God on earth"—a view based on nineteenth-century doctrine of historical optimism— Bonhoeffer argued now that "the forgiveness of sins . . . remains the sole ground of all peace!" (pp. 168–69). Forgiveness of sins is therefore the "ultimate ground on which all ecumenical work rests" precisely because the "broken character of the order of peace" results from human rebellion against God.

21. Paul Althaus and Emanuel Hirsch cited in Rasmussen, "Editor's Introduction to the English Edition," p. 20, note 69; see also Bethge, *Dietrich Bonhoeffer: A Life in Pictures*, p. 54.

22. "The ecumenical sphere in contemporary usage includes cooperation between the two major Western churches, the Roman Catholic and the Protestant. The ecumenical movement of the 1930s was intra-Protestant: Roman Catholic doctrine regarded Protestantism as an [inauthentic?] representation." See Schlingensiepen, *Dietrich Bonhoeffer*, p. 81.

23. Bonhoeffer, *No Rusty Swords*, pp. 123–24.

24. Bethge, *Bonhoeffer*, p. 44.

25. The scholar Ernst-Albert Scharffenorth is correct to say that Hitler's appointment as chancellor of the Reich gives "this particular phase in Bonhoeffer's life its unique character." But Scharffenorth simplifies Bonhoeffer's situation in 1931–33 in saying that the political events "set into motion a dynamic in Bonhoeffer's own life that might allow us to characterize his life from this point onward as "sharing Germany's destiny." Scharffenorth, "Editor's Afterword to the German Edition," p. 483.

26. Klaus Bonhoeffer cited in Rasmussen, "Editor's Introduction to the English Edition," p. 4.

27. Rößler cited in Bonhoeffer, *No Rusty Swords*, 73.

28. See Bonhoeffer cited in Bethge, *Dietrich Bonhoeffer: A Biography*, p. 173.

29. Bonhoeffer, *DBW*, vol. 12, p. 69.

30. Ibid., pp. 118–20.

31. Bosanquet, *The Life and Death of Dietrich Bonhoeffer*, p. 101.

32. Dietrich Bonhoeffer to Erwin Sutz, in Bonhoeffer, *DBW*, vol. 12, p. 102. In a letter to Paul Lehmann six months earlier, Bonhoeffer commented on the state of affairs in the universities: "A prelude to what can be expected from the National Socialists at the university is taking place right now in Halle, where the students (and not only the theology students) refuse to continue studying if a recently called pacifist professor of theology, who is an extraordinarily capable man, is not fired immediately [a reference to Dehn]. The intellectual level now entering the universities is simply dreadful." Letter of November 5, 1931, to Paul Lehmann, in Bonhoeffer, *DBW*, vol. 11, p. 116a.

33. Bonhoeffer, *No Rusty Swords*, p. 123.

34. Green, "Editor's Introduction to the English Edition," p. 36.

35. Bonhoeffer, *No Rusty Swords*, pp. 123–24.
36. Wendebourg, "Dietrich Bonhoeffer und die Berliner Universität."
37. Found in "13. Sermon on John 8:32. Berlin, Ninth Sunday after Trinity (Worship Service at the end of the Semester), July 24, 1932," in Bonhoeffer, *DBW*, vol. , 11, p. 471.
38. Bonhoeffer, *No Rusty Swords*; Ibid., p. 140.
39. Ibid., pp. 125–32.
40. Found in "5. Sermon on Matthew 24:6-14, Berlin, Reminiscere (Memorial Day), February 21, 1932," in Bonhoeffer, *DBW*, vol. 11, p. 426.
41. Found in "Devotions on John 8:31-32. Berlin, Technical College, Beginning of Summer Semester 1932," in ibid., pp. 433–34.
42. Bethge, *Dietrich Bonhoeffer: A Biography*, p. 204.
43. Bonhoeffer, *No Rusty Swords*, p. 140.
44. Ibid., p. 150.
45. Ibid., p. 151.
46. Ibid., p. 140.
47. Ibid., p. 37.
48. Ibid., p. 151.
49. During his three months in Wedding, Bonhoeffer received a copy of Karl Barth's new book, *Fides Quaerens Intellectum (Faith Seeking Understanding)*. In this slim but explosive volume, Barth plumbed Saint Anselm's well-traveled ontological argument for the existence of God and reached new insights on the naming of God as "that than which nothing greater can be conceived." Barth argued that the argument depended on a prayer; according to some scholars of his thought, the book lay the methodological foundations for the Church Dogmatics. *Fides Quaerens Intellectum* further signaled Barth's robust commitment to academic theology at precisely the time Bonhoeffer had begun gravitating toward practical ministry—although Bonhoeffer found Barth's book a splendid read.
50. Bonhoeffer, *DBW*, vol. 12, p. 76.
51. This phrasing comes from Inge Scholl's memoir, *The White Rose*.
52. Bethge, *Dietrich Bonhoeffer: A Biography*, pp. 203–6.
53. Zimmermann, "Years in Berlin," pp. 58–59.
54. Ibid., p. 61.
55. Ibid., pp. 61–62.
56. Ibid., p. 61.
57. Ibid.
58. Ibid., pp. 61–62.
59. Ibid., p. 62.
60. Ibid.
61. Bethge, *Dietrich Bonhoeffer: A Biography*, p. 207.
62. Zimmermann, "Years in Berlin," p. 62.
63. Ibid.
64. Ibid.
65. Busing, "Reminiscences of Finkenwalde," p. 1108.

66. Bethge, *Dietrich Bonhoeffer: A Life in Pictures*, p. 53.
67. Although he kept the apartment in Berlin, he lived in the town of Güstow/Inselsee.
68. Barlach remained, in any case, an expressionist whose primary language was "the human figure" and the objects "through which and in which he lives, suffers, rejoices, feels, thinks." He once complained that he could feel no compassion in Kandinsky's "dots, specks, lines and smudges." Werner, "When Artists Protest," p. 627.
69. Bonhoeffer, *Christ the Center*, p. 1004.
70. Zimmermann, "Years in Berlin," p. 67.
71. De Gruchy, "Editor's Introduction to the English Edition," *DBW*, vol. 3, p. 1.
72. Bonhoeffer, *DBW*, vol. 3, p. 30.
73. Ibid., pp. 30–31.
74. Ibid., p. 81.
75. De Gruchy, "Editor's Introduction to the English Edition," in ibid., p. 3.
76. Bonhoeffer cited in Bethge, *Dietrich Bonhoeffer: A Biography*, p. 173.
77. Bonhoeffer cited in Schlingensiepen, *Dietrich Bonhoeffer*, p. 93.
78. Bonhoeffer, *DBW*, vol. 13, p. 217.

CHAPTER EIGHT Theological Storm Troopers On the March

1. Bonhoeffer to Erwin Sutz, October 8, 1931, cited in Bonhoeffer, *No Rusty Swords*, p. 124.
2. Vladimir Nabokov, cited in Otto Friedrich, *Before the Deluge: Portrait of Berlin in the 1920's* (New York: Harper Collins, 1995), while living in Berlin had spoken of the "hopeless, godless vacancy of satisfied faces." p. 90.
3. The description comes from Thomas Merton, *Raids on the Unspeakable* (New York: New Directions Publishing, 1966), p. 67.
4. Also known as the Faith Movement, not to be confused with the German Faith Movement. Regarding Luther's influence on the German Christians, Doris Bergen writes, "Heroes of German history proved more amenable to manly revision than biblical figures. For many German Christians Martin Luther exemplified the fusion of manliness, Christianity, and Germanness. Although he was not a soldier, Luther's rejection of monasticism and celibacy gave him solid potential as a paragon of manliness. In a publication of the German Christian Women's Service in 1937, a leading German Christian described Luther's marriage as a 'defiant declaration of war on a totally mistaken kind of piety.' Luther, that author maintained, demonstrated no sultry sensuality,' only 'healthy, straightforward, strong masculinity.' Another German Christian blamed the emasculation of the church in Germany on neglect of Luther. He described the 'effeminacy' that had invaded the church through 'sentimental' sermons, 'religious kitsch,' the 'overly sweet picture of Jesus

that the Nazarenes and others have produced,' and a 'pious English sing-song' form of church music. Since the German Enlightenment, he argued, appreciation of Luther had declined and, in his view, that was why the church had 'lost so many men.'" Bergen, *The Twisted Cross*, p. 75.

5. The scholar and theologian Keith Clements writes, "The German Church Struggle was very much shaped by the historical complexities of the German church scene. Since the Reformation, Protestantism in Germany had comprised many wholly autonomous regional churches [the *Landeskirchen*]. Such churches had been formed on the principle of *cuius regio, eius religio*, that is, the religion of a population within a given region was determined by the ruler of government of that territory. Of the twenty-eight regional churches that existed in 1933, twenty were Lutheran in confession, two Reformed and the remaining six were United—among them the Old Prussian Union Church, established in 1817, which was by far the largest and included eight provincial churches. While some forms of cooperation among them had been devised, one could speak only very loosely of the 'German Evangelical Church' as an umbrella terms for these churches collectively." Bonhoeffer, *DBW*, vol. 13, p. 4.

6. Scharffennorth notes this notation on the lecture: "Lic. Dr. Bonhoeffer (Dietrich) Rund[funk-] Vortrag Funk-St[un]de am 1.2. [1933 um] 17.45 Uhr" ([Dr. Bonhoeffer [(Dietrich]) Radio Lecture *Funkstunde* on February 1, 1933, at 5:45 p.m.),] in *DBW*, vol. 12, p. 268.

7. These scripts were titled "The Führer and the Individual in the Younger Generation."

8. Stern, *Dreams and Delusions*, p. 144.

9. Bonhoeffer cited in ibid., p. 144.

10. Almost immediately after Hitler became chancellor on January 30, 1933, Bonhoeffer began to send messages abroad about the German situation. Victoria Barnett, "The Rise and Fall of the Confessing Church," Lecture, University of Virginia, February 9, 2009.

11. Intended originally to hold communists, trade unionists, and political dissidents, the medieval town twenty kilometers northeast of Munich would become a symbol of the horrific actions carried out against Jews within the camp's walls, and more generally for the existence of radical evil.

12. 1940, Oxford; 1947, returned to Göttingen; 1951–71, judge in the federal constitutional court, Karlsruhe.

13. Scharffennorth in Bonhoeffer, *DBW*, vol. 12, pp. 506–8.

14. Bonhoeffer to Reinhold Niebuhr in Bonhoeffer, *DBW*, vol. 12, p. 94.

15. In fact, the Reich conference of the German Christians in Berlin, a week before the Reichstag passed the Aryan paragraph, had issued a demand for the "synchronization of church and state."

16. "Leaders in the existing church administration countered with a proposal to draft a new constitution and organize a single Evangelical Church in

place of the twenty-eight independent regional churches." Bonhoeffer, *DBW*, vol. 12, pp. 100–1.

17. Ericksen, *Theologians Under Hitler*, p. 47.
18. Ibid.
19. Bonhoeffer, *DBW*, vol. 12, p. 264.
20. Zimmermann, "Years in Berlin," p. 63.
21. Bonhoeffer, *DBW*, vol. 12, pp. 373–74. No transcript of Bonhoeffer's words at this public exchange exists. Quotations come from writings of spring 1933.
22. Scholder, *Churches and the Third Reich*, vol. 1, pp. 446–47.
23. Ibid.
24. Keith Clements, "Forward," in Bonhoeffer, *DBW*, vol. 13, p. 3ff. Gertrud Staewen's recently discovered correspondence reveals the "story of her important connections with Bonhoeffer from the early 1930s, including opening his mind to the importance of urban youth work, then risking her life in the process of hiding Berlin Jews and helping others escape deportation."
25. Shelley Baranowski, "Church History: The 1933 German Protestant Church Elections: Machtpolitik or Accommodation?," *Church History* 49 (1980): 304.
26. Bonhoeffer, *DBW*, vol. 12, p. 101.
27. Glenn Stassen, conversation with author.
28. Regarding the number of Jewish Christians in the Reich, the historian Aleksandar-Sasa Vuletic estimates that in 1933 there were 350,000 non-Aryan Christians in Nazi Germany. These were Christians classified by the Nazis as either full Jewish, half Jewish, or quarter Jewish, thus non-Aryan; many of these—although the exact number is not known—were children and grandchildren of marriages between Christians and Jews who had been baptized. Vuletic, *Christen judischer Herkunft im Dritten Reich: Verfolgung und organisierte Selbsthilfe 1933–1939*, Veröffentlichungen des Instituts für Europäische Geschichte, Abteilung Universalgeschichte, no. 169 (Mainz: Philipp von Zabern, 1999), pp. x, 368.
29. See Stern, *Dreams and Delusions*, p. 186.
30. Bethge, *Dietrich Bonhoeffer: A Biography*, pp. 275–76.
31. Bonhoeffer, *DBW*, vol. 13, p. 42.
32. Robert McAfee Brown, "1984: Orwell and Barmen." Robert McAfee Brown, whose name is symbolic for engaged theologian and ethicist, is perhaps best known for being able to write clearly—in, for example, in *Theology in a New Key: Responding to Liberation Theology* and *Saying Yes and Saying No: On Rendering to God and Caesar*. His "1984: Orwell and Barmen" article is adapted from a *Christian Century* lecture delivered in Seattle in April 1984. This article appeared in the *Christian Century*, August 15–22, 1984, p. 770. Copyright by the Christian Century Foundation and used by permission.
33. "One important phrase is drawn verbatim from Karl Barth's *Theologische*

Existenz Heute (June 1933, p. 52) as well as Barth's conclusion: "If the German Evangelical Church excludes Jewish Christians or treats them as second-class Christians, it ceases to be a Christian church."

34. "A Christian Church cannot exclude from its communion a member on whom the sacrament of baptism has been bestowed, without degrading baptism to a purely formal rite to which the Christian communion that administers it is indifferent. It is precisely in baptism that God calls man into this concrete Church and into its communion." Bonhoeffer, *DBW*, vol. 12, p. 372.

35. As in "The Church and the Jewish Question," this second statement, "The Jewish Christian Question as Status Confessionis," while affirming the responsibility of the church, was to help all victims of the Nazi repression, the call to a *status confessionis* pertained only to the church's adoption of the Aryan paragraph. Nowhere does he say that this "state of confession"—an intense and public solidarity with the church's indispensible convictions—also bears on the state's treatment of non-Christian Jews.

36. Rasmussen, "Editor's Introduction to the English Version," *DBW*, vol. 12, p. 30.

37. Ibid.

38. Jack Forstman, *Christian Faith in Dark Times: Theological Conflicts in the Shadow of Hitler* (Louisville, KY: Westminster/John Knox, 1992), p. 12.

39. See Rasmussen, "Editor's Introduction to the English Version." A principle enforced by the bishop of Berlin/German Evangelical Church. See also Gerlach, *And the Witnesses Were Silent*, pp. 36–38, 77–78.

40. Victoria J. Barnett, "Dietrich Bonhoeffer's Ecumenical Vision," *Christian Century*, April 26, 1995, pp. 454–57.

41. My discussion of Bonhoeffer and the Jews is indebted to the Ruth Zerner's excellent analysis, "Dietrich Bonhoeffer and the Jews." Jewish Social Studies. Summer/Fall75, Vol. 37 Issue 3/4, pp. 235-50.

42. "A shameful part of the record of many church leaders, even in the Confessing Church, was their support for allowing congregations to decide whether they could 'handle' a 'Jewish Christian' pastor." Rasmussen, "Editor's Introduction to the English Version," in *DBW*, vol. 12, p. 373.

43. Two early works that documented this were *Judaism and Christianity Under the Impact of National Socialism*, ed. Otto Dov Kulka and Paul Mendes-Flohr (Jerusalem: Historical Society of Israel and Zalman Shazar Center for Jewish History, 1987), and *The Grey Book: A Collection of Protests Against Anti-Semitism and the Persecution of Jews, Issued by Non-Roman Church Leaders During Hitler's Rule*, ed. Johan Snoek (New York: Humanities Press, 1970). Armin Boyens's two-volume work, *Kirchenkampf und Ökumene: Darstellung und Dokumentation* (Munich: Christian Kaiser Verlag, 1969 and 1973) also provides detailed historical background.

44. The lectures were later edited by Eberhard Bethge from student notes and published originally under the title *Christ the Center*.

45. The published lectures are based on the notes of students Gadow, Pfeiffer, Sperling, and Zimmermann, among which there is extensive agreement.

46. Leith, "Introduction," *Creeds of the Churches*, p. 1.

47. Larry Rasmussen continues: "It is not too much to say that Bonhoeffer's Christology was not only the theological ground for his critique of National Socialism; it was the basis for his efforts to find a way beyond the church crisis and beyond the church itself." "Editor's Introduction to the English Edition," in *DBW*, vol. 12, pp. 37–38.

48. Bonhoeffer, *DBW*, vol. 12, p. 359.

49. Cited in Davies, *Infected Christianity*, p. 43.

50. Bonhoeffer, *DBW*, vol. 12, p. 356.

51. Ibid., p. 314.

52. Available at http://www.nybooks.com/articles/archives/1988/jun/16/heidegger-and-the-nazis/?pagination=false (accessed February 17, 2013).

53. See Safranski, *Martin Heidegger*, p. 228.

54. Heidegger cited in ibid., p. 228. The image of the autumn suns comes from Heidegger's tribute to Albert Leo Schlageter, given on May 26, 1933.

55. Koonz, *The Nazi Conscience*, p. 55.

56. Martin Heidegger, "Declaration of Support for Adolf Hitler," November 11, 1933.

57. Bonhoeffer probably wrote at the request of his sister Christine and her husband, Hans von Dohnányi, who knew Landshut from Hamburg.

58. Correspondence with Victoria Barnett, March 3, 2014; *DBWE*, vol. 12, p. 589.

59. The line is from Heine's 1821 play, *Almansor*. The original reference is to the burning of the Quran during the Spanish Inquisition.

60. The few exceptions, besides Bonhoeffer, were the older professors who "openly disliked the brown regime, Deißmann above all, who saw the fruits of decades of ecumenical work vanish. But critical statements could be heard only in small circles. Others, especially the younger ones, offensively took the other side." Wendebourg, "Dietrich Bonhoeffer und die Berliner Universität."

61. Wendebourg writes that Seeberg had been "by far the most active, aggressive and most influential propaganda-maker in terms of publications of the total war" among the Protestant professors of theology during World War I, and contributed "with all his power to the destabilization" of the Weimar Republic. Ibid.

62. Ibid.

63. Bonhoeffer, *DBW*, vol. 12, p. 104. It shows more than a little naïveté that Bonhoeffer turned to Erich Seeberg for help in saving Tillich from dismissal. Bonhoeffer told Seeberg, "Even just my own gratitude for what I have learned from Tillich on many occasions gives me the courage to turn to you, and ask if you might initiate such a process among the faculty." Seeberg politely declined to intervene.

64. Rasmussen, "Introduction to the English Version," *DBW*, vol. 12, p. 24.
65. Cited in Conway, *The Nazi Persecution of the Churches*, p. 46.
66. Bonhoeffer, *DWB*, vol. 12, p. 134.
67. He also claimed this for the ideas of the world and the self, but my purpose here is not to provide a summary of Kant's epistemology. That can be found in my doctoral dissertation "Philosophy and Community in the Early Thought of Dietrich Bonhoeffer," chapter 4, University of Virginia, 1989.
68. Schleiermacher, *On Religion*, p. 39.
69. Ibid., p. 43.
70. Barth, *The Humanity of God*, pp. 25–26.
71. Ibid.
72. "Minutes of Meeting 'The Struggle for the Church,'" in Bonhoeffer, *DBW*, vol. 12, pp. 123–25.
73. Julius Rieger in Bonhoeffer, *DBW*, vol. 13, p. 48.
74. Ibid.
75. "The Reich law that set the date for these elections [the church elections set for July 23, 1933] was newly enacted and controversial (the state had not previously been involved in church elections); this was the basis for the subsequent argument by the church opposition that the elections were not legitimate," writes Larry Rasmussen in Bonhoeffer, *DBW*, vol. 12, p. 140. See also Helmreich, *German Churches Under Hitler*, pp. 140–41.
76. Baranowski, "Church History," p. 298.
77. Schlingensiepen, *Dietrich Bonhoeffer*, p. 131.
78. Ibid.
79. Bonhoeffer, *DBW*, vol. 13, p. 30.
80. On July 14, 1933, the Reich had enacted the Law for the Prevention of Children with Hereditary Diseases (Gesetz zur Verhütung erbkranken Nachwuchses), which gave the government the right to subject according to which certain persons with mental and physical disabilities inherited diseases were subject to compulsory sterilization. By the end of the decade, the grounds, gardens, and spacious interiors of the Bethel Clinic would become an extension of Hitler's T4 euthanasia program.
81. Bonhoeffer, *DBW*, vol. 12, p. 157.
82. Dietrich Bonhoeffer, "The Barmen Confession," in Kelly and Nelson, eds., *A Testament to Freedom*, p. 143.
83. Ernst-Albert Scharffennorth, the editor of Bonhoeffer's 1932–33 papers, explains that if one accepts Gerhard Stratenwerth's handwritten notes—Stratenwerth was a colleague of Bodelschwingh's in Bethel—those responsible for the various sections of the August version of the Confession are "I. Bonhoeffer and Sasse; II. Merz; III. Bonhoeffer; IV/1 through VI/2. Bonhoeffer and Fischer; VI/3a. Stratenwerth; VI/3b. Merz; VI/4–5. Stratenwerth; VI/6. Vischer and Merz; VI/7. Stratenwerth." (HA Bethel, 2/39–209), 12; facsimile reprint in Carter, *Confession at Bethel*, p. 295. See also Bonhoeffer, *DBW*, vol. 12, p. 362.

84. Bonhoeffer to Karl Barth, September 9, 1933, in Bonhoeffer, *DBW*, vol. 12, p. 165.
85. Bonhoeffer to Helmut Rößler, December 25, 1932, *DBW*, vol. 12, p. 83.
86. Barth to Bonhoeffer, September 11, 1933, in Bonhoeffer, *DBW*, vol. 12, p. 166.
87. Rasmussen cited in ibid."Editor's Note," *DBW*, vol. 12, p. 163.
88. Sasse writing in agreement with Bonhoeffer, in *DBW*, vol. 12, p. 169.
89. Rasmussen, "Editor's Introduction to the English Version," p. 42.
90. Julius Richter had become a professor at the University of Berlin, author of the five-volume *History of Missions*, and, since his involvement in the 1910 Edinburgh World Missionary Conference, a loyal ecumenist.
91. Victoria J. Barnett, "Dietrich Bonhoeffer's Relevance for Post-Holocaust Theology," *Studies in Jewish-Christian Relations* 2, no. 1 (2007): 55.
92. "Statement by the Executive Committee of the World Alliance for Promoting International Friendship Through the Churches," in Bonhoeffer, *DBW*, vol. 12, pp. 174–75.
93. Bonhoeffer, *DBW*, vol. 12, p. 492.
94. See Wendebourg, "Dietrich Bonhoeffer und die Berliner Universität."
95. Karl Clodius, professor in Berlin, economist, and Balkans expert, worked with the German delegation in Sofia. Barnett, "Dietrich Bonhoeffer's Relevance for Post-Holocaust Theology," p. 55. Despite the claim of the official report from the German Legation in Sofia, there is no evidence that Bonhoeffer told German officials that he "had tried to prevent the adoption of the resolution condemning the Aryan laws in general." Bonhoeffer, *DBW*, vol. 12, p. 177.
96. Cited in ibid., p. 179.
97. Ibid., p. 31.
98. Rasmussen, in ibid., p. 318.
99. Cited in Bethge, *Bonhoeffer*, p. 319.
100. Cited in Scholder and Bowden, eds., *The Churches and the Third Reich*, vol. 1, p. 491.
101. Cited in Barnett, *For the Soul of the People*, p. 4.
102. Scholder and Brown, eds., *The Churches and the Third Reich*, vol. 1, p. 491.
103. Bonhoeffer, *DBW*, vol. 12, p. 140.
104. The German Christians had come to regard the paragraph as an international liability and avoidable distraction. Their focus became politics and power. For more on this, see Scholder and Brown, eds., *The Churches and the Third Reich*, vol. 1, pp. 488–91.
105. Ibid.
106. Fischer cited in Bonhoeffer, *DBW*, vol. 12, p. 511.
107. Merz cited in ibid., p. 512.
108. In fact, Merz blamed Bonhoeffer for the breakdown: "I can at most say that, in a way, I saw it coming," though "it's Bonhoeffer's own fault for having gone at this thing too precipitately and for having let go of it too

hastily. Nothing good can come from such treatment. But we won't be able to make this clear to him because he is simply too young and slipped into academia too early and too one-sidedly." Ibid.

109. Bethge, *Dietrich Bonhoeffer: A Biography*, p. 303.

110. Althaus cited in Ericksen, *Theologians Under Hitler*, p. 100.

111. Klaus Scholder, in his seminal study *The Churches and the Third Reich*, noted that Bonhoeffer's "August Version" of the Bethel Confession might well be remembered as a clear and forceful statement of the hope that still existed in the summer of 1933, that effective organizing and theological protest could arrest the church's realignments. "While ponderous in form, burdened with numerous proof texts from the Bible, from Luther, and above all from the confessions," the Bethel Confession was, in many respects, "theologically and *politically clearer and more precise*" than the more famous Barmen Declaration drafted the following year.

112. Wendebourg, "Dietrich Bonhoeffer und die Berliner Universität."

113. Erich Seeberg in Bonhoeffer, *DBW*, vol. 12, p. 159.

114. Gertrud Staewen's communication of September 25, 1933, to Charlotte von Kirschbaum: "Bonhoeffer is extremely depressed about the situation in the church. Obviously, as he says, *almost* all those who a short time ago were willing to stand fast on 'G[erman] C[hristian]' matters are now in retreat, so that one can only fear the worst for the National Synod." Letter located in the Karl Barth-Archiv, Basel.

CHAPTER NINE Crying in the Wilderness

1. Whitburn, "Bonhoeffer Without His Cassock," p. 81.

2. Bethge, *Dietrich Bonhoeffer: A Life in Pictures*, p. 72.

3. Clements, *Bonhoeffer and Britain*, pp. 22–24.

4. Schlingensiepen, *Dietrich Bonhoeffer*, pp. 144–45.

5. Ibid., p. 144.

6. Zimmermann, "Some Weeks in London," p. 77.

7. Schlingensiepen, *Dietrich Bonhoeffer*, p. 145.

8. Clements, *Bonhoeffer and Britain*, p. 26; Dietrich Bonhoeffer, *DBW*, vol. 13, p. 251.

9. Schlingensiepen, *Dietrich Bonhoeffer*, p. 145.

10. Ibid., p. 146.

11. "Welcome to Our Church," *Dietrich Bonhoeffer Church, Sydenham*, 1999, p. 15. Publication of the Dietrich Bonhoeffer Church, Sydenham; nd.

12. Schlingensiepen, *Dietrich Bonhoeffer*, p. 146.

13. Bosanquet, *The Life and Death of Dietrich Bonhoeffer*, p. 97.

14. Bonhoeffer, *DBW*, vol. 13, p. 39. Bonhoeffer's exchanges with Barth in the fall of 1933 marked a shift in the relationship, or perhaps more precisely clarified the relationship. The scholar Mark Brocker is correct that

Bonhoeffer and Barth's association remained always "fitful" and never developed fully into friendship. "Their minds never completely met," wrote Brocker, "but passed by one another . . . a hair's breadth apart."

15. Citations from a letter from Karl Barth to Bonhoeffer, written on November 20, 1933, in Bonhoeffer, *DBW*, vol. 13, pp. 39–41.

16. Letter from Bonhoeffer to Karl Barth written on October 24, 1933, in ibid., pp. 21–24. He wrote to explain his decision: "I found myself in radical opposition to all my friends; I was becoming increasingly isolated with my views of the matter, even though I was and remain personally close to these people. All this frightened me and shook my confidence, so that I began to fear that dogmatism might be leading me astray—since there seemed no particular reason why my own view in these matters should be any better, any more right, than the views of many really good and able pastors whom I sincerely respect."

17. Bonhoeffer, *DBW*, vol. 10., p. 64. See note 28.

18. Schlingensiepen, *Dietrich Bonhoeffer*, p. 147.

19. Bonhoeffer, *DBW*, vol. 13, pp. 134–36.

20. See ibid., pp. 429–31.

21. See ibid., p. 118, editor's note 2, pp. 121–22.

22. Ibid., pp. 121–22; Bethge, *Dietrich Bonhoeffer: A Biography*, pp. 364–66.

23. Schlingensiepen, *Dietrich Bonhoeffer*, p. 147.

24. Bonhoeffer, *DBW*, vol. 13, p. 81.

25. See ibid., pp. 27–28; Clements, *Bonhoeffer and Britain*, p. 36.

26. Bonhoeffer, *DBW*, vol. 13, p. 41.

27. Ibid., p. 56.

28. Ibid., pp. 22–23. See note 10.

29. Zimmermann, "Some Weeks in London," p. 78.

30. Stephen Plant, in *Bonhoeffer, Christ and Culture*, edited by Keith L. Johnson and Timothy L. Larsen (Downers Grove, IL: Intervarsity Press, 2012), p. 78.

31. Zimmermann, "Some Weeks in London," p. 78.

32. Ibid., p.78 Alan Jacobs: "It turns out that while many of the early cinemas were converted stage theaters, there was an explosion of purpose-built cinemas in London at the end of the twenties and beginning of the thirties (despite the Depression). The two chief architects were Oscar Deutsch, who worked primarily in an Art Deco style, and George Coles, who specialized in building ersatz Egyptian temples. Probably the largest of Coles's cinemas was the Troxy in Stepney Green, just down Mile End Road from Whitechapel. It seated over 3,000 and was quite an attraction. Since it opened in 1933 (first film shown there: *King Kong*) I can't imagine that Bonhoeffer wouldn't have known it well." Correspondence with the author.

33. "History," St. George's German Lutheran Church, n.d., http://www.stgeorgesgermanchurch.org.uk/page1.html (accessed June 15, 2008).

34. Clements, *Bonhoeffer and Britain*, p. 26.

35. Zimmermann, "Some Weeks in London," pp. 77–78.
36. Clements, *Bonhoeffer and Britain*, p. 22.
37. Bonhoeffer, *DBW*, vol. 13, p. 151.
38. Bonhoeffer, *No Rusty Swords*, p. 182.
39. Bonhoeffer, *DBW*, vol. 13, p. 135.
40. Clements, *Bonhoeffer and Britain*, pp. 67, 66.
41. Bonhoeffer, *DBW*, vol. 13, pp. 337, 341.
42. Ibid., pp. 339–41.
43. Ibid., pp. 383, 392.
44. Clements, *Bonhoeffer and Britain*, p. 67.
45. Bonhoeffer, *DBW*, vol. 13, p. 382.
46. See "The German Evangelical Pastors in London to the Reich Church Government," note 2, and "49. Friedrich Wehrhan to the Reich Church Government," in Bonhoeffer, *DBW*, vol. 13, p. 77.
47. See "54. To Karl Friedrich Bonhoeffer," in Bonhoeffer, *DBW*, vol. 13, p. 81.
48. Ibid., p. 392.
49. Ibid., p. 395.
50. See ibid., p. 32, note 18.
51. Bell asked Bonhoeffer to meet him in Brighton, where he had a meeting with area clergy. Trains left Victoria Station for Brighton every quarter of an hour, and Bell's driver and his assistant would be waiting for Bonhoeffer up at the station. The two men would have tea at the Church House, after which they would drive on to Chichester together and talk further. See ibid., p. 37. Bell's book, which had appeared originally in English in 1929, was published in winter 1934 under the title *Die Anglikanische Kirche*.
52. Clements, *Bonhoeffer and Britain*, pp. 29–33.
53. See Bonhoeffer, *DBW*, vol. 13, pp. 43–44, 87–89. Part of the success of his appeals to Bell lay in his flattering estimation of the bishop as the most influential voice of the ecumenical movement. Coupled with Bonhoeffer's repeated claim that the German church was "no longer an internal issue" but "the question of [the] existence of Christianity in Europe," indeed the decisive test of the ecumenical movement's credibility upon which the fate of "the whole world of Christianity" depended, Bell readily took up the mantle of international ambassadorship of the dissident German church. Ibid., p. 118.
54. See ibid., p. 36, note 2.
55. Bethge, *Dietrich Bonhoeffer: A Biography*, p. 335.
56. Schlingensiepen, *Dietrich Bonhoeffer*, pp. 147–48.
57. Cited in Poewe, *New Religions and the Nazis*, p. 104.
58. Bergen, "Storm Troopers of Christ," p. 50.
59. Other theologians and religion scholars on the board were Karl Fezer, Helmuth Kittel, Hanns Rückert, Friedrich Karl Schumann, Otto Weber, and Arthur Weiser. Bonhoeffer, *DBW*, vol. 13, p. 69, note 4.

60. Bethge, *Dietrich Bonhoeffer: A Biography*, pp. 338–39.
61. "GERMANY: New Heathenism," *Time*, November 27, 1933, http://www.time.com/time/magazine/article/0,9171,746354,00 .html#ixzz1uIKz4WFQ (accessed October 10, 2013).
62. Cited in Bergen, *Twisted Cross*, p. 65.
63. Clements, *Bonhoeffer and Britain*, p. 39.
64. See Bethge, *Dietrich Bonhoeffer: A Biography*, p. 355. After the war, Hossenfelder was able to maintain his employment in the church and given the influential job of overseeing and assigning the placements of ministers in congregations from 1954 to 1969.
65. The Oxford Group was not affiliated with the Oxford Movement of the nineteenth century. In an interview in "Hitler or Any Fascist Leader Controlled by God Could Cure All Ills of World," *New York World-Telegram*, August 25, 1936, Buchman was quoted as saying, "I thank heaven for a man like Adolf Hitler."
66. Driberg, "Thank Heaven for Hitler," p. 69.
67. Niebuhr, *Christianity and Power Politics*, pp. 160–62. In other words, a Nazi social philosophy has been a covert presumption of the whole Oxford Group enterprise from the very beginning. "We may be grateful to the leader for revealing so clearly what has been slightly hidden. If it would content itself with preaching repentance to drunkards and adulterers one might be willing to respect it as a religious revival method which knows how to confront the sinner with God. But when it runs to Geneva, the seat of the League of Nations, or to Prince Starhemberg or Hitler, or to any seat of power, always with the idea that it is on the verge of saving the world by bringing the people who control the world under God-control, it is difficult to restrain the contempt which one feels for this dangerous childishness." After that Buchman would be nominated for two Nobel Peace Prizes and would be affiliated with Alcoholic's Anonymous.
68. Hossenfelder returned to Germany a disgraced man. On December 20, 1933, he was forced to relinquish his church offices as well as his more cherished role as Reich leader of the German Christian movement; see Scholder, *The Churches and the Third Reich*, vol. 1, pp. 570–71; see also Bonhoeffer, *DBW*, vol. 13, p. 106, note 10.
69. See Scholder, *The Churches and the Third Reich*, vol. 1, pp. 570–82.
70. Rasmussen, "Editor's Introduction to the English Edition," *DBW*, vol. 12, p. 6.
71. Theodor Heckel to the German Congregations and Pastors Abroad, January 31, 1934, in Bonhoeffer, *DBW*, vol. 13, pp. 91–92.
72. Ibid., p. 77. Bethge, *Dietrich Bonhoeffer: A Biography*, p. 352. When Heckel was pressed by dissenting German pastors in England on how the Reich Church could justify the assimilation of church youth groups into the Hitler Youth, he responded with the banal defense that "the incorporation of the Evangelical Youth into the Hitler Youth had been accom-

plished in some places without any friction." Bonhoeffer, *DBW*, vol. 13, p. 108.

73. Bonhoeffer, *DBW*, vol. 13, pp. 91, 118, note 2, 128–30.

74. "The Declaration by the Pastors in Great Britain," found in ibid., p. 112. This decree was written on February 9, 1934, and stated that: (1) The Evangelical Church stands on the ground of the Reformation. (2) It is founded on the Holy Scriptures of the Old and New Testaments. (3) The Aryan paragraph is not recognized by the German Evangelical pastors in Great Britain, and they expect it not to be implemented anywhere by the Reich Church. (4) The German Reich Church does not dismiss any pastor in Germany who accepts the above points, except in the case of other, serious offenses against discipline. (5) The pastors declare that, following the dissolution of the Church Federation, they have no further obligation to the Reich Church; they are nevertheless prepared, on the basis of the above and in Christian love and fellowship, to remain in the Reich Church. (6) The German Evangelical churches in Great Britain, declaring themselves prepared to be members of the new Reich Church, nevertheless declare specifically that, as is already the case, they have the right to resign their membership in this association of churches at any time.

75. Clements, *Bonhoeffer and Britain*, p. 45.

76. Ibid., p. 45.

77. See "85. From the Diary of Julius Rieger," in Bonhoeffer, *DBW*, vol. 13, p. 124.

78. Bonhoeffer, *DBW*, vol., p. 175.

79. "146. From the Diary of Julius Rieger," September 11, 1934, in ibid., pp. 216, note 5.

80. Ibid., p. 216.

81. "143. From the Minutes of the Session of the Reich Council of Brethren," in ibid., p. 212, note 7.

82. See ibid., pp. 307–10.

83. Bethge, *Dietrich Bonhoeffer: A Life in Pictures*, p. 82.

84. He was disappointed by the poor turnout of Confessing Church leaders, who he later learned had been intimidated by superiors. Bethge, *Dietrich Bonhoeffer: A Biography*, p. 391.

85. Ibid., p. 389.

86. Bonhoeffer, *DBW*, vol. 12, p. 260–68.

87. Bonhoeffer, *DBW*, vol. 13, pp. 289–90.

88. Paul Althaus cited in Tödt, Tödt, Feil, and GreenIlse Todt et al., "Editors' Afterword to the German Edition," in *DBW*, vol. 6, p. 290; Ericksen, *Theologians Under Hitler*, p. 79. By all reports, Althaus had been, over the years, an amiable colleague and generous to students. He had always demanded "a certain pontifical respect," which was not unusual in German academe. After 1933, however, he insisted that students rise to their feet after he entered the classroom and join him with right hand held high

in the *"Sieg Heil!"*—but that was no longer unusual either. With a "narrow head (praised as 'Nordic' in the Third Reich)," piercing eyes, and "a fresh complexion," Althaus gave National Socialism religious respectability. He promoted German nationalism in the doctrine of the orders of creation and a Hegelian fondness for synthesizing the singularities of experience into a perfect unity, which in 1934 meant integrating the Nazi doctrines of blood and soil, nation and race into Lutheran thought. Althaus did not seek to identify Christianity and Germanism vis-à-vis the German Faith Movement, but the results were equally catastrophic. In 1934, he signed the Ansbach Recommendation, which repudiated the Barmen Declaration and conferred on Hitler the blessings of the Protestant churches and theological faculties: "As believing Christians we thank the Lord our God for giving our nation in its time of distress the Führer to be our 'pious and loyal sovereign' and for wishing to establish good governance with discipline and honor through the National Socialist system of government." Totalitarianism as realized in Hitler constituted "a perfectly satisfactory form of government."

89. Webster, *Karl Barth*, p. 29.
90. Cited in Bonhoeffer, *DBW*, vol. 6, p. 15, note 58.
91. Bonhoeffer, *DBW*, vol. 13, p. 292.
92. Ibid., pp. 284–85. Karl-Friedrich had studied biochemistry with Max Planck and undertaken research on heavy water. Unwilling, however, to take part in the Nazi government's experiments in nuclear energy, he shifted his focus to "the interaction between leaves and air." He had been the most politically outspoken of the Bonhoeffer children, but because he had served alongside his fallen brother Walter in World War I, he "enjoyed a certain prestige in the house."
93. "152. George Bell to Edward Keble Talbot," in ibid., p. 224. In this letter of October 16, 1934, Bell said that Bonhoeffer was likely to leave England by the end of 1934, but he remained until December 1935 and visited these Christian communities in March of that year. E. K. Talbot was the son of E. S. Talbot, the first warden of Keble College, Oxford; in addition, Bonhoeffer spoke with Father Tribe O'Brien, Reverend Eric Graham, principal of Wycliffe Hall (Oxford), and Canon Tomlin of St. Augustine's, Canterbury.
94. Christopher Howse, "The Levelling of Mirfield Church," Telegraph.co.uk, November 13, 2009, http://www.telegraph.co.uk/comment/columnists/christopherhowse/6562705/The-levelling-of-Mirfield-church.html (accessed September 10, 2008).
95. Clements, *Bonhoeffer and Britain*, p. 86.
96. Bethge, *Dietrich Bonhoeffer: A Biography*, p. 412.
97. Clements, *Bonhoeffer and Britain*, p. 79.
98. Ibid., pp. 83–84.
99. Ibid., p. 84.
100. Rieger, "Contacts with London," pp. 97–98.

101. Clements, *Bonhoeffer and Britain*, p. 83.
102. "114a. Hardy Arnold to Eberhard Arnold," Birmingham, June 14, 1934, and "114b. Hardy Arnold to Edith Boker," Birmingham, June 15, 1934, in Bonhoeffer, *DBW*, vol. 13. pp. 158–63.
103. Ibid.; Arnold, *Innerland*, p. 311. Eberhard Arnold noticed another worrisome pattern in Bonhoeffer's presentation. He said nothing about the Holy Spirit. He spoke only about Jesus. In his summation of a community permeated by the Sermon on the Mount, Bonhoeffer held forth gloriously on "religious exercises and serious study, and the process of conforming to the essential core of the truth of Christ." But without an appreciation of the Holy Spirit, a spiritual leader—itself a problematic notion for Arnold—would eventually replace Jesus Christ with a hardened rule, and the rule would be set by the whims of a single person—which in this case meant Bonhoeffer. Arnold thought that Bonhoeffer may have even been too much influenced by Barth in this regard, identifying "spirit-filled Christians" with Pietists and navel-gazers. Eberhard Arnold, Hardy Arnold's father, said this in an exchange: "The belief in unanimous community is so amazingly unknown everywhere, because the third article of the Apostles' Creed, that of faith in the Holy Spirit and the work of the Spirit, has been totally lost to Christendom in general. Even in the case of Dietrich Bonhoeffer, who has not yet come to see us here although we telephoned him, the foundation of the renunciation of private property and holding of goods in common, as well as nonviolence, still seems to me, like many another such undertakings, to be quite far from the calling of the community by the Spirit of Jesus Christ." See "115a & 115b. Eberhard to Hardy Arnold," in Bonhoeffer, *DBW*, vol. 13, pp. 164–66.
104. Rieger, "Contacts with London," p. 98.
105. Bonhoeffer's letter to Gandhi had been preceded by a formal introduction by Archbishop George Bell, who in a letter of October, 22, 1934, described Bonhoeffer as "a friend of mine . . . who wants to study community life as well as methods of training." Bell "heartily commend[ed]" the young German pastor to Gandhi, calling him a "very good theologian" and a "most earnest man." See "154. George Bell to Mahatma Gandi," October 22, 1934, in Bonhoeffer, *DBW*, vol. 13, p. 225.
106. "158. From Mahatma Gandi," November 1, 1934, in Bonhoeffer, *DBW*, vol. 13, pp. 229–30. In original English, printed in and photocopied from *The Collected Works of Mahatma Gandhi*, vol. 59 (September 16–December 15, 1934) (Ahmedabad: Navajivan Trust; published in Delhi by the director, Publications Division, Ministry of Information and Broadcasting, Government of India; printed by Shantilal Harjivan Shah, 1974). Bonhoeffer's travel companion would have been either Julius Rieger or Herbert Jehle; both later said they had made plans to travel to India with Bonhoeffer. The Anglican priest, Charles Freer Andrews, had very likely given Bonhoeffer details on India; Andrews had spent most of his life in India and immersed himself deeply in Indian culture and Gandhian

spirituality. Andrews also encouraged Bonhoeffer to visit Woodbrooke and to speak with Horace Alexander at Selly Oak. From Charles Freer Andrews, April 29, 1934, in Bonhoeffer, *DBW*, vol. 13, pp. 136–37 and 137, note 2.

107. Reinhold Niebuhr told the ethicist Larry Rasmussen in a 1968 interview that he had advised Bonhoeffer not to study with Gandhi, saying that Gandhi was "an ethical liberal with philosophical footings at great distance from the Weltanschauung of a sophisticated German Lutheran; furthermore, Nazi Germany was no place for attempting the practice of nonviolent resistance. . . . Hitler's creed and deeds bore no resemblance to British ways and means. The Nazis would suffer none of the pains of conscience about using violence which the British did, and organized passive resistance would end in utter failure." Rasmussen, *Dietrich Bonhoeffer*, p. 213. Bonhoeffer nevertheless pursued his plans for India; see Bonhoeffer, *DBW*, vol. 13, p. 225. 4.

108. Rieger, *Bonhoeffer in England*, p. 27.

109. Bonhoeffer, *DBW*, vol. 13, p. 370. Hardy Arnold had been delighted to tell a colleague that Bonhoeffer shared the Bruderhof view that Gandhi's movement was "without doubt the most positive living example today in the area of individual mysticism and the monastic thinking connected to that." "114b. Hardy Arnold to Edith Boker," Birmingham, June 15, 1934, in ibid., p. 163.

110. When Bonhoeffer told George Bell that the issues at stake in the *Kirchenkampf* were not simply internal church matters but ones that raised inescapable questions about the future of Christianity, he was affirming Christian internationalism and asking whether Western Christianity had run aground.

111. Bonhoeffer, *DBW*, vol. 13, p. 81.

112. Ibid., p. 152. Bonhoeffer "was haunted by the question about the will of God hic et nunc.," and he turned to Gandhi with his teachings on passive resistance and the soul-force of agapeic love did not represent God's will for the nations. Jacobi, "Drawn Towards Suffering," p. 73.

113. Bonhoeffer, *DBW*, vol. 13, p. 370.

114. Ibid., p. 22.

115. Ibid., p. 151.

116. Ibid., p. 74.

117. Leith, ed., *Creeds of the Churches*, p. 517.

118. See Barth and Green, *Karl Barth*, pp. 148–51.

119. Barth cited in Busch and Bowden, *Karl Barth*, p. 248: "But that does not excuse me for not having at least gone through the motions of fighting."

120. Bonhoeffer, *DBW*, vol. 13, p. 135.

121. In her lecture at the University of Virginia on the Confessing Church ("The Rise and Fall of the Confessing Church"), Victoria Barnett explained that, despite its story being widely praised among contem-

porary church people, and indeed in some Protestant circles granted near-canonical status, "the Barmen Declaration moves in two different directions." On the one hand, it can be read "as a retreat inward to a pure Christian message that will remain untainted by the politics of the world"; on the other hand, it issues an outward "challenge to the world and its attempts to stifle the conscience and the spirit." In fact, the declaration was "read in both directions at the time, even by the more than 100 Protestant leaders who voted in Barmen to affirm it. As a condemnation of German Christian ideology, of the attempt to create an ideological Christianity that conformed to National Socialism, the Barmen Declaration was a clear statement to the world, a real 'here I stand' moment. But the basis of the Christianity it proclaimed—a return to the scriptures, to the claim to follow Christ alone (not any worldly führer)—could also be read as a move inward, a call to 'let the church be the church,' to withdraw from the tumultuous political world toward institutional purity, to 'render unto Caesar.' This was actually the most widespread interpretation at the time."

122. Cited in Bonhoeffer, *DBW*, vol. 6, p. 344, note 22.
123. Bonhoeffer, *DBW*, vol. 13, p. 179.
124. Dietrich Bonhoeffer, "The Church Is Dead," sermon presented at the various ecumenical conferences, Germany, Czechoslovakia, and Switzerland, 1932.
125. Bonhoeffer, *DBW*, vol. 13, p. 135.
126. Ibid., p. 129.
127. Ibid., p. 309.
128. Bonhoeffer, *DBW*, vol. 6, p. 163.
129. Bonhoeffer cited in: Clements, *Bonhoeffer and Britain*, 76.
130. Bonhoeffer, *DBW*, vol. 13, p. 29.

CHAPTER TEN "A New Kind of Monasticism"

1. Bonhoeffer, *DBW*, vol. 9, p. 138.
2. Bethge, *Dietrich Bonhoeffer: A Biography*, p. 347.
3. Ibid., p. 425. During World War II, there were several industrial companies that were of military importance and in which thousands of people were employed. In 1940, the prisoner-of-war camp Stalag Luft I was built. Ten thousand members of the Royal Air Force and of the U.S. Air Force were handed over there until April 1945. From November 1943 to 1945, there was a KZ, or *Konzentrationslager* (concentration camp), on the site of the military airfield, a branch of the Ravensbrück concentration camp for women. About seven thousand women and men from twenty-one nations were forced to work for the Heinkel airplane factory; more than two thousand prisoners died.

4. Pejsa, *Matriarch of Conspiracy*, p. 207.

5. Bonhoeffer to Ernst Cromwell, June 1935, letters in possession of Stephen Plant, Cambridge, England.

6. Mary Glazener, *A Cup of Wrath: The Story of Dietrich Bonhoeffer's Resistance to Hitler* (Macon, GA: Smyth and Helwys, 1993), p. 113.

7. Bethge, *Dietrich Bonhoeffer: A Life in Pictures*, p. 145.

8. Bonhoeffer to Ernst Cromwell, July 2, 1935, in *Letters to London*, edited by Stephen J. Plant and Toni Burrowes-Cromwell (London, SPCK, 2013), pp. 60–1.

9. Pejsa, *Matriarch of the Conspiracy*, p. 208.

10. Cited in Zimmermann and Smith, eds., *I Knew Dietrich Bonhoeffer*, p. 115.

11. Cited in ibid., p. 116.

12. Bonhoeffer made every effort to stay in touch with his former students at Finkenwalde, but restrictions on his correspondence required further circumventions of official policy. He often responded to questions large and small in the circular letters but through indirection.

13. Cited in Zimmermann and Smith, eds., *I Knew Dietrich Bonhoeffer*, p. 117.

14. Cited in ibid., "Life Together," p. 153.

15. Dietrich Bonhoeffer, *The Way to Freedom: Letters, Lectures and Notes, 1935–39*, edited and introduced by Edwin H. Robertson, translated by Edwin H. Robertson and John Bowden. (London: Collins, 1966), p. 34.

16. Schönherr, "The Single-Heartedness of the Provoked," p. 126.

17. Glazener, *A Cup of Wrath*, p. 113.

18. Bonhoeffer, *Life Together*, p. 49.

19. Schönherr, "The Single-Heartedness of the Provoked," p. 128.

20. Cited in Robert O. Smith, "Bonhoeffer and Musical Metaphor," *Word and World*, vol. 26, no. 2, (2006), p. 198.

21. Zimmermann and Smith, eds., *I Knew Dietrich Bonhoeffer*, pp. 107–11.

22. Dietrich Bonhoeffer, *The Way to Freedom*, p. 30.

23. Staats, "Editors' Afterword to the German Edition," in, *DBW*, vol. 10, p. 614.

24. William Richard Russell, *Berlin Embassy* (New York: Dutton, 1941), p. 41.

25. Busing, "Reminiscences of Finkenwalde," p. 1108.

26. He aligned himself with the Confessing Church out of respect for the Old Prussian Union and his father's high regard for independent regional churches.

27. In his biography of Eberhard Bethge, John de Gruchy explains, "As momentous as both Barmen and Dahlmen were for the church, they were not explicitly acts of political resistance but acts of faith and confession. Nor did they address the Nazi persecution of the Jews. Nonetheless, they had serious consequences for Eberhard Bethge and fourteen of his fellow theological students in Wittenberg, who courageously took the risk of publicly identifying with the Confessing Church. Mindful of Luther's own fateful step in nailing his 'ninety-five theses' to the Wittenberg Cas-

tle Church door in 1517, fifteen candidates for the ministry wrote a terse letter to the secretary of the Reichsbishop on 28 October 1934, informing him that they had shifted their allegiance to the Council of Brethren of the Confessing Church. At the insistence of the Reich Church authorities in Berlin, they were immediately expelled from the seminary and thus lost the possibility of sitting [for] their second theological examination, which was necessary for ordination." In *Daring, Trusting Spirit*, p. 12.

28. Bonhoeffer, *DBW*, vol. 7, p. 100.

29. Vibrans cited in de Gruchy, *Daring, Trusting, Spirit*, p. 17.

30. Bonhoeffer, *DBW*, vol. 8, p. 200.

31. Bonhoeffer, *The Way to Freedom*, p. 31.

32. Zimmermann and Smith, eds., *I Knew Dietrich Bonhoeffer*, p. 107.

33. The phrase is Bonhoeffer's own. See "The First Year at Finkenwalde," in *The Way to Freedom*, p. 31.

34. Zimmermann and Smith, eds., *I Knew Dietrich Bonhoeffer*, p. 107.

35. Ibid., p. 111.

36. Ibid., p. 108.

37. Bonhoeffer, *Christ the Center*, trans. John Bowden (New York: Harper and Row, Publishers, 1960), p. 27.

38. Cited in Zimmermann and Smith, eds., *I Knew Dietrich Bonhoeffer*, Jensen, "Life Together," p. 153.

39. Ibid. These meditations offered Jensen the soul-care he needed after being confined to a Gestapo prison; he had preached a sermon that related the story of the Good Samaritan to German Jews. "There are still some marginal comments to the psalms in my Bible which date from the Gross-Schlönwitz time, for instance, the date 10th November 1938, the 'Crystal Night,' beside Psalm lxxiv, 8: 'They burned all the meeting places of God in the land.'" While the Old Testament was vilified, mocked, and quite often rejected by the Deutsche Christen, Bonhoeffer encouraged his students to reclaim the Psalms as the prayers of the church, promises of presence amid suffering.

40. Ibid., p. 155.

41. Cited in Bethge, *Dietrich Bonhoeffer: A Biography*, pp. 592–93.

42. Zimmermann and Smith, eds. *I Knew Dietrich Bonhoeffer*, p. 110.

43. Cited in ibid., p. 125.

44. From the lecture notes of Joachim Kanitz, 1935, *NL* B 10, 6, pp. 22ff. See also the reference to Kierkegaard in *DBWE*, vol. 4, pp. 61ff.

45. Bonhoeffer, *DBW*, vol. 4, p. 57.

46. At the same time, Karl Barth pursued the the work of the Christian dogmatics as an exercise in *nachdenken*: a thinking after the language of scripture and tradition so as to revivify the faith with new energies and fresh perspective. Barth's astonishing achievement was nothing less than the "lengthy, even leisurely unfolding" of a theological universe, as Yale theologian Hans Frei explained, an utterly necessary remedy to the exhaustion of Christian language. Barth was "restating or re-using a language

that had once been accustomed talk, both in first-order use in ordinary or real life, and in second-order technical theological reflection, but had now for a long time, perhaps more than two hundred and fifty years, been receding from natural familiarity, certainly in theological discourse." Karl Barth, in the tradition of Reformed theology, held that divine revelation endows Christians with the gifts to think God's thoughts after him. Bonhoeffer had no serious qualms with this basic conviction. But with church people marching in lockstep to the drumbeats of the führer, a different aspect would need to be emphasized. *Nachdenken* without *nachfolgen* was a beautiful castle built on sand.

47. Kuske and Tödt, "Editors' Afterword to the German Edition," *DBW*, vol. 4. p. 290.

48. Stephen Plant, *Bonhoeffer* (London: Continuum, 2004), p. 98.

49. Bethge, *Bonhoeffer*, p. 456.

50. Bonhoeffer, *DBW*, vol. 4, p. 99.

51. Jørgen Glenthøj, Ulrich Kabitz, and Wolf Krötke write, "According to Jutta Jochimsen, this is probably a reference to the performance by the Berlin Vocal Academy and the Berlin Philharmonic conducted by Fritz Stein on March 22, 1940, Good Friday, in the Berlin Garrison Church (information provided to the German editor by Jutta Jochimsen, August 25, 1988)." In Bonhoeffer, *DBW*, vol. 16, p. 39.

52. Lehmann, "Paradox of Discipleship," pp. 41–45.

53. Oetinger's translation of Swedenborg into German brought him into conflict with ecclesial authorities, but his friendship with the Duke of Würtenburg protected him from suspension or excommunication.

54. Bethge, *Dietrich Bonhoeffer: A Life in Pictures*, p. 145.

55. Cited in Zimmermann and Smith, eds., *I Knew Dietrich Bonhoeffer*, p. 149.

56. De Gruchy, *Daring, Trusting Spirit*, p. 29.

57. Outside of Berlin, very little changed. In one town where Bonhoeffer gave a talk, members of the German Christians hung a sign in the bookstore: "After the Olympics we will beat the Confessing Church to jam"; "When we will throw the Jews out, the Confessing Church will be over."

58. Koonz, *The Nazi Conscience*, p. 232.

59. Large, *Berlin*, pp. 293–96.

60. Cited in David Large, *Berlin*, p. 295.

61. Ibid., p. 296.

62. David Clay Large, *Nazi Games: The Olympics of 1936* (New York: Norton, 2007), p. 142.

63. De Gruchy, *Daring Trusting, Spirit*, p. 33.

64. Ibid.

65. Bonhoeffer correspondence with Eberhard Bethge, July 28, 1936, translated by Ingrid Müller and Charles Marsh; unpublished.

66. De Gruchy, *Daring, Trusting Spirit*, p. 30.

67. Bonhoeffer, *DBW*, vol. 14, pp. 224–27, emphasis mine.

68. De Gruchy, *Daring, Trusting Spirit*, p. 30.

69. While in Switzerland, Bonhoeffer had been disappointed to learn of Barth's unavailability in Basel but delighted that he was finally able to introduce Bethge to Sutz, his New York classmate. Bonhoeffer found time to write Barth an update on his book *Discipleship* and appears to have been too busy to fret over Barth's curt response. Bethge, *Dietrich Bonhoeffer: A Biography*, p. 555.

70. Eberhard's cousin Vibrans returned to his pastorate in Rosian, "and the misunderstandings of the Chamby journey were apparently soon forgotten. Vibrans remained in his pastorate until it became impossible for 'illegal' pastors to avoid conscription. In May 1940 he was drafted into the army, serving in France, then the Balkans and finally on the Russian front, where his unit was involved in the invasion in June 1941. He was killed in action on February 3, 1942. Throughout this period Vibrans remained Bethge's close friend, as well as a friend of Bonhoeffer and others from his Finkenwalde days. Bethge preached at his memorial service in Rosian on March 22, 1942, reminding those gathered not only of Gerhard's life and witness as a Christian and pastor of the Confessing Church, but of his love of music and especially poetry, and his longing for community, friendship and love. Thus, sadly, Bethge's friendship with his cousin, which had begun in boyhood and lasted for so many years, came to an end. After the war, Vibrans's widow, Elisabeth, married Christoph Bethge, Eberhard's younger brother." De Gruchy, *Daring, Trusting Spirit*, p. 32.

71. The book was published in 1939 by Christian Kaiser Verlag as Heft 61 in the series *Theologische Existenz Heute*.

72. Bonhoeffer, *DBW*, vol. 5, pp. 29-29.

73. Dietrich Bonhoeffer, *Life Together: A Discussion of Christian Fellowship* (New York: Harper, 1992), pp. 18–20, 30, 39.

74. Albrecht Schönherr cited in Zimmermann and Smith, eds., *I Knew Dietrich Bonhoeffer*, p. 146.

75. Wilhelm Niesel, cited in ibid., p. 146.

76. W. H. Auden, cited in Edward Callan, "Exorcising Mittenhofer," *London Magazine* 14, no. 1 (1974): 79. Here was an example of Auden's prophecy for a civilization in dissolution, that "in elite lands your generation may be called upon to opt for a discipline that out-peers the monks, a Way of obedience, poverty and—good grief—perhaps chastity."

77. Wilhelm Niesel, cited in Zimmermann and Smith, eds., *I Knew Dietrich Bonhoeffer*, p. 145.

78. Bonhoeffer, *Life Together*, trans. John W. Doberstein (New York: Harper and Row, Publishers, 1954), p. 86.

79. Bosanquet, *The Life and Death of Dietrich Bonhoeffer*, p. 185.

80. Karl Barth cited in Bethge, *Dietrich Bonhoeffer: A Life in Pictures*, p. 146.

81. For Bonhoeffer, "the Psalms, and also the entire Old Testament, were the Book of Christ." The Old Testament should therefore be read in the light of both the incarnation and the cross. A scholarly exposition of this vantage point has been offered recently by Martin Kuske of East Ger-

many, *The Old Testament as the Book of Christ: An Appraisal of Bonhoeffer's Interpretation* (Philadelphia: Westminster, 1976).

82. Bethge, *Dietrich Bonhoeffer: A Biography*, p. 589. Earlier abuses of religious leaders held as prisoners had created some concern among Nazi political leaders regarding public perception, so there was some laxity in prosecution in this area.

83. Thomas E. Leuze, "The Collective Pastorates of the Confessing Church: A Model for Ministerial Preparation," unpublished paper, Chapman Seminary, Oakland City University, Oakland City, Indiana.

84. Bosanquet, *The Life and Death of Dietrich Bonhoeffer*, p. 34.

85. Friedrich Onnasch's son Fritz served as inspector of studies for the group. Previously he had studied at the preachers' seminary in Finkenwalde under Bonhoeffer. Bethge, *Dietrich Bonhoeffer: A Biography*, p. 590.

86. Ibid., p. 590.

87. Quoted in *Informationsdienst*, no. 4, DC Landesleitung Nassau-Hese, Frankfurt am Main/M (January 30, 1937).

88. Bethge, *Dietrich Bonhoeffer: A Biography*, pp. 590–94.

89. Bosanquet, *The Life and Death of Dietrich Bonhoeffer*, p. 197.

90. Victoria Barnett, "The Rise and Fall of the Confessing Church," University of Virginia Lecture, March 2009. Barnett said, "Throughout the 1930s, each year is marked by major political events as well as—on the subterranean level, not frequently traced in general historical works of the period—by ongoing church conversations and reactions and debates and—people going to church and sending their kids to bible studies and ministers preaching sermons: 1933—34—35—36—37—38—39. The story of the Confessing Church usually peters out by 1935 or so, and yet it continued. It was part of the reality of thousands of German Protestants."

CHAPTER ELEVEN "I Must Be a Sojourner and a Stranger"

1. Bethge, *Dietrich Bonhoeffer*, p. 620.

2. On the history and mission of the Eisenach Institute, see Susannah Heschel's *The Aryan Jesus: Christian Theologians and the Bible in Nazi Germany* (Princeton: Princeton University Press, 2008).

3. Hitler quoted in Victoria Barnett, *For the Soul of My People*, p. 124.

4. Cited in Bosanquet, *The Life and Death of Dietrich Bonhoeffer*, pp. 201–3.

5. See text on Dohnányi in Höhne, *Canaris: Hitler's Spy*, pp. 265–66.

6. Bethge, *Dietrich Bonhoeffer: Theologian, Christian, Contemporary*, p. 504.

7. Bethge, *Dietrich Bonhoeffer: Theologian, Christian, Contemporary*, pp. 504–5.

8. Luther's doctrine was based on St. Paul's remark in his letter to the Romans, that "everyone must submit himself to the governing authorities," for "the *authorities that exist* have been established by God" (Romans 13:1–2, my emphasis).

9. Bethge, *Dietrich Bonhoeffer: Theologian, Christian, Contemporary*, pp. 504–5.

10. Rainer Bucher, *Hitler's Theology*, p. 77.

11. I am grateful to my colleague Alon Confino for his clarification of this larger purpose.

12. Bonhoeffer would have read the report's grim details in the solitude of his dorm room in New York City in the summer of 1939. These documents appear to be from the files of Charles Roden Buxton; a slip of paper reading "With Mrs. Charles Roden Buxton's Compliments" is found in the third folder of Box 25. Charles Roden Buxton (November 27, 1875–December 16, 1942) was an English philanthropist and politician, born in London, the third son of Sir Thomas Buxton, 3rd Baronet. His elder brother Noel Buxton was a prominent figure in British politics, as was his cousin Sidney Buxton.

13. "List of Confessional Pastors Subject to Measures of Oppression by Police and Church Authorities as of June, 1939." Dietrich Bonhoeffer Archives, Staatsbibliothek Berlin.

14. From Bethge, *Bonhoeffer: A Biography*, p. 601.

15. Cited in Victoria Barnett, "Dietrich Bonhoeffer: Relationship between Judaism and Christianity," http://www.ushmm.org/museum/exhibit/online/bonhoeffer/?content=5 (accessed June 10, 2010). See also Christine-Ruth Müller, *Dietrich Bonhoeffers Kampf gegen die nationalsozialistische Verfolgung und Vernichtung der Juden* (Munich: Christian Kaiser Verlag, 1990), pp. 213–22.

16. "Children of Bethlehem" and "innocent children of Bethlehem" are found in Bonhoeffer's letter to the Finkenwalde Brothers, December 20, 1937, Bonhoeffer, *DBW*, vol. 5, p. 23. The others appear in Bonhoeffer's address (and later as a circular letter) given by DB to the "Illegal Young Brothers" in Pomerania on October 26, 1938, in Bonhoeffer, *DBW*, vol. 15, pp. 407–31. For the reference to "church and synagogue," see *DBW*, vol. 15, pp. 435–36, footnote 115. In *Ethics*, Bonhoeffer writes of the Jews as the "most defenseless brothers and sisters of Jesus Christ." *Ethics*, Guilt Justification Renewal, *DBW*, vol. 6, page 139. "The church confesses that it has witnessed the arbitrary use of brutal force, the suffering in body and soul of countless innocent people, that it has witnessed oppression, hatred and murder without raising its voice for the victims and without finding ways of rushing to help them," in Bonhoeffer, *DBW*, vol. 6, pp. 138. "She is guilty of the deaths of the weakest and most defenceless brothers of Christ," in Bonhoeffer, *Ethics*, trans. Neville Horton Smith (New York: MacMillan, 1955), p. 50.

17. Keith Clements, *The SPCK Introduction to Bonhoeffer* (London: SPCK, 2010), p. 18.

18. Bonhoeffer, *DBW*, vol. 15, p. 161.

19. Bonhoeffer, *DBW*, vol. 14, pp. 157–58.

20. Ibid., p. 157.

21. Bosanquet, *The Life and Death of Dietrich Bonhoeffer*, p. 206.
22. Sabine Dramm, *Dietrich Bonhoeffer and the Resistance*, p. 7.
23. Richard Fox, *Reinhold Niebuhr*, p. 178.
24. Charles Calvin Brown, *Niebuhr and His Age: Reinhold Niebuhr's Prophetic Role and Legacy* (London: T and T Clark, 2002), p. 96.
25. Ursula M. Niebuhr, *Remembering Reinhold Niebuhr: Letters of Reinhold and Ursula M. Niebuhr* (San Francisco: Harper SanFrancisco, 1991), p. 19.
26. In Niebuhr's mind there were other benefits in bringing Bonhoeffer to Union as a member of the faculty. One was the opportunity to reinvigorate the public mission of the seminary, which in his opinion had become worrisomely rarefied since the fashionable émigré theologian Paul Tillich had replaced Scotch Calvinist John Baillie. Bonhoeffer's presence, Niebuhr wrote, "would be valuable for our sake as well as for his." It might sound odd to hear Niebuhr endorsing the "Barthian voice" and "the spirit of the struggle," but he saw Bonhoeffer as an antidote to the vexing popularity of Tillich's trendy sobriquets: "ground of being," "the question of being," "ultimate concern," "the structure of being," "the courage to be," "the new being." Enough with all the talk about being: it was time for deliberate and steady action. And while Niebuhr may have never been so blunt, he had come to despise Tillich's predatory sexual habits. A half century after his death, it may seem implausible that a philandering miscreant, given to interminable pontifications, with no obvious interest in the American prospect, had once been the darling of the religious left. But this was Tillich's genius: he captivated American audiences with his bipartite and tripartite abstractions and his lumbering prose. Henry Sloane Coffin, the Union president who hired Tillich, later told an interviewer that he never understood a word Tillich said, although he gathered "that what [Tillich] said was important."

  Tillich's existential search for the "transcendent sphere" required the services of attractive and provocative women. And his reputation for extramarital relationships preceded his arrival in New York. Prodding his wife, Hannah, into sexual dalliances with other men and women, Tillich had commenced his assault on "legal and conventional" marriage as early as their wedding night. After Paul was dismissed from his teaching post in Göttingen for his socialist views and opposition to Nazism, the Tilliches moved into one of the seminary's spacious faculty apartments on Broadway and 121st Street. From the start, both did little to hide their contempt for American Protestant sexual conventions, hosting pornography nights in their faculty apartment and forays to Harlem strip clubs.

  Although Niebuhr and Tillich had worked amiably enough for the five years of Tillich's tenure, their collegiality had recently cooled dramatically as a result of the "Tilliches' moral intransigence." It was not only that Tillich was unfaithful to his wife and that his wife reciprocated such infidelities as she could on occasion arrange with younger men. Tillich was exuberantly, compulsively promiscuous. Their falling out began after Niebuhr referred a female student to Tillich for office hours. Tillich welcomed her warmly, closed the door, arranged his chair next to the woman, and moved his hands onto her thighs. The student returned to Niebuhr in tears, and Niebuhr never forgave Tillich this betrayal. But neither did he report Tillich's behavior.

27. Bonhoeffer, "American Diary," 1939, in Bonhoeffer, *DBW*, vol. 15, pp. 217–37.

28. A year earlier Houghton and Mifflin had licensed the London-based Reynal and Hitchcock for the rights to publish a complete translation. A thirty-one-page pamphlet also appeared in the summer of 1939 under the title *Mein Kampf: An Unexpurgated Digest*, by the Political Digest Press of New York. The book was translated by a committee from the New School for Social Research in New York and appeared on February 28, 1939. An abridged version had been published in English in 1933. James Murphy, an Irishman, began work on an authorized version in Berlin in the fall of 1936 after spending some time as the official translator for the Propaganda Ministry, mostly working to translate Hitler's speeches. For reasons as of yet fully unknown, Murphy was taken off the task in the early months of 1937. After he returned to London, a battle ensued between the London publishers and Berlin concerning Murphy's translation. Against the ministry's wishes, Hurst and Blackett went forward with Murphy's translation, publishing the work on March 20, 1939. This was two weeks after two new (also unauthorized) translations were published in America. Central Germany, May 7, 1936,—Confidential—A Translation of Some of the More Important Passages of Hitler's Mein Kampf (1925 edition) British Embassy in Berlin 11 Germany's Foreign Policy as Stated in Mein Kampf by Adolf Hitler FOE pamphlet n.38

29. Bonhoeffer also had read the German theologian Hermann Sasse's account during his 1925–26 year at Hartford Seminary, which Sasse had included as the foreword to his book *Here We Stand*. See Sasse, *The Lonely Way*, p. 23.

30. He also received an invitation from the Boerickes, his relatives in Philadelphia.

31. Bonhoeffer cited in *The Way to Freedom: Letters, Lectures and Notes, 1935–1939*, trans. Edwin H. Robertson and John Bowden (New York: Harper and Row, Publishers,1966), p. 228.

32. Dramm, *Dietrich Bonhoeffer and the Resistance*, p. 7.

33. The 1939 film *Juarez* (directed by William Dieterle), with Paul Muni in the role of Benito Pablo Juárez.

34. Bonhoeffer cited in *The Way to Freedom*, p. 228.

35. Bethge, *Dietrich Bonhoeffer: A Biography*, p. 658.

36. "Later this will eventually be a center of resistance long after Riverside Church will have become a temple of idolatry. I was very pleased about this sermon."

37. Martin Luther King Jr. would echo this sentiment three decades later

when he called Niebuhr's Jesus "a pure abstraction," not "the Jesus of history who walked in Jerusalem."

38. Martin Sasse cited in "German Martyrs," *Time*, Monday, December 23, 1940.

39. Mark S. Brocker, "Editor's Introduction to the English Edition," *DBW*, vol. 16, p. 1.

40. Ibid., p. 5.

41. Brocker, "Editor's Introduction to the English Edition," DBW, vol. 16, Ibid. p. 4.

42. Bonhoeffer, *DBW*, vol. 16, p. 26.

43. Ibid., p. 47.

44. Ibid., p. 49.

45. Bonhoeffer, *DBW*, vol. 16, Ibid., p. 112.

46. Brocker, "Editor's Introduction to the English Edition," DBW, vol 12, pp. 1–6.

47. Ibid.

48. Victoria Barnett, "The Rise and Fall of the Confessing Church." [VB—P]

49. Bonhoeffer, *DBW*, vol. 5, p. 23–26; *Ethics*, pp. 46–49.

50. Brocker, "Editor's Introduction to the English Edition," *DBW*, vol. 16.

51. Ibid.

52. Bonhoeffer, *DBW*, vol. 16, pp. 474–75. "For Bonhoeffer's understanding of the assumptio carnis, or "assumption of the flesh," see his "Reflection on the Ascension," 2/2.

CHAPTER TWELVE "Christmas in the Ruins"

1. Bonhoeffer, *Werke*, vol. 16, pp. 109–10. (Author's translation from the original German.)

2. Jørgen Glenthøøj, et al., "Editors' Afterword to the German Edition," in *DBW*, vol. 16 , pp. 651.

3. Schlingensiepen, *Dietrich Bonhoeffer*, p. 239.

4. Bonhoeffer, *DBW*, vol. 16, pp. 96–97.

5. Ibid., p. 60.

6. Schlingensiepen, *Dietrich Bonhoeffer*, p. 245.

7. De Gruchy, *Daring, Trusting Spirit*, p. 53.

8. Bonhoeffer, *DBW*, vol. 16, p. 81.

9. Jørgen Glenthøøj, et al., "Editors' Afterword to the German Edition," in ibid, p. 651.

10. Bonhoeffer, *DBW*, vol. 16, p. 95. (Author's translation from the original German.)

11. Ibid., p. 82.

12. Mark Brocker, "Editor's Introduction to the English Edition," in ibid., p. 18.

13. Bonhoeffer, *DBW,* vol. 16, p. 86.

14. Mark Brocker, "Editor's Introduction to the English Edition," in ibid., p. 18; Bonhoeffer, *DBW*, vol. 16, p. 89.

15. Bonhoeffer, *DBW*, vol. 16, p. 87.

16. Jørgen Glenthooj, et al., "Editors' Afterword to the German Edition," in ibid., p. 650.

17. Bonhoeffer, *DBW*, vol. 16, pp. 105, 109–10.

18. Ibid., p. 86.

19. Ibid., p. 89; author's translation of a quote from the monastery's 1996 printing of the brochure: *Benediktinerabtei Ettal* (Oberammergau: H. Weixler, 1996), N.P.

20. Bonhoeffer, *DBW*, vol. 16, pp. 89–90.

21. Ibid., p. 87.

22. Ibid., p. 92.

23. While writing his biography of Eberhard Bethge, the South African theologian John de Gruchy discovered that Bethge had himself received the UK exemption given to pastors and that when this exemption was revoked in September 1942 he was given a temporary *Abwehr* assignment by Dohnányi. See ibid., p. 57.

24. Ibid., p. 95.

25. Ibid., pp. 97–101.

26. Ibid., p. 101.

27. Ibid., p. 105.

28. Ibid., p. 111.

29. Ibid., p. 113.

30. Ibid., p. 105.

31. Mark Brocker in ibid., pp. 106–7.

32. Bonhoeffer, in ibid., pp. 106–7.

33. Ibid., pp. 108.

34. Ibid., pp. 205–7.

35. Ibid., p. 92.

36. Ibid., pp. 104.

37. Ibid., pp. 112, 168.

38. Ibid., p. 137.

39. Ibid., p. 140.

40. Ibid., p. 133.

41. Ibid., p. 282.

42. Although Bonhoeffer does not specify the edition he preferred, this seems the most likely of the three available translations: Ludwig Tieck; an anonymous translation revised by Konrad Thorer; and Ludwig Braunfels.

43. Ibid., pp. 138–40.

44. Bonhoeffer, *DBW*, vol. 8, p. 394.

45. Although the protest of Barth against natural theology had made sense to the younger Bonhoeffer as an effective means of jamming a wedge between the state and the church (the German Christians employed the

category of the natural to justify the legitimacy of the Nazi state), he now recognized an urgency to reclaiming the natural—the bodily, the physical, the human—from its colossal disfigurations.

46. Bonhoeffer, *DBW*, vol. 10, pp. 501–2.
47. Bonhoeffer, *The Cost of Discipleship* (New York: The Macmillan Company, 1967), p. 272; Bonhoeffer, *DBW*, vol. 6, p. 185.
48. Bonhoeffer, *DBW*, vol. 6, p. 187.
49. Ibid., pp. 187–88.
50. Bonhoeffer, *DBW*, vol. 16, p. 156.
51. Ibid., p. 128.
52. Ibid., pp. 129, 132, 141, 146.
53. Ibid., p. 156. (Author's translation from the original German.)
54. Mark Brocker, "Editor's Introduction to the English Edition," in ibid., p. 11.
55. Bonhoeffer, *DBW*, vol. 16, in ibid., p. 139.
56. Ibid., pp. 156, 126.
57. Ibid., pp. 134, 139.
58. Bonhoeffer, *DBW*, vol. 7, p. 131.
59. Bonhoeffer, *DBW*, vol. 16, p. 136.
60. Ibid, pp. 138–39.
61. Ibid, p. 159.
62. Ibid, p. 155.
63. Ibid, p. 161.
64. Ibid, p. 162.
65. Bonhoeffer, *DBW*, vol. 16, p. 168.
66. Ved Mehta, *The New Theologian*, pp. 128–29.
67. Bonhoeffer, *DBW*, vol. 8, p. 50.
68. Bonhoeffer, *DBW*, vol. 16, p. 208.
69. Ibid., p. 192. (Author's translation from the original German.)
70. Bonhoeffer, *DBW*, vol. 8, pp. 447–48.
71. Wilhelm Ihde in Bonhoeffer, *DBW*, vol. 16, pp. 180–81.
72. Bonhoeffer in ibid., pp. 186–88.
73. Wilhelm Ihde in ibid., pp. 189–90.
74. Bonhoeffer, *Ethics* (New York: The Macmillian Company, 1955), p. 181.
75. Ibid., p. 178.
76. Ibid.; "theologian in the resistance" is a concept developed by Sabina Drumm in *Dietrich Bonhoeffer and the Resistance*.
77. W. Lovin, New Studies in Bonhoeffer's Ethics "Biographical Context," pp. 90–91.
78. Bonhoeffer, *DBW*, vol. 8, p. 333.
79. Bonhoeffer, *Ethics* (New York: The Macmillian Company, 1955), p. 193.
80. Leibholz-Bonhoeffer, *The Bonhoeffers*, pp. 22–23.
81. Bonhoeffer, *DBW*, vol. 7, p. 103.
82. Ibid., p. 126.
83. Bonhoeffer, *DBW*, vol. 16, p. 330.

84. As Jørgen Glenthøøj, et al., wrote in the "Editors' Afterword to the German Edition" (in ibid., pp. 657–58): "Subsequent scholars have debated whether those at the center of the conspiracy should have taken such a risk, since precisely this action did indeed prove to be the undoing of its initiators through a series of fateful developments. Bonhoeffer's defense letters to the lead investigator, Dr. Roeder, during his imprisonment show the role that Operation 7 played in the interrogations. However, there is no doubt that both Dohnányi and Bonhoeffer felt that what they were able to do in this regard was too little rather than too much. The motto of 1933, 'Open your mouth for the dumb,' is countered at the end of 1942 by the admission, 'We have been silent witnesses of evil deeds.' "

85. Mark Brocker, the scholar who edited the eight-hundred-page English translation of Bonhoeffer's writings in and around the conspiracy, explained, "During Dohnányi's arrest, interrogator Manfred Roeder found notes that discussed plans for a journey on April 19, 1943, by Bonhoeffer and Josef Müller to Rome, where they would explain to church leaders why the assassination attempt on Hitler in March had failed. Roeder's initial interrogations of Dohnányi focused on these notes, which were evidence of highly treasonous behavior. Dohnányi, Oster, and Canaris successfully argued that these papers were official coded Military Intelligence materials, and Roeder temporarily dropped this line of interrogation. Roeder's interrogations then turned to Operation 7. The fourteen 'non-Aryans' in Operation 7 had been smuggled into Switzerland under the pretext that they were working for Military Intelligence," Brocker, "Editor's Introduction to the English Edition," in ibid., vol. 16, p. 14.

86. Ibid.

87. Bonhoeffer, *DBW*, vol. 16, pp. 352–53.

88. Ibid., p. 231.

89. Bonhoeffer's recommendation letter for Dohnányi did, however, come into Koechlin's possession. See Marikje Smid, *Hans von Dohnanyi, Christine Bonhoeffer: Eine Ehe im Widerstand gegen Hitler* (Munich: Gütersloher, 2002), pp. 301–2.

CHAPTER THIRTEEN Killing the Madman

1. The recent publication of his *Prayerbook of the Bible* had provoked the attention of the Reich Chamber of Literature.

2. Bonhoeffer, *DBW*, vol. 16, pp. 228, 226.

3. Ibid., p. 228.

4. Ibid., pp. 225–26.

5. Ibid., pp. 230, 212.

6. Ibid., pp. 226–27.

7. Bonhoeffer, *DBW*, vol. 16, p. 227.

8. Roger Moorhouse, "Germania: Hitler's Dream Capital," *History Today* 62, no. 3 (2012).

9. Ibid., p. 240.

10. Ibid., pp. 224, 253.

11. Orte der Erinnerung 1933–1945, "House of the Wannsee Conference: Memorial and Education Site," http://www.orte-der erinnerung.de/en/institutions/institutions_liste/house_of_the_wannsee_conference_memorial_and_educational_site/ (accessed February 20, 2013).

12. Jewish Virtual Library, "Reinhard Heydrich," http://www.jewishvirtu allibrary.org/jsource/Holocaust/Heydrich.html (accessed February 20, 2013).

13. Mark Roseman, *The Villa, the Lake, the Meeting: Wannsee and the Final Solution* (London: Penguin Books, 2003), p. 55.

14. Mark Roseman explains, "What we have is the Protocol, or in other words Eichmann's glossary of the notes, which he claimed was in turn heavily edited by Heydrich." Cited in ibid., p. 109.

15. *The Wannsee Conference and the Genocide of the European Jews*, trans. Caroline Pearce (Berlin: House of the Wannsee Conference, Memorial and Educational Site, 2007), p. 1.

16. Roseman, *The Villa, the Lake, the Meeting*, p. 67.

17. Ibid., p. 1.

18. Ibid., p. 101.

19. Bonhoeffer, *DBW*, vol. 16, pp. 52, 38.

20. Bosanquet, *The Life and Death of Dietrich Bonhoeffer*, p. 233.

21. Dramm, *Dietrich Bonhoeffer and the Resistance*, pp. 6, 233.

22. See Victoria Barnett's review of Sabine Dramm, *V-Mann Gottes und der Abwehr? Dietrich Bonhoeffer und der Widerstand* (Gütersloh: Gütersloher Verlagshaus, 2005). (The review appeared first in the *Zeitschrift für Kirchengeschichte*, 2007/2.)

23. Dramm, *Dietrich Bonhoeffer and the Resistance*.

24. Both scholars find support for their intuitions in Bethge's 1969 biography, which, while it may have helped to shape the heroic picture in its various forms, at the same time offered only the most modest statements on Bonhoeffer's role in the resistance, and which today, in Sabine Dramm's view, should for this reason be noted "all the more carefully." "Bonhoeffer's position in the Resistance Movement was of no great importance politically," Bethge later explained—although his modest estimation of Bonhoeffer's resistance activities was largely ignored until recent years. "Regarding the planning for a future Germany and its constitutional forms Bonhoeffer's share in the conspiracy was comparatively small." In ibid., p. 234.

25. Bethge cited in ibid., p. 234.

26. Lovin, "Biographical Context," p. 88.

27. Glenthoøj et al., "Editors' Afterword to the German Edition," pp. 654–55.

28. Bonhoeffer, *DBW*, vol. 16, pp. 278.
29. Glenthøøj et al., "Editors' Afterword to the German Edition," p. 655.
30. Brocker, "Editor's Introduction to the English Edition," p. 10.
31. Busch and Bowden, *Karl Barth*, p. 315.
32. Cited in Bonhoeffer, *DBW*, vol. 16, p. 279.
33. Schlingensiepen, *Dietrich Bonhoeffer*, pp. 289–90.
34. Bonhoeffer cited in ibid. This is also found in Bonhoeffer, *DBW*, vol. 16, p. 286.
35. Winston Churchill, "Blood, Toil, Tears and Sweat," speech to the House of Commons, May 13, 1940, cited in *Memoirs of the Second World War* (Boston: Houghton Mifflin Company Reprint, 1991), p. 245.
36. Victoria Barnett, "Dietrich Bonhoeffer: Resistance and Execution," http://www.ushmm.org/information/exhibitions/online-features/special-focus/dietrich-bonhoeffer/resistance-and-execution (accessed November 2, 2013).
37. Bonhoeffer's 1936 visit to Sweden with the students of Finkenwalde introduced him to friends and contacts who would continue playing roles in his ecumenical and resistance work throughout the years—for example, Erling Eidem, the Swedish archbishop of Uppsala, and Nils Kalstrom, who facilitated the diplomatic necessities of getting Bonhoeffer and friends to Sweden.
38. Björn Ryman, "Dietrich Bonhoeffer and Sweden," unpublished paper, Sigtuna Bonhoeffer Conference, p. 7.
39. Ibid., pp. 2–3.
40. Dramm, *Dietrich Bonhoeffer and the Resistance*, pp. 190–91.
41. Ryman, "Dietrich Bonhoeffer and Sweden," p. 11.
42. Bonhoeffer, *DBW*, vol. 16, p. 318.
43. Bell cited in Ryman, "Dietrich Bonhoeffer and Sweden," p. 11: "It was a definite attempt to secure an early peace. It would have never been made if there had been no ecumenical movement."
44. Ibid., p. 12.
45. Mark Brocker explains further: "On March 18, 1957, Eberhard Bethge sent these diary fragments to Bishop Bell with an accompanying letter, saying: 'I enclose the pretended diary of 1942 which Dietrich wrote that the Gestapo should find it on his desk. They did' (Bell Papers, vol. 42). The fictitious diary fragments apparently played no role in the cases against Bonhoeffer, Dohnányi, and Oster." In Bonhoeffer, *DBW*, vol. 16, p. 400.
46. Ryman, "Dietrich Bonhoeffer and Sweden," p. 12.
47. Bonhoeffer cited in Lovin, "Biographical Context," p. 96.
48. Bonhoeffer in Bonhoeffer, *DBW*, vol. 16, pp. 402–3.
49. Bethge, "Dietrich and Maria," p. 12.
50. Bonhoeffer in Bonhoeffer, *DBW*, vol. 16, p. 329.
51. Ibid., pp. 329–30. He said he "sensed how an opposition to all that is 'religious' is growing in me. Often into an instinctive revulsion—which is

surely not good either. I am not religious by nature. But I must constantly think of God, of Christ; authenticity, life, freedom, and mercy mean a great deal to me. It is only that the religious clothes they wear make me so uncomfortable."

52. Ibid., pp. 374–75.

53. Ibid., p. 376.

54. In Bethge's biography of Bonhoeffer, January 17, 1943, is identified as the date of the engagement. Since Wedemeyer accepted Bonhoeffer's proposal of marriage in writing on January 13, 1943, that date is now considered the day of the engagement. See Bethge, *Dietrich Bonhoeffer: A Biography*, p. 790.

55. Bonhoeffer in Bonhoeffer, *DBW*, vol. 8, pp. 91–92.

56. Brocker, "Editor's Introduction to the English Edition," p. 21.

57. Bonhoeffer, *DBW*, vol. 16, p. 375.

58. De Gruchy, *Daring, Trusting Spirit*, p. 66. Bonhoeffer kissed Maria on the cheek, in front of the public prosecutor, Manfred Roeder, on her second visit to Tegel prison. That appears to be the only time they kissed. After a later visit, Maria told Dietrich it made her sad that he did not leave his hand on hers. "And it was so good, your warm hand, I wished that you would leave there. . . . A stream flowed from it all over me, it filled me completely, leaving no space for thought. But you took it away. You don't like being romantic, do you?" Cited in Margarete Nürnberger, "Maria von Wedemeyer: Fiancée [sic] of Dietrich Bonhoeffer," *Journal of Theology for Southern Africa*, no. 127 (March 2007): 123.

59. Wedemeyer-Weller, *The Other Letters from Prison*, pp. 103–13.

60. Maria von Wedemeyer cited in Bonhoeffer cited in Brownjohn, trans., *Love Letters from Cell 92*, p. 30. In September 1977, before her death two months later, Maria von Wedemeyer imposed the condition that these manuscripts might be consulted after her death or after twenty-five years, whichever would come later. Having contemplated publishing the correspondence with Bonhoeffer herself, she gave copies of the manuscripts and other papers, including her own letters to Bonhoeffer, to her sister, Ruth-Alice von Bismarck. Bismarck collaborated with Ulrich Kabitz, and in 1992 the German edition of the correspondence was published and eventually translated and published in Britain in 1994 as *Love Letters from Cell 92: Dietrich Bonhoeffer Maria von Wedemeyer 1943–45*. A slightly revised American edition was published in 1995. As implied by its title, the book was confined to the correspondence with Bonhoeffer "during his imprisonment."

61. Ibid., p. 27.

62. Scott Paradise, "Eulogy for Maria Friedricka von Wedemeyer Weller, 18 November 1977," *International Bonhoeffer Newsletter: English Language Section*, no. 82 (summer 2003): 4.

63. Bethge, "Dietrich and Maria," p. 12.

64. De Gruchy, *Daring, Trusting Spirit*, p. 66. More than sixty thousand

German Jews immigrated to Palestine during the 1930s, most under the terms of the Haavara (Transfer) Agreement.

65. Bethge cited in de Gruchy, *Daring, Trusting Spirit*, pp. 66–67.
66. Bonhoeffer, *DBW*, vol. 8, p. 240.
67. Bethge cited in de Gruchy, *Daring, Trusting Spirit*, p. 66.
68. Bonhoeffer, *DBW*, vol. 8, p. 248.
69. Zimmermann, "A Meeting in Werder," p. 191.
70. Ibid., pp. 191–92.
71. Cited in Dramm, *Dietrich Bonhoeffer and the Resistance*, p. 214.
72. Ibid.
73. On August 15, 1944, Haeften's older brother, Hans-Berndt von Haeften, a diplomat in the Foreign Office in Berlin and member of the Kreisau Circle, suffered a similar fate, only hours after he was pronounced guilty by the People's Court as a conspirator. Zimmermann and Smith, eds., *I Knew Dietrich Bonhoeffer*, pp. 190–93.
74. Bonhoeffer, *DBW*, vol. 8, p. 52.
75. Bonhoeffer, *DBW*, vol. 6, pp. 181–82.
76. Bonhoeffer, *Letters and Papers from Prison*, ed. Eberhard Bethge, p. 25.
77. Bonhoeffer, *DBW*, vol. 8, p. 52.
78. Ibid., p. 37.
79. Ibid., pp. 38–39.
80. Ibid., pp. 42–44. Bonhoeffer's remedy began not with the acquisition of knowledge, however, in education or instruction, but in the proper "fear of the Lord." The spell can be broken—and "liberation from stupidity" achieved—only from a source *beyond* the individual, the community, the *Volk*, the nation. The wisdom gleaned from the Hebrew Bible and the New Testament proclaims "that the internal liberation of human beings to live the responsible life before God" is the only genuine way to overcome stupidity. Liberation from stupidity enlivens the moral senses.
81. Ibid., p. 48.
82. Ibid., pp. 48–49.
83. Ibid., p. 50.
84. Bethge, *Costly Grace*, p. 114.
85. Scholl, *The White Rose*, pp. 22, 86.
86. Schlabrendorff managed to retrieve the intact bomb the next day without being caught, but he was arrested on July 20, 1944, following the failure of the July 20 assassination attempt on Hitler at Wolf's Lair, and sent to a Gestapo prison. Between February and May 1945, Schlabrendorff was moved from the Gestapo prison on Prinz-Albrecht-Strasse to the Sachsenhausen, Flossenbürg, Dachau, and Innsbruck concentration camps. In late April 1945, he was transferred to Tyrol, together with about 140 other political prisoners, but the SS left the prisoners behind shortly before the Fifth U.S. Army liberated the camp on May 5, 1945.
87. Brocker, "Editor's Introduction to the English Edition," p. 15.

88. Bishop of Chichester, "The Background of the Hitler Plot," *Contemporary Review* 16 (July/December 1945): 208.
89. Victoria Barnett writes, "[Bonhoeffer's] role in the actual resistance may have been minor, and his colleagues in that resistance may have been nationalists and monarchists. But his theological reflections on the challenges that confronted Christians under Nazism, including his reflections on the role of the Church in an ideological dictatorship and the consequences this has for the Church's very identity, are powerful reminders to all Christians of the dangers of an alliance between Christianity, state authority, and ideology." Review of Sabine Dramm, *V-Mann Gottes und der Abwehr? Dietrich Bonhoeffer und der Widerstand* (Gütersloh: Gütersloher Verlagshaus, 2005). (This review appeared first in the *Zeitschrift für Kirchengeschichte*, 2007/2, and is reprinted with the kind permission of the author.)
90. Bethge cited in Mehta, *The New Theologian*, p. 198.
91. Bonhoeffer and Bethge cited in ibid., p. 201.

CHAPTER FOURTEEN
"The Greatest of Feasts on the Journey to Freedom"

1. Schlingensiepen, *Dietrich Bonhoeffer, 1906–1945*, p. 435.
2. Eberhard Bethge, cited in Bonhoeffer, *DBW*, vol. 8, p. 194, note 1. "These prayers belong to the most profound expressions of Bonhoeffer's spirituality. They were not jotted down spontaneously but were composed after extended meditation and experienced discipline." De Gruchy in Bonhoeffer, *DBW*, vol. 8, p. 94.
3. Bonhoeffer, *DBW*, vol. 8, p. 56.
4. John de Gruchy, "Editor's Introduction," *DWB*, vol. 8, p. 13. No first name is given for Knobloch in the scholarly literature. According to de Gruchy, "These, together with a photograph of Bonhoeffer taken in the yard of Tegel prison, were kept by Bethge's mother in her home in Kade until after the war. At the same time, Bonhoeffer gave the letters Bethge had sent him to his parents during their prison visits. Nonetheless, several letters, both from Bonhoeffer and from others, were lost; some had never reached their destination in the first place, some were misplaced in the chaos of the times, and others, notably Bonhoeffer's letters to Bethge in September 1944, were destroyed for security reasons." Three photographs from Tegel survived. Another guard, Linke, who brought the baptism letter to the parents, was also familiar to the Bonhoeffers, although, unlike Knobloch, Linke had to be bribed. Dietrich's gold watch was the cost for the delivery of Bonhoeffer's baptism letter for young Dietrich Bethge on May 21, 1944. Renate and the family knew he was receiving letters from Dietrich. In January 1944, Bethge's unit was sent to Rignano, north of Rome.

5. Ibid.
6. De Gruchy, *Daring, Trusting Spirit*, p. 76.
7. On Christmas Day 1943, Bethge was garrisoned in Lissa, Poland, where earlier that year he had been briefly deployed with military intelligence.
8. Bonhoeffer, *DBW*, vol. 8, p. 221.
9. Since all his writings now had to be approved by the censors, they had to be readable, and he had to plan exactly what to write. Bonhoeffer composed *Ethics* in Gothic script or on a typewriter. Eberhard Bethge, interview with author, May 1992, Villiprot-Bonn, Germany.
10. Hannah Arendt refers to Rahel Varnhagen's remark that Goethe's works are "fragments of a great confession." See Arendt, "Berlin Salon," p. 61.
11. Bonhoeffer, *DBW*, vol. 8, p. 344.
12. Cited in Zimmermann and Smith, eds., *I Knew Dietrich Bonhoeffer*, p. 222.
13. *Apocalypse* is a series of fifteen woodcuts Albrecht Dürer made depicting various scenes from the book of Revelation, published in 1498. Bonhoeffer's was a reproduction printed by the *Deutsche Allgemeine Zeitung* of the woodcut *St. Michael Battling the Dragon*. See Bonhoeffer, *DBW*, vol. 8, p. 66. *St. Michael Battling the Dragon* is Dürer's rendering of Revelation 12:7, when war broke out in heaven; Michael leads the angels against the seven-headed dragon, all set against a peaceful landscape. "And war broke out in heaven; Michael and his angels fought against the dragon. The dragon and his angels fought back, but they were defeated, and there was no longer any place for them in heaven" (Revelation 12:7).
14. Barth, *Church Dogmatics*, II/2, p. 318.
15. In volume II/2, Barth turned his attention to the doctrine of the salvation, and in particular the contentious issue of predestination, that God elected some people to salvation and some to eternal damnation. Although Barth rejected the moniker of universal salvation, the effect was the same. Barth recast the doctrine of the salvation to show that all humanity has been saved by the vicarious work of Jesus Christ. No finite reality can finally resist God's mercy and grace.
16. Bonhoeffer, *DBW*, vol. 16, p. 425.
17. Bonhoeffer had written a number of letters and follow-up notes to Roeder related to his UK classification. Volume 16 of *DBW* also includes Bonhoeffer's "camouflage letter" (*Tarnbrief*), which he wrote at Dohnányi's request to disguise the true course of events.
18. Bonhoeffer, *Letters and Papers from Prison*, ed. Eberhard Bethge, pp. 56–57.
19. Walter Benjamin cited in Wayne Whitson Floyd Jr., "Style and Critique of Metaphysics: The Letter as Form in Bonhoeffer and Adorno," in Wayne Whitson Floyd Jr. and Charles Marsh, *Theology and the Practice of Responsibility: Essays on Dietrich Bonhoeffer* (Philadelphia: Trinity Press International, 1994), p. 239.
20. Bonhoeffer, *DBW*, vol. 8, p. 110.
21. Bosanquet, *The Life and Death of Dietrich Bonhoeffer*, p. 251.

22. Edwin Robertson, *The Shame and the Sacrifice* (New York: Macmillan, 1988), p. 230.
23. Bonhoeffer cited in Bosanquet, *The Life and Death of Dietrich Bonhoeffer*, p. 249.
24. Ibid., p. 263.
25. Robertson, *The Shame and the Sacrifice*, p. 235.
26. From Floyd, "Style and Critique of Metaphysics," p. 249.
27. Bonhoeffer speaks of the day "when people will once more be able to speak the word of God with renewing and redemptive power. But on that day, Christians will have learned to speak a new language—perhaps quite nonreligious language, but liberating and redeeming like Jesus's language . . . the language of a new righteousness and truth, a language proclaiming that God makes peace with humankind and that God's kingdom is drawing near; and liberating and hope-inspiring like the language of the Hebrew prophets. On that day 'They shall fear and tremble because of all the good and all the prosperity I provide for them' (Jer. 33:9)."
28. Although *Letters and Papers from Prison* was published in an abridged English version in 1953, it was not until the publication of John A. T. Robinson's *Honest to God* in 1963 that Bonhoeffer's theology became known to popular audiences. As the theological inspiration of the Anglo-American "Death of God" movement of the late 1960s, Bonhoeffer's prison writings offered phrases and ideas well suited to a generation of disenchanted church people—"the world come of age," "religionless Christianity," and "living in the world as if there is no God." And the Death of God movement, for fifteen minutes, stimulated conversations in the universities and churches on the church in the secular city, even though the movement's riff on selected prison writings (and its indifference to most everything else in Bonhoeffer's corpus) led to distorted, if not at times comically flawed, interpretations. Still, these boyish theologians and "a/theologians," as some came to be called, leveled important and unsettling questions against the floundering Protestant mainline and brought daring and passion to American academic theology; as I have said elsewhere, they should be forgiven their excesses.
29. Bonhoeffer, *DBW*, vol. 11, p. 285.
30. Bethge, *Dietrich Bonhoeffer: A Biography*, p. 883.
31. Bonhoeffer, *Letters and Papers from Prison*, ed. Eberhard Bethge, p. 312.
32. Aside from the Barcelona sermon, there are only five mentions of the Song of Solomon in Bonhoeffer's writings. One appeared in a London sermon; another was from Barcelona. The rest are found in the prison writings.
33. John de Gruchy, conversation with the author.
34. Bethge does not mention this visit in his biography. Ibid.
35. Bonhoeffer, *DBW*, vol. 8, p. 412.
36. See the "Editors' Afterword to the German Edition," *DBW*, vol. 6, pp. 307–9.

37. This confession proved deeply unsettling to those who knew Bonhoeffer from the Finkenwalde years. Many of these pastors were disturbed by this question of whether, "in the end, Finkenwalde might have been only a temporary phase" in Bonhoeffer's spiritual journey. Members of Bonhoeffer's family, on the other hand, felt relief upon reading the prison letters after the war, concluding that the strenuous theology of his writings in the 1930s had been superseded by the meditations on religionless Christianity.

38. De Gruchy in Bonhoeffer, *DBW*, vol. 8, p. 374.

39. Edward Callan, "Exorcising Mittenhofer," *London Magazine* 14, no. 1 (1974): 73.

40. W. H. Auden, "Epistle to a Godson," cited in ibid., p. 74.

41. In Bonhoeffer's fictional piece, "A Quiet Forest Pond," the young German aristocrat ponders the fate of Christianity in the time beyond the war and reimagines Christianity in the form of a "new elite of people."

42. Schlabrendorff, *The Secret War Against Hitler*, p. 318.

43. Bosanquet, *The Life and Death of Dietrich Bonhoeffer*, p. 264.

44. Bonhoeffer, *DBW*, vol. 16, p. 405.

45. See Mark Brocker's excellent introduction to the English-language edition of *DBW*, vol. 16, pp. 1–30.

46. Schlingensiepen, *Bonhoeffer*, p. 359.

47. Bosanquet, *The Life and Death of Dietrich Bonhoeffer*, p. 267.

48. John de Gruchy, correspondence with the author.

49. Ibid.

50. *The "House Prison" at the Gestapo Headquarters in Berlin* (Berlin: Topography of Terror Foundation, 2005), p. 50.

51. Schlabrendorff, *I Knew Dietrich Bonhoeffer*, p. 228.

52. Schlabrendorff, *The Secret War Against Hitler,* pp. 329–35.

53. Fabian von Schlabrendorff, cited in *The "House Prison" at the Gestapo Headquarters in Berlin*, p. 53.

54. Bosanquet, *The Life and Death of Dietrich Bonhoeffer*, p. 267.

55. Sack cited in ibid., p. 256.

56. Bonhoeffer, *Letters and Papers from Prison*, ed. Eberhard Bethge, p. 326.

57. Stifter seems an unlikely guide to the human psyche; after a failed romance and an unhappy marriage he committed suicide in 1868 by slashing his neck with a razor.

58. Bonhoeffer, *DBW*, vol. 8, p. 397.

59. In the poem "The Past," written in summer 1944, Bonhoeffer heralded the recovery of an earthy richness, faded and dissolved—"comfortless, distant . . . past"—and enriched now by prayer, thought, and love. The past returned to him in a dream at daybreak, "pure, free, and whole." Was this not how grace should feel? "The past coming to you once again, and becoming your life's enduring part, through thanks and repentance." Bonhoeffer stretched out his hands in solitude and prayed. "A new thing now I hear," he said amid the silences of the hour.

60. Karl and Paula were not allowed to visit Dietrich in the Gestapo prison; fortuitously, Bonhoeffer's prosecutor was fond of Maria and made a few exceptions for her. Renate Bethge and Nancy Lukens, "By Powers of Good," in Association of Contemporary Church Historians (*Arbeitsgemeinschaft kirchlicher Zeitgeschichtler*), vol. 12, special issue on Dietrich Bonhoeffer, ed. John S. Conway (February 2006): 74. Compare with this the note from Lukens: "The handwritten original is part of Bonhoeffer's December 19, 1944, letter from the Prinz-Albrecht-Straße prison in Berlin to Maria von Wedemeyer."

61. Ibid., p. 77.

62. Ibid., p. 79.

63. Text of the children's song, titled "Abendgebet" (evening prayer), in *Des Knaben Wunderhorn*. ("When at night I go to bed, fourteen angels round my stead.") See also Martin Luther, Sermon on Michaelmas, September 29, 1531: "I should soon accustom a child from the youngest age on to say: Dear child, you have an angel; when you pray in the morning and the evening, this angel will be by you, will sit by your little bed, will be dressed in a little white cloak, and will take care of you, rock you and keep you safe."

64. Christoph Gestrich, conversation with the author, March 2011, Berlin.

65. No contemporaneous documents were preserved from the events leading to the April 9 executions. However, the account given by English secret service officer Payne Best, first in his letter of March 2, 1951, to Gerhard Leibholz, and then in his 1953 book *The Venlo Incident*, has been generally accepted by most scholars. "Officer Best was part of the group of prisoners that was housed in the special barracks at the Buchenwald concentration camp and then transported to Schönberg in the Bavarian forest." "His soul really shone in the dark desperation of our prison. He was one of the very few men I have ever met to whom God was real and ever close to him." Best wrote that when Bonhoeffer was taken away by prison guards, he "remained calm and normal, seemingly perfectly at his ease," and that he approached him directly, grasped his hand, and whispered, "Will you give this message from me to the Bishop of Chichester, 'tell him that this is for me the end, but also the beginning—with him I believe in the principle of our Universal Christian brotherhood which rises above all national hatreds and that our victory is certain—tell him, too, that I have never forgotten his words at our last meeting.'" London, Bell Papers, vol. 42; typewritten; in original English, including errors; excerpt from S. Payne Best's letter of October 13, 1953. Here Captain Best, who was transported together with Bonhoeffer up until their stay in the schoolhouse in Schönberg in the Bavarian forest, conveyed to the bishop the full text of Bonhoeffer's parting message as he was summoned for court martial in the Flossenbürg concentration camp on April 8, 1945. In a preceding letter to Bell on September 23, 1953, Best wrote, "I remember that the thought flashed through my mind, that perhaps the

message was a prearranged code which only you would understand." To this Bell responded on October 5, 1953, "You will see that the message was short; and it was not a pre-arranged code." For further reading, see Best, *Venlo Incident*, pp. 180, 191, 200; DB-ER, 921–28; and the Best/Bell correspondence in Glenthøj, "Zwei neue Zeugnisse," 99–111. [DBWE, vol., 16, pp. 467–69.]

66. In the same letter he asked for "some toothpaste a few coffee beans, and a laxative."

67. Karl Bonhoeffer cited in Bosanquet, *The Life and Death of Dietrich Bonhoeffer*, p. 269.

68. Schlingensiepen, *Dietrich Bonhoeffer*, p. 368.

69. Bethge, *Dietrich Bonhoeffer: A Biography*, p. 927.

70. Toni Siegert, "Concentration Camp Flossenburg," UTS Bonhoeffer Primary Sources, Serie 3, Box 1, Folder 7, p. 1.

71. Bethge, *Dietrich Bonhoeffer: A Biography*, p. 927.

72. Schlabrendorff, *The Secret War Against Hitler*, p. 330.

73. Clements, *Bonhoeffer*, p. 24.

74. For details see Rainer Mayer and Peter Zimmerling, eds., *Dietrich Bonhoeffer Aktuell: Biografie, Theologie, Spiritualität* (Gießen: Brunnen Verlag, 2001), pp. 92–93.

75. "In the postwar years, when the Nazi atrocities still had news value, the information circulated that Canaris was hanged by the string of a violin to prolong the strangulation, which meant that, when death was facing, he was brought back to consciousness only to be re-strangled. The victim was killed more than once. This information about the string is untrue." Cited in ibid.

76. "The atmospheric account of Bonhoeffer's hour of death by the camp physician is thus wholly devoid of truth. Moreover, the physician would have had to have ability to see the cell compound as well as the washing rooms through the open door, to observe Bonhoeffer kneeling. Besides, the executioner would never have permitted Bonhoeffer to interrupt the normal procedure. Regarding the knee praying pause taken by Bonhoeffer before ascending the gallows, it suffices to say that there were neither gallows nor steps to the gallows. One situation is conceivable where H. Fischer Hüllstrung would have been able to witness Bonhoeffer's final hour; in case the doctor—as he had done before—had accompanied the group of prisoners. This would have made sense in this particular situation, since he was to resuscitate the semi-strangled prisoners. Normally, the tasks assigned to the camp doctor were more banal e.g. oversee that the prisoners sentenced to death were stripped of their dental crowns. This would explain why he waited ten years before parting with these contorted details. Still, the story has a bright side: Family and friends of Bonhoeffer could learn from the letter that Bonhoeffer had exhibited such worthy conduct until the very end, which even managed to impress a cynical camp doctor. One can pray deeply without kneeling or without

clasping one's hands as they are tied in the back." Jørgen L. F. Morgensen cited in ibid.

77. "Chaplain Leslie Thompson Recalls Flossenbürg; A Personal Memory of Flossenburg by Leslie A. Thompson," January 14, 1989, http://milewis .wordpress.com/chaplain-leslie-thompson-flossenbuerg/ (accessed October 13, 2013).

78. From von Hase, "'Turning Away from the Phraseological to the Real,'" pp. 591–604.

79. Maria von Wedemeyer cited in Bonhoeffer, *DBW*, vol. 8, p. 556

SELECTED BIBLIOGRAPHY

~

1. ARCHIVAL SOURCES AND PRIVATE COLLECTIONS

Bildagentur für Kunst, Kultur und Geschichte, Berlin; and Art Resource, New York

Papers of Dietrich Bonhoeffer, Papers of Eberhard Bethge, Staatsbibliothek zu Berlin

Dietrich Bonhoeffer Sources, Burke Library, Union Theological Seminary, New York

KZ-Gedenkstätte Flossenbürg Archive

Archives of the Dietrich Bonhoeffer Church, Sydenham, London

Bundesarchiv Berlin-Lichterfelde (BA Berlin-Lichterfelde)

Karl Barth-Archiv, Basel, Switzerland

Museum der Dinge Archives, Berlin

Reinhold Niebuhr Papers, Library of Congress

Visual History Archive of the USC Shoah Foundation, Free University of Berlin

House of the Wannsee Conference, Memorial and Educational Site, Berlin

World Council of Churches Library and Archives, Geneva, Switzerland

2. PRIMARY LITERATURE

The seventeen-volume Dietrich Bonhoeffer Werke, published in English translation by Fortress Press, Minneapolis (sixteen volumes).

Bonhoeffer, Dietrich. *Dietrich Bonhoeffer Werke*. 17 vols. Edited by Eberhard Bethge et al. Munich: Chr. Kaiser/Gütersloher Verlagshaus, 1986–99. Translated as *Dietrich Bonhoeffer Works* (*DBW*), edited by Victoria J. Barnett, Wayne Whitson Floyd Jr., and Barbara Wojhoski (general editors). 17 vols. (Minneapolis: Fortress Press, 1996–).
    Vol. 1: *Sanctorum Communio: Eine dogmatische Untersuchung zur Soziologie der Kirche*. Edited by Joachim von Soosten. Munich: Chr. Kaiser Verlag, 1986. Translated by Reinhard Krauss and Nancy Lukens as *Sanctorum Commu-*

nio: A Theological Study of the Sociology of the Church, edited by Clifford J. Green (Minneapolis: Fortress Press, 1998).

Vol. 2: *Akt und Sein: Transzendentalphilosophie und Ontologie in der systematischen Theologie*. Edited by Hans-Richard Reuter. Munich: Chr. Kaiser Verlag, 1988. Translated by Martin Rumscheidt as *Act and Being: Transcendental Philosophy and Ontology in Systematic Theology*, edited by Wayne Whitson Floyd Jr. (Minneapolis: Fortress Press, 1996).

Vol. 3: *Schöpfung und Fall: Theologische Auslegung von Genesis 1–3*. Edited by Martin Rüter and Ilse Tödt. Munich: Chr. Kaiser Verlag, 1989. Translated by Douglas Stephen Bax as *Creation and Fall: A Theological Exposition of Genesis 1–3*, edited by John W. de Gruchy (Minneapolis: Fortress Press, 1996).

Vol. 4: *Nachfolge*. Edited by Martin Kuske and Ilse Tödt. Munich: Chr. Kaiser Verlag, 1989; 2nd ed., Gütersloh: Chr. Kaiser/Gütersloher Verlagshaus, 1994. Translated by Barbara Green and Reinhard Krauss as *Discipleship*, edited by Geffrey B. Kelly and John D. Godsey (Minneapolis: Fortress Press, 2001).

Vol. 5: *Gemeinsames Leben: Das Gebetbuch der Bibel*. Edited by Gerhard Ludwig Müller and Albrecht Schönherr. Munich: Chr. Kaiser Verlag, 1987. Translated by Daniel W. Bloesch and James H. Burtness as *Life Together* and *Prayerbook of the Bible*, edited by Geffrey B. Kelly (Minneapolis: Fortress Press, 1996).

Vol. 6: *Ethik*. Edited by Ilse Tödt, Heinz Eduard Tödt, Ernst Feil, and Clifford Green. Munich: Chr. Kaiser Verlag, 1992; 2nd ed., Gütersloh: Chr. Kaiser/Gütersloher Verlagshaus, 1998. Translated by Reinhard Krauss and Charles West, with Douglas W. Stott, as *Ethics*, edited by Clifford J. Green (Minneapolis: Fortress Press, 2004).

Vol. 7: *Fragmente aus Tegel*. Edited by Renate Bethge and Ilse Tödt. Gütersloh: Chr. Kaiser/Gütersloher Verlagshaus, 1994. Translated by Nancy Lukens as *Fiction from Tegel Prison*, edited by Clifford J. Green (Minneapolis: Fortress Press, 2000).

Vol. 8: *Widerstand und Ergebung*. Edited by Christian Gremmels, Eberhard Bethge, and Renate Bethge, with Ilse Tödt. Gütersloh: Chr. Kaiser/Gütersloher Verlagshaus; Minneapolis: Fortress Press, 1998. Translated by Isabel Best, Lisa E. Dahill, Reinhard Krauss, and Nancy Lukens as *Letters and Papers from Prison*, edited by John W. de Gruchy (Minneapolis: Fortress Press, 2010).

Vol. 9: *Jugend und Studium: 1918–1927*. Edited by Hans Pfeifer, with Clifford Green and Jürgen Kaltenborn. Munich: Chr. Kaiser Verlag, 1986. Translated by Mary Nebelsick, with the assistance of Douglas W. Stott, as *The Young Bonhoeffer: 1918–1927*, edited by Paul Matheny, Clifford J. Green, and Marshall Johnson (Minneapolis: Fortress Press, 2001).

Vol. 10: *Barcelona, Berlin, Amerika: 1928–1931*. Edited by Reinhard and Hans-Christoph von Hase, with Holger Roggelin and Matthias Wünsche.

Munich: Chr. Kaiser Verlag, 1991. Translated by Douglas W. Stott as *Barcelona, Berlin, New York: 1928–1931*, edited by Clifford J. Green (Minneapolis: Fortress Press, 2008).

Vol. 11: *Ökumene, Universität, Pfarramt: 1931–1932*. Edited by Eberhard Amelung and Christoph Strohm. Gütersloh: Chr. Kaiser Verlagshaus, 1994. Translated by Isabel Best, Nicholas S. Humphry, Marion Pauck, Anne Schmidt-Lange, and Douglas W. Stott as *Ecumenical, Academic, and Pastoral Work: 1931–1932*, edited by Victoria J. Barnett, Mark Brocker, and Michael B. Lukens (Minneapolis: Fortress Press, 2012).

Vol. 12: *Berlin: 1932–1933*. Edited by Carsten Nicolaisen and Ernst-Albert Scharffenorth. Gütersloh: Chr. Kaiser/Gütersloher Verlagshaus, 1997. Translated by Isabel Best, David Higgins, and Douglas W. Stott as *Berlin: 1932–1933*, edited by Larry L. Rasmussen (Minneapolis: Fortress Press, 2009).

Vol. 13: *London: 1933–1935*. Edited by Hans Goedeking, Martin Heimbucher, and Hans-Walter Schleicher. Gütersloh: Chr. Kaiser/Gütersloher Verlagshaus, 1994. Translated by Isabel Best as *London, 1933–1935*, edited by Keith W. Clements (Minneapolis: Fortress Press, 2007).

Vol. 14: *Illegale Theologenausbildung: Finkenwalde 1935–1937*. Edited by Otto Dudzus and Jürgen Henkys, with Sabine Bobert-Stützel, Dirk Schulz, and Ilse Tödt. Gütersloh: Chr. Kaiser/Gütersloher Verlagshaus, 1996. Translated by Douglas W. Stott as *Theological Education at Finkenwalde: 1935–1937*, edited by H. Gaylon Barker and Mark Brocker (Minneapolis: Fortress Press, 2013).

Vol. 15: *Illegale Theologenausbildung: Sammelvikariate: 1937–1940*. Edited by Dirk Schulz. Gütersloh: Chr. Kaiser/Gütersloher Verlagshaus, 1998. Translated by Claudia D. Bergmann, Peter Frick, and Scott A. Moore as *Theological Education Underground: 1937–1940*, edited by Victoria J. Barnett (Minneapolis: Fortress Press, 2011).

Vol. 16: *Konspiration und Haft: 1940–1945*. Edited by Jørgen Glenthøj, Ulrich Kabitz, and Wolf Krötke. Gütersloh: Chr. Kaiser Gütersloher Verlagshaus, 1996. Translated by Lisa E. Dahill as *Conspiracy and Imprisonment: 1940–1945*, edited by Mark Brocker (Minneapolis: Fortress Press, 2006).

Vol. 17: *Register und Ergänzungen* (Index and supplements). Edited by Herbert Anzinger and Hans Pfeifer, assisted by Waltraud Anzinger and Ilse Tödt. Gütersloh: Chr. Kaiser/Gütersloher Verlagshaus, 1999. No English translation available.

Individual Works by Bonhoeffer

Bonhoeffer, Dietrich. *Akt und Sein: Tranzendentalphilosophie und Ontologie in der systematischen Theologie*. Beiträge zur Förderung christlicher Theologie 34. Gütersloh: C. Bertelsmann, 1931.

———. *Akt und Sein: Tranzendentalphilosophie und Ontologie in der systematischen*

Theologie. Edited by Ernst Wolf. Theologische Bücherei 5. Munich: Chr. Kaiser, 1956; 4th ed., 1976. Translated by Bernard Noble as *Act and Being*, with an introduction by Ernst Wolf (New York: Octagon Books, 1983).

———. *Christ the Center*. New translation by Edwin H. Robertson. San Francisco: Harper and Row, 1978.

———. *Ethik*. Arranged and edited by Eberhard Bethge, 1949, restructured 1963. 6th ed. Munich: Chr. Kaiser Verlag, 1985. Translated by Neville Horton Smith as *Ethics* (New York: Macmillan, 1955, paperback edition, 1965; New York: Simon and Schuster, 1995).

———. *Fragmente aus Tegel: Drama und Roman*. Edited by Eberhard and Renate Bethge. Munich: Chr. Kaiser, 1978. Translated by Ursula Hoffmann as *Fiction from Prison: Gathering Up the Past* (Philadelphia: Fortress Press, 1981).

———. *Gemeinsames Leben*. 1939; Munich: Chr. Kaiser, 1986. Translated by John W. Doberstein as *Life Together* (1954; London: SCM Press, 1986).

———. *Gesammelte Schriften* (Collected works). Edited by Eberhard Bethge. 6 vols. Munich: Chr. Kaiser, 1958–74.

———. *Letters and Papers from Prison*. Translated by Reginald H. Fuller, edited by Eberhard Bethge, translation revised by Frank Clarke et al., additional material translated by John Bowden for the enlarged edition published in London (London: SCM, 1971; New York: Macmillan, 1972; New York: Simon and Schuster, 1997).

———. *Nachfolge*. Munich: Chr. Kaiser, 1937, 1940. Reprint, 1961; reprinted with an afterword by Eberhard Bethge, 1985. Translated by Reginald H. Fuller as *The Cost of Discipleship*, with a foreword by Bishop George K. A. Bell of Chichester and a memoir by Gerhard Leibholz (London: SCM, 1948); with a preface by Reinhold Niebuhr (New York: Macmillan, 1949). (Both the 1948 and the 1949 editions were abridged.) Second unabridged edition with translation revised by Irmgard Booth (London: SCM, 1959; New York: Macmillan, 1960; paperback edition [with different pagination], New York: Macmillan, 1963; London: SCM, 1964; first Touchstone edition, New York: Simon and Schuster, 1995).

———. *No Rusty Swords: Letters, Lectures, and Notes, 1928–1936*. Translated by Edwin H. Robertson and John Bowden. London: Collins; New York: Harper and Row, 1965.

———. *Prayers from Prison: Prayers and Poems*. Interpreted by Johann Christoph Hampe. Philadelphia: Fortress Press, 1978.

———. *Predigten—Auslegungen—Meditationen* (Sermons, interpretations, meditations). 2 vols. Vol. 1: *1925–1935*. Vol. 2: *1935–1945*. Edited by Otto Dudzus. Munich: Chr. Kaiser, 1984, 1985.

———. *The Prison Poems of Dietrich Bonhoeffer*. Translated and with a commentary by Edwin Robertson. Guilford, Surrey, UK: Eagle, 1998.

———. *Sanctorum Communio*. Translated by R. Gregor Smith from the third German edition. (London: William Collins Sons and Co., Fortress Press

Ltd., 1963). Published in the United States as *The Community of Saints* (New York: Harper and Row, 1963).

———. *Sanctorum Communio: Eine dogmatische Untersuchung zur Soziologie der Kirche* (The community of saints: A theological study of the sociology of the church). 26th Stück der neuen Studien zur Geschichte der Theologie und der Kirche. Edited by Reinhold Seeberg. Berlin: Trowitzsch, 1930.

———. *Schöpfung und Fall: Eine theologische Auslegung von Genesis 1–3*. 5th ed. Munich: Chr. Kaiser, 1968. Translated by John C. Fletcher and Kathleen Downham as *Creation and Fall/Temptation* (New York: Macmillan, 1959).

———. *Zettelnotizen für eine "Ethik"* (Working notes for an "Ethics"). Edited by Ilse Tödt. Supplementary volume to *DBW*, vol. 6. Gütersloh: Chr. Kaiser, 1993.

3. SECONDARY LITERATURE, INCLUDING WORKS USED BY BONHOEFFER

Adams, James Luther. *Not Without Dust and Heat: A Memoir*. Chicago: Exploration Press, 1995.

Althaus, Paul. *Kirche und Volkstum: Der völkische Wille im Lichte des Evangeliums*. Gütersloh: C. Bertelsmann, 1928.

Arendt, Hannah. "Berlin Salon." In *Essays in Understanding, 1930–1954*, edited by Jerome Kohn. New York: Harcourt, Brace and Co., 1994.

Arnold, Eberhard. *Innerland: A Guide into the Heart of the Gospel*. Farmington, PA: Plough Publishing House, 1999.

Baigent, Michael, and Richard Leigh. *Secret Germany: Claus von Stauffenberg and the Mystical Crusade Against Hitler*. London: Jonathan Cape, 1994.

Balkow-Gölitzer, Harry, Rüdiger Reitmeier, Bettina Biedermann, and Jörg Riedel. *Prominente in Berlin-Grunewald und ihre Geschichten*. Berlin: Be.bra Verlag GmbH, 2006.

Barnett, Victoria. *Bystanders: Conscience and Complicity During the Holocaust*. Westport, CT: Greenwood Press, 1999.

———. Correspondence with the author. June 19, 2011.

———. *For the Soul of the People: Protestant Protest Against Hitler*. Oxford: Oxford University Press, 1998.

———. "The Rise and Fall of the Confessing Church." Lecture delivered at the University of Virginia, February 9, 2009.

Barth, Karl. *Against the Stream: Shorter Post-War Writings, 1946–1952*. New York: Philosophical Library, 1954.

———. *The Doctrine of the Word of God: Prolegomena to Church Dogmatics*. Edinburgh: Clark, 1936.

———. *The Epistle to the Romans*. Oxford: Oxford University Press, 1960.

———. *Fides quaerens intellectum: Anselms Beweis der Existenz Gottes im Zusammenhang seines theologischen Programms*. Forschungen zur Geschichte und

Lehre des Protestantismus, series 4, volume 3. Munich: Chr. Kaiser, 1931. Translated by Ian W. Robertson as *Anselm: Fides Quaerens Intellectum; Anselm's Proof of the Existence of God in the Context of His Theological Scheme* (London: SCM Press; Richmond: John Knox Press, 1960; Pittsburgh: Pickwick Press, 1985).

———. *The Humanity of God.* Richmond: John Knox Press, 1960.

———. *Theologische Existenz Heute!* Issue no. 2 of *Zwischen den Zeiten.* Munich: Chr. Kaiser, 1933. Translated by R. Birch Hoyle as *Theological Existence Today: A Plea for Theological Freedom* (London: Hodder and Stoughton, 1933; Lexington, KY: American Theological Library Association, 1962).

———. *The Word of God and the Word of Man.* Translated by Douglas Horton. Gloucester, MA: Peter Smith, 1978.

Barth, Karl, and Rudolf Karl Bultmann. *Karl Barth–Rudolf Bultmann Letters, 1922–1966.* Edited by Bernd Jaspert and Geoffrey William Bromiley. Translated by Geoffrey Bromiley. Grand Rapids, MI: Eerdmans, 1981.

Barth, Karl, and Eduard Thurneysen. *Revolutionary Theology in the Making: Barth-Thurneysen Correspondence, 1914–1925.* Translated by James D. Smart. English edition. Richmond: John Knox Press, 1964.

Bassewitz, Gert von, und Christian Bunners. *Auf den Spuren von Dietrich Bonhoeffer.* Hamburg: Ellert und Richter Verlag, 2006.

Bell, G. K. A. *The Kingship of Christ: The Story of the World Council of Churches.* Westport, CT: Greenwood Press, 1979.

Bell, G. K. A., and Gerhard Leibholz. *On the Brink of Divided Europe: The Correspondence Between George Bell and Gerhard Leibholz 1939–1951.* Edited by Eberhard Bethge and Ronald Jaspers. 1st edition. Stuttgart: Kreuz Verlag, 1974.

Benjamin, Walter. *Illuminations: Essays and Reflections.* Edited by Hannah Arendt. Translated by Harry Zohn. New York: Schocken Books, 1968.

Bergen, Doris L. *Twisted Cross: The German Christian Movement in the Third Reich.* Chapel Hill, NC: University of North Carolina Press, 1996.

———. *War & Genocide: A Concise History of the Holocaust.* Lanham, MD: Rowman and Littlefield, 2003.

Bernanos, Georges. *Under Satan's Sun.* Translated by J. C. Whitehouser. Lincoln, NE: University of Nebraska Press, 2001.

Best, S. Payne. *The Venlo Incident.* London: Hutchinson, 1950.

Bethge, Eberhard. *Bonhoeffer: An Illustrated Introduction in Documents and Photographs.* Translated by Rosaleen Ockenden. London: Collins, 1979.

———. "Der Freund: Dietrich Bonhoeffer und seine theologische Konzeption von Freundschaft" (The friend: Dietrich Bonhoeffer and his theological conception of friendship). In Gremmels and Huber, *Theologie und Freundschaft*, pp. 29–50. English translation in Bethge, *Friendship and Resistance*, pp. 80–105.

———. "Dietrich and Marie." *International Bonhoeffer Society Newsletter*, no. 78 (February 2002).

———. *Dietrich Bonhoeffer: A Biography.* Edited by Edwin Robertson and

Victoria Barnett. Translated by Eric Mosbacher, Peter Ross, Betty Ross, Frank Clarke, and William Glen-Doepel. Revised edition. Minneapolis: Augsburg Fortress Press, 2000.

———. *Dietrich Bonhoeffer: Man of Vision, Man of Courage*. New York: Harper and Row, 1970.

———. *Dietrich Bonhoeffer: Theologe—Christ—Zeitgenosse*. 4th edition. Munich: Chr. Kaiser Verlag, 1978.

———. *Dietrich Bonhoeffer: Theologian, Christian, Contemporary*. London: Collins, 1970.

———. *Friendship and Resistance: Essays on Dietrich Bonhoeffer*. Grand Rapids, MI: Wm. B. Eerdmans, 1995.

———. *In Zitz gab es keine Juden: Erinnerungen aus meinen ersten vierzig Jahren* (There were no Jews in Zitz: Memories of my first forty years). Munich: Chr. Kaiser, 1989.

———. "Mein Freund" (My friend). In Gremmels and Huber, *Theologie und Freundschaft*, pp. 13–28.

Bethge, Renate. *Dietrich Bonhoeffer: A Life in Pictures*. Centenary edition. Minneapolis: Fortress Press, 2006.

———. "Editor's Afterword to the German Edition." In *DBW*, vol. 7, pp. 205–33. English edition. Minneapolis: Fortress Press, 2000.

Birchall, Frederick T. "Olympics Leave Glow of Pride in the Reich." *New York Times*, August 16, 1936.

Bismarck, Ruth Alice, and Ulrich Kabitz, eds. *Brautbriefe Zelle 92: Dietrich Bonhoeffer–Maria von Wedemeyer, 1943–1945*. Munich: C. H. Beck'sche Verlagsbuchhandlung, 1992. Translated by John Brownjohn as *Love Letters from Cell 92: The Correspondence Between Dietrich Bonhoeffer and Maria von Wedemeyer, 1943–1945*, with a postscript by Eberhard Bethge (London: HarperCollins, 1994; Nashville: Abingdon Press, 1995).

Bonhoeffer, Emmi. *Essay, Gespräch, Erinnerung*. Berlin: Lukas Verlag, 2004.

———. "Professors' Children as Neighbors." In Zimmermann and Smith, eds., *I Knew Dietrich Bonhoeffer*, pp. 34–37.

Bosanquet, Mary. *The Life and Death of Dietrich Bonhoeffer*. New York: Harper and Row, 1968.

Brocker, Mark. "Editor's Introduction to the English Edition." In *DBW*, vol. 16.

Buber, Martin. *I and Thou*. Translated by Ronald Gregor Smith. Edinburgh: T and T Clark, 1937.

Bucher, Rainer. *Hitler's Theology: A Study in Political Religion*. Translated by Rebecca Pohl. New York: Continuum, 2011.

Burgsmüller, Alfred, and Rudolf Weth. *Die Barmer theologische Erklärung: Einführung und Dokumentation* (The Barmen theological declaration: Introduction and documentation). Edited by Eduard Lohse. 2nd edition. Neukirchen-Vluyn: Neukirchener Verlag, 1984.

Busch, Eberhard, and John Bowden. *Karl Barth: His Life from Letters and Autobiographical Texts*. Grand Rapids, MI: Wm. B. Eerdmans, 1994.

Busing, Paul F. W. "Reminiscences of Finkenwalde." *Christian Century* 78, no. 38 (spring 1961): 1108–11.

Carter, Guy Christopher. *Confession at Bethel, August 1933: Enduring Witness; The Formation, Revision and Significance of the First Full Theological Confession of the Evangelical Church Struggle in Nazi Germany*. PhD dissertation, Marquette University, 1987.

Clements, Keith. *Bonhoeffer*. London: SPCK, 2010.

Clements, Keith W. *Bonhoeffer and Britain*. London: Churches Together in Britain and Ireland, 2006.

Cochrane, Arthur C., ed. *The Church's Confession Under Hitler*. Philadelphia: Westminster Press, 1962.

Cocks, Geoffrey. *Psychotherapy in the Third Reich: The Göring Institute*. New Brunswick: Transaction Publishers, 1997.

Conway, John S. *The Nazi Persecution of the Churches, 1933–45*. New York: Basic Books, 1968.

Cresswell, Amos S., and Maxwell G. Tow. *Dr. Franz Hildebrandt: Mr. Valiant-for-Truth*. Bodmin: Gracewing, 2000.

Davies, Alan T. *Infected Christianity: A Study of Modern Racism*. Kingston, Canada: McGill-Queen's University Press, 1988.

De Gruchy, John W. *Christianity and Democracy: A Theology for a Just World Order*. Cambridge: Cambridge University Press, 1995.

———. *Daring, Trusting Spirit: Bonhoeffer's Friend Eberhard Bethge*. Minneapolis: Fortress Press, 2005.

———. "Editor's Introduction to the English Edition." In *DBW*, vol. 3.

De Gruchy, John W., ed. *The Cambridge Companion to Dietrich Bonhoeffer*. Cambridge: Cambridge University Press, 1999.

De Lange, Frits. *Waiting for the Word: Dietrich Bonhoeffer on Speaking About God*. Translated by Martin N. Walton. Grand Rapids, MI: William B. Eerdmans Publishing Company, 1995.

Dohnányi von, Ilona. *Ernst von Dohnányi: A Song of Life*. Edited by James A. Grimes. Bloomington, IN: Indiana University Press, 2002.

Dorrien, Gary J. *Soul in Society: The Making and Renewal of Social Christianity*. Minneapolis: Fortress Press, 1995.

Driberg, Tom. *The Mystery of Moral Re-armament*. New York: Alfred A. Knopf, 1965.

———. "Thank Heaven for Hitler." In Driberg, *The Mystery of Moral Re-armament*.

Du Bois, W. E. B. *The Souls of Black Folks*. New York: Modern Library, 1993.

Dudzus, Otto, and Jiirgen Henkys. "Editors' Afterword to the German Edition." In *DBW*, vol. 14.

Duke, David Nelson. "The Experiment of an Ethic of Radical Justice: The Formative Experiences of Bonhoeffer's American Education." In *Bonhoeffer Group*. Archives on the Burke Library at Union Theological Seminary, New York, 1996.

————. *In the Trenches with Jesus and Marx: Harry F. Ward and the Struggle for Social Justice*. Tuscaloosa, AL: University of Alabama Press, 2003.

Dunbar, Anthony. *Against the Grain: Southern Radicals and Prophets, 1929–1959*. Charlottesville, VA: University of Virginia, 1981.

Eddy, George Sherwood. *Facing the Crisis: A Study in Present Day Social and Religious Problems*. New York: G. H. Doran, 1922.

Egerton, John. *Speak Now Against the Day: The Generation Before the Civil Rights Movement in the South*. New York: Alfred A. Knopf, 1994.

Ein neues Lied: Ein Liederbuch für die deutsche evangelische Jugend (A new song: A songbook for German Protestant youth). Berlin: Reichsverband weiblicher Jugend, 1933.

Ericksen, Robert P. *Complicity in the Holocaust: Churches and Universities in Nazi Germany*. Cambridge: Cambridge University Press, 2012.

————. *Theologians Under Hitler: Gerhard Kittel, Paul Althaus, and Emanuel Hirsch*. New Haven, CT: Yale University Press, 1985.

Ericksen, Robert P., and Susannah Heschel, eds. *Betrayal: German Churches and the Holocaust*. Minneapolis: Fortress Press, 1999.

Evangelisches Gesangbuch für Brandenburg und Pommern (Protestant hymnbook for Brandenburg and Pomerania). Berlin: Provinzialkirchenräte von Brandenburg und Pommern, 1931.

Faye, Emmanuel. *Heidegger: The Introduction of Nazism into Philosophy in Light of the Unpublished Seminars of 1933–1935*. Translated by Michael B. Smith. New Haven, CT: Yale University Press, 2009.

Feil, Ernst. *The Theology of Dietrich Bonhoeffer*. Translated by Martin Rumscheidt. Philadelphia: Fortress Press, 1985.

Fishbane, Michael, and Judith Glatzer Wechsler, eds. *The Memoirs of Nahum N. Glatzer*. Cincinnati, OH: Hebrew Union College Press, 1997.

"Flossenbürg Concentration Camp, 1938–1945." Catalogue of the Permament Exhibition. Flossenbürg: Flossenbürg Memorial/Bavarian Memorial Foundation.

Floyd, Wayne Whitson. "The Search for an Ethical Sacrament from Bonhoeffer to Critical Theory." *Modern Theology* 7, no. 9 (1991): 175–93.

Fosdick, Harry Emerson. *Christianity and Progress*. New York: Fleming H. Revell, 1922.

Fox, Richard Wightman. *Reinhold Niebuhr: A Biography*. 1st edition. New York: Pantheon Books, 1985.

Frei, Hans W. *Types of Christian Theology*. Edited by George Hunsinger and William C. Placher. New Haven: Yale University Press, 1994.

Frick, Peter. *Bonhoeffer's Intellectual Formation: Theology and Philosophy in His Thought*. Tübingen: Mohr Siebeck, 2008.

Friedländer, Saul. *Nazi Germany and the Jews: Volume 1—The Years of Persecution, 1933–1939*. New York: HarperCollins, 1997.

Friedrich, Otto. *Before the Deluge: A Portrait of Berlin in the 1920s*. New York: Harper and Row, 1972.

Gandhi, Mahatma. *The Essential Gandhi*. Edited by Louis Fischer. New York: Vintage Books, 1983.

Gay, Peter. *Education of the Senses: The Bourgeois Experience: Victoria to Freud*. New York: Oxford University Press, 1984.

———. *My German Question: Growing Up in Nazi Berlin*. Illustrated. New Haven: Yale University Press, 1998.

———. *Weimar Culture: The Outsider as Insider*. New York: Harper and Row, 1970.

Gerlach, Wolfgang. *And the Witnesses Were Silent: The Confessing Church and the Persecution of the Jews*. Translated and edited by Victoria J. Barnett. Lincoln, NE: University of Nebraska Press, 2000.

Gestrich, Christof, und Johannes Neugebauer, eds. *Der Wert menschlichen Lebens: Medizinische Ethik bei Dietrich Bonhoeffer und Karl Bonhoeffer*. Berlin: Wichern-Verlag, 2006.

Giardina, Denise. *Saints and Villains: A Novel*. New York: W. W. Norton and Company, 1998.

Godsey, John D. *Barth and Bonhoeffer: The Basic Difference: Presidential Address, American Theological Society, April 4, 1986*. N.d.

Goebel, Johannes. "When He Sat Down at the Piano." In Zimmermann and Smith, eds., *I Knew Dietrich Bonhoeffer*, pp. 107–11.

Goethe, Johann Wolfgang von. *Goethe's Travels in Italy: Together with His Second Residence in Rome and Fragments on Italy*. Translated by Alexander James William Morrison and Charles Nisbet. English edition. London: George Bell and Sons, 1911.

———. *Italian Journey, 1786–1788*. London: Penguin, 1992.

Gogarten, Friedrich. *Politische Ethik: Versuch einer Grundlegung* (Political ethics: Toward a foundation). Jena: Diederichs, 1932.

Goggin, James E., and Eileen Brockman Goggin. *Death of a "Jewish Science": Psychoanalysis in the Third Reich*. West Lafayette, IN: Purdue University Press, 2001.

Gordon, Mel. *Voluptuous Panic: The Erotic World of Weimar Berlin*. Los Angeles: Feral House, 2000.

Gorringe, Timothy. *Karl Barth: Against Hegemony*. Oxford: Oxford University Press, 1999.

Green, Clifford J. "Editor's Introduction to the English Edition." In *DBW*, vol. 10.

Green, Clifford J. *Bonhoeffer: A Theology of Sociality*. Revised edition. Grand Rapids, MI: Wm. B. Eerdmans Publishing, 1999.

———. "Bonhoeffer's Concept of Religion." *Union Seminary Quarterly Review* 19 (1963): 11–21.

———. "Editor's Introduction to the English Edition." In *DBW*, vol. 6.

———. "Pacifism and Tyrannicide: Bonhoeffer's Christian Peace Ethic." *Studies in Christian Ethics* 18, no. 3 (December 2005): 31–47. (doi:10.1177/0953946805058796.)

———. "Two Bonhoeffers on Psychoanalysis." In *A Bonhoeffer Legacy: Essays in Understanding*, edited by A. J. Klassen, pp. 58–75. Grand Rapids, MI: Eerdmans, 1981.

Gregor, Brian, and Jens Zimmermann, eds. *Bonhoeffer and Continental Thought: Cruciform Philosophy*. Bloomington, IN: Indiana University Press, 2009.

Gremmels, Christian, and Wolfgang Huber. *Theologie und Freundschaft: Wechselwirkungen, Eberhard Bethge und Dietrich Bonhoeffer*. Gütersloh: Kaiser, 1994.

Gumaer, David Emerson. "Apostasy—The National Council of Churches." *Studies in Reformed Theology*, 1998, available at http://www.reformed-theology.org/html/issue07/apostasy.htm (accessed May 2, 2011).

Gustafson, Susan E. *Men Desiring Men: The Poetry of Same-Sex Identity and Desire in German Classicism*. Detroit, MI: Wayne State University Press, 2002.

Handy, Robert T. *A History of Union Theological Seminary in New York*. New York: Columbia University Press, 1987.

Harnack, Adolf von. *Das Wesen des Christentums: Sechzehn Vorlesungen vor Studierenden aller Fakultäten im Wintersemester 1899/1900 an der Universität Berlin Gehalten* (The essence of Christianity: Sixteen lectures to students of all faculties in the winter semester 1899/1900 held at the University of Berlin). Edited by Claus-Dieter Osthövener. Tübingen: Mohr Siebeck, 2012.

Harnack, Adolf von, and Wilhelm Herrmann. *Essays on the Social Gospel*. Translated by G. M. Craik. New York: G. P. Putnam's Sons, 1907.

Hase, Hans-Christoph von. " 'Turning Away from the Phraseological to the Real': A Personal Recollection." In *DBW*, vol. 10.

Hegel, Georg Wilhelm Friedrich. *Vorlesungen über die Philosophie der Religion*. Based on the extant manuscripts completely revised by G. Lasson. Pt. 1: *Begriff der Religion*. Vol. 12 of *Sämtliche Werke*. Leipzig: Felix Meiner, 1925. Translated by Ebenezer Brown Speirs and J. Burdon Sanderson as vol. 1 of *Lectures on the Philosophy of Religion* (London: Kegan Paul, Trench, Trubner, 1895).

Heidegger, Martin. *Sein und Zeit*. 9th edition. Tübingen: M. Niemeyer, 1960. Translated by John Macquarrie and Edward Robinson as *Being and Time* (San Francisco: Harper and Row, 1962).

Heilbut, Anthony. *Exiled in Paradise: German Refugee Artists and Intellectuals in America from the 1930's to the Present*. New York: Viking, 1983.

Heine, Heinrich. *The Harz Journey and Selected Prose*. Translated and edited by Ritche Robertson. London: Penguin Books, 2006.

Heschel, Susannah. *The Aryan Jesus: Christian Theologians and the Bible in Nazi Germany*. Princeton, NJ: Princeton University Press, 2008.

Hildebrandt, Franz. *And Other Pastors of My Flock: A German Tribute to the Bishop of Chichester*. Cambridge: Cambridge University Press, 1942.

———. *Theologie für Refugées: Ein Kapitel Paul Gerhardt* (Theology for refugees: A chapter on Paul Gerhardt). London: Finsbury, 1940.

"History." *St. George's German Lutheran Church*. Available at http://www.st georgesgermanchurch.org.uk/page1.html (accessed December 31, 2011).

"Hitler or Any Fascist Leader Controlled by God Could Cure All Ills of World." *New York World-Telegram*, August 25, 1936.

Hodgson, Leonard. *The Second World Conference on Faith and Order, Held at Edinburgh, August 3–18*. New York: Macmillan, 1938.

Hofmann, Klaus, ed. *Awake My Heart: Bach Chorale Collection and Settings for the Eucharist*. Stuttgart: Carus Verlag, 2000.

Hoffmann, Peter. *Widerstand-Staatsstreich-Attentat: Der Kampf der Opposition gegen Hitler*. 2nd revised and enlarged edition. Frankfurt am Main: Ullstein, 1970. Translated by Richard Barry as *The History of the German Resistance, 1933–1945* (Cambridge, MA: MIT Press, 1977).

Höhne, Heinz. *Canaris: Hitler's Master Spy*. Translated by Maxwell Brownjohn. Garden City, NJ: Doubleday, 1979.

Hölderlin, Friedrich, and Eduard Mörike. *Selected Poems*. Translated by Christopher Middleton. Chicago and London: University of Chicago Press, 1972.

Holl, Karl. "Die Kulturbedeutung der Reformation." In *Gesammelte Aufsätze zur Kirchengeschichte*. Vol. 1: *Luther*, pp. 359–413. Tübingen: J. C. B. Mohr, 1921. Translated by Karl Hertz, Barbara Hertz, and John H. Lichtblau as *The Cultural Significance of the Reformation*, with an introduction by Wilhelm Pauck (New York: Meridian Books, 1959).

Horton, Myles, Judith Kohl, and Herbert R. Kohl. *The Long Haul: An Autobiography*. New York: Doubleday, 1990.

The "House Prison" at the Gestapo Headquarters in Berlin. Berlin: Topography of Terror Foundation, 2005.

Howard, Thomas Albert. *Protestant Theology and the Making of the Modern German University*. Oxford: Oxford University Press, 2009.

Howse, Christopher. "The Levelling of Mirfield Church." *Telegraph.co.uk*, November 13, 2009.

Humphreys, Fisher, and Philip Wise. *A Dictionary of Doctrinal Terms*. Nashville, TN: Broadman Press, 1983.

Jakle, John A., and Keith A. Sculle. *Motoring: The Highway Experience in America*. Athens, GA: University of Georgia Press, 2008.

Jensen, Hans-Werner. "Life Together." In Zimmermann and Smith, eds., *I Knew Dietrich Bonhoeffer*, pp. 152–55.

Jones, Ernest. *The Life and Works of Sigmund Freud: Years of Maturity, 1901–1919*. Vol. 2. New York: Basic Books, 1955.

Jungel, Eberhard. *Gott als Geheimnis der Welt*. Tübingen: J. C. B. Mohr, 1977. Translated by Darrel L. Guder as *God as the Mystery of the World* (Grand Rapids, MI: Eerdmans, 1983).

Kant, Immanuel. *Sämtliche Werke*. 6 vols. Leipzig: Insel Verlag, 1921–24. Translated as *The Cambridge Edition of the Works of Immanuel Kant*, edited by Paul Guyer and Allen W. Wood (Cambridge: Cambridge University Press, 1992).

Kelly, Geffrey B. "An Interview with Jean Lasserre." *Union Seminary Quarterly Review* 27, no. 3 (spring 1972): 149–60.

———. "'Unconscious Christianity' and the 'Anonymous Christian' in the

Theology of Dietrich Bonhoeffer and Karl Rahner." *Philosophy and Theology: Marquette University Quarterly Review* 9, nos. 1–2 (1995): 117–49.

Kelly, Geffrey B., and F. Burton Nelson, eds. *A Testament to Freedom: The Essential Writings of Dietrich Bonhoeffer*. San Francisco: HarperSanFrancisco, 1995.

Kittel, Gerhard. "Das Urteil des Neuen Testamentes über den Staat" (The view of the New Testament on the state). *Zeitschrift für Systematische Theologie* 14 (1937): 651–80.

Klassen, Abram John. *A Bonhoeffer Legacy: Essays in Understanding*. Grand Rapids, MI: Eerdmans, 1981.

Klemperer, Klemens von. *German Resistance Against Hitler: The Search for Allies Abroad, 1938–1945*. New York: Clarendon Press; Oxford: Oxford University Press, 1992.

Klemperer, Victor. *I Will Bear Witness: The Diaries of Victor Klemperer, 1933–1941*. 2 vols. New York: Random House, 1998.

Knight, Eric. *This Above All*. New York: Grosset and Dunlap, 1942.

Koch, Werner. "Dietrich Bonhoeffer in Pomerania." In Zimmermann and Smith, eds., *I Knew Dietrich Bonhoeffer*, pp. 112–22.

Koonz, Claudia. *The Nazi Conscience*. Cambridge: Harvard University Press, 2003.

Krieg, Robert A. *Catholic Theologians in Nazi Germany*. New York: Continuum Publishing, 2004.

Kuske, Martin. *The Old Testament as the Book of Christ: An Appraisal of Bonhoeffer's Interpretation*. Philadelphia: Westminster Press, 1976.

Kuske, Martin, and Ilse Tödt. "Editors' Afterword to the German Edition." In *DBW*, vol. 4.

Ladd, Brian. *The Ghosts of Berlin: Confronting German History in the Urban Landscape*. Chicago: University of Chicago Press, 1997.

Large, David Clay. *Berlin*. New York: Basic Books, 2000.

———. *Nazi Games: The Olympics of 1936*. New York: W. W. Norton and Company, 2007.

Lassels, Richard. *The Voyage of Italy or a Compleat Journey Through Italy in Two Parts*. Vol. I. Paris: Starkey, 1670.

Lehel, Ferenc. "Seen with the Eyes of a Pupil." In Zimmermann and Smith, eds., *I Knew Dietrich Bonhoeffer*, pp. 68–70.

Lehmann, Paul. "Paradox of Discipleship." In Zimmermann and Smith, eds., *I Knew Dietrich Bonhoeffer*, pp. 41–45.

Leibholz, Sabine. "Childhood and Home." In Zimmermann and Smith, eds., *I Knew Dietrich Bonhoeffer*, pp. 19–33.

———. "Letter of May 19, 1946." Series 3, Box 1, Folder I. Union Theological Seminary Primary Sources.

Leibholz-Bonhoeffer, Sabine. *The Bonhoeffers: Portrait of a Family*. Translated and edited by F. Burton Nelson. Chicago: Covenant Publications, 1994.

———. *Weihnachten in Hause Bonhoeffer*. Reprint. Gütersloh: Gütersloher Verlagshaus, 2005.

Leith, John H., ed. *Creeds of the Churches: A Reader in Christian Doctrine, from the Bible to the Present.* 3rd edition. Atlanta: John Knox Press, 1982.

Leuze, Thomas E. "The Collective Pastorates of the Confessing Church: A Model for Ministerial Preparation." Unpublished paper, Chapman Seminary, Oakland City University, Oakland City, Indiana.

Levenson, Thomas. *Einstein in Berlin.* New York: Bantam Books, 2003.

Lewis, Alan. *Between Cross and Resurrection: A Theology of Holy Saturday.* Grand Rapids, MI: W. B. Eerdmans, 2001.

Liukkonen, Petri. "Ernst Barlach (1870–1938)." *Books and Writers,* 2008, available at http://kirjasto.sci.fi/barlach.htm.

Locke, Hubert G. *The Barmen Confession: Papers from the Seattle Assembly.* Toronto: Edwin Mellen Press, 1986.

Lossky, N., Jose Miguez Bonino, John Pobee, and Tom F. Stransky, eds. *Dictionary of the Ecumenical Movement.* Geneva: WCC Publications, 2002.

Lovin, Robin W. "Biographical Context." In *New Studies in Bonhoeffer's Ethics,* edited by William J. Peck and Clifford J. Green. Vol. 30. Toronto Studies in Theology, Bonhoeffer Series 3. Lewiston, NY: Edwin Mellen Press, 1987.

Löwith, Karl. *My Life in Germany Before and After 1933.* Translated by Elizabeth King. London: Athlone Press, 1994.

Lukens, Nancy. *Who Am I?* Edited by John S. Conway. Association of Contemporary Church Historians (Arbeitsgemeinschaft kirchlicher Zeitgeschichtler), University of British Columbia. Vol. 12: Special Issue on Dietrich Bonhoeffer, February 2006, p. 77.

Lütgert, Wilhelm. *Die Religion des deutschen Idealismus und ihr Ende* (The religion of German idealism and its end). Vol. 1: *Die religiöse Krisis des deutschen Idealismus* (The religious crisis of German idealism). 2nd edition. Gütersloh: C. Bertelsmann, 1923.

———. *Ethik der Liebe* (Ethics of love). Vol. 39. Beiträge zur Förderung Christlicher Theologie 2. Gütersloh: C. Bertelsmann, 1938.

Luther, Martin. *Luther's Works.* Vol. 35: *Word and Sacrament.* Edited by Pelikan. St. Louis, MO: Concordia Pub. House, 1986.

Maltusch, Gottfried. "When the Synagogues Burnt." In Zimmermann and Smith, eds., *I Knew Dietrich Bonhoeffer,* pp. 150–51.

Marienburger Allee 43: Begleitheft zur Ausstellung (Marienburger Allee 43: Exhibition guide). Berlin: Curatorium of the Bonhoeffer-Haus, 1988.

Marty, Martin E. *Dietrich Bonhoeffer's "Letters and Papers from Prison": A Biography.* Princeton: Princeton University Press, 2011.

Matheson, Peter, ed. *The Third Reich and the Christian Churches.* Grand Rapids, MI: William B. Eerdmans Publishing Company, 1981.

Mayer, Rainer. *Dietrich Bonhoeffer, Mensch hinter Mauern—Theologie und Spiritualität in den Gefängnisjahren* (Dietrich Bonhoeffer: Person behind walls—Theology and spirituality in the prison years). Giessen: Brunnen Verlag, 1993.

McCarraher, Eugene. *Christian Critics: Religion and the Impasse in Modern American Social Thought*. Ithaca, NY: Cornell University Press, 2000.

Mehta, Ved. *The New Theologian*. New York: Harper and Row, 1966.

Meyer, Beate, Hermann Simon, and Chana Schütz. *Jews in Berlin: From Kristallnacht to Liberation*. Chicago: University of Chicago Press, 2009.

Meyer, Dietrich, und Eberhard Bethge. *Nachlaß Dietrich Bonhoeffer: Ein Verzeichnis, Archiv, Sammlung, Bibliothek*. München: Christian Kaiser Verlag, 1987.

Meyer, Winfried. *Unternehmen Sieben: Eine Rettungsaktion für vom Holocaust Bedrohte aus dem Amt Ausland/Abwehr im Oberkommando der Wehrmacht* (Operation Seven: A rescue action on behalf of those threatened by the Holocaust conducted by the Foreign Office of Military Intelligence in the Armed Forces High Command). Frankfurt am Main: Verlag Anton Hain, 1993.

Middleton, Christopher, ed. *Friedrich Hölderlin and Eduard Mörike, Selected Poems*. Chicago: University of Chicago Press, 1972.

Moltke, Helmuth James von. *Briefe an Freya: 1939–1945*. Edited by Beate Ruhm von Oppen. Munich: Beck, 1988. Translated and edited by Beate Ruhm von Oppen as *Letters to Freya: 1939–1945* (New York: Knopf, 1990).

Mommsen, Hans. *Alternatives to Hitler: German Resistance Under the Third Reich*. Translated by Angus McGeoch. Princeton: Princeton University Press, 2003.

Moser, Hans Joachim. *Heinrich Schütz: A Short Account of His Life and Works*. London: Faber and Faber, 1967.

Moses, John Anthony. *The Reluctant Revolutionary: Dietrich Bonhoeffer's Collision with Prusso-German History*. New York: W. W. Norton and Company, 2009.

Moskopp, Dag, and Dorothea Jäkel. *Karl Bonhoeffer: Ein Nervenarzt*. Berlin: Wichern-Verlag, 2009.

Nelson, F. Burton. "Friends He Met in America." *Christian History* 10, no. 4 (1991): 37.

———. "The Relationship of Jean Lasserre to Dietrich Bonhoeffer's Peace Concerns in the Struggle of Church and Culture." *Union Seminary Quarterly Review* 8, nos. 1–2 (1985): 71–84.

Nicholls, William. *Christian Antisemitism: A History of Hate*. Northvale, NJ: Jason Aronson, Inc., 1993.

———. *Systematic and Philosophical Theology*. Middlesex: Penguin Books, 1971.

Niebuhr, Reinhold. *Beyond Tragedy: Essays on the Christian Interpretation of History*. New York: C. Scribner's Sons, 1938.

———. *Christianity and Power Politics*. Hamden, CT: Archon Books, 1969.

———. *The Essential Reinhold Niebuhr: Selected Essays and Addresses*. Edited by Robert McAfee Brown. New Haven, CT: Yale University Press, 1987.

———. *Moral Man in Immoral Society: A Study in Ethics and Politics*. New York: Scribner, 1932.

Niebuhr, Ursula M., ed. *Remembering Reinhold Niebuhr: Letters of Reinhold and Ursula M. Niebuhr.* San Francisco, CA: HarperSanFrancisco, 1991.

Niesel, Wilhelm. "From Keelson to Principal of a Seminary." In Zimmermann and Smith, eds., *I Knew Dietrich Bonhoeffer*, pp. 145–48.

———. *Kirche unter dem Wort: Der Kampf der bekennenden Kirche der altpreussischen Union 1933–1945* (Church under the word: The struggle of the Confessing Church of the Old Prussian Union 1933–1945). Arbeiten zur Geschichte des Kirchenkampfes. Supplemental series 11. Göttingen: Vandenhoeck und Ruprecht, 1978.

Nürnberger, Margarete. "Maria von Wedemeyer: Fiancée [sic] of Dietrich Bonhoeffer." *Journal of Theology for Southern Africa* 127 (March 2007): 116–31.

Ott, Heinrich. *Reality and Faith: The Theological Legacy of Dietrich Bonhoeffer.* Philadelphia: Fortress Press, 1971.

Pangritz, Andreas. "Aspekte der 'Arkandisziplin' bei Dietrich Bonhoeffer" (Aspects of "arcane discipline" in Dietrich Bonhoeffer). *Theologische Literaturzeitung* 119 (1994): 755–68.

———. *Karl Barth in the Theology of Dietrich Bonhoeffer: A Clarification Whose Time Has Come.* Edited by Barbara Rumscheidt and Martin Rumscheidt. Grand Rapids, MI: William B. Eerdmans, 1999.

———. "Mystery and Commandment in Leo Baeck's and Dietrich Bonhoeffer's Thinking." *European Judaism: A Journal for the New Europe* 30 (autumn 1997): 44–57.

———. "Point and Counterpoint—Resistance and Submission. Dietrich Bonhoeffer on Theology and Music in Times of War and Social Crisis." In *Theology in Dialogue: The Impact of the Arts, Humanities, and Science on Contemporary Religious Thought: Essays in Honor of John W. de Gruchy*, edited by Lyn Holness and Ralf K. Wüstenberg. Grand Rapids, MI: William B. Eerdmans, 2002.

———. *Polyphonie des Lebens: Zu Dietrich Bonhoeffers "Theologie der Musik"* (Polyphony of life: On Dietrich Bonhoeffer's "theology of music"). Dahlemer Heft 13. Berlin: Alektor Verlag, 1994.

———. "Who Is Jesus Christ for Us, Today?" In *The Cambridge Companion to Dietrich Bonhoeffer*, edited by John W. De Gruchy, pp. 134–53. Cambridge: Cambridge University Press, 1999.

Paret, Peter. *An Artist Against the Third Reich: Ernst Barlach, 1933–1938.* Cambridge: Cambridge University Press, 2003.

Paton, William. *The Church and the New Order.* London: SCM Press, 1941.

Pejsa, Jane. "Dietrich Bonhoeffer's Letter to an Unknown Woman." *Newsletter, International Bonhoeffer Society, English Language Section* 52 (1993): 3ff.

———. *Matriarch of Conspiracy: Ruth von Kleist, 1867–1945.* Cleveland, OH: Pilgrim Press, 1991.

Pelikan, Jaroslav. *Bach Among the Theologians.* Eugene, OR: Wipf and Stock Publishers, 1973.

Pfeifer, Hans. "An Aesthetic Voyage: Dietrich Bonhoeffer's Gradual Approach

Towards Full Reality, and Eberhard Bethge's Contribution to It." *Journal of Theology for Southern Africa* 127 (March 2007): 63–68.

———. "Editor's Afterword to the German Edition." In *DBW*, vol. 9., pp. 563–78.

———. "Learning Faith and Ethical Commitment in the Context of Spiritual Training Groups: Consequences of Dietrich Bonhoeffer's Post Doctoral Year in New York City, 1930–31." *Dietrich Bonhoeffer Jahrbuch* 3 (2007/2008): 251–78.

Plant, Stephen J., and Toni Barrowes-Cromwell. *Dietrich Bonhoeffer: Letters to London*. London: SPCK, 2013.

Poewe, Karla O. *New Religions and the Nazis*. New York: Psychology Press, 2006.

"Rabbi Stephen Wise (1874–1949)." *The American Experience: America and the Holocaust, People & Events*. Available at http://www.pbs.org/wgbh/amex/holocaust/peopleevents/pandeAMEX101.html (accessed October 11, 2011).

Rahner, Karl. *Encyclopedia of Theology: The Concise Sacramentum Mundi*. New York: Seabury Press, 1975.

Rasmussen, Larry L. *Dietrich Bonhoeffer: Reality and Resistance*. Louisville, KY: Westminster John Knox Press, 2005.

———. "Editor's Introduction to the English Edition." In *DBW*, vol. 12.

———. "Introduction: A Public Theologian." In *Reinhold Niebuhr: Theologian of Public Life*. Making of Modern Theology series. Minneapolis: Fortress Press, 1991.

Rauschenbusch, Walter. *Christianity and the Social Crisis*. New York: Macmillan, 1907.

———. *Christianizing the Social Order*. Boston: Pilgrim Press, 1912.

———. *A Theology for the Social Gospel*. New York: Macmillan, 1917.

Read, Anthony, and David Fisher. *Berlin Rising: Biography of a City*. London: Pimplico, 1988.

Rebiger, Bill. *Jewish Berlin: Culture, Religion, Daily Life Yesterday and Today*. Berlin: Jaron Verlag, 2005.

Rieger, Julius. *Bonhoeffer in England*. Berlin: Lettner-Verlag, 1966.

———. "Contacts with London." In Zimmermann and Smith, eds., *I Knew Dietrich Bonhoeffer*, pp. 95–103.

Rilke, Rainer Maria. *The Selected Poetry of Rainer Maria Rilke*. New York: Vintage Books, 1989.

Ritter, Gerhard. *Machtstaat und Utopie: Vom Streit um die Dämonie der Macht seit Machiavelli und Morus*. 2nd edition. Munich: N.p., 1941. Translated by F. W. Pick as *The Corrupting Influence of Power*, with a foreword by G. P. Gooch (Westport, CT: Hyperion Press, 1979).

Rorty, Richard. *Achieving Our Country: Leftist Thought in Twentieth Century America*. Cambridge, MA: Harvard University Press, 1998.

Roth, Andrew and Michael Frajman. *The Goldapple Guide to Jewish Berlin*. Berlin: Goldapple Publishing, 2000.

Rumscheidt, Martin, ed. *The Way of Theology in Karl Barth: Essays and Comments*. Allison Park, PA: Pickwick Publications, 1986.

Rürup, Reinhard. *Topography of Terror: Gestapo, SS and Reichssicherheitshauptamt on the "Prinz-Albrecht-Terrain"—A Documentation*. Translated by Werner T. Angress. Berlin: W. Arenhövel, 1989.

Ruter, Martin, and Ilse Tödt. "Editor's Afterword to the German Edition." In *DBW*, vol. 3.

Sabev, Todor, ed. *The Sofia Consulation*. Geneva: World Council of Churches, 1982.

Safranski, Rüdiger. *Martin Heidegger: Between Good and Evil*. Cambridge, MA: Harvard University Press, 1998.

Santayana, George. *The Last Puritan*. 1st Scribner/Macmillan Hudson River edition. New York: Macmillan, 1936.

Sasse, Hermann. *The Lonely Way: Selected Essays and Letters, 1927–1939*. Translated by Matthew C. Harrison. Vol. 1. St. Louis, MO: Concordia Publishing House, 2001.

Scharffenorth, Ernst-Albert. "Editor's Afterword to the German Edition." In *DBW*, vol. 12.

Schlabrendorff, Fabian von. *The Secret War Against Hitler*. Translated by Hilda Simon. New York: Pitman Publishing, 1965.

Schleiermacher, Friedrich. *On Religion: Speeches to Its Cultured Despisers*. Translated by John Oman. 1st Westminster/John Knox Press edition. Louisville, KY: Westminster/John Knox Press, 1994.

Schlingensiepen, Ferdinand. *Dietrich Bonhoeffer, 1906–1945: Martyr, Thinker, Man of Resistance*. London: T and T Clark International, 2010.

Smid, Marikje. *Hans von Dohnanyi, Christine Bonhoeffer: Eine Ehe im Widerstand gegen Hitler*. Gütersloh: Gütersloher Verlagsshaus, 2002.

Schmitt, Carl. *The Concept of the Political*. Translated by George Schwab. New Brunswick, NJ: Rutgers University Press, 1976.

Schmitt, Stefanie. *"Für eine Weile in die Wüste gehen": Dietrich Bonhoeffer in London, 1933–1935*. London: Kirchenvorstand der Dietrich-Bonhoeffer Kirche, 2005.

Schneider, Reinhold. *Macht und Gnade: Bilder und Werte der Geschichte* (Power and grace: Pictures and values from history). Leipzig: Insel Verlag, 1940.

Scholder, Klaus. *The Churches and the Third Reich*. Vol. 1: *1918–1934*. Philadelphia: Fortress Press, 1988.

———. *The Churches and the Third Reich*. Vol. 2: *The Year of Disillusionment 1934, Barmen and Rome*. Philadelphia: Fortress Press, 1988.

Scholder, Klaus, and John Bowden, eds. *The Churches and the Third Reich: Preliminary History and the Time of Illusions, 1918–1934*. Philadelphia: Fortress Press, 1988.

Scholl, Inge, and Dorothee Sölle. *The White Rose: Munich, 1942–1943*. Middletown, CT: Wesleyan University Press, 1983.

Schönherr, Albrecht. *Lutherische Privatbeichte* (Lutheran private confession). Göttingen: Vandenhoeck and Ruprecht, 1938.

———. "The Single-Heartedness of the Provoked." In Zimmermann and Smith, eds., *I Knew Dietrich Bonhoeffer*, pp. 126–29.

Schweitzer, Albert. *The Mysticism of Paul the Apostle.* Prefatory note by F. C. Burkitt. 1931; New York: Seabury Press, 1968.

Seeberg, Reinhold. *Christliche Dogmatik* (Christian dogmatics). Vols. 1 and 2. Erlangen: Deichert, 1924.

———. *Grundriss der Dogmatik* (Outline of dogmatics). Leipzig: Deichert, 1932.

———. *Lehrbuch der Dogmengeschichte.* 3rd edition. Vols. 1–4. Leipzig: A Deichert, 1917–23. *NL-Bibl.* 2 C 4 44. Translated by Charles E. Hays as *Textbook of the History of Doctrines.* 2 vols. (Grand Rapids, MI: Baker Book House, 1977).

Sifton, Elisabeth. *The Serenity Prayer: Faith and Politics in Times of Peace and War.* 1st edition. New York: Norton, 2003.

Smylie, James H. "Pastor, Educator, Ecumenist: Henry Sloane Coffin (1877–1954)." *Presbyterian Outlook*, June 13, 2005. Available at http://www.pres-outlook.com/reports-a-resources/presbyterian-heritage-articles/1683-pastor-educator-ecumenist-henry-sloan-coffin-1877-1954.html.

Soosten, Joachim von. "Editor's Afterword to the German Edition." In *DBW*, vol. 1.

Steigmann-Gall, Richard. *The Holy Reich: Nazi Conceptions of Christianity, 1919–1945.* Cambridge: Cambridge University Press, 2003.

Steinbach, Peter, and Johannes Tuchel. *Widerstand gegen den Nationalsozialismus.* Berlin: Akademie Verlag, 1994.

Steiner, Robert. "Desire and Transgression: Dietrich Bonhoeffer in Occupied Tripoli." *Journal of Theology for Southern Africa* 127 (March 2007): 22–42.

Stern, Fritz. *Dreams and Delusions: National Socialism in the Drama of the German Past.* New York: Vintage, 1987.

Stern, Fritz, and Elisabeth Sifton. *No Ordinary Men: Dietrich Bonhoeffer and Hans von Dohnányi: Resisters Against Hitler in Church and State.* New York: New York Review of Books Collections, 2013.

Stifter, Adalbert. *Indian Summer.* Translated by Wendell Frye. 3rd edition. New York: Peter Lang, 2006.

Ströhle, Andreas, Jana Wrase, Henry Malach, Christof Gestrich, and Andreas Heinz. "Karl Bonhoeffer (1868–1948)." *American Journal of Psychiatry* 165, no. 5 (May 2008): 575–76.

Taylor, Ronald. *Berlin and Its Culture: A Historical Portrait.* New Haven: Yale University Press, 1997.

Thielicke, Helmut. *Notes from a Wayfarer: The Autobiography of Helmut Thielicke.* St. Paul, MN: Paragon House, 1995.

Thum, Gregor. *Uprooted: How Breslau Became Wroclaw During the Century of Expulsions.* Translated by Tom Lampert and Allison Brown. Princeton, NJ: Princeton University Press, 2011.

Tillich, Paul. *My Travel Diary: 1936.* Edited by Maria Pelikan. New York: Harper and Row, 1970.

Times, Guido Enderis. "Fascists Make Big Gains in Germany." *New York Times*, September 15, 1930.

Tödt, Heinz Eduard. "The Bonhoeffer-Dohnányi Circle in Opposition and Resistance to Hitler's Regime of Violence: Interim Report on a Research Project." In Heinz Eduard Tödt, *Authentic Faith: Bonhoeffer's Theological Ethics in Context*. Translated by David Stassen and Ilse Tödt. Grand Rapids, MI: Eerdmans Publishing, 2007.

Tödt, Ilse, ed. *Dietrich Bonhoeffers Hegelseminar: Nach Aufzeichnungen von Ferenc Lehel* (Dietrich Bonhoeffer's Hegel seminar: From the notes of Ferenc Lehel). Internationales Bonhoeffer Forum: Forschung und Praxis 8. Munich: Chr. Kaiser, 1988.

Tödt, Ilse, Heinz Eduard Tödt, Ernst Feil, and Clifford J. Green. "Editors' Afterword to the German Edition." In *DBW*, vol. 6, pp. 409–49.

Treece, Patricia. *A Man for Others: Maximilian Kolbe the Saint of Auschwitz in the Words of Those Who Knew Him*. San Francisco: Harper and Row, 1982.

Visser 't Hooft, Willem Adolph. *The Background of the Social Gospel in America*. St. Louis, MO: Bethany Press, 1962.

The Wannsee Conference and the Genocide of the European Jews. Berlin: House of the Wannsee Conference, Memorial and Educational Site, 2007.

Ward, Harry Frederick. *The New Social Order: Principles and Programs*. New York: Macmillan, 1923.

———. *Our Economic Morality and the Ethic of Jesus*. New York: Macmillan, 1929.

———. *The Social Creed of the Churches*. New York: Abingdon Press, 1916.

———. *Which Way Religion?* New York: Macmillan, 1931.

Warren, Heather A. *Theologians of a New World Order: Reinhold Niebuhr and the Christian Realists: 1920–1948*. New York: Oxford University Press, 1997.

Watkins, T. H. *The Great Depression: America in the 1930s*. New York: Back Bay Books, 1993.

Watson, Peter. *The German Genius: Europe's Third Renaissance, the Second Scientific Revolution, and the Twentieth Century*. New York: HarperCollins, 2010.

Weber, Max. *The Protestant Ethic and the Spirit of Capitalism*. Mineola, NY: Dover Publications, 2003.

Wedemeyer, Ruth von. *In des Teufels Gasthaus: Eine preussische Familie 1918–1945* (In the inn of the devil: A Prussian family 1918–1945). Moers: Brendow, 1993.

Weinreich, Max. *Hitler's Professors*. New Haven: Yale University Press, 1999.

Weitz, Eric D. *Weimar Germany: Promise and Tragedy*. Princeton, NJ: Princeton University Press, 2007.

Weizsäcker, Carl Friedrich von. "Thoughts of a Nontheologian on Dietrich Bonhoeffer's Development." In *The Ambivalence of Progress: Essays on Historical Anthropology*. English translation. New York: Paragon, 1988.

"Welcome to Our Church." *Dietrich Bonhoeffer Church, Sydenham*, 1999.

Wendebourg, Dorothea. "Dietrich Bonhoeffer und die Berliner Universität" (Dietrich Bonhoeffer and the Berlin University). *Berliner Theologische*

Zeitschrift 23 (2006): 285–312. Translation by Ingrid Mueller and Charles Marsh.

Whitburn, Lawrence B. "Bonhoeffer Without His Cassock." In Zimmermann and Smith, eds., *I Knew Dietrich Bonhoeffer*, 79–81.

Wise, Stephen A. "Righteous Gentile? Bonhoeffer and the Policies of Yad Vashem, or Why Isn't Bonhoeffer Honored at Yad Vashem?" *Christian Century* 115, no. 6 (February 1998): 202–04.

Wise, Stephen S. *Stephen S. Wise: Servant of the People*. Edited by Carl Herman Voss. Philadelphia: Jewish Publication Society of America, 1969.

Wolfgang, Huber. "Answering for the Past, Shaping the Future: In Memory of Dietrich Bonhoeffer." *Ecumenical Review* 47, no. 3 (July 1995): 252–62.

Wolin, Richard. *Heidegger's Children: Hannah Arendt, Karl Löwith, Hans Jonas, and Herbert Marcuse*. Princeton, NJ: Princeton University Press, 2003.

Zahn-Harnack, Agnes von. *Adolf von Harnack*. 2nd edition. Berlin: W. de Gruyter, 1951.

Zehnpfund, Dieter. *Die Familie Bonhoeffer und Friedrichsbrunn*. Katalog zur Ausstellung. Halberstadt, 2006.

Zerner, Ruth. "Dietrich Bonhoeffer's American Experiences: People, Letters, and Papers from Union Seminary." *Union Seminary Quarterly Review* 31, no. 4 (1976): 261–82.

———. "Dietrich Bonhoeffer and the Jews: Thoughts and Actions, 1933–1945." *Jewish Social Studies* 37, no. 2–4 (summer-fall 1975): 235–50.

Zimmerman, Jens, and Brian Gregor. *Being Human, Becoming Human: Dietrich Bonhoeffer and Social Thought*. Eugene, OR: Pickwick Publications, 2010.

Zimmermann, Wolf-Dieter. "A Meeting in Werder." In Zimmermann and Smith, eds., *I Knew Dietrich Bonhoeffer*.

———. "Some Weeks in London." In Zimmermann and Smith, eds., *I Knew Dietrich Bonhoeffer*.

———. "Years in Berlin." In Zimmermann and Smith, eds., *I Knew Dietrich Bonhoeffer*.

Zimmermann, Wolf-Dieter, and Ronald Gregor Smith, eds. *I Knew Dietrich Bonhoeffer*. New York: Harper and Row, 1966.

INDEX

~

Page numbers in *italics* refer to illustrations.

PHOTOGRAPHIC CREDITS

Art Resource, N.Y.: 4, 5, 10, 19, 35, 43, 55, 66, 70, 74, 109, 113, 117, 141, 143, 153, 188, 195, 214, 219, 220, 228, 230, 256, 262, 265, 266, 270, 276, 287, 303, 320, 321, 336, 356, 358, 391; Album, 136; bpk, Berlin, 154; Schomburg Center, NYPL, 115

Courtesy of the Author: 28–9, 296, 393

Dietrich Bonhoeffer Manuscript Collection, Burke Library Archives, Columbia University Libraries, at Union Theological Seminary, New York: 119, 129, 130, 275

Library of Congress: 106, 132

Mississippi Department of Archives and History: 133

A NOTE ABOUT THE AUTHOR

Charles Marsh is the Commonwealth Professor of Religious Studies at the University of Virginia and director of the Project on Lived Theology. He is the author of seven previous books, including *The Last Days*, and *God's Long Summer: Stories of Faith and Civil Rights*, which won the 1998 Grawemeyer Award in Religion. He was a recipient of a Guggenheim Fellowship in the Creative Arts and was named the 2010 Ellen Maria Gorrissen Fellow at the American Academy in Berlin, and he has served as the Dietrich Bonhoeffer Visiting Professsor at Humboldt University in Berlin. He lives in Charlottesville, Virginia.

A NOTE ON THE TYPE

This book was set in Janson, a typeface long thought to have been made by the Dutchman Anton Janson, who was a practicing type-founder in Leipzig during the years 1668–1687. However, it has been conclusively demonstrated that these types are actually the work of Nicholas Kis (1650–1702), a Hungarian, who most probably learned his trade from the master Dutch typefounder Dirk Voskens. The type is an excellent example of the influential and sturdy Dutch types that prevailed in England up to the time William Caslon (1692–1766) developed his own incomparable designs from them.

Composed by North Market Street Graphics,
Lancaster, Pennsylvania

Printed and bound by Berryville Graphics,
Berryville, Virginia

Designed by Betty Lew